Communications in Computer and Information Science 1654

More information about this series at https://link.springer.com/bookseries/7899

Constantine Stephanidis · Margherita Antona ·
Stavroula Ntoa · Gavriel Salvendy (Eds.)

HCI International 2022 – Late Breaking Posters

24th International Conference on Human-Computer Interaction
HCII 2022, Virtual Event, June 26 – July 1, 2022
Proceedings, Part I

Editors
Constantine Stephanidis
University of Crete and Foundation for
Research and Technology – Hellas (FORTH)
Heraklion, Crete, Greece

Margherita Antona
Foundation for Research and Technology
Hellas (FORTH)
Heraklion, Crete, Greece

Stavroula Ntoa
Foundation for Research and Technology
Hellas (FORTH)
Heraklion, Crete, Greece

Gavriel Salvendy
University of Central Florida
Orlando, FL, USA

ISSN 1865-0929 ISSN 1865-0937 (electronic)
Communications in Computer and Information Science
ISBN 978-3-031-19678-2 ISBN 978-3-031-19679-9 (eBook)
https://doi.org/10.1007/978-3-031-19679-9

This Springer imprint is published by the registered company Springer Nature Switzerland AG
The registered company address is: Gewerbestrasse 11, 6330 Cham, Switzerland

Foreword

Human-computer interaction (HCI) is acquiring an ever-increasing scientific and industrial importance, as well as having more impact on people's everyday life, as an ever-growing number of human activities are progressively moving from the physical to the digital world. This process, which has been ongoing for some time now, has been dramatically accelerated by the COVID-19 pandemic. The HCI International (HCII) conference series, held yearly, aims to respond to the compelling need to advance the exchange of knowledge and research and development efforts on the human aspects of design and use of computing systems.

The 24th International Conference on Human-Computer Interaction, HCI International 2022 (HCII 2022), was planned to be held at the Gothia Towers Hotel and Swedish Exhibition & Congress Centre, Göteborg, Sweden, during June 26 to July 1, 2022. Due to the COVID-19 pandemic and with everyone's health and safety in mind, HCII 2022 was organized and run as a virtual conference. It incorporated the 21 thematic areas and affiliated conferences listed on the following page.

A total of 5583 individuals from academia, research institutes, industry, and governmental agencies from 88 countries submitted contributions, and 1276 papers and 275 posters were included in the proceedings that were published just before the start of the conference. Additionally, 296 papers and 181 posters are included in the volumes of the proceedings published after the conference, as "Late Breaking Work". The contributions thoroughly cover the entire field of human-computer interaction, addressing major advances in knowledge and effective use of computers in a variety of application areas. These papers provide academics, researchers, engineers, scientists, practitioners, and students with state-of-the-art information on the most recent advances in HCI. The volumes constituting the full set of the HCII 2022 conference proceedings are listed in the following pages.

I would like to thank the Program Board Chairs and the members of the Program Boards of all thematic areas and affiliated conferences for their contribution and support towards the highest scientific quality and overall success of the HCI International 2022 conference; they have helped in so many ways, including session organization, paper reviewing (single-blind review process, with a minimum of two reviews per submission) and, more generally, acting as good-will ambassadors for the HCII conference.

This conference would not have been possible without the continuous and unwavering support and advice of Gavriel Salvendy, Founder, General Chair Emeritus, and Scientific Advisor. For his outstanding efforts, I would like to express my appreciation to Abbas Moallem, Communications Chair and Editor of HCI International News.

July 2022   Constantine Stephanidis

HCI International 2022 Thematic Areas and Affiliated Conferences

Thematic Areas

- HCI: Human-Computer Interaction
- HIMI: Human Interface and the Management of Information

Affiliated Conferences

- EPCE: 19th International Conference on Engineering Psychology and Cognitive Ergonomics
- AC: 16th International Conference on Augmented Cognition
- UAHCI: 16th International Conference on Universal Access in Human-Computer Interaction
- CCD: 14th International Conference on Cross-Cultural Design
- SCSM: 14th International Conference on Social Computing and Social Media
- VAMR: 14th International Conference on Virtual, Augmented and Mixed Reality
- DHM: 13th International Conference on Digital Human Modeling and Applications in Health, Safety, Ergonomics and Risk Management
- DUXU: 11th International Conference on Design, User Experience and Usability
- C&C: 10th International Conference on Culture and Computing
- DAPI: 10th International Conference on Distributed, Ambient and Pervasive Interactions
- HCIBGO: 9th International Conference on HCI in Business, Government and Organizations
- LCT: 9th International Conference on Learning and Collaboration Technologies
- ITAP: 8th International Conference on Human Aspects of IT for the Aged Population
- AIS: 4th International Conference on Adaptive Instructional Systems
- HCI-CPT: 4th International Conference on HCI for Cybersecurity, Privacy and Trust
- HCI-Games: 4th International Conference on HCI in Games
- MobiTAS: 4th International Conference on HCI in Mobility, Transport and Automotive Systems
- AI-HCI: 3rd International Conference on Artificial Intelligence in HCI
- MOBILE: 3rd International Conference on Design, Operation and Evaluation of Mobile Communications

Conference Proceedings – Full List of Volumes

http://2022.hci.international/proceedings

24th International Conference on Human-Computer Interaction (HCII 2022)

The full list with the Program Board Chairs and the members of the Program Boards of all thematic areas and affiliated conferences is available online at:

http://www.hci.international/board-members-2022.php

HCI International 2023

The 25th International Conference on Human-Computer Interaction, HCI International 2023, will be held jointly with the affiliated conferences at the AC Bella Sky Hotel and Bella Center, Copenhagen, Denmark, 23–28 July 2023. It will cover a broad spectrum of themes related to human-computer interaction, including theoretical issues, methods, tools, processes, and case studies in HCI design, as well as novel interaction techniques, interfaces, and applications. The proceedings will be published by Springer. More information will be available on the conference website: http://2023.hci.international/.

General Chair
Constantine Stephanidis
University of Crete and ICS-FORTH
Heraklion, Crete, Greece
Email: general_chair@hcii2023.org

http://2023.hci.international/

Contents – Part I

Accessibility, Usability, and UX Design

HCI Research and Design Across Cultures

Cultural Heritage Experience Design

HCI for Health and Wellbeing

Virtual, Augmented, and Mixed Reality

Design Case Studies

Contents – Part II

Interactive Technologies for Learning

Digital Transformation in Business, Government, and Organizations

Automated Driving and Urban Mobility

Robots, Agents, and Intelligent Environments

AI in HCI: Methods, Applications, and Studies

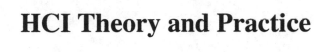

HCI Theory and Practice

Can Eye Tracking with Pervasive Webcams Replace Dedicated Eye Trackers? an Experimental Comparison of Eye-Tracking Performance

Parviz Asghari[1]([✉]) [iD], Maike Schindler[1] [iD], and Achim J. Lilienthal[2] [iD]

[1] University of Cologne, DE-50923 Cologne, Germany
{parviz.asghari,maike.schindler}@uni-koeln.de
[2] Örebro University, SE-701 82 Örebro, Sweden
achim.lilienthal@oru.se

Abstract. Eye tracking (ET) is increasingly used in cognitive science and human-computer interaction research. Currently, however, expensive ET devices are required, which limits their pervasive application, for example, as a tool for digital learning. The emergence of low-cost Artificial Intelligence (AI)-based consumer-grade webcam eye tracking, partially already available as open-source software, promises to change this situation. It is currently unclear (1) what performance in terms of, e.g., tracking accuracy, calibration stability and real time sampling rate stability can be achieved with webcam ET (wcET) in comparison to using expensive dedicated hardware eye tracking (dhET); and (2) how the expected performance degradation affects ET-based applications. In this work, we address the first question and present a wcET system, which we developed based on open source code and publicly available data sets. We ran this system with a consumer-grade Logitech BRIO Ultra HD Pro webcam that provides a stream of HD images 60 Hz simultaneously to a commercial remote eye tracker, the Tobii Pro X3-120, which delivers tracked gaze points at a rate of 120 Hz. Based on recordings of 20 participants (age: 27.0±4.5 years), we assessed the data quality in terms of accuracy, precision, and sampling rate stability. The observed performance of the wcET system (accuracy: $2.5° ± 0.7°$, precision: $0.3° ± 0.3°$) is, as expected, worse than the performance of the dhET system (accuracy: $0.9° ± 0.9°$, precision: $0.7° ± 0.8°$), which it is sufficient for many applications, especially if the stimulus can be designed and adapted to the gaze tracking quality correspondingly. Running the wcET system in real-time, we obtained a sampling rate of 26.3±1.03 Hz, i.e., nearly the frequency with which the camera provides images.

Keywords: Eye tracking · Webcam eye tracking · Eye-tracking hardware · Performance evaluation

This project has received funding by the Federal Ministry of Education and Research a part of the program KI-ALF [01NV2123]. The responsibility for the content of this publication remains with the authors.

C. Stephanidis et al. (Eds.): HCII 2022, CCIS 1654, pp. 3–10, 2022.
https://doi.org/10.1007/978-3-031-19679-9_1

1   Introduction

Eye tracking (ET) is frequently used, for example, in behavioral research and human-computer interaction. Eye movement patterns can reveal detailed information about the user's cognitive processes, their attention level, or decision-making processes [3,12]. Applications and research based on ET require reliable and robust data [9]. Traditionally, this requires dedicated hardware with high-resolution cameras and infrared illumination to detect corneal reflections [7]. However, dedicated hardware is expensive and thus limits the pervasive use in real-world applications. This situation may change since, propelled by recent advances in deep learning, appearance-based gaze estimation methods that deliver promising results based on low-cost consumer-grade camera inputs start to emerge [2,10,11,21]. These approaches learn to estimate gazes from a video stream based on large-scale data sets and provide 3D gaze vectors or corresponding 2D gaze locations on a screen. Furthermore, they do not require any specific external devices and can be used with standalone computers, laptop built-in webcams, or mobile device consumer-grade cameras. This opens up the possibility of developing affordable automated intelligent ET solutions for research, commerce, and the general public. On the way to realize this ambition, webcam ET (wcET) has to address several challenges including gaze estimation accuracy, gaze estimator prediction time, and that gaze estimation quality can be affected by user movements [11]. This paper aims to contribute to the first step toward utilizing wcET as a low-cost pervasive technology by validating the data quality of a state-of-the-art wcET approach in comparison to the performance of an established, commercially available dedicated eye tracking (dhET) system. Accordingly, we address the following research question in our work: How does the gaze estimates of wcET differ from dhET in practical settings regarding accuracy, precision, and sampling rate? We will further discuss how the limitations of the data quality may affect the performance of wcET applications.

There are previous works that have compared wcET with dhET using commercial eye trackers. Robal et al. [15] use the agreement between the number of gaze detections with wcET and dhET on a screen as a measure to evaluate attention tracking performance. Although this metric might be useful for specific applications, application-agnostic metrics are more desirable. Xu et al. [18] proposed a method that trains a gaze estimator from participant data and then evaluates the estimated gaze direction. However in this study, the participants used a chin rest, which positively affects the wcET data quality (since it limits head movements) and is therefore not fully representative of real-world application scenarios. Zhang et al. [20] used pre-recorded videos to evaluate the performance that can be achieved offline with a wcET approach. In comparison to [20], the focus of our research is on the gaze tracking rate as a crucial parameter for ET applications that respond to gaze patterns online. We have developed an AI-based wcET system based on available software, trained on publicly available data sets, and investigate its data reliability in terms of accuracy, precision, and sampling rate stability in comparison to a popular remote (screen-based) commercial eye tracker [17]. We used both systems simultaneously with 20 participants in a semi-controlled, practical educational setup.

- We evaluate wcET data quality in a practical, realistic setting in terms of accuracy, precision, and sampling rate.
- We propose a modular eye tracking framework that can be used with various gaze estimation and calibration techniques.

2   Related Work

The first video-based eye-tracking study was conducted in the 1940s s to analyze pilot behavior [4]. Not least because of increasing computing power, real-time eye trackers became available in the 1990s. Baluja et al. [1] proposed an artificial neural network-based appearance-based eye tracker for non-intrusive gaze tracking in 1993, for example. Eye trackers differ among others along two dimensions: the imaging device and the gaze estimation method used. Accordingly, we will discuss various imaging devices and gaze estimation techniques below, followed by common ET applications and their requirements.

Imaging Devices. Various imaging devices such as RGB [13], RGBD [14], and IR cameras are used for ET. RGBD cameras use extra depth information ("D") to predict the gaze direction based on RGB images. The corneal reflection technique can be used with IR cameras to predict the gaze direction. Besides that, a variety of setups such as multiple cameras, different camera positions (near-eye, around the screen, on glasses), as well as active and passive light are used [7]. Most of works attempt to use a single RGB camera that is compatible with cameras integrated into laptops and mobile devices.

Gaze Estimation. The computation of the direction in 3D space or the area on a 2D screen the foveal area of the eye is directed to is known as gaze estimation. Gaze estimation techniques can be divided into three major groups: feature-based, model-based, and appearance-based. Feature-based methods extract eye region features such as eye corners and other eye landmarks to predict the gaze direction. In model-based approaches, gaze direction is determined using a 3D model of the eyeball and geometry calculations. These methods usually need a high-resolution image of the eye region to reach satisfactory results. Appearance-based models, try to find a mapping function between raw image input and gaze [7]. With progress in AI, appearance-based gaze estimation reached promising results with low-resolution camera inputs [12]. This has kick-started the use of low-resolution single RGB cameras also in ET research [8]. One of the interesting data sets to test these methods' performance is MPIIGaze [21], which has been captured with regular web cameras without restrictions of head movements and under naturally occurring different light conditions. Appearance-based methods can reach an accuracy of around 4° on this data set, which is promising for some real-world applications of ET.

Applications of Webcam-Based Eye Tracking. Several wcET studies have recently been conducted in fields such as marketing [19], code development [16], and digital learning [15]. Yang et al. [19] conducted an online study with the Web-Gazer eye tracker to examine customer decision-making behavior. Thilderkvist and Dobslaw [16] used ET for visual processing of source code. They note that applications such as text reading with small AOIs (Areas of Interest), require more accurate gaze tracking. Another important point is temporal stability [5, 16], i.e. that gaze estimates are delivered at an approximately constant rate.

Calibration. All gaze estimation methods need to determine a set of parameters through calibration. For 3D gaze-vector prediction some works use model-based ET to reduce calibration requirements. However, estimating the gaze point within the 2D coordinate system of a screen in front of the subject requires a second calibration layer (screen calibration) for each participant [7]. Traditional models use geometry calibration to map the gaze to a point on the screen. Also, some machine learning-based methods try to learn a regression function to calibrate the system. Gudi et al. [6] propose a hybrid approach that uses machine learning to learn geometry calibration parameters.

3   Webcam Eye Tracking and Evaluation Method

System Design. The wcET system that we propose has three distinct blocks, see Fig. 1. First, the participant's image is captured by the webcam. This is done through Logitech Brio 60 Hz webcam as imaging device. Second, a deep learning appearance-based gaze estimation model. Then, the gaze model uses the pre-processed and normalized raw image to estimate a 3D gaze vector. We use resnet 18 trained on the MPIIgaze data set. Finally, based on the participants' calibration, the 3D gaze vector is mapped to a 2D point on the screen. To this end, we use a modified version of the hybrid screen calibration technique discussed in [6].

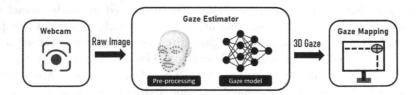

Fig. 1. Proposed Webcam-based ET method.

Participants. Our study included 20 adults (gender: 10 men, 10 women - age: 27.0 ± 4.5 years). One of the participants wore glasses during the trial, and none wore make-up.

Calibration/Validation (wcET). For the initial calibration and the subsequent validation, we asked the participants to move the mouse to calibration points shown on the screen. In this way we realized a fast calibration method and made sure that the participants fixated the points. For each calibration point, first, a red circle with 30 pixels radius was displayed around the central calibration point on the black screen. As soon as the users hovered over the circle with the mouse, we assumed that they looked at the circle; and the system recorded the related gazes. We did this for six different calibration points twice in order to obtain a stable calibration. Then we validated the calibration result with nine points and the same procedure. Six of these nine points were the same points as in calibration, and three additional points were chosen.

Eye Tracker, Computer, and Screen (dhET). For comparison to wcET, we used the Tobii Pro x3-120 screen-based (IR) eye-tracker 120 Hz sampling rate. The experiment was run on a desktop computer (Intel Core i7-11700k @ 3.60 GHz, 32 GB RAM, Windows 11) and the task stimuli were presented on a screen (53 x 30 cm, 60 Hz refresh rate, 1920 × 1080 pixels).

Experiment. We used two screens to run both ET systems at the same time, one screen for controlling both systems and the other for displaying tasks. We first launched the Tobii eye-tracker, followed by the wcET system after the calibration/validation phase, see Fig. 1. We used the calibration start point timestamp and the start time of dhET as a general offset between the two systems, since both were measured to the global clock.

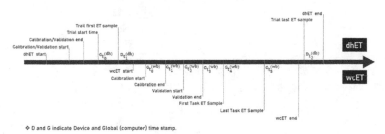

Fig. 2. Experiments' timeline, indicating the timestamps used for data synchronization.

4   Results

Precision. For wcET we found a precision of $0.3° \pm 0.3°$ and for dhET a precision of $0.7° \pm 0.8°$. In terms of precision wcET can be comparable to dhET. This could be partially caused by the lower frame rate of wcET.

Accuracy. For the dhET we observed an accuracy of $0.9° \pm 0.9°$. The wcET accuracy was $2.5° \pm 0.7°$. Although the accuracy we observed for our wcET system may not be sufficient for applications such as text reading or route map scanning where the given stimulus requires a high accuracy, it can be sufficient for a variety of applications where the stimulus or tasks can be designed, including for example decision-making research or digital learning applications (Fig. 3). As Fig. 4 shows the accuracy for all participants in our study. Despite some outliers, dhET had overall a higher accuracy than wcET. One key reason is likely that dhET is more robust to head movements in comparison with wcET.

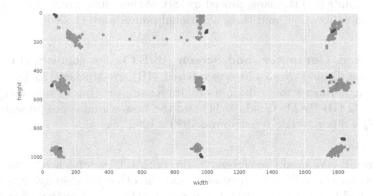

Fig. 3. Validation of gaze estimation with 9 points for one participant. Ground truth (green dots), dhET (red dots), and wcET (blue dots). (Best viewed in the electronic version of this paper in colour.)

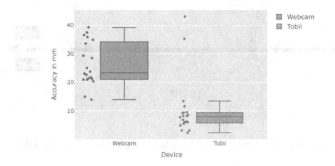

Fig. 4. Participants accuracy distribution in mm.

Sampling Rate Stability. Another important aspect for real-world applications is that gaze estimates should be delivered with a stable sampling rate during interaction with the system. Therefore, we computed the gaze sampling frequency during the experiments. We calculated the average sampling frequency over intervals with 30 samples. For wcET we measured an average sampling rate of 26.3 Hz, which shows that the proposed wcET system is fast enough on a standard laptop for webcams with frame rate 30 Hz. For dhET we measured an average sampling rate 107 Hz considering just valid samples (the sampling rate for all samples 120 Hz), see Table 1. wcET STD is 1.03 Hz which is comparable with dhET (0.2 Hz). This indicates wcET sampling rate is stable enough for tracking eye movements.

Table 1. Mean and STD sampling rate (Hz).

Device/Sampling rate	Mean	STD
wcET	26.3	1.03
dhET valid samples	107.3	18.22
dhET all samples	120	0.2

5   Discussion and Future Work

In future work we plan to evaluate wcET holistically as part of AI systems. We expect that wcET can be sufficient for supervised or unsupervised machine learning dependent on stimulus and data representation. This opens up the possibility for applications in a wide range from research to commercial systems. For some applications, especially when the stimulus cannot be adopted accordingly, the accuracy of wcET may be still too low, however. Another currently limiting factor is the much lower sampling rate compared to dhET. To address this issue, future work may also look into the development of fixation detection algorithms that work with low frame rate input.

References

1. Baluja, S., Pomerleau, D.: Non-intrusive gaze tracking using artificial neural networks. In: Proceedings of the 6th International Conference on Neural Information Processing Systems, NIPS 1993, pp. 753–760. Morgan Kaufmann Publishers Inc., San Francisco, CA, USA (1993). https://doi.org/10.5555/2987189.2987284
2. Cheng, Y., Wang, H., Bao, Y., Lu, F.: Appearance-based gaze estimation with deep learning: A review and benchmark (2021). https://doi.org/10.48550/ARXIV.2104.12668
3. Duchowski, A.T.: A breadth-first survey of eye-tracking applications. Behav. Res. Methods Instrum. Comput. **34**(4), 455–470 (2002)
4. Fitts, P.M., Jones, R.E., Milton, J.L.: Eye movements of aircraft pilots during instrument-landing approaches. Aeronaut. Eng. Rev. **9**(2), 1–6 (1950)
5. Gómez-Poveda, J., Gaudioso, E.: Evaluation of temporal stability of eye tracking algorithms using webcams. Expert Syst. Appl. **64**, 69–83 (2016)
6. Gudi, A., Li, X., van Gemert, J.: Efficiency in real-time webcam gaze tracking. In: Bartoli, A., Fusiello, A. (eds.) ECCV 2020. LNCS, vol. 12535, pp. 529–543. Springer, Cham (2020). https://doi.org/10.1007/978-3-030-66415-2_34
7. Hansen, D.W., Ji, Q.: In the eye of the beholder: A survey of models for eyes and gaze. IEEE Trans. Pattern Anal. Mach. Intell. **32**(3), 478–500 (2010)

8. He, J., et al.: On-device few-shot personalization for real-time gaze estimation. In: 2019 IEEE/CVF International Conference on Computer Vision Workshop (ICCVW), Seoul, Korea (South) , pp. 1149–1158. (2019). https://doi.org/10.1109/ICCVW.2019.00146

9. Holmqvist, K., Nyström, M., Mulvey, F.: Eye tracker data quality: What it is and how to measure it. In: Proceedings of the Symposium on Eye Tracking Research and Applications, . ETRA 2012, pp. 45–52. Association for Computing Machinery, New York (2012). https://doi.org/10.1145/2168556.2168563

10. Kar, A., Corcoran, P.: A review and analysis of eye-gaze estimation systems, algorithms and performance evaluation methods in consumer platforms. IEEE Access **5**, 16495–16519 (2017)

11. Krafka, K., et al.: Eye tracking for everyone. In: Proceedings of the IEEE Conference on Computer Vision and Pattern Recognition (CVPR), Las Vegas, pp. 2176–2184 (2016). https://doi.org/10.1109/CVPR.2016.239

12. Li, Y., Kumar, R., Lasecki, W.S., Hilliges, O.: Artificial intelligence for hci: A modern approach. In: CHI EA 2020, pp. 1–8. Association for Computing Machinery, Honolulu (2020). https://doi.org/10.1145/3334480.3375147

13. Lian, D., et al.: Multiview multitask gaze estimation with deep convolutional neural networks. IEEE Trans. Neural Netw. Learn. Syst. **30**(10), 3010–3023 (2019)

14. Lian, D., et al.: Rgbd based gaze estimation via multi-task cnn. In: Proceedings of the AAAI Conference on Artificial Intelligence, vol. 33(01), pp. 2488–2495 (2019)

15. Robal, T., Zhao, Y., Lofi, C., Hauff, C.: Webcam-based attention tracking in online learning: A feasibility study. In: 23rd International Conference on Intelligent User Interfaces, IUI 2018, pp. 189–197. Association for Computing Machinery, Tokyo (2018). https://doi.org/10.1145/3172944.3172987

16. Thilderkvist, E., Dobslaw, F.: On current limitations of online eye-tracking to study the visual processing of source code. Available at SSRN 4051688. https://doi.org/10.2139/ssrn.4051688

17. Tobii: Tobii pro x3–120 eye tracker. computer hardware (2017). http://www.tobiipro.com/

18. Xu, P., Ehinger, K.A., Zhang, Y., Finkelstein, A., Kulkarni, S.R., Xiao, J.: Turkergaze: Crowdsourcing saliency with webcam based eye tracking (2015). https://doi.org/10.48550/ARXIV.1504.06755

19. Yang, X., Krajbich, I.: Webcam-based online eye-tracking for behavioral research. Judgm. Decis. Mak. **16**(6), 1485–1505 (2021)

20. Zhang, X., Sugano, Y., Bulling, A.: Evaluation of appearance-based methods and implications for gaze-based applications. In: Proceedings of the 2019 CHI Conference on Human Factors in Computing Systems, pp. 1–13. Association for Computing Machinery, Glasgow (2019). https://doi.org/10.1145/3290605.3300646

21. Zhang, X., Sugano, Y., Fritz, M., Bulling, A.: Mpiigaze: Real-world dataset and deep appearance-based gaze estimation. IEEE Trans. Pattern Anal. Mach. Intell. **41**(1), 162–175 (2019)

The Orientation to Physicality and Physical Objects in the Digitalized World

Selva Özkal$^{(\boxtimes)}$ ⓘ and AdviyeAyça Ünlüer ⓘ

Yildiz Technical University, 34220 Istanbul, Turkey
`selva.ozkal@std.yildiz.edu.tr`

Abstract. Despite the advanced possibilities of our age, people may show a tendency towards product production, usage techniques and communication techniques that are far from all necessities, whether nostalgic or not. There are still common unnecessary interactions such as pen pals and lighting candles. People form an emotional bond with such issues. In addition, there are technological tools such as VR and Metaverse that directly transfer the real environment to the virtual environment. The fact that technology, which provides opportunities for the individual in every way, does not make people forget the old methods is a situation worth discussing. This situation is a situation in which the person establishes an emotional connection in the psychological, sociological and biological context and has taken place in design as an area of emotional design. It is an issue that can be examined in more than one subject such as personal preferences, globalization, art, design, experience design, fashion, industrialization and culture. In addition, the following questions remain relevant: How much more can our mental model adapt to the digital world? Are we ergonomically prone to this? Digitization increases freedom, but does it increase originality and productivity? Does digitalization in communication connect or divide us? In this study, it is desired to examine the orientation to physicality and physical objects in the digitalized world. The issue of usability of digital and analog techniques in art and design can also be included in the study.

Keywords: Analog world · Virtual world · Digitalization

1 Physical and Virtual Environments

1.1 Comparison of Analog and Digital

According to Hayashi mental models are known to have a powerful impact upon one's personality and intercultural communication style (Ono 2018). Although the concept of analog and digital is usually used in the field of technology, these terms can also be used to describe an individual's way of perception. Hayashi mentions that the operating mode of analog is feeling and that of digital is thinking (Fig. 1) (Ono 2018).

C. Stephanidis et al. (Eds.): HCII 2022, CCIS 1654, pp. 11–16, 2022.
https://doi.org/10.1007/978-3-031-19679-9_2

What is Analog? What is Digital?

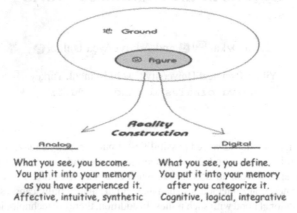

Fig. 1. Inroduction to analog and digital perception and communication.

When we make a comparison from the point of view of the user, we come across the following distinction:

Analog: Robustness - Limited possibilities, Limited options - Low user experience - There is a possibility of wastage of raw materials.

Digital: Sensitivity - Many possibilities, Many options - High user experience - Looking at the screen for a long time and using limited motor skills can turn into a tiring experience.

So, digitization increases freedom, but does it increase originality and productivity? In a 1995 study, Sheena Iyengar a professor of business at Colombia University and author of "The Art of Choosing" raised the hypothesis that people might find more and more choices to actually be debilitating. Iyengar and her research assistants set up a booth with samples of jam. Every few hours, they have switched from offering a sample selection of 24 jams to only 6 jams. 30% of customers who stopped at the small selection of jams, decided to buy one, while only 3% of those who stopped at the booth containing 24 jams, decided to buy one (Iyengar and Lepper 2000) (Fig. 2). As a result, the fact that there are many options in the digital environment can bring indecision and loss of time in some cases. Also, accessibility options have increased with digitalization as a communication tool too. This brings to mind the question of whether digitalization in communication unites or separates people.

Analogue vs digital comparison is basically based on experience. An experience is the intersection of emotion and context. Experience is what happened, and how it made us feel (Uwa 2021). When we compare the experience with simply digital and analog note-taking techniques, we come across the following research: Pam Mueller's research, which tested how hand-held note-taking affects learning compared to computer-based notes, concluded: "When people take notes by hand, they tend to write down as much as possible what they have learned. In our studies, students who took long-form notes were more successful. Thinking speed was higher than writing speed. Students who took

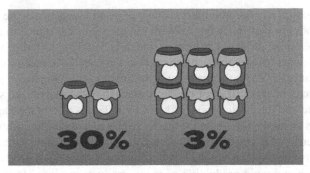

Fig. 2. The visualization of research result at The 10 Biggest Time Wasters - Are You Guilty? Video by Psych2Go.

notes because of the high number of students processed the learned material more in their brains, which caused the two groups to get different results in the same exams" (Mueller and Oppenheimer 2014). Another example of the studies on the subject is the report published by South Texas College of Law professor Kevin Yamamoto in the Journal of Legal Education on the prohibition of laptop computer use during class in 2007. Yamamoto's research shows that students who take notes by hand can follow the lessons more easily and learn more (Yamamoto 2007). Necati Inceoglu, the author of Sketches, Thinking by Drawing, Drawing by Thinking, said the following about the sketching technique: "Sketches are mostly linear speech of the person making it to himself/herself. A speech whose words and words are lines. Thinking by drawing, like thinking by humming. It is important for design students to acquire this habit. This linear humming gives them the opportunity to research different things, not just the first thing that comes to their mind" (Inceoglu 2012).

2   Survey Method and Data

AN average of 600 people participated in the online survey, dated December 2020, in order to measure the interest in the analog-digital distinction and the situations associated with the sense of touch in the society. The average gender, age and location information of the participants are as follows;

% 74 Woman %26 Male
%28 18−24 years old
%42 25−34 years old
%17 35−44 years old
Location: Turkey

The aims of the questions asked are as follows; 'How do you prefer to take your notes?' With the question, it was desired to reach a general opinion by reaching the data of how the participants took their notes in daily life. Digital drawing or traditional drawing closer to you? With the question, it was aimed to reach the information about which participants prefer because their average age and interests may be related to art. PDF (digital book) or paperback book? With the question, it is aimed to reach the data of the usage preference of the PDF format, which is widely used today, which is more convenient and easier to carry than a normal book. Do you like to receive a letter with an envelope or a message? With the question, it is aimed to learn the usage preferences of the letter system, which is still emotionally connected with the message system, which is easier to write and reach. So, do you like to write letters or text messages? With the question, it was desired to test how the participant understood the difference between liking and preferring. Do you believe that handmade works are more valuable? With the question, it was aimed to measure the level of interest in handmade products as a result of the fabrication and rapid production of many products produced today. There are 2 postcards in the same shapes, one is handmade and the other is digital print. Both are affordable and you like it very much. Would you rather buy it even if the handmade one is more expensive than the other? With the question, it was desired to learn how much your interest in handmade products is preferred compared to digital in financial terms. Do you enjoy unpacking something new? With the question, it is aimed to process the interest in the moment of 'accommodating' the product between a new product acquired in the virtual environment and a product acquired in the real environment. Finally, do you think that although digitalization makes our lives easier, interacting with things by "touching" does not lose its importance? With the question, the subject, which is the main target of the research, was directed directly to the participant.

As a result of the survey, the following data were obtained:

How do you prefer to take your notes? The number of people who answered the question as 'Notebook' was 508, and the number of people who answered 'Digital' was 73. The percentage rate is 87% 'Booked' and 13% 'Digital'.

Digital drawing or traditional drawing closer to you? The number of people who answered the question as 'Traditional' is 442, and the number of people who answered as 'Digital' is 116. The percentage rate is 79% 'Traditional' and 21% 'Digital'.

PDF (digital book) or paperback book? The number of people who answered the question 'Paperback' was 551, and the number of people who answered 'PDF' was 64. The percentage rate is 90% 'Paperback', 10% 'PDF'.

Do you like to receive a letter with an envelope or a message? The number of people who answered the question as 'Letter' is 477, and the number of people who answered as 'Message' is 127. The percentage rate is 79% 'Letter', 21% 'Message'.

So, do you like to write letters or text messages? The number of people who answered the question as 'Letter' is 344, and the number of people who answered as 'Message' is 245. The percentage rate is 58% 'Letter', 42% 'Message'.

Do you believe that handmade works are more valuable? The number of people who answered the question "Yes" is 585, and the number of people who answered 'No' is 19. The percentage rate is 97% 'Yes' and 3% 'No'.

There are 2 postcards in the same shapes, one is handmade and the other is digital print. Both are affordable and you like it very much. Would you rather buy it even if the handmade one is more expensive than the other? The number of people who answered the question 'Yes' is 452, and the number of people who answered 'No' is 107. The percentage rate is 81% 'Yes' and 19% 'No'.

Do you enjoy unpacking something new? The number of people who answered the question "Yes" was 597, and the number of people who answered 'No' was 20. The percentage rate is 97% 'Yes' and 3% 'No'.

Although digitalization makes our lives easier, do you think that interacting with things by "touching" does not lose its importance? The number of people who answered the question 'Yes' was 444, and the number of people who answered 'No' was 106. The percentage rate is 81% 'Yes' and 19% 'No'.

In addition, an empty space was left for the participants to report the reasons for their answers and their views on the subject. The answers given in this area were generally about the feelings about the importance of touch and that digitalization cannot change this. In the written feedback given at the end of the survey, the following opinions come to the fore; opinions on the fact that things have their own energy, the importance of tactile memory, the negative impact of digital life on the act of touching, the relationship between touching and feeling, the importance of feeling, the problem of not being able to provide the pleasure of the sense of touch in the digital environment, the excitement of correspondence, the touch as a language/being seen as a form of communication, seeing digital techniques as the easy way, art being related to the technique (like touching the pen), the perception that digital environments make life difficult even though it seems to make life easier, the belief that something cannot be fully grasped without a sense of touch, the senses work in an integrated way, touch Activating the area in the brain that allows feeling and causing the amygdala to work with a more intense/longer hormone release, the tactile technique provides a experience with the material, the idea that touching gives a therapeutic feeling, the fact that touch is a tangible connection, the view that digitalization is at the center of our lives, the digital environment is preferred because of its practicality, but the traditional is preferred in the same way, the tendency to not want some items to remain in the past even if they are old, the feeling of living life in interaction with touch the feeling of being watched in digital interaction, the thought that more meaning is attached to the touched object, the view that longing for the past is in human nature, the idea that vision comes second after the ability to touch, the fact that the textures on the real floor are not available in the digital environment, The Z generation can study with PDF format on the differences between Z and Y generations, but the Y generation cannot study without printing the page, the fact that there is no real substance in the digital environment and therefore energy cannot be mentioned, a designer's drawings made on the computer do not replace the real model, during the pandemic period The problem of not being able to meet the need for touch, the work done by touching and putting effort gives a feeling of satisfaction, the work done by touching increases the focus, the gifts that can be given in the real environment are preferred, while traditional environments are preferred in terms of 'pure art', the digital environment is preferred for design, the practical and emotional negative aspects of increasing the accessibility of the digital environment, the fact that other sensory environments such as smell are activated in the real environment, the thought that social media addiction distances people from the real world, the prevalence of applications similar to analog techniques (For example, camera applications that give similar results to 35 mm cameras), the idea that people who use second-hand goods interact indirectly with the previous owners of the goods, packaging of all products in city life and taking them away from nature, body language tending to touch as a sign of love. In addition to all these answers, there were also participants who defended the digital environment.

Solution Examples. As it is known, with the new age, the interaction of the children born in that age is different from the previous generation. Each generation is more exposed to the digital world than the previous one, and its interaction with analog products and nature is decreasing. In addition, with the digitalization of work areas for adults, it is now difficult to take an active part off the screen. Motor skills need to be used for physical health. At the same time, techniques to increase creativity give more efficient results when done with analog techniques. As a solution to these issues, combining the opportunities offered by the digital world with analog and physical techniques can contribute to increasing motor skills (Fig. 3).

Fig. 3. Physically distributed ambient storytelling, BloodBank and DarkLight, University of Geneva, Faculty of Art and Design, Department of Media Design graduate students, 2017

References

Ono, K.: Analog and digital intercultural perception the cultural impact on pedagogical decisions of foreign teachers in Japan. Matsuyama University, Studies in Language and Literature, vol. 38, no. 1-1 (2018)

Iyengar, S.S., Lepper, M.R.: When choice is demotivating: can one desire too much of a good thing? J. Pers. Soc. Psychol. **796**, 995–1006 (2000)

The 10 Biggest Time Wasters Are You Guilty? Psych2Go. https://youtu.be/n6ZefKSyYuI. Accessed 18 Mar 2022

Uwa, R.: V' R' Storytellers - designing experiences: considerations for analog and virtual worlds. https://youtu.be/MdBV1wNsBIw. Accessed 18 Mar 2022

Mueller, P.A., Oppenheimer, D.M.: The pen is mightier than the keyboard: advantages of longhand over laptop note taking. Psychol. Sci. **25**, 1159–1168 (2014)

Yamamoto, K.: Banning laptops in the classroom: is it worth the hassles? J. Legal Educ. **57**(4), 477–520 (2007)

Inceoglu, N.: Sketches, Thinking by Drawing, Drawing by Thinking. 2nd edn. YEM, Istanbul (2012)

University of Geneva, Faculty of Art and Design, Department of Media Design graduate students, BloodBank and DarkLight, Physically distributed ambient storytelling project (2017)

Extended, Distributed, and Predictive: Sketches of a Generative Theory of Interaction for HCI

Jacob T. Browne[1,2]([✉]) [iD] and Ignacio Garnham[3]

[1] Philips Experience Design, Eindhoven, The Netherlands
jacob.browne@philips.com
[2] Delft University of Technology, Delft, The Netherlands
[3] Aarhus University, Aarhus, Denmark
igarnham@cc.au.dk

Abstract. This paper blends work in extended mind, distributed cognition, and predictive processing to provide a novel generative theory of interaction. This dovetailing offers an emerging picture of cognition that HCI stands to benefit from: our cognition is extended, distributed, and constantly trying to predict incoming sensory stimuli across social, cultural, and temporal scales. We develop a sketch of a generative theory of interaction for HCI and offer some directions for future work.

Keywords: Extended mind · Predictive processing · Distributed cognition · HCI · Artificial Intelligence · Generative theory of interaction

1 Introduction

HCI has a long history of borrowing concepts from other sciences to guide HCI research. In a synthesis of the histories of HCI Theory, Rogers traces different theories that have come to fruition over the classical, modern, and contemporary stages of HCI [31]. Rogers reflects that importing and building on theories is crucial to HCI: that creating a transdisciplinary agenda will further our impact on society [31].

As our technologies become more complex, it becomes more apparent that the boundaries between mind and technology are blurring. This has spiked concerns in HCI around how to design for and study these complex technologies [12]. Human-centered design and contemporary models in HCI are rendered incompetent to deal with these questions regarding ontological uncertainty: we're struggling to keep up with what is being empirically observed [12]. Frauenberger puts it nicely, "HCI may not yet be in a state of serious crisis, but it is certainly cracking and squealing, struggling to make sense of computers, humans and interfaces in the face of rapid technological progress, coupled with profound social change" [12]. Theoretical and empirical work in predictive processing, extended mind, and distributed cognition similarly point in this direction.

In this paper, we will outline the basics of extended mind, distributed cognition, and predictive processing. A blending of these theories is presented. Then, we will offer some preliminary theoretical implications for HCI, offering an early form of a generative

C. Stephanidis et al. (Eds.): HCII 2022, CCIS 1654, pp. 17–24, 2022.
https://doi.org/10.1007/978-3-031-19679-9_3

theory of interaction [1]. This paper makes two contributions: a rendering of a developing picture of cognition for HCI and a direction for a new generative theory of interaction.

2 Extended Mind, Distributed Cognition, and Predictive Processing

This section will present a brief sketch of each body of work. The intent is not to serve as an all-encompassing review or to argue for specific flavors of each respective body of work. Instead, we aim to present what might be most crucial to understand for HCI researchers for each body of work.

2.1 Extended Mind

The extended mind thesis (EMT) maintains that, under certain conditions, cognitive states and processes can be distributed across brain, body, and world [7]. This means that, should an artifact or prop be used in the right way, it would constitute a literal part of one's mind. This thesis stands against cognitivist intracranialism and poses a new "active externalism". Recently, Chalmers (with Clark's approval) presents a refined version of the thesis: "A subject's cognitive processes and mental states can be partly constituted by entities that are external to the subject, in virtue of the subject's sensori-motor interaction with these entities" [2]. Chalmers places a focus on what's most interesting about the thesis: how an intercranial implant wouldn't be much of a surprise to constitute an extension but using a notebook to remember an address or moving tiles on a rack during a Scrabble game do count as extensions [2, 7, 26]. Extensions do not need to replicate neural functioning or have the same dynamics but could complement our cognitive abilities [33]. The extended mind is a soft assembly made up of whatever elements are needed to accomplish the task an agent faces [25]. While this has profound ontological and epistemological implications, we will avoid them for now.

Clark has stated that HCI can be seen as a sort of nascent science of the extended mind [3]. In this direction, Heersmink offers us a multidimensional framework for understanding the degree of extendedness to guide empirical research [14]. The different dimensions include information flow, reliability, durability, trust, procedural transparency, informational transparency, individualization, and transformation [14]. Systems can ebb and flow between degrees of cognitive extendedness, varying in time and by need. The higher the scores across dimensions, the denser the integration [14].

2.2 Predictive Processing

Predictive processing (PP) is a "framework involving a general computational principle which can be applied to describe perception, action, cognition, and their relationships in a single, conceptually unified manner" [36]. Our brain is seen as a prediction machine [5]. It's constantly attempting to match incoming sensory information with top-down predictions through a probabilistic generative model [5]. This is to reject the standard passive, stimulus-driven view of perception, action, and the brain, instead viewing it as highly active and predictive of incoming stimuli, a controlled, online hallucination [5, 8, 36].

Any unpredicted elements are propagated as information back into the predictions in the form of prediction errors [5]. Through active inference, actions are then recruited to improve the state of information within the environment and reduce future prediction error, reducing free energy (known as epistemic actions) [5, 13, 27, 30]. Prediction error minimizing is constantly modulated by precision weighting, adjusting the gain on specific error units, or unexplained sensory units, until an error signal is suppressed [30]. There is a great deal of traffic between interoceptive and exteroceptive information as well, where bodily states (e.g., hunger) can modulate what information in the environment is salient (e.g., food) [8]. PP is particularly alluring given it unifies the mechanics of action, perception, attention, emotion, language, and learning into one unified framework, while bridging empirical and theoretical work [6, 30, 36].

2.3 Distributed Cognition

Distributed cognition (DCog) is a branch of cognitive science, a perspective that seeks to understand cognitive systems by extending the unit of analysis for cognition beyond the boundaries of the skin or skull [16–18]. DCog takes the body, social, and material world as fundamental to understanding cognition: "a [functional] system that can dynamically configure itself to bring subsystems into coordination to accomplish various functions... delimited by the function; relationships among the elements that participate in it, rather than by the spatial colocation of the elements" [16, 17, 21]. DCog has historically been adopted to study human activity 'in the wild', noting how cognitive processes are distributed across people, time, and internal/external structures [16, 17]. It recognizes that "humans create their cognitive powers in part by creating the environments in which they exercise those powers", as ecological assemblies [17, 22]. Cognition doesn't only happen in the brain, rather it is distributed between people and technology, across time in the development of social and material contexts.

A profound element of DCog is its realization of culture. DCog renders culture as "a process that accumulates partial solutions to frequently encountered problems", and "a complex cognitive ecosystem that includes, in addition to the brain, a large number of somatic and extrasomatic processes" [16, 19]. Cultural practices are "the things people do and their [learned] ways of being in the world... [that] organize the action in situated action. Emergent products of dynamic distributed networks of constraints" [20]. Culture serves to reduce entropy at multiple scales [22]. Our cultural practices shape our perception as active ways of "seeing" the world by indicating what to pay attention to and what to perceive [19]. For instance, seeing a constellation of stars is a process enacted via cultural practices which enable you to give visual attention in that specific way to see the constellation [23]. Our environment itself consists of dynamic products nearly entirely due to prior cultural activity [20]. High-level cognitive outcomes are born through the coordination of the mechanisms of distributed cognitive systems within these cultural practices [23].

The questions distributed cognition asks concern "the relations among the elements [of the cognitive system], and how cognitive processes arise from interactions among those elements" [22]. It looks for principles that might apply across scales and cognitive systems (e.g., all cognitive systems are characterized by "local regions of high interconnectivity separated by regions of lower interconnectivity") [22]. DCog doesn't assume a center for any cognitive system. Instead, the centers are determined by the "relative density of information flow across a system" [22]. This is to say that some systems have an obvious center, others several centers, others no center. It all depends on the scaling in question.

3 Dovetailing Sketches of Cognition and Implications for HCI

HCI isn't new to many of these ideas. For instance, distributed cognition has been used to understand complex sociotechnical systems in a variety of contexts and was borne from researchers in HCI [16, 31]. These different theories complement each other and are relatively consistent in principle. According to the authors, this would be the first attempt to mesh these ideas together to form a coherent generative theory of interaction. So, what is this composite depiction of cognition?

3.1 Extended, Distributed, and Predictive: A Low-Fidelity Prototype

Recent compositions of extended mind, predictive processing, active inference, and cognitive niche construction are seen by Constant et al. in their work on "extended active inference" and Veissière et al. in their work on "thinking through other minds" (TTOM) [9, 34]. A complete review of these works is beyond the scope of this paper, and instead we'll point out some relevant aspects.

Constant et al. depict a cognitive niche (externally realized cause-and-effect models) where epistemic cues and affordances are proliferated throughout our inherited environments, reducing uncertainty through ecological legacies, as a shared generative model [9]. Veissière et al. depict "regimes of attention", which highlight different contextually relevant actions as particularly important and aid agents in learning to adapt to their local niche, shaping these epistemic cues [34]. Cognitive niche construction is shown as a "shared cognitive function enabling organisms to track—often implicitly and at low cost—cause–effect relationships otherwise difficult" [9]. This is especially apparent in cases where causal structures are volatile or too complex to be learned by the agents own sensory mechanisms [9, 34].

Learning to use these epistemic cues reduces the complexity of our own generative models, increasing our performance. Constant et al. call the leveraging and optimizing of this shared generative model "extended active inference" (EAI), where active inference is "optimizing an organism's generative model about the cause of its sensations" through action [9]. This leads to the maximization of model evidence through perception, and selective sampling of expected sensory sensations through action. Cognitive niche construction is a cognitive function: uploading and offloading into the niche. Once uploaded into the environment, cognitive extensions can be shared by other agents, as the "scaffolding of complex networks of shared expectations encoded across brains, bodies, constructed environments, and other agents, which modulate attention, guide action, and entail the learning of patterned behaviours" [34]. The environment can be seen as a generative model of the agent. As Constant et al. state, "…one can treat the environment as inferring the cause of the "sensations" it receives from being acted upon by its denizens", or as Veissière puts it, "that the affordances of the–environment and the capacities of an individual are inextricably interwoven, and co-determining" [9, 34]. The cognitive niche and the agent are constantly trying to optimize their generative models of each other.

3.2 Implications for a Generative Theory of Interaction in HCI

HCI can make use of this blending of theories through a new generative theory of interaction [1]. Following Beaudouin-Lafon et al., a generative theory of interaction is:

- Grounded in a theory of human activity and behavior with technology [1]
- Involves analytical ("a description of current use and practice"), critical ("assesses both the positive and negative aspects of a system"), and constructive lenses ("inspires new ideas relative to the critique") [1]
- Provides tools that allow examination of the design space related to a research problem [1].

In the next section, we'll briefly sculpt out how blending predictive processing, extended mind, and distributed cognition might fit into a generative theory of interaction.

Theoretical Grounding
We can see that our blending of predictive processing, distributed cognition, and extended mind is well grounded in theory. Through predictive processing and active inference lenses, we're able to render distributed cognition and extended mind through similar principles. Extended mind provides the basis for blurring the boundary between technology and the brain, laying the groundwork for extending the mind beyond the boundaries of the skull. Distributed cognition provides the temporal and cultural lenses to view these extensions. Predictive processing provides the computational principles which govern the different scales. This is to render culture, environments, tools, brains, bodies, and other generative models as mechanisms for uncertainty reduction [32]. Cultural practices can be seen as shaping epistemic cues: highlighting affordances, uploading cognitive functions, extending precision weighting, shared across time and people through cognitive niches. Our cognitive capacities constitute our tools, culture, environment, etc.: "ontologically inseparable from the start" [24]. As Herbert Simon is said to remark, "Most human intelligence is artificial intelligence anyway".

We can surface some early concepts (cognitive extensions, temporality) and principles (as adopted from Heersmink: information flow, reliability, durability, trust, procedural transparency, informational transparency, individualization, and transformation) to examine analytical, critical, and constructive lenses [1, 14].

Analytical, Critical, and Constructive Lenses
Analytically, we can begin to look at how well certain extensions extend cognition and how this might vary across time by [14, 15]. How well do these cognitive functions embed into the cognitive niche? How does it increase uncertainty reduction across different time scales? Critically, we can begin looking at who gets the opportunity to extend their minds with different extensions and how has that access propagated across society, in what forms? Who has more power to design the cognitive niches and what types

of cognitive niches are most dominant [10]? Constructively, we can begin to consider how we could better extend people's minds, increase access to different extensions, or increase people's ability to design their cognitive niche. We believe that Heersmink's dimensions of integration offer a good starting point to consider different principles to evaluate cognitive systems upon (information flow, reliability, durability, trust, procedural transparency, informational transparency, individualization, and transformation) [14].

4 Conclusion

In this paper, we sought to present a developing generative theory of interaction through blending extended mind, distributed cognition, and predictive processing into a single account. We chose these theories given how well they complement each other, and how they lack directly actionable principles to guide HCI research. For future work, we'll more closely develop this generative theory of interaction by offering more insight into a theoretical grounding, offering well-defined principles and concepts to look at this theory through, and develop questions that can be asked by looking at different lenses (as depicted by Beaudouin-Lafon et al.) [1]. We hope that we've offered a starting point for others to more directly consider how we can bring these theories into HCI and open channels for transdisciplinary work with these fields.

Acknowledgements. This work is part of the DCODE project. The project has received funding from the European Union's Horizon 2020 research and innovation programme under the Marie Skłodowska-Curie grant agreement No. 955990.

References

1. Beaudouin-Lafon, M., et al.: Generative theories of interaction. ACM Trans. Comput. Hum. Interact. **28**(6), 1–54 (2021). https://doi.org/10.1145/3468505
2. Chalmers, D.J.: Extended cognition and extended consciousness. In: Andy Clark and His Critics, pp. 9–20. Oxford University Press (2019)
3. Clark, A.: Memento's revenge: the extended mind, extended. In: The Extended Mind, pp. 43–66. The MIT Press (2010)
4. Clark, A.: Natural-Born Cyborgs: Minds, Technologies, and the Future of Human Intelligence. Oxford University Press, New York (2004)
5. Clark, A.: Surfing Uncertainty: Prediction, Action, and the Embodied Mind. Oxford University Press, New York (2019)
6. Clark, A.: Whatever next? Predictive brains, situated agents, and the future of cognitive science. Behav. Brain Sci. **36**(3), 181–204 (2013). https://doi.org/10.1017/s0140525x12000477
7. Clark, A., Chalmers, D.: The extended mind. Analysis **58**(1), 7–19 (1998). https://doi.org/10.1111/1467-8284.00096
8. Clark, A.: Consciousness as generative entanglement. J. Philos. **116**(12), 645–662 (2019). https://doi.org/10.5840/jphil20191161241
9. Constant, A., et al.: Extended active inference: constructing predictive cognition beyond skulls. Mind Lang. Mila. 12330 (2020). https://doi.org/10.1111/mila.12330

10. Costanza-Chock, S.: Design Justice: Community-Led Practices to Build the Worlds We Need. MIT Press, London (2020)
11. Engel, A.K., et al.: Dynamic predictions: oscillations and synchrony in top–down processing. Nat. Rev. Neurosci. **2**(10), 704–716 (2001). https://doi.org/10.1038/35094565
12. Frauenberger, C.: Entanglement HCI the next wave? ACM Trans. Comput. Hum. Interact. **27**(1), 1–27 (2020). https://doi.org/10.1145/3364998
13. Friston, K., et al.: Active inference and agency: optimal control without cost functions. Biol. Cybern. **106**(8–9), 523–541 (2012). https://doi.org/10.1007/s00422-012-0512-8
14. Heersmink, R.: Dimensions of integration in embedded and extended cognitive systems. Phenomenol. Cogn. Sci. **14**(3), 577–598 (2014). https://doi.org/10.1007/s11097-014-9355-1
15. Heersmink, R.: The cognitive integration of scientific instruments: information, situated cognition, and scientific practice. Phenomenol. Cogn. Sci. **15**(4), 517–537 (2015). https://doi.org/10.1007/s11097-015-9432-0
16. Hollan, J., et al.: Distributed cognition: toward a new foundation for human-computer interaction research. ACM Trans. Comput. Hum. Interact. **7**(2), 174–196 (2000). https://doi.org/10.1145/353485.353487
17. Hutchins, E.: Cognition, distributed. In: International Encyclopedia of the Social & Behavioral Sciences, pp. 2068–2072. Elsevier (2001)
18. Hutchins, E.: Cognition in the Wild. MIT Press, Cambridge (1994)
19. Hutchins, E.: Cognitive ecology. Top. Cogn. Sci. **2**(4), 705–715 (2010). https://doi.org/10.1111/j.1756-8765.2010.01089.x
20. Hutchins, E.: Enculturating the supersized mind. Philos. Stud. **152**(3), 437–446 (2011). https://doi.org/10.1007/s11098-010-9599-8
21. Hutchins, E.: Imagining the cognitive life of things. https://citeseerx.ist.psu.edu/viewdoc/download?doi=10.1.1.104.6035&rep=rep1&type=pdf. Accessed 18 Mar 2022
22. Hutchins, E.: The cultural ecosystem of human cognition. Philos. Psychol. **27**(1), 34–49 (2014). https://doi.org/10.1080/09515089.2013.830548
23. Hutchins, E.: The role of cultural practices in the emergence of modern human intelligence. Philos. Trans. R. Soc. Lond. B Biol. Sci. **363**(1499), 2011–2019 (2008). https://doi.org/10.1098/rstb.2008.0003
24. Introna, L.D.: Towards a post-human intra-actional account of sociomaterial agency (and morality). In: Kroes, P., Verbeek, P.-P. (eds.) The Moral Status of Technical Artefacts. PET, vol. 17, pp. 31–53. Springer, Dordrecht (2014). https://doi.org/10.1007/978-94-007-7914-3_3
25. Kirchhoff, M.D., Kiverstein, J.: Extended Consciousness and Predictive Processing: A Third Wave View. Routledge, London (2019)
26. Kirsh, D.: The intelligent use of space. Artif. Intell. **73**(1–2), 31–68 (1995). https://doi.org/10.1016/0004-3702(94)00017-u
27. Kirsh, D., Maglio, P.: On distinguishing epistemic from pragmatic action. Cogn. Sci. **18**(4), 513–549 (1994). https://doi.org/10.1207/s15516709cog1804_1
28. Marshall, P., Necker, E.H.: Theories of embodiment in HCI. In: The SAGE Handbook of Digital Technology Research, pp. 144–158. SAGE Publications Ltd., London (2014)
29. Menary, R. (ed.): The Extended Mind. The MIT Press, Cambridge (2010)
30. Nave, K., et al.: Wilding the predictive brain. Wiley Interdiscip. Rev. Cogn. Sci. **11**(6), e1542 (2020). https://doi.org/10.1002/wcs.1542
31. Rogers, Y.: HCI Theory: Classical, Modern, and Contemporary. Morgan & Claypool, San Rafael (2012)
32. Sterelny, K.: Minds: extended or scaffolded? Phenomenol. Cogn. Sci. **9**(4), 465–481 (2010). https://doi.org/10.1007/s11097-010-9174-y
33. Sutton, J.: Exograms and interdisciplinarity: history, the extended mind, and the civilizing process. In: The Extended Mind, pp. 189–225. The MIT Press (2010)

34. Veissière, S.P.L., et al.: Thinking through other minds: a variational approach to cognition and culture. Behav. Brain Sci. **43**, e90 (2020). https://doi.org/10.1017/s0140525x19001213
35. Verbeek, P.-P.: Beyond interaction: a short introduction to mediation theory. Interactions **22**(3), 26–31 (2015). https://doi.org/10.1145/2751314
36. Wiese, W., Metzinger, T.K.: Vanilla PP for philosophers: a primer on predictive processing. (2017). https://doi.org/10.15502/9783958573024
37. Wilson, R.A., Clark, A.: How to situate cognition: Letting nature take its course. In: Aydede, M., Robbins, P. (eds.) The Cambridge Handbook of Situated Cognition, pp. 55–77. Cambridge University Press, Cambridge (2009)

Leveraging Temporal Causal Discovery Framework to Explore Event-Related EEG Connectivity

Shao-Xun Fang[1,6] , Tsai-Feng Chiu[2,6] , Chih-Sheng Huang[3,4,5] ,
and Chun-Hsiang Chuang[6,7(✉)]

[1] Department of Computer Science and Engineering, National Taiwan Ocean University,
Keelung, Taiwan
11057039@mail.ntou.edu.tw
[2] Department of Computer Science, National Yang Ming Chiao Tung University,
Hsinchu, Taiwan
[3] College of Artificial Intelligence and Green Energy, National Yang Ming Chiao
Tung University, Taipei City, Taiwan
[4] College of Electrical Engineering and Computer Science, National Taipei University
of Technology, Taipei City, Taiwan
[5] Artificial Intelligence Research and Development Department, ELAN Microelectronics
Corporation, Hsinchu, Taiwan
[6] Research Center for Education and Mind Sciences, College of Education,
National Tsing Hua University, Hsinchu, Taiwan
cch.chuang@gmail.com
[7] Institute of Information Systems and Applications, College of Electrical Engineering
and Computer Science, National Tsing Hua University, Hsinchu, Taiwan

Abstract. Deciphering the cause-and-effect relationships between brain regions
not only can provide insights into the mechanism of brain networking but also
facilitate the development of the brain-computer interface. Numerous studies have
adopted effective connectivity measurements such as transfer entropy or multivariate autoregressive model to investigate the synchronous neuronal coupling
across brain regions. Recent successes with representation learning in deep neural
networks deserve further investigation on their capability for causal discovery. To
this end, this study modified the Temporal Causal Discovery Framework (TCDF)
with a sliding-window approach to explore the event-related intra-brain electroencephalogram (EEG) dynamics. The TCDF used a convolution neural network with
an attention mechanism to predict causal direction among multi-channel time
series data. The resultant array of attention scores was used to gauge the causality
magnitude. The TCDF was first validated through a simulation study, followed by
real EEG data collected in a virtual reality-based multitasking experiment. Results
showed that the time-varying causality magnitudes were positively correlated with
the predefined regression coefficients of simulated data, and the TCDF could successfully capture the coupling between brain regions, particularly for adjacent
channels. However, some issues were raised in modeling as the number of channels increased or the causal order became larger. The current findings might shed
some light on the development of deep learning-based causality analysis.

C. Stephanidis et al. (Eds.): HCII 2022, CCIS 1654, pp. 25–29, 2022.
https://doi.org/10.1007/978-3-031-19679-9_4

Keywords: Cause-and-effect relationships · TCDF · Attention score · Multitasking

1 Introduction

Many deep-learning-based predictive models [1, 2] have been developed to predict time series data and have been successfully applied in various fields. However, most of the models make predictions based on correlations, not causation [3], making the models challenging to investigate the cause-and-effect relationships of time series data.

Attention mechanism [4] in deep learning has been proven to enhance the performance of the encoder-decoder models in machine translation, automatic speech recognition, image caption, etc. [5, 6]. The attention mechanism enables the model to distinguish and explain what the model has learned and gains an insight into how deep learning behaves. It's hypothesized that the attention mechanism may facilitate an accurate exploration of coupling among time series data.

This study used the Temporal Causal Discovery Framework (TCDF) [7] to discover causality in EEG data and used simulation data to verify the model's ability to discover underlying causality. Finally, this study applied TCDF to brain signals, i.e., EEG, to explore event-related coupling among brain regions.

2 Methods

2.1 Temporal Causal Discovery Framework and Attention Score

One of the deep-learning-based models recently developed to explore causality between time series data is the Temporal Causal Discovery Framework (TCDF). The TCDF is composed of a number of attention-based convolutional neural network (CNN) models. Each submodel is with the same architecture trained to depict the relationship between the input time series and the target time series by minimizing the loss between them. By a depthwise separable convolution, different kernels are applied to input time series independently to avoid mixing them. Adequate size of the receptive field R is critical to discovering the delay between cause and effect. Therefore, a dilation approach is employed to make the convolution operate on a coarser scale. The resultant size of the receptive field is:

$$R = 1 + \sum_{l=0}^{L}(K - 1) \cdot c^l$$

where L and K are numbers of hidden layers and kernel size, respectively. The dilation factor is c^l, where c is the dilation coefficient. This study set the parameters, L, K, and c, set to 1, 4, and 4. Therefore, the size of the receptive field was 16. The discovered delay was then determined by the position of the highest kernel weight.

The causality among the EEG channels of interest was then estimated by the attention scores obtained in TCDF. For N-channel EEG data, the attention score $a_{i,j}$ depicts the causal effect of the j th channel time series, x_j, on the i th channel x_i.

2.2 Experiment: Simulation Data

The first test data used to validate the effectiveness of the TCDF in modeling the time-varying causality was generated through a built-in data simulation function in SIFT [8]. This simulated dataset consisted of 100 segments of time series. Each segment was a 2-channel time series containing 500 data points (Fig. 1a). The coupling between two channels occurred from 201 to 300, and the causal magnitude from channel 1 to channel 2 was set to 1. The self-causal magnitudes of channels 1 and 2 were 0.618 and 0.6643 (Fig. 1b).

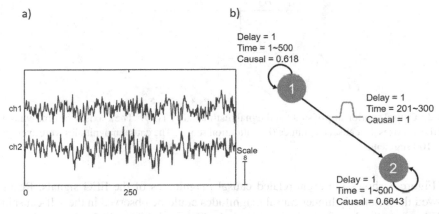

Fig. 1. Simulated data for model validation. a) A segment of simulated time series data. b) The simulated causality diagram (ground truth), where gray nodes represent two simulated time series signals. The curved arrow represents the self-causality within time series. The straight arrow shows the causal relationship between two simulated signals.

2.3 Experiment: Real EEG Data

The second test data was a 32-ch EEG dataset collected from 36 subjects performing psychomotor vigilance test (PVT) during a multitasking task. The sampling rate was 500 Hz. To analyze the event-related intra-brain connectivity, this study extracted EEG segments from 1 s before to 2 s after the PVT event. Each segment contained 500 data points. Thirty segments were collected from each subject. The EEG channels at the midline, Fz, Cz, Pz, and Oz, were selected. The EEG signals were processed with the independent component analysis [9] to remove artifacts. The TCDF was then applied to each 100-point nonoverlapping subsegment.

3 Result

Figure 2 displays the time-varying causal magnitudes estimated by the attention scores in TCDF. Results showed that the magnitudes of the self-causality were greater than those of other links. Additionally, the causal magnitudes of channel 1 to channel 2 increased between 201 and 300 (the left-bottom panel in Fig. 2), evidencing that TCDF could capture the causality as expected (Fig. 1).

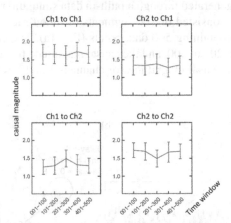

Fig. 2. Causal relationship of simulated signals estimated by TCDF. The x-axis is the time window, and the y-axis is the causal magnitude (i.e., attention score). The causal magnitudes were averaged over 100 segments.

Figure 3 shows the event-related causal magnitudes of the EEG signals. Results showed that relatively higher causal magnitudes could be observed in the self-causality and the causality between adjacent channels. The causal magnitudes between source and sink channels were proportional to the distance between them. However, the TCDF failed to capture the PVT-related changes in the causal magnitude.

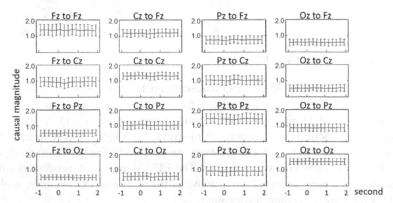

Fig. 3. Causal magnitudes between distinct brain regions while subjects performed a sustained-attention test (i.e., PVT).

4 Conclusion

This study demonstrated the feasibility of TCDF in capturing the causality underlying time series data. Results showed that the causal relationship could be successfully modeled for the simulated signals but partially for the EEG data. It's necessary to investigate the model behavior of TCDF to improve its performance in the effective connectivity analysis.

Acknowledgement. This work was supported by the Ministry of Science and Technology, Taiwan (project numbers: MOST 111-2636-E-007-020 and 110-2636-E-007-018), by the Research Center for Education and Mind Sciences, National Tsing Hua University, and by Yin Shu-Tien Educational Foundation.

References

1. Elman, J.L.: Finding structure in time. Cogn. Sci. **14**(2), 179–211 (1990)
2. Shi, X., Chen, Z., Wang, H., Yeung, D.-Y., Wong, W.-K., Woo, W.-C.: Convolutional LSTM network: a machine learning approach for precipitation nowcasting. Adv. Neural. Inf. Process. Syst. **28**, 802–810 (2015)
3. Kleinberg, S.: Why: A guide to finding and using causes. O'Reilly Media, Inc. (2015)
4. Vaswani, A., et al.: Attention is all you need. Adv. Neural. Inf. Process. Syst. **30**, 6000–6010 (2017)
5. Watanabe, S., Hori, T., Kim, S., Hershey, J.R., Hayashi, T.: Hybrid CTC/attention architecture for end-to-end speech recognition. IEEE Journal of Selected Topics in Signal Processing **11**(8), 1240–1253 (2017)
6. Xu, K., et al., Show, attend and tell: Neural image caption generation with visual attention. In: International Conference on Machine Learning, pp. 2048–2057. PMLR (2015)
7. Nauta, M., Bucur, D., Seifert, C.: Causal discovery with attention-based convolutional neural networks. Machine Learning and Knowledge Extraction **1**(1), 312–340 (2019)
8. Delorme, A., Makeig, S.: EEGLAB: an open source toolbox for analysis of single-trial EEG dynamics including independent component analysis. J. Neurosci. Methods **134**(1), 9–21 (2004)
9. Makeig, S., Bell, A., Jung, T.-P., Sejnowski, T.J.: Independent component analysis of electroencephalographic data. Adv. Neural. Inf. Process. Syst. **8**, 145–151 (1995)

Mirror Neurons as a Potential Confounder in Thought-Based Device Control Using Brain Computer Interfaces with fNIRS

Anja Filippi, Maximilian Kraus[✉], Philipp Ulsamer, and Nicholas Müller

University of Applied Sciences Würzburg-Schweinfurt, Sanderheinrichsleitenweg 25,
97074 Würzburg, Germany
`maximilian.kraus@fhws.de`

Abstract. Brain Computer Interfaces (BCI) have so far been used primarily in the medical context. The question arises whether an interface between brain and user device could be established as an innovative technology in everyday life and which potential disruptive factors would have to be taken into account.

The investigations conducted for this paper intend to show whether the mirror neuron effect is a confounding factor for BCI with fNIRS as a means of thought-based device control for people with uninhibited motor skills. A further aim was to gain insights into whether there is a difference in the mirror neuron effect between looking at a stranger and looking at oneself while performing a waving movement.

The conducted research showed that the subjects' reactions to a seen movement were stronger than the reactions to an imagined movement. Thus, the mirror neuron effect represents a confounding factor for thought-based device control via fNIRS.

Furthermore, no significant difference was found between the responses to a stranger waving and the subjects themselves carrying out the motion. Although the subjects' reactions to seeing themselves were slightly increased, the available data does not allow for definite conclusions in this matter.

Keywords: Mirror neurons · Brain-computer interface · fNIRS

1 Motivation

A researcher at the University of California, Los Angeles first investigated the real possibility of an interface between the human brain and a terminal device in 1973 by connecting subjects to an EEG and using light and touch to provide stimuli that caused distinct, neural responses [1]. They developed a theoretical system in which these responses could be deliberately caused and used for thought-based control of a terminal device and named it the Brain Computer Interface (BCI). Although the state of technology the 1970s made it impossible to put this design into practice, they suggested that it would only be a matter of time before such an interface became a reality.

Today, BCI are predominantly used in the medical field [2], where they are mainly applied in work with motor-impaired individuals [3, 4]. In this context, BCIs that utilized

C. Stephanidis et al. (Eds.): HCII 2022, CCIS 1654, pp. 30–38, 2022.
https://doi.org/10.1007/978-3-031-19679-9_5

the thought of movement (motor imagery) as a signal have achieved success in thought-based terminal control [5].

The question arises whether people with uninhibited motor skills also benefit from thought-based terminal control via motor imagery in everyday life in the future. Since BCI systems have so far been tested mainly in controlled laboratory environments, there is little evidence whether the technology researched so far is at all suitable for working with mobile devices, or whether already known interfering factors such as the mirror neuron effect could lead to problems [6].

2 Neuroscientific Foundations

2.1 Motor Imagery

The planning of a movement to be performed is usually a subconscious process in the brain that takes place before the actual movement [7]. However, under certain circumstances, these processes can be consciously initiated by imagining movement, and corresponding signals can be released in the brain [8].

The ability to imagine movement varies from person to person, and the type of imagination also affects signaling. So far, the "first-person perspective" has proven to be the most effective method for eliciting a signal trigger in the motor cortex through thought: The subject imagines performing a movement themself. This process is referred to as *Motor Imagery* [7].

Motor Imagery is one of the few mental activities that can be executed and stopped consciously, thus enabling motionless signaling [5].

2.2 Neurovascular Coupling

The term *Hemodynamics* generally refers to the nature and movement of blood [9]. In the context of BCI systems, hemodynamic describes the measurement of blood flow and the associated oxygenation (oxygen saturation) of the blood in specific areas of the brain [10].

When the action potential is transmitted to the different areas of the brain, the activity of the local neurons and glial cells increases, and so does the oxygen and glucose demand in the affected area. At the same time, the cells of the brain are unable to store these nutrients within themselves [11]. Therefore, as soon as an area of the brain becomes particularly active (e.g., the motor cortex when complex movements are performed), a hemodynamic response occurs: Blood supply increases by between 10% and 40% to compensate for the sudden increase in nutrient consumption in that area [12]. The response is so pronounced that the relative oxygen saturation of the blood in the affected area rises well above the resting state saturation despite the increased consumption.

The direct correlation between increased, electrical potential, and increased blood oxygen saturation is called *neurovascular coupling* and is the basis of the hemodynamic measurement method. The relationship was first noted in studies on humans [13] and shortly thereafter described in more detail through experiments on dogs [12]. More profoundly, neurovascular coupling was explored from the middle of the 20th century. It is now considered a fundamental principle of neuroscience [11].

Although measurements using the hemodynamic method generate time-delayed data and are not accurate down to microvascular levels, the measurement results obtained are still sufficient to detect brain activation at a regional level [11].

In addition, measurement of blood oxygen saturation does not require invasive procedures or high-precision placements on the skull of the subjects, which offers increased mobility in BCI work [10].

2.3 Functional Near-Infrared Spectroscopy

Functional near-infrared spectroscopy (fNIRS) describes a non-invasive, hemodynamic measurement method that uses light in various wavelengths near the infrared spectrum to measure changes in blood flow within the brain [14].

The light is emitted from light sources (emitter) located on the scalp. It penetrates various tissue layers (scalp, skullcap, etc.) before reaching the neuronal tissue (Fig. 3). There, it is partially reflected and collected by detectors also adjacent to the scalp [14, 15].

Tissue that is perfused by highly oxygenated blood absorbs a particularly large amount of light but causes little light scattering. Brain areas with high neuronal activity show an increased oxygen saturation in the blood according to the principle of *neurovascular coupling* and consequently have a high absorption rate. If a tissue has a low blood supply, it absorbs little light but causes more light scattering [15].

Combining the principles of *neurovascular coupling* and *motor imagery* with the *fNIRS* technology makes it possible for subjects to consciously evoke brain activity that can be captured, measured, and used as a signal generator to control arbitrary external devices.

2.4 Mirror Neuron Effect

As established, planning, performing and imagining a motor-action triggers increased activity in the neurons of the motor cortex. Some neurons are additionally activated when an action is performed by a counterpart and merely observed in a passive state. This effect is referred to as the *mirror neuron effect* [16]. It was first demonstrated in studies on the motor cortex of a macaque [17]. The monkey was presented with objects with which it performed set motor actions. After it had performed the desired action, it was rewarded with food.

During the experiment, the monkey happened to see an object being placed that was irrelevant to the experiment. Without the animal performing any of the previously requested actions, some neurons were then activated in the brain regions that were also active during the previous measurements. It was found that some neurons in the motor cortex of the macaque could be activated by only observing a movement performed by humans in the animal's field of view. Furthermore, different triggers for activation were defined: The motor cortex responded when one of the actions previously demanded of the animal was performed (e.g., grasping or turning an object). It was also activated by movements that were only indirectly related to the experimental setup (e.g., placing the object near the monkey) [17].

Like in monkeys, the mirror neuron effect is also evident in humans, especially when observing actions and reactions [18] and contributes to a better understanding of the movement or emotion seen [16, 19]. Additionally, the mirror neuron effect in humans is enhanced when the motion sequence is familiar to the observer or has been performed before [20].

3   Experimental Design

Humans are permanently confronted with movement in everyday life without consciously perceiving it. The brain's natural reaction to an observed movement could lead to functional limitations when working with BCI for thought-based terminal control via Motor Imagery. The tests conducted in this paper aim to show whether and to what extent the mirror neuron effect is detectable in measurements with fNIRS and whether it represents a confounding factor in thought-based device control via BCI with fNIRS.

Specifically, the comparison between a subject's response to *Motor Imagery* and the possible influence of the mirror neuron effect was addressed. Furthermore, these trials sought to provide information on whether a difference in the intensity of the mirror neuron effect could be determined when the subjects observed themselves or a stranger performing motor-actions.

Since the *mirror neuron effect* in measurements of neuronal activity with EEG has so far been demonstrated mainly with movement of the extremities [21], in this experiment a waving, beckoning movement with the arms was specified as the movement under consideration. The choice of the arm was left to the subjects.

The test was composed of passive and active sections designed to show the brain's normal response to movement as well as to visualize the response to imagined and seen movement. In addition, a possible difference in the expression of the mirror neuron effect between looking at a stranger and oneself while performing a waving movement was investigated.

3.1   Setup and Equipment

The experiment was conducted in a neutral, low-stimulus environment. The room could be darkened by opaque curtains and allowed little to no external noise to enter. Each subject participated individually in the study.

Two laptops, the fNIRS device *Brite 24* from the supplier artinis, and the associated analysis software *Oxysoft* from the same supplier were used for the experiment.

In Fig. 1, at location (1), the subject is shown wearing the fNIRS device during the experiment. While they were viewing an automated slide show on a laptop (3) and performing the required actions, another laptop (2) received the data measured by the fNIRS device via Bluetooth and processes them in the *Oxysoft* evaluation software.

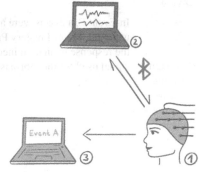

Fig. 1. An overview of the equipment used for this experiment.

3.2 Slide Show

The slide show consisted of a 30-s resting phase Event A, as well as the ten-second phases Event B, C, D, and E, which were separated by 30-s resting periods (see Table 1).

Table 1. Slide show events with descriptions.

Event	Description
II A) Resting	The initial resting period in Event A represents a regulated period of time during which the natural activity in the oxygen saturation of the subjects was to be observed. It also served as an opportunity for the subjects to focus and calm down
B) Active waving	Event B, in which the subjects were asked to perform an actual angular movement, was used as a benchmark for the analysis of the results described below and further served as a control for the correct functioning of the fNIRS device
C) Viewing a video of a person waving	In Event C, subjects were shown a repetitive video of a stranger waving. The brains response to Event C should show whether and to what extent viewing a strange person could activate mirror neurons and how it affected oxygen saturation
D) Viewing a video of the subject waving	Event D consisted of a recorded video of the respective subject. The purpose of this event is the same as that of Event C. In addition, however, the use of the subject's video was intended to determine whether a difference between the response of the motor cortex to the movement of an unfamiliar person and a movement of the subject themself is detectable
D) Imagine a waving movement with motor imagery	In Event E, subjects were asked to imagine a self-performed angular movement using the Motor Imagery Principle and to avoid actually moving. In this event, the response to an imagined movement is measured, which would also be the signal used for thought-based device control via BCI

In order to avoid sequence effects, the order of phases B, C, D, and E was randomly generated for each subject.

3.3 Data Processing and Evaluation

The evaluation and analysis software *Oxysoft* allows data transfer in real time. Via Bluetooth, the data measured during the trials was transferred directly to *Oxysoft* and visualized as graphs depicting the time curve of oxygen saturation in the subject's motor cortex.

Markers representing the start and end of a given phase were placed in the graph and a moving gaussian filter was applied in order to obtain the moving average of the raw signal in windows of three and six seconds duration. With these filters in place, natural fluctuations in blood pressure, as well as heartbeat, could be smoothed in the recording and changes in oxygen saturation, caused by external stimuli became more visible (see Fig. 2).

Fig. 2. A graph without applied filter, with moving gaussian with window width 3 s and with moving gaussian with window width 6 s (left to right).

The data were evaluated visually by comparing the responses, i.e., the increase in oxygen saturation, to the individual events.

A significant response was evaluated if the graph showed signs of *neurovascular coupling,* i.e., it dropped at the beginning of the event and shortly afterwards rose above the value before the drop (Fig. 3). In addition, rises without a preceding drop were also noted as a response, if their occurrence was comparable in time to the response in Event B.

If a graph remained unchanged or at one level with regular, slight fluctuations during the event, this was considered a weak response of the motor cortex, because oxygen saturation did not increase detectably but did not decrease further either (Fig. 4).

A steady decrease in oxygen saturation without a subsequent increase was interpreted as no response of the motor cortex (Fig. 5).

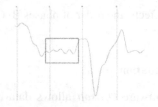

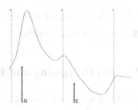

Fig. 3. Example from a subject measurement, which was classified as a clear response due to the initial drop and subsequent rise.

Fig. 4. Compared to the subject's responses to the other events, no significant decrease or increase occurs in the marked section.

Fig. 5. Around the increase in reference Event B, there is a steady decrease in Event E, indicating no response.

4   Results

The evaluation of the data collected in this thesis is based on visual comparisons of the results and should therefore be regarded as approximations and reproductions of trends, as they were not subjected to a detailed, statistical evaluation. Twenty-five subjects between the ages of 20 and 64 participated in this study.

4.1   Data

During the initial resting phase in event A, 56% of the subjects showed a stable to slightly decreasing oxygen saturation. In 28%, saturation increased slightly, and 16% of subjects experienced a sharp increase in oxygen saturation.

The actual waving motion elicited a significant response in all subjects. In 80% of the subjects, moreover, the reaction to event B was the most pronounced compared to the other events.

Of 25 subjects, all 25 had a response to events C or D, i.e., showed increased oxygen saturation when looking at a stranger or themselves while performing a waving movement. 92% of the subjects showed a reaction to both events, 4% reacted only to event C, 4% only to event D.

When performing *motor imagery* (event E), 68% of subjects responded with increased oxygen saturation, 12% with unchanged oxygen saturation. In 20% of the subjects, there was no discernible response.

4.2   Interpretation

To determine whether the mirror neuron effect is a confounding factor when working with *Motor Imagery* as a thought-based control method in BCI with fNIRS, the response to a seen movement and the response to an imagined movement of the subjects must be compared. Therefore, to answer the research question, the vascular responses of the subjects to events C and D were compared with each other, as well as with the responses to event E.

The data shows that looking at a stranger, as well as looking at oneself while performing a movement, triggered neurovascular reactions in the subjects. The mirror neuron effect can therefore be clearly demonstrated with fNIRS devices. There is no direct difference between the two events C and D, but it can be seen that event D triggered more strong reactions in the subjects with almost 64% than event C with 36%. Also, the reaction to event D was the most significant of all other events for 8% of the subjects, whereas none of the subjects showed a strongest reaction to event C.

Comparing the subjects' reactions to events C and D with their reactions to event E, the reactions to event E tended to be weaker on average. Thus, imagining a movement triggers a smaller increase in oxygen saturation in the subjects than passively viewing a movement.

Answering the Research Question. Imagining a movement elicited a smaller response than watching a movement in most subjects. If motor imagery is to be used as a thought-based control in everyday life, observed motion could interfere with signaling. The mirror neuron effect must therefore be considered as a confounding factor in thought-based terminal control when working with BCI with fNIRS.

References

1. Vidal, J.J.: Toward Direct Brain-Computer Communication (1973)
2. Cervera, M.A., et al.: Brain-computer interfaces for post-stroke motor rehabilitation: a meta-analysis. Annals of clinical and translational neurology **5**(5), 651–663 (2018)
3. Brumberg, J.S., Nieto-Castanon, A., Kennedy, P.R., Guenther, F.H.: Brain-computer interfaces for speech communication. Speech communication **52**(4), 367–379 (2010). https://doi.org/10.1016/j.specom.2010.01.001
4. Mellinger, J., et al.: An MEG-based brain-computer interface (BCI). NeuroImage **36**(3), 581–593 (2007)
5. Leeb, R., Friedman, D., Müller-Putz, G.R., Scherer, R., Slater, M., Pfurtscheller, G.: Self-Paced (Asynchronous) BCI Control of a Wheelchair in Virtual Environments: A Case Study with a Tetraplegic. Computational Intelligence and Neuroscience **2007**(2), 1–8 (2007)
6. Ulsamer, P., Fertig, T., Kraus, M., Pfeffel, K., Müller, N.H.: Motor Imagery to Control Mobile Applications. An fNIRS Study (2020)
7. Jeannerod, M.: Mental imagery in the motor context (1995)
8. Li, S., Kamper, D.G., Stevens, J.A., Rymer, W.Z.: The effect of motor imagery on spinal segmental excitability. The Journal of neuroscience: the official journal of the Society for Neuroscience 24 (43), 9674–9680 (2004)
9. Piper, W.: Innere Medizin. 2. Aufl. Springer (2013)
10. Sorger, B., et al.: Another kind of 'BOLD Response': answering multiple-choice questions via online decoded single-trial brain signals. In: Coma Science: Clinical and Ethical Implications, Bd. 177: Elsevier (Progress in Brain Research), pp. 275–292 (2009)
11. Iadecola, C.: The neurovascular unit coming of age: a journey through neurovascular coupling in health and disease. Neuron **96**(1), 17–42 (2017). https://doi.org/10.1016/j.neuron.2017.07.030
12. Roy, C.S., Sherrington, C.S.: On the Regulation of the Blood-supply of the Brain (1890)
13. Mosso, A.: Ueber den Kreislauf des Blutes im menschlichen Gehirn: Veit & Comp. (1881)

14. Naseer, N., Hong, K.-S.: fNIRS-based brain-computer interfaces: a review. Frontiers in human neuroscience **9**, 3 (2015)
15. Herold, F., Wiegel, P., Scholkmann, F., Müller, N.G.: Applications of Functional Near-Infrared Spectroscopy (fNIRS) Neuroimaging in Exercise–Cognition Science: A Systematic, Methodology-Focused Review. Journal of clinical medicine **7**(12) (2018). https://doi.org/10.3390/jcm7120466
16. Fabbri-Destro, M., Rizzolatti, G.: Mirror Neurons and Mirror Systems in Monkeys and Humans (2008)
17. Di Pellegrino, G., Fadiga, L., Fogassi, L., Gallese, V., Rizzolatti, G.: Understanding motor events: a neurophysiological study (1992)
18. Hari, R., Forss, N., Avikainen, S., Kirveskari, E., Salenius, S., Rizzolatti, G.: Activation of human primary motor cortex during action observation: a neuromagnetic study. Proceedings of the National Academy of Sciences of the United States of America **95**(25), 15061–15065 (1998)
19. Calvo-Merino, B., Grèzes, J., Glaser, D. E., Passingham, R.E., Haggard, P.: Seeing or doing? Influence of visual and motor familiarity in action observation. Current biology: CB **16**(19), 1905–1910 (2006)
20. Cross, E.S., Hamilton, A.F. de C., Grafton, S.T.: Building a motor simulation de novo. Observation of dance by dancers (2006)
21. Carrillo, M., Han, Y., Migliorati, F., Liu, M., Gazzola, V., Keysers, C.: Emotional Mirror Neurons in the Rat's Anterior Cingulate Cortex. Current biology: CB **29**(8), 1301–1312.e6 (2019). https://doi.org/10.1016/j.cub.2019.03.024

An Experimental Method for Studying Complex Choices

Nikolos Gurney[1]([✉]) [ID], Tyler King[2], and John H. Miller[3,4]

[1] University of Southern California, Los Angeles, CA 90094, USA
gurney@ict.usc.edu
[2] Cornell University, Ithaca, NY 14850, USA
ttk22@cornell.edu
[3] Carnegie Mellon University, Pittsburgh, PA 15213, USA
JM7T@andrew.cmu.edu
[4] Santa Fe Institute, Santa Fe, NM 87501, USA

Abstract. The promise of computational decision aids, from review sites to emerging augmented cognition technology, is the potential for better choice outcomes. This promise is grounded in the notion that we understand human decision processes well enough to design useful interventions. Although researchers have made considerable advances in the understanding of human judgment and decision making, these efforts are mostly based on the analysis of simple, often linear choices. Cumulative Prospect Theory (CPT), a famous explanation for decision making under uncertainty, was developed and validated using binary choice experiments in which options varied on a single dimension. Behavioral science has largely followed this simplified methodology. Here, we introduce an experimental paradigm specifically for studying humans making complex choices that incorporate multiple variables with nonlinear interactions. The task involves tuning dials, each of which controls a different dimension of a nonlinear problem. Initial results show that in such an environment participants demonstrate classic cognitive artifacts, such as anchoring and adjusting, along with falling into exploitive traps that prevent adequate exploration of these complex decisions. Preventing such errors suggest a potentially valuable role for deploying algorithmic decision aids to enhance decision making in complex choices.

Keywords: Complex choice · Judgment and decision making · Behavioral economics · Decision aids

1 Introduction

From buying groceries to the purchase of a house, and from choosing a course schedule to accepting a job offer, individuals often confront complex choices. The necessity to integrate information across multiple dimensions is a key feature of these choices. For example, in the purchase of a car, one must pick how the car is powered, how many passengers it can carry, expected mileage, top speed, quality,

C. Stephanidis et al. (Eds.): HCII 2022, CCIS 1654, pp. 39–45, 2022.
https://doi.org/10.1007/978-3-031-19679-9_6

price, and so on. If the dimensions do not interact, then choices are relatively easy as they can be made one dimension at a time. Such linear scenarios, however, are typically the exception rather than the rule. Most choice dimensions have nonlinear interactions (for example, to carry more passengers you need a larger car and that impacts the performance of the motor, etc.) We investigate this realm of decision making over complex choices to both explore how individuals approach them as well as suggest a productive role for computational assistance.

We consider a choice complex when it involves multiple variables with nonlinear interactions. This includes mundane choices, such as deciding what groceries to buy, as well as monumental, i.e. high resource, choices over cars, houses, and life events from jobs to marriage. Given the nature of complex choices, there may be a role for computational decision aids (CDAs), i.e. digitally mediated information sources that are frequently, but not always, supported by machine learning. CDAs can improve choice making in these complex environments by implementing insights from behavioral science (e.g. [2,9,10]). A growing body of research also examines how people make use of CDAs once they are deployed, how they impact choices, and even how to regulate them (e.g. [1,3,7]). However, the underlying theories of human judgment and decision making that inform the design of CDAs are almost entirely grounded in the analysis of simple, often linear, choices. For example, Cumulative Prospect Theory (CPT) was developed and validated using binary choice experiments in which options varied on a single, linear dimension [13]. CPT and the behavioral predictions that emerge from it are widely cited, applied, and adapted in CDA research (e.g. [4,6,11]) even though choices rarely look like those from the original research.

2   Methodology

Our methodology generates continuous, n-dimensional search spaces that are explored using a digital interface. We take inspiration from complexity science and adapt the *fitness landscape* metaphor to represent choice sets. Fitness landscapes were originally used as a means of describing the relationship between the genetics of an organism, represented by a location in its "fitness landscape," and its success in the world, represented by the elevation of that location [14]. If the landscape is relatively smooth, then it is easy for slight, uni-dimensional changes to result in climbs to higher elevations. As the landscape becomes more rugged, that is, more nonlinear, the impact on elevation of moving along a single dimension becomes much harder to predict. Such landscapes are characterized by many local optima, with numerous peaks and valleys, that increase the difficulty of finding the highest peak. Classically, if one wants to climb to the top of a mountain in a fog, it is far easier to climb Mount Fuji than a rugged expanse of, say, the Rocky Mountains.

A popular generalized formal model of fitness landscapes, the NK model [5], has been used to describe complex settings from biology [12] to business operations [8]. The basic concept of the NK model is that each of an object's N dimensions contributes to its overall fitness, but that contribution is contingent on K interactions with the other dimensions.

2.1   Procedural Generation of Landscapes

We use a proof-of-concept model for procedurally generating N-dimensional choice landscapes.[1] The landscapes that we generate are continuous over their edges, meaning that if, say, you go above the upper limit of a dimension you are placed at its lower limit. A two-dimensional landscape would thus wrap its upper side to its lower, and its left side to its right—equivalent to an ant wandering around on a floating donut (aka a torus).

We generate a set of elevation points for such a landscape. Here, we ensure a certain degree of continuity between adjacent points, though this is easily changed. First, we define the underlying parameters for the landscape, for example, its width, height, maximum elevation, number of "peaks" (local maxima), and the steepest acceptable slope between two points. Next, we randomly place the peaks in the landscape and check that they are in compatible locations, namely, that they are far enough apart that one peak will not be subsumed by another. Finally, a smoothing algorithm fills in the remaining points in the landscape. This algorithm ensures that all of the peaks are separated by intervening "valleys."

2.2   User Interface

Users move about a landscape by setting rotating dials akin to those found on combination locks or analog radios (see Fig. 1). Once the user has decided on the dial settings, the system is queried and the user receives a report of the landscape's elevation at that setting. Thus, two dials are needed to explore a 3-dimensional landscape, one of which can be thought of as controlling the east-west dimension (longitude) while the other determines the north-south dimension (latitude). While we implemented discrete dials, continuous-valued dials are also possible. The reported elevation, captured in an onscreen history of past dial settings and their associated elevation, can be manipulated in various ways, for example, it can have added noise, be re-scaled so that elevations are negative (to explore loss aversion), and so on.

3   Experimental Design

Participants are tasked with tuning the available dials to achieve a stated (and incentivized) goal. The goals are designed for gaining insights about decision making in such environments. For example, maximizing (or minimizing in a loss domain) the final elevation. Such goals are motivated by an associated narrative and incentive structure. For example, when trying to recover economic choice behavior, researchers can introduce an incentive structure in which participants earn more rewards for discovering better dial settings.

---

[1] A tutorial is available at http://nmgurney.com/complex-choice-landscape-maker/.

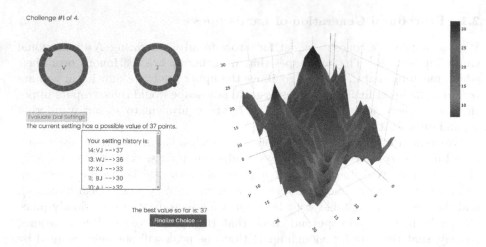

Fig. 1. The user interface is presented on the left. Note the two dials with orange handles. Users click and drag the handles to adjust the dials. The "Evaluate Dial Settings" button allows users to get feedback on a dial setting. The dial setting history is displayed below as well as a submission button, which finalizes their effort on a task. The right image is a rendering of an underlying 3-dimensional landscape. The global optimum is the yellow peak set in the middle-top and the minimum is located in the dark blue valley in the middle bottom of the image.

3.1 Pilot Study Design

302 participants (Mechanical Turk workers) each completed nine dial tuning tasks for a total of 2718 observations. Each of the nine tasks had a unique three-dimensional, discrete search space comprised of 24 points in each tunable dimension, implying 576 possible locations. The search spaces (landscapes) varied in their ruggedness, having either one, two, or four peaks. Metaphorically, a landscape with four peaks is more rugged than one with two peaks, and thus finding, say, the global maximum should be more challenging. The experiment design crossed each level of ruggedness with three levels of feedback accuracy: no noise, low noise, and high noise. When a task provided noisy feedback, a random integer on a fixed interval (either $[-1,1]$ or $[-3,3]$) was drawn and added to the underlying elevation value each time the dial settings were checked. For each task, a participant could tune the dials and sample unique locations as many times as they wished. The last dial tune submitted became their chosen setting for a given task. The order of the nine different tasks for each participant was randomized. Each participant was paid a bonus based on her or his performance in one of the nine tasks (drawn at random) in addition to a base payment for participation. To further incentivize effort, each participant's performance across all nine tasks was totaled and became entries in a lottery for one of five large cash prizes. Finally, note that participants were not informed of the global maximum that they could obtain in a given task, so such information would have to be gained during the course of exploration.

3.2 Results

Please note that we did not formalize any hypotheses prior to data collection, thus we view these results as exploratory and present them as a means of demonstrating the ability of the methodology to generate behavioral insights. Additionally, we report linear models for simplicity and leave more robust approaches to future work.

A multiple linear regression model revealed evidence supporting the notion that the final value that participants submitted for the initial dial tuning task served as an aspiration, or anchor, level in the subsequent tasks ($F(9, 2408) = 70.40, p < 0.001, R2 = 0.21, \beta_{anchor} = 0.394, p < 0.001$). We also analyzed the effect of explore and exploit strategies on attainment in the first round and subsequent rounds. Performance in the first round was highly correlated with exploration ($F(9, 292) = 10.54, p < 0.001, R2 = 0.22, \beta_{explore} = 0.670, p < 0.001$), which we define as a location shift of greater than two positions (Manhattan distance) as was performance across missions ($F(9, 2408) = 41.10, p < 0.001, R2 = 0.22, \beta_{explore} = 0.531, p < 0.001$). In general, participants tended to fall into exploitive traps that, by limiting exploration early on in the process, limited their potential gains. However, when participants used a strategy of exploring early and then later exploiting local information in a given task, they tended to perform much better ($F(9, 2408) = 39.32, p < 0.001, R2 = 0.12, \beta_{exploreExploit} = 4.485, p < 0.001$).

Across our models, we controlled for landscape complexity and consistently saw that the 2-peaked landscape was correlated with worse performance than both the 1-peaked and 4-peaked landscapes. Further investigation revealed that this is likely an artifact of the fixed landscape size, as adding more peaks increases the average value in the plain. This means that, without correcting for average elevation, performance on a 4-peaked landscape looks better because participants are simply more likely to land on a higher location than the other landscapes. An ANOVA ($F(2, 293) = 4.192, p = 0.016$) looking at performance in the first task with performance adjusted for average elevation, for example, suggests that the 4-peaked landscapes were, in fact, the hardest. A Tukey's HSD test for multiple comparisons found that the mean value of corrected submissions was significantly lower for 4-peaked than 1-peaked landscapes ($p = 0.014, 95\%C.I. = [-5.155, -0.463]$).

4 Conclusion

Most of the choices we face in the world involve multiple, interacting dimensions. Such choices are fundamentally difficult because movement across one dimension can alter how prior decisions across other dimensions impact the value of the choice. We found that when facing such choices, participants fall into previously identified decision failures such as anchoring. Moreover, many of the subjects tended to focus far more on the exploitation of what was known rather than on the exploration of the unknown—which is particularly damaging early on when little is known about the choice landscape. While such a strategy works well in a linear world of single-peaked landscapes, it fails in nonlinear worlds with multiple peaks.

The paradigm we develop provides a tractable way to begin to explore human decision making in the realm of complex choice. We argue that complex choices tend to be the norm for the real-world problems that face most individuals. Understanding better how humans confront such choices is not only important but essential to developing a more complete appreciation for the human condition. More pragmatically, the work also suggests a potential role for deploying computational decision aids to improve outcomes. For example, such aids can help users avoid the usual decision traps caused by faulty heuristics or search strategies. People have, for millennia, successfully navigated complex choices. Studying what allows us to succeed in the face of such choices will empower us to build resources to continue to flourish in an increasingly complex world.

References

1. Cai, C.J., Winter, S., Steiner, D., Wilcox, L., Terry, M.: "hello ai": Uncovering the onboarding needs of medical practitioners for human-ai collaborative decision-making. In: Proceedings of the ACM on Human-Computer Interaction 3(CSCW), pp. 1–24 (2019)
2. Dietvorst, B.J., Simmons, J.P., Massey, C.: Algorithm aversion: people erroneously avoid algorithms after seeing them err. J. Exp. Psychol. Gen. **144**(1), 114 (2015)
3. Green, B., Chen, Y.: The principles and limits of algorithm-in-the-loop decision making. In: Proceedings of the ACM on Human-Computer Interaction 3(CSCW), pp. 1–24 (2019)
4. Grgic-Hlaca, N., Engel, C., Gummadi, K.P.: Human decision making with machine advice: an experiment on bailing and jailing. In: Proceedings of the ACM on Human-Computer Interaction 3 (2019)
5. Kauffman, S.A., Weinberger, E.D.: The nk model of rugged fitness landscapes and its application to maturation of the immune response. J. Theor. Biol. **141**(2), 211–245 (1989)
6. Lee, M.C., Park, J.: There is no perfect evaluator: an investigation based on prospect theory. Hum. Factors Ergon. Manuf. Serv. Ind. **28**(6), 383–392 (2018)
7. Lee, M.K., Jain, A., Cha, H.J., Ojha, S., Kusbit, D.: Procedural justice in algorithmic fairness: leveraging transparency and outcome control for fair algorithmic mediation. In: Proceedings of the ACM on Human-Computer Interaction 3(CSCW), pp. 1–26 (2019)
8. Levinthal, D.A.: Adaptation on rugged landscapes. Manage. Sci. **43**(7), 934–950 (1997)
9. Logg, J.M., Minson, J.A., Moore, D.A.: Algorithm appreciation: people prefer algorithmic to human judgment. Organ. Behav. Hum. Decis. Process. **151**, 90–103 (2019)
10. Poursabzi-Sangdeh, F., Goldstein, D.G., Hofman, J.M., Wortman Vaughan, J.W., Wallach, H.: Manipulating and measuring model interpretability. In: Proceedings of the 2021 CHI Conference on Human Fctors in Computing Systems, pp. 1–52 (2021)
11. Quinn, P., Cockburn, A.: Loss aversion and preferences in interaction. Hum.- Comput. Inter. **35**(2), 143–190 (2020)

12. Romero, P.A., Arnold, F.H.: Exploring protein fitness landscapes by directed evolution. Nat. Rev. Mol. Cell Biol. **10**(12), 866–876 (2009)
13. Tversky, A., Kahneman, D.: Advances in prospect theory: cumulative representation of uncertainty. J. Risk Uncertain. **5**(4), 297–323 (1992)
14. Wright, S., et al.: The roles of mutation, inbreeding, crossbreeding, and selection in evolution (1932)

Gaze-Enhanced User Interface for Real-Time Video Surveillance

Jutta Hild[✉], Gerrit Holzbach, Sebastian Maier, Florian van de Camp, Michael Voit, and Elisabeth Peinsipp-Byma

Fraunhofer Institute of Optronics, System Technologies and Image Exploitation IOSB, 76131 Karlsruhe, Germany
jutta.hild@iosb.fraunhofer.de

Abstract. Image analysis is a demanding task, particularly, if real-time analysis of motion imagery is required. Hence, the human image analysts needs assistance by a customized software system. In this contribution, a user interface for real-time video surveillance is proposed. The objective is to provide a concept that enables a single user to perform sensor operation and basic observation and detection tasks at the same time. In order to provide efficient and comfortable support, our approach enhances the typical joystick input with gaze input and automated image exploitation algorithms; an alternative concept uses a gamepad instead of the joystick. First qualitative assessment by expert video analysts identified different advantages of the different concepts.

Keywords: User interface · Gaze input · Video surveillance

1 Introduction

Image analysis is a common task in various application domains like geosciences, medicine or safety and security. Particularly demanding are applications, which require the real-time analysis of motion imagery throughout a longer period. This is for example the case in the domain of traffic control or environmental surveillance.

In this contribution, we address the situation of a human operator performing real-time video surveillance using a UAV (unmanned aerial vehicle). The objective is to provide a user interface that, first, allows sensor operation for recording of meaningful video material, and, second, allows the annotation of relevant objects in the video. As a result, such a system would enable a single human operator to perform sensor operation and basic observation and detection tasks at the same time.

According to expert video analysts, sensor operation using a joystick over hours can be manually and cognitively stressful. If the human operator in addition must accomplish observation and detection tasks, the required stronger attention focus occupies additional perceptive and cognitive resources. Hence, the human operator needs support by a user interface that keeps their resources required for interaction with the system to a minimum.

C. Stephanidis et al. (Eds.): HCII 2022, CCIS 1654, pp. 46–53, 2022.
https://doi.org/10.1007/978-3-031-19679-9_7

In our approach, we propose a user interface that supports the human operator in two ways. (1) We propose to utilize gaze-based interaction. (2) We propose to incorporate automated video analysis algorithms.

Gaze-based interaction has proved to be an efficient interaction method. Early research showed the potential as an alternative to mouse input or touch for static object selection [1–3]. The introduced gaze interaction methods typically utilize the current gaze position provided by an eye-tracker for pointing, and a key press or dwell time on an object for selection actuation. Evaluation results showed that gaze interaction was very fast, intuitive and easy to use as well as manually less stressful. The main drawback was that due to technical and physiological issues the eye-tracker provides a noisy signal allowing robust selection only for objects of a size starting with 2° of visual angle. Providing a zoom mechanism can help but requires an additional interaction step before object selection which, in turn, increases the total selection time. If selection objects are moving, gaze-based selection is not only fast, intuitive and manually less stressful, but achieves similar effectiveness as mouse input [4, 5]; Hild et al. [4] reported up to 40% shorter selection time for moving object selection in video data captured by a UAV. Besides moving object selection, gaze-based interaction is also intuitive for navigation in a scene. Velloso et al. [6] reported this for gaming applications and Hild et al. [7] for navigation in a UAV-based video.

Automated image analysis algorithms like object detection or object classification assist the human image analysts' perception and cognition. Considering real-time video surveillance applications, motion detection and object classification algorithms might help finding relevant objects; object tracking algorithms assist in keeping track of relevant objects. However, automated algorithms are never perfect. Therefore, the human operator with their deep understanding of situations due to long-time experience as well as the ability of creative reasoning still play a key role in image analysis, particularly, in safety and security applications. However, an evaluation with 12 participants showed that the availability of automated motion detection and vehicle classification reduced the mean error rate in a visual object search and selection task up to 50% [5]. An evaluation with 18 expert video analysts on initializing automated object tracking on vehicles in full motion video showed that using a gaze-based selection method (gaze pointing + ENTER key press) provides the same low error rate and is significantly faster in difficult selection situations (objects partly occluded, turbulent image motion) than mouse input [8].

In the following, Sect. 2 describes the advanced image exploitation station, an experimental system we implemented to develop and test novel concepts for improved operator support in the domain of traffic or environmental surveillance. One of its components is a UAV overflight simulation comprising the typical sensor operation using a joystick. Section 3 describes the concepts we implemented to support a single human operator to perform sensor operation and basic observation and detection tasks at the same time.

2 Advanced Image Exploitation Station

The Advanced Image Exploitation Station is an experimental system used to develop and test novel concepts for improved operator support. Figure 1 shows the setup. It provides several systems that are used in the domain of imaging reconnaissance and surveillance:

a common operational picture including sensor mission planning (1), (video) image recording from a (simulated) UAV (2), software for image exploitation (3), and an image exploitation assistance system (4). Each system is provided on a separate flat screen; the three vertical screens are attached on a Dataflex Viewlite mount on a table with a size of 2 m × 1 m. The overall realization regards, on the one hand, the state-of-the-art of user interfaces; in particular, considering novel input methods. On the other hand, the setup incorporates requirements of image exploitation systems as shaped in discussion with expert image analysts.

In this paper, we focus on a user interface supporting a single human operator to perform sensor operation and basic observation and detection tasks at the same time during a drone flight (Fig. 1, no. 2). The drone flight simulation is realized as web application using the CESIUM library for 3D presentation of the world. CESIUM was used because in contrast to other simulation frameworks it provides a world model; and real data like aerial images can be easily integrated. Moreover, objects of all kinds can be defined, e.g., vehicles on the ground with individual movement trajectories.

The simulation features typical UAV characteristics as flight altitude and flight speed. Within the drone flight simulation, a sensor is defined that can be operated during the simulation using a Logitec Extreme 3D Pro joystick. Tilting the joystick moves the sensor focus, turning the joystick sidelong zooms the sensor, and pressing the fire button saves a single image frame of the current scene (see the green arrows in Fig. 2). The simulation features two sensor types, a pan-tilt sensor and a tilt-roll sensor. The tilt-roll control allows relocating the sensor focus with a simple, linear movement that combines the linear tilt movement and the linear roll movement. The pan-tilt control is more complex as it combines the linear tilt movement with a rotating pan movement. The advantage of pan-tilt sensors is that they provide the horizon continuously at top of the display.

3 Gaze-Enhanced User Interface for Video Surveillance

To enable a single human operator to perform improved video surveillance the user interface of the drone flight simulation was extended in order to allow sensor operation and basic observation and detection tasks at the same time. To accomplish this, we discussed with expert video analysts, which functions to add to the user interface. As a result, we came up with the integration of three additional functions:

1. Automated motion detection
2. Automated single object tracking
3. Annotated single frame

Figure 2 shows the basic interaction realization for the six system functions, using the joystick in a traditional way for sensor control; the three additional functions utilize additional joystick keys and an eye-tracker for the required pointing operations as to keep the additional manual intervention at a minimum.

The automated motion detection can be switched on/off by pressing a specified joystick key. If switched on, all moving objects in the scene are highlighted by a semi-transparent, red overlay.

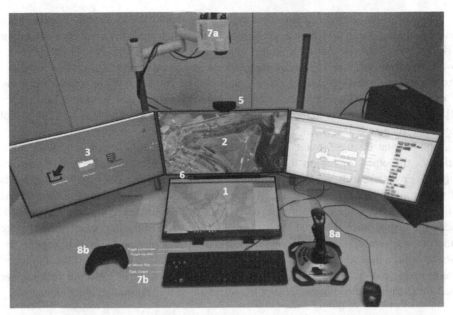

Fig. 1. The Advanced Image Exploitation Station. The setup integrates several systems necessary for imaging reconnaissance and surveillance. 1: Common operational picture for sensor mission planning (touchscreen) 2: Drone flight simulation 3: Image exploitation software 4: Image exploitation assistance 5: Webcam for user authentication 6: Eyetracker providing gaze position on screen and head pose 7a/b: Beamer for annotation of specific key assignments 8a/b: Joystick and gamepad for operation of drone flight simulation.

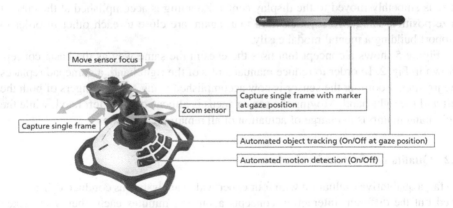

Fig. 2. Basic interaction realization for the six system functions using joystick and eye-tracker.

The automated single object tracking provides a semi-transparent violet overlay to highlight the object selected for tracking (see Fig. 3). The selection is accomplished by pressing a specified joystick key while gaze pointing at the wanted object. Gaze pointing is realized using the Tobii 4C eye-tracker mounted at the bottom of the screen displaying the drone flight simulation (see Fig. 1, no. 6).

The Tobii 4C device is a low-cost eye-tracker that costs about 150$. It has been developed for gaming and, hence, is able to cope with a broad variety of users and their different eye characteristics (e.g., color, shape). The sampling rate of 90 Hz is similar to lower sampling rates for high-cost eye-trackers, which proved being suitable for gaze-based interaction in dynamic selection situations [4]. The accuracy appears to be about 1° of visual angle [8] (we did not find any accuracy information from the manufacturer [9]) which is slightly worse than the accuracy of high-cost eye-trackers (0.5° of visual angle is typical).

The annotated single image function records a single image together with an annotation of the object or region the human operator considers currently highly relevant (Fig. 3). From research, we know that the gaze position is a reliable proxy for the focus of visual attention [10]. Hence, we assume that the operator's gaze is directed to this point of high relevance in the image, and, hence, utilize the current gaze position provided by the eye-tracker for the annotation. The actuation of the annotated single image function is accomplished by pressing a specified joystick button. In order to support the user to build a mental model of the various input functions, we allocated the annotated single image button close to the simple single image button; in a similar fashion, we used joystick keys close to each other for actuation of the automated algorithms.

3.1 Alternative Interaction Concepts Reducing Manual Stress

In order to reduce manual stress even more, we propose two alternative interaction realizations. Figure 4 shows a concept that utilizes only the keys of the joystick and avoids any manual tilting or rotating of the joystick. Moving the sensor focus is now accomplished by gaze interaction only: The image region where the user directs their gaze is smoothly moved to the display center. Zooming is accomplished at the current gaze position using two joystick keys that, again, are close to each other in order to support building a mental modal easily.

Figure 5 shows a concept that uses the eyes in the same way as the basic concept shown in Fig. 2. In order to reduce manual stress of the right hand, a gamepad replaces the joystick. Zooming the sensor is now accomplished using several fingers of both the left and the right hand. Moving the sensor focus is allocated to the left hand, while the right hand thumb is in charge of actuation of all remaining functions.

3.2 Qualitative System Evaluation

So far, a qualitative evaluation with four expert video analysts was conducted. The users tried out the different interaction concepts about ten minutes each; they were asked afterwards for their preferred realization.

As a result, none of the concepts was clearly preferred. Actually, the users emphasized that each concept had its benefits. The basic concept has the advantage of familiarity. The concept using only the joystick keys has the advantage of reduced manual stress. The concept using the gamepad has the advantage of distributing the manual stress to both hands; moreover, the younger generation of expert video analysts has often long-time experience using gamepads rather than joysticks.

Fig. 3. Annotated single frame: the red box shows where the operator's gaze was directed. The semi-transparent violet overlay marks an object tracked by the automated tracking algorithm at the same time. (Color figure online)

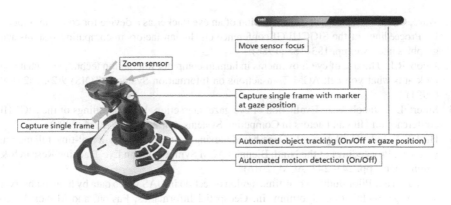

Fig. 4. Alternative interaction realization reducing manual stress of the right hand using joystick keys and an eye-tracker.

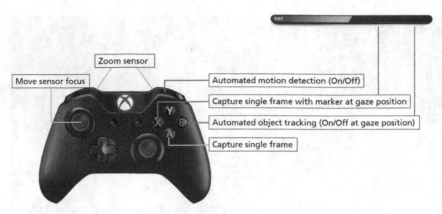

Fig. 5. Alternative interaction realization reducing manual stress of the right hand using a gamepad and an eye-tracker.

4 Future Work

First, a quantitative evaluation of the interaction concepts in a controlled user study would be beneficial. Another idea is extending the drone flight simulation by providing an image exploitation assistance for object recognition as an overlay.

References

1. Ware, C., Mikaelian, H.H.: An evaluation of an eye tracker as a device for computer input2. In: Proceedings of the SIGCHI/GI conference on Human factors in computing systems and graphics interface, pp. 183–188 (1986)
2. Jacob, R.J.: The use of eye movements in human-computer interaction techniques: what you look at is what you get. ACM Transactions on Information Systems (TOIS) 9(2), 152–169 (1991)
3. Sibert, L.E., Jacob, R.J.: Evaluation of eye gaze interaction. In: Proceedings of the SIGCHI conference on Human Factors in Computing Systems, pp. 281–288. ACM (2000)
4. Hild, J., Kühnle, C., Beyerer, J.: Gaze-based moving target acquisition in real-time full motion video. In: Proceedings of the Ninth Biennial ACM Symposium on Eye Tracking Research & Applications, pp. 241–244. ACM (2016)
5. Hild, J., et al.: Pilot study on real-time motion detection in UAS video data by human observer and image exploitation algorithm. In: Geospatial Informatics, Fusion, and Motion Video Analytics VII, vol. 10199, p. 1019903. International Society for Optics and Photonics (2017)
6. Velloso, E., Carter, M.: The emergence of eyeplay: a survey of eye interaction in games. In: Proceedings of the 2016 annual symposium on computer-human interaction in play, pp. 171–185. ACM (2016)
7. Hild, J., et al.: A Pilot Study on Gaze-Based Control of a Virtual Camera Using 360°-Video Data. In: Harris, D. (ed.) EPCE 2018. LNCS (LNAI), vol. 10906, pp. 419–428. Springer, Cham (2018). https://doi.org/10.1007/978-3-319-91122-9_34
8. Hild, J., Peinsipp-Byma, E., Voit, M., Beyerer, J.: Suggesting gaze-based selection for surveillance applications. In: 16th IEEE International Conference on Advanced Video and Signal Based Surveillance, pp. 1–8. IEEE (2019)

9. Tobii homepage: https://help.tobii.com/hc/en-us/articles/360008539058-What-s-the-differ ence-between-Tobii-Eye-Tracker-4C-and-5-, last accessed 18 March 2022
10. Zhai, S.: What's in the Eyes for Attentive Input. Commun. ACM **46**(3), 34–39 (2003)

Cyber Security Table-Top Exercise Gamification with Dynamic Scenario for Qualification Assessment

Gabrielė Kvietinskaitė, Linas Bukauskas(✉)[iD], and Virgilijus Krinickij

Cyber Security Laboratory, Institute of Computer Science, Vilnius University, Vilnius, Lithuania
{linas.bukauskas,virgilijus.krinickij}@mif.vu.lt

Abstract. Today, information technology is used to fight the virus and perform various daily activities like teleworking and learning from home. It is essential to ask within the cyber community how to acquire and build competencies during the pandemic that would span beyond technological skills. Digitally made online tabletop environments are especially relevant in this crucial time. Tabletop exercises help professionals learn and analyse different scenarios of human behaviour and prepare for real-life situations. In particular, it is essential to use tabletop exercises with gamification capabilities for agile adaptation to learners' competencies. Gamification elements in education are used when simulating static or dynamic incidents and scenarios. Depending on the scenario at hand, different competencies are evaluated. This poster describes a prototype developed by the cyber security roles and competencies assessment. It is a comprehensive analysis and implementation process. The prototype introduces some specialised roles that can be chosen. Based on the role, the difficulty of a scenario is set, and the game begins. The poster demonstrates how implemented prototype puts a varying effort on the cyber domain, general communication and organisational skills.

Keywords: Table-top exercises · Gamification · Competences · Assessment

1 Introduction

The rapid development of technology and changes within the community using digital assets puts in perspective a traditional learning environment ever before. The heavy use of computerized systems questions how we learn and build competencies from the digital world. Digital table-top environments are especially relevant in this post-COVID-19 time to minimize large gatherings and support interpersonal communication bubbles.

The need for specialists, especially in Information Technologies, is proliferating. In different professions, security skill permeates qualification assessment in all aspects of a business. A gamification process is used to simulate incidents and

© The Author(s), under exclusive license to Springer Nature Switzerland AG 2022
C. Stephanidis et al. (Eds.): HCII 2022, CCIS 1654, pp. 54–62, 2022.
https://doi.org/10.1007/978-3-031-19679-9_8

scenarios leading to these incidents. Depending on the scenario at hand, different competencies are evaluated. Also, the table-top Gamification method is used to evaluate competencies and is a training tool. Training while playing spikes cognitive skills and inspiration in one's efforts to learn and finish the game [6].

Standard learning methods while being in the same room or location are restricted for the foreseeable future. The need for drastic measures to assess competencies of different physical locations is very viable now. Using the digitized version of table-top exercises makes it possible to work with a more significant number of people and their competencies in parallel. A digital version of such a platform would enable uninterrupted operation even without the possibility of physically entering the place where such inspections would occur. In general, table-top games are suitable for everyone to straighten relationships, increase brain function, enhance creativity and self-confidence.

The work aims to show the work on developing cyber security table-exercise implementation and application in the dynamic scenario for specialist qualification assessment.

2 Related Work

There is a significant bias when it comes to a person's thoughts when the topic is security. To mitigate or remediate complex attacks requires an excessive amount of knowledge, skills and abilities from many fields. Overall, the progress of Information Technologies invokes a more profound training in competence development [9]. A vast amount of experts are required to undertake these tasks. In the U.S. alone, a workforce of twenty to thirty thousand skilled specialists is in demand. Such a considerable demand became needed only in the last decade because of ever-increasing cyber events [5]. In the next several years, supply will slightly soften the market demand for specialists [3].

Significant research is established to find more efficient ways for people to learn cyber security. Highly receptive people who learned cyber security more easily and quickly through gamification were students [1,6]. One solution was a gamified cyber event data logging and partial theoretical assessment given to students as an experiment. The results were a mass of collected data throughout the gameplay that could be used for competence, cyber event awareness and stress level evaluation.

Based on one research, a system was developed that is called Experience Accelerator (ExpAcc) [10], for assessing competencies for system engineers, which, as described, are in huge demand. The described system contemplates a competence taxonomy distributed in two groups: system thinking and critical thinking. System thinking describes the systemic and systematic thinking, while critical thinking lets the person see the product from a management side. These requirements must meet technical analytical, technical leadership, technical management, and general professional project management. The first three describe the technical aspects that the engineer must meet, and the second describes the management part. The given method can be used for inexperienced candidates to become engineers and for current workers to evaluate their competencies.

One of the proposed models for competence assessment in [7] research is to model competencies based on Bayesian networks. The research is proposing a model mainly to evaluate student competencies. First, the proposed method's primary step is to establish the Bayesian network topology. The second step is to evaluate the student's knowledge and skills. The third step is to update the probabilities of the Bayesian network. The main idea of the research is to focus on a given problem, testing student knowledge and updating the knowledge base. That would trigger possible competencies via probability updating of the network.

The research in [4] provides a better view when comparing competencies of professionals who work in the field and non-professionals in [9] research. The research strongly suggests evaluating the skills of non-IT and IT people over time by gathering the needed criteria presented on an IPad application. The research provides scenarios for both groups of people to handle. Evaluation is described as accumulating the needed declarative knowledge, procedural knowledge, automaticity, and skill over time, producing competence.

Another way to try and build competencies in cyber security is through the TTX (Table-Top Exercises) or the TTXWE (Table-Top Exercise Web Environment). This TTX environment is used to simulate high-level scenarios through the gamified TTXWE not only to raise competencies but to assess the ones already obtained [2].

The cyber security workforce framework created by NIST (National Institute of Standards and Technology) is the basis for categorizing, organizing and describing cyber security work into categories, specialities, job role tasks, knowledge, skills and abilities. This system provides organizations with a common, consistent lexicon that classifies and describes cyber security work. Academic institutions can also use the framework to develop CS programs that better prepare students for current and anticipated cybercrime security workforce need [8].

3 Proposed Prototype Model for Competency Assessment

The representation of core model is in Fig. 1 of the qualification assessment states that a user first needs to authenticate and derive his already claimed competences.

The US National Institute of Standards and Technology was chosen to use the developed system led by the National Cyber Security Education Initiative (NICE) cyber security workforce framework positions and competencies. A total of 52 positions and 60 competencies is saved in the database. Each role is assigned to the appropriate competencies. The same competencies can be assigned to more than one role. Before running a script that runs the scenario, each logged-in system user must select a role that describes the player. A player will assume some role based on the scenario while playing the game. They are displayed in a drop-down list. As seen in Fig. 1 the roles are given based on the competency

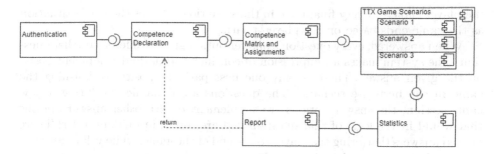

Fig. 1. Competence assessment model

matrix. All selections are saved in the database. The choice of roles will later determine which scenario the system will offer the player to run.

An appropriate scenario is given based on the previous parameters. Then data is processed using the Bayesian network. The results accumulated while playing the scenario are reported back in the form of a structured document. The report is a PDF whose content consists of general information about the game and various types of charts. For the scenario we chose SCADA system where an engineer is working at a water supply company. In Fig. 2 you can see a generalised snippet of an expanding scenario. The script consists of 254 questions and 253 answer options. Questions have 0 to 4 answers options. Some questions have a dead end because of possible negative outcomes to the system based on

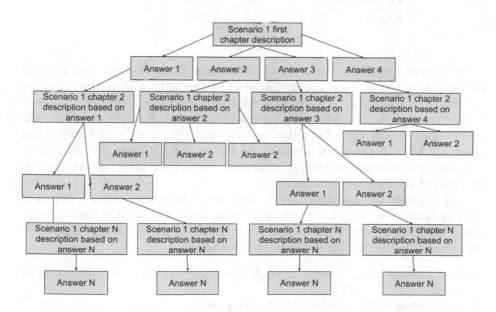

Fig. 2. Scenario for competency assessment in SCADA systems

the player choices. Every final node in the scenario describes the whole situation as the game ends based on the player's path.

When answered, every question's answer option gives a different further question. The system makes an impression of continued scenario development based on the given answer. There is only one best path for positively finishing the game in the best-case scenario. The questions are dynamic, so during a new game session, the answer options are supplemented with other answer options that would fit the logic of that question and are sorted in random order. There are red answers that bring the player to the end of the game, while yellow answers assume that your part in this scenario is over and some other party steps in to continue the job. Having a plethora of possibilities in one scenario it is imperative to note that the possible level of the player playing the scenario may vary. That is why we propose a 5 level distinction between the players in this model (Table 1).

Table 1. Player levels and points needed to achieve a certain level

Level	Points from	Points to	Minimal amount of points to achieve a level
Novice	0	10	5
Proficient	11	20	15
Advanced	21	30	25
Professional	31	40	35
Expert	41	50	45

The given scenario is set for novice level users. Based on the different levels of the player the scenario could change. The competence is assigned for the question and the answer is assigned a value that determines whether the player has or acquires the competence being tested in the question. At each step, the calculations update the information and increase the chance that a player can reach the level of the given scenario. At the end of the game, all the results obtained are summed and then it is checked whether the player corresponds to the level of the executed scenario.

For example, when a player selects a scenario, the first question is displayed "While monitoring the water pressure in the monitor and coordinating the computer on (level 3) you notice that the first pipe's pressure starts rising. What will you do?". You get 3 possible answers variants:

1. Send message to supervisory computer level (level 2) to release pressure/open pipe.
2. Keep watching the monitor. Maybe the pressure will go down on its own.
3. Send a message to level 2 to stop all of the water flow.

As mentioned before this will continue until the play is over. The given data in the questions and answers is linear and the given links influence one another. Meaning that depending on the clicked answer, the scenario will continue based on that answer. Another scenario description or step appears to continue the scenario. The scenario itself is a continuous Bayesian network. Every answer in the question is a variable that we present with a small amount of weight based on the scenario level. This weight is summed and the sum is the points needed for the player to get and achieve some level. The weight is distributed according the logic of the question and it's answers. Meaning that based on the answers weight we determine how much points per answer a player gets to achieve the needed minimum or maximum for that level.

Throughout the game, calculations are performed using Bayesian theorem for each question and answer option selected. At each step, the calculations update the information and increases the chance that the player can reach the level of the scenario. At the end of the game, all the results obtained are summed up and then it is checked whether the player matches the level of the executed scenario.

$$allPoints = \sum_{i=1}^{n} \frac{P(question_i \mid answer)\, P(answer)}{P(question_i)} \tag{1}$$

In (1) Equation to get all the points after the game is played. Here, $P(question|i)$ or $P(q|a)$—hypothesis is true given the event, $P(answer)$ or $P(a)$—prior probability the hypothesis was true,

When the play is finished the results provided in the generated PDF are as fallows:

1. Player login name.
2. What scenario was played and scenario level.
3. Player level before and after the game.
4. Date and time when the scenario was started and when it was finished.
5. Statistical evaluation information.

The scenario takes additional parameters to evaluate a person. The given parameters after calculating provide a total score that says how you did overall in your job. The parameters describe:

SA ability to maintain the *service availability* through out the whole playtime of the scenario.

BI *Business impact* to the business while the business was suffering from the attack.

DAA *Defence against an attack* estimates the defensive time while scenario was ongoing even if the event is a false positive.

R *Reporting* indicates if the incident was reported to the relevant recipients during the whole playtime of the scenario.

O *Others* is a parameter describing other possible circumstantial third party or internal human factor cases that possibly could not be accounted for.

The expert chosen weights are used to calculate the final result:

$$result = 0.45 \cdot SA + 0.2 \cdot BI + 0.2 \cdot DAA + 0.1 \cdot R + 0.05 \cdot O \tag{2}$$

4 Results

Table 2 shows that the player has selected the *Asset/Inventory Management competency*, which was evaluated during the game's initial phase. Unfortunately, the player did not appear to have this competence, as the system indicates that the player does not have/did not acquire this competence. You can see this in the competency check column, where a triplet based formula of predicates is shown. The predicates consist of checked chosen and achieved. We would check during the game if the competence was achieved by the player that chose that competence. Another competency was tested in the system, but the player did not choose it—*Computer Forensics*. When the scenario is executed, the system indicates that the player can have or acquire this competence, although the player does not think so. The last competency chosen by the player, but not checked by the system, was *Computer Languages*. As the system did not check this competence during the game, it is unknown if the player really has it.

Table 2. Competency assesement report

Competence	Description	Competency check
Asset / Inventory Management	This area contaisn KSA that relate to the process of developing, operating, maintaining, upgrading and disposing of assets	True, True, False
Computer Forensics	This area contains KSA that relate to the tools and techniques used in data recovery and preservation of electronic evidence	True, False, True
Computer Languages	This area contains KSA that relate to computer languages and their applications to enable a system to perform specific functions	False, True, False

The graph of the frequency of answers and the answers chosen by the player in Fig. 3 shown as heat-map. In this case, based on the scenario and the level the starting answer point is the same.

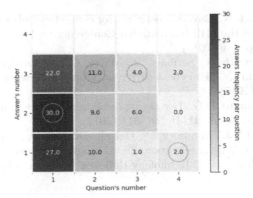

Fig. 3. Frequency of responses and response options chosen by the player

5   Conclusions

High level of cyber vulnerability has been observed due to the lack of workforce and general cyber security knowledge, skills and abilities. The proposed methods enable easier to cope with global pandemic as it became an additional factor which accelerated the need for more cyber security specialists and overall security awareness. The proposed methodology tooling is applicable among many organizations and cyber security actors to help enforce better stability in the cyber space.

References

1. Boopathi, K., Sreejith, S., Bithin, A.: Learning cyber security through gamification. Indian J. Sci. Technol. **8**(7), 642–649 (2015)
2. Brilingaitė, A., Bukauskas, L., Krinickij, V., Kutka, E.: Environment for cybersecurity tabletop exercises. In: ECGBL 2017 11th European Conference on Game-Based Learning, pp. 47–55. Academic Conferences and publishing limited (2017)
3. Catota, F.E., Morgan, M.G., Sicker, D.C.: Cybersecurity education in a developing nation: the Ecuadorian environment. J. Cybersecurity **5**(1), tyz001 (2019)
4. Fink, G., Best, D., Manz, D., Popovsky, V., Endicott-Popovsky, B.: Gamification for measuring cyber security situational awareness. In: Schmorrow, D.D., Fidopiastis, C.M. (eds.) AC 2013. LNCS (LNAI), vol. 8027, pp. 656–665. Springer, Heidelberg (2013). https://doi.org/10.1007/978-3-642-39454-6_70
5. Gasiba, T., Lechner, U., Pinto-Albuquerque, M., Zouitni, A.: Design of secure coding challenges for cybersecurity education in the industry. In: Shepperd, M., Brito e Abreu, F., Rodrigues da Silva, A., Pérez-Castillo, R. (eds.) QUATIC 2020. CCIS, vol. 1266, pp. 223–237. Springer, Cham (2020). https://doi.org/10.1007/978-3-030-58793-2_18
6. László, K., András, N., Ákos, O., András, S.: Structuration theory and strategic alignment in information security management: Introduction of a comprehensive research approach and program. AARMS-Acad. Appl. Res. Mil. Publ. Manage. Sci. **16**(1), 5–16 (2017)

7. Le, N.T., Pinkwart, N.: Bayesian networks for competences-base student modeling. In: Proceedings of the 11th International Conference on Knowledge Management, Osaka, Japan, pp. 4–6 (2015)
8. Newhouse, W., Keith, S., Scribner, B., Witte, G.: National initiative for cybersecurity education (NICE) cybersecurity workforce framework. NIST Spec. Publ. **800**(2017), 181 (2017)
9. Pfleeger, S.L., Caputo, D.D.: Leveraging behavioral science to mitigate cyber security risk. Comput. Secur. **31**(4), 597–611 (2012)
10. Squires, A., Wade, J., Dominick, P., Gelosh, D.: Building a competency taxonomy to guide experience acceleration of lead program systems engineers. Technical report, Stevens Institute of Technology Hoboken NJ School of Systems and Enterprises (2011)

Motivating Subscription of Video-on-Demand in Mainland China: A Push-Pull-Mooring Perspective

Lili Liu, Bingyun Jin(✉), Yajun Shi, Linwei Hu, Jingping Yang, and Chuanmin Mi

College of Economics and Management, Nanjing University of Aeronautics and Astronautics, Nanjing, China

{llili85,shiyajun,yangjingping,Cmmi}@nuaa.edu.cn,
1649362574@qq.com

Abstract. Majority of Chinese video websites failed to make profit from subscription of Video-on-Demand, partially due to the fact that Chinese audiences either easily find alternative free videos elsewhere, or switch to a competing video website with minimal effort. The inability to retain existing subscribers would gravely imperil the survival of video websites. Therefore, it is critical to understand why audiences subscribe the Video-on-Demand in order to maintain the sustainability of Chinese video websites. In light of the push-pull-mooring theory, we develop a research model to investigate the determinants of audiences' subscription behavior. We conducted an online survey to collect data. SmartPLS 3.33 was adopted to analyze data. Results indicating that: (1) subscribe intention positively affect subscription behavior; (2) push factors and pull factors have positive impacts on subscribe intention; (3) mooring factors: fans enthusiasm positively influence subscribe intention, while price cost negatively affect intention. Potential contributions and limitations are discussed.

Keywords: Video-on-demand · Push-Pull-Mooring theory · Subscription behavior

1 Introduction

Chinese video websites have gradually adopted the "Pay Wall" mode since 2010, in which users have privileges through paid membership services of different levels, such as skipping advertising and watching exclusive movies [26]. At present, Chinese online video market is dominated by three tech giants: Baidu (iQiyi), Alibaba (Youku), and Tecent (Tecent video), collectively known as BAT. Chinese video websites make great efforts to develop paid contents in order to enrich the business mode. According to Statista report, the average revenue per Chinese user in the Video-on-Demand segment is projected to reach US$32.00, user penetration will be 27.5% in 2021 (Video-on-Demand - China | Statista Market Forecast). Although number of subscribers and their spend are rising, majority of Chinese video websites stuck in a state of loss, and fail to make profit from the subscription mode, including BAT video websites [25]. This

C. Stephanidis et al. (Eds.): HCII 2022, CCIS 1654, pp. 63–71, 2022.
https://doi.org/10.1007/978-3-031-19679-9_9

dilemma is easy to understand when we make a comparison between China and United States. U.S. has one-fifth of China's population, yet the total revenue in the Video-on-Demand segment reaches THREE times that of China. In addition, U.S. average revenue per user in the Video-on-Demand segment is projected to be US$167.44, user penetration will be 64.7% in 2021, far ahead of China (Video-on-Demand - United States | Statista Market Forecast).

Many Chinese video websites failed to make profit from subscription of Video-on-Demand, partially due to the fact that Chinese audiences either easily find alternative free videos elsewhere, or switch to a competing video website with minimal effort. The inability to retain existing subscribers would gravely imperil the survival or thrival of video websites. Therefore, it is critical to understand why audiences subscribe the Video-on-Demand in order to attract new subscribers and retain existing subscribers and ultimately, the sustainability of video websites. However, little research attention has been devoted to understating Chinese video websites audiences, and their subscription behavior. The objective of this paper is, therefore, to shed light on the determinants of audiences' subscription behavior. We thus ground our research in the migration theory, more specifically, the push-pull-mooring theory (hereinafter referred to as "PPM") to develop a research model that would enhance our understanding of audiences' subscription motivations.

2 Theoretical Background

PPM theory was originally designed for human migration studies, which has been widely used in many disciplines. PPM theory summaries determinants of user migration behavior into three dimensions: push factors that encourage emigration, pull factors that attract immigrants, and mooring factors that may promote or inhibit migration, and has been proposed with the expectation to explain the migration phenomenon more thoroughly [1]. The PPM theory has been applied to the marketing domain, with strong predictive power in consumer behavior literature. For instance, Chen and Zhu adopt PPM theory to investigate key determinants of users' mobile reading behavior [3], while Liu applies PPM theory to investigate consumers' online purachase behavior [14]. Accordingly, in our study, the PPM theory is applied as the overarching theory to develop the research framework and investigates the drivers of Chinese video websites audiences' subscription behavior.

Drawing on PPM theory, we define independent variables and classify them into three aspects that affect consumer's subscription of Video-on-demand services. Specifically, push factors (time cost and functional deprivation), pull factors (perceived enjoyment and non-substitutability) and mooring factors (consumer devotion and price cost) are the antecedents of consumers' intention to subscribe, which in turn directly affects subscription behavior.

3 Research Model and Hypotheses

The research model is presented below in Fig. 1. Additionally, corresponding hypotheses are discussed in the following section.

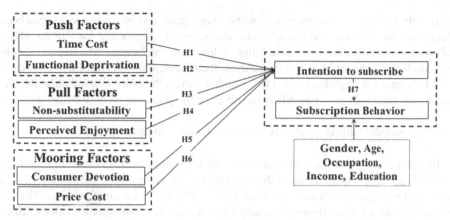

Fig. 1. Research model

Many studies have demonstrated a strong relationship between the time cost and consumer activities. For instance, Chocarro et al. find that the potential of saving time and 24-h shopping are conducive to promoting consumers to shop online [5]. Users of a Social Network Site may not change if they have to spend a lot of time switching to new SNSs [11]. From economic perspective, if audiences are able to find alternative free videos (e.g., Hit TV series) elsewhere with low time cost, they would switch to using other video sources rather than subscribe current video-on-demand services. On the other hand, when consumers have to spend more time in searching for alternative free videos, they will be more likely to give up the searching activities and pay the subscription fee. Therefore, we propose:

H1. Time cost positively affects audiences' intention to subscribe.

Functional deprivation refers to the deprivation of practical or technical benefits perceived by users from a service or product [24]. According to Chinese video website operation policy, audiences have to pay the subscription fee to enjoy exclusive privileges, such as watching videos on multiple devices, skipping ads, high quality videos (1080p and 4k), and content only available for VIP members (including trending drama, variety show, movie and anime). Without subscription, audiences are merely able to access limited videos, and have to watch 30 ~ 120 s ads before the video. In this case, audiences may consider it a waste of time to watch ads, though the videos are free of charge. In short, functional deprivation may impair audiences' experience of watching videos, which may incentivize them start to subscribe the VIP services [20]. Accordingly, we assume:

H2. Function deprivation positively affects audiences' intention to subscribe.

Non-substitutability refers to users' perception, preference and evaluation of the heterogeneity and monopoly of online videos. A non-substitutable video cannot be found elsewhere and replaced by other videos, which is exclusively provided by a particular video website [22]. For instance, a trending drama produced by Tecent video has been released on the website, and the full episodes are merely accessable for VIP members. According to the high non-substitutability of this drama, audiences have to pay the subscription fee if they would like to watch the full episodes, since it is impossible for them to find alternatives anywhere else [10]. In other words, the more non-substitutable the videos are, audiences are more likely to subscribe the prime services. We thus propose:

H3. Non-substitutability positively affects audiences' intention to subscribe.

Perceived enjoyment is a primary driver of technology and service adoption [13]. Studies have demonstrated that audiences pay for the subscription fee if they believe they could be pleased by watching online videos [15]. Subscription of prime services of a video website allow audiences to watch all of the ads-free, high quality videos, which enhances their enjoyment. Therefore, we make the following assumption:

H4. Perceived enjoyment positively affects audiences' intention to subscribe.

Consumer devotion represents audiences' strongest attitudinal bonding with a product or service, or "a state of passionate dedication" [17]. Comsumer devotion theory reveals the religious behavior characteristics of fans, which constantly stimulates fans' feelings for the things they are infatuated with, and then forms a strong willingness to consume [23]. For instance, devotion is the highest form of love, sometimes predicts irrational consumption and loyalty [12]. Audiences of video websites, especially young generation, may subscribe the prime service to support their favorite actors or idols, because the dramas or varieties starring their idols are broadcasted on certain video websites. Hence, we hypothesize:

H5. Consumer devotion positively affects audiences' intention to subscribe.

Researchers have proven that price cost is the primary factor affecting users' adoption of services [19], it has a negative impact on the user's attitude towars purchasing [6]. Apparently, before paying for a product or service, consumers would evaluate whether it worth buying, and whether the price is affordable. If consumers feel that the subscription fee is too high and exceeds a certain budget, they will stop paying for VIP services offered by video websites. Accordingly, we argue:

H6. Price cost negatively affects audiences' intention to subscribe.

Intention to subscribe is described as the possibility of a video website audience's subscription behavior [7]. Venkatesh et al. prove that a user's behavioral intention and actual behavior are different variables, and users will first form an intention to adopt a system or service before actual usage [21]. Prior research has verified that intention to subscribe has positive influence on subscription behavior [2]. Hence, we propose:

H7. Intention to subscribe positively affects audiences' subscription behavior.

4 Research Methodology

4.1 Data Collection

Data collection was carried out via Sojump.com, a Chinese online survey platform. The questionnaire consists of two parts: demographic information and measurement items of variables in the research model, including 64 questions. All items in the questionnaire were adopted from prior studies and measured with 7-likert scale ranging from 1 (strongly disagree) to 7 (strongly agree). A total of 167 valid responses were collected. Detailed demographic information was shown in Table 1:

Table 1. Respondent demographics

Measure	Item	Frequency	Percentage(%)
Gender	Male	94	56.29
	Female	73	43.71
Age	18–20	12	7.19
	21–30	153	91.62
	31–40	0	0.00
	41–50	2	1.20
	>51	0	0.00
Education	Middle school or below	1	0.60
	High school	3	1.80
	College	49	29.34
	Bachelor	108	64.67
	Master and above	6	3.59
Occupation	Professional	20	11.98
	Service	1	0.60
	Freelance	47	28.14
	Worker	1	0.60
	Public institutions	34	20.36
	Others	64	38.32
Income	< = 2000	37	22.16
	2001–5000	16	9.58
	5001–8000	49	29.34
	8001–10000	41	24.55
	> = 10001	24	14.37

4.2 Data Analyses and Results

Smart PLS 3.33 [18] and partial least squares structural equation model (PLS-SEM) [16] were used to verify the research model and corresponding hypotheses. Following a two-step method, data analysis was conducted [4]. First, reliability was evaluated by checking composite reliability and Cronbach's α values. Results indicated that composite reliability values of this study ranging between 0.662 and 0.879, most of which are greater than the suggested value of 0.70 [9]. Besides, internal consistency was verified by checking Cronbach's α values, which were all greater than 0.818, exceeding the threshold of 0.70 [8].

Discriminant validity of the measurement model was evaluated by comparing the square root of AVE with correlations among the measurement items. The results in Table 2 showed that the value of each AVE square root was greater than the correlation between any pair of corresponding structures. To conclude, our measurement model had acceptable reliability, convergence validity and discriminant validity.

Table 2. Discriminant validity

Variables	Time Cost	Functional Deprivation	Non-substitutability	Percived Enjoyment	Consumer Devotion	Price Cost	Intention to Subscribe	Subscription Behavior
Time Cost	0.772							
Functional Deprivation	0.622	0.825						
Non-substitutability	0.522	0.549	0.775					
Percived Enjoyment	0.681	0.812	0.65	0.789				
Consumer Devotion	0.618	0.693	0.663	0.785	0.898			
Price Cost	-0.376	-0.322	-0.478	-0.526	-0.428	0.844		
Intention to subscribe	0.716	0.827	0.699	0.632	0.849	-0.53	0.841	
Subscription Behavior	0.578	0.783	0.739	0.785	0.821	-0.52	0.729	0.89

Notes: The diagonal elements dipict the square root of the AVE

We then tested the structural model and hypotheses. As shown in Fig. 2, The results showed that: (1) intention to subscribe positively affected subscription behavior (β = 0.880, t = 7.535); (2) the push factors (time cost and function deprivation) had positive impacts on intention to subscribe (β = 0.081, t = 1.658; β = 0.408, t = 7.648); (3) pull factors (perceived enjoyment and non-substitutability) positively influenced intention to subscribe (β = 0.213, t = 3.061; β = 0.073, t = 2.504); (4) mooring factors: consumer devotion had positive impact on intention to subscribe (β = 0.253, t = 9.589), while price cost had negative impact on the intention (β = −0.111, t = 2.744). Finally, the push, pull and mooring factors jointly explained 94.5% variance of intention to subscribe, which in turn explained 77.1% variance of subscription behavior. Thus proving that the model had high degree of fit and strong prediction ability.

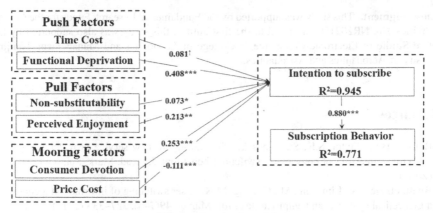

Fig. 2. Structural model

5 Conclusions

In mainland China, research on subscription of video-on-demand remains in its infancy, and a holistic perspective for understanding audiences' subscription behavior has yet to be formulated. In this study, drawing on PPM theory, we develop a research model to investigate factors afffectiong audiences' subscription intention and behavior in Chinese video websites. The results supported all of the hypotheses and strongly supported the proposed model. This study contributes to the emerging literature on subscription of Video-on-Demand in the following ways. First, limited research effort has been directed at the Chinese audiences' Video-on-Demand subscription behavior. To the best of our knowledge, this work is among the first to provide theoretical insights into understanding factors that influence the subscription intention and behavior of Chinese video websites audiences. Second, while the PPM theory has been previously used to investigate technology discontinuance and switching behaviors, this research extends the application of this theory by adapting it to explain users' subscription motivations in the Video-on-Demand context. Finally, our study is expected to provide valuable insights to online video websites administrators who urgently seek to improve audiences' subscription intention and actual revenue.

This study also has some limitations that create future research opportunities. For instance, we explored audiences' subscription intention and behavior, but failed to distinguish novice (who pay the subscription fee for the first time) or experienced subscribers (who have paid the subscription fee before). Prior research indicates that the determinants of user behavior and intention are affected by the preadoption and postadoption stages in innovation. Hence, future studies can separately analyze the subscription intention and behavior of novice and experienced users. In addition, we recruited Chinese university students as survey participants, the reults might be limited to this population. Researchers may generalize current findings to other population or culture by re-collecting data in the future.

Acknowledgment. This study was supported by the Fundamental Research Funds for the Central Universities No. NR2021003 awarded to the first author; this study was also supported by the Creative Studio of Electronic Commerce in College of Economics and Management, Nanjing University of Aeronautics and Astronautics.

References

1. Bansal, H.S., Taylor, S.F., St. James Y.: "Migrating" to new service providers: Toward a unifying framework of consumers' switching behaviors. J. Acad. Mark. Sci. 33(1), 96–115 (2005)
2. Bhattacherjee, A., Limayem, M., Cheung, M.K.: User switching of information technology: a theoretical synthesis and empirical test. Inf. Manag. 49(7–8), 327–333 (2012)
3. Chen, Y., Zhu, Y.Q.: Research on the influence factors of user transfer behavior from paper reading to mobile reading from the perspective of PPM theory. Res. Libr. Sci. 2, 70–80 (2020)
4. Chin, W.W., Marcolin, B.L., Newsted, P.R.: A partial least squares latent variable modeling approach for measuring interaction effects: results from a Monte Carlo simulation study and an electronic-mail emotion/adoption study. Inf. Syst. Res. 14(2), 189–217 (2003)
5. Chocarro, R., Cortiñas, M., Villanueva, M.L.: Situational variables in online versus offline channel choice. Electron. Commer. Res. Appl. 12(5), 347–361 (2013)
6. Chu, C.W., Lu, H.P.: Factors influencing online music purchase intention in Taiwan: an empirical study based on the value-intention framework. Internet Res. 17(2), 139–155 (2007)
7. Dodds, W.B., Monroe, K.B., Grewal, D.: Effects of price, brand, and store information on buyers' product evaluations. J. Mark. Res. 28(3), 307–319 (1991)
8. Fornell, C., Larcker, D.F.: Evaluating structural equation models with unobservable variables and measurement error. J. Mark. Res. 18(1), 39–50 (1981)
9. Hair, J.F., et al.: Multivariate Data Analysis With Reading. Prentice-Hall, Inc. (1995)
10. Himma-Kadakas, M., Kõuts, R.: Who is willing to pay for online journalistic content? Media Commun. 3(4), 106–115 (2015)
11. Hsieh, J.K., et al.: Post-adoption switching behavior for online service substitutes: a perspective of the push–pull–mooring framework. Comput. Hum. Behav. 28(5), 1912–1920 (2012)
12. Li, K.H.: Fan consumption and the construction of fan economy. Henan Soc. Sci. (7), 72–78 (2016)
13. Lieberman, J.N.: Playfulness: Its Relationship to Imagination and Creativity. Academic Press (2014)
14. Liu, M.W.: Research on channel migration behavior of consumers from offline to online: based on PPM theory. Henan Coll. Financ. Tax 32(1), 34–40 (2018)
15. Moon, J.W., Kim, Y.G.: Extending the TAM for a World-Wide-Web context. Inf. Manag. 38(4), 217–230 (2001)
16. Pavlou, P.A., Liang, H., Xue, Y.: Understanding and mitigating uncertainty in online exchange relationships: a principal-agent perspective. MIS Quarterly 105–136 (2007)
17. Pimentel, R.W., Reynolds, K.E.: A model for consumer devotion: Affective commitment with proactive sustaining behaviors. Acad. Mark. Sci. Rev. 1 (2004)
18. Ringle, C.M., Wende, S., Will, A.: Smart PLS 2.0 (beta). SmartPLS, Hamburg (2005)
19. Shin, D.H.: An empirical investigation of a modified technology acceptance model of IPTV. Behav. Inf. Technol. 28(4), 361–372 (2009)
20. Tzeng, J.Y.: Perceived values and prospective users' acceptance of prospective technology: the case of a career eportfolio system. Comput. Educ. 56(1), 157–165 (2011)

21. Venkatesh, V., et al.: User acceptance of information technology: toward a unified view. MIS Q. **27**(3), 425–478 (2003)
22. Wang, D.H., Zhang, S.: Research on influencing factors of online content payment willingness: the regulatory effect based on users' free psychology. Modern Communication (Journal of Communication University of China) **41**(11), 122–129 (2019)
23. Wang, X.Y., Liu, H.C.: Enthusiasm formation mechanism of online fans and its impact on consumption intention. Enterprise Economy **36**(2), 129–135 (2017)
24. Zhao, Y.X., Peng, X.X, Zhu, Q.H.: Investigating user switching intention for mobile instant messaging application: taking WeChat as an example. Comput. Hum. Behav. 64, 206–216 (2016)
25. Zhu, H.T.: Research on the difficulties and countermeasures of the development of domestic video websites. West China Broadcast. TV **41**(16), 33–35 (2021)
26. Zhu, X.Y.: Analysis on the transformation of user payment model of domestic video websites. J. News Res. **8**(8), 43–44 (2017)

Targeted Training Improves Security Culture

Jacopo Paglia[1]([✉]), Gregor Petrič[2], Anita-Catrin Eriksen[1], Thea Mannix[1], and Kai Roer[1]

[1] KnowBe4 Research AS, Kristian Augustsgate, 13, Oslo, Norway
research@knowbe4.com
[2] University of Ljubljana, Faculty of Social Sciences,
Kardeljeva ploscad 5, 1000 Ljubljana, Slovenia

Keywords: Phishing · Social engineering · Industry · Security culture

1 Introduction

A growing reliance on information technology has resulted in an increasingly higher proportion of cyber attacks aimed at human targets. The manner in which people understand the methods of such attacks and take action to defend themselves and their organizations is fast becoming an important factor in human computer interactions. While IT based defences such as firewalls have been commonplace in organizational IT systems, there is a growing trend of implementing security awareness training amongst employees to build a human element of defense. Research has demonstrated that providing people with knowledge about threats and appropriate actions reduces their risk of falling victim to forms of social engineering such as phishing attacks, given the right training approach [3, 4].

Factors that influence the efficiency of security awareness training are a popular topic of investigation in the behavioral research field of infosec [5–7]. Targeted training, whereby training is individually tailored to weaknesses in knowledge or behaviours that have been previously assessed, has been demonstrated to improve security behaviours [3], however the literature specifically examining targeted training is sparse. Moreover, to our knowledge it has not yet been empirically tested how targeted training impacts the security culture of an organization. Here we present a case study examining whether assessing areas of specific weakness in knowledge, followed by targeted training, has a greater impact on security culture assessment scores compared with generalised training regimens.

2 Methods

2.1 Materials

The analysis made use of data collected using the Security Culture Survey [2]. The Security Culture Survey was developed to measure dimensions of security

Supported by KnowBe4, inc.

culture by use of validated measures assessing users across 7 dimensions of security culture (Attitudes, Behaviors, Cognition, Responsibility, Norms, Communication, and Compliance) [8]. The survey uses 28 5-point Likert scale items that ask respondents to express their degree of (dis)agreeing with statements related to the 7 dimensions.

2.2 Participants

663 employees from an organization of approx. 3000 total employees affiliated with the energy industry were selected for analysis. Consent for the use of anonymised survey data was given via the participants' organisation upon collaboration with KnowBe4 Inc. All respondents were informed that their responses are anonymous prior to taking the survey. No demographic information regarding participants is included in the data set. Employees were selected as participants based on the criteria that they were employed by the selected organization and completed the survey during the two time periods selected for the analysis.

2.3 Data Collection

Data used for the analysis were collected via a third party organization as a customer of KnowBe4 Inc. The Security Culture Survey is deployed through KnowBe4's security awareness training platform. Organizations decide when to offer the survey to their employees, where upon completion the organization receives information regarding their employees performance. Data stored by KnowBe4, and thus used here, is anonymised upon collection by use of unique numerical identifiers.

663 respondents completed the survey in June 2020 where base scores were established for each dimension (Attitudes, Compliance, Behaviors, Cognition, Responsibility, Norms, Communication and Compliance), in addition to an aggregated baseline score determining overall security culture per respondent. Of these, 194 employees were found to specifically lack knowledge regarding password security by scoring comparably low on password specific questions, and were assigned specific training targeting this weakness. Targeted training was completed by employees over the course of the following 12 months. For comparison purposes, 469 other employees from the same organization who had received general, non-targeted training in the same 12 month period were assigned to the not targeted training group. All employees received equal training within group. Employees from both groups (Targeted/Not Targeted) then completed the survey a second time post-training in June 2021.

3   Results

Overall survey scores for pre-training and post-training were separated by group and then analysed using dependent samples t-tests. Figure 1 shows the distribution of the test scores before and after targeted training, and demonstrates

Table 1. Descriptives.

N	Group	Pre-training		Post-training	
		Mean	SD	Mean	SD
194	Targeted	66.8	9	68.8	9.3
469	Not targeted	73.1	9.4	71.6	9.1

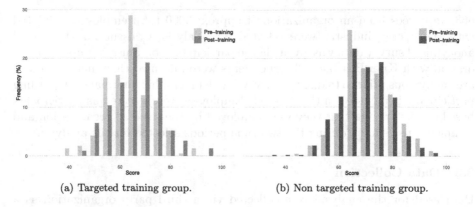

(a) Targeted training group.   (b) Non targeted training group.

Fig. 1. Distribution of the security culture scores of the survey for the pre-training and post-training for the targeted training group and non targeted training group.

a consistent shift towards higher scores for the post training responses. This is also evident from the mean score values presented in Table 3.

To examine the significance of the difference in security culture scores between the targeted groups' pre and post training means, we performed a dependent t-test using a significance level of $\alpha = 0.05$. The analysis revealed significant differences between the two means ($t(385) = -2.14$, $p = 0.03$, $d = 0.33$), (see Table 2). The effect size calculation using Cohen's d revealed a low to moderate effect size (0.3), which can be explained by the relatively small data sample used in the analysis.

Table 2. t-test results.

	t-value	df	p-value	95% CI	Cohen's d
Targeted	−2.14	385.54	0.03	[−3.81, −0.16]	0.33
Not targeted	2.48	935.5	0.01	[0.31, 2.68]	0.16

Further analysis revealed that some dimensions showed particularly large improvements following targeted training. The greatest improved average score was within the Cognition dimension, with an average improvement of 8.8. A second t-test examining this change revealed this difference to be significant ($p < 0.001, d = 0.66$). Among the survey's items that constitute the Cognition

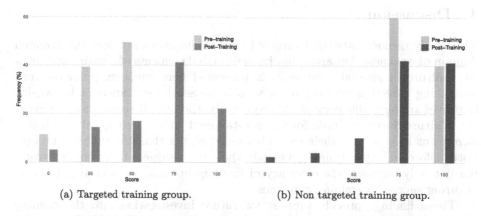

(a) Targeted training group.   (b) Non targeted training group.

Fig. 2. Distribution of the pre and post training scores of the password-specific item for the targeted training group and non targeted training group.

Table 3. Summary of statistical outcomes per item and overall score.

	Targeted			Not targeted		
	Pre	Post	p-value	Pre	Post	p-value
Attitudes	71.5	75.1	0.01	76.8	78.2	0.1
Behavior	73.4	75.5	0.14	77.2	76.7	0.54
Cognition	53.4	62.2	< 0.01	69.7	66.9	< 0.01
Communication	66.2	63.1	0.04	69.7	67.1	< 0.01
Compliance	71.8	70.6	0.42	75.3	72.3	< 0.01
Norms	65.3	67.1	0.19	70.6	69.2	0.13
Responsibility	65.8	67.6	0.17	72.8	71.1	0.07
Overall security culture score	66.8	68.8	0.03	73.1	71.6	0.01

dimension, the largest improvement was found with the passwords item directly related to the topic of the training (see Fig. 2), with an average increase of 30.7. Statistical analysis revealed this difference to be highly significant with a large effect size ($p < 0.001, d = 1.3$).

Analysis of pre and post training scores for the not targeted training group also revealed significant differences ($t(935) = -2.48$, $p = 0.01$, $d = 0.16$). Contrary to the targeted group, those who had received general training in the previous 12 month period saw a reduction in average overall score (see 2). Within-group comparison for the non-targeted group on pre and post training scores for the Cognition dimension revealed a significant reduction in average score of -2.8 ($p < 0.01$), as well as a significant reduction of -6 in the average password-specific item.

4   Discussion

This study demonstrates that targeted training improves not only the targeted domain of weakness, but also other human-related elements of security and security culture in general. The analysis presented here supports previous work suggesting targeting training to previously assessed weak areas of knowledge improves training efficiency [3]. Unexpectedly, the overall score from the Security Culture Survey reduced for the non-targeted training group, although it is important to note that their scores remained higher than the targeted groups' both before and after training. Overall, these data suggest that targeted training not only improves the efficiency of training but may be a vital element in ensuring successful training outcomes.

These findings provide support for future investigation into the positive effects of targeted training on security awareness training efficiency. In order for training to be efficient they need to be tailored and targeted, as general training might do more harm than good. Furthermore, organizations that are interested in the effects of training should consider measuring the impact of training not only on the domain that was addressed as a weakness, but on other security-related domains. Future work should consider examining the effectiveness of targeted training on actual behaviors. It is important to note that the data presented here has some limitations with regards to generalizability, as analysis included a sample of employees from a single organization within a single industry and country, and did not include a 'no training' control group. Future work should consider addressing these limitations.

5   Conclusion

Assessing areas of poor knowledge and targeting security awareness training based on specific areas of weakness may improve training efficiency, while not providing tailored training programs to employees may be detrimental to training efficiency. Additionally, different methods of tailoring to weaknesses in different domains of security culture can improve the overall security culture of an organization. Those responsible for training programs should consider these benefits when contemplating the trade off in time and cost for targeted training.

References

1. Roer, K., Eriksen, A., Pterič, G.: The Security Culture Report 2020. KnowBe4 Research (2020). https://www.knowbe4.com/hubfs/Security-Culture-Report.pdf
2. Roer, K., Eriksen, A., Pterič, G.: The Security Culture Report 2021. KnowBe4 Research (2021). https://www.knowbe4.com/organizational-cyber-security-culture-research-report
3. Schütz, A., Weber, K., Fertig, T.: Analyze before you sensitize: preparation of a targeted ISA training (2020)
4. Al-Daeef, M.M., Basir, N., Saudi, M.M.: Security awareness training: a review. In: Lecture Notes in Engineering and Computer Science (2017)

5. Chen, C.C., Medlin, B.D., Shaw, R.S.: A cross-cultural investigation of situational information security awareness programs. In: Information Management & Computer Security(2008)
6. Hassanzadeh, M., Jahangiri, N., Brewster, B.: A conceptual framework for information security awareness, assessment, and training. In: Emerging Trends in ICT Security, 99–110, (2014). Morgan Kaufmann
7. Bauer, S., Bernroider, E.W., Chudzikowski, K.: Prevention is better than cure! Designing information security awareness programs to overcome users' non-compliance with information security policies in banks. Comput. Secur. **68**, 145–159 (2017)
8. Petrič, G., Roer, K.: The impact of formal and informal organizational norms on susceptibility to phishing: combining survey and field experiment data. Telematics Inf. **67**, 101766 (2021)

Identification of Physical-Digital Ecosystem Personalization Factors

Alberts Pumpurs[✉]

Department of Management Information Technology, Riga Technical University, Riga, Latvia
alberts.pumpurs@rtu.lv

Abstract. This research paper investigates prior work on physical-digital product ecosystem personalization and seeks to find answers on how to personalize physical-digital product ecosystems and what personalization factors matter. A literature overview is used to find relevant research to identify gaps, and a future research plan is proposed.

Keywords: Ecosystems · Personalization factors

1 Introduction

Physical-digital product ecosystems, consisting of multiple digital and physical products connected, have become an important discussion topic. Combining multiple products with a common aim but different functional capabilities provides more benefits than a single product [1–3]. Moreover, ecosystems are developed by one or more firms, serving as a foundation upon which many organizations can build additional complementary products and innovations to generate a network effect [2]. An example is Apple's ecosystem, where it has hardware supported by software, which allows third-party developers to add even more value through external software or hardware services.

The undeniable success of Apple's physical-digital product ecosystem shows what a combination of multiple products in the ecosystem can do for users and the company. Companies such as Google, Microsoft, Meta, and others use a similar physical-digital product ecosystem approach to increase value for their users. For other companies to compete with existing product ecosystems or join them - they need to introduce that also provide value. Personalization is considered an advantage that helps customers receive the most suitable solution to their needs from the vast product offer. At the same time, businesses can reduce acquisition costs and increase revenues and marketing efficiency.

Ecosystems are essential as users, before making a purchase decision, now tend to review not only single products features and capabilities but also what integrations and connections it has with other products and ecosystems [4]. That is why it is essential to personalize not only one standalone product but do that with a digital-physical product ecosystem context in mind.

To create a digital-physical product ecosystem personalization approach considering the ecosystem in play – it is necessary to review existing scientific research on digital-physical products and ecosystem personalization approaches. Unfortunately, there is not

C. Stephanidis et al. (Eds.): HCII 2022, CCIS 1654, pp. 78–85, 2022.
https://doi.org/10.1007/978-3-031-19679-9_11

much research that directly analyzes ecosystem personalization factors and approaches. There is a gap that would provide a better understanding of personalizing products connected with ecosystems. This gap can be filled by answering RQ1: *Which methods and results have been tried in ecosystem personalization research prior to this work?* Furthermore, RQ2: *Which personalization factors matter in physical-digital product personalization?* A systematic literature overview will answer these questions and help sketch out future research perspectives.

This research paper proposes a future research design and highlights the road to developing ecosystem personalization methods using personalization factors. The rest of the paper is organized as follows: Sect. 2 reviews available research on ecosystem personalization to identify approaches and factors. Section 3 identifies the research gap in digital-physical product ecosystem personalization and proposes a future research approach, expected outcome, and challenges.

2 Methods and Results

During the research, qualitative methods were used – the analysis and systematic literature analysis methods – literature overview. Applying the overview method, more than 300 articles were considered to choose 17 full-text articles for in-depth analysis. In addition, scientific articles were selected from databases IEEE Explore and Web of Science.

The systematic literature analysis method overview is based on a chronological and thematic analysis of the literature to summarize the most relevant and specific according to research questions. Most relevant literature was found by searching scientific databases using carefully selected keywords – physical-digital product ecosystems, ecosystem personalization, digital product personalization, and physical product personalization.

As a result, 17 entries were selected for inclusion in the literature overview. Scientific publication is selected chiefly as well as some conference materials. According to the applied literature overview done in Table 1, Table 2 is an example of notable studies in product ecosystem personalization attempts and factors that impact digital-physical product personalization. Further, RQ1 and RQ2 have been reviewed in the Ecosystems and Personalization factors chapters.

2.1 Ecosystems

Ecosystems are large and complex systems – it is hard to define where they start or where they end. That depends on the observer's viewpoint. Furthermore, each ecosystem contains many residents with dynamic, interconnected relationships that can change. Because of their size, complexity, and dynamism, it is challenging to describe, model, and simulate them formally. Therefore, it is essential to seek research methods that would help to understand better ecosystems and how personalization methods could be applied to them.

Researchers and industry practitioners have used the term product ecosystems to signify multiply related, often interconnected products, retail environments, and usage contexts in coherent processes compared to the conventional viewpoint of static, isolated products [4]. The concept has evolved from nature because of its complex and inter-dependent connections [5].

Ecosystem analogy is essential in other domains because it helps to understand the better value in the complex interaction of populations of subjects in the same environment [6]. For example, bringing the ecosystem analogy to digital-physical product ecosystems holds the potential to ease life for businesses [7–9]. When introducing new products or improving existing ones, the outcome must fit in the ecosystem to successfully use existing ecosystem resident open interfaces [2], At the same time, providing the opportunity for other residents to use theirs further to provide more excellent value to the

Table 1. Summary of notable studies in ecosystems related to personalization

Source	Method	Research aim	Conclusion
[1]	Case studies	What and how the ecosystems are shaped and how the design of the ecosystem is shaped depending on its surrounding conditions	The ecosystem design – actors, business model, and resource sharing is dependent on orchestrators existing knowledge of the domain of technology and ecosystems business model
[11]	Laboratory research	Examine the fundamental issues underlying the product ecosystem design and its implications for ecosystem ambiance, UX, users' affect, and cognition	People have different responses, physiological and cognitive-based on environment configuration and ambiance. Environment setting affects user experience
[4]	Literature review	To envision affective and cognitive design perspective to mass personalization to make better-informed decisions and improve customer satisfaction	Mass personalization can better solve user needs and thus increase their UX. A designer should view user needs from an affective-cognitive perspective and not separately as it was previously accustomed to. Due to many products and services, it is beneficial to look at ecosystem theory in mass personalization to achieve better UX
[12]	Data mining and data analysis	Create technical approach to elicit user wants and needs in product ecosystem	The research resulted in the preposition to use ecosystem product-service relationship understanding to build better outcomes

whole ecosystem, resulting in greater ecosystem productivity and thus profitability [1, 5, 12]. To better understand what has been done previously on ecosystem personalization and what was uncovered - a literature review is performed and represented in Table 1.

Lingens et al. [1] researched what shapes ecosystem architecture based on its surrounding factors. Researchers identified the potential that ecosystems have and the gap in how ecosystems are designed. Researchers did a case study conducting multiple interviews with ecosystem originators and participants to address this gap. As a result, they discovered and proposed the concept of ecosystem effective distance – an ecosystem orchestrator existing knowledge on used technologies, activities, actors, and knowledge of relevant ecosystems field of business. The shorter this distance is, the better orchestrators were able to define ecosystems' values, activities, and skills to further evolve the ecosystem to their plans. Because of that, the ecosystems were less flexible than ones where effective distance was larger, and ecosystem co-orchestrators had more say in ecosystem evolvement and value creation.

The product ecosystem, design, ambiance, and cognitive and affective user experience (UX) are explored in [12]. n this work, ambiance can be seen as what Bernhard Lingens referred to as an ecosystem surrounding factors [1]. Through the literature review, Feng Zhou defined that user experience – a person's perceptions and responses that result from the use or anticipated use of a product, system, or service [13] – affects the ecosystems perception of its users and primarily that is based on user cognitive processes and affective states. Empirical research results showed that when designing an environment that can also be called an ecosystem – designers must consider environmental factors, user cultural differences, ability to cope and fulfill the given tasks, and affective and cognitive needs [11].

Zhou et al. [14] did extensive literature research on user affective and cognitive needs in a mass personalization context to propose a framework that would help designers make better-informed decisions to increase customer satisfaction. While this was not direct ecosystem-related research, they concluded that new product development in consumer-oriented markets has been incredibly celebrated, and they have become dependent on each other in user experience. Therefore, ecosystem thinking should be applied for product innovation and personalization.

Based on existing theoretical frameworks on user need elicitation [11, 14], the follow-up research [12] aims to analyze customer needs of a product ecosystem – which in turn would give information to improve business strategy and profits. The authors do not specifically mention the personalization of products or ecosystems, but what is possible with knowledge of users' needs in a product ecosystem structured in the Kano model [15]. They concluded that understanding individual ecosystem products and services associated with them makes it possible to improve user experience and satisfaction of the product ecosystem. Also, to better understand the customer needs within the product ecosystem, the characteristics and interrelationships between products and services and the whole ecosystem should be studied.

2.2 Personalization

The conventional argument for personalization demands is that it is necessary to diversify the functions and features of products and services to satisfy more customers who have different needs [16]. In the context of this research aim and lack of detailed research in digital-physical product ecosystem personalization, it is valuable to review existing research in personalization seeking answers on what factors impact levels of personalization.

Table 2. Digital-physical product personalization factors

Source	Method	VS	PEC	HE	UE	PE	BP	PM
[20]	Framework based on literature review and case study	X	X	X	X			
[21]	Case study with surveys			X	X			
[20]	Proposed framework tested it on user feedback	X	X			X	X	
[22]	Technical framework and method			X	X	X		X
[21]	User interviews and focus groups	X	X					
[22]	Focus Group interviews	X		X	X			X
[23]	Personalisation framework via literature review and case study						X	
[24]	Literature review with architecture as proposal				X			
[25]	Customer research using interviews	X			X			
[26]	Conceptual framework and user questionnaire		X	X		X	X	

VS – Visual stimulation and aesthetics, PEC – Past experience and culture; HE – Hedonic and emotional pleasure, UE – Utilitarian and functional, PE – personality aspects, BP – Behavioural patterns, PM – Product materials.

An attempt to identify and collect digital-physical personalization factors was made based on the current literature review, and the results are in Table 2. Multiple authors claim that user-centric personalization factors fall under two major categories: hedonic – pleasurable personalization factors and utilitarian – functional ones [17–19]. Visually stimulating and aesthetical design, industrial or digital as a user interface, also creates a sense of personalization when found pleasing by a user [20, 21]. Physical product materials can also be part of the visual preference category, but it also provides tactile sensations, creating a sense of personalization [19, 22]. Via user interviews and case studies, it was uncovered that sense of personalization differs from culture to culture and differs based on users' experience [17, 20, 21]. At the same time, the experience was affected by behaviour [20] which is affected by the user's personality and personality traits [20, 22].

3   Discussion and Future Research Directions

There is limited targeted research that would address physical-digital product ecosystem personalization, methods, approaches, and factors. While searching for an answer on RQ1 in Table 1. is worthy for understanding product ecosystem personalization, it does not uncover what factors impact the physical-digital product ecosystem personalization. There is a lack of practical knowledge and methods on applying personalization in the ecosystems to make them and the products more valuable to users.

As the physical-digital product ecosystem consists of digital and physical products, Table 2. Concludes an answer on RQ2 on personalization factors commonly used in physical-digital product personalization. Literature analysis shows that broad product category personalization provides broad personalization factors, and research specifically targeted to a specific product and service categories provides very niched personalization factors.

Combining knowledge from both research questions, we can conclude that digital-physical product ecosystem personalization fulfills users' affective-cognitive needs in an ecosystem design of actors, business model, resource sharing, and ambiance. That can be achieved by eliciting user needs on a specific product and fulfilling his visual stimulation and aesthetic needs. Matching his experience and cultural factors and providing expected hedonic pleasure and functionality while acknowledging his personality, behavioral patterns, and physical material preferences. The literature review implies that analysis of interconnected product relationships potentially is a vital ecosystem personalization factor [1, 11], which requires further investigation.

Future research is proposed to fill the research gap on the ecosystem personalization approach involving using ecosystem factors combined with product factors and internal product relationships based on user-generated content. Future research will seek methods to define the observable ecosystem, its factors, product connections, user fulfilled and unfulfilled needs, and how these different factors can come together to create knowledge on better personalization.

Motivation and significance	Problem formulation	Research methods	Outcome
Digital-physical product ecosystems	Ecosystem factor elicitation for personalization	Ecosystem personalization framework	Set of processes and executable ecosystem personalization methods
Digital-physical product personalization	Product factor elicitation for personalization	Use case study on ecosystem perception	User generated content as guiding information to personalyze digital-physical products and ecosystem itself
Ecosystem personalization	User cognitice and affective need elicitation	Product and ecosystem factor elicitation from user generated contet with ML algorithms	
		Interconected product relationship mining and sensemaking	

Fig. 1. Proposed future research design

A future research design (Fig. 1) is proposed to outline necessary steps from research motivation to the outcome. Following these steps, research will fulfill the gap in physical-digital ecosystem personalization methods that can be applied to make personalized products and product ecosystems. The proposed approach starts with identifying research significance and a literature review of existing ecosystem personalization, digital-physical product personalization, and digital-physical ecosystems. Reviewing what has been tried practically and the outcome will help identify limitations, challenges, and opportunities in user need elicitation and personalization factors in digital-physical product ecosystems. Based on identified knowledge - best practice or a potential new one could be used for user need elicitation from user-generated content in product ecosystems and interconnected product relationship extrapolation. With the case study research on user perception in ecosystems, the resulting outcome would be a set of methods and processes to use on user-generated content and available ecosystem information to create individual digital-physical products personalized within its ecosystem. It is expected that such a framework and set of methods will allow product developers to create more targeted and financially successful products and eliminate resource wasting during the product creation process.

Proposed future research differs from existing ecosystem research with an approach to include ecosystem factors in product personalization decisions. For example, current research in terms of personalization does not include interrelated product relationships, ecosystem orchestrator factors, ecosystem's purpose, and product soft and hard factors in the context of other products. These and other uncovered ecosystem factors that would propose value to personalization will be researched in future work.

The challenges the future research will need to address are the uniqueness of each digital-physical product ecosystem and whether the proposed personalization method will apply to other ecosystems. In addition, the quality of user needs elicitation and evaluation from user-generated content, which is text, is limited to algorithmic capabilities of parsing natural language.

References

1. Lingens, B., Miehé, L., Gassmann, O.: The ecosystem blueprint: how firms shape the design of an ecosystem according to the surrounding conditions. Long Range Plan. **54**(2), 102043 (2021). https://doi.org/10.1016/j.lrp.2020.102043
2. Zhou, F., Ji, Y., Jiao, R.J.: Industry platforms and ecosystem innovation. J. Prod. Innov. Manag. **31**, 417–433 (2014). https://doi.org/10.1111/jpim.12105
3. Pilinkienė, V., Mačiulis, P.: Comparison of different ecosystem analogies: the main economic determinants and levels of impact. Procedia. Soc. Behav. Sci. **156**, 365–370 (2014). https://doi.org/10.1016/j.sbspro.2014.11.204
4. Zhou, F.: Affective-cognitive design of product ecosystems for user experience
5. Mars, M.M., Bronstein, J.L., Lusch, R.F.: The value of a metaphor: organizations and ecosystems. Organ. Dyn. **41**, 271–280 (2012). https://doi.org/10.1016/j.orgdyn.2012.08.002
6. Durst, S., Poutanen, P.: Success factors of innovation ecosystems: A literature review Success factors of innovation ecosystems-Initial insights from a literature review1 *
7. Williams, T.: Product Ecosystems: Extrinsic Value in Product Design. PhD by Publication. Queensland University of Technology (2019)
8. Iansiti, M., Levien, R.: Strategy as Ecology. Harv. Bus. Rev. **82** (2004)
9. Dass, M., Kumar, S.: Bringing product and consumer ecosystems to the strategic forefront. Bus. Horiz. **57**, 225–234 (2014). https://doi.org/10.1016/j.bushor.2013.11.006
10. Miguel, J.C., Casado, M.Á.: GAFAnomy (Google, Amazon, Facebook and Apple): The big four and the b-Ecosystem. In: Gómez-Uranga, M., Zabala-Iturriagagoitia, J.M., Barrutia, J. (eds.) Dynamics of Big Internet Industry Groups and Future Trends, pp. 127–148. Springer, Cham (2016). https://doi.org/10.1007/978-3-319-31147-0_4
11. Zhou, F., Xu, Q., Jiao, R.J.: Fundamentals of product ecosystem design for user experience. Res. Eng. Design **22**, 43–61 (2011). https://doi.org/10.1007/s00163-010-0096-z

12. Ayoub, J., Zhou, F., Xu, Q., Yang, J.: Analyzing customer needs of product ecosystems using online product reviews. In: Proceedings of the ASME Design Engineering Technical Conference. American Society of Mechanical Engineers (ASME) (2019)
13. Mirnig, A.G., et al.: A formal analysis of the ISO 9241–210 definition of user experience. In: Conference on Human Factors in Computing Systems - Proceedings, pp. 437–446. Association for Computing Machinery (2015)
14. Zhou, F., Ji, Y., Jiao, R.J.: Affective and cognitive design for mass personalization: status and prospect. J. Intell. Manuf. 24(5), 1047–1069 (2012). https://doi.org/10.1007/s10845-012-0673-2
15. Hinterhuber, H.: The Kano Model: How to Delight Your Customers Top Management Team Heterogeneity and Technological Diversification: A Study of Relatedness View Project National Strategy for Tourism View project Elmar Sauerwein h&z Management Consulting (1996)
16. Kaneko, K., Kishita, Y., Umeda, Y.: Toward developing a design method of personalization: proposal of a personalization procedure. Procedia CIRP 69, 740–745 (2018). https://doi.org/10.1016/j.procir.2017.11.134
17. Personalization: A Case Study. In: Procedia CIRP, pp. 2–7. Elsevier B.V.
18. Candi, M., van den Ende, J., Gemser, G.: Benefits of customer codevelopment of new products: the moderating effects of utilitarian and hedonic radicalness. J. Prod. Innov. Manag. 33, 418–434 (2016). https://doi.org/10.1111/jpim.12286
19. Bruseberg, A., McDonagh-Philp, D.: New product development by eliciting user experience and aspirations. Int. J. Hum. Comput. Stud. 55, 435–452 (2001). https://doi.org/10.1006/ijhc.2001.0479
20. Tseng, M.M., Jiao, R.J., Wang, C.: Design for mass personalization. CIRP Ann. Manuf. Technol. 59, 175–178 (2010). https://doi.org/10.1016/j.cirp.2010.03.097
21. Fossdal, M., Berg, A.: The relationship between user and product: durable design through personalisation
22. Kajtaz, M., et al.: An approach for personalised product development. Procedia Technol. 20, 191–198 (2015). https://doi.org/10.1016/j.protcy.2015.07.031
23. Al-Khanjari, Z.A.: Developing a common personalization framework for the e-application software systems
24. Germanakos, P., Belk, M., Constantinides, A., Samaras, G.: The personaweb system: personalizing E-commerce environments based on human factors
25. Mpinganjira, M.: Understanding online repeat purchase intentions: a relationship marketing
26. Pappas, I.O.: User experience in personalized online shopping: a fuzzy-set analysis. Eur. J. Mark. 52, 1679–1703 (2018). https://doi.org/10.1108/EJM-10-2017-0707

Design of a Portable Interface for Vibrotactile Feedback Applications

Blanca Topón Visarrea[1]([envelope]) [iD], Christian Iza[1] [iD], Gerardo Arteaga[1] [iD], and Byron Remache[1,2] [iD]

[1] SISAu Research Group, Facultad de Ingeniería y Tecnologías de la Información y la Comunicación, Universidad Tecnológica Indoamérica, Machala y Sabanilla, Ecuador
blancatopon@uti.edu.ec
[2] Departamento de Electrónica, Universidad de Málaga, 29071 Malaga, Spain

Abstract. In this project we developed a portable haptic interface for vibro-tactile feedback applications. Currently, commercial systems similar to the proposed interface have high costs with applications in specific areas, and there is no variety of these devices in Ecuador. For this reason, we propose to develop a portable vibrotactile feedback system that will allow the user to perceive movement. The illusions that were used to validate the interface are read through a micro_SD card connected to a controller, and the algorithm used transmits information through a pair of coil type actuators, generating the tactile illusion. Finally, an experiment was conducted to demonstrate its functionality, which resulted in the Funneling illusion being the one that is best perceived in the device, in addition to the fact that the participants reported perceiving a directionality in each illusion. It is expected that this system will be a support tool in urban mobility applications, due to its advantages in terms of portability, reduced weight, low cost compared to other commercial options, reproducible using the drawings and specifications of the system.

Keywords: Interface · Vibrotactile illusion · Portability

1 Introduction

A haptic interface is a tool that allows a person to manipulate, feel or perceive objects in a virtual environment. These systems are becoming more and more immersed in daily activities, which is why the development of projects in this area must continue to advance. There are applications in different fields, for example, communication, navigation, mobile devices, vehicles, medicine, among others [1]. However, the interfaces that currently exist have a high cost, which makes implementation and experimentation difficult [2], so the design of a low-cost interface that is easily transportable for urban mobility applications is proposed.

Vibrotactile feedback devices seek to deliver sensations in unusual contexts, for example, in this case, we seek to generate a system that allows to perceive an illusion of directionality when a vehicle is being used. Vibrotactile illusions can be used to improve

C. Stephanidis et al. (Eds.): HCII 2022, CCIS 1654, pp. 86–90, 2022.
https://doi.org/10.1007/978-3-031-19679-9_12

the visualization of information through mechanical devices [3, 4]. The interface will allow to generate a physical sensation in the hands through tactile illusions. The illusions that will be used to validate the interface in the experiments are Cutaneous "Rabbit" (CR), which presents a smooth progression of jumps in this case from one hand to another [5]. Phantom Motion (PM), which allows to perceive a continuous movement from one hand to another, without being interconnected [6], and Funneling (Fun), which allows to perceive continuous jumps from one hand to another [7]. The final product will be a portable vibrotactile feedback system based on illusions and designed for any vehicle.

2 Method

2.1 Proposed Algorithm

ESP8266 Controller. The controller has been programmed in the arduino IDE software. In this platform it is necessary to declare the libraries of recognition of the devices, LCD screen I2C and MP3 module. The first thing the controller does is to verify that the MP3 module has the SD card with the illusions, the next step is to print on the screen a welcome message to the interface and the list of available illusions. To select the illusions, press a button, the signal will be activated indefinitely until the stop button is pressed (See Fig. 1).

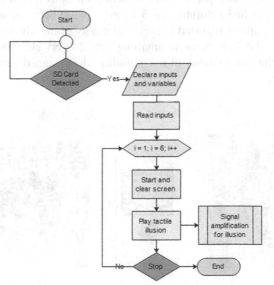

Fig. 1. Control logic of the haptic interface

XH M543 Amplifier. Once the signal is selected, it will go through an amplification stage so that the actuators can create the illusion, which is powered by a portable battery.

Reading of Tactile Illusions. The tactile illusions PM right – left, PM left – right CR right – left, CR left – right, Fun right – left and Fun left – right, are stored on an SD card, the information of the illusions is processed through an MP3 module with amplified output.

MP3 Module. The MP3 module will be in charge of reading the.wav files of the tactile illusions. The module will be controlled through an ESP8266 card.

2.2 Experimental Evaluation

To verify the operation of the portable interface, an experiment was conducted with the participation of 10 volunteers from the Indo-American University community. The experiment consisted of generating tactile illusions through mechanical-type vibratory stimuli on the skin with the designed portable interface. Using questionnaires, the participants reported the perception of the illusions.

The main objective of the experiment was to verify the performance of the portable vibrotactile feedback interface. To validate the interface, PM, CR, Fun illusions with left right and right left location changes were used. The system will be functional if the participants are able to perceive the movement from one hand to the other with the generation of the different illusions through the actuators.

Procedure. All the participants of the experiment signed a letter of consent for their voluntary participation. Afterwards, the type of stimulus to be sent was explained to them. Then, they were placed in a comfortable place and earplugs were placed to avoid any type of distraction. Each participant was sent 3 illusions with different changes of location, each illusion had a duration of 5 s, and a pause between sessions of 2 min. At each pause, participants reported the level of clarity of the illusion, the rating scale was 0 to 4 where 0 "I did not perceive anything" and 4 "Very clear motion perception" and also reported the directionality of the stimulus. The designed handheld interface is presented in Fig. 2.

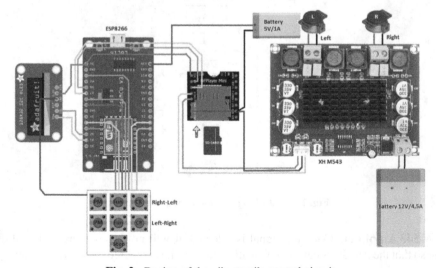

Fig. 2. Design of the vibrotactile control circuit

The coil-type actuators were designed and implemented based on [8], the encapsulation of which was performed with 3D printing at Indoamerica University (Fig. 3).

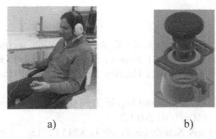

a)   b)

Fig. 3. a) Participant during experimentation, b) Coil type actuators implemented in Indoamerica University.

3 Results

Through a statistical analysis, the data reported by the participants regarding the level of perception of the tactile illusions sent can be appreciated. In the interval graph, the mean and standard deviation of the data are analyzed with a 95% confidence interval, showing the dispersion of the results. Figure 4 shows that the Fun illusion (M = 3.8, SD = 0.414) is the best perceived, because the dispersion of the data is closer to the mean of 3.8, which corresponds to the maximum value of the perception scale which is 4, CR (M = 3.65, SD = 0.617) and PM (M = 3.533, SD = 0.640). Moreover, it can be seen how dispersed the data for each illusion are. Thus validating the designed vibrotactile interface.

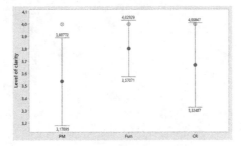

Fig. 4. Interval Chart – clarity levels of vibrotactile illusions

4 Conclusions

The participants of the experiment were able to perceive the 3 illusions sent through the portable interface with the coil type actuators. According to the results, the illusion that the respondents perceived the most is Funneling, however, the 3 illusions have a high level of perception. The validation of the haptic interface has been successful because it has been able to transmit tactile illusions with a medium level of clarity with a reliability of 95%, having as main features the portability, a reduced size of 15 × 15 × 15 cm, weight of the complete system of 1 kg, and a mechanical adaptation has been made in the housing so that it can be attached to the handlebars of a bicycle, with the aim of conducting studies of urban mobility using vibrotactile feedback.

References

1. Choi, S., Kuchenbecker, K.J.: Vibrotactile display: perception, technology, and applications. Proc. IEEE **101**(9), 2093–2104 (2013). https://doi.org/10.1109/JPROC.2012.2221071.(2013)
2. Bengoechea, E., Sánchez, E.: Palanca Háptica Versátil de Bajo Coste para Simuladores de Conducción y Entrenamiento. (2016)
3. Lederman, S.J., Jones, L.A.: Tactile and haptic illusions. IEEE Trans. Haptics **4**(4), 273–294 (2011). https://doi.org/10.1109/TOH.2011.2
4. Hayward, V.: Tactile illusions. Scholarpedia **10**(3), 8245 (2015)
5. Geldard, F.A.: Cutaneous rabbit – perceptual illusion. Science **178**, 178 (1972)
6. Pittera, D., Obrist, M, Hand-to-hand: an intermanual illusion of movement. In: Proceedings of the 19th ACM International Conference on Multimodal Interaction (ICMI'17). Association for Computing Machinery, New York, NY, USA, pp. 73–81 (2017). https://doi.org/10.1145/3136755.3136777
7. Lee, J., Kim, Y., Kim, G.J.: Rich pinch: perception of object movement with tactile illusion. IEEE Trans. Haptics **9**(1), 80–89 (2016). https://doi.org/10.1109/TOH.2015.2475271
8. Boer, L., Vallgårda, A., Cahill, B.: Giving form to a hedonic haptics player. In: DIS 2017 – Proceedings of the 2017 ACM Conference on Designing Interactive Systems, pp. 903–914 (2017). https://doi.org/10.1145/3064663.3064792

Predicting Gender via Eye Movements

Rishabh Vallabh Varsha Haria(✉) [iD], Sahar Mahdie Klim Al Zaidawi[iD],
and Sebastian Maneth[iD]

Department of Informatics in University of Bremen, Bremen, Germany
{haria,saharmah,maneth}@uni-bremen.de

Abstract. In this paper, we report the first stable results on gender
prediction via eye movements. We use a dataset with images of faces as
stimuli and with a large number of 370 participants. Stability has two
meanings for us: first that we are able to estimate the standard deviation (SD) of a single prediction experiment (it is around 4.1%); this is
achieved by varying the number of participants. And second, we are able
to provide a mean accuracy with a very low standard error (SEM): our
accuracy is 65.2%, and the SEM is 0.80%; this is achieved through many
runs of randomly selecting training and test sets for the prediction. Our
study shows that two particular classifiers achieve the best accuracies:
Random Forests and Logistic Regression. Our results reconfirm previous
findings that females are more biased towards the left eyes of the stimuli.

Keywords: Gender prediction · Eye movements data · Machine
learning

1 Introduction

A lot of research has been spawned by the advent of new eye tracking devices.
Recordings of eye movements can be used for a variety of purposes; for instance,
to detect particular diseases, to identify persons (biometrics), or to study cognitive developments in children. Previous studies on using machine learning
classifiers for gender prediction via eye movements have achieved accuracies of
64% [13] and 70% [22], respectively. One drawback of these results, however, is
their instability in these two respects: either an unknown or large standard deviation (SD), or a low number of participants. The first study does not mention
the SD while the second states an SD of 13.22% and these studies use 52 and 45
users, respectively. Here, we present the first stable results for gender prediction:
our employed dataset features 370 users. Our results show a mean accuracy of
65.2% based on 50 runs, with a standard error (SEM) of 0.80%, and we estimate the SD of a single prediction experiment to be around 4.1% by varying the
number of participants.

Our method segments eye movement trajectories into fixations and saccades
by using the I-VT algorithm [3,8,14]. A small number of statistical features are

---

R. Haria and S. Al Zaidawi contributed equally to the work.

C. Stephanidis et al. (Eds.): HCII 2022, CCIS 1654, pp. 91–100, 2022.
https://doi.org/10.1007/978-3-031-19679-9_13

then computed. We use two separate classifiers of the same kind, one for fixation's and another for saccade's. Different ML classification algorithms were examined, and we found that Logistic Regression [12] and Random Forest [15,16] performed best. We find that the best accuracy is obtained when we use the Nelder-Mead algorithm [10] to weight the fixation and the saccade classifiers. We observe increased accuracy when fixation weights are higher.

Another highlight of our results is the fact that our best accuracies are obtained by using only two features: the maximum angular velocity (this is applied to fixations) and the saccade ratio (maximum angular velocity divided by the duration; this is applied to saccades). We consider such a small number of features an advantage.

Our main contributions in this paper are:

- We present the first stable results for gender prediction using 50 runs and we achieve an accuracy of 65.2% with SEM of 0.80%.
- We compare our approach to the best previously known accuracy of 70% with an SD of 13.22% [22] and we show that in their setting (45 users and 5 runs) we achieve an accuracy of 77.5% with an SD of only 4.00%.
- We are also able to confirm previous findings that females are biased towards the left eye [17,21,28] and have a more explorative gaze behavior when compared to males [2,3,22] (the stimuli of our dataset are pictures of human faces) and we show that these differences are statistically significant.

2   Proposed System

This section describes our gender prediction architecture including the employed dataset, data preprocessing and segmentation methods, feature extraction, machine learning classifiers, and the accuracy metric used in this study.

2.1   Dataset

In our study we use the *gaze on faces* (GOF)[1] dataset. This dataset [20] comprises eye movement recordings of 405 participants aged 18–72 years. There were 27 participants whose data was erratic or absent so they were eliminated. After eliminating the participants the age group changed to 20–72 years. The GOF dataset comprised of 370 users with 185 females and 185 males. The stimuli employed in this dataset are faces of actors. The recordings were produced in 2016 at the Science Museum of London, UK. The eye tracker was an EyeLink 1000 eye-tracker running 250 Hz. The distance of the seated participants was 57 cm from an LCD screen of 19 inch (1280 × 1024 pixels). The stimuli's height and width was 429 × 720 pixels. Overall, eight actors were used as stimuli consisting of four females and four males. During the start and end of the video clip, the actor gazed towards the bottom of the screen for half a second.

---

[1] The GOF dataset can be found here [1].

The minimum recording duration for each participant is two minutes. We capped all recordings to two minutes (a few recordings were slightly longer). During the dataset recording each participant had 32 individual trials. The participants looked at multiple images of a single actor gazing towards them for varying durations (0.1 s to 10.3 s) in all the 32 different trials. This two minute trajectory is the concatenation of all the 32 trails of each participant. We always merge the last point of the first trial with the first point of the next trial. Figure 1 shows an example stimulus and the trajectories of one female and one male participant.

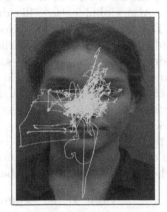

(a) Female participant   (b) Male participant

Fig. 1. Example stimulus with gaze trajectories of a female and a male participant.

2.2   Data Processing and Segmentation

There is noise in the raw data. To reduce this, a Savitzky-Golay filter [6,19] is used with polynomial order of 6 and a frame size of 15. We use the same parameters for the Savitzky-Golay filter as used in [8,24].

For several prediction tasks, segmentation has shown to be beneficial [3,8,22]. Hence, we segment the eye movement trajectories into fixations and saccades. We use the version of the *identification by velocity threshold* (I-VT) algorithm used in [8] and [3] to segment eye movements into fixations and saccades. It uses two parameters: the *velocity threshold* (VT) and the *minimum fixation duration* (MFD). Any segment of the trajectory for which the velocity is below the VT, and the length is longer than the MFD is classified as a fixation; all other segments are classified as saccades. The standard MFD value of 100 ms is chosen and changing this value (e.g. to 0 ms or 200 ms) has no impact on the accuracy in our study. We choose a VT value of 20 °/s for the dataset. By selecting the VT parameter, it is ensured that each participant has a non-zero number of fixations which is around the mean of the maximum number of fixations over all participants. In previous experiments of [14], this way of choosing the VT has been shown to give the best accuracies of certain classification tasks.

2.3   Feature Extraction

In the work of [3] they show that, contrary to previous research, gender prediction is possible in prepubsecent children with 64% of accuracy using machine learning. As a result of this promising approach, we calculate the sixty-seven features mentioned in [3].

The work of [27] mentions that a rich amount of information is present in saccades about the dynamics of the oculomotor plant. Hence, we extract the saccade amplitude and saccadic ratio. The temporal properties are leveraged by using the distance and the angle with the previous fixation and saccade as features. Also, global features like duration, dispersion, and path length are computed. The derivatives, such as velocity and acceleration are computed using the "forward difference method". Earlier work [18] suggests that different areas of the brain generate fixations and saccades in horizontal and vertical directions. Therefore, we generate versions in x and y directions of our features. Various statistical features (M3S2K) mean, median, maximum, SD (standard deviation), skewness, and kurtosis of the trajectories are computed for velocities and accelerations.

We pick the top eight features (see Table 1) in order of their ANOVA scores [7, 26]. We only consider a maximum of eight features since the accuracy started to drop when we increased the number of features beyond eight.

Table 1. Top features ranked using ANOVA scores.

Fixation features	Saccade Features
1) Maximum angular velocity	1) Saccade ratio
2) SD angular velocity	2) Mean angular velocity
3) Minimum angular acceleration	3) Mean angular acceleration
4) Mean angular velocity	4) SD angular velocity

2.4   Machine Learning Classifiers and Performance Metrics

According to our study on gender prediction, the following classifiers are the most effective:

- Logistic Regression (LogReg) [12]
- Random Forest (RF) [15,16]

We also tried Support Vector Machines (SVM) [9], Radial Basis Function Networks (RBFN) [8,25], and Naïve Bayes (NB) [5], but their results were worse than LogReg and RF. During the experiments, the ratio of male to female is always balanced. We perform hyper-parameter tuning for RF using grid search.

For every experiment, we perform cross-validation using 50 runs. Here, cross-validation refers to selecting training and test sets for the prediction randomly for each new run. In our work, we use the ratio of 80:20 meaning we use 80% participants for training and the remaining 20% for testing.

Our performance metric is the accuracy. Together with each accuracy, we also report the *standard error of the mean* (SEM), $\sigma_\mu = \frac{\sigma}{\sqrt{n}}$, where σ is the *standard deviation* (SD) and n is the number of runs. This is done using the notation x $\pm$ y%, where x is the accuracy (in percentage points) and y is the SEM. Section 4 is the only section in which we also report the standard deviation (SD).

3   Gender Prediction Experiments

In this section, we describe our experiements for gender prediction. We chose an equal number of fixation and saccade features since we have two classifiers, one for fixations and one for saccades. We perform the experiments using an incremental number of features (see Table 1) from two to eight and show the achieved accuracies with different classifiers in Table 2. We observe that both classifiers peak with *two* features (one "fixation" and one "saccade" feature). In our study we call these two top features as the "pipeline features". The LogReg classifier gives us the best accuracy of 63.7 $\pm$ 0.60% followed by the RF classifier with an accuracy of 63.4 $\pm$ 0.70%.

Table 2. Accuracies with SEM using top two to eight features over 50 runs.

No. of features	LogReg	RF
2 (1 Sac 1 Fix)	63.7 $\pm$ 0.60%	63.4 $\pm$ 0.70%
4 (2 Sac 2 Fix)	61.8 $\pm$ 0.70%	62.8 $\pm$ 0.80%
6 (3 Sac 3 Fix)	61.3 $\pm$ 0.70%	62.6 $\pm$ 0.80%
8 (4 Sac 4 Fix)	59.3 $\pm$ 0.80%	62.8 $\pm$ 0.80%

3.1   Optimizing Weights for the Fixation and Saccade Classifiers

The Nelder-Mead Method [10] is used to find the optimal weights for the fixation and saccade classifiers. In a survey of black box optimization methods [11] for low-dimensional problems, it outperformed the other methods. Table 3 presents the accuracy and weights for fixations and saccades using equal weights as well as weight-optimized approaches. According to the research of [23], the fixation classifier is more important for gender prediction and they found this by optimizing the weights manually. Our study also revealed the same with the fixation classifier being more important for this task.

The weights increase the accuarcy by 1.5% (see Table 3) for the best performing experiment using two features for the LogReg classifier and by 0.6% for the RF classifier.

Table 3. Accuracies with SEM using Nelder-Mead method over 50 runs.

No. of features	LogReg weights Sac/Fix	LogReg	RF weights Sac/Fix	RF
Two (1 Sac 1 Fix)	0.5/0.5	63.7 ± 0.60%	0.5/0.5	63.4 ± 0.70%
Two (1 Sac 1 Fix)	0.304/0.696	65.2 ± 0.80%	0.454/0.546	64.0 ± 0.70%

4   Comparison with State-of-the-Art

Only in this section we use standard deviation (SD) with the accuracy as our metric. To the best of our knowledge, the study of [22] has the highest accuracy which uses machine learning classifiers to predict gender using eye movements. They report an accuracy of 70% with an SD of 13.22% using 5 runs. The demographics of the study is as follows: 20 females and 25 males aged 25–34 years. Indoor images are used as stimuli from the Change Blindness database. An Eyelink 1000 plus eye-tracker is used at 1000 Hz.

In order to compare our pipeline features with the state-of-the-art features we perform a similar experiment (SOTA) using the same number of participants and also using 5 runs. We use two types of features for the experiment. We use our pipeline features and the features of [22]. The state-of-the-art features include six features in total. These features are fixation duration, spatial density feature, RFDSD (ratio fixation duration to saccade duration), number of saccades, saccade amplitude, and path length. The results are shown in Table 4. For the pipeline features, we achieve the best accuracy of 72.5% with an SD of 9.35% using the RF classifier. And using state-of-the-art features we achieve an accuracy of 55.0% with an SD of 11.00% with the RF classifier.

Table 4. Accuracies with SEM using pipeline and state-of-the-art features over 5 runs.

Feature type	No. of features	LogReg	RF
Pipeline	Two	62.5% with an SD of 13.69%	72.5% with an SD of 9.35%
SOTA	Six	52.5% with an SD of 4.36%	55.0% with an SD of 11.00%

We then optimize the weights for the best accuracy experiment using the Nelder-Mead Method and we find it increases the accuracy by 5% (see Table 5).

Table 5. Accuracies with SEM using Nelder-Mead method over 5 runs.

Feature type	No. of features	RF weights Sac/Fix	RF
Pipeline	Two	0.5/0.5	72.5% with an SD of 9.35 %
Pipeline	Two	0.219/0.781	77.5% with an SD of 4.00%

4.1   Relation Between SD and Number of Users

Because we are using SD in this subsection, we wanted to know if there is a correlation between SD and the number of users. The Fig. 2 illustrates how, by increasing the number of users, the SD approaches a value at around 4.10%. According to our experiments, the standard deviation is lower in an environment with more users, and it must approach a constant value as more users are added.

On the other hand, we found that when the number of runs is increased (200 runs), the SEM approaches a value of 0.31% with accuracy of 63.9% using the LogReg classifier. This means that in 95.4% of repeating our 50 runs experiment, the resulting mean accuracy will be within the range of (63.3%, 64.5%). This is a known statistical fact [4]. We consider these numbers as stable.

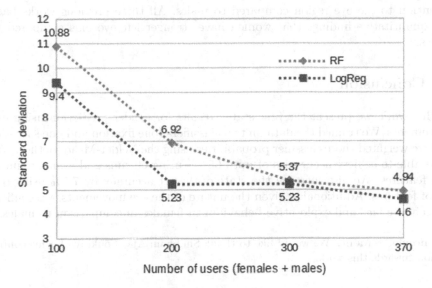

Fig. 2. Standard deviation (SD) for LogReg and RF classifier against number of users with two features and over 50 runs.

5   Statistics and Quantitative Observations

In this section we discuss some statistics and quantitative differences between female and male eye movements based on the existing literature [2,3,22].

We want to verify whether the statistics of the data as mentioned in [20] are the same. They found saccade amplitudes smaller and fixation duration longer for males than for females. With our findings (see Table 6) we confirm that the saccade amplitudes are smaller and total number of fixations is larger for males. We also find that the path lengths are longer for females. This indicates that females are more explorative than males.

The mean number of fixations (in percentage points) in eye region for females and males is shown in Table 6. It can be seen that females have more fixations on

Table 6. Mean values for females and males.

Gender	Path length	Saccade amplitude	Left eye	Right eye
Males	990.6 ± 1605.1	308.2 ± 1567.0	66.4 ± 5.2	96.2 ± 8.3
Females	2996.6 ± 14748.8	2064.5 ± 14741.0	89.5 ± 5.6	65.7 ± 7.2

the left eye of the stimuli. Males on the other hand make more fixations on the right eye. Previous research of this kind shows very strong left eye bias during the first 250 ms of exploration in women [21]. The study of [28] found that female participants focused their attention more on the left eye of the stimulus than male participants. It is observed by the work of [17] that females have a greater attention to the eye region compared to males. All these previous works back our quantitative findings that women have stronger left eye bias compared to males.

6   Conclusion

In this work, we present the first stable results for gender prediction using eye movements. We trained the data on two classifiers (one fixation and one saccade) and we weighted those classifier probabilities using the Nelder-Mead method. We were able to achieve accuracies of upto 65.2% using 50 runs and a maximum of two features. We also increase the state-of-the-art accuracy by 7.5% using our set of features. Additionally, given the nature of the eye movements, we confirm the left eye bias and explorative behaviour in females in comparison to males.

Acknowledgement. We would like to thank Shubham Ajay Soukhiya for his contribution towards this work.

References

1. Files - uncloud. https://uncloud.univ-nantes.fr/index.php/s/8KW6dEdyBJqxpmo. Accessed on 21–28 2020
2. Li, C., Xue, J., Quan, C., Yue, J., Zhang, C.: Biometric recognition via texture features of eye movement trajectories in a visual searching task. PLoS One **13**(4), e0194475 (2018)
3. Al Zaidawi, S.M.K., Prinzler, M.H., Schröder, C., Zachmann, G., Maneth, S.: Gender classification of prepubescent children via eye movements with reading stimuli. In: Companion Publication of the 2020 International Conference on Multimodal Interaction, pp. 1–6 (2020)
4. Lee, D.K., In, J., Lee, S.: Standard deviation and standard error of the mean. Korean J. Anesthesiol. **68**(3), 220 (2015)
5. Bayes, T.: Naive bayes classifier. In: Article Sources and Contributors, pp. 1–9 (1968)
6. Press, W.H., Teukolsky, S.A.: Savitzky-golay smoothing filters. Comput. Phys. **4**(6), 669–672 (1990)

7. de Souza Jacomini, R., do Nascimento, M.Z., Dantas, R.D., Ramos, R.P.: Comparison of PCA and ANOVA for information selection of CC and MLO views in classification of mammograms. In: Yin, H., Costa, J.A.F., Barreto, G. (eds.) IDEAL 2012. LNCS, vol. 7435, pp. 117–126. Springer, Heidelberg (2012). https://doi.org/10.1007/978-3-642-32639-4_15

8. George, A., Routray, A.: A score level fusion method for eye movement biometrics. Pattern Recogn. Lett. **82**, 207–215 (2016)

9. Cortes, C., Vapnik, V.: Support-vector networks. Mach. Learn. **20**(3), 273–297 (1995). https://doi.org/10.1007/BF00994018

10. Powell, M.J.: An efficient method for finding the minimum of a function of several variables without calculating derivatives. Comput. J. **7**(2), 155–162 (1964)

11. Hansen, N., Auger, A., Ros, R., Finck, S., Pošík, P.: Comparing results of 31 algorithms from the black-box optimization benchmarking bbob-2009. In: Proceedings of the 12th Annual Conference Companion on Genetic and Evolutionary Computation, pp. 1689–1696 (2010)

12. Bishop, C.M.: Multiclass logistic regression. In: Pattern Recognition and Machine Learning, chapter 4.3.4, pp. 209–210. Springer (2006)

13. Mercer Moss, F.J., Baddeley, R., Canagarajah, N.: Eye movements to natural images as a function of sex and personality. PLoS One **7**(11), e47870 (2012)

14. Mahdie Klim Al Zaidawi, S., Prinzler, M.H., Lührs, J., Maneth, S.: An extensive study of user identification via eye movements across multiple datasets. arXiv e-prints pp. arXiv-2111 (2021)

15. Breiman, L.: Random forests. Mach. Learn. **45**(1), 5–32 (2001). https://doi.org/10.1023/a:1010933404324

16. Breiman, L.: Bagging predictors. Mach. Learn. **24**(2), 123–140 (1996). https://doi.org/10.1007/BF00058655

17. Sæther, L., Van Belle, W., Laeng, B., Brennen, T., Øvervoll, M.: Anchoring gaze when categorizing faces' sex: evidence from eye-tracking data. Vision. Res. **49**(23), 2870–2880 (2009)

18. Harwood, M.R., Herman, J.P.: Optimally straight and optimally curved saccades. J. Neurosci. **28**(30), 7455–7457 (2008)

19. Schafer, R.W.: What is a savitzky-golay filter? [lecture notes]. IEEE Signal Process. Mag. **28**(4), 111–117 (2011)

20. Coutrot, A., Binetti, N., Harrison, C., Mareschal, I., Johnston, A.: Face exploration dynamics differentiate men and women. J. Vis. **16**(14), 16–16 (2016)

21. Leonards, U., Scott-Samuel, N.E.: Idiosyncratic initiation of saccadic face exploration in humans. Vision. Res. **45**(20), 2677–2684 (2005)

22. Sargezeh, B.A., Tavakoli, N., Daliri, M.R.: Gender-based eye movement differences in passive indoor picture viewing: an eye-tracking study. Physiol. Behav. **206**, 43–50 (2019)

23. Soukhiya, S.: Investigation of improvement of user and gender prediction accuracy via eye-movement by using ensemble classifier and weighting fixations and saccades. (2021). https://doi.org/10.13140/RG.2.2.26461.90080

24. Schröder, C., Al Zaidawi, S.M.K., Prinzler, M.H., Maneth, S., Zachmann, G.: Robustness of eye movement biometrics against varying stimuli and varying trajectory length. In: Proceedings of the 2020 CHI Conference on Human Factors in Computing Systems, pp. 1–7 (2020)

25. Broomhead, D.S., Lowe, D.: Radial basis functions, multi-variable functional interpolation and adaptive networks. Technical report, Royal Signals and Radar Establishment Malvern (United Kingdom) (1988)

26. Weerahandi, S.: Anova under unequal error variances. Biometrics **51**(2), 589–599 (1995)
27. Komogortsev, O.V., Jayarathna, S., Aragon, C.R., Mahmoud, M.: Biometric identification via an oculomotor plant mathematical model. In: Proceedings of the 2010 Symposium on Eye-Tracking Research & Applications, pp. 57–60 (2010)
28. Sammaknejad, N., Pouretemad, H., Eslahchi, C., Salahirad, A., Alinejad, A.: Gender classification based on eye movements: a processing effect during passive face viewing. Adv. Cogn. Psychol. **13**(3), 232 (2017)

Creative Design Diffusion Model Under Agglomerate Effect—Transformation of Creative Clusters From Weak Connection to Strong Connection

Yuwei Wu[✉] [iD]

Tongji University, Yangpu District, 1239 Siping Road, Shanghai, China
18982930786@163.com

Abstract. The emergence of creative groups aims to make the city better, solve the "persistent diseases" of the city and bring more vitality to the city through creativity. However, due to the viscosity of the group, there is a centripetal force that attracts economic activities to a certain area, forming an aggregation effect. This is also the basic factor leading to urbanization. Creativity is generated from the central area and gradually diffuses outward. In this process, different clusters participate according to the order, but the more late participating groups are, the less economic benefits brought by creativity. At this time, barriers between groups arise. According to the theory of "weak connection advantage", the information exchange of communication network is negatively correlated with two factors: one is the similarity of communication, the other is the homogeneity. In other words, the farther the distance, the more valuable the information is. As an important carrier of creativity, the diffusion process of design can intuitively reflect the interaction between creative clusters and other groups in order to find deficiencies. At the same time, the diffusion process of creative design is also a neglected field of design. The research on this can also supplement the cognition of design and provide more valuable information feedback to design creators. Therefore, the premise of this paper is to let different groups participate in the diffusion process of creative design in the context of spatial aggregation, expand the interaction mode between creative clusters and other clusters to more diversified fields, and realize the transformation from weak connection to strong connection between clusters.

Creative cluster refers to the group that creates economic value with creativity within a certain space. Its elements include not only people, but also activities and space (material space and non-material space). Diffusion has different meanings in different disciplines. In this study, the innovation diffusion theory in the field of communication is introduced as the cognitive basis, and it is modified to adapt to the research situation. This paper will introduce how to include different clusters more closely in the diffusion process of creative design, and explore the advantages and disadvantages of the diffusion process of the famous creative cluster cases through case studies. The research results will provide a multi-directional interactive creative design diffusion model, which shows that the diffusion process of creative design is not one-way and linear, but a circular process. The study is still at an early stage and aims to trigger discussion on how to strengthen the interaction between creative clusters and other clusters.

Keywords: Creative cluster · Creative city · Creative design diffusion model ·
Group interaction · Aggregation effect

1 Creative Clusters Under Aggregation Effect

1.1 Positive Impact of Agglomeration Effect on Creative Clusters

With the continuous growth of creative groups, the economic effects produced by the spatial concentration of various industries and economic activities and the centripetal force to attract economic activities to a certain area lead to the agglomeration effect. The aggregation effect also brings positive feedback of a virtuous circle within the creative cluster: first, they can reduce operating costs by sharing public infrastructure [1]. At the same time, the aggregation of creative talents also makes the division of labor clearer and more flexible, improves the efficiency of creative production [2], and even brings knowledge spillover [3]. The centripetal force generated by aggregation is like a vortex, and aggregation will aggravate aggregation. The agglomeration of enterprises has cultivated and attracted a large number of skilled labor, reduced the cost of labor mobility, and formed a labor market with sufficient supply. The strong centripetal force within the cluster can form a "regional brand effect" that cannot be formed by a single enterprise [4], strengthen trust [5], and then increase the cooperation among enterprises.

1.2 Negative Impact of Aggregation Effect on Creative Groups

However, the creative group has been regarded as an isolated and privileged group in the development process of these two decades, which is not conducive to the workers [6]. On the one hand, these creative clusters have benefited the creative groups in them. On the other hand, creative content has become the added value of products, rapidly pushing up the local cost of living, diluting the income of other groups, and forcing them to leave their original living areas. At this time, the distance of physical space weakens the activities between clusters and intensifies the incomprehension and mistrust between clusters. In essence, it is caused by unfair opportunities and message lag between clusters. Creativity is generated from the central area and gradually diffuses outward. In this process, different clusters participate according to the order, but the more late participating groups are, the less economic benefits brought by creativity.

1.3 Impact of Aggregation Effect on Physical Space

Due to the growth of creative groups, they have the same pursuit of inclusiveness and diversity, so creativity is always attracted to a specific geographical location [7]. This also leads to different geographical distribution of different groups. Physical space is endowed with different attributes by different groups, which also reflects the "concentration of creativity" to a certain extent. The distance in space has become a natural barrier for creativity to spread among different groups. Different distances represent different social relations. For example, public distance can reach 360 cm [8]. In fact, the physical distance between creative clusters and other clusters is far more than that, which also leads to the weakening of their interaction.

2 New Understanding of Creative Clusters

By using the vosviewer document measurement tool and taking the core collection of web of science database from 2000 to 2022 as the data source, this paper analyzes the knowledge map of creative cluster research. Descriptive analysis of the evolution process, core strength and knowledge base, including the research status, focusing on the analysis of research hotpots, hot spot evolution process, core themes and research frontiers.

2.1 Knowledge Map Analysis

Knowledge map is an image that takes knowledge domain as the object and shows the development process and structural relationship of scientific knowledge. The visual map reveals the relationship between knowledge and the evolution law of knowledge [9]. In this paper, vosviewer is used to analyze the knowledge map of literature data in the field of creative clusters, using the functions of organization, author cooperation network analysis, keyword co-occurrence, keyword clustering, document co citation analysis, emergent words and so on.

2.2 Data Collection and Sorting

The data of this paper comes from wos database platform English literature in the core collection of. First, the search conditions set in the core collection of wos database are: TS = "creative cluster", where TS is the subject and the file type is "article". Secondly, the time span is 1986-2022 (1986 is the starting time of the journals included in the core collection), and the retrieval time is May 1, 2022. A total of 1761 articles were retrieved in this search, of which the earliest appeared in 2000. Finally, the effective documents are exported in TXT format according to the processing requirements of vosviewer software, transcoding and document splitting are carried out to form the required creative cluster research sample database. 332 words related to creative clusters that appeared more than 15 times in each article were retrieved, and 10 terms unrelated to this study were deleted. Among them, hot words include creative subject, creative class, creative economy, creative talents, creative industry, creative city, creative community, etc., and these terms are defined, analyzed and classified by concept mapping, so as to clarify the connotation of creative cluster. The four quadrants of concept mapping select two groups of contradiction points concerned in this paper: aggregation and diffusion, surrounding and environment.

The creative industry refers to the place where creative economic activities take place [7] and creative economic groups as the core. Therefore, creative clusters include three elements: people, activities and places. With the development of network technology, the place where creativity takes place has also changed from a single physical space to a mixed space online and offline. Therefore, the place elements of creative clusters should be extended to the field of physical space and non physical space (environment) [10]. Surround is the "environing circles" of our life - the physical feeling around us that is consistent with our life process. They can be anything we think is outside of ourselves, with unknown but potential personal significance. When we as a person intentionally stay in a space for some reason or purpose, the environment appears. Human intention transforms the surrounding environment into an environment of experience and action [11]. Therefore, surrounding here refers to the physical space of the real world, and environment refers to the spiritual space and virtual space that throw out the physical space (Figs. 1 and 2).

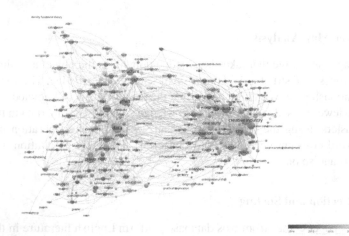

Fig. 1. Vosviewer hot vocabulary data analysis

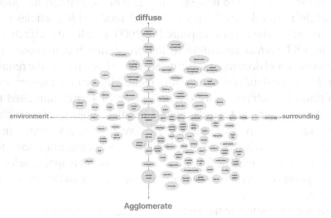

Fig. 2. Cluster concept mapping

3   Research Issues and Objectives

Question ① what is the diffusion model of creative design under the aggregation effect?
Question ② how does the connection between clusters change?

This paper hopes to improve the stage of innovation based on the original innovation diffusion model, and take the influence of aggregation and diffusion as reference factors to form a more and perfect creative design diffusion model.

4   Linkages Between Clusters

4.1   Adaptability of Innovation Diffusion Theory

As an important subject in the creative cluster, designers' innovation and creativity have always been deeply concerned by them [12]. Creativity is generally considered to occur in the process of interaction between the originator and the receiver of an idea [13]. In the diffusion research in the field of communication, the term "innovator" does not refer to the creator of the solution, but refers to the initial category of adopters in the S-shaped or S-shaped diffusion curve, followed by early, late adopters and laggards [14]. Therefore, it is necessary to clarify the different meanings of creativity and innovation, and clarify the micro and macro links between them. At the same time, the theory reminds us that in the process of innovation diffusion, we should combine mass communication with interpersonal communication, give full play to the timely, rapid and extensive communication advantages of mass media at the initial stage of communication, and when people have a full understanding of new things, try to mobilize the enthusiasm of interpersonal channels, and spread persuasive information with the help of interpersonal networks, so as to produce the expected results. However, the theory has some limitations due to the lack of feedback and inconsistency with the actual situation. And this model is more suitable for promoting sexual communication from top to bottom and from outside to inside; If it is from bottom to top, adoption is the initiative of the user, and diffusion is the result of natural propagation, the applicability of this model is poor. Therefore, this paper will modify the original innovation diffusion theory to make it more perfect.

4.2   Group Classification in the Process of Innovation Diffusion

According to the "innovation diffusion theory", the diffusion process includes four groups: brave innovators, respected early adopters, cautious ordinary people, skeptical late receivers, and conservative traditional laggards [7]. However, it ignores the diffusion process from the creator to the innovator, that is, the process from the creation of ideas to the first acceptance. Generally, this process includes at least three steps: expert judgment, popularity recognition and peer recognition [15, 16]. So this process should include five groups. In order to better understand the activity process between them, the five groups need to be simplified. To this end, attributes of all stakeholders are summarized through the research sector map, and×2 to determine different groups. There are different relationships among different groups, and these relationships were reclassified at noon in this study. The six different types of stakeholders are sorted out and divided into three groups: designers, opinion leaders and adopters. Designers are the creators and producers of ideas, and they transform ideas into knowledge and include them in the repository. The design process includes generating alternative solutions by learning (knowledge measurement) or imitating other designers (cognitive measurement). The resulting ideas are adopted by the first to receive and identify with. Their pursuit of aesthetics, novelty, quality and surprise makes them always attracted by creativity [17]. They become the opinion leaders of the public and greatly promote the diffusion of creativity. When ideas reach the public, these social groups will choose to accept or reject them in the follow-up process. At this stage, they will reflect the popularity and satisfaction of the design and judge whether the design is creative. In this framework, the three different groups interact with each other to make the diffusion of ideas flow among the three[1] (Fig. 3).

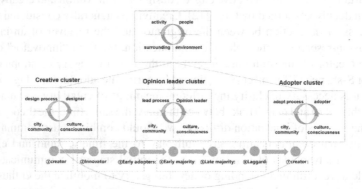

Fig. 3. Group classification

4.3 "Weak Connection Advantage" Theory

Stanford University professor granovetter [18] put forward the theory of weak joint advantage in 1973. This theory points out that a person often only establishes close relationships with those who have strong similarities with himself in all aspects, but the information they have is not different from the information they have; On the contrary, those who are relatively distant from this person are more likely to have access to helpful information that this person has no chance to get because of their significant differences with this person. Therefore, the weak relationship between people is an essential factor for individuals to integrate into society or community. It can bring unexpected information and opportunities to people, and has the ability to contact different social circles. Therefore, the farther the communication distance is, the more valuable the information fed back by the groups with larger gap is. Because they have different living environment, educational background and cultural media, the repetition of information is greatly reduced.

---

[1] Research partition map.

5   Research Methods

5.1   Case Study

No. 8 Bridge creative industry park consists of four phases, with a total construction area of about 60000 Sq.m.

Phase I is located at No. 8, Jianguo Middle Road, Huangpu District, Shanghai, and phases II, III and IV are located at No. 436, 555 and 457, jumen Road, Huangpu District, Shanghai, respectively [26]. No. 8 bridge was built by Qike group founded by Huang Hanhong. It controls all links such as planning, transformation, investment promotion and operation management. Adhering to the concept of "creating a quality living space", it has successfully built the creative industry brand of No. 8 bridge [19].

5.2   Quantitative Analysis

Based on the analysis of the location data of Douban exhibition in Shanghai, exhibition is an important means of communication [20], and many design prototypes are widely known in the form of exhibition. Today's exhibition mode has formed a mature form of online ticket sales due to the impact of the Internet and the epidemic. Therefore, this study crawls through the data of Douban exhibition in Shanghai, All offline exhibition data of Shanghai in recent 5 years have been collected, and their locations and coordinates have been found. Data visualization has been carried out through GIS, i.e. geographic information system, to intuitively reflect the distribution of exhibition activities in physical space. Through the frequency analysis of the data, it can be seen that the Shanghai New International Expo Center located in Pudong New Area accounts for 27.66%.Then came the Shanghai Contemporary Art Museum, No. 678, miaojiang Road, Huangpu District, 1.7%, the art warehouse Art Museum, No. 4777, Binjiang Avenue, Pudong New Area, 0.85%, the yudeyao Art Museum, Xuhui District, 0.85%, the Longyang Road, Pudong New Area, 2345, 0.85%, and the Shangnan Road, Pudong New Area, 205, 0.85% (see Fig. 4).

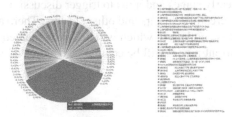

Fig. 4. Visual analysis diagram

6 Creative Design Diffusion Model Under the Aggregation Effect

Why is there a sequence of participation? Because this is a process, it has a starting point and an ending point. With a starting point and an ending point, the process will naturally have a sequence. At the same time, there is a limiting factor in this process, that is, one-way communication, which exacerbates the "tiger head and snake tail" economic flow. At the same time, they have no interaction between each stage. There are two main factors that lead to these problems: time and distance. So let me focus on the diffusion process that is not controlled by time and distance. I think diffusion means that different objects contact each other and enter each other when they collide freely. But in fact, diffusion in communication means that innovation spreads among members of a certain social group through a specific channel over a period of time. It is a special type of communication, which contains information related to new ideas. Diffusion is a special type of propagation. The information transmitted is about a new idea, and the novelty of the idea gives diffusion a special purpose. New means that there are some uncertain factors in the diffusion. Diffusion is a kind of social change, which can be defined as the process in which the structure and function of a social system change. The whole process is controlled by time and distance (see Fig. 5). So I think it is precisely because of this understanding. I hope to establish a new model to understand this problem.

Fig. 5. Design diffusion interaction mechanism

7 Discuss

The study is still in its early stages and aims to trigger discussion on how to strengthen the interaction between creative clusters and other clusters. There are some deficiencies in data collection and case collation, which will be supplemented and improved in the future research. The current model will be continuously adjusted in the process of data improvement.

References

1. Weber: Industrial location theory, The Commercial Press, China, Beijing (1997)
2. Porter. m.e. cluster and the new economy of competition. Harvard business review **11**, 77–90 (1998)
3. Piore, M.J., Sabel, C.F.: The Second Industrial Divide: Possibilities for Prosperity. Basic Books, New York (1984)
4. Shouhua, W., Bihua, S.: A study on the competitive advantages of enterprise clusters. China Industrial Economics **1**, 59–65 (2002)

5. Marshall: Principles of Economics, The Commercial Press, China, Beijing (1997)
6. Henderson, A.: David Brooks argues that the urban 'creative class' has screwed working-class America (2021)
7. Richard, F.: The of the creative class: and how it's transforming work Leisure, community and everyday life Canadian public policy-analysis de policies, Canada (2003)
8. Edward, H.: The Hidden Dimension, Peter Smith Publisher Inc, America (1992)
9. Chen, Y., et al.: Methodological function of Cite Space knowledge graph. Science research 33(2), 242-253 (2015)
10. John, H.: The creative economy. Penguin, America (2002)
11. Richard, B.: Surrounds and environments in fourth order design. Design Issues 35(1), 4-22 (2019)
12. Gardner, H.: Creating Minds: an Anatomy of Creativity Seen Through the Lives of Freud, Einstein, Picasso, Stravinsky, Eliot, Graham and Gandhi. Basic Books, New York (1993)
13. Eysenck, H.J.: Dimensions of personality. Personality and Individual Differences 12, 773–90 (1991)
14. Von Stamm, B.: Managing innovation Design and creativity. Wiley, London (2003)
15. Høgni Kalsø H., Niedomysl, T.: Migration of The Creative Class: Evidence from Sweden. Journal of Economic Geography (4), 12-16 (2008)
16. Mrogers, E.: Diffusion of Innovations, 1st edn. The Free Press, New York (1983)
17. Runco, M., Pritzker, S.: Encyclopedia of creativity. Academic Press, San diego (1999)
18. Simon, D.K.: Creative development as acquired expertise: theoretical issues and an empirical test, developmental review (20), 283-318 (2000)
19. Zhang, Y., Yu, X.: Urban tourism and the politic of creative class: a study of the chefs in macao, International Journal of Tourism Sciences (2), 23–25 (2018)
20. Jingjing, Z., Jianqiang, Y.: Interpretation system: a new exploration to strengthen the communication effect of museum exhibitions. The southeast culture 2(250), 119–128 (2016)

Riemannian Classification and Regression for EEGEyeNet

Derrick Zhen[✉] and Guy Berreby

Swarthmore College, Swarthmore, USA
dzhen1@swarthmore.edu

Abstract. In this paper, we use emerging Riemannian geometry based classifiers and regressors to perform eye-tracking tasks over a 2021 dataset: EEGEyeNet. The classification task we attempt is determining Left/Right eye movement, and the regression task we attempt is determining absolute eye position on a Cartesian plane. We find that Riemannian methods are not more accurate than traditional ML techniques, and offer suggestions for future improvement.

Keywords: Riemannian geometry · EEG · Eye tracking

1 Introduction

1.1 Problem Statement

In the past decades, EEG based BCIs have seen an explosion in popularity. However, mainstream adoption of BCIs remains largely untenable due to the general lack of robustness of EEG classification in uncontrolled environments beyond the research laboratory. To deal with these difficulties, a new research paradigm focusing on robust algorithm development has been proposed. Obeid and Picone (2013) One of the most exciting candidates for a robust, adaptive, universal EEG decoder has been Riemannian geometry classifiers (RGC), which have reached state of the art performances on multiple BCI problems. Lotte et al. (2018)

In this paper, we apply these Riemannian classifiers, and newly developed Riemannian regressors, to the EEGEyeNet dataset, a 2021 dataset containing 47 h of synchronized eye tracking (ET) and EEG measurements; focusing on a motor-imagery (MI) task of identifying saccades from antisaccades using RGCs trained on EEG data. Kastrati et al. (2021) We will attempt to outperform traditional ML models benchmarked in the EEGEyeNet paper, and discuss conceptual advantages and drawbacks of RGCs in classifying MI trials and RGRs for gaze prediction, as well as analyze potential optimizations for Riemannian geometry classifiers and regressors.

C. Stephanidis et al. (Eds.): HCII 2022, CCIS 1654, pp. 110–118, 2022.
https://doi.org/10.1007/978-3-031-19679-9_15

1.2 Literature Review

When trying to compare the distance between two points on a sphere, such as two cities on Earth's surface, a naive approach would be to use the Euclidean distance, which measures the length of the straight line between two points. This measure of distance, however, is nonsensical. Since the Earth is (allegedly) a sphere, traveling in a straight line between those two cities would require boring a tunnel straight through the Earth! No one travels this way, meaning that we need a different method to calculate distances between points on Earth. To do this, we have to take into account the curvature of the Earth's surface, and how that effects the distances of paths along the surface. Luckily for us, the field of differential geometry gives us the tools to solve this problem. More specifically, if we can show that some shape or surface in any dimensions satisfies certain constraints, then we can find a mathematical expression which gives us the geodesic, or the shortest path along the curve of the shape, between two points. The set of constraints needed are those needed for what is called a Riemannian Manifold. The proper definition of a Riemannian manifold is quite technical, and we do not need to know the specific details for this paper, so we will not discuss it here. The study of Riemannian manifolds is known as Riemannian geometry, which is the namesake of the algorithms we are using.

There is one more important concept to have an intuitive grasp of, which is that of the tangent space. Despite the fact that Earth is a sphere, when walking around in our day-to-day lives, it appears to be mostly flat. Namely, approximating the local area you are currently in as a 2-dimensional Cartesian grid and then measuring the distance between two points on that grid using the euclidean metric will give you a distance that is almost exactly correct. When on the scale of two points within a single square mile, the distance calculated will be the same as the geodesic distance to any reasonable degree of precision.

This then tells us that for two points close enough on a shape or surface, it is possible to get a good calculation for the distance between those points by treating that space as being flat. We have to choose a single point on the surface which we will treat as the basis for where the flatness is starting, since technically due to the shape's curvature there is a distinct flat plane which we can use for approximations at each point on the shape. This flat plane at a point on the surface is known as the tangent space. To look at relationship between points on the surface that are close together, we can do an operation called projection, which tells us what points on the tangent space the points on the surface correspond to. Then, since the points are now in the tangent space, and the tangent space is flat (another word for Euclidean), we can now apply any algorithms that are designed to work in Euclidean space on those points. This includes many machine learning algorithms, which will be one of the main features of this paper. Working on data in the tangent space of a surface is a middle ground between looking just at the intrinsic structure of the data and just assuming the data is Euclidean, as it allows us to use regular machine learning techniques while still preserving some sense of the data's structure.

How does this relate to gaze prediction using EEG data? Well, many machine learning algorithms often implicitly assume the the input data is structured in a Euclidean way, i.e. some blob lying in n-dimensional space, where n is the number of features the data has. However, for some data, this assumption fails to hold, such as data distributed over the surface of a sphere. In order to deal with this more structured data, we need to use more sophisticated techniques

This is the situation we face when working with EEG data, or more specifically, the covariance matrices of EEG data. When using an EEG with n-electrodes on someone, we get n different streams of numbers corresponding to the value of electric waves around each electrode at different points in time. Using these n different streams of numbers, we can take each block of numbers across the n streams corresponding to a single second in time, and turn that block into what is called a covariance matrix. The covariance matrix is $n \times n$, with the (i, j)th component of the matrix being the covariance between the ith and jth data streams. Since the covariance between two random variables is same regardless of order of input, and due to other properties beyond the scope of this paper, the covariance matrix constructed here will always be symmetric and positive definite (SPD). [CITEME] Due to the work of others, it is known that the covariance matrices constructed from EEG data retain releven spatial and temporal information that can be used for classification. Additionally, it turns out that the set of all $n \times n$ SPD matrices has the structure of a Riemannian manifold Bhatia (2007). This means that to properly work with classifying and regressing on these covariance matrices, we need to construct algorithms which take advantage of this Riemannian structure.

The most basic RGC is a Minimum Distance to Mean (MDM) classifier. In a MDM, pre-processed and labeled time-series data are transformed into covariance matrices and mapped onto a geometrical space. Each trial is a point in space, and the center of mass for each class is computed based on the positions of its constituent trials. Classification on unknown trials then follows by estimating the Riemannian distance between the new point and the existing centers. Congedo (2013) Since covariance matrices encode spatial information, it suffices in classifying motor-imagery (MI) BCI data, since MI trials of different classes produce different scalp patterns. Indeed, MDMs have been shown to outperform conventional models (like CSP+LDA) on competition motor-imagery datasets Congedo (2013). This works as covariance matrices are positive-definite and symmetric. It has been shown that the set of all positive-definite matrices has the structure of a manifold, allowing for the application of tools from differential geometry to problems using these matrices Förstner and Moonen (2003).

Tangent space mapping classifiers work as follows: at each point in a Riemannian manifold, there exists a tangent space which is similar to euclidean space, like elaborated on previously. Looking at the tangent space at the point representing the geometric mean of the EEG trials done, we can then apply traditional classification techniques on data projected onto that tangent space, such as Linear Regression. Barachant et al. (2010)

A Riemannian kernel works similarly, taking in points (as covariance matrices) and mapping them to the tangent plane. When this is done, the projected points can be manipulated and used in SVM classification. Jayasumana et al. (2013).

In our paper, for regression we will be focusing on the Minimum Distance to Riemannian Mean classifier and Riemannian SVM proposed by Barachant et al. (2013). These algorithms have shown promising results when compared to other state of the art classifiers Kalunga et al. (2016). There have been no papers published studying RGRs, so our work will be pioneering that area.

1.3   Purpose of Study

The purpose of this study is to apply RGCs and RGRs on EEGEyeNet, a novel dataset with MI tasks and benchmarks. For classification, we will attempt several variations on the simplistic MDM algorithm, including tangent space mappings and Riemannian kernel-based SVMs. For regression, we will use a modified KNN regression which checks distances using a Riemannian geodesic, and apply classic regression algorithms in the tangent space. Based on the results of our benchmarks, we will discuss the viability of RGCs in classifying eye tracking data and the effectiveness of RGRs in gaze prediction.

1.4   Research Question

In this work, we would like to answer the following questions: How do Riemannian classifiers and regressors compare with traditional ML classifiers and DL methods used in the EEGEyeNet paper benchmark?

2   Dataset

The EEGEyeNet dataset includes simultaneous EEG and Eye tracking data from 356 different subjects with a temporal resolution of 500 HZ. The EEG data contains 128 channels and the eye tracking has an instrument spatial resolution of less than .01° RMS of the distances between each sample. 3 experimental paradigms were employed. The first measured pro and anti saccades - eye movements shifting gaze towards and away from stimulus. The second paradigm was a large grid trial, in which participants fixated their gaze on dots within a grid. And the final paradigm was Visual Symbol search, which is a clinical assessment measuring processing speed.

3   Experimental Design

The purpose of our study is to compare existing SoTA algorithms employed in the EEGEyeNet manuscript to emerging Riemannian geometry based methods.

Accuracy and runtime will be evaluated using the Left-Right task and Absolute Position task for classification and regression respectively. We will be using Riemannian MDM as well as a Riemannian-kernel based SVMs for the binary classification task and Riemannian KNN and Linear Regression performed in the tangent space to perform the regression task.

4   Methods

4.1   Classifier Methods

The classification task we are tackling is the Left-Right task, which consists of determining the direction of the subject's gaze along the horizontal axis using data from the first experimental paradigm (Pro/Antisaccade). Performance is measured in terms of accuracy, with a naive baseline of 52.3% given by the majority class Kastrati et al. (2021). We will be using Riemannian MDM as well as a Riemannian-kernel based SVMs for this binary classification task.

Due to hardware limitations, we were unable to perform classification over the entire concatenated Pro/Antisaccade dataset. In order to bypass this limitation, we instead performed classification on data from 7 subjects out of a total 329 subjects. By sampling data from specific subjects, we were also able to explore inter-subject performance, which will be discussed in the next section. Our experimental paradigm is visualized in Fig. 1.

The raw, unconcatenated subject data is available on the EEGEyeNet website as .mat files. We then used Kastrati's data preparation module on each each subject's .mat file to produce subject specific .npz files fit for manipulation in Python.Covariance matrices are computed using the PyRiemann package, and 5- fold cross validation is performed with a test-train split of 20–80.

4.2   Regressor Methods

Our regression task is the Absolute Position task, wherein the position of the subject's gaze fixation on a XY plane is predicted based on data from the second experimental paradigm (Large Grid Fixation). Performance is measured by the millimeter distance between the estimated gaze position and the actual position. Our naive baseline to beat is a model that outputs the mean position of the recorded fixations for every regression, which corresponds to an average distance of 123.3mm Kastrati et al. (2021). We will be using Riemannian KNN and Linear Regression performed in the tangent space to perform the regression task.

For the regression task, we did the following steps. First, we went to the EEGEyenet data website, and downloaded the Position_task_with_dots_ synchronised_min.npz file, which we used as our data. To load this data in properly, we used the config and IOHelper files from the EEGEyenet github repos.

Once loaded in, the data was sampled, so that only 2000 of the 21000 datapoints and only 30 of the 129 electrodes are used. Then, the sampled data was turned into covariance matrices using the PyRiemann package. From here, the covariance matrices were used to train a variety of models. Most of these models were trained in the tangent space of the geometric mean of the covariance matrix data, as projecting to the tangent space allows for the use of conventional machine learning algorithms. The algorithms used in the tangent space were all taken from the SciKit learn library, and included ElasticNet , Bayesian Ridge, and Support Vector Regression with linear and RBF kernels. In addition, we created a Riemannian Geometry based KNN regression algorithm, which makes predictions by looking at the K-closest neighbors according to the given Riemannian metric.

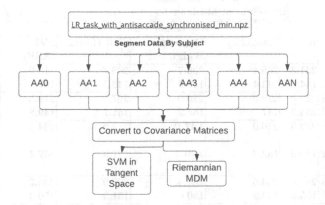

Fig. 1. Experimental paradigm

5   Results

We notice several trends from the classification results. **First**, Riemannian SVM outperformed MDM. The SVM trained on the concatenated data from 7 subjects was 66% accurate, compared to the MDM's 48% accuracy. **Secondly**, training evaluating over each individual subject results in more accurate models. In particular, training subject-unique SVMs yielded mean and median accuracies of 79% and 81% respectively, compared to the concatenated data's accuracy of 66%.

For the regression task, we used a Riemannian-geometry based KNN algorithm, alongside a variety of standard regression algorithms applied in the tangent plane of the geometric mean of the covariance matrices. For all of these algorithms, the results were near random, with all having an RMS of roughly 230–250 pixels for the X-position of the eye, and an RMS of 145–155 pixels for the Y-position (Fig. 2).

When doing regression on each individual, the results stay near random, with the best performing algorithm being ElasticNet, having an X RMS of 197 and a Y RMS of 129.5 when working on subject EP14. This, however, is still not a significant result.

Classification Task		
Subject	MDM	SVM
AA0	0.55	0.86
AA1	0.63	0.84
AA4	0.53	0.68
AA5	0.45	0.78
AA7	0.66	0.63
AA8	**0.35**	**0.96**
AA9	**1.0**	**0.90**
Concatenated	**0.48**	**0.66**
Inter-Subject Mean	0.58	0.79
Inter-Subject Median	0.54	0.81

Regression Task						
Subject	KNN	ElasticNet	**Bayesian Ridge**	SVR (Linear)	SVR (RBF)	Linear SVR
EP10 X RMS	231.3	206.4	206.7	208.7	213.9	231.5
EP10 Y RMS	144.8	142.4	142.6	148.3	157.8	153.1
EP12 X RMS	230.0	219.3	220.0	227.6	219.5	267.6
EP12 Y RMS	154.3	147.5	148.2	151.2	149.8	166.9
EP14 X RMS	233.5	216.0	**197.0**	212.9	234.4	281.7
EP14 Y RMS	149.3	132.2	**129.5**	127.9	147.4	132.6
EP18 X RMS	249.6	233.6	236.4	239.9	236.2	272.3
EP18 Y RMS	155.9	149.9	150.4	151.5	150.3	160.1
EP23 X RMS	249.3	240.8	247.1	250.0	234.3	284.0
EP23 Y RMS	154.1	142.5	145.1	149.0	144.9	152.6

Regression Task (Aggregate)		
Model Name	X RMS	Y RMS
KNN RMS	248.29	151.20
ElasticNet RMS	**233.55**	**144.59**
Bayseian RMS	234.11	145.17
SVR (Linear) RMS	237.63	152.21
SVR (RBF) RMS	234.96	145.03
Linear SVR RMS	247.30	152.55
Naive Baseline	123.3	123.3

Fig. 2. Results

6 Discussion

For classification, the Riemannian methods we attempted did not outperform traditional machine learning algorithms benchmarked in the EEGEyeNet manuscript, which were up to 98.8% accurate. However, it's worth noting that in the EEGEyeNet benchmark, Kastrati et al. performed classification on feature extracted EEG data, while we ran the Riemannian classifiers over the entire dataset.

Instead, RGCs may be suited for online BCIs, where raw data is being fed into the model directly. In this scenario, we also find an additional optimization:

that RGCs trained on individual subjects greatly outperform RGCs trained on a pool of subjects.

For regression, our results did not yield any good results. There may be several ways to explain why this is. First, it is important to note that in the original EEGEyenet paper, all classical ML models similarly failed to do well on this dataset, achieving essentially random accuracy. Only the deep learning models did better than random, meaning that our results are actually in line with those of classical ML models.

Many of the regression models revolved around applying classic regressors to the tangent space mapping of the data's covariance matrices. This is because the tangent space is just a local approximation of the manifold of symmetric positive-definite matrices at a certain point, meaning that if the data has a high variance its possible for tangent space projections to not give a good representation of the true distances between points, causing regressors to not do as well.

For future improvement of both the classification and regression tasks, we could employ more dimension reduction techniques. Currently, we aren't even able to use all of the dimensions of the data anyways, as that causes the covariance matrices to be singular. By using dimension reduction, we could incorporate more of the important information encoded in the EEG data when constructing the covariance matrices, possible increasing our general accuracy.

An area which future research could examine is using neural networks in the tangent space for both regression and classification. The EEGEyeNet benchmark found that neural networks performed the best on almost all tasks, so it is possible that trying to leverage them using Riemannian methods could create further improvement. To do this, one would first apply a tangent space projection to the data, and then train and test neural networks on that projected data.

7   Conclusion

Overall, Riemannian-geometry based classifiers and newly developed regressors did not outperform classifical ML techniques on the EEGYEyenet benchmark. Despite this, neither should be discounted for future use, and there are a variety of further directions with which to take these algorithms.

References

Barachant, A., Bonnet, S., Congedo, M., Jutten, C.: Riemannian geometry applied to BCI classification. In: Vigneron, V., Zarzoso, V., Moreau, E., Gribonval, R., Vincent, E. (eds.) LVA/ICA 2010. LNCS, vol. 6365, pp. 629–636. Springer, Heidelberg (2010). https://doi.org/10.1007/978-3-642-15995-4_78

Barachant, A., Bonnet, S., Congedo, M., Jutten, C.: Classification of covariance matrices using a Riemannian-based kernel for BCI applications. Neurocomputing 112, 172–178 (2013)

Bhatia, R.: Positive definite matrices. Princeton University Press (2007). ISBN 9780691129181. http://www.jstor.org/stable/j.ctt7rxv2

Congedo, M.: EEG source analysis. PhD thesis, Université de Grenoble (2013)

Förstner, W., Moonen, B.: A metric for covariance matrices. In: Geodesy-the Challenge of the 3rd Millennium, pp. 299–309. Springer, Cham (2003). https://doi.org/10.1007/978-3-662-05296-9_31

Jayasumana, S., Hartley, R., Salzmann, M., Li, H., Harandi, M.: Kernel methods on the Riemannian manifold of symmetric positive definite matrices. In: proceedings of the IEEE Conference on Computer Vision and Pattern Recognition, pp. 73–80 (2013)

Kalunga, E.K., Chevallier, S., Barthélemy, Q., Djouani, K., Monacelli, E., Hamam, Y.: Online SSVEP-based BCI using Riemannian geometry. Neurocomputing 191, 55–68 (2016)

Kastrati, A., et al.: EEGEyeNet: a simultaneous electroencephalography and eye-tracking dataset and benchmark for eye movement prediction. arXiv preprint arXiv:2111.05100 (2021)

Lotte, F., et al.: A review of classification algorithms for EEG-based brain-computer interfaces: a 10 year update. J. Neural Eng. 15(3), 031005 (2018)

Obeid, I., Picone, J.: Bringing big data to neural interfaces. In: Proceedings of the Fifth International Brain-Computer Interface Meeting (2013)

BrainActivity1: A Framework of EEG Data Collection and Machine Learning Analysis for College Students

Zheng Zhou[1]([✉])(iD), Guangyao Dou[1](iD), and Xiaodong Qu[1,2](iD)

[1] Brandeis University, Waltham, MA 02453, USA
{zhengzhou,guangyaodou}@brandeis.edu
[2] Swarthmore College, Swarthmore, PA 19081, USA
xqu1@swarthmore.edu

Abstract. Using Machine Learning and Deep Learning to predict cognitive tasks from electroencephalography (EEG) signals has been a fast-developing area in Brain-Computer Interfaces (BCI). However, during the COVID-19 pandemic, data collection and analysis could be more challenging than before. This paper explored machine learning algorithms that can run efficiently on personal computers for BCI classification tasks. Also, we investigated a way to conduct such BCI experiments remotely via Zoom. The results showed that Random Forest and RBF SVM performed well for EEG classification tasks. The remote experiment during the pandemic yielded several challenges, and we discussed the possible solutions; nevertheless, we developed a protocol that grants non-experts who are interested a guideline for such data collection.

Keywords: Brain-machine interface · Machine learning · Ensemble methods · Remote BCI · Interpretable AI

1 Introduction

Previous research in Computer Science, Neuroscience, and Medical fields has implemented EEG-based Brain-Computer Interfaces (BCI) in several ways, [1, 13, 14, 19, 21, 23, 25, 33–35], such as diagnosis of Alzheimer's, emotion recognition, mental workload, motor imagery tasks [3–5, 15, 22, 26]. Machine learning, deep learning, and transfer learning algorithms have demonstrated the great potential in such biomarker data analysis [2, 6, 7, 16, 17, 20, 24, 27, 28, 31, 37–41].

However, EEG datasets' size is still relatively small compared with peers in Computer Vision and Natural Language Processing [13, 23, 36].

Our **research questions** are: 1. Can we develop a larger dataset with data from a larger audience? for example, college students? 2. Can we design easy-to-use BCI experiments to collect EEG data with consumer-grade devices for college students? 3. Can we develop a step-by-step guide for such a data collection and machine learning analysis process?

© The Author(s), under exclusive license to Springer Nature Switzerland AG 2022
C. Stephanidis et al. (Eds.): HCII 2022, CCIS 1654, pp. 119–127, 2022.
https://doi.org/10.1007/978-3-031-19679-9_16

Fig. 1. College students using EEG devices

2   Methods

As [11,18,30,32] mentioned, several affordable (less than three hundred dollars) non-invasive consumer-grade EEG headsets are commercially available. As shown in Fig. 1, we have pilot-tested several clinical and non-clinical EEG devices with college students. The Top left cell in Fig. 1 showed an example of the wearing of a clinical device while others demonstrated the consumer-grade devices. Muse Headset were used as an example for demonstration, followed by more details in the 6-page full-length page.

As shown in Fig. 2, first, we installed the data collection software or application. The following method section was formulated based on the example of using Muse Headset. We have used this device since 2016. First, the end user's OS version must match the version of the EEG recording application. If the end-user had a newer Macbook or the latest version of Muse headset, they ought to use the Mind Monitor Application to record EEG signals. Otherwise, the end-user may still use the Muselab application for EEG recording.

Two individuals, the EEG coach, and the end-user, were usually required to complete the data acquisition of such non-invasive EEG signals via Muse

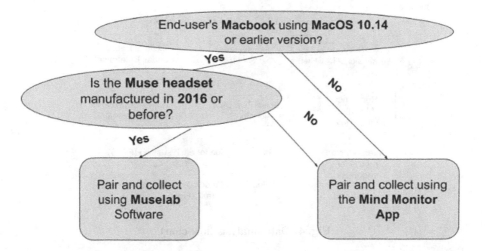

Fig. 2. Data collection app selection

headset and Muse Recording software, As shown in Fig. 3. First, the EEG Coach introduced the Muse Headset and Muse recording application to the end-user. Then the EEG coach explained the details of a specific experiment. Next, the EEG coach and the end-user started the experiment to collect the data. The data was saved as a MUSE file. The end-user then summarized the experimental feedback to the EEG coach. Together with the research team, the EEG coach

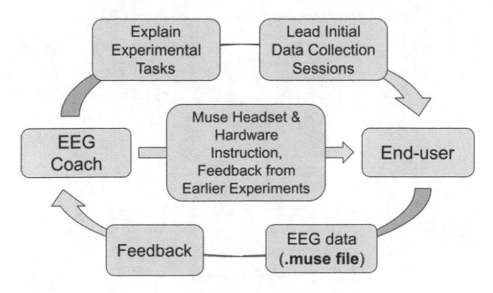

Fig. 3. Data collection flow chart, user and coach

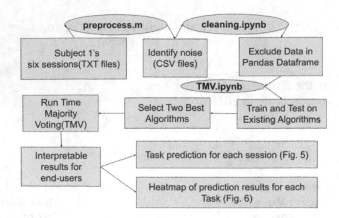

Fig. 4. Data analysis flow chart

generated visual feedback to the End-user. Such feedback may contribute to the development of future experiments.

If the end-user was interested, they could learn the data analysis themselves, which took two hours on average for students who major in computer science.

Most EEG recording applications came with a toolset to convert the recording files to TXT or CSV files. Afterward, we could pick the subset of data we planned to use for further analysis; we recommended starting with the absolute value of the EEG signals.

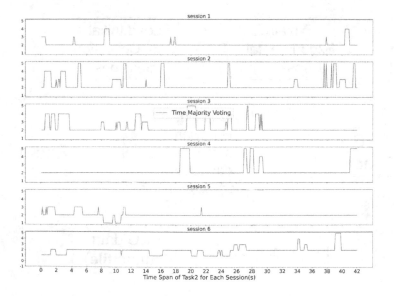

Fig. 5. Subject 1 task 2 prediction for all six sessions

We implemented several machine learning algorithms commonly used in the field [8–10, 12] from the scikit-learn [29]. For example, Linear Classifiers, Nearest Neighbors, Decision Tree, and Ensemble Methods.

As shown in the Fig. 4, once we had six TXT files for all six sessions of data, we first executed a Matlab program - preprocess.m - to identify the noises and turn all the TXT files into separate CSV files. Then, we ran the Clean.ipynb to exclude these data in the Pandas Dataframe for further analysis. Next, we executed the TMV.ipynb to train and cross-validate existing machine learning algorithms such as the Random Forest, SVM, and KNN. Then we selected the top two best-performing algorithms and used these two algorithms to perform Time Majority Voting. In our case, these two algorithms were Random Forest and RBF SVM. Lastly, the TMV.ipynb would generate a visualization of task predictions for end-users. Figure 5 and a heatmap for all six sessions (Fig. 6). These two figures are examples of task one's prediction results for all six sessions of subject 1 in the TCR Experiment.

3   Results

As shown in Fig. 5, sessions designed task were clearly recognized. All six sessions of subject 1's task 2 showed consistent patterns. Such visual feedback was provided to the EEG coach and end-user who collected this set of data. From the experiment notes, we ran into a signal issue behind the right ear of the end-user throughout the session, then we recorded this case and potential solutions to improve future experiments.

As shown in Fig. 6, the X-Axis is the designed tasks, the Y-Axis is the predicted tasks. The diagonal means the designed tasks matched the prediction. Such visual feedback also helped the research team and the end-users better understand what task pairs were easy to be confused with each other.

4   Discussion

This paper proposed an approach for non-export independent researchers to collect EEG-based BCI data with affordable non-clinical devices. When performing test trials with Muse headsets, we provided a general guideline, as shown in Figs. 2 and 3, which showed promising result in many EEG data collections performed by naive EEG end-users. This general guideline demonstrated a decision tree for non-expert researchers to acquire data collection hardware and software. We also presented our data collection flow, which formed a closed loop between the researchers and the experimental subjects. In addition, we elaborated our data-cleaning analysis procedures.

Significant progress has been made in user-training for EEG-based BCI studies, while the framework proposed in this paper serves as a stepping stone for further improved training programs in future research. However, some limitations were identified along the course of our project. Our project spanned from pre-pandemic to post-pandemic time. We found that in-person data collection

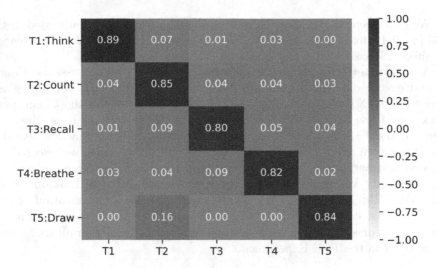

Fig. 6. Subject 1's TMV heatmap for all six sessions

trials were significantly more efficient than trials that took place virtually during the global pandemic. We ought to explore more strategies and updated methods that could grant us the efficiency when data collection has to be completed in a virtual environment.

Even though as much detail and trial and error experience we managed to include in our guideline, there are chances that individual cases develop distinct issues. Our future work includes research/EEG coach-based student study/work community, in which they can learn and discuss their experience with non-clinical devices collecting EEG-based data and possibly establish solutions to various issues after the encounter.

5   Conclusion

This paper investigated the data collection for EEG-based BCI to develop larger datasets. We explored the possibility of collecting EEG data from college students with affordable devices. The results demonstrated that the proposed framework could simplify the process and contribute to developing a larger EEG dataset.

References

1. Appriou, A., Cichocki, A., Lotte, F.: Modern machine-learning algorithms: for classifying cognitive and affective states from electroencephalography signals. IEEE Syst. Man Cybern. Mag. **6**(3), 29–38 (2020)

2. Basaklar, T., Tuncel, Y., An, S., Ogras, U.: Wearable devices and low-power design for smart health applications: challenges and opportunities. In: 2021 IEEE/ACM International Symposium on Low Power Electronics and Design (ISLPED), p. 1. IEEE (2021)

3. Bashivan, P., Bidelman, G.M., Yeasin, M.: Spectrotemporal dynamics of the EEG during working memory encoding and maintenance predicts individual behavioral capacity. Eur. J. Neurosci. 40(12), 3774–3784 (2014)

4. Bashivan, P., Rish, I., Heisig, S.: Mental state recognition via wearable EEG. arXiv preprint arXiv:1602.00985 (2016)

5. Bashivan, P., Rish, I., Yeasin, M., Codella, N.: Learning representations from EEG with deep recurrent-convolutional neural networks. arXiv preprint arXiv:1511.06448 (2015)

6. Bhat, G., Tuncel, Y., An, S., Lee, H.G., Ogras, U.Y.: An ultra-low energy human activity recognition accelerator for wearable health applications. ACM Trans. Embed. Comput. Syst. (TECS) 18(5s), 1–22 (2019)

7. Bird, J.J., Manso, L.J., Ribeiro, E.P., Ekart, A., Faria, D.R.: A study on mental state classification using EEG-based brain-machine interface. In: 2018 International Conference on Intelligent Systems (IS), pp. 795–800. IEEE (2018)

8. Breiman, L.: Bagging predictors. Mach. Learn. 24(2), 123–140 (1996)

9. Breiman, L.: Random forests. Mach. Learn. 45(1), 5–32 (2001)

10. Breiman, L.: Classification and regression trees. Routledge (2017)

11. Cannard, C., Wahbeh, H., Delorme, A.: Validating the wearable muse headset for eeg spectral analysis and frontal alpha asymmetry. In: 2021 IEEE International Conference on Bioinformatics and Biomedicine (BIBM), pp. 3603–3610. IEEE (2021)

12. Chevalier, J.A., Gramfort, A., Salmon, J., Thirion, B.: Statistical control for spatio-temporal MEG/EEG source imaging with desparsified multi-task lasso. arXiv preprint arXiv:2009.14310 (2020)

13. Craik, A., He, Y., Contreras-Vidal, J.L.: Deep learning for electroencephalogram (EEG) classification tasks: a review. J. Neural Eng. 16(3), 031001 (2019)

14. Darvishi, A., Khosravi, H., Sadiq, S., Weber, B.: Neurophysiological measurements in higher education: a systematic literature review. Int. J. Artif. Intell. Educ. 32, 1–41 (2021). https://doi.org/10.1007/s40593-021-00256-0

15. Devlaminck, D., Waegeman, W., Bauwens, B., Wyns, B., Santens, P., Otte, G.: From circular ordinal regression to multilabel classification. In: Proceedings of the 2010 Workshop on Preference Learning (European Conference on Machine Learning, ECML), p. 15 (2010)

16. Dongare, S., Padole, D.: Categorization of EEG using hybrid features and voting classifier for motor imagination. In: 2021 International Conference on Recent Trends on Electronics, Information, Communication & Technology (RTEICT), pp. 217–220. IEEE (2021)

17. Gu, J., et al.: Multi-phase cross-modal learning for noninvasive gene mutation prediction in hepatocellular carcinoma. In: 2020 42nd Annual International Conference of the IEEE Engineering in Medicine & Biology Society (EMBC), pp. 5814–5817. IEEE (2020)

18. Ienca, M., Haselager, P., Emanuel, E.J.: Brain leaks and consumer neurotechnology. Nat. Biotechnol. 36(9), 805–810 (2018)

19. Jamil, N., Belkacem, A.N., Ouhbi, S., Guger, C.: Cognitive and affective brain-computer interfaces for improving learning strategies and enhancing student capabilities: a systematic literature review. IEEE Access (2021)

20. Kaya, M., Binli, M.K., Ozbay, E., Yanar, H., Mishchenko, Y.: A large electroencephalographic motor imagery dataset for electroencephalographic brain computer interfaces. Sci. Data **5**(1), 1–16 (2018)

21. Lotte, F.: A tutorial on EEG signal-processing techniques for mental-state recognition in brain–computer interfaces. In: Miranda, E.R., Castet, J. (eds.) Guide to Brain-Computer Music Interfacing, pp. 133–161. Springer, London (2014). https://doi.org/10.1007/978-1-4471-6584-2_7

22. Lotte, F.: Signal processing approaches to minimize or suppress calibration time in oscillatory activity-based brain-computer interfaces. Proc. IEEE **103**(6), 871–890 (2015)

23. Lotte, F., et al.: A review of classification algorithms for EEG-based brain-computer interfaces: a 10 year update. J. Neural Eng. **15**(3), 031005 (2018)

24. Lotte, F., Congedo, M., Lécuyer, A., Lamarche, F., Arnaldi, B.: A review of classification algorithms for EEG-based brain-computer interfaces. J. Neural Eng. **4**(2), R1 (2007)

25. Lotte, F., Guan, C.: Regularizing common spatial patterns to improve BCI designs: unified theory and new algorithms. IEEE Trans. Biomed. Eng. **58**(2), 355–362 (2010)

26. Lotte, F., Jeunet, C.: Towards improved BCI based on human learning principles. In: The 3rd International Winter Conference on Brain-Computer Interface, pp. 1–4. IEEE (2015)

27. Lotte, F., Jeunet, C., Mladenović, J., N'Kaoua, B., Pillette, L.: A BCI challenge for the signal processing community: considering the user in the loop (2018)

28. Miller, K.J.: A library of human electrocorticographic data and analyses. Nat. Hum. Behav. **3**(11), 1225–1235 (2019)

29. Pedregosa, F., et al.: Scikit-learn: machine learning in Python. J. Mach. Learn. Res. **12**, 2825–2830 (2011)

30. Portillo-Lara, R., Tahirbegi, B., Chapman, C.A., Goding, J.A., Green, R.A.: Mind the gap: state-of-the-art technologies and applications for EEG-based brain-computer interfaces. APL Bioeng. **5**(3), 031507 (2021)

31. Qian, P., Zhao, Z., Chen, C., Zeng, Z., Li, X.: Two eyes are better than one: exploiting binocular correlation for diabetic retinopathy severity grading. In: 2021 43rd Annual International Conference of the IEEE Engineering in Medicine & Biology Society (EMBC), pp. 2115–2118. IEEE (2021)

32. Qu, X., Hall, M., Sun, Y., Sekuler, R., Hickey, T.J.: A personalized reading coach using wearable EEG sensors-a pilot study of brainwave learning analytics. In: CSEDU (2), pp. 501–507 (2018)

33. Qu, X., Liu, P., Li, Z., Hickey, T.: Multi-class time continuity voting for EEG classification. In: Frasson, C., Bamidis, P., Vlamos, P. (eds.) BFAL 2020. LNCS (LNAI), vol. 12462, pp. 24–33. Springer, Cham (2020). https://doi.org/10.1007/978-3-030-60735-7_3

34. Qu, X., Liukasemsarn, S., Tu, J., Higgins, A., Hickey, T.J., Hall, M.H.: Identifying clinically and functionally distinct groups among healthy controls and first episode psychosis patients by clustering on EEG patterns. Front. Psychiatry, 938 (2020)

35. Qu, X., Mei, Q., Liu, P., Hickey, T.: Using EEG to distinguish between writing and typing for the same cognitive task. In: Frasson, C., Bamidis, P., Vlamos, P. (eds.) BFAL 2020. LNCS (LNAI), vol. 12462, pp. 66–74. Springer, Cham (2020). https://doi.org/10.1007/978-3-030-60735-7_7

36. Qu, X., Sun, Y., Sekuler, R., Hickey, T.: EEG markers of stem learning. In: 2018 IEEE Frontiers in Education Conference (FIE), pp. 1–9. IEEE (2018)

37. Roy, Y., Banville, H., Albuquerque, I., Gramfort, A., Falk, T.H., Faubert, J.: Deep learning-based electroencephalography analysis: a systematic review. J. Neural Eng. **16**(5), 051001 (2019)

38. Xu, K., et al.: Multi-instance multi-label learning for gene mutation prediction in hepatocellular carcinoma. In: 2020 42nd Annual International Conference of the IEEE Engineering in Medicine & Biology Society (EMBC), pp. 6095–6098. IEEE (2020)

39. Zhang, X., Yao, L., Wang, X., Monaghan, J.J., Mcalpine, D., Zhang, Y.: A survey on deep learning-based non-invasive brain signals: recent advances and new frontiers. J. Neural Eng. **18**(3), 031002 (2020)

40. Zhao, Z., Chopra, K., Zeng, Z., Li, X.: Sea-net: squeeze-and-excitation attention net for diabetic retinopathy grading. In: 2020 IEEE International Conference on Image Processing (ICIP), pp. 2496–2500. IEEE (2020)

41. Zhao, Z., Xu, K., Li, S., Zeng, Z., Guan, C.: MT-UDA: towards unsupervised cross-modality medical image segmentation with limited source labels. In: de Bruijne, M., et al. (eds.) MICCAI 2021. LNCS, vol. 12901, pp. 293–303. Springer, Cham (2021). https://doi.org/10.1007/978-3-030-87193-2_28

Accessibility, Usability, and UX Design

Kick-Starting Ready-to-Go Assets to Speed Up Motion Design Development for Mobile Devices

Andrii Bogachenko[1]([✉]) [iD], Daria Voskoboinikova[1] [iD], Inna Bondarenko[1] [iD], Yevhenii Buhera[1] [iD], Dongjoo Ko[2] [iD], and Svitlana Alkhimova[1] [iD]

[1] Samsung R&D Institute Ukraine (SRK), 57, Lva Tolstogo Str., Kyiv 01032, Ukraine
{an.bogachenk,d.voskoboyni,i.bondarenko,y.buhera,
s.alkhimova}@samsung.com
[2] Samsung Electronics, Seoul R&D Campus, 33 Seongchon-gil, Seoul 06765, Seocho-gu, Korea
dongjoo.ko@samsung.com

Abstract. Animated design elements make the interaction between mobile devices and users more easy and enjoyable. Ready-to-go assets generated directly from the designer's environment might be used immediately by designers as high-fidelity prototypes or by developers as precisely implemented animations. It is essential to ensure the correctness of generated assets on the target device. In this study, we propose an approach that allows verifying ready-to-go assets on the target mobile device with the Android operating system. It is based on parsing and reconstructing assets on a canvas that offers a set of features to verify the animation. To investigate the performance of the proposed approach we conduct a comparison with the existing approach, qualitative analysis, and survey of designers and developers. The results indicate that the proposed approach is effective and delivers new prospects to prototype and implement animation directly on a target mobile device.

Keywords: Animation · Motion design · Interaction design · Designer-developer collaboration · Software development · Human-computer interaction

1 Background

Nowadays, animations or motion graphics are a great way to connect users with mobile devices in an impactful and memorable way. Animated design elements are considered as a core component that can keep users engaged, make an application attractive and memorable, clarify activity, progress, and relationships between elements showing on the screen, and they are used to provide feedback on gesture-based operations, virtual tours, and visual comfort and aesthetic [1, 2]. Usage of animations in design of mobile user interfaces have shown to be able to give benefits, both functionally and aesthetically [3–5].

Addressing the process of creating an animation, it is possible to state that it is complex, time-consuming and includes many phases from ideas generation to production

C. Stephanidis et al. (Eds.): HCII 2022, CCIS 1654, pp. 131–138, 2022.
https://doi.org/10.1007/978-3-031-19679-9_17

[6]. To be sure that the animation is adding value to the user's experience, it is important to prototype and test animations on the target device [7]. This is an iterative process. In terms of development of digital products on mobile platforms it is complicated by the fact that testing is performed on a mobile, while prototyping is performed on a desktop. On the other hand, not only careful prototyping of animations is crucial but also precise implementation. As developers make animation a reality, misunderstanding during design handoff to developers can heavily influence the efficiency of animation implementation [8–10].

Prototype and communicate animations between designers and developers can be done in many ways. Besides the variety of tools (e.g., Zeplin[1], InVision[2], ProtoPie[3], Web VI guide [11]), the output can vary from video files enhanced with test guides to frame-accurate artifacts to clarify implementation for developers. More technically experienced designers can create their own code to be more in control of the details of animation implementation. Nowadays, this requires a designer to have a comfort level with HTML, CSS, and JavaScript and a good grasp of how development goes in a modern development environment. High-fidelity prototypes can be created using motion pattern libraries such as Velocity[4], GreenSock[5], Material[6], but relying on built-in motion patterns may limit the solution and result in bland outcomes. Therefore, the most promising solution for creating an animation proposes to generate ready-to-go assets directly from the designer's environment [12]. Such an approach is able to provide animation assets, which are self-contained code targeted to the specific platform. As a result, ready-to-go assets might be used by designers as prototypes that work like the actual digital product or by developers as precisely implemented animations. However, the process of generating and immediately utilizing of ready-to-go assets increases the risk of animation mistakes. To ensure the animation works as expected, it is important to add a verification step of generated assets on the target device before handoff to developers.

In the current study, we present the approach for conducting a quick verification process of ready-to-go assets on the target mobile device. The performance of the proposed approach was assessed through a comparison with the existing approach, qualitative analysis, and survey of designers and developers.

2   Proposed Approach

The focus of the current study is Android operating system (OS) due to its open-source availability and popularity on the mobile device market.

The traditional approach to verify assets and test animation on Android device is based on creating a demo project in Android Studio. Following this approach, two options are possible. The first one requires from designer to create and configure an

---

[1] https://zeplin.io/.
[2] https://www.invisionapp.com/.
[3] https://www.protopie.io/.
[4] http://velocityjs.org/.
[5] https://greensock.com/
[6] https://material.io.

Android project, add assets correctly to the project using interpreters or web browser components, build the project, and run obtained application on a target device. The second one relies on collaboration with developers. As developers can create an application using platform-specific languages, tools, and technologies, such a solution renders native user interfaces and communicates with Android specific features without the need for an abstraction layer. However, negotiation about possible issues and mistakes during the iterative process of animation testing can be frustrating for both the developers and designers involved.

Since ready-to-go assets are self-contained code of animations, it is more preferred to test them by checking the result in a sandbox or player. This approach is quite useful compared to the traditional one. It does not require any specific skills from designers and offers the possibility of testing the animations on a mobile device without involving developers. As a result, designers can tweak and test the animation through multiple iterations before handoff to developers.

Implementation of animations on the Android OS is possible in various ways, from both designer and developer points of view [13, 14]. Despite that, Adobe After Effects[7] (AAE) is still one of the most powerful tools to design animated elements. In our previous study [12], we developed a web extension for exporting AAE animations into ready-to-go assets in a format of the Android Vector Drawable (AVD), which is a native animation format for Android. Accordingly, the approach proposed in the current study aims to verify ready-to-go assets in AVD based format (Fig. 1).

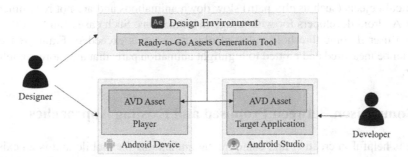

Fig. 1. Schematic presentation of the proposed approach.

The proposed approach to verify assets on the target devices can be divided into three main stages: assets loading, graphics reconstruction, and animation preview.

Originally, assets in AVD based format can be stored in the form of an XML file. During application build, the XML files are compiled alongside with the source code to create an Android application. Therefore, AVD assets can be as XML files or separately pre-compiled resources to be used in the proposed approach. Depending on the asset format, the loading and graphic reconstruction stages may differ fundamentally.

Pre-compiled assets loading emulates native Android application behavior, i.e., assets are compiled into a final binary file. This guarantees that animation will work absolutely

---

[7] https://www.adobe.com/products/aftereffects.html.

the same way as expected. Loaded assets require minimal efforts to be reconstructed on the canvas. In this case, Android high-level methods and classes from the Android Graphics package are used for that. Usage of the pre-compiled assets is reliable and simple to implement, but it has two significant constraints. The first one is an extra step of asset compilation. The second is that runtime loading of the pre-compiled assets can only be made with the Resource Loader package added since Android version 11.

In the case of XML file usage, loading requires parsing the file, building a separate data structure, and reconstructing the graphics on the canvas. Reconstruction is performed sequentially drawing one object after another with the usage of standard Android classes from low level Graphics Drawable package. Implementation of such loading requires more effort, but it provides more opportunities for prototyping as assets can be edited directly on the device.

Finally, after loading and graphics reconstruction on the canvas user can preview animation to verify generated asset.

All the stages described above are embodied in Android application with all necessary functionality to verify ready-to-go assets on the target mobile device.

To improve the verification process and increase its accuracy, the proposed approach allows the implementation of additional features using standard Android API. To manage the animation preview, convenient features like control of playback speed, progress information display, and animation trimming can be implemented. Android API allows implementing even more advanced functionality that supports designers with information about the features (i.e., graphical objects, effects, styles) used for specific effects. Graphical objects (such as clip-path) slow down animations and are not recommended by the Android developers for wide usage in animations. Such cases can be tracked to notify a user if some threshold value of objects usage is exceeded. Frame rendering time can be measured and plotted to highlight animation parts that are more complex to render.

3   Comparison Between Proposed and Existing Approaches

Lottie is helpful in creating and customizing animations for mobile and is an existing approach for preparing ready-to-go assets nowadays [15, 16]. Lottie uses assets in JSON based format that are exported from the AAE by Bodymovin[8] extension. Detailed review of pros and cons of Lottie animations can be found in our previous study [12].

As might be expected, Lottie provides users a way to preview generated assets on the mobile device. To assess usability through available features a comparison of Lottie and proposed approaches was conducted.

Animation sample was prepared in the AAE version CC2021. Bodymovin extension version 5.6.5 and AAE extension developed in our previous study [12] were used to generate ready-to-go assets from the sample in JSON and AVD based formats, respectively.

---

[8] https://aescripts.com/bodymovin/.

We used Lottie Android application[9] (below referred to as *Sample App*) version 5.0.1 and Android application developed according to the proposed approach (below referred to as *Player*) to verify generated assets.

As the target device, we used Samsung Galaxy Note 10 with Android 11.

In this case, the list of analyzed features was obtained through merging lists of available functionality supported by *Sample App* and *Player*. Actions commonly used by users to test animation on a mobile device were applied to assess usability of each analyzed feature. Thus, we obtained cases when features were fully, partially supported, or unsupported at all (Fig. 2).

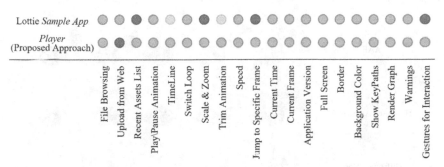

Fig. 2. Comparison of supported features between Lottie *Sample App* and *Player*. Green circles are fully supported feature, yellow circles are partially supported features, and red circles are unsupported features.

From the obtained results, it is concluded that each approach has its own pros and cons. *Player* does not have an opportunity to load files from the web, while *Sample App* has this feature. Loading files from the web by Lottie *Sample App* is not a verification of animations so much as an asset market for animation sharing.

At the same time, *Player* has such advances in usability as the list of recently browsed files, the possibility to jump directly to a specific frame, and the variety of gestures for interacting with an asset. This set of features improves the verification process and increases its accuracy.

It was indicated that Lottie *Sample App* suffers from issues in actions commonly used by users to test animation on a mobile device. Among them dragging issues during animation playback for the TimeLine feature and user input issues for the Trim Animation feature. In addition, the Scale & Zoom feature was completely removed in the latest release and was partially supported only on earlier versions.

4 Qualitative Analysis

To carry out qualitative analysis, 10 animation samples with different levels of complexity were prepared in the AAE version CC2021. Each sample has the same resolution of 450 x 300 pixels. Samples contain different numbers of animated objects, from 3 to 11.

---

[9] https://play.google.com/store/apps/details?id=com.airbnb.lottie.

AAE extension developed in our previous study [12] was used to generate ready-to-go assets from the samples in AVD based format. The duration of the animations from the generated assets was the same for all samples.

We used the same device (i.e., Samsung Galaxy Note 10 with Android 11) as for that the comparison was conducted.

As a quality metric, we analyzed per pixel difference of frames obtained from AAE samples and from the corresponding animations reproduced in *Player* using generated assets. Frames were captured at the same moments of time.

In Fig. 3, five exemplary frames from one animation (for both AAE and *Player*) are displayed together with per pixel difference maps.

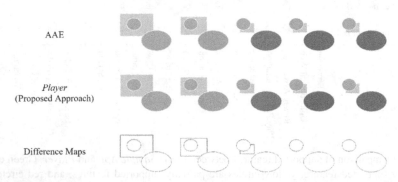

Fig. 3. Example animation frames with per pixel difference maps used for quantitative analysis.

Obtained difference resulting in an average 4.06% of different pixels (SD 2.84%) with a range from 1.1% to 7.29%. This result may be explained by different anti-aliasing technics that are applied on different platforms to remove the aliasing effect, i.e., jaggies [17].

5   Designers and Developers Survey

We conducted a survey asking designers and developers about their satisfaction with the proposed approach.

We involved 12 participants (9 Male, 3 Female). The age ranged from 25 to 54 years with an avg. Age of 34.2 years. We involved equal number of designers (6 participants) and developers (6 participants). The process of creating an animation was a direct duty for all the participants. All of them have wide experience working with ready-to-go assets development and utilization. Participants were not compensated.

Participants were briefed on how to use the proposed approach to ensure the animation works as expected. Designers used *Player* as verification step of generated assets on the target device before handoff to developers. After trials, the participants were asked to assess the proposed approach by taking an online survey.

The closed questions were defined using the Likert scale [18] to tell about participants experience on ready-to-go assets verification and to determine the degree of satisfaction with the proposed approach.

Addressing the necessity to provide code inspection of the generated asset, 67% of participants assumed that it might be required in case when there was no verification on the target device. At the same time, 33% of participants answered that code modification of the generated ready-to-go assets is necessary to make them display correctly on the device. In Fig. 4, a more detailed answers distribution is available.

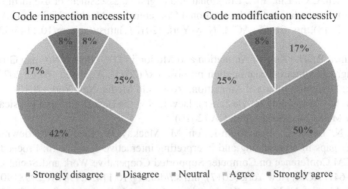

Fig. 4. Necessity of code inspection and modification for generated ready-to-go assets.

More than half of participants (59%) said that they usually spend hours to negotiate details of the animation implementation, while 33% of participants said it might require the whole day or even more. Only 8% of participants said it is a matter of a few minutes.

The majority of participants noted that sharing ready-to-go assets without verification often (33% of participants) or sometimes (50% of participants) leads to possible issues and mistakes in animation implementation that could cause delays in the software development process. Only 17% of participants noted that it rarely leads to mentioned effects.

Answering the questions whether the proposed approach simplifies the animation creation process and improves collaboration between designers and developers, all the participants (100%) agreed with the statement.

6 Conclusions

In the current study, we proposed an approach to get quick and easy verification of ready-to-go assets on the target mobile device with Android OS. From the performance assessment results, it is concluded that the proposed approach simplifies the workflow of animation prototyping and design handoff to developers. Furthermore, it allows kick-starting ready-to-go assets more quickly and considerably improves design-developer collaboration, providing a human-computer interaction solution for this domain.

References

1. Chalbi, A.: Understanding and designing animations in the user interfaces. Dissertation, Université de Lille (2018)

2. Sosa-Tzec, O., Bergqvist, E.S.: Delight by motion: investigating the role of animation in microinteractions. In: Coorey, J., Murnieks, A., Rinnert, G., Shaw, H., Tegtmeyer, R. (eds.) Motion Design Education Summit 2021 Edited Conference Proceedings, 10–13 Jun 2021
3. Chang, B.W., Ungar, D.: Animation: from cartoons to the user interface. In: Proceedings of the 6th annual ACM symposium on User interface software and technology (UIST'93), pp. 45–55. ACM, New York (1993). https://doi.org/10.1145/168642.168647
4. Ma, J., Chen, C.C., Lin, Y.C.: Emotional and cognitive assessment of use of functional animation. In: Proceedings of the International Conference on Machine Vision and Applications (ICMVA 2018), pp. 61–65. ACM, New York (2018). https://doi.org/10.1145/3220511.3220516
5. Laubheimer, P.: The Role of Animation and Motion in UX. Nielsen Norman Group. https://www.nngroup.com/articles/animation-purpose-ux/ (2021). Accessed 16 Feb 2022
6. Head, V.: Designing Interface Animation. Rosenfeld Media, New York (2016)
7. McElroy, K.: Prototyping for Designers: Developing the Best Digital and Physical Products. O'Reilly Media Inc., Sebastopol, CA (2016)
8. Maudet, N., Leiva, G., Beaudouin-Lafon, M., Mackay, W.: Design breakdowns: designer-developer gaps in representing and interpreting interactive systems. In: Proceedings of the 2017 ACM Conference on Computer Supported Cooperative Work and Social Computing, pp. 630–641. ACM, New York (2017). https://doi.org/10.1145/2998181.2998190
9. Leiva, G., Maudet, N., Mackay, W., Beaudouin-Lafon, M.: Enact: reducing designer-developer breakdowns when prototyping custom interactions. ACM Trans. Comput.-Hum. Interact. 26(3), 1–48 (2019). https://doi.org/10.1145/3310276
10. Walny, J., et al.: Data changes everything: challenges and opportunities in data visualization design handoff. IEEE Trans. Visual Comput. Graphics 26(1), 12–22 (2019). https://doi.org/10.1109/TVCG.2019.2934538
11. Bogachenko, A., et al.: All you need is web: visual interaction with no graphic background. In: Stephanidis, C., Antona, M. (eds.) HCII 2020. CCIS, vol. 1224, pp. 3–10. Springer, Cham (2020). https://doi.org/10.1007/978-3-030-50726-8_1
12. Bogachenko, A., Bondarenko, I., Voskoboinikova, D., Buhera, Y., Ko, D., Alkhimova, S.: Transform motion design into ready-to-go assets. In: Stephanidis, C., Antona, M., Ntoa, S. (eds.) HCII 2021. CCIS, vol. 1419, pp. 3–11. Springer, Cham (2021). https://doi.org/10.1007/978-3-030-78635-9_1
13. Biørn-Hansen, A., Grønli, T.M., Ghinea, G.: Animations in cross-platform mobile applications: an evaluation of tools, metrics and performance. Sensors 19(9), 2081 (2019). https://doi.org/10.3390/s19092081
14. Rufo, P.: Experimenting with motion in Android. Medium. https://medium.com/snapp-mobile/experimenting-with-motion-in-android-9283962ae0ef (2019). Accessed 16 Feb 2022
15. Gladkiy, S.: Native Animation for mobile apps using lottie. https://dzone.com/articles/native-animation-for-mobile-app-using-lottie/ (2019). Accessed 16 Feb 2022
16. Hidayat, T., Sungkowo B.D.: Comparison of memory consumptive against the use of various image formats for app onboarding animation assets on Android with Lottie JSON. In: 2020 3rd International Conference on Computer and Informatics Engineering (IC2IE). IEEE (2020). https://doi.org/10.1109/IC2IE50715.2020.9274612
17. Ivanova, B.N., Rusev, R.: Improving computer-generated images – methods for realistic depiction. In: The 3rd International Conference on Applied Research in Engineering, Science and Technology, Vilnius (2020)
18. Joshi, A., Kale, S., Chandel, S., Pal, D.K.: Likert scale: explored and explained. British J. Appl. Sci. Technol. 7(4), 396–403 (2015). https://doi.org/10.9734/BJAST/2015/14975

LICOR: Beyond the Design System. A Proposal to Empower Teams to Develop Software in Compliance with the Principles of Accessibility, Usability, and Privacy by Design in the Extreme Contexts and Challenging Domains Post-COVID-19

Deivith Silva Matias de Oliveira[1]([⊠]) [iD], Francisco C. M. B. Oliveira[1] [iD],
Cláudia A. C. Pernencar[2] [iD], Breno S. de Morais[1], João W. Silva[1],
Antonio R. B. Costa[1], Joaquim B. C. Pereira[3], and Inga F. Saboia[4] [iD]

[1] Department of Computer Science, State University of Ceará, Fortaleza, Ceará, Brazil
deivith.oliveira@aluno.uece.br, fran.oliveira@uece.br,
{breno.morais,weslley.silva,rootedy}@ffit.com.br
[2] NOVA Institute of Communication, Nova University Lisbon, Lisbon, Portugal
claudiapernencar@fcsh.unl.pt
[3] Institute UFC Virtual, Federal University of Ceará, Fortaleza, Ceará, Brazil
[4] Department of Communication and Art, Aveiro University, Aveiro, Portugal
inga@virtual.ufc.br

Abstract. During the pandemic, people were asked to stay at home, which increased the demand for software. The quality of the software is improving as a result of this trend. In response, companies have accelerated their digitization processes to provide better quality software that is more accessible, user-friendly, and secure. Since the pandemic, software development teams around the world have struggled to meet deadlines during uncertain times. This poster addresses the difficulties developers and designers face in developing and managing digital health software. This is due to the growing appeal of low and no-code platforms that are becoming more accessible and user-friendly to non-programmers. The goal of this project is to develop and evaluate a prototype digital health component library known as LICOR. This software development kit contains integrated digital components designed specifically for the digital health industry. It helps even non-experts create effective digital health products. The design approach was developed by combining various theories and techniques such as design system principles, domain-oriented design, micro front-ends, and microservices. The methodology is based on the design-based research approach, which combines theoretical research with working and coded software artifacts to enable real-world testing. We are interested in contributions from the community and would be happy to discuss ethical concerns, bias, and illiteracy in digital health with academics. Finally, we discuss future research opportunities and the difficulties of connecting the design phase with the development phase in digital health software development.

Keywords: Digital health · Software development · HCI

1 Introduction and Context

With post-Covid-19, the world as we knew it has collapsed in a matter of weeks. Reality presents itself as a fragile, anxious, non-linear and incomprehensible world - the so-called BANI world [1]. The current crisis has reached proportions not seen since the Great Depression [2].

At the same time, the pandemic has increased demand for software products as people have been encouraged to stay home. People are not just demanding more software - they are demanding better software. Accessibility, usability, and privacy have become key requirements in today's world.

The pandemic also had a severe economic impact on businesses in general, forcing many companies to close their doors. The context COVID -19 has accelerated the digital transformation of businesses and entire industries such as retail, hospitality, and education [2]. Other businesses are increasingly impacted by digital technologies such as the Internet, mobile connectivity, cloud computing, Big Data, machine learning, artificial intelligence (AI), blockchain, and the Internet of Things (IoT) [2].

At the same time, consumers now have many more choices [2]. Customers are increasingly intrigued by digital technologies, forcing traditional businesses to seek digital transformation. With new or renewed value propositions based on digital technologies, other companies are moving from one sector to another. As a result, IT teams are under significant pressure to develop increasingly advanced applications with shorter deadlines.

Software engineering teams should be adaptable, especially when it comes to structuring the development and design phases [3]. In recent years, large companies have developed and implemented their own design systems to solve this problem [4, 5].

Design systems became popular because they focus on scaling design decisions and accelerating code implementation while ensuring software quality and code reuse. [6, 7]. However, unfortunately, because they became so popular as simple UI example libraries, they are generally misused in this way. [8]. The goal of a design system is to support the development of software by providing guidelines that impact the overall user experience and software development process [9]. Therefore, it is important that everyone on the team is familiar with these ideas and principles.

To make developers' jobs easier, libraries such as PrimeFaces [10] ocus on existing, reusable microservices that are connected to other services, such as an API. This process promotes more efficient long-term development [11].

On the other hand, most of these libraries are generalists. There are no specific standards for certain domains such as digital health, which is a major gap. This is a critical issue since the main role of software is to solve problems relevant to the user's domain and situation.

If these fundamental concepts, such as resistance to adoption or even outright exclusion of people due to non-compliance with accessibility standards, are not recognized by users [12, 13], it can affect their experience.

The rapid pace at which developers and designers are required to become near experts in such specialized areas has led to a lack of competent responsed [12]. However, design techniques can help teams organize their products during development [12].

In the next section, we will detail the primary and secondary objectives of this research. Just reinforcing that this is still an ongoing project and more detailed results (as well with your dear participation) will be available soon.

1.1 Objectives

The goal of this study is to develop and evaluate a prototype LICOR component library that combines theoretical and practical aspects of Design Systems [4, 6], Domain-Driven Design (DDD) [12, 14], Microservices [15] and Micro-Frontends [16] for building digital health applications..

The specific objectives are:

1. Learn how to use micro front-end approaches with Design Systems, DDD, and other methodologies.

   a. Identify the most common micro-scenarios of interaction in the health industry;
   b. Design and produce the micro front-ends.
   c. Create two different apps that utilize the same domain, one for a medical consulting and one for medical auditing, utilizing these tiny front-ends;
   d. Analyze the characteristics of these applications with consumers;
   e. With this new approach, discuss the building procedure with designers and developers.

2. Propose other courses of action based on the study's findings.
3. Investigate how accessibility, usability, and privacy can be integrated into library components in the user domain.
4. Examine the software to determine whether domain information affects its compliance with code reuse, user experience, usability, accessibility, and privacy.

In the following section, we'll describe the LICOR library prototype.

1.2 Introducing the LICOR Library Prototype

Our prototype is based on the Material Design System [17]. Due to copyright compliance, it will be used only for study and internal experimentation only.

The software development process will be the focus of our study, with designers, coders, clients, and other stakeholders all included. We'll be able to compare the various viewpoints like this.

We will create all artifacts, phases, and necessary activities based on Driven Domain Design [18], which is focused on the digital health sector. Mapping and construction of the domain, including bounded context, general language, context maps, context architecture, and domain model patterns are a few examples.

All about our day-to-day equipment now. The Figma [19] program is being used to create and improve our design system. We're utilizing Storybook [20] for the code components library. We're always trying out new tools, like as Anima [21] or Zeroheigh [22], and seeing how they impact the way we do research.

We're also inviting seasoned experts from areas like privacy, accessibility, usability, and ethics to review and offer constructive criticism on our theoretical framework as well as the quality of our pre-formatted beta goods.

We must declare that failing quickly is an important goal for us, too. As everyone who faces the risks of innovation understands, we aim to fail fast in order to learn more quickly. You will find out what research methods we are utilizing in certain parts of this paper.

In the following section, we'll show you a tiny but carefully chosen sample of what libraries of digital interface components can do for you.

2 Related Works

There are some open resources that companies and professionals are using today to achieve some of these goals, such as scalability and product consistency.

Popular design systems such as Google's Material Design [23] and Ant Design [24] provide a huge repository of design guidelines and materials, components, and templates, complemented by solid documentation that guides both designers and developers in their use and implementation.

Moreover, these design systems support various device types, not only the most popular mobile and desktop devices but also wearable devices and some IoT products.

In addition, these design systems support some widely used technologies used in digital products, such as popular JavaScript frameworks like React and React Native.

In some cases, such as digital health, the requirements are so stringent that these resources are not sufficient to enable the development of digital products that meet users' needs.

In the following section, we'll give a quick rundown of our prominent theoretical references as they assist us in our study.

3 Theoretical Reference

3.1 Design Systems

A design system is a set of interrelated elements that are organized in such a way as to assist the objectives of digital products [5]. The components we use to construct an interface are known as patterns: Processes, interactions, buttons, text boxes, icons, colors, typography, and so on...

One of the most popular design systems today is Material Design, maintained by Google - currently in its third version [23]. Other examples include Microsoft's Fluent [25], IBM's Carbon [27] and Ant Design, from the Alibaba Group [24].

Digital Health

According to [28], Digital Health is the combination of information and communication technologies (ICT) to generate and deliver trusted information about a person's health when it is needed.

The term "digital health" is broader than e-health and also includes more recent technological advances such as social media concepts and applications, the Internet of Things (IoT), artificial intelligence (AI), and others. Health IT projects aim to identify, prioritize, and integrate health programs, projects, and policies, as well as information and communication services and systems. The goal is to turn the vision of ESD into reality by using digital health for its integration [28].

The Conecte SUS program is a Brazilian federal government program that supports access to health information and promotes digital engagement between patients and health professionals. Despite the detailed program and action level, the document itself notes the need to consider the integration of new information services such as artificial intelligence (AI), analytics, Big Data, IoT, and other emerging technologies for knowledge discovery in healthcare. In addition to providing services such as expanding telemedicine and consolidating clinical terminology, the document also addresses improving telemedicine interoperability and regulating smart healthcare [28].

Looking at the Brazilian scenario, the question is whether all these efforts are compatible with a global strategy for digital health, as promoted by The World Health Organization (WHO). An example of this is the WHO 'Recommendations on digital interventions for health system strengthening' to promote the integration of technology worldwide for advances in health [29].

The WHO promotes the use of digital learning and training methods in the health professions so that they can be used alongside, rather than in place of, traditional training methods. WHO [30] advocates the use of cell phones for births, deaths, inventory reporting, commodity management, telemedicine, targeted patient communication, decision support for health workers, and digital tracking of health status and performance in specific situations.

According to WHO, any digital health tool or technology should be developed and implemented according to digital development principles. It also provides advice on how to create an enabling environment to promote the adoption of digital healthcare.

There are many issues in the digital health space that can be addressed, as you can see. We'll discuss how microservices and domain-driven design connect in the following section.

3.2 Microservices and Domain-Driven Design

A microservice is a small service that provides a tiny number of functions. Microservice designs are gaining popularity as a means of building cross-platform applications based on service-oriented architectures [31].

The Domain-Driven Design pattern provides concepts for subdividing microservices. Domain-Driven Design (DDD) is a software development methodology that focuses on modeling a domain based on contributions from domain experts [32].

Microservices use bounded contexts to identify microservices. Domain-driven design provides concepts, patterns, and activities for building a domain model in its pure form. However, it does not provide a step-by-step development approach. [31].

There is a lot of uncertainty about how to create programming interfaces for web applications for microservices. Microservices effectiveness requires application participation. [31].

The domain-driven design approach emphasizes that the core domain logic of microservices should be determined by the application, while the user interface is considered when creating specific web APIs. In a microservice, there is no graphical user interface, although there is one for a technical purpose. For a domain, you need to consider a variety of use cases. [31].

Although the use of Domain-Driven Design may vary in practice, there are several advantages. The layered architecture required by Domain-Driven Design distinguishes the domain from other concerns. DDD is a framework that provides fundamental ideas and processes for developing applications based on a microservice architecture. DDD is about breaking down a software system into smaller components, and microservices is about how they are divided. One of the main advantages of DDD and microservices is the ability to reuse existing functionality. With the Web API, you can find and reuse microservices [31].

You saw why we decided to try combining Domain-Driven Design with Microservices to provide a new way for digital healthcare. In the section that follows, we'll go over how design systems and micro front-ends are related.

3.3 Micro Front-Ends and Design System

It is critical to understand the LICOR experiment's micro frontend approach in light of its definition and benefits within the software development process.

Many projects are divided into numerous components, team structures, and technologies to mitigate the problem of collaboration between teams and coworkers growing more complicated and difficult as the size of a project and team membership grows, according to [11]. A front-end team and one or more back-end teams may be used to build horizontal layers.

Micro frontends provide a unique viewpoint. The application is sliced into vertical sections. Each slice is developed from the database to the user interface and carried out by a separate team. The client's browser is used to link the various team front-ends together [11]. Individual backend teams can now work on and modify system elements independently, which enhances their long-term development prospects. Also, because small services are more manageable than monolithic systems, their effective development in growing teams becomes more likely in the long run [9].

The service, as you may recall, is made up of a number of smaller services. It also includes several advantages that are particularly useful for team growth and product development [9]. This method is connected to microservices architecture. The major distinction is that the service now includes a user interface as well. This addition to the service eliminates the need for a central front-end staff. Micro front-ends attempt to keep things simple by lowering the complexity of each front-end while also adding complexity to the architecture's organizational layer, ensuring that subsystems are linked to the overall system. This entails activities such as autonomous deployment methods for continuously integrating and testing new micro frontend systems, or establishing failover procedures in case a piece becomes unavailable for any reason. Improve customer satisfaction. Customers receive everything they need directly from the vendor. There are no API specialists or operational staff involved.

Let's look at some of the organizational and technological advantages of this design after you've learned what micro front-ends are [9]. Optimize for the creation of new features. The primary motivation for employing a micro front-end is to improve development speed. In addition, everyone working on a feature in the micro-front-end approach works on the same team and communication is easier. The unified front end will no longer be present. Modern architectures don't have a concept of scaling front-end development, as far as I know. The application is divided into smaller vertical systems with micro frontends.

As a result, a micro frontend is [9]: Concentrates risk in a smaller area, making it easier to understand; Has a smaller codebase that is easier to refactor or replace when necessary.

Let's look at the design of systems in the micro front-end environment based on their features and a stakeholder analysis [9]: The connection between design systems and frameworks. Frameworks are frequently used in web development to embed an application within a supporting framework that aids the software's growth. A design system is a framework for creating user interfaces that adhere to principles, patterns, and a design language. Because a compatible design system is required for the development of a frontend, its framework has an impact on how it develops. However, because the design system was built for a specific technology stack and is not framework-agnostic, it would be unusable for various stacks.

4 Materials and Methodology

4.1 Evaluation Methodology Plan

We will hold a workshop with representatives of a software development team to learn about their reactions during the activities and receive anonymous evaluations at the end.

The researchers will conduct this workshop in different steps following the evaluation strategy used by Oran et al. [26].

The study will randomly divide participants into two groups and have them use LICOR components in real-time development.

For this task, groups are to create an interactive UX / UI prototype for a local health problem. The two groups will need to create a prototype in one hour, one with access to LICOR UI components and the other with access to a free library.

After the time is up, 10 people will be randomly selected to use a prototype and evaluate it based on SUS (System Usability Scale) (Table 1).

Table 1. Distribution of groups, scenarios, and specifications

Group	Scenario	Library
Group A	A simple digital health specific domain app	LICOR library
Group B		Google material design library

5 Results and Discussion

This study is a work in progress. All results will be published in the full paper along the year. A long-term study will assess how adopting the LICOR library may influence the Brazilian software companie's success in the second half of 2022.

6 Conclusion

A widespread problem is that digital health disparities exist and they must be addressed to provide consistent benefits [29]. To really identify genuine needs and introduce effective changes in the software development process to support a constant, adaptable, and successful digital health solution, we've established a scientific production calendar for 2022/2023. Researchers are invited to submit a Systematic Literature Review, A/B testing results, and software development process analysis.

Acknowledgement. To all of the HCII 2022 personnel, my Master Professor Dr. Fran Oliveira and my family who encouraged me while I was writing this study.

References

1. de Godoy, M.F., Filho, D.R.: Facing the BANI World. Int. J. Nutrology **14**, e33–e33 (2021). https://doi.org/10.1055/s-0041-1735848
2. Soto-Acosta, P.: COVID-19 pandemic: shifting digital transformation to a high-speed gear. Inf. Syst. Manag. **37**, 260–266 (2020). https://doi.org/10.1080/10580530.2020.1814461
3. Varajão, J.: Software development in disruptive times. Queueing Syst. **19**, 94–103 (2021). https://doi.org/10.1145/3454122.3458743
4. Abdi, M.: Fundamentals of design systems. https://iconline.ipleiria.pt/handle/10400.8/5839 (2021)
5. Kholmatova, A., Magazine, S.: Design Systems (Smashing eBooks). Smashing Media AG (2017)
6. Fessenden, T.: Design Systems 101. https://www.nngroup.com/articles/design-systems-101/ (2021)
7. Gu, Q.: Design system as a service. http://urn.fi/URN:NBN:fi:aalto-202106217676 (2021)
8. Nguyen, D.: Why design systems are a single point of failure. https://www.chromatic.com/blog/why-design-systems-are-a-single-point-of-failure/ (2020)
9. Klimm, M.C.: Design systems for micro frontends – an investigation into the development of framework-agnostic design systems using Svelte and Tailwind CSS. https://epb.bibl.th-koeln.de/frontdoor/index/index/docId/1666 (2021)

10. PrimeTek: PrimeFaces.org, www.primefaces.org (2021). Accessed 21 Oct 2021
11. Geers, M.: Micro Frontends in Action. Manning Publications, New York, NY (2020)
12. Evans, E.: Domain-Driven Design: Tackling Complexity in the Heart of Software. Addison-Wesley Professional (2003)
13. Fowler, M.: Domain Driven Design. https://martinfowler.com/tags/domain%20driven%20design.html (2021). Accessed 21 Oct 2021
14. Cycle, F.: Aprenda DDD (Domain Driven Design) do jeito certo. https://www.youtube.com/watch?v=eUf5rhBGLAk (2021). Accessed 21 Oct 2021
15. Richardson, C.: Microservices From Design to Deployment (2021). Accessed 21 Oct 2021
16. Geers, M.: Micro Frontends, micro-frontends.org (2021). Accessed 21 Oct 2021
17. Google: Material Design (2021). Accessed 21 Oct 2021
18. Evans, E., Evans, E.J.: Domain-driven Design: Tackling Complexity in the Heart of Software. Addison-Wesley Professional (2004)
19. Figma: https://www.figma.com/contact/ (2022). Accessed 4 Jun 2022
20. Storybook: UI component explorer for frontend developers. https://storybook.js.org/ (2022). Accessed 4 Jun 2022
21. Anima: Design to code: https://www.animaapp.com/. Accessed 4 June 2022
22. Zeroheight: document your design systems, together: https://zeroheight.com/ (2022). Accessed 4 Jun 2022
23. Material Design: https://material.io/ (2022). Accessed 3 Jun 2022
24. Ant Design: https://ant.design/ (2022). Accessed 3 Jun 2022
25. Microsoft Design: https://www.microsoft.com/design/fluent/#/ (2022). Accessed 3 Jun 2022
26. Oran, A.C., Nascimento, E., Santos, G., Conte, T.: Analysing requirements communication using use case specification and user stories. In: Proceedings of the XXXI Brazilian Symposium on Software Engineering (SBES 2017), pp. 214–223. Association for Computing Machinery, New York, NY, USA (2017). https://doi.org/10.1145/3131151.3131166
27. Carbon Design System: https://carbondesignsystem.com/ (2022). Accessed 3 Jun 2022
28. de Oliveira, A.C.S.F.M.G.N.N.J.P. de S.Z.M.L. dos S.C.M.E.M. da S.M.L.D.: Brazil's 2019–2023 National digital health strategy action, monitoring and evaluation plan. SUS (Executive Secretary of the Ministry of Health) IT Department (2019)
29. Jandoo, T.: WHO guidance for digital health: What it means for researchers. Digit Health. **6**, 2055207619898984 (2020). https://doi.org/10.1177/2055207619898984
30. Labrique, A., Agarwal, S., Tamrat, T., Mehl, G.: WHO digital health guidelines: a milestone for global health. NPJ Digit Med. **3**, 120 (2020). https://doi.org/10.1038/s41746-020-00330-2
31. Steinegger, R.H., Giessler, P., Hippchen, B., Abeck, S.: Overview of a domain-driven design approach to build microservice-based applications. In: The Thrid International Conference on Advances and Trends in Software Engineering. Unknown (2017)
32. Vernon, V.: Implementing Domain-Driven Design. Addison-Wesley (2013)

Design for Positive UX: From Experience Categories to Psychological Needs

Vera Fink[1], Katharina M. Zeiner[2(✉)], Marc Ritter[1], Michael Burmester[3], and Maximilian Eibl[4]

[1] University of Applied Sciences Mittweida, Technikumplatz 17, 09648 Mittweida, Germany
{fink,ritter}@hs-mittweida.de
[2] Siemens AG, Werner-von-Siemens-Straße 1, 80333 München, Germany
katharina.zeiner@siemens.com
[3] Hochschule der Medien, Nobelstraße 10, 70569 Stuttgart, Germany
burmester@hdm-stuttgart.de
[4] University of Technology Chemnitz, Straße der Nationen 62, 09110 Chemnitz, Germany
maximilian.eibl@informatik.tu-chemnitz.de

Abstract. One challenge students or other novices face when designing for positive User Experience can be taking the step from finding out all about users' needs and then identifying them before turning it into concepts that reflect those needs rather than simply developing concepts and retroactively mapping them to needs in general. In this late breaking work, we describe an approach to familiarizing students with psychological needs and their identification. The sections in the paper are accompanied by a classification in the design process to give an overview of how we applied the methods and in which order. In the process, needs were identified and worked with in all further process phases. The personas were expanded to include needs. All described use cases were developed from the needs. Or rather, a mapping of the functions to the identified needs was created. In this article we described the transfer from Experience categories directly to the needs. This simplifies the work of identifying the needs.

Keywords: Human computer interaction · User experience · Psychological needs · Eudaimonia

1 Introduction

The field of human computer interactions (HCI) has traditionally focused on creating usable products and interfaces. However, over the last twenty years more and more authors have pointed out that simply creating usable products is not enough and we have observed a shift towards aiming to fulfill users' needs. Amongst them have been Stephanidis and colleagues [1]. Looking ahead, as the technology landscape is changing

Desmet, P., Fokkinga, S.: Beyond Maslow's pyramid: introducing a typology of thirteen fundamental needs for human-centered design. Multimodal Technol. Interaction **4**(3), 38 (2020). https://doi.org/10.3390/mti4030038

© The Author(s), under exclusive license to Springer Nature Switzerland AG 2022
C. Stephanidis et al. (Eds.): HCII 2022, CCIS 1654, pp. 148–155, 2022.
https://doi.org/10.1007/978-3-031-19679-9_19

dramatically, Stephanidis and colleagues describe 7 grand challenges for living and interacting in technology-augmented environments. These challenges include:

- Human-technology symbiosis
- Human-environment interactions
- Ethics, privacy & security
- Well-being, health & eudaimonia
- Accessibility & universal access
- Learning & creativity
- Social organization & democracy

They point out that HCI will need to shift its focus, to stop simply talking about user experience towards focusing on user eudaimonia. This late breaking work describes an approach where experience interviews are used in conjunction with design thinking methods. We will describe several student projects, how the two methodologies were combined and how students were able to confidently pinpoint users' needs during experience interviews.

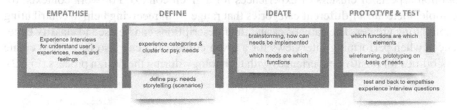

Fig. 1. Overview experimental approach

Furthermore, the article gives a general introduction to the methods of Experience Interviews and Experience Categories in the Empathize phase. The next section describes how the transfer between the categories and needs took place (Define). On this basis, the Ideation Phase collected ideas on how to implement the defined and identified needs and then how the ideas found their use at the prototype stage.

1.1 Positive Computing

This is aligned with positive computing [2] and positive design [3] both fields within HCI that focus on developing technologies that support users' wellbeing and by creating eudemonic experiences through products or services.

A problem that arises when focusing on user eudaimonia is that it is purely subjective and therefore harder to measure and define (see also Gilhooly et al. 2009 [4]). The field of positive user experience (positive UX) offers a way past this – by assuming that positive user experience is created in situations that fulfill users' psychological needs [5] then we can assume that a product or service that is designed to fulfill a given need might create the opportunity for an individual to experience eudaimonia while using it. Subsequent paragraphs, however, are indented.

1.2 Psychological Needs

Psychological needs as described by Desmet and Fokkinga [6] are repeatedly mentioned in the literature when searching for 'positive User Experience'. However, even in interviews using the laddering technique it can be very difficult to get participants to talk about positive experiences in everyday life, let alone about needs. Many cannot name needs, and if they are able to, the knowledge of what it means is imprecise. If we focus more on psychological needs, we find that in the descriptions of needs elaborated by Desmet and Fokkinga, there is also a category or statement to describe the respective needs and associated sub-needs.

1.3 Experience Interviews and Experience Categories

Experience Interviews were developed by two of the authors and colleagues [7] as an interview technique that focuses on understanding positive experiences in a given context. After interviewing 349 participants about positive experiences in work contexts, we started noticing clusters in the descriptions of positive experiences. These clusters laid the basis for what we now call experience categories [8]. Experience categories describe common aspects of clusters of experiences for a given context. For work contexts, for example, there are 17 different categories that range from receiving help to contributing to something greater. The categories and their descriptions can be used to classify experiences when performing interviews for a given context but can also be used to create possibilities for positive experiences with technology during the design process (Fig. 2).

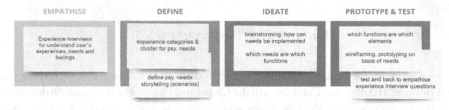

Fig. 2. The first step empathise and define

2   Method

As part of her doctoral thesis the primary author (VF) worked with experience interviews. The initial research question was "How can psychological needs be identified?". She piloted a selection of methods from IDEO, interviews and workshops, the result was that end users only talk about their needs all the time. The only drawback: "We have to listen carefully", but how?

To look at how well students are able to work with psychological needs, we observed their practical work over the course of a semester. The students got the framework of the Design Thinking process for their projects with the extension of the experience interview, a method from the field of positive UX. Their goal was to design applications according to psychological needs they extracted using the interviews.

Over 45 students participated in this field study in 2021 as part of their course work. They all took a course on HCI which had the goal of them getting to know, apply, name, and analyze different methods from HCI You should be able to get to know, apply, name, and analyze methods from the HCI. The project itself was part of a university project on robotic shopping assistance in the supermarket [9].

Table 1. Exercise structure in semester '21

Date and weeks	Focus	Description
29.03–11.04 2 weeks	Unit 0: Kickoff – Overview Event – UCD process, getting to know each other, finding groups 4–5 students	Registration in Thematic Groups
12.04–09.05 4 weeks	Unit 1 empathize: Experience Interviews for Research Requirements, Persona, Use Cases, Flow Charts (UML[a])	Task: Research in the context of robotic shopping assistance
10.05–09–05 4 weeks	Unit 2 Define & Ideate & Prototype & Test: identify needs, storytelling, interaction concept, low-fidelity paper prototype and mini-evaluation	Task: theme specific analysis Tools: LucidChart, Conceptboard, Stormboard, Sketch Tools, Paper pen and scissors
07.06–02.07 4 weeks	Unit 3 Ideate & Prototype & Evaluate: brainstorming, high-fidelity prototype, evaluation	Tools: Axure RP, Balsamiq Mockups, Just-in-mind, Adobe XD, proto.io, Figma
05.07.2021	Unit 4; closed session: presentations	

[a] Unified Modelling Language.

2.1 Realization

The semester was divided into blocks according to the steps in the Design Thinking process. The first phase included the methods of the empathize phase (Table 1). This is where students conducted the interviews. For this purpose, each group member went into the survey phase in individual work and interviewed his persons from the target groups. Students wrote down every comment of the respondents in order to be able to classify the needs as precisely as possible. It was found out that the target groups sometimes found it difficult to answer all questions concretely. Especially with the positive experience, some interviewees had to think very intensively. The interviews took an average of 30 min. The knowledge gained was independently evaluated by each group member and assigned to the needs. Here are some excerpts to answer the question:

What was your last positive experience while shopping?:

– Ferrero Rocher ice cream was very cheap, cheap t-shirt – Favorite cream, which otherwise had to be ordered, was available in the store – bought high quality camera – found a new variety of favorite wine – supermarket had again a certain seasonal product in the assortment – all products I wanted to buy in one store available – found a bargain / offer and bought it – used self-checkout for the first time -

How did you feel in that moment?:

– surprised, satisfied, happy (especially because of right size) – joy – euphoria – larger selection provides more variety – the product is only available in spring – time saving – enthusiastic – satisfied with himself and time saved -

If we look at some of the statements, the individual statements can be clustered.

2.2 Transfer

If we look at the individual statements, they can be generalized and clustered. For example, many of the statements went in the direction of creating shopping lists, using them, ticking them off as a memory aid. Or another example is getting offers, even personalized ones, sent to the email inbox, finding things in the store, or buying something if available. So, in summary, searching for products, their current availability, product information and description, and even saving them to ones' favorites (Fig. 3).

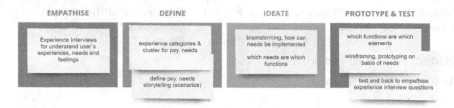

Fig. 3. Transfer from clustering categories to users' needs

Because the students worked in small project groups, the groups were able to work with the individual statements of the interviewees. Accordingly, the categories themselves were based on the results in each group. The groups were told to work independently from the other groups, at first independently of each other and to then bring things together in their group. The students took the statements and approached the needs according to Fig. 1. The transfer took place in the group directly through the statements of the interviewees (these were the categories) according to the table of needs.

3 Results

The most astonishing thing was that similar statements like: – see on the tablet where the products are – no long search for the product – knowing what offers are currently available – digital shopping cart for self-checkout – in all groups the same need was assigned quite accurately, the comfort. The area of comfort includes all functions that make the purchasing process more efficient (Fig. 4).

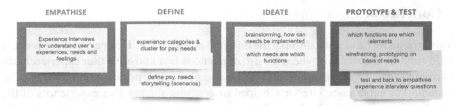

Fig. 4. The last part, prototype, and test

The student groups then used these findings to create prototypes. Based on the design elements from these statements, interaction concepts such as a planned route through the market based on the supermarket floor plan were created to indicate where products are located. If a product was searched for, it could immediately be visually displayed on the map to save time by searching the market. The customer could be informed by the application which offers are currently available on things they have in their shopping list (with the consent of the customer). The digital shopping cart was found to be very comfortable with the possibility to pay yourself with PayPal, or credit card (also without profile) to save the time at the checkout to pay. Thus, it is even faster to do the shopping.

Fig. 5. Prototyping functions best route, product search, offers showing

As a final circle, the evaluations, due to the pandemic, took place digitally e. g. via the Discord platform, in which the screen of the respective person was transmitted. The experiment was explained to the participants and how they could interact with the prototype. They were observed and questions were asked afterwards.

They found the "shortest route" function, budget, and preferences very good. The ability to filter products with the preferences function was felt to be very important and good, as there are many different dietary options and restrictions/allergies in today's world. Subsequently, the test persons were still asked about their need improvement. It was answered that it is very comfortable, and it facilitates the purchase, if one does not know the supermarket and/or this is very large.

Consequently, "comfort" was identified as the most important need across all target groups. Accordingly, the app should primarily contribute to making shopping more comfortable. In addition, the needs "autonomy" and "stimulation" were also counted among the top 3 needs in the shopping experience. Consequently, these were also considered in the development of the prototype.

4   Conclusion

In this article, we have gone through the different phases of the Design Thinking process (Fig. 5) and have described where the use of methods from positive user experience can contribute to the development of an intuitive and innovative prototype for a purchasing assistant. The experience interview helped to get from the positive experiences of the individual interviewees to the detailed categories in the purchasing process and to identify the needs. Based on the needs, functions were implemented in wireframes. And as feedback in the tests, it was examined which needs the prototype met individually for the test person and thus could have a positive effect on the experience of the purchasing process [10] (Fig. 6).

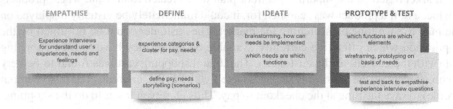

Fig. 6. Overview experimental approach

We have found that it is not only possible for the experts to accurately determine the needs, but also for the novices (students). And the step to the needs can happen much faster than expected. We have found that this lends itself specially to work with students and other novices because the prototypes can be evaluated afterwards to check if functions can be assigned to the different needs. Since even our novices were able to accurately identify the different needs, this can even be done in class.

References

1. Stephanidis, C., et al.: Seven HCI grand challenges. Int. J. Human-Comput. Interact. **35**(14), 1229–1269 (2019). https://doi.org/10.1080/10447318.2019.1619259
2. Calvo, R.A., Peters, D.: Positive Computing: Technology for Wellbeing and Human Potential. MIT Press (2014)
3. Desmet, P.M., Pohlmeyer, A.E.: Positive design: an introduction to design for subjective well-being. Int. J. Des. **7**(3), 5–19 (2013)
4. Gilhooly, M.L., Gilhooly, K.J., Jones, R.B.: Quality of life: Conceptual challenges in exploring the role of ICT in active ageing, pp. 49–76. IOS Press, Amsterdam, The Netherlands (2009)
5. Burmester, M., Zeiner, K.M., Laib, M., Hermosa Perrino, C., Queßeleit, M.L.: Experience design and positive design as an alternative to classical human factors approaches. In: INTERACT 2015 Adjunct Proceedings, pp. 153–160 (2015)
6. Desmet, P., Fokkinga, S.: Beyond Maslow's pyramid: introducing a typology of thirteen fundamental needs for human-centered design. Multimodal Technol. Interact. **4**(3), 38 (2020). https://doi.org/10.3390/mti4030038
7. Zeiner, K.M., Laib, M., Schippert, K., Burmester, M.: Das Erlebnisinterview–Methode zum Verständnis positiver Erlebnisse. Tagungsband der Mensch und Computer (2016)

8. Zeiner, K.M., Laib, M., Schippert, K., Burmester, M.: Identifying experience categories to design for positive experiences with technology at work. In: Proceedings of the 2016 CHI Conference Extended Abstracts on Human Factors in Computing Systems (CHI EA'16), pp. 3013–3020. Association for Computing Machinery, New York, NY, USA (2016). https://doi.org/10.1145/2851581.2892548

9. Fink, V., Börner, A., Eibl, M.: Living-lab and experimental workshops for design of I-RobEka assistive shopping robot: ELSI aspects with MEESTAR. In: Conference: Ro-Man The 29th IEEE International Conference on Robot & Human Interactive Communication. 31 Aug–04 Sep 2021. https://doi.org/10.1109/RO-MAN47096.2020.9223507

10. Fink, V., Langer, H., Ritter, M., Burmester, M., Eibl, M.: Positive user experience: novices can assess psychological needs. In: 2022 IEEE 9th International Conference on Computational Intelligence and Virtual Environments for Measurement Systems and Applications (CIVEMSA) – Regular Sessions (2022)

Do ICT Competence in and ICT Service Use Affect Life Satisfaction? Focusing on Mobile ICT Services

Seonglim Lee[1] , Jaehye Suk[2](✉) , Jinsook Kim[2] , Jinu Jung[3] ,
and Jinju Kim[1]

[1] Department of Consumer Science, Convergence Program for Social Innovation,
Sungkyunkwan University, Seoul, South Korea
[2] Convergence Program for Social Innovation, Sungkyunkwan University, Seoul, South Korea
[3] Department of Consumer Science, Sungkyunkwan University, Seoul, South Korea
jaehye.s@skku.edu

Abstract. This study examines how consumer competence in using information and communication technology (ICT) affects mobile ICT service use and how they relate to life satisfaction. We used data from the 2020 Survey on Digital Divide conducted by the Korean National Information Society Agency. The Survey collects information on access to and using mobile devices and services. Among 7,000 nationally representative survey participants, we selected 6,359 mobile ICT service users for analysis. A confirmatory factor analysis was conducted to check the reliability and validity of measurements. Structural equation model analysis was conducted to examine the mediation effect of mobile ICT service use in the relationship between competence in using mobile ICT and life satisfaction. The major results were as follows. First, more mobile ICT use competence was positively associated with more uses of the three types of mobile ICT services. Second, more competence in mobile ICT uses was positively associated with life satisfaction. Third, using mobile social networking and economic activity services positively affected, but using mobile trading & e-governance services negatively affected life satisfaction. The use of the three types of mobile ICT services partially mediated the relationship between mobile ICT competence and life satisfaction. The implications for the ICT service industry were suggested based on the results.

Keywords: ICT competence · ICT service use · Life satisfaction

1 Introduction

Information and Communication Technology (ICTs) is defined as technical tools and resources required to transmit, store, create, share, and exchange information [1], including computers, the Internet, live technology, recording technology, and mobile phones. As we enter the Web 2.0 era, where user participation is centered, the ability to use ICT

C. Stephanidis et al. (Eds.): HCII 2022, CCIS 1654, pp. 156–163, 2022.
https://doi.org/10.1007/978-3-031-19679-9_20

has become a critical ability. Furthermore, the amount and quality of information available to users vary greatly depending on their ability to use ICT. Therefore, the ability to use ICT has a significant impact on the overall qualtiy of life, in terms of individual ability development, human relationship formation, and increased well-being [2].

As of 2021, 95.7% of Korean consumers had mobile devices [3]. The spread and use of digital devices have become common, and access to ICT has been sufficiently satisfied in Korea. Since smartphones were first released in Korea, mobile devices have rapidly become common and spread to consumers' daily lives. Mobile devices' mobility and connectivity lead time and place-independent Internet access have, consequently, led to the mobilization of everyday life [4, 5]. The use of mobile devices may contribute to enhancing the quality of life through the increase in the amount and speed of information acquisition, the increase in the convenience of daily life, the expansion of social networks and communication, and the increase in participation in various leisure or social activities [6].

Mobile ICT refers to the use of digital devices such as mobile phones or tablet PCs while moving to transmit, store, create, and share information. New information and communication technologies such as smartphones and mobile Internet may positively impact individuals' lives. However, in reality, these devices inevitably have negative consequences that make it impossible for all consumers to enjoy the same benefits of the new technology equally [7]. Consumers who freely handle mobile devices such as smartphones and consumers who encounter difficulty with them cannot enjoy the same convenience provided by various mobile-based living services. Furthermore, the level of use of mobile-based living services may be differentiated depending on the ability to users' mobile devices.

Previous research on the ICT competency has focused on specific demographic groups such as students and older people [8–11] or its influence on social network activities such as SNS use [12, 13] despite its enormous potential impact on a wide range of human life. Thus, this study aims to examine how consumers' mobile ICT competence affects the utilization of various mobile ICT services and how they relate to overall life satisfaction.

2 Methods

2.1 Sample

We used data from the 2020 Survey on Digital Divide conducted by the National Information Society Agency. The Survey collects information on access to and using ICT devices and services. Among 7,000 nationally representative survey participants, we selected 6,359 mobile ICT service users for analysis. The descriptive characteristics of the sample are shown in Table 1.

Table 1. Descriptive statistics *(N = 6,359, Weighted)*

Variables		Freq.	(%)
Gender	Male	3,234	(50.86)
	Female	3,125	(49.14)
Age	10 s	781	(12.28)
	20 s	995	(15.65)
	30 s	1,029	(16.18)
	40 s	1,181	(18.57)
	50 s	1,213	(19.08)
	≥60 s	1,160	(18.24)
Education	≤Middle school	903	(14.20)
	High school	3,045	(47.88)
	≥College	2,411	(37.91)
Work status	Working	4,074	(64.07)
	Unemployed	1,100	(17.30)
	Students	1,185	(18.64)
Region	City	6,012	(94.54)
	Country	347	(5.46)
Income (KRW)[1]	(1) <0.5 million KRW	4	(0.06)
	(2) 0.5–0.99 million KRW	29	(0.46)
	(3) 1–1.49 million KRW	61	(0.96)
	(4) 1.5–1.99 million KRW	102	(1.60)
	(5) 2.0–2.49 million KRW	285	(4.48)
	(6) 2.5–2.99 million KRW	344	(5.41)
	(7) 3.0–3.49 million KRW	805	(12.66)
	(8) 3.5–3.99 million KRW	863	(13.57)
	(9) 4.0–4.99 million KRW	1,647	(25.90)
	(10) 5.0–5.99 million KRW	1,410	(22.17)
	(11) ≥6 million KRW	809	(12.72)

Notes: [1] KRW 1 million = USD 785.09, Freq = Frequency

2.2 Measures and Analysis

The dependent variable was life satisfaction, which was measured with four items on a 4-point Likert scale ranging from 1 (not at all) to 4 (very much). The independent variable was consumers' competence in using mobile ICT, which was measured with seven items on a 4-point Likert scale. The mediation variable was the three types of mobile ICT service use: social networking, trading & e-governance, and economic activity. Each type of mobile ICT service use was measured with four items on a 4-point Likert scale, from 1 = totally disagree to 4 = totally agree.

2.3 Data Analysis

We used the R 4.1.0 environment with the lavaan package, R 4.1.0, for the data analysis. We conducted confirmatory factor analysis (CFA) to identify the latent variables and structural equation modeling (SEM) to test the impact of consumers' ICT competence on using the three types of ICT services as well as how they relate to life satisfaction.

3 Results

3.1 Measurement Model

CFA was used to assess the efficacy of the model structure. The resulting measurement model produced an excellent fit ($\chi^2 = 4697.101$, df = 179, CFI = 0.931, TLI = 0.919, RMSEA = 0.063 (CI 90% [.061, .065]), SRMR = 0.043). The convergent validity of the measurement model was tested by standardized factor loadings, average variation extracted (AVE), and composite reliabilities (CR). As shown in Table 2, all factor loadings were larger than 0.4. Also, all CRs and AVEs exceed 0.7 and 0.4, respectively. AVE is less than 0.5, but CR is higher than 0.6, and the convergent validity of the construct is adequate [14]. Thus, the model achieved a good fit, and all indicators related to potential factors showed significant differences.

We evaluated the discriminant validity of the results of each factor. As the square roots of the AVE were higher than the maximum correlation between constructs(the shared variance between the two constructs), they satisfied the criteria to have the discriminant validity [15], as shown in Table 3.

3.2 The Results of the Structural Equation Model

The results of SEM analysis are presented in Table 4. The fitness index of the structural model was $\chi^2 = 4136.710$ (p = 0.000), df = 176, CFI = 0.940, TLI = 0.928, RMSEA = .059(CI 90% [.058, .061]), SRMR = 0.041, thus indicating that the model was acceptable. ICT competence positively affected the use of all three types of ICT services (i.e., social networking, trading & e-governance, and economic activities) and life satisfaction ($\beta = .222$, p < .001). In addition, the results showed that using mobile social networking ($\beta = .192$, p < .01), and economic activity services ($\beta = .112$, p < .001) had a significant and positive effect on the life satisfaction. Meanwhile, using mobile trading & e-governance services ($\beta = .181$, p < .001) had a negative effect on the life satisfaction.

As indicated in Table 5, we found a positive indirect effect of ICT competence on life satisfaction through using mobile social networking ($\beta = .119$, p < .001, 95% CI: [.079, .152]) and economic activity services ($\beta = .043$, p < .001, 95% CI: [.024, .061]), but a negative indirect effect on life satisfaction through using mobile trading & e-governance services ($\beta = -.019$, p < .001, 95% CI: [−.142, −.069]).

Table 2. Results of Confirmatory Factor Analysis for Measurement

Construct	Item	Mean (SD)	FL	CR	AVE	Cα
ICT competence	Controlling divice settings	3.051 (.662)	.522	.898	.561	.895
	Connecting wireless network (Wi-fi)		.559			
	Transferring files between mobile and PC		.749			
	Transferring files and photo to others		.526			
	Instolling/deleting/updating mobile app		.648			
	Inspecting/deleting malicious code		.719			
	Writing documents with mobile devices		.686			
Using social network services	Using Social Network Services (SNS)	2.446 (.693)	.720	.788	.553	.785
	Using blog services		.754			
	Using community services		.749			
Using trading & E-government services	Using e-commerce services	2.582 (.740)	.869	.832	.626	.825
	Using e-banking services		.839			
	Using e-governance services		.649			
Using economic services	For Job-seeking	1.890 (.794)	.764	.856	.599	.856
	For Internet marketing		.694			
	For Financial management		.743			
	For Cost-saving shopping		.739			
Life satisfaction	In most cases, my life is close to my ideal	2.695 (.527)	.480	.786	.481	.783
	The conditions of my life are very good		.571			
	I am content with my life		.436			
	If I lived my life again, I would hardly change anything		.480			

Notes: SD = standard deviation, FL = Factor Loading, CR = composite reliability, AVE = average variation extracted, Cα = cronbach's α

Table 3. Results of Discriminant Validity

Construct	1	2	3	4	5
1. ICT Competence	**.75**				
2. Using social network services	.610 (.010)	**.74**			
3. Using trading & E-governance	.599 (.011)	.725 (.010)	**.79**		
4. Using economic services	.377 (.011)	.633 (.011)	.676 (.009)	**.77**	
5. Life satisfaction	.264 (.014)	.270 (.015)	.168 (.016)	.197 (.015)	**.69**

Notes: Bold values on the diagonal are the square root of AVE, while others are correlations. Robust standard error is shown in parentheses

Table 4. Results of Structural Equation Modeling

Path	B	(S.E)	β	Results
H1. ICT Competence → Social networking	.891	(.024)***	.619	Supported H1
H2. ICT Competence → Trading & E-governance	1.049	(.026)***	.604	Supported H2
H3. ICT Competence → Economic activity	.589	(.021)***	.385	Supported H3
H4. Social networking → Life satisfaction	.128	(.020)**	.192	Supported H4
H5. Trading & E-governance → Life satisfaction	−.100	(.018)***	−.181	Rejected H5
H6. Economic activity → Life satisfaction	.071	(.015)***	.112	Supported H6
H7. ICT Competence → Life satisfaction	.213	(.022)***	.222	Supported H7

Notes: Robust standard error is shown in parentheses. $^*p < .05$, $^{**}p < .01$, $^{***}p < .001$

Table 5. Indirect Effects on Life Satisfaction by Bootstrapping

Path	Effect	Boot S.E	β	95% CI	
				Lower	Upper
ICT Competence → Social networking → Life Satisfaction	.114***	.019	.119	.079	.152
ICT Competence → Trading & E-governance → Life Satisfaction	−.105***	.019	-.109	−.142	−.069
ICT Competence → Economic activity → Life Satisfaction	.042***	.009	.043	.024	.061

Notes: Based on 5,000 bootstrap samples. CI = confidence interval. $^*p < .05$, $^{**}p < .01$, $^{***}p < .001$

4   Conclusion

This study investigated the effects of consumers' ICT competence on mobile ICT service use and how it relates to life satisfaction using data from the 2020 Survey on Digital Divide collected by the National Information Society Agency. The major results were as follows. First, mobile ICT competency was positively associated with using mobile social networking, trading & e-government, and economic activity services, while mobile ICT competency was positively associated with life satisfaction. Second, while using mobile social networking and economic activity services positively affected life satisfaction, using mobile trade and e-governance services had a negative effect on life satisfaction.

First, mobile ICT competency was positively associated with the use of mobile social networking, trading & e-government, and economic activity services. Mobile ICT competency also had a positive direct effect on life satisfaction. The results indicated that using mobile-based ICT services is bound to vary depending on consumers' ability to use mobile devices and services. Disadvantaged consumers who are not familiar with or have difficulty using mobile devices and services may not be able to fully utilize various ICT services. In particular, the ability to use ICT also directly affects consumers' quality of life and life satisfaction.

Second, more use of mobile social networking and economic services was related to more life satisfaction. However, more use of mobile trading and e-governance services was related to less life satisfaction. Life satisfaction increases with positive social relationships as people meet and express their opinions. Consumers who actively interact and experience connectivity with people might feel happier, thus using SNS contributes to greater life satisfaction [16]. More use of mobile services for various economic purposes led to more life satisfaction. The result was supported by the previous studies that showed the usage of fintech applications led to an increase in financial well-being [17], and job searching online is associated with significantly shorter unemployment spells, an important factor that has a positive impact on life satisfaction [18, 19]. Using e-banking, e-commerce, and e-government may represent conducting daily chores. Using mobile services for more daily chores might result in less life satisfaction. The results suggested that consumers are happier with increasing their use of mobile services for purposive activities, including those related to social relationships and economic benefits. The use of mobile services as a tool for performing daily life tasks did not lead to life satisfaction.

The results of this study provided important policy implications. First, ICT competence itself affects life satisfaction. Therefore, improvement in ICT competency enhances people's life satisfaction. Public and private policy efforts for continuing ICT education to clarify how to handle and use mobile devices may be necessary. Second, mobile services that support consumers' purposive activities are more effective for improving consumer satisfaction than those that are used as a convenient tool for accomplishing daily tasks. The development of mobile ICT applications for consumers should focus on serving meaningful activities rather than providing a convenient and effective way of doing them.

References

1. UNESCO Institute for Statistics: Guide to measuring information and communication technologies (ICT) in education (2009). https://unesdoc.unesco.org/ark:/48223/pf0000186547. Accessed 21 May 2022
2. Hargittai, E.: The digital reproduction of inequality. In: The Inequality Reader, 2nd edn. Routldege, NY (2018)
3. Korean National Information Society Agency: 2021 Survey on the Internet Usage (2022). https://www.nia.or.kr/site/nia_kor/ex/bbs/View.do;jsessionid=9328331D61558BC47BFDC F2F5A523B53.34b4204634c806361195?cbIdx=99870&bcIdx=24378&parentSeq=24378. Accessed 28 May 2022
4. Middleton, C., Scheepers, R., Tuunainen, V.K.: When mobile is the norm: researching mobile information systems and mobility as post-adoption phenomena. Eur. J. Inf. Syst. **23**(5), 503–512 (2014)
5. Hwang, R.J., Shiau, S.H., Jan, D.F.: A new mobile payment scheme for roaming services. Electron. Commer. Res. Appl. **6**(2), 184–191 (2007)
6. Kim, M.Y., Jun, H.J.: The effects of smartphone use on life satisfaction in older adults: the mediating role of participation in social activities. Korean J. Gerontological Soc. Welfare **72**(3), 343–370 (2017)
7. Ye, L., Yang, H.: From digital divide to social inclusion: a tale of mobile platform empowerment in rural areas. Sustainability **12**(6), 2424 (2020)
8. Zhao, L., Liang, C., Gu, D.: Mobile social media use and trailing parents' life satisfaction: social capital and social integration perspective. Int. J. Aging Hum. Dev. **92**(3), 383–405 (2021)
9. Kim, S.-K., Shin, H.-R., Kim, Y.-S.: Accessibility to digital information of middle-aged and elderly people, and its impact on life satisfaction level: sequential mediation effects on online social engagement and online network activity. J. Dig. Convergence **17**(12), 23–34 (2019). https://doi.org/10.14400/JDC.2019.17.12.023
10. Jun, W.: A study on the current status and improvement of the digital divide among older people in Korea. Int. J. Environ. Res. Public Health **17**(11), 3917 (2020). https://doi.org/10. 3390/ijerph17113917
11. Jara, I., et al.: Understanding factors related to Chilean students' digital skills: a mixed methods analysis. Comput. Educ. **88**, 387–398 (2015)
12. Han, S., et al.: The effect of using SNS to interpersonal relation and quality of life: focused on the moderating role of communication capability. The J. Inform. Syst. **22**(1), 29–64 (2013)
13. Wang, J.L., Jackson, L.A., Gaskin, J., Wang, H.Z.: The effects of social networking site (SNS) use on college students' friendship and well-being. Comput. Hum. Behav. **37**, 229–236 (2014)
14. Fornell, C., Larcker, D.F.: Structural equation models with unobservable variables and measurement error: Algebra and statistics. J. Mark. Re. **18**(3), 382 (1981). https://doi.org/10.2307/3150980
15. Fornell, C., Larcker, D.F.: Evaluating structural equation models with unobservable variables and measurement error. J. Mark. Res. **18**(1), 39–50 (1981)
16. Valkenburg, P.M., Peter, J., Schouten, A.P.: Friend networking sites and their relationship to adolescents' well-being and social self-esteem. Cyberpsychol. Behav. **9**(5), 584–590 (2006)
17. Frame, W.S., Wall, L., White, L.J.: Technological Change and Financial Innovation in Banking: Some Implications for FinTech, 3rd edn. Oxford University Press. NY, Oxford (2019)
18. Kuhn, P., Mansour, H.: Is internet job search still ineffective? Econ. J. **124**(581), 1213–1233 (2014). https://doi.org/10.1111/ecoj.12119
19. Grün, C., Hauser, W., Rhein, T.: Is any job better than no job? Life satisfaction and re-employment. J. Lab. Res. **31**(3), 285–306 (2010)

Understanding Users' Perception of Cute Aesthetics in Mobile Interface Design

Chei Sian Lee[1]([✉]), Dion Hoe-Lian Goh[1], Shermine Shimin Lau[2], Wei Yan Low[2], and Shu Fan[1]

[1] Wee Kim Wee School of Communication and Information, Nanyang Technological University, Singapore, Singapore
{leecs,ashlgoh,N2107150D}@ntu.edu.sg
[2] School of Social Sciences, Nanyang Technological University, Singapore, Singapore
{SLAU014,P180026}@ntu.edu.sg

Abstract. Despite growing interest in interface designs for mobile applications, research on the use of cute aesthetics in mobile interface design has largely been unexplored. Hence, this research aims to fill this gap by studying perceptions of cute aesthetics in mobile interface designs. Here, cute aesthetics refer to the use of cute design elements and bright colors in the interface designs as they are deemed to be attractive and appealing. A total of 166 participants were recruited to participate in a study to evaluate three sets of cute aesthetic designs. Findings revealed that participants responded favorably toward cute aesthetics and suggest that cute aesthetics is a plausible approach to engaging online mobile users. This study contributes to a better understanding of the conceptualization of cute aesthetics to be used in mobile interface design for the masses.

Keywords: Cuteness · Cute aesthetics · Mobile devices · Interface design

1 Introduction

Designing apps that are appealing is an essential step as aesthetics influence usage intention and engagement [1, 2]. Hence, it is not surprising that many studies have reported the relevance and importance of aesthetics in interface designs. Interfaces with aesthetic designs were found to be more effective at fostering positive attitudes than unaesthetic designs [3] and the inclusion of aesthetic design can improve online user experience [4]. In the context of mobile interfaces, aesthetic designs affect usability perceptions [5] and aesthetically pleasing interfaces can result in higher usage as well as better user performance [6, 7]. Collectively, aesthetics determine the pleasing qualities of a design [8], and factoring aesthetics into mobile interfaces can be an effective approach to influence behaviors [9].

Separately, cuteness has been cited as one of the pervasive aesthetic trends of the new millennium [10, 11]. Cuteness is often perceived as non-threatening, invoking a sense of comfort in users [12, 13]. In the context of Human-Computer Interaction (HCI), cuteness is believed to create a pleasurable user experience [14]. Specifically, research has shown

© The Author(s), under exclusive license to Springer Nature Switzerland AG 2022
C. Stephanidis et al. (Eds.): HCII 2022, CCIS 1654, pp. 164–171, 2022.
https://doi.org/10.1007/978-3-031-19679-9_21

that the appeal of cute characters provides reassurance and motivates prosocial behaviors [15]. Thus, incorporating cuteness in aesthetic design on mobile interfaces appears to be a viable approach in mobile interface designs for the masses for everyday use as it helps users to make sense of everyday information [16, 17]. Particularly, it has been reported that such use of cute aesthetics makes information that is typically seen as complex and tedious more palatable [18].

Despite the proliferation of cute aesthetics, the perception of cute aesthetics in mobile interface design is not well understood. Here, cute aesthetics refer to the use of cute design elements and bright colors in the interface designs as they are deemed to be attractive and appealing [19]. Put differently, it is unclear how adult users perceive cute aesthetics and their usage in their everyday mobile information environment. To fill this gap, this study seeks to understand the perception of cute aesthetics on mobile interfaces by examining how users describe their responses and perceptions. The contribution of this work is two-fold. First, it enhances our understanding of how cute visual elements can be blended onto the mobile interface for the masses. Second, it presents the implications of an exploratory study that elicited users' perception of cute aesthetics on mobile interfaces by examining their responses in terms of adjectives and visual elements. The finding will contribute to defining and conceptualizing cute aesthetics for mobile interfaces in future research.

2   Related Work

As a general concept, cuteness is most directly tied to the physical characteristics of humans, animals, and objects. A related development in this field is the concept of "kawaii" – the Japanese term to describe cute entities and objects [20, 21]. Since then, scholars have accounted for a new set of adjectives to describe cuteness including fun, playful and mischevious [22]. Sherman and Haidt [15] suggested that cuteness is a social engagement response, and it evokes engagement or affiliative motives. Following this line of argument, cuteness has its appeal and can be used for collective and social good. Specifically, Wang et al. [23] found that appeals to cuteness can be used to promote prosocial behaviors. In the context of HCI, Lin et al. [24] reported that cuteness in avatar significantly reduces users' perceived severity of software error taking. Taken together, prior works indicate that understanding perceptions of cuteness is valuable to shed light on how it can be blended in a mobile information environment for the masses.

The study of cute aesthetics in the HCI domain is a relatively new phenomenon and evaluating aesthetics is still a subjective and challenging process. The most related field of cute aesthetics is in the stream of research known as "Cuteness Engineering". Here, cuteness is defined as "a characteristic of a product, person, thing, or context that makes it appealing, charming, funny, desirable, often endearing, memorable, and/or (usually) non-threatening" [18, p. 8]. Cute aesthetic designs were found to appeal to certain demographic profiles [16] or cultures [25]. Hence, the appropriateness of cute aesthetics and their subsequent effectiveness may also be contingent on the context. Recently, Medley et al. [26] reported that cute aesthetics in inappropriate contexts may lead to cognitive dissonance. Notably, usable and attractive designs for interfaces define universally accepted norms. In the case of cute aesthetics, personal preference for cute aesthetics can be strongly influenced by perceptions of appropriateness and thus this study aims to examine this issue.

3   Methodology

A total of 166 participants were recruited to take part in the study. Participants attended a presentation where they were briefed about the purpose of the original mobile application prototype [17]. Specifically, the mobile application was developed as a software prototype to allow adult users in a community to volunteer, help, share and retrieve comments about everyday happenings in their community. Following the presentation, participants were shown three sets of mobile interface designs with cute aesthetics and a set of designs without cute aesthetics (the original interface). The main theme of interface design 1 is the use of a cute typeface with pastel colors while interface design 2 focuses on cute shapes (round edges) with bright colors. Finally, cute icons with a warm color tone were the emphasis in interface design 3 (refer to Figs. 1, 3 and 5). Participants were asked to answer a survey with questions pertaining to their perceptions and evaluation of the three designs. Demographic information of the participants was also collected. There were 104 female participants (63%) and the majority of the participants were in the 21–30 age group (84%). Participants received $5 SGD in compensation for their participation.

4   Results

4.1   Visualizing Using Word Clouds

Word clouds were used to visualize the words provided by the participants for the three interfaces (refer to Figs. 2, 4, and 6) and they show that participants responded differently to the three designs. Overall, results indicate that cute aesthetics appeal to the participants in particular Interfaces 2 and 3 appealed to the liking of most of the participants.

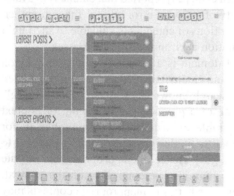

Fig. 1. Interface design 1

Fig. 2. Description of design 1

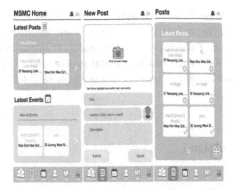

Fig. 3. Interface design 2

Fig. 4. Description of design 2

Fig. 5. Interface design 3

Fig. 6. Description of design 3

4.2 Describing Cute Aesthetics Based on Frequency Count Analysis

Frequency count analysis was further conducted. Figure 7 show frequency counts of the most frequently used adjectives to describe interface design 1. While some commented they liked the cute design others had negative views of the design. Participant 27 shared that *"The colours in design 1 appeal to me personally most as it seems the most friendly and wholesome"* and participant 75 thought that *"Design 1 is clear and have [has] cute touch"*. However, participant 108 felt that *"Design 1 is too casual, cute but [and] cannot be taken seriously"* and participant 115 further commented that it is *"messy, and cluttered"*. Figure 8 shows the adjectives used by the participants to describe interface design 2. Most participants considered interface design 2 to be cute, warm, and simple. Hence, it is not surprising that this design was the most preferred design. Here are some quotes. Participant 22 commented that *"I think design 2 gives the warm vibes, which is in line with what volunteering means to me - to be warm to others"* and this is echoed by Participant 37, *"It looks simple and easy to navigate. It also gives me a warm feeling."* Fig. 9 shows the adjectives to describe interface design 3. Most participants were attracted by the yellow shade and the bee theme which provided a feeling of fun and positivity while encouraging usage. Participant 58 highlighted that *"... a striking yellow-orange colour which is more striking. The use of white background makes it more simplistic and the whole application looks more welcoming for volunteering."* Participant 98 further commented that *"I like the bee-themed design. The bright colours and cute bee icons make me want to explore the app further (P98)."* The same sentiment is also shared by participant 164, *"I like the colour yellow and design 3 appeals to me because it looks engaging."*

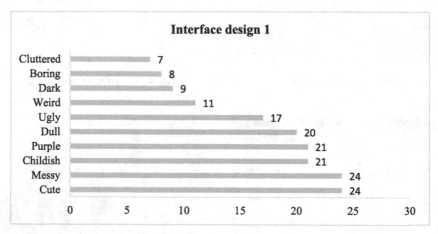

Fig. 7. Top 10 adjectives of interface design 1 (N = 166)

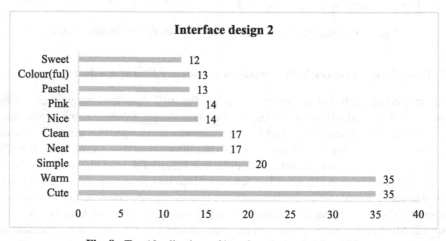

Fig. 8. Top 10 adjectives of interface design 2 (N = 166)

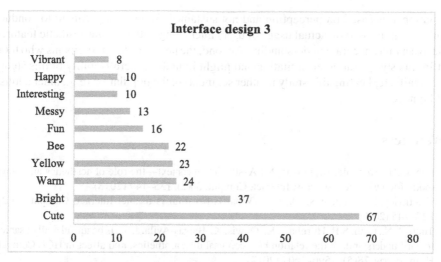

Fig. 9. Top 10 adjectives of interface design 3 (N = 166)

5 Discussion

The results of our exploratory work yielded the following preliminary findings. First, blending cute aesthetics is a balancing act. Specifically, the findings suggest that there is a great need to balance cuteness with professionalism for mobile interfaces for the masses. Notably, several participants voiced that such viewpoints could be a matter of users' age group. For instance, Participant 59 explained that "*Design 1 and 3 may appeal to the younger audiences, Design 3 appears playful and seems the cutest due to the use of icons and the matching colour scheme*". Participant 18 also recognized that "*interface 3 have more picture and there is a striking balance in between the background and the words. For interface 2, it has slightly more variation in the shape as compared to interface 1.*" Participant 29 concluded that "*2nd one (interface) is the best balance of cute and professional enough*". Second, the idea of using a theme for cute aesthetic design was well-received by the participants. The theme must be aligned with the purpose and expected actions of the users. Several participants expressed their liking for the cute icons (with the bee theme) in interface 3. Participant 1 noted that "*The bees amplify the cuteness*". Participant 12 reiterated that "*As a user, the bee theme is eye catching and I would tend to use the interface more because it gives a very user-friendly outlook at a glance*".

6 Limitations and Future Work

This exploratory study shows that cute aesthetic design in mobile interface design is a viable approach to appeal to the masses. We extend prior work in aesthetics design by exploring the use of cute design elements in a mobile interface design. Our findings reveal how users describe cute aesthetics and how different cuteness elements can be blended appropriately. The caveats to this study should also be noted. First, the user evaluation was based on perception and not sustained usage. It is pertinent to conduct future research based on actual usage of users interacting with the cute aesthetic features to derive a more accurate understanding. Second, the profile of the participants who took part in this study is another limitation and might limit the generalizability of this study. Specifically, replicating this study in other segments of the population (e.g., older adults) will be necessary.

References

1. Iten, G.H., Troendle, A., Opwis, K.: Aesthetics in context—the role of aesthetics and usage mode for a website's success. Interact. Comput. **30**(2), 133–149 (2018)
2. Tractinsky, N., Katz, A.S., Ikar, D.: What is beautiful is usable. Interact. Comput. **13**(2), 127–145 (2000)
3. Tuch, A.N., Roth, S.P., Hornbæk, K., Opwis, K., Bargas-Avila, J.A.: Is beautiful really usable? toward understanding the relation between usability, aesthetics, and affect in HCI. Comput. Hum. Behav. **28**(5), 1596–1607 (2012)
4. Silvennoinen, J., Vogel, M., Kujala, S.: Experiencing visual usability and aesthetics in two mobile application contexts. J. Usability Stud. **10**(1), 46–62 (2014)
5. Goh, D.H.L., Lee, C.S., Zhou, Q., Guo, H.: Finding trafficked children through crowdsourcing: a usability evaluation. Aslib J. Inf. Manag. **73**(3), 419–435 (2021). https://doi.org/10.1108/AJIM-08-2020-0254
6. Sonderegger, A., Sauer, J.: The influence of design aesthetics in usability testing: effects on user performance. Appl. Ergon. **403–410**, 2 (2009)
7. Chopdar, P.K., Balakrishnan, J.: Consumers response towards mobile commerce applications: S-O-R approach. Int. J. Inf. Manag. **53**, 102106 (2020). https://doi.org/10.1016/j.ijinfomgt.2020.102106
8. Chow, A.: The usability of digital information environments: planning, design and assessment. Trends Disc. People Digital Age **2**, 13–37 (2013)
9. Chakraborty, A.: The aesthetic-usability effect: why beautiful-looking products are preferred over usable-but-not-beautiful ones (2017). https://medium.com/@coffeeandjunk/design-psychology-aesthetic-usability-effect-494ed0f22571
10. Dale, J.P., Goggin, J., Leyda, J., McIntyre, A.P., Negra, D.: The Aesthetics and Affects of Cuteness. Routledge, Abingdon (2016). https://doi.org/10.4324/9781315658520
11. Marcus, A., Ma, X.: Cuteness design in the UX: an initial analysis. In: Marcus, A. (ed.) DUXU 2016. LNCS, vol. 9747, pp. 46–56. Springer, Cham (2016). https://doi.org/10.1007/978-3-319-40355-7_5
12. Pellitteri, M.: Kawaii aesthetics from Japan to Europe: theory of the Japanese "Cute" and transcultural adoption of its styles in Italian and French comics production and commodified culture goods. Arts **7**(3), 24 (2018)
13. Takamatsu, R.: Measuring affective responses to cuteness and Japanese kawaii as a multidimensional construct. Curr. Psychol. **39**(4), 1362–1374 (2020)
14. Marcus, A.: The cult of cute: The challenge of user experience design. Interactions **9**(6), 29–34 (2002). https://doi.org/10.1145/581951.581966
15. Sherman, G.D., Haidt, J.: Cuteness and disgust: the humanizing and dehumanizing effects of emotion. Emot. Rev. **3**(3), 245–251 (2011)
16. Lee, C.S., Tian, S., Xu, A., Liu, Y., Goh, D.H.L., Seah, N.C.: Investigating the influence of cute aesthetics in community crowdsourcing. Proc. Assoc. Inf. Sci. and Technol. **58**(1), 765–767 (2021)

17. Lee, C.S., Goh, D., Zhou, Q., Sin, S.-C.J., Theng, Y.L.: Integrating motives and usability to examine community crowdsourcing. Proc. Assoc. Inf. Sci. Techno. **57**, e53 (2020). https://doi.org/10.1002/pra2.353

18. Marcus, A., Kurosu, M., Ma, X., Hashizume, A.: Cuteness Engineering: Designing Adorable Products and Services, vol. 3. Springer, Heidelberg (2017). https://doi.org/10.1007/978-3-319-61961-3

19. Cheok, A.D.: Kawaii/cute interactive media. In: Art and Technology of Entertainment Computing and Communication. Springer, London. https://doi.org/10.1007/978-1-84996-137-0_9

20. Nittono, H.: The two-layer model of 'kawaii': a behavioural science framework for understanding kawaii and cuteness. East Asian J. Pop. Cult. **2**(1), 79–95 (2016). https://doi.org/10.1386/eapc.2.1.79_1

21. Nittono, H., Lieber-Milo, S., Dale, J.P.: Cross-cultural comparisons of the cute and related concepts in Japan, the United States, and Israel. SAGE Open **11**(1), 2158244020988730 (2021). https://doi.org/10.1177/2158244020988730

22. Nenkov, G.Y., Scott, M.L.: "So cute I could eat it up": priming effects of cute products on indulgent consumption. J. Cons. Res. **41**(2), 326–341 (2014). https://doi.org/10.1086/676581

23. Wang, T., Mukhopadhyay, A., Patrick, V.M.: Getting consumers to recycle NOW! When and why cuteness appeals influence prosocial and sustainable behavior. J. Public Policy Mark. **36**(2), 269–283 (2017)

24. Lin, Y.T., Doong, H.S., Eisingerich, A.B.: Avatar design of virtual salespeople: mitigation of recommendation conflicts. J. Serv. Res. **24**(1), 141–159 (2021). https://doi.org/10.1177/1094670520964872

25. Dydynski, J., Mäekivi, N.: Multisensory perception of cuteness in mascots and zoo animals. Int. J. Mark. Sem. **6**(1), 2–25 (2018)

26. Medley, S., Zaman, B., Haimes, P.: The role of cuteness aesthetics in interaction. In: Rousi, R., Leikas, J., Saariluoma, P. (eds.) Emotions in Technology Design: From Experience to Ethics. HIS, pp. 125–138. Springer, Cham (2020). https://doi.org/10.1007/978-3-030-53483-7_8

The Impact of Personality on Gamification Interfaces

Viktoriya Limonova[1]([✉]) [iD], Gustavo Barradas[1] [iD], and Sandra Gama[2] [iD]

[1] Instituto Superior de Tecnologias Avançadas, 1750-142 Lisbon, Portugal
{viktoriya.limonova,gustavo.barradas}@my.istec.pt
[2] INESC-ID and Instituto Superior Técnico, 1049-001 Lisbon, Portugal
sandra.gama@tecnico.ulisboa.pt

Abstract. Gamification has been used to improve engagement in a variety of settings while improving overall results, which makes it a popular research topic nowadays. Notwithstanding, gamified systems must be designed carefully, correctly balancing game elements. Nevertheless, one-size-fits-all approaches are limited and do not guarantee absolute success. In fact, gamification can affect individuals differently. This may be explained by individual differences presented by players, such as their player type or gaming styles, which cannot be dissociated from personality. Such traits can be measured and, when used in relevant manners, may play a very important role in the design of more personalized gamification systems. This paper presents our study on the influence of personality in gamification design. We present an interface for gamifying Kanban methodologies, with its underlying mechanisms. Its appearance has been varied through the use of a restricted color palette. We then present the study we have designed to measure individuals' responses to different interfaces regarding personality and gaming profiles.

Keywords: Gamification · Agile methodologies · Kanban · Human-computer interaction · Human factors in HCI

1 Introduction

Gamification, the use of game elements in non-game contexts [1], is nowadays a widely popular research topic. Not only has it proven to enhance motivation and fun [1], but it has also shown promising results in terms of technology adoption, teaching-learning processes, among other settings. Some of the most commonly adopted game mechanisms are Points, Badges, and Leaderboards (PBL). Nevertheless, the elements present in gamification are not just part of a balanced and carefully designed system. While a combination of game elements may positively impact the performance of an individual, it may also negatively influence the motivation of another [4], which emphasizes the shortcomings of one-size-fits-all gamification approaches.

Studies associated with personality and behavior have demonstrated how gamification can affect different groups of individuals who have a significant number of characteristics in common regarding their player type, personality traits, or gaming styles.

C. Stephanidis et al. (Eds.): HCII 2022, CCIS 1654, pp. 172–179, 2022.
https://doi.org/10.1007/978-3-031-19679-9_22

Both personality traits and player types aim to observe differences between players and explain distinctions in their behaviors and attitudes [5]. Several authors and specialists in diverse fields of psychology helped to conclude different ways of measuring behaviors, including unique patterns of thought or feeling. These characteristics can be classified as personality traits and can be measured by applying different types of tools and techniques. Personality is designated as a set of characteristic patterns related to behavior, opinions, and emotions. This aggregation of factors defines the exceptionality of each person, especially in certain relevant situations. It is believed to arise from within an individual and remains consistent throughout life [1]. Based on the collection of the spontaneous facets and the state of the user, physiological computing has been expanding and increasingly applying approaches associated with the interaction between humans and computers [2], which allows the creation of a largely unconscious channel between the two. The concept related to player types manifests the existence of different phenomena, correlated with the characteristics of each player. These can be classified based on different factors regarding their motivations, playing style, behavior, and other types of preferences. As such, this grouping of unique factors can be further grouped into typologies, taxonomies, or categories [3].

With our work, we study the influence of personality in gamification design. To that end, we created a gamification interface and varied its appearance through the use of different colors. We will measure how individuals respond to the different interfaces regarding their personality and gaming profiles. While we will rely on self-reported preferences through questionnaires, we will also take advantage of neurophysiological signals to corroborate our results. This paper is organized as follows. In Sect. 2, we frame our research into its related work. We then present our gamification interface, together with the game mechanisms we have adopted. In Sect. 4 we describe our study, followed by its expected findings. We then draw some conclusions, together with future work we intend to develop in the context of our research.

2 Related Word

2.1 Gamifying Kanban Methodologies

In project management, it is necessary to control and adjust a project's every detail, from its initial drafts to completion. Agile methodologies adoption has been popular among team managers, Alexandra Altvater[1] points out the reason for its popularity being that the main objective of these life cycle programs is to obtain the best possible result in a short period of time, at the lowest cost, by identifying and removing redundancies. Through Gamification, it is possible to create a video game environment in an Agile context. This allows a new user experience that can lead to added value for both managers and development members.

In the following case study, Manal Alhammad and Ana M. Moreno [6], created several groups working in different methodologies such as Scrum and Scrumban, where they applied different gamification mechanics to better understand which combinations provide the best results. In the end, the authors determined that mechanics such as points

---

[1] https://stackify.com/what-is-sdlc/.

and badges were favorites among the test groups and that overall, the results are promising. Additionally, other solutions where gamification provided positive results, Murat Yilmaz and Rory O'Connor [7], implemented gamification to a Scrumban solution, and concluded that the mechanics introduced, improved the developer's motivation and engagement in the solution. Rita Marques et al. [8], also used gamification to address the low motivation levels in agile adoption, and concluded, that after its implementation, there were improvements in users' long-term engagement.

2.2 The Role of Personality in Interfaces

Personality and player profile play a crucial role in gamification and contribute in a very positive way increasing motivation and improving the user experience, especially in gamified interfaces [9]. The applicability of certain elements may awaken extrinsic or intrinsic motivation and improve their use. Player profiling can help in classifying different types of players and the customization of certain features and functionality in applications and games. Several authors have used biofeedback techniques to more accurately assess a variety of characteristics present not only in player profiles but also in gamification. A great number of authors have proposed the adaptation of different types of visual techniques such as color differentiation [2], cosmetic options [3], real-time feedback [4], goals and objectives [5]. Thanks to a development of a gamified management system [10] it was possible to analyze more deeply the motivation of its users, including the application of different badges and awards based on their performance. Certain elements are strongly related to psychological needs. Performance graphs, leaderboards, and badges can positively affect the satisfaction of participants, improve their skills, and increase social relationships and a sense of relevance [11]. The link between different personalities and gamification elements can help creating appealing designs [12]. Avoiding overlapping screens effect, using the entire working area effectively, and minimizing icon usage, are some of the important factors to take into consideration. According to Mitov et al. [13], personality demographics should be taken in place to improve color design techniques, typography, and information display. Many authors defend solutions that follow the user preferences and their personality since they tend to be more efficient and increase satisfaction during task completion [14].

Personality traits can strongly influence the information process, Kostov and Fukuda found that users performed better when they interacted with an interface that matched their personality [15]. As mentioned by several authors [16–18], one of the most important aspects when designing an interface is to elaborate solutions based on personality and apply a variety of elements, such as buttons [19], colors, information density [20] and font styles [21]. As determined by Arockiam and Selvaraj [22], extraverts can easily collect data written in blue with "Times" as font style, while neurotics prefer it in green.

3   A Gamification Interface

To overcome the adhesion challenges of agile, a gamified solution was created around the agile methodology Kanban. This solution implements mechanics that allow users to take advantage of the Kanban methodology while ignoring some of the less desirable challenges that it alone creates. The mechanics implemented in the solution is aimed at the users' extrinsic motivation. Thus, it ensures that the user keeps using the agile solution and be rewarded by it. To not exhaust users, only a small portion of all the available gamification mechanics were implemented. This permits a clean interface, without the concern of straying away from the original Kanban template. The implemented mechanics are: (i) points; (ii) badges; (iii) leaderboards; (iv) progression bars and (v) awards. Inside the gamified interface there are two types of users, managers and development members. The users who interact the most with the gamification mechanics are the development members, as they can receive points from completed projects, badges, trade points for awards, and see their progress towards the next objective (Fig. 1).

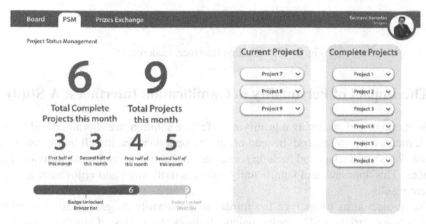

Fig. 1. Gamification interface, project status management

In many video games, players are very competitive with each other, and to take advantage of this factor, from time to time, there will be a project that is not assigned to any development member and is open to be taken by whoever wants it. This means the hoarding of more points to be later exchanged for awards. This will provide a small and healthy competitive environment among the members since these projects will have little value in points. The managers, on the other hand, have control over the interface, and of the gamified mechanics, they can assign points to a determined project, visualize the current leaderboards of all the dev members, and add new badges and awards (Fig. 2). It may seem that the development members have the most "fun" in this solution and can benefit more from the points and awards system.

However, with this solution, managers can benefit from a better overview of all current projects' status, a more dedicated and content team of development members, and a better perception, of what types of "players" they have on their teams.

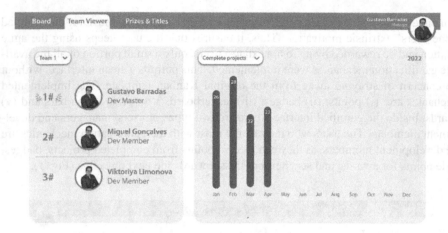

Fig. 2. Gamification interface, leaderboard

4 The Impact of Personality in Gamification Interfaces: A Study

When planning and designing a gratifying effective solution, we should consider some key elements for it to succeed, instead of relying on a one-size-fits-all model and being limited. We should adapt and include some personalization according to individual differences. This approach can significantly enhance motivation and enjoyment and lead to great results.

Our project aims to analyze the impact of personality on gamification interfaces through color variation. The color palette follows the values of the hue-saturation-brightness (HSB) color system (red, yellow, green, and blue). These can be seen in Fig. 3, which also includes the corresponding values, only the saturation and brightness were adjusted to provide a friendly view and cause less eye strain.

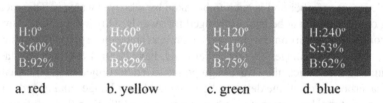

H:0°	H:60°	H:120°	H:240°
S:60%	S:70%	S:41%	S:53%
B:92%	B:82%	B:75%	B:62%
a. red	b. yellow	c. green	d. blue

Fig. 3. Hue-saturation-brightness (HSB) color palette. (Color figure online)

For the trait classification, two different models were applied, NEO Personality Inventory-Revised model (NEO PI-R) [23] for the measurement of the five traits (openness, conscientiousness, extraversion, agreeableness, and neuroticism) related to the Five-Factor Model [24], and gamification user types Hexad, destined for the categorization of player types (socializers, free spirits, achievers, philanthropists, players, and disruptors) [25]. The structure of the study consists of two essential parts, each one responsible for acquiring important information regarding personality and its impact.

The first phase is composed by a questionnaire, divided into several chapters whose questions are responsible for the categorization of personality, player type and acquiring information about color preference and general opinion about the interface. At this stage, participants will have a first contact with the interface, with a random color from the color palette presented in Fig. 3. Furthermore, each participant will be invited to participate in the second phase of the investigation consisting of an experience with BITalino[2] device. Neuroscience and physiological computing will be the main allies, including electrodes and capture of biosignals (Heart Rate and Electroencephalography), which may lead to an interesting conclusion, and a starting point for new knowledge and ideas in future research.

5 Expected Findings

Emotionality and colors are extremely associated with psychology, the impact of colors on the user experience can significantly change user behavior. It is estimated that about eighty percent of the information processed by the brain is acquired through vision, which makes color one of the essential elements for gamification. Each color has a different meaning and can be strongly associated with a personality trait.

With our first questionnaire, we expect to find different kinds of personalities and player types, and which color preferences can or cannot coincide with such traits. We expect to see some connection between the personality traits, player types, and color preference, and understand what kind of relationship might exist between them. However, this relation can be analyzed with more accuracy in the second phase, responsible for the visualization of a gamified interface together with the capture of biosignals and measurement of participants' valence and arousal. Depending on the answers, we may be able to observe which of the traits and player types stand out and study their behavior during the questionnaire. If possible, we hope to group our participants according to their common attributes and analyze their responses to understand if they match the results from biofeedback. With our study, we might be able to discover how users with different player types and personalities respond to different colors and in which way can biosignals be used to help examine the participant's response regarding the gamified interfaces. Also, we expect to study the effect of color on our gamification interface, analyzing several important factors, namely, to understand what kind of roles can personality and player types play and their influence.

6 Conclusions and Future Work

Although there are already cases where gamification has been successfully implemented in agile methodologies such as Scrum and Scrumban, this study seeks to create a gamified solution to the Kanban methodology and to understand if the applied mechanics help overcome the difficulties of adherence and maintain users' motivation long term. The interface presented in this study will hopefully help future researchers who want to apply gamification to Kanban, and how some of its mechanics can be implemented without

---

[2] https://www.pluxbiosignals.com/.

major changes in the methodology template. Personality plays an important role in gamification, it allows for classifying different types of individuals based on common characteristics, which makes it possible to analyze certain preferences. These interests can significantly help during the design phase of gamified solutions, especially when the main purpose collides with the personalization of certain elements, which in turn, can arouse motivation and certain actions from users. As mentioned before, we should not only choose a single option for every user, but rather a more flexible one, in this way, we can broaden our horizons and reach more individuals, which in turn, contributes to more interesting and relevant results.

Our future work will comprise an experimental phase alongside BITalino, a biosignal open-source platform designed for academic purposes, which contains sensors and electrodes capable of measuring the valence and arousal of our participants. Once more, the participants will examine the same interface and answer a variety of questions. These results will be further analyzed and compared with the results obtained from the first questionnaire and will help to conclude what kind of impact the personality exerts on gamification. Data from our study can significantly help in future research, studies, or books related to the effect of color on gamification, and about the roles that personality and player types play and their influence. With our study we hope to motivate future authors to research more about personality, gamification, or even color psychology. Due to the lack of studies related to the impact of personality on gamification, we believe that our study will contribute to enhance new ideas, thoughts, and hopefully will be a starting point for new research, especially with the evolution of physiological computing over the years.

References

1. Sheldon, L.: The Multiplayer Classroom: Designing coursework as a game. Course Technology/Cengage Learning, Boston (2012)
2. Korn, O., Muschick, P., Schmidt, A.: Gamification of Production? A Study on the Acceptance of Gamified Work Processes in the Automotive Industry. In: Chung, W.J., Shin, C.S. (eds.) Advances in Affective and Pleasurable Design, pp. 433–445. Springer International Publishing, Cham (2017). https://doi.org/10.1007/978-3-319-41661-8_42
3. Donatiello, L., Morotti, E., Marfia, G., Di Vaio, S.: Exploiting immersive virtual reality for fashion gamification. In: 2018 IEEE 29th Annual International Symposium on Personal, Indoor and Mobile Radio Communications, pp. 17–21 (2018). https://doi.org/10.1109/PIMRC.2018.8581036
4. Liu, M., Huang, Y., Zhang, D.: Gamification's impact on manufacturing: enhancing job motivation, satisfaction and operational performance with smartphone-based gamified job design. Hum. Factors Man. **28**, 38–51 (2018). https://doi.org/10.1002/hfm.20723
5. Roh, S., et al.: Goal-based manufacturing gamification: bolt tightening work redesign in the automotive assembly line. In: Schlick, C., Trzcieliński, S. (eds.) Advances in Ergonomics of Manufacturing: Managing the Enterprise of the Future, pp. 293–304. Springer International Publishing, Cham (2016). https://doi.org/10.1007/978-3-319-41697-7_26
6. Alhammad, M.M., Moreno, A.M.: What is going on in agile gamification? In: International Conference on Agile Software Development: Companion. Association for Computing Machinery, New York, USA, Article 36, pp. 1–4 (2018). https://doi.org/10.1145/3234152.3234161

7. Yilmaz, M., O'Connor, R.: A Scrumban integrated gamification approach to guide software process improvement: a Turkish case study. Tehnicki Vjesnik (2016)
8. Marques, R., Costa, G., Silva, M.M., Gonçalves, D., Gonçalves, P.: Using Gamification for Adopting Scrum. ISD (2018)
9. Toda, A.M., Klock, A.C.T., Oliveira, W., et al.: Analysing gamification elements in educational environments using an existing Gamification taxonomy. Smart Learn. Environ. **6**, 16 (2019). https://doi.org/10.1186/s40561-019-0106-1
10. Aseriskis, D., Damaševičius, R.: Gamification of a project management system. In: ACHI (2014)
11. Sailer, M., Hense, J.U., Mayr, S.K., Mandl, H.: How gamification motivates: an experimental study of the effects of specific game design elements on psychological need satisfaction. Comput. Hum. Behav. **69**, 371–380 (2017). https://doi.org/10.1016/j.chb.2016.12.033
12. Jia, Y., Xu, B., Karanam, Y., Voida, S.: Personality-targeted gamification: a survey study on personality traits and motivational affordances. In: Conference on Human Factors in Computing Systems (2016). https://doi.org/10.1145/2858036.2858515
13. Mitov, I., et al.: Ergonomic design of the graphical user interface of integrated software systems for business management (2016)
14. Alves, T., Natálio, J., Henriques-Calado, J., Gama, S.: Incorporating personality in user interface design: a review. Pers. Individ. Diff. **155**, 109709 (2019)
15. Kostov, V., Fukuda, S.: Development of man-machine interfaces based on user preferences. In: 2001 IEEE International Conference on Control Applications, pp. 1124–1128 (2001). https://doi.org/10.1109/CCA.2001.974022
16. Berrais, A.: Knowledge-based expert systems: user interface implications. Adv. Eng. Softw. **28**(1), 31–41 (1997). https://doi.org/10.1016/S0965-9978(96)00030-0
17. Schlegel, T.: Model-based user interface generation from process-oriented models. In: Human-Computer Interaction. IntechOpen, London (2009). https://doi.org/10.5772/7718
18. McTear, M.F.: Intelligent interface technology: from theory to reality?, In: Interacting with Computers, pp. 323–336 (2000). https://doi.org/10.1016/S0953-5438(99)00002-8
19. Kane, S.K., et al.: Getting off the treadmill: evaluating walking user interfaces for mobile devices in public spaces. In: Mobile HCI (2008)
20. Reinecke, K., Bernstein, A.: Knowing what a user likes: a design science approach to interfaces that automatically adapt to culture. MIS Q. **37**, 427–453 (2013)
21. Evett, L., Brown, D.J.: Text formats and web design for visually impaired and dyslexic readers - clear text for all. Interact. Comput. **17**(4), 453–472 (2005)
22. Arockiam, L., Selvaraj, J.: User interface design for effective e-learning based on personality traits. Int. J. Comput. Appl. **61**, 28–32 (2013)
23. McCrae, R.R., Costa, Jr., P., Martin, T.A.: The NEO-PI-3: a more readable revised NEO personality inventory J. Personality Assess. 84(3), 261–270 (2005). https://doi.org/10.1207/s15327752jpa8403_05
24. McCrae, R.R., John, O.P.: An introduction to the five-factor model and its applications. J Pers. **60**(2), 175–215 (1992). https://doi.org/10.1111/j.1467-6494.1992.tb00970.x
25. Diamond, L., Tondello, G., Marczewski, A., Nacke, L., Tscheligi, M.: The HEXAD gamification user types questionnaire: background and development process (2015)

Human-Computer Interaction Challenges and Opportunities in the Arab World Design Education

Reejy Atef Abdelatty Mikhail$^{(\boxtimes)}$ (iD)

Design Department, Politecnico di Milano, Milan, Italy
`reejyatef.mikhail@polimi.it`

Abstract. The Arab world is constantly evolving in the field of human-computer interaction. However, HCI's involvement in design education in Arab institutions faces many different challenges than in the West. A single disciplinary study, industry-academia separation, Arabic language, and limited HCI research resources are seen as major barriers to HCI integration, backed by examples of the Egyptian education system. This poster proposes five solutions to be implemented in the Arab world to help introduce HCI concepts and principles to students, academia, and industry researchers. These solutions encourage improving interdisciplinary collaboration, increasing awareness of the importance of HCI education, creation of research databases for students and researchers, policies and activities organization, improving teaching systems, and discovery of language opportunities. The adoption of such solutions creates an environment in which the corporate sector, philanthropy, and the general public can all contribute to general academic education and research, especially HCI-related projects.

Keywords: Arab World · Human-Computer Interaction HCI · Design Education · Interdisciplinary Studies · User Experience

1 Introduction

The Arab world, which stretches from the Atlantic coast of northern Africa in the west to the Arabian Sea in the east, and from the Mediterranean Sea in the north to Central Africa in the south, is one of the world's most strategic domains. With numerous religious, ethnic, and linguistic groups inhabiting the same region, the Arab World is rich in diversity. Apart from speaking the same language, Arab countries have a common history that is dominated by early colonialism [1].

Another distinguishing trait of this region is devotion to cultural values that range from traditional as in Saudi Arabia to modern and secular as in Lebanon. Since the Arab Spring, there has been a growing interest in the Arab world's use of technology, as seen by the involvement of social media in the Arab uprising [2]. Finally, the region's rates and ratios of technology adoption were influenced by economic activity and growth. Consider that Saudi Arabia ranks eighth in the world in terms of social media accounts per capita [1].

© The Author(s), under exclusive license to Springer Nature Switzerland AG 2022
C. Stephanidis et al. (Eds.): HCII 2022, CCIS 1654, pp. 180–187, 2022.
https://doi.org/10.1007/978-3-031-19679-9_23

In the realm of Human-Computer Interaction, the Arab world is always evolving (HCI). However, in the context of the Arab World, this development faces a particular set of challenges that are distinct from those in the West. HCI is a multidisciplinary field that encompasses behavioral sciences, computer science, and design. The Arab World's design educational system, on the other hand, is not interdisciplinary in nature. As a result, numerous examples of user experience (UX) research and design practices research in HCI contexts have been found outside of academia, such as in non-governmental organizations (NGOs), Fabrication Labs, and digital media civil society activity.

In this position poster, the roots of the main HCI challenges in the Arab world are explored, and some practical solutions are given for the future to bring the HCI field closer to academics and, eventually, closer to local communities across the Arab World. The challenges and solutions have been explored through four lenses which are the education system, language, research, and industry (see Fig. 1).

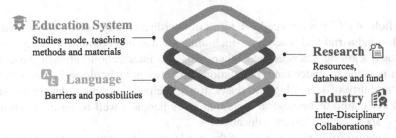

Education System
Studies mode, teaching
methods and materials

Language
Barriers and possibilities

Research
Resources,
database and fund

Industry
Inter-Disciplinary
Collaborations

Fig. 1. Research lenses for exploring HCI challenges and opportunities

2   HCI and the Future of Education

The OECD has recently provided an educational model that attempts to show the relationship between knowledge, skills, attitudes, values, and competencies. Knowledge, skills, attitudes, and values are considered intertwined and interact to develop actionable competencies [3]. Competency is not limited to the acquisition of knowledge and skills. It involves mobilizing knowledge, skills, attitudes, and values to meet complex needs [4] (see Fig. 2).

Students will require broad and specialized knowledge to be future-ready. Disciplinary knowledge, as well as the ability to think across fields and "connect the dots," will continue to be critical. Understanding how something is done or manufactured – the sequence of processes or actions taken to achieve a goal – is how procedural knowledge is acquired. Some procedural knowledge is domain-specific, whereas others can be transferred between them. Design thinking and systems thinking are two methods for developing it [4]. Education's aims have shifted as a result of this focus on these characteristics. As teachers and students become more familiar with digital literacy development tools, pedagogy has evolved as well [5].

Different global aspects, such as economics and entrepreneurship, globalization, migration, and changes in labor needs, have a substantial impact on education reform goals. These educational goals provide an overview of the necessity of interdisciplinary approaches in educational systems in order to meet the social, economic, and industrial needs of the twenty-first century. Furthermore, accomplishing these aims will need a focus on collaboration between the public sector and civil society, the commercial sector, philanthropy, and foreign affairs.

Fig. 2. The future of education and skills: OECD education 2030 framework

The field of HCI has emerged as a result of interdisciplinary research work in different fields—industrial and academic—including engineering, computer science, design, psychology, learning sciences, and others [6]. The intersection between these fields makes it possible to understand the relationship between technology, human behavior, and the usability of technology products. It also helps in planning, designing, studying, and evaluating technological tools that serve people's well-being in different life practices (sport, health, leisure, education).

This interdisciplinary is a result of the needs of the industry on one hand, and the needs of researchers from all these fields to collaborate for the sake of developing research-based products that are relevant to daily life uses and solve real-world problems [7].

3   The Arab World's HCI Design Educational Challenges

HCI has a particular set of challenges in the context of the Arab World. While some of these issues are shared by all educational systems, others are particular to the Arab world.

3.1   Single Discipline Studies

The lack of multidisciplinary programs in HCI design education poses a global challenge to students seeking rich instruction in a sector that is rapidly evolving and growing [8]. In the Arab World, design education is more traditional. Colleges and universities, for example, are notorious for their lack of collaboration, and majors and specialties are often divided. It draws clear borders between engineering and science and the humanities, resulting in engineering and science students undervaluing humanities courses putting HCI research on the back burner [9, 10]. Humanities research in the Arab world is primarily undertaken in Arabic and is not often archived online, in contrast to Engineering, where English is the predominant language of instruction [2].

In addition, the efforts of HCI educators are exacerbated by several challenges, including the lack of a localized HCI curriculum that addresses contextual details, such as low literacy rates and limited access to technology. In addition, educators suffer from overcrowded classrooms and a lack of opportunities for proper professional development. They also teach using educational resources that are not written in their native language and do not address the details of non-Western culture [11].

3.2 Industry and Academia Disconnection

The public and private sectors work separately from academia and rarely communicate. This limits multidisciplinary research, which is critical in an area like HCI. There are a few examples of philanthropy and tech businesses supporting the co-development of initiatives in academia, for example. Collaboration between corporations and universities is critical for discovering new ways to promote science, design, and education. Businesses will be able to build models or goods that bring them greater profit, while research, knowledge, and education advance. Furthermore, multidisciplinary and collaborative approaches provide a new set of tools and lay the foundation for innovation, which we believe has technical and strategic benefits for both businesses and universities [12].

3.3 The Arabic Language: Its Linguistics and Digitalization

In the Arab world, there are also linguistic challenges. There are substantial distinctions in colloquial dialects throughout the Arab world, and Arabic is separated into literary and colloquial languages. The quality of digital content is influenced by many of these languages. Algorithms that can recognize and distinguish dialects should be built in order to improve digital material. The usage of literary dialects as the primary dialect has hampered the creation of more user-friendly information. This is a fact that must be acknowledged and embraced in order to improve digital content that is appropriate for Arabic-speaking consumers in various regions with various slang dialects [12].

3.4 Limitations of HCI Research Resources

According to the CHI metric, the number of Arabs who have attended CHI conferences in the last four years is so limited. This covers the percentage of publications by Arabic-related scholars and the presence of Arab researchers on the Program Committee as members and/or peer reviewers. Over the last two years, Arab countries' research has been confined to five papers in partnership with international laboratories at the CHI conference [1].

Due to a multitude of challenges associated with HCI education, Arabs are underrepresented in HCI research. Lack of multidisciplinary research is one of them, and collaboration is difficult for engineers and computer scientists who have never conducted qualitative or ethnographic research. The lack of such research methodologies conducts design-based research, assesses, and incorporates users in the design process, which can contribute greatly to the creation of effective HCI techniques. This results in resource limitations (so-called participatory design).

The existing publications, on the other hand, are primarily published in unknown or low-ranking journals. There are various frameworks or models for designing in Arabic, however, they have not been tested and require further research. Unfortunately, fresh academics create new frameworks rather than validating or studying current frameworks. Furthermore, research that provides recommendations for systems or algorithms for Arabic searches is limited [13].

Additionally, researchers who desire to use well-known participatory methodologies face problems such as over-centralized institutional structures imposing top-down research agendas, the lack of ethical committees, and the unappreciated importance of citizen involvement and participation. Finally, when it comes to HCI projects, budgets are limited. As a result, graduate students or post-docs are more likely to interact with the CHI community while abroad [2].

4 Egypt's Challenges as a Case Study

One of the key challenges facing HCI research and practice in Egypt, for example, is the technical community's lack of awareness of the present body of HCI knowledge [4]. To explore and better understand the issues they confront, semi-structured interviews were conducted by a group of researchers with some of the pioneers in the HCI sector in both academia and industry. Participants came from all backgrounds and had varying levels of formal education, with the majority holding master's, Ph.D., and MBA degrees. The lack of awareness and knowledge of the sector is a significant issue, according to all participants, since few managers recognize its value [14].

They also emphasized the importance of public and private training institutions in supporting HCI. It is also frequently difficult to obtain necessary information. For example, one participant stated that it was difficult to obtain authorization to test an intervention inside the educational framework of a university during her master's studies. Many teachers were opposed to testing or data collection in their classes because they believed the researchers were spying on them. This could be due to Egyptian culture's high "uncertainty avoidance," in which people are wary of danger, such as the chance of an observer misusing observational data or breaking confidentiality pledges [14].

For exploring what challenges undergraduate students faced when it came to HCI research, a survey was prepared and circulated in previous research among students in order to determine where they were having difficulties with their studies. They stated that HCI is becoming more prominent in their colleges and that more individuals are becoming interested in the topic. They did agree, however, that lab and field investigations are the most difficult due to a lack of effective recruitment routes and compensation mechanisms. They also stated that it is more difficult to find participants for long-term testing and evaluations in which they must appear multiple times [14].

5 Recommendations and Future Research

5.1 Enhancement of Inter-disciplinary Collaborations

In the Arab world, HCI has enormous potential. This field has the potential to address the difficulties associated with encouraging interdisciplinarity in higher education. Individuals have the capacity to make a significant change in the world through education and the development of cross-border contacts, not only inside the country but also between academic subjects and professions. With research projects, both the technology industry and academics must collaborate. User experience research (UX), for example, is undervalued in the academic discipline of communication, but this form of study can substantially aid in the understanding of HCI.

To facilitate collaborations, three ecosystem-related solutions are proposed: (a) Involving industry IT and UX specialists in the development and research design process. (b) Developing relationships with philanthropies. (c) Integrating design-based research and participatory design by including civil society and the public sector (For example Citizen Science, Sensr Project [15], Designing for Syrian Refugees, Health Applications for Refugees [16], Digital Storytelling Workshops [17], Design and Participation Patterns in Makerspaces and FabLabs [18].

5.2 Raising Awareness of the Importance of HCI Education

At the grassroots level, changing the status quo of HCI design education entails raising awareness of its importance to society and developing a curriculum for local HCI teachers [19]. Two communities have emerged in African and Arab nations in recent years that fulfill these two purposes by arranging events to improve local HCI research and practice; the events also address cultural challenges [1, 20]. A change in local HCI design education programs would also necessitate a culture shift by developing solutions that address the issues educators experience in their classrooms, which is more than simply establishing a curriculum based on recognized standards and exams [21]. Educators adopting a reflective practice is a critical enabler for such a shift in learning about best practices "in context" [11].

In both interviews and a survey done in recent research, participants have been asked to offer solutions to these issues. They claimed that raising awareness of the relevance of the HCI field is the first step toward making all other solutions work. Seminars and workshops in both industry and academics could be used to accomplish this. Collaboration between industry and academia would also be advantageous in terms of new recruitment and feedback channels [14].

5.3 Research Database, Guidelines, and Activities for Researchers

A database of existing works and scholars engaging in this field of study is needed. This can be accomplished through a crowdsourcing effort that will help to foster community among researchers. It is critical to hold workshops to discuss HCI design research and education in the Arab world, as well as to publish the material provided at these workshops. Researchers should also look into making recommendations for search systems and algorithms, as well as building or modifying existing ones to make them more useful for Arabic searches [13].

5.4 Educational System Improvement

Students in HCI should be taught using real-life examples or contemporary websites and apps so that they can improve or criticize them. It is critical to have HCI materials that are appropriate for the Arab world. Students must comprehend the significance of involving users at various levels. Students should also be taught about the necessity of usability principles and testing [13]. It is necessary to create and develop guidelines and standards for designing interactive systems. Previous research [22] has also suggested this. Furthermore, researchers might collaborate to collect and generate materials that could aid in the improvement of present systems and the development of well-designed systems [13].

5.5 Linguistic Opportunities

Finally, while the linguistic challenges outlined above offer a barrier to the current state of HCI in the Arab World, they hold considerable promise for developing powerful AI and machine learning systems. Such methods could someday be incorporated into designs that appeal to a wider range of people.

6 Conclusion

This position poster briefly describes the current state of HCI's involvement in design education in the Arab world. The obstacles discussed should not be seen as a hindrance to the development of this field, but as a stepping stone to opportunities for creativity, interdisciplinary collaboration, and scientific and educational contributions. Political instability in some Arab countries should not be seen as deterrence. Existing technologies enable cross-border collaboration and open up the possibility of creating the coveted "educated design" that equitably supports the development of research and education around the world.

References

1. Alabdulqader, E., Abokhodair, N., Lazem, S.: Human-computer interaction across the Arab world, pp. 1356–1359 (2017)
2. Alabdulqader, E., et al.: With an eye to the future: HCI practice and research in the Arab world1. In: Extended Abstracts of the 2019 CHI Conference on Human Factors in Computing Systems, Glasgow, Scotland, UK, p. Paper W02. Association for Computing Machinery (2019)
3. Lucas, B.: International perspectives on how education offers solutions to tackle skills mismatches and shortages (2018)
4. Co-operation, O.f.E., D.D.f. Education, and Skills, The future of education and skills: Education 2030, p. 21. OECD, Paris (2018)
5. Ananiadou, K., Claro, M.L.: 21st Century Skills and Competences for New Millennium Learners in OECD Countries (2009)
6. Zimmerman, J.: Position Paper on Design in HCI Education. Human-Computer Interaction Institute (2003)
7. Mubin, O., Alnajjar, F., Arsalan, M.: HCI research in the Middle East and North Africa: a bibliometric and socioeconomic overview. Int. J. Hum.-Comput. Interact. 1–17 (2021)
8. Churchill, E.F., Bowser, A., Preece, J.: The future of HCI education: a flexible, global, living curriculum. Interactions 23(2), 70–73 (2016)

9. Lazem, S.: A case study for sensitising Egyptian engineering students to user-experience in technology design. In: Proceedings of the 7th Annual Symposium on Computing for Development, Nairobi, Kenya, Article no. 12. Association for Computing Machinery (2016)

10. Lazem, S., Dray, S.: Baraza! human-computer interaction education in Africa. Interactions **25**(2), 74–77 (2018)

11. Lazem, S.: Championing HCI education to CS undergraduates at a grassroots level: a case study in Egypt. J. Usability Stud. **15**(1), 8–22 (2019)

12. Areej Mawasi, S.Z.: Human-computer interaction in the Arab world: challenges and opportunities. In: 2017 Design4Arabs Workshop at DIS 2017 - Designing Interactive Systems, UK (2017)

13. Alarfaj, A.: Challenges and opportunities in designing interactive systems in the Arab region (2019)

14. Galal-Edeen, G.H., et al.: HCI of Arabia: the challenges of HCI research in Egypt. Interactions **26**(3), 55–59 (2019)

15. Kim, S., Mankoff, J., Paulos, E.: Sensor: evaluating a flexible framework for authoring mobile data-collection tools for citizen science. In: Proceedings of the 2013 Conference on Computer Supported Cooperative Work, San Antonio, Texas, USA, pp. 1453–1462. Association for Computing Machinery (2013)

16. Talhouk, R., et al.: Refugees and HCI SIG: the role of HCI in responding to the refugee crisis. In: Proceedings of the 2016 CHI Conference Extended Abstracts on Human Factors in Computing Systems, San Jose, California, USA, pp. 1073–1076. Association for Computing Machinery (2016)

17. Sawhney, N.: Voices beyond walls: the role of digital storytelling for empowering marginalized youth in refugee camps. In: Proceedings of the 8th International Conference on Interaction Design and Children, Como, Italy, pp. 302–305. Association for Computing Machinery (2009)

18. Bar-El, D., Zuckerman, O.: Maketec: a makerspace as a third place for children. In: Proceedings of the TEI 2016: Tenth International Conference on Tangible, Embedded, and Embodied Interaction, Eindhoven, Netherlands, pp. 380–385. Association for Computing Machinery (2016)

19. Stachowiak, S.: Pathways for Change: 10 theories to inform advocacy and policy change efforts. The ORS Impact (2013)

20. Bidwell, N.J.: Decolonising HCI and interaction design discourse: some considerations in planning AfriCHI. XRDS **22**(4), 22–27 (2016)

21. Fullan, M.: Change theory as a force for school improvement, pp. 27–39 (2007)

22. Alsadi, A., Parry, D., Carter, P.: Usability considerations for educational tablet applications using an Arabic interface (2014)

A Novel System Based on a Smart Toy Responding to Child's Facial Expressions: Potential Use in Early Treatment of Autism Spectrum Disorders

Francesco Montedori[✉], Francesca Romana Mattei, Beste Özcan,
Massimiliano Schembri, Valerio Sperati, and Gianluca Baldassarre

Institute of Cognitive Sciences and Technologies, National Research Council of Italy,
via San Martino Della Battaglia 44, 00185 Roma, Rome, Italy
francesco.montedori@istc.cnr.it
http://www.istc.cnr.it

Abstract. We present the first working implementation of a novel technological system, potentially helpful in the early intervention of Autism Spectrum Disorders (ASD), to reinforce some basic social competencies in children. The system, composed of several components, allows an interactive toy to produce rewarding outputs (as coloured lights and amusing sounds), in response to specific child's facial expressions relevant for social interaction, like a smile or eye contact towards the therapist. The toy rewarding patterns could be used in future tests to improve the social engagement between an ASD child and the therapist. The system relies on a wearable camera, arranged on the therapist's chest, which captures frontal images of the child during play activities, and sends them to a central computer; this unit extracts, through standard computer vision algorithms, relevant social information from the child's face; finally, the information is sent to the interactive toy which accordingly produces rewarding outputs. The prototype was successfully tested in a lab environment. The real-time communication between the various components, all based on wireless technology, proved to be reliable for a field test, which is planned to be run in the next months in actual therapy sessions involving ASD children.

Keywords: Autism Spectrum Disorders · Interactive technology ·
Early intervention · Neural network · Computer vision · PlusMe ·
Transitional Wearable Companion

1 Introduction

Autism Spectrum Disorders (ASD) are a set of neurodevelopmental conditions characterised by important life-long behavioural impairments, mainly in social interaction, which is generally limited or atypical [1]. Early intervention (possibly before the complete onset of the symptoms, in early childhood) proved to be beneficial to ameliorate the severity of the condition through behavioural activities aiming to reinforce social competencies [5,16].

In this respect, devices exploiting new technologies (e.g., robotics, interactive toys, virtual reality, tablet Apps based on Artificial Intelligence) demonstrated to be particularly interesting tools, since they improve children's engagement during therapeutic activities [4,15]. Although their usage in clinical settings is generally still experimental, interactive technologies — by providing interesting feedback for ASD children and therefore eliciting a high degree of motivation — can be used to promote and train the development of key social skills as imitation, eye contact, and joint attention.

Within this promising research field, we present a novel prototype system that provides an interactive soft toy, the Transitional Wearable Companion *PlusMe* specifically designed for early ASD treatment [10], with a novel capability. In particular, the new system allows the *PlusMe* to respond to *socially relevant* child's facial expressions (e.g. smiling or looking *towards* the therapist) producing rewarding outputs as amusing sounds and coloured lights. The main contribution of the work is the particular integration of the multiple system components, and the solutions developed to support their wireless communication, that allow the system to smoothly process and elaborate the continuous stream of camera data thus making them usable online. These features make the system usable for applications as those required by ASD children therapy where both the camera/therapist should be able to freely move in the environment. For example, the system could be used to enhance the child's involvement in the therapy play-based activities by reinforcing the child-therapist eye contact through online reinforcing reactions of the *Plusme*.

In the next sections, after a brief overview on the related works Sect. 2), we first describe the functioning of the system, and in particular all the set of solutions we devised to allow a smooth wireless-based online functioning of the system (Sect. 3); we then illustrate the tests we run to validate the system and show its potential for therapeutic use. Finally (Sect. 4), we foresee possible improvements to overcome the current limitations of the system and enhance it for a future field test with ASD children.

2   Related Work

In this section we provide a brief overview of the use of technological toys as support tools in therapy activities (Subsect. 2.1), and about the use of Computer Vision in ASD research (Subsect. 2.2). Both research fields are relevant for the proposed system.

2.1   Interactive Toys for ASD Research

Smart toys have been developed for early ASD intervention in several promising works. Here we do not focus on classical, complex robots, characterised by many degrees of freedom and many interesting features: such devices, because of their intrinsic complexity, generally require the intervention of specialised researchers and complex settings [2], a practical side that still limits their use. Rather we bring attention to simpler — yet still interesting — interactive devices, able to arouse curiosity and engagement in ASD children.

Keepon [7] is a small funny robotic toy able to orient its gaze to a child's face; this behaviour was shown to intrigue the children, who in turn learn to look back at *Keepon* eyes, thus stimulating the eye contact behaviour (although towards an artificial agent). *COLOLO* [9] is a set of two paired, wirelessly connected spheres, able to sense the user's manipulation and produce rewarding visual feedback when certain rules of manipulation are respected; this feature is designed to support social games involving child and therapist (each one handling one sphere), based on *turn-taking*, an ability often impaired in ASD. *PlusMe* [13] is a soft sensorised panda, which produces coloured lights and sounds when touched on the paws; since the toy behaviour depends on both the child (who touches the paws and trigger the sensory outputs) and the therapist (who can select the colour hue and the type of sound through a control tablet), this *shared* control can stimulate some social interactions from the child towards the therapist, to obtain a *desired* output.

In the current work, we have used the *PlusMe*[1], since its technical characteristics are suitable to the requirements of the proposed system. More specifically we provided the toy with the novel ability to produce rewarding feedback in response to socially relevant facial expressions, a feature relying on Computer Vision and Machine Learning.

2.2 Computer Vision for ASD Research

In the current state of the art, there are several reports about the development of computer vision approaches in autism research [3]. To date, computer vision shows reliable performances, comparable to a human analyst, in analysing different ASD children's behaviour [11]. The performance rate increases further by moving to deep learning techniques, compared to traditional computer vision approaches [8]. A challenge met here is the comparison of the performance of the eligible techniques due to the lack of standard datasets usable for benchmarking deep learning systems [14]. Overall, however, computer vision approaches seems to be usable to identify and quantify autistic behaviour, in particular by supporting the development of non-invasive, objective, and automatic tools for ASD therapy and research [6].

3   The Proposed System

The integrated system we developed can be used for multiple applications needing to (a) collect a video streaming through a camera (b) communicate it wirelessly to a computer that has the sufficient computational power to perform the

---

[1] A video about *PlusMe* features is available at the link https://vimeo.com/259130096.

online computational-intensive processing needed by facial expressions, and (c) broadcast the information on the detected expression to downstream devices that use such information. In the particular application to the *PlusMe*, considered in detail here, the information on the detected facial expression is broadcasted to a tablet with which the therapist can control and monitor the *PlusMe*: this information can be used by the terapist and/or sent to the *PlusMe* to support its reactions to the child's behaviour.

3.1   Architecture

The whole system is composed of the following components (Fig. 1):

- A webcam wired to a self-powered *Raspberry Pi 4* board, whose goal is to record a user's face; in the application to the *PlusMe*-based therapy, the webcam-board will be worn by the therapist on the chest and the webcam will point to the child's face.
- A central computer, in charge of processing the video and performing the Facial Expression Recognition (FER); this component hosts the the bulk of the computational power and memory is concentrated, ensures a smooth online processing of the video streaming and its storing when needed.
- The downstream device using the outcome of the face processing. In the application considered here this is the *PlusMe* toy and its control tablet.

Since the system should be usable in dynamic scenarios, as those involved in play-based therapy, the interaction between the three components is based on wireless communication to ensure a maximum freedom of movement in space to the users and elements, for example the therapist carrying the camera and the *Plusme*/tablet using the processed information.

The communication protocols and the main contents of data exchange are listed below (the same order outlined in Fig. 1 is used):

- The *Raspberry* board sends the video captured by the webcam to the central computer, using the ZeroMQ TCP/IP protocol[2], which is a common protocol relying on a wireless Internet connection. The video stream was set to provide a frame resolution of 480×480 pixels, and a speed of 14 Frame Per Second (FPS);
- The central computer, when a face is detected, performs FER on the received image and categorises the user's expression in 3 classes (namely *Negative, Positive, Neutral*). Then, it sends the detected class information to the *PlusMe* control tablet, via BLE protocol. Details about FER implementation are given in the next Sect. 3.2;
- The control tablet acts then as a bridge and broadcasts the information to the *PlusMe* device, which produces a rewarding pattern in case of detection of a positive facial expression. For this purpose, both the control App and the toy firmware have been partially rewritten.

---

[2]   https://zeromq.org.

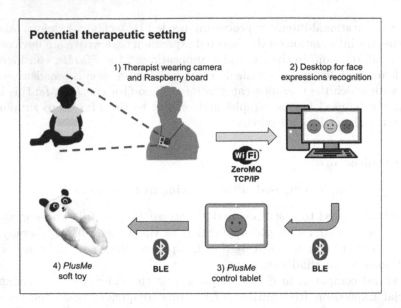

Fig. 1. System architecture as it could be employed in a therapeutic setting: when an interesting child's facial expression (e.g., a smile towards the therapist) is detected by the camera arranged on the therapist's chest, the interactive toy *PlusMe* produces in real-time a rewarding feedback (e.g., coloured lights and sounds). Computer vision processing is provided by a central computer running in real-time the *face traits* analysis; wireless data flow is supported by Wi-Fi (from Raspberry to central computer) and Bluetooth Low Energy (from central computer to control tablet and from tablet to toy).

The speed of the system depends both on the quality of the Internet connection and on the specifics of the machine where the algorithms run. We achieved a speed of 14 FPS using an Asus gaming laptop (Intel core i7 10th generation and NVIDIA RTX 2080 Super GPU) and being connected to the GARR national network[3].

Our test shows how this performance is indeed enough to make the toy respond in real-time to facial expressions (Fig. 2). A brief video demo is available at the link https://bit.ly/3z2bUli. For sake of clarity, in the video the toy changes colours according to all three detected emotions.

3.2   Implementation of Facial Expression Recognition

The real-time FER algorithm, processing the webcam images, is performed using a Neural Network (NN) whose output is a vector that describes the probability associated with each one of the six emotions (happy, sad, surprise, disgust, fear, anger) plus neutral. The element of the vector with the highest probability corresponds to the emotion that better reflects the user's expression at that moment.

---

[3] https://www.garr.it/en/infrastructures/network-infrastructure/our-network.

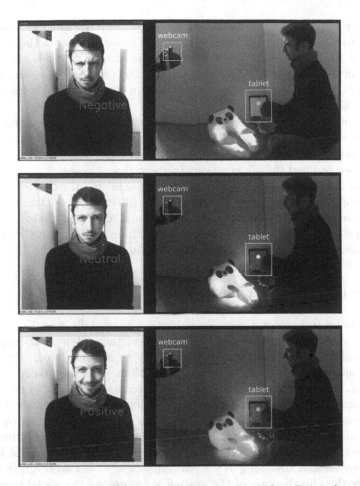

Fig. 2. Three frames extracted from the demonstration video. For each row, the left panel shows the image captured by a frontal fixed webcam (to be worn on the therapist's chest in the future implementation); the panel also displays the detected bounding box, the selected facial landmarks and the detected facial expression, as processed by FER algorithm. The right panel presents the experimental setup; for sake of clarity, *PlusMe* changes colour according to all three detected emotion.

Specifically we used a customised convolutional multilayer network, featuiring a new type of architecture called Amending Representation Module to deal with the padding erosion problem as a substitute for the pooling layer [12] . This network has been trained with square cropped images that show only the face of the subjects in order to ignore the background and reduce the noise. For this reason, a face detection algorithm is required to identify the face inside the image and return the bounding box that surrounds it. In this way, we send to the NN only cropped faces, increasing classification accuracy (Fig. 2, left panels).

In order to ensure that FER is performed exclusively when the user's face is frontal to the camera (simulating the child looking towards the therapist), we decided to compute face landmarks[4] on the image. We then calculate the distance between the eye and the temple landmarks on each side, and compute the ratio of these two lengths: this value is used to decide whether a frame should be processed or not.

Since our main purpose is to potentially detect the child's positive engagement, it is enough to identify whether the user's expression corresponds to a positive (happy, surprise), negative (fear, sad, disgust, angry), or neutral emotion; thus we grouped the six emotions in these three classes.

For the training of the NN, we used the general facial expressions dataset (mainly containing adult faces), the Real World Affective State Database - RAF-DB[5]. We are aware this is a potential limitation in an actual clinical setting, as we expect a lower accuracy when the system will be used with ASD children; a possible solution is then discussed in the conclusions.

4   Conclusions and Future Work

We presented a technological prototype system, potentially useful as a support tool in the ASD early intervention. The value of the system is its capacity to collect a video stream, communicate wirelessly to a central computer able to perform computationally heavy processes, like those needed by facial expression recognition, and then to communicate the outcome (wireless) to downstream devices using it. The wireless nature of the communication allows full freedom of movement to the person/devices hosting the camera and of the downstream devices using the facial recognition outcome. Since the lab test described in this work seemed technically feasible, we are now planning to run a pilot test in a real therapy session involving ASD participants aged between 30–48 months, to evaluate the effectiveness of the system in improving the social engagement between the child and the therapist. In such tests, as illustrated in Fig. 1 a wearable webcam will be arranged on the therapist's chest.

We are aware of the various limitations which still characterise the system, in the first place the "goodness" of video data, on which the whole system is based; in this regard, a preliminary test during a therapy session (Fig. 3) is indeed promising, as it shows how the wearable camera position and the concurrent therapist's position (generally sit in front of the child playing with *PlusMe*) are likely to capture the child's face during most of the therapy session.

We then propose further implementations and improvements:

– Concerning the Machine Learning performance, we are going to train the current NN with a new dataset specific for ASD children, the *Multimodal Dyadic Behaviour Dataset (MMDB)*[6]. This should greatly improve the facial

---

[4] https://github.com/vardanagarwal/Proctoring-AI.
[5] http://www.whdeng.cn/raf/model1.html.
[6] https://cbs.ic.gatech.edu/mmdb/.

expressions detection, as MMDB provides behavioural data collected during tabletop play interactions between therapists and ASD children aged 15–30 months (ages comparable to our target). Moreover, with the progress of experimentation, we plan to collect data during the therapy session in order to build our own dataset.

– Concerning the wearable webcam, we are planning to run a new test, placing it on the therapist's head. This new position should increase the probability that, when the child's face is detected as frontal, he/she is likely looking in the eyes of the therapist. Moreover, we intend to replace the standard wearable camera with an action camera (*GoPro* or *Insta360*), that ensures very stable images, even in presence of therapist's natural body movements.

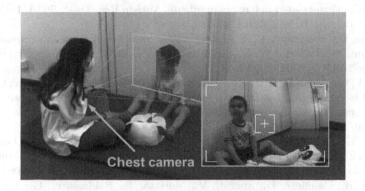

Fig. 3. Example of a typical therapeutic session with *PlusMe*. The box in the right corner shows the video input taken by the therapist's chest camera. The result confirms a good quality of the input image for computer vision tasks, and the feasibility of the proposed system for the next experiments with actual children.

We expect that such new features will improve the system performance and its potential for research on ASD.

Acknowledgments. We wish to thank N. Faedda and G. Cavalli (researchers from the Department of Human Neuroscience, Section of Child and Adolescent Neuropsychiatry, University of Rome *La Sapienza*), and F. Giocondo (researcher from ISTC-CNR) for their help in the preliminary tests about the feasibility of the chest camera.

This work has received funding from the European Union's Horizon 2020 Research and Innovation program under grant agreements No. 945887 (project *PlusMe: Transitional Wearable Companions for the therapy of children with Autism Spectrum Disorders*) and No. 952095 (project *IM-TWIN: from Intrinsic Motivations to Transitional Wearable INtelligent companions for autism spectrum disorder*).

References

1. American Psychiatric Association: Diagnostic and Statistical Manual of Mental Disorders: DSM-5. Washington DC, 5th edn. (2013). https://doi.org/10.1176/appi.books.9780890425596

2. Begum, M., Serna, R.W., Yanco, H.A.: Are robots ready to deliver autism interventions? a comprehensive review. Int. J. Soc. Robot. **8**(2), 157–181 (2016). https://doi.org/10.1007/s12369-016-0346-y

3. de Belen, R.A.J., Bednarz, T., Sowmya, A., Del Favero, D.: Computer vision in autism spectrum disorder research: a systematic review of published studies from 2009 to 2019. Transl. Psychiatry **10**(1) (2020). https://doi.org/10.1038/s41398-020-01015-w

4. Boucenna, S., et al.: Interactive technologies for autistic children: a review. Cogn. Comput. **6**(4), 722–740 (2014). https://doi.org/10.1007/s12559-014-9276-x

5. Dawson, G.: Early Intensive Behavioral Intervention Appears Beneficial for Young Children with Autism Spectrum Disorders. J. Pediatr. **162**(5), 1080–1081 (2013). https://doi.org/10.1016/j.jpeds.2013.02.049

6. Hashemi, J., et al.: Computer vision tools for low-cost and noninvasive measurement of autism-related behaviors in infants. Autism Res. Treat. **2014**, 1–12 (2014). https://doi.org/10.1155/2014/935686

7. Kozima, H., Nakagawa, C.: Social robots for children: practice in communication-care. Int. Workshop Adv. Motion Control AMC **2006**, 768–773 (2006). https://doi.org/10.1109/AMC.2006.1631756

8. Leo, M., Carcagnì, P., Mazzeo, P.L., Spagnolo, P., Cazzato, D., Distante, C.: Analysis of facial information for healthcare applications: a survey on computer vision-based approaches. Information (Switzerland) **11**(3), 128 (2020). https://doi.org/10.3390/info11030128

9. Nunez, E., Matsuda, S., Hirokawa, M., Yamamoto, J., Suzuki, K.: Effect of sensory feedback on turn-taking using paired devices for children with ASD. Multimodal Technol. Interact. **2**(4), 1–18 (2018). https://doi.org/10.3390/mti2040061

10. Özcan, B., Caligiore, D., Sperati, V., Moretta, T., Baldassarre, G.: Transitional wearable companions: a novel concept of soft interactive social robots to improve social skills in children with autism spectrum disorder. Int. J. Soc. Robot. **8**(4), 471–481 (2016). https://doi.org/10.1007/s12369-016-0373-8

11. Rehg, J.M.: Behavior Imaging: Using Computer Vision to Study Autism. Tech. rep. http://www.cbs.gatech.edu

12. Shi, J., Zhu, S., Liang, Z.: Learning to Amend Facial Expression Representation via De-albino and Affinity (2021). http://arxiv.org/abs/2103.10189

13. Sperati, V., et al.: Acceptability of the transitional wearable companion +me in children with autism spectrum disorder: a comparative pilot study. Front. Psychol. **11**, 1–9 (2020). https://doi.org/10.3389/fpsyg.2020.00951

14. Thabtah, F.: Machine learning in autistic spectrum disorder behavioral research: a review and ways forward (2019). https://doi.org/10.1080/17538157.2017.1399132

15. Virnes, M., Kärnä, E., Vellonen, V.: Review of research on children with autism spectrum disorder and the use of technology. J. Spec. Educ. Technol. **30**(1), 13–27 (2015). https://doi.org/10.1177/016264341503000102

16. Webb, S.J., Jones, E.J., Kelly, J., Dawson, G.: The motivation for very early intervention for infants at high risk for autism spectrum disorders. Int. J. Speech Lang. Pathol. **16**(1), 36–42 (2014). https://doi.org/10.3109/17549507.2013.861018

Assistive Technology on Demand (AToD) + Morphic 2.0 - Changing What is Possible with Assistive Technologies and Who Can Benefit

Gregg Vanderheiden[1]([⊠]) [iD], Christopher Walker[2] [iD], and J. Bern Jordan[2] [iD]

[1] University of Maryland, College Park, MD 20740, USA
GreggVan@umd.edu
[2] Raising the Floor – US, Washington, DC 20002, USA

Abstract. Access to and use of computers has become essential for almost all aspects of life. Yet some people cannot use computers directly and need to use an assistive technology. But what if they need assistive technologies to use a computer but don't own a computer? What if the only computers available to them are shared-use computers at their school, the library, or a community program? Or they need to borrow someone else's; their tutor's or gramma's or a friend's? It usually is not possible to install their AT on each of these computers. As a result, the strategies that all of their peers (who don't have their own computers) use to access computers will not work for them. As a result, they have to use the computers without AT (if they can), not use one at all, or only have access to one during some hours in some locations. They are either severely disadvantaged compared to their peers or they are cut off from computers most (or all) of the time and consequently not be able to participate, compete, develop, or exhibit their potential and abilities. To address this, Raising the Floor working with the Trace Center and other researchers has developed a new capability for AT users. Called Assistive Technology on Demand (AToD), the new capability, along with Morphic, allows assistive technologies to appear on any computer an AT user sits down to. The software is now complete and in testing for deployment in universities and disability programs nation-wide.

Keywords: Personalization · Ubiquitous · Assistive technology · Disability

1 Introduction

1.1 Morphic – Part 1 of the Solution

Morphic is a free open-source tool that has been developed to make computers easier for those who use assistive technologies – as well as for those who just have trouble using computers.

© The Author(s), under exclusive license to Springer Nature Switzerland AG 2022
C. Stephanidis et al. (Eds.): HCII 2022, CCIS 1654, pp. 197–201, 2022.
https://doi.org/10.1007/978-3-031-19679-9_25

Computer access is increasingly critical for all aspects of life (education, employment, daily living, health, almost all types of participation). Yet many face barriers due to disability, literacy, or digital literacy. Although the problems faced by individuals with disabilities have received focus for some time, the problems faced by people who just have difficulty in using technologies has not. However, this unrecognized problem is many times larger than most other accessibility barriers. Although Morphic was originally not designed to address this problem, our field placements exposed the magnitude of this problem – and so Morphic's features were expanded to address this as well. We have dubbed this problem "low digital affinity."

1.2 Digital Affinity

Digital affinity is a term we use to refer to innate ability that a person has for learning and using digital technologies. Whereas *digital literacy* is a skill and something that one can acquire (like reading or singing or drawing or athletics), *digital affinity* is a talent (like singing, drawing or athletic talent). Something that a person has a certain amount of – and if they have no talent (are tone deaf, cannot draw, or are naturally neurologically clumsy), they will never be good at something (singing, drawing or athletics).

Often digital affinity is equated with intelligence. There may be some relationship between the two, but it is more like the relationship between height and athletic ability, or breath-capacity and singing. There is some relationship, but they are not closely correlated. There are many short people who are great athletes, and many tall people who have no athletic talent at all. And great breath-capacity does not mean that one can even sing on tune. In the same manner, digital affinity and IQ are not necessarily closely correlated. There are many people who are extremely bright, blazingly brighter than we are, who just can't grasp their technologies or learn new technologies like many of us can.

So just as we need to keep people who are very short in mind when we design things (and people who have very little vision, very little hearing, etc.), we need to keep those who have very little ability to understand and learn technologies in mind as we design our technologies -- especially those technologies that society is now requiring for education, employment, health, and communication.

One of the key features of Morphic is both the ability to make it easier to discover and use accessibility and usability features built into computers – but also the ability to create very simple custom interfaces for basic features and functions of the computer.

1.3 Auto-personalization

A second function of Morphic, and the function it was originally created for, is auto-personalization. Auto-personalization is the ability to have a computer automatically configured for a person when they sit down to it. With Morphic this includes:

- Configuring all of the built-in accessibility features to match user's needs and preferences
- Configuring all of the built-in usability features of the computer to match the user's preferences

- Configuring all of the assistive technologies to match the needs and preferences of the users.

  With Morphic this is accomplished in the following way.

1. The person sets up a computer (that has Morphic installed on it) to match their needs and preferences. This includes installing and setting up any assistive technologies they want or need to use.
2. The individuals then use Morphic to do a 'capture' of all of the settings using the "save setup" command on the Morphic menu.
3. They are asked to sign into their Morphic cloud account (or set one up if they do not have one.) (Morphic accounts are free.)
4. The captured settings are then saved to the cloud using any name the user wants to use to name the setup. (Users can save multiple setups to the cloud and apply any of them at any time to a computer.)

Once this is done, the user can sit down to any other computer anywhere that has Morphic installed on it, sign in, and have that computer and its assistive technologies set up exactly like the original computer.

2 Assistive Technology on Demand (AToD)

2.1 Morphic and AToD

As long as the computer has all of the assistive technologies the user needs on it – the above process works fine. However, if the user sits down to a computer that does not have their assistive technologies on it – the auto-personalization would fall short. It could only configure the software that was on the computer. This is where Assistive Technology on Demand (AToD) comes in.

Assistive Technology on Demand (AToD) is a separate service being developed by Raising the Floor that works with Morphic to set up computers just as the user needs them. With AToD a person can sign into Morphic on a computer as described above. If Morphic determines that assistive technologies that a person needs are not on the computer, AToD will download special installation packages for each of the assistive technologies and install them on the computer. This occurs even if the computer is locked down so that users are not (otherwise) able to install things on the computer. Once all the required assistive technologies are installed on the computer, Morphic then takes over again and configures the assistive technologies to match the user's needs and preferences.

2.2 Installation Security

All of the installation packages are scanned in advance for malware and are signed. In addition, organizations can, if they wish, host the installation packages on their own servers. In this manner the IT departments have complete control of the packages being auto-installed on their computer, as well as the ability to pre-scan them themselves for malware.

Organizations that do not have the ability themselves to do security scans can rely on both the scanning done by Raising the Floor, and the scans done by other larger universities or organizations since the same signed packages are used by all locations. The packages can be hosted at the individual locations or they can be downloaded directly from the central Morphic servers at Raising the Floor (though installations are faster for locally cached packages).

2.3 Benefits of Installation on Demand (IoD)

The IoD service provides a number of benefits to users and organizations:

1. The most obvious is to users who use AT – especially those who do not have their own computer. For the first time they can use AT because it can appear on any computer they are presented with (at school, home, tutor, testing, library, etc.) and any computer they borrow or is loaned to them.
2. For all AT users however it is a benefit, even if they have their own computer. There are always times when they will need to use some other computer; to take a controlled test, because it has special software they need that they cannot install on their computer, because their computer is down, because their computer is not with them, etc.
3. For libraries, it provides an easy way to ensure their computers are accessible. Rather than having to buy many different types of assistive technology in order to have any AT that any of their patrons need, they can pay a flat fee to "borrow" any AT they need at any time, and to "borrow" as many copies they need at any time, to meet the needs of patrons in the library at any time. They also do not need to worry about constantly upgrading AT or figuring out which versions will work on their computers and whichever version of the operating system they are running.
4. For all organizations, AToD represents the first time that people who need assistive technologies can experience true digital equity. AToD, for the first time, lets the organization make all of their computers, in all locations, rooms, labs, and programs accessible to AT users. For the first time an AT user can sit down to any computer that anyone else can and be able to use it (rather than only being able to use one or a few computers in a resource room somewhere in the library – that may not even be available at all hours).
5. It is also the first time that it is practical for organizations to provide access to the full range of assistive technologies rather than just a couple of the most popular.
6. Small libraries or organizations, that see few people with disabilities, and who could not otherwise afford the cost of buying the different AT in case a patron came in, can now afford to make a full spectrum of AT available on all of their computers because it is only installed, and they only pay for it, on the occasion that a patron needs it.
7. Users can purchase their AT through the AToD program and have that AT available not only on their personal computer but also on any other computer (that has Morphic on it and is in a location that supports AToD). Note that that location does not need to pay for AT, and Morphic is free. If they choose to not make any AT available to their patrons, they can still, at no cost, allow users to be able to use their AT on the organization's (e.g., library's) computers.

3   Status to Date

Morphic is now installed in thousands of computers in universities, disability, and reha-bilitation programs across the US. Among the organizations that are installing Morphic on their shared computers across their organizations are the University of Maryland, University of Michigan, Ann Arbor, University of Illinois, University of Wisconsin System, Olympic College, Washington, Guelph University, Canada, Barrie Public Library, Easter Seals of Great Houston, and ServiceSource with programs in 32 states. It is also estimated to be installed on over 1000 individual computers. (Exact counts are difficult since the program can be downloaded and installed free and only those who sign up for accounts are countable.)

The Assistive Technology on Demand (AToD) has now been completed in prototype form and will enter into testing at University of Maryland and University of Michigan this summer – for deployment later in the year. It will be available for demonstration as part of the poster session.

We look forward to feedback and suggestions at HCII, both to the overall concepts and to the implementation.

Acknowledgements. Assistive Technology on Demand (AToD) was created with funding from the grant H133E130028/90RE500 from the National Institute on Disability, Independent Living, and Rehabilitation Research, Administration for Community Living (ACL), Department of Health and Human Services (HHS) and from the Automated Personalization Computing Project (APCP) grant #H421A150006 from the U.S. Department of Education.

Morphic was created with funding from the Automated Personalization Computing Project (APCP) grant #H421A150006 from the U.S. Department of Education, grants H133E080022 and H133E130028/90RE500 from the National Institute on Disability, Independent Living, and Rehabilitation Research, Administration for Community Living (ACL), Department of Health and Human Services (HHS), the European Union's Seventh Framework Programme (FP7/2007-2013) grant agreement n° 289016 and 610510, by the Flora Hewlett Foundation, the Ontario Ministry of Research and Innovation, and the Canadian Foundation for Innovation, by Adobe Foundation and the Consumer Electronics Association Foundation.

This work does not necessarily represent the policy of the funding agencies, and no endorsement by the Funders should be assumed.

Research on the Design of Series Emoticons Based on the User Cognition Experiment

Jiarui Wang[✉] and Ye Qiu

Xi'an Mingde Institute of Technology, Xian, China
wangjiarui1012@foxmail.com

Abstract. Under the background of the Visual Culture, the popularity of emoticons is important evidence of the Pictorial Turn in network communication. Previous research on emoticons mostly focuses on the fields of communication and semiotics, and there remains a blank about the design principle and user habits of emoticons from the perspective of design. Therefore, this paper is trying to explore the design principles of different emoticons via a User Cognition Experiment. Through exploratory statistical analysis methods such as multi-dimensional scale analysis and correspondence analysis, this paper explores corresponding emoticons classification and design principles. With the help of emoticon design principles, this original design practice will help designers do better emoticons design.

Keywords: Emoticon · Cognition experiment · Multidimensional scale analysis · Modeling design · Style characteristics

1 Introduction

With the rapid development of the Internet, people have created various network communication terms as well as visual emoticons. As a supplement and substitute for nonverbal information, emoticons play an important role in emotional sharing in online communication [1]. Emoticons refer to the image or symbol with the function of simulating expression which is an expansion of the forms of network communication. In the process of its development, some images and stickers gradually show a series of common characteristics, which gave birth to the concept of the emoticons package [2]. With commercial success and the lower production threshold of emoticons, a raft of emoticon packs has gradually become the focus of discussion in recent years.

C. Stephanidis et al. (Eds.): HCII 2022, CCIS 1654, pp. 202–216, 2022.
https://doi.org/10.1007/978-3-031-19679-9_26

In this study, 100 emoticon packages are selected as samples from the WeChat emoticon open platform which is the Chinese largest instant message App by subscribers. Then the users with professional knowledge about design are invited to participate in the user cognition experiments. After the data collection, the classification standard of emoticon packages can be figured out through multi-dimensional scale analysis [3]. As it is seeking to figure out the design principle of typical emoticons, this research uses the morphological analysis method to disassemble and encode one sector of emoticons with a cute style. Through deconstructing the overall image into different sub graphic elements, the Researcher tries to explore the impact of different shapes of each part on the perception of the whole emoticon [4].

2 Literature Review

Heidegger, the famous German philosopher, first asserted that human beings would enter the "image age" in 1930 [11]. His claim argues that the world should be evaluated as an image because it marks the essence of modernity [12]. The American scholar W.J.T. Mitchell was the first to put forward the term "pictorial turn". She advocated the image as an important part of cultural studies, and the research scope should not be limited to traditional painting or visual arts. This claim has also become the theoretical foundation of the "picture reading age". There is an emotional reaction with the image communication that people cannot get with the words. Words are abstractions of experience, usually with metaphorical qualities. While the image is a straightforward expression and direct pursuit of visual stimulation. Therefore, Neil Postman pointed out that words are for ideas and images are for entertainment [11]. With the development of the internet and technology, the form of images and pictures are diversified.

Psychologist Albert Melabian once proposed a quantitative formula. He believes that when expressing emotions and attitudes, language itself provides only 7% of the information, and the rest is composed of 38% of voice and intonation and 55% of body movements [1]. Based on the lack of nonverbal information in network communication, the transmission and perception of emotion is a major challenge in the process of network instant messaging. Doris Graber pointed out that human being tended to use characters to convey abstract information, but now this phenomenon has given way to establishing the reality and feelings brought by image communication [7]. The utility of network emoticons is not limited to helping users express their emotions, but also includes other aspects, such as improving communication efficiency and increased interestingness.

On September 19 in 1989, Professor Scott Farman at Carnegie Mellon University first used punctuation to form emoji:-), emoji began to become an important symbol of the Internet age [8]. To ensure that the messages were not misunderstood, scientists at Carnegie Mellon University decided to develop a method to distinguish jokes from other types of informational content [9], the practice of using emojis to symbolize emotion soon became widespread use. This early form of network emoji is a non-verbal symbol that simulates emotions formed by some character combinations and later evolved into small colored anthropomorphic icons. As technology and graphic technology developed, emojis evolved into the popular cartoon stickers that are popular among online chatting users. When a pack of emojis has the same pictorial characteristics, people group them and call them a set of emoticon packages [10]. The Oxford dictionary once included the Internet emoticons that broke tears into laughter into the annual vocabulary for the first time in 2015, which marked the trend that Internet emoticons began to gradually replace text symbols in the process of information dissemination and exchange [5]. Moreover, all the users can participate in the process of creating their pictures and emoticons online. This interactive model of communication sprouts the popularity of emoticons.

3   Research Method and Data Collection

The traditional design process believes that image creation is based on the inspiration of the creator. While this research tries to find a universal principle for the emoticon design through a quantitative research method.

3.1   Sample Acquisition

Firstly, the researcher selects the data sample of emoticons from the WeChat platform, which allows users to upload a complete set of emoticons designed by themselves. 100 emoticons are collected as the stimulus for user cognition experiments (Fig. 1). After deleting the emoticons with high coincidence, the research ultimately gets 49 stimulus emoticons for the cognition experiments.

Fig. 1. Example of emoticon sample

3.2   Correlation Matrix

Users with professional design knowledge are asked to evaluate the similarity of different emoticons and grades from 1 to 9 by their correlation to get the correlation matrix (Table 1). The scoring criteria are based on the professionals' understanding of the emoticon design style. Then the classification of emoticon styles will be extracted via SPSS after analyzing the score results.

Table 1. The correlation score matrix of 49 emoticons (part)

Name of emoticons	Number	1	2	3	4	...	49
Yi Yi	1	1	9	2	5	1	1
The Puff	2	9	1	8	9	8	9
The little pig	3	2	8	1	5	4	3
The cute baby	4	5	9	5	1	4	4
Sweet panda	5	1	8	4	4	1	2
...	...	1	9	3	4	2	1
Clever duck	49	9	1	9	9	9	9

3.3   Code of Emoticon Morphologic

To explore the impact of different emoticon features of each part on the overall style perception, firstly one typical emoticon style is selected (the cute group with 24 samples) and the researcher use the morphological analysis method to disassemble and encode the sector of emoticons within this group (Fig. 2).

Feature Group	Sectors	Number	Description	Illustration	Sample
General look	Head (A)	01	Circle		
		02	Ellipse		
		03	Pear-shape		
	Proportion (B)	04	1 : 1		
		05	1 : 2		
		06	2 : 1		
	Arm (C)	07	Rounded rectangle		
		08	wedge		
		09	Humanoid		
	Leg (D)	10	Rounded rectangle		
		11	wedge		
		12	Humanoid		

a) Coding table of general look

Fig. 2. (a) Coding table of general look; (b) Coding table of constitutions info; (c) Coding table of facial features

Feature Group	Sectors	Number	Description	Illustration	Sample
Constitutions info	Color (E)	13	White		
		14	Grey		
		15	Brown		
	Line (F)	16	penciling lines		
		17	Smooth lines		
	GUI (G)	18	Cubic		
		19	Flat		
	Decoration (H)	20	Accessory	scarf, hat etc.	
		21	Tools	pencil, box	
		22	None		

b) Coding table of constitutions info

Fig. 2. (*continued*)

Feature Group	Sectors	Number	Description	Illustration	Sample
Facial features	Eyes (I)	23	dot (big)	● ●	
		24	dot (small)	··	
		25	cartoon	ၜၜ	
	Blush (G)	26	round (big)	●	
		27	round (small)	●	
		28	ellipse	⬤	
		29	lines	///	
		30	None		
	Mouse (K)	31	line	———	
		32	ellipse	O	
	ears (L)	33	with auricle	A	
		34	without auricle	∩	
		35	None		

b) Coding table of facial features

Fig. 2. (*continued*)

Then 9 users participate in the style perception process and scored on a 9-point scale ranging from "significant negative correlation" to "significant positive correlation" for the cognition experiment (Table 2). Through deconstructing the overall image into different sub graphic elements, the Researcher tries to explore the impact of different shapes of each part on the perception of the whole emoticon through the Chi-square test.

Table 2. Score of cognition experiment for style perception (part)

Users' no	Emoticons' no	Perception score	Head	Arm	Leg	Color	⋯	Line
1	1–1	9	4	9	11	13	16	19
1	1–2	7	2	4	7	10	15	17
⋯	⋯	⋯	⋯	⋯	⋯	⋯	⋯	⋯
1	1–24	3	2	4	7	10	13	17
2	1–1	8	4	9	11	13	16	19
⋯	⋯	⋯	⋯	⋯	⋯	⋯	⋯	⋯
9	1–1	8	4	9	11	13	16	19
⋯	⋯	⋯	⋯	⋯	⋯	⋯	⋯	⋯
9	1–24	4	2	4	7	10	13	17

4 Data Analyze

4.1 Classification and Analysis of Emoticon Style

Based on the correlation matrix data in Table 1, the reliability analysis is done and the value of Cronbach's alpha reaches 0.965, indicating good data reliability (Table 3).

Table 3. Reliability analysis results of correlation matrix

Cornbach's alpha	Items
0.965	49

According to the dendrogram obtained by clustering analysis and artificial clustering results from professional users, 49 emoticons are divided into 11 groups and the description is in Table 4 (Figs. 3 and 4).

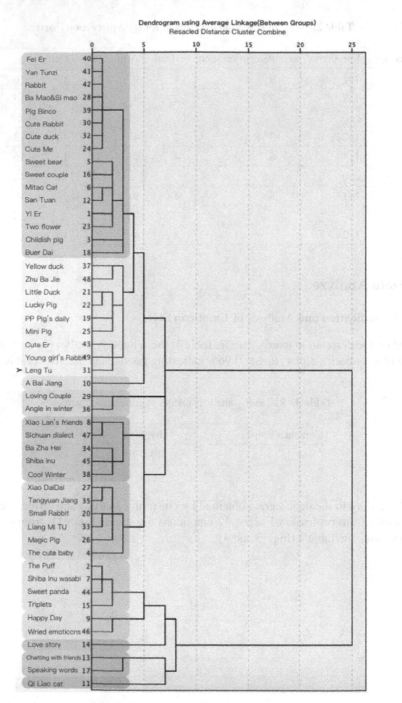

Fig. 3. Dendrogram of emoticons groups

Table 4. Style features and design features of 11 groups of emoticons

Group no	Style	Description
G1	Soft and cute	Animal-shaped such as bears and rabbits. The facial features are blurry, creating a soft feeling, and the color is mainly white
G2	Delicate and cute	Animal-shaped such as bear, pig and duck, with clear facial features and details, with a certain color as the main tone
G3	Abstract and concise	Anthropomorphic, simple stroke modeling, simple lines and colors
G4	Cartoon character	Depicting more details, such as hair, facial expression, etc.
G5	Funny cute type	Design with complex lines and bright colors, expressing emotions in a hilarious way
G6	Small and hilarious	Design with simple lines and colors, small content images and less changes, add words to express emotions
G7	Film and television screenshot	Intercept realistic characters or animals in a variety of shows or photos
G8	Chromatic flower type	Flowers and plants with low pixels, hearts and other shapes, usually accompanied by blessing words
G9	Cartoon couple type	Bust figures similar to QQ show, with rich and gorgeous colors
G10	Text type	All kinds of handwritten or designed fonts, the content is a cyber expression or commonly used short words
G11	Rampant comic style	Mostly exaggerated and mischievous, mostly expressing a sarcastic tone

4.2 General Design Principle for Style Perception

To further explore the design principles of each group of emoticons, taking the soft and cute G1 type emoticon with the largest number of expression packs in the group as an example, nine users are invited to score the differences of 24 emoticons in G1. Due to the different evaluation criteria of each user, the researcher uses the multidimensional scale analysis method based on the optimal scale (PROXSCA). Considering the individual differences, each space is calculated for each distance matrix, and the different weights of different individuals are automatically based on the comprehensive results.

After several times of exploration, it is found that when the dimension is set to 2, the initial stress of the data is 4.9%, the percentage value of dispersion is 0.95, and the overall fitting degree is acceptable (Fig. 5).

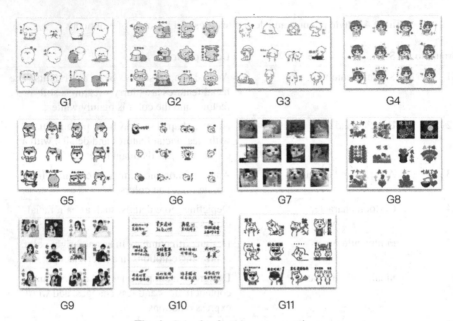

Fig. 4. Samples for 11 group emoticons

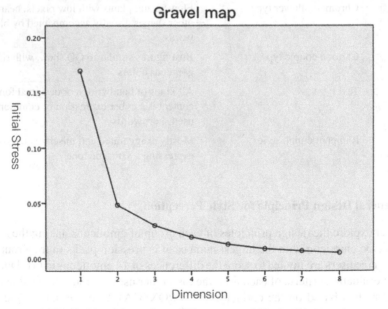

Fig. 5. Plots of emoticons difference matrix in the G1 group

By locating emoticons in the G1 group in two-dimensional space we can get the spatial cognitive map of G1. It can be found that the overall distribution of 12 sets of emoticons is evenly distributed, indicating that there are great differences in the direction of the first and the second dimension (Fig. 6).

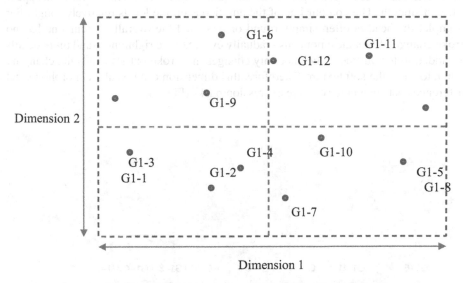

Fig. 6. Cognitive map of emoticons in the G1 group

Projecting the emoticons in the G1 in the first-dimension direction to get the distribution of them in this dimension. It is obvious that the color change from the left side to the right side. On the left side, the color is mainly black and dark brown. When evolving to the right, it can be found that the outline of the expression gradually becomes lighter, and the overall color of the emoticons also tends to be pure white or light pink. Therefore, this dimension can reveal the color changes between cute soft emoticons (Fig. 7).

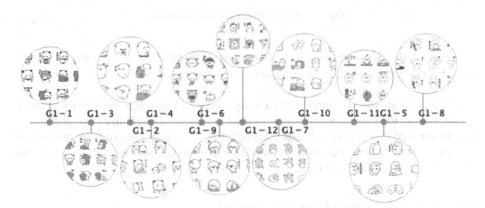

Fig. 7. Changes in the first dimension

Projecting the emoticons in G1 in the second-dimension to get the distribution of them in this direction. The emoticons in this direction have obvious differences in morphology. The emoticons close to the left present a clear outline, while those close to the right appear soft and smooth. The contour line of the emoticons on the left is relatively rough. For example, the head is often simply round or oval, and the overall contour line has no stroke change. When the emoticons gradually evolve to the right, more and more details are added to the outline, which not only changes the stroke but also adds the changing radian to show the soft texture. Therefore, this dimension can reveal the morphological differences between cute soft cute expression packs (Fig. 8).

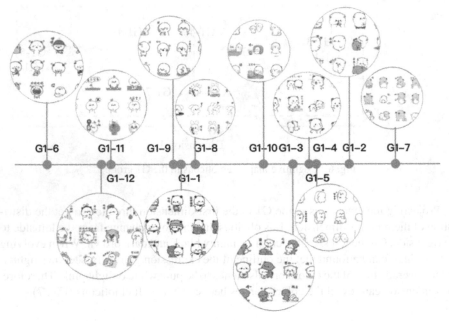

Fig. 8. Changes in the second dimension

Based on the above analysis, it can be concluded that the cute soft emoticons should have the following design features in the overall shape:

(1) The color should be simple, with a unique main color. When the non-white color is used as the main color, the contour color needs to be bright to distinguish.
(2) In terms of shape, the head body ratio of 2:1 or 1:1 is adopted to outline the overall shape with smooth lines, which can add stroke changes and rich radian changes to increase details and soft texture.

4.3 Detail Design Principle for Style Perception

Based on Fig. 2, each emoticon can be divided into 3 parts, namely the general look, constitutions info, and facial features. Through the Pearson's chi-square test of correlation and coefficient table of different parts' perception of the overall modeling, as shown in Table 2, it can be found that Proportion, line type, and ear shape are the three sub-features that most affect the overall style perception (Table 5).

Table 5. Correlation of different shapes and overall cognition

Feature group	Sectors	Coding	Pearson's chi-squared test
General look	Head	A	0.051
	Proportion	**B**	**0.000**
	Arm	C	0.021
	Leg	D	0.025
Constitutions info	Color	E	0.211
	Line	**F**	**0.000**
	GUI	G	0.003
	Decoration	H	0.051
Facial features	Eyes	I	0.057
	Blush	J	0.044
	Mouse	K	0.666
	Ears	**L**	**0.000**

According to the above data analysis, every emoticon style has its own different design principles. Taking the soft cute type as the example in this research, this research summarizes several design guiding principles. When creating a cute lovely emoticon, the basic images should meet the following three criteria:

Rule 1.0: the overall color should be simple and the white color is recommended. When the non-white color is used as the main color, the contour color needs to be bright to distinguish. The shape mostly adopts the head body ratio close to 1:1, and the pear-shaped head contributes the most to the perception of loveliness;
Rule 2.0: the shape of limbs should adopt an oblong shape to represent hands and feet, which reflects the soft and cute texture, and can appropriately increase the facial shadow to create a three-dimensional visual effect. The shape is outlined with smooth lines, and the chances of strokes and rich radians can be added to increase the details and soft texture;
Rule no. 3: dot-shaped eyes and blusher are recommended for the facial feature to increase the perception of loveliness. The details of the ears, body decoration, or auxiliary props can be added to make the image more vivid.

5 Conclusion

With the popularity of visual culture, it is more common for people to choose nonverbal information for online communication, where the emoticons are become more and more important. Emoticons provide a method to visualize the language and information through anthropomorphic elements, which makes up for the lack of being unable to convey nonverbal information in the network environment, enriches the interactive behavior of network social interaction, and improves the efficiency and quality of communication. While most of the research on emoticons is about the field of communication and semiotics, and few people study users' habits in the use of emoticons from the perspective of design. Therefore, this study aims to explore the relevant design principles of emoticons in quantitative methods.

Through cluster analysis, it can be found that the emoticons of the same category have similar design forms. Specific to each emoticon, different detailed design features can distinguish different types of emoticons. It can be found that except for the three groups of G7 (film and television screenshot), G8 (Chromatic flower type), and G10 (text type), the other eight groups have specific anthropomorphic images. Taking the cute and soft emoticons of group G1 as an example, this research summarizes that the cute and soft emoticons should have the following design rules: choose the correct color and shape, add detailed information such as facial features and decorations to increase the perception of loveliness;

When the design pattern conforms to the above rules, the users who prefer the cute and soft emoticons are more likely to like these emoticons. The above methods of exploring specific style design principles can also be applied to the research of other design style rules exploration and can help designers to put forward more operational design principles and do better design work.

References

1. Yuan, K.: Perception and expression in instant messaging: the influence of emotion icons. Ph.D. thesis, Central China Normal University (2014)
2. Liu, S., Pan, Y.: The rise and development trend of network emoticons. J. Beijing Univ. Posts Telecommun. Soc. Sci. Ed. **05**, 12–16 (2017)
3. Zhang, W., Dong, W.: Advanced Course of SPSS Statistical Analysis. Higher Education Press, Beijing (2013)
4. Zhang, H.: Research on modeling design and evolution method of animation toys combined with user preference image. Master thesis, Zhejiang University (2011)
5. Zheng, M.: The popularity of Internet expression package and the turn of discourse space. Friends of Editors, pp. 42–46 (2016)
6. Zhou, Z.: The influence of "expression package" on network public opinion. Audio Visual 118–120 (2017)
7. Brosius, H.B., Unkel, J.: Processing the News: How People Tame the Information Tide. By von Doris A. Graber (1984) Schlüsselwerke der Medienwirkungsforschung (2016)
8. Garber, M.: Today, the Emoticon Turns 30 :-) (2016). http://www.theatlantic.com/technology/archive/2012/09/today-the-emoticon-turns-30/262571/. Accessed January 15
9. Garber, M.: How to Tell a Joke on the Internet (2016). http://www.theatlantic.com/magazine/archive/2013/05/how-to-tell-a-joke-on-the-internet/309293/. Accessed January 13
10. Dimson, T.: Emojineering Part 1: Machine learning for emoji trends. Instagram Engineering Blog (2015)
11. Du, J.: Research on image communication of the WeChat. Reporter, pp. 76–77 (2018)
12. Wang, J.: Research on the WeChat image communication and audience. Master thesis, Yangzhou University (2015)

Empathy Between Designers in the Design Synthesis Stage

Xiuxiu Wu⊙, Kin Wai Michael Siu(✉), and Jörn Bühring

School of Design, The Hong Kong Polytechnic University, Hung Hom, Hong Kong
`21050591r@connect.polyu.hk`

Abstract. Design synthesis is the most challenging stage of the design process because the problem and solution need to be linked to discover the best solution. Designers need to use convergent thinking to ensure the usefulness and practicality of the ideas generated by divergent thinking in other stages. Handling the pressure of an argumentative and judgmental atmosphere is challenging and involves persuasion and compromise to reach a common goal. If not handled properly, this will generate more arguments and increase cognitive pressure, resulting in a diminished design outcome.

Empathy plays an essential role in design research and practice. There are multiple ways to improve designers' empathy involving research techniques, communication skills, and self-reflection. Empathy-related measurement tools or assessment questions are used as assessment criteria when companies recruit and evaluate new product development. While most studies have emphasized end-users, how designers' empathy affects the design process has been seldom explored, particularly in relation to the pressure and disagreements associated with design synthesis. This paper draws upon previous studies to consider the entanglement of empathy among designers during the design synthesis stage and how it affects design outcomes. We conclude that empathy is a way to alleviate pressure in the design synthesis stage, but it compromises the design outcome by putting the spotlight on designers instead of on end-users or on the problem itself. In this regard, designers need to overcome the impulse to alleviate pressure even when under cognitive pressure in an argumentative environment. The reason for this behavior is that convergence based on deliberative reasoning and cooperation is more convincing towards design outcomes.

Keywords: Empathy · Cognitive empathy · Designers · Design synthesis

1 Introduction

Design synthesis is the design stage in which the solution and problem need to be linked. Studies have shown that designers feel the most confusion and intense emotion during this stage [1, 2]. Synthesis requires convergent thinking to narrow down the problem and solution and distill the best insights from divergent thinking. Thus, designers need to use persuasion and compromise to reach a common understanding while under high cognitive pressure. The complicated synthesis process involves selecting and comparing

© The Author(s), under exclusive license to Springer Nature Switzerland AG 2022
C. Stephanidis et al. (Eds.): HCII 2022, CCIS 1654, pp. 217–224, 2022.
https://doi.org/10.1007/978-3-031-19679-9_27

information and results in a contentious and judgmental environment [1, 3]. Designers experience discomfort when encountering controversial design opinions from team members [2]. Managing uncomfortable emotions is crucial to producing rational and valuable design outcomes. At the same time, empathy has been viewed as occupying a central position in design. Empathy in design research involves a comprehensive, empathic understanding of others' experiences including the truthfulness, intimacy, and precepted problem of a particular situation [4]. In human-centered design, empathy is generally considered to be the capacity to stand in others' shoes to feel what they feel and experience. In the Stanford design thinking process, it includes empathize, define, ideate, prototype and test. Empathy is the first stage and has a strong influence on the loop. There are several ways to improve designer empathy as a research technique, as a communication skill, and as a method of self-reflection [5]. In addition, empathy-related measurement tools or assessment questions are applied as criteria for recruiting and evaluating new product development in companies. Building empathy with potential users to understand user desires and needs is considered a crucial early step in the design process [5]. In teamwork, empathy has been proven to reduce conflict between in- and out-group members, facilitating collaboration with different perspectives even in conflict situations [6].

However, the link between designers' empathy toward each other and the design synthesis stage remains inconclusive. Our analysis is based on a vast amount of research on empathy related to design, neuroscience, and philosophy. The study contributes to recent research on empathy and the design process in three ways:

- We show why design synthesis is essential for revealing the transformation from divergent thinking to convergent thinking.
- We demonstrate how empathy between designers becomes entangled during this design synthesis stage, which has unintended consequences.
- We discuss how designers should handle empathy in the design synthesis stage.

We first briefly discuss the design synthesis stage and why it is essential. We then analyze designers' empathy in the design synthesis stage and how it affects design outcomes. We end with a discussion of how the proper operation of empathy can facilitate design.

2 Design Synthesis Stage

Five stages of design thinking have been observed in real design projects: understanding the challenge, synthesizing information to connect the problem with the solution (synthesis stage), generating ideas (ideation), testing with target users, and refining the prototype [1]. Semantic analysis of transcripts has shown that designers have different emotions in the different stages: generally, there is an optimistic atmosphere in the four-stage with positive emotional expression, but there is a sharp decline in the design synthesis stage [1]. Moreover, both experienced and less experienced designers have been shown to feel confused emotions expressed with high pitch voices in the synthesis stage [2].

In the synthesis stage, ideas need to be filtered and organized to match the problem. Designers need to persuade and compromise to reach a consensus on the solution to move to the next stage. Compared with divergent thinking in design thinking, "synthesis" requires convergent thinking to narrow down the problem and scenarios to distill the best insights from primary or secondary research. It is a way to focus on massive amounts of information [1]. Discussion in the synthesis stage involves intuitive thinking and deliberative reasoning to balance the demands of different stakeholders.

Generating ideas is not challenging for designers. Traditional methods such as brainstorming with unlimited post-it notes enable designers to create countless ideas in a short time. The real challenge is how to initiate a good question and a good solution that is inclusive for all related stakeholders.

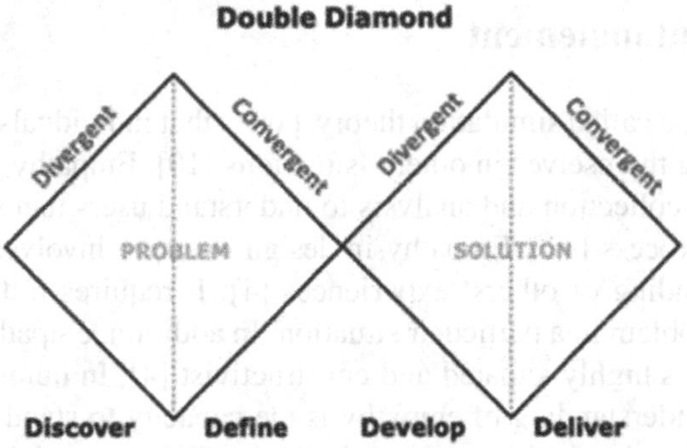

Double Diamond

Fig. 1. Double diamond process developed by Phillip Dyrberg [7]

In the double diamond design process (Fig. 1), divergent thinking is emphasized in the "discover" stage, but convergent thinking is more important in the "define" stage. Similarly, convergent thinking in the synthesis stage, along with a transformation of thinking style, entails the clustering, comparison, and selection of target problems and design ideas, which generates a more contentious and judgmental environment resulting in more contradictions [1, 3]. Designers have been found to show discomfort when encountering controversial design opinions from team members [2]. Handling and weighing these conflicts requires more mental effort than generating new ideas or solutions [1, 8]. This creates a dilemma. Conflict is valuable for generating creative solutions because innovation requires discordance and uncertainty, and indecisive conversation is beneficial for an open and inspirational process [1, 9]. However, conflict makes it difficult to achieve the best performance when defining design challenges and realizing complex solutions, especially given the different backgrounds and personalities of designers.

Designers must overcome uncertainty and suppress a strong desire to alleviate tension. The need for accordance and discordance in the synthesis stage results in emotional fluctuations, and strong emotional involvement can lead to a change in the design frame [2]. How emotions are handled in the synthesis stage differs between designers. Experienced designers tend to leverage emotions to design a better outcome, but less experienced designers tend to detach their emotions from the design process as a way to be professional and objective [2]. Detaching emotions is a way to depersonalize the process and circumvent potential biases. However, experienced designers are advanced synthesizers and demonstrate excellent performance in the synthesis stage [1, 18].

Emotion is essential during the design process. Neither extremely negative nor extremely positive emotions are good for design; mid-level emotional arousal is optimal for changing the design frame [2]. Smoothly transferring from divergent thinking to convergent thinking with a suitable level of emotion is a challenge. Besides, emotional experience drives empathy. In design, empathy has been emphasized as an approach to understanding end-users and a way to generate understanding between team members to solve team conflict [5]. The following section considers how empathy entanglement among designers in the synthesis stage can better tackle conflict, leading to a better design outcome.

3   Empathy Entanglement

Empathy theory, also called simulation theory, posits that individuals can predict others' behavior by putting themselves in others' situations [10]. Empathy can also be considered a way of data collection and analysis to understand users that should exist during the entire design process [11]. Empathy in design research involves a comprehensive, empathic understanding of others' experiences [4]. It requires truthfulness, intimacy, and a precepted problem in a particular situation. In addition, empathy is a specific type of knowledge that is highly situated and constructivist [4]. In human-centered design, a more common understanding of empathy is the capacity to stand in others' shoes to feel what they feel and experience. Empathy is the first stage of the Standford design thinking process and has a powerful influence on the loop. However, studies of empathy in design have focused on empathy with end-users [4–6, 12, 14]. How designers' empathy affects other designers and design outcomes remains uncertain. It is widely accepted that empathy building using methods such as interviews or observation is an essential part of the design process [12]. In addition, empathy is valuable for building a positive connection with customers and for transforming less experienced designers into professional designers [12]. There are two routes to empathy, the mirroring route and the "reconstructive" route [13], which are approaches to "emotional empathy" and "cognitive empathy, respectively [14, 15]. Which strategy will be adopted is based on the specific situation, but both strategies can be inadequate.

3.1   Mirroring Route to Emotional Empathy

The mirroring route involves low-level stimulation, which can occur automatically, even involuntarily. The certain parts of the brain, including the anterior insula and the cingulate cortex, are active both when we feel pain and when we watch someone else feel pain [15, pp.48]. Empathizing with someone in pain activates the same areas of the brain that are activated when directly experiencing pain [15]. Similarly, when team members exhibit anxiety and nervousness, other team members may feel the same emotions. This is part of a dynamic experience in which individuals empathize with others based on the similarity of emotional and physical responses [14]. The mirroring route is based on information-poor inference and does not require much information to build empathy.

If the target is part of the group, the mirroring route is plausible because it saves cognitive effort. Empathy can occur when the target has a similar background in terms of age, gender, hobbies, or beliefs. When individuals attend to only superficial similarities, an inappropriate object will emerge but the differences will not be noticed. The mirroring route is also constrained by neural system differences. As Bloom [15, pp. 50] mentioned, "Watching someone getting slapped in the face doesn't make your cheek burn, and watching someone get a back rub doesn't make your aches disappear. We may feel the pain of someone else in a limited sense, but in another sense, we don't. Relative to real experience, empathic resonance is pallid and weak."

3.2 Reconstructive Route to Cognitive Empathy

The reconstructive route to cognitive empathy requires deliberative effort and is cognitively demanding. It entails taking others' perspectives and replicating their experience [5]. Self-awareness is required to understand and recognize others' thoughts, feelings, and experiences, such as their joy, humiliation, or pride, without necessarily experiencing them. This understanding of cause and effect can generate a profound understanding and guide people to the right decision for long-term benefits [14, 15]. Individuals use deliberative thinking when they perceive an event as distant or when the information is ambiguous [14, 16]. The reconstructive route is an information-rich inference that includes the target's circumstances, context, and background, all of which need to be organized to fully understand the target's mental state.

When using this strategy, the empathic experience will be affected by the information needed to understand the situation fully [15]. Even when sufficient detail is available, complex principles are required to understand others successfully, and observed behavior is caused by many different mental states. This process can involve being misled or defaulting to stereotypes. Stereotypical assumptions can be involved in the empathic understanding of others via how we understand ourselves and make assumptions about others' emotions, values, and knowledge [14]. Confirmation bias, which leads individuals to conform to preconceived ideas by seeking and interpreting information based on pre-existing opinions, is common in both deliberative and intuitive processes in empathy [17]. Moreover, when self-interest is involved, empathy is compromised.

4   Discussion

In the design synthesis stage, empathy is both powerful and problematic [12]. Empathy acts like a spotlight to draw attention to specific individuals, which may lead to excluding the experiences and feelings of the majority of people and ignoring statistical data because in most cases empathy is intuitive and spontaneous [15]. Various laboratory studies have shown that empathy prioritizes concrete targets [15]. If designers empathize with their colleagues in the design synthesis stage, they will pay attention to how team members think, which will ignore other factors essential to the design outcome and end-users. Managing empathy in the synthesis stage is crucial for managing cognitive pressure and conflict because empathy may compromise the design outcome and ignore long-term effects. Empathizing with other designers in the team can quickly lead to consensus because understanding why individuals argue in a certain way makes it easier to accept their statements. This aligns with the finding that empathy reduces conflict between in- and out-group members, facilitating collaboration with different perspectives even in a conflict situation [6]. A team is more harmonious when designers can think from other perspectives. The drawback is that thinking from another perspective can cause the absence of the designer's own perspective, which compromises the design outcome due to inadequate design concepts or ideas [20]. It is difficult to empathize with two people because, by nature, empathy is like a spotlight, as noted above [15]. Therefore, focusing on the design issue itself through deliberative reasoning instead of using empathy to alleviate pressure is essential to generate long-term benefits. Otherwise, the design outcome will be diminished because long-term goals often require inflicting short-term conflicts [15].

Designers need to control their emotional empathy while practicing their cognitive empathy. In this way, team members can understand each other better and consider the real costs and benefits for all stakeholders in the synthesis stage. Letting go of empathy is not easy because it is easier than deliberative reasoning. Empathy is essential to understand the mental state of another person for the benefit of social interaction, but a person who generates stronger emotion and empathy than warranted may behave negatively. They may want to escape the situation by deciding on a quick and easy conclusion. Dealing with empathy requires the wisdom to restrain unconscious impulses. Designers work under intense cognitive pressure in the design synthesis stage, which requires the transformation from divergent thinking to convergent thinking, but working creatively involves continually navigating and negotiating uncertainty and ambiguity [1, 12]. Dealing with ambiguity is an essential part of a creative personality [19]. Processing ambiguous dialogue and scenarios is challenging but necessary for designers.

Last, the convergence of conclusions or judgments in the design stage is not enough to tackle the conflict in the synthesis stage. Reaching an agreed statement is not the goal, as being approved does not necessarily mean being worthy of approval [20]. Agreement confirmed by empathy does not offer a suitable justification for convergence. Thus, convergence based on the deliberative cooperation of designers is more convincing. Convergence is not simply required in the deliberative process, but is a matter of cooperative integration by exchanging information and arguments in discussion, so that the reason is shared [20].

5   Conclusion

Designers can use cognitive empathy to understand others, but more important is to use deliberative reasoning to make a decision. Both emotional empathy and cognitive empathy can be inadequate for understanding others. The design outcome is closely related to the design process, and the design synthesis stage involves the most intense emotions. Empathy is a way to alleviate pressure, but it compromises the design outcome by putting the spotlight on designers instead of on end-users or on the problem itself. In this regard, empathy may mislead moral judgments in the same way prejudice does: it limits resonance with more people and is insensitive to statistical data [15].

To conclude, designers need to overcome the impulse to alleviate pressure even when under cognitive pressure in an argumentative environment. Convergence based on deliberative reasoning and cooperation is more convincing towards design outcomes. In the design synthesis process, it is best to eliminate empathy between team members or use it wisely so that attention can be focused on design issues.

Acknowledgements. We would like to thank the research support of the postgraduate research fund provided by the PolyU. We also acknowledge the support of the Eric C. Yim Endowed Professorship and the partially support of the Wuhan University of Technology.

References

1. Ewald, B., Menning, A., Nicolai, C., Weinberg, U.: Emotions along the design thinking process. In: Meinel, C., Leifer, L. (eds.) Design Thinking Research. UI, pp. 41–60. Springer, Cham (2019). https://doi.org/10.1007/978-3-319-97082-0_3
2. Ge, X., Leifer, L., Shui, L.: Situated emotion and its constructive role in collaborative design: a mixed-method study of experienced designers. Des. Stud. **75**, 101020 (2021)
3. Hollingshead, A.B.: Communication, learning, and retrieval in transactive memory systems. J. Exp. Soc. Psychol. **34**(5), 423–442 (1998)
4. Surma-aho, A., Hölttä-Otto, K.: Conceptualization and operationalization of empathy in design research. Des. Stud. **78**, 101075 (2022)
5. Heylighen, A., Dong, A.: To empathise or not to empathise? empathy and its limits in design. Des. Stud. **65**, 107–124 (2019)
6. Tuomala, E.K.S., Baxter, W.L.: Design for empathy: a co-design case study with the finnish parliament. In: Proceedings of the Design Society: International Conference on Engineering Design, vol. 1, no. 1, pp. 99–108). Cambridge University Press (2019)
7. Double diamond: a design process model. http://wiki.doing-projects.org/index.php/Double_diamond:_A_design_process_model. Accessed 10 May 2022
8. Shehab, H.M., Nussbaum, E.M.: Cognitive load of critical thinking strategies. Learn. Instr. **35**, 51–61 (2015)
9. Christensen, B.T., Ball, L.J.: Fluctuating epistemic uncertainty in a design team as a metacognitive driver for creative cognitive processes. In: CoDesign, Special Issue on Designing Across Cultures, pp. 1–20 (2017)
10. Gordon, R.M.: Folk psychology as simulation. Mind Lang. **1**(2), 158–171 (1986)
11. Segal, L.D., Suri, J.F.: The empathic practitioner: measurement and interpretation of user experience. Proceedings of the Human Factors and Ergonomics Society Annual Meeting **41**(1), 451–454 (1997)
12. Bennett, C.L., Rosner, D.K.: The promise of empathy: design, disability, and knowing the "other". In: Proceedings of the 2019 CHI Conference on Human Factors in Computing Systems (2019)
13. Goldman, A.I.: Joint Ventures: Mindreading, Mirroring, and Embodied Cognition Oxford University Press Oxford (2013). 9780190869564
14. Myllylä, M.: Empathy in technology design and graffiti. In: International Conference on Human-Computer Interaction, pp. 278–295. Springer, Cham (2021). https://doi.org/10.1007/978-3-030-77411-0_19
15. Bloom, P.: Against Empathy: The Case for Rational Compassion, 1st edn. Ecco, an imprint of HarperCollins, New York (2016). ISBN 9780062339348
16. Fuchs, T.: The brain–A mediating organ. J. Conscious. Stud. **18**(7–8), 196–221 (2011)

17. Shannon, S.: Cognitive empathy. In: Maibom, H.L. (eds) The Routledge Handbook of Philosophy of Empathy, p. 2223. New York: Routledge (2017). ISBN 9780367254933
18. Goldschmidt, G., Tatsa, D.: How good are good ideas? Correlates Des. Creativity. Des. Stud. **26**(6), 593–611 (2005)
19. Tracey, M.W., Hutchinson, A.: Uncertainty, reflection, and designer identity development. Des. Stud. **42**, 86–109 (2016)
20. Bianchin, M., Heylighen, A.: Just design. Des. Stud. **54**, 1–22 (2018)

Model Proposal of Designerly Ways of Material Thinking from the Viewpoints of Sustainable Transitions

Ye Yang[✉] [iD], Hongtao Zhou[✉], and Hanfu He

College of Design and Innovation, Tongji University, Shanghai 200092, China
yeyang_design@tongji.edu.cn, lifeisfurniture@gmail.com

Abstract. The history of design education has experienced the progress from materiality to immateriality. Dissociating and alienating from actual materials has become an evident characteristic of current design activities. Physical materials are passively selected or accepted at the end restricted to mass production. However, this fixed status is entering into an indeterminate situation resulting from the increasingly deteriorating ecological problems. An increasing number of designers are beginning to create degradable materials, especially biomaterials or recreate wasted materials in the monodisciplinary or interdisciplinary form at the very beginning of the design process. The paper aims to construct an inquiry to transform the indeterminate situation into the determinate one by reflecting on the Material Thinking among designers for sustainable transitions. We dated back to the origin and nature of Material Thinking, and redefine it in Design. We proposed a new concept of Designerly Ways of Material Thinking, and presented the proposed constructing model from the viewpoints of sustainable transitions.

Keywords: Material thinking · Designerly Ways of Material Thinking · Sustainable transitions · Transition Design

1 Background

1.1 The History of Design Education Tracing Back: From Materiality to Immateriality

Before the renascence of Modern Design, artisans were seen as early designers who actively studied and dialogued with materials, and materials played an essential role throughout the whole design activities [1]. Modern Design emerged in the 1900s based on two practice methods following the Second Industrial Revolution. One was Prototyping, and the other was Drawing or Draftsmanship [2]. The prototyping approach limited the trials within the easily shaped materials that were away from actual physical materials to test the usability of products in a short time. Drawing or Draftsmanship method made the conceiving process get away from hand-making and disassembled a product into parts that could be assembled simultaneously. Both approaches induced Industrial manufacturing processes such as division of labor, assembly line and product assembly,

C. Stephanidis et al. (Eds.): HCII 2022, CCIS 1654, pp. 225–232, 2022.
https://doi.org/10.1007/978-3-031-19679-9_28

which significantly accelerated mass production. At that time, design practice in education started to be separated from manufacturing, breaking away from the practice of traditional artisans, from the active exploration for materials at the very beginning to passive acceptance in the end [1].

In addition, another critical factor in design history to trigger this trend is the movement of scientizing design practice that was popular in the 1960s, e.g., the first 'Conference on Design Methods' held in London in 1962, the Seminar on 'The design methods' held in Birmingham in 1965, etc. Such activities aimed to define a clear, rational and systematic approach to design practice [3]. At that time, scholars saw the process of 'making with materials' as more intuitive and sensitive. The educational reform of Ulm School of Design was the most representative in 1956[4], wiping off the curriculum of focusing on making with materials in Bauhaus [5, 6]and starting to apply mind and soul-oriented scientific methods to design education. After that, with the development of science and technology, in the 1990s, the birth of CAD (Computer-Aided Design) accentuated the immaterial practice further in design education. Furthermore, the rapid development of Artificial Intelligence has strengthened and consolidated the immaterial design process in education since 2000.

1.2 Emerging Phenomena Calling on the Return of Materiality in Design Education

Materials originally come from nature, but it causes great harm and pollution when humans end their lives and discard them in the environment. Since the 21st century, the human-earth crisis has become more severe. The dematerialization of the design process in design education began to be questioned. A series of phenomena have emerged, like Maker Movement, DIY materials, Material-driven Design, etc., showing designers start to explore materials at the beginning of the design process proactively. In this way, the fixed mainstream design education mode that material is selected or accepted in the end is becoming indeterminate [7]. The relationship between designers and materials is changing from passive acceptance to proactive understanding, collaboration and creation.

Through the past research based on the Grounded Theory methodology [8], Ye Yang and Hongtao Zhou studied the reasons behind these phenomena. They explored the differences between the emerging Material-oriented Artefact Design practice (MAD) and the current mainstream Problem-oriented Artefact Design practice (PAD). They demonstrated the unique values of MAD, especially in the era of sustainable transitions. MAD has its special functions not only for the design practice in the post-industrial era but also for changing the relationship between humans and non-humans from hierarchy to flat, which facilitates the progress of ecological civilization.

Given that, in this paper, we tried to follow the discussions before by researching the thinking mode of designers in these emerging phenomena to redefine the relationship between designers and materials in design education and contribute an alternative approach to design practice for sustainable transitions. We proposed the primary research question here: *What is the thinking mode of designers who explore and develop materials aimed at promoting sustainable transitions?*

2 The Philosophical Base Analysis for Material Thinking in Design

2.1 The Epistemology of Material Thinking Tracing Back

Paul Carter first addressed Material Thinking in his book Material Thinking: The Theory and Practice of Creative Research [9]. Carter depicted vivid examples depending on his personal experiences to illustrate how the artists' abstract ideas are translated into physical works. He tried to explain the roles of materials and constructed the philosophical base for the transformations between materiality and immateriality. As an interdisciplinary scholar and artist, Carter emphasized that 'collaboration' occupied the critical status of Material Thinking. Carter invoked a metaphor from Thomas de Quincey: A collaborative project is likened to a series of journeys plotted on a map. Where the plots of all individual or singular journeys that have been taken intersect, they gather, coagulate, and ultimately produce a blot on the map. The individual journeys are arrested in the swelling of this blot. Employing the metaphor, Carter captured how collaborations can bump into indistinguishable results. Carter claimed that a new artwork is composed of memory and emergence. Materials bunch memories and emergent phenomena in new ways and act as mediators to enable mediation between known and unknown, which is the activity of Material Thinking.

Carter argued that Material Thinking is the creative research in artistic activities, discussing the relationship between artists and materials through the constructive position, which can be concluded as the epistemology—'makingly-known' [10]. In philosophical inquiries, ontology means the form and nature of reality. Epistemology is constrained by the ontological question, which means the nature of the relationship between the knower and what can be known. In terms of constructive paradigm, ontology is relativism, and epistemology is transactional [11]. In this way, 'makingly-known' can be explained that a knower can gain and create new knowledge simultaneously through making. Here, 'making' means the 'collaborating process' when artists or designers work jointly with materials. If 'making' can produce knowledge, 'thinking' must be existed when 'making.' So here, in order to further elaborate on the nature of Making Thinking, we need to analyze the relationship between 'making' and 'thinking.' The materiality left during the 'making' process embodies the 'thinking' process. Just like the discussion from Carter, Material Thinking is performed in making—'making thinking' or 'thinking making', indicating its commutative functions afforded by the term [12]. On account of that, 'thinking' can occasionally happen anytime during the 'making' process. It might act as the mediation during craft or as the judgment in response to what is made [13]. In this way, we concluded and define this cognitive activity as 'thinking exchanging with making.'

2.2 Rethink and Redefine the Epistemology of Material Thinking in Design

Material Thinking claimed by Carter is focused on artistic activities. The objective of Material Thinking is to create and understand 'the third apprehension.' However, the goal of design activities is more than apprehensions and lies in creating new functions [10]. For quite a long time, artifact design has become a tool to promote products and make profits. The function is mainly about the formal structure of products to become usable, useful and desirable for users with the character of utility. The traditional artifact design approach has caused evident threats to the planet, and human beings are now undertaking warnings and even retributions from nature. Function in a new context extends beyond original meanings, and it extends into the individual, social, and cultural life of human beings, especially considering ethics issues [14]. Sustainability is a strategy for humans and their generations to survive on the planet. Superficially, it aims to solve problems of ecological crisis, but actually, the critical problem to tackle is the moral and spiritual crisis of human beings (e.g., consuming habits, lifestyles, etc.). In view of that, constructing a new material culture is far more essential today. Designers should pay more attention to inner new meaning creations of the products for ecological civilization. 'Meaningfulness' stresses the spiritual and ethical aspects of 'function', which should be the core objective for designers to pursue. Overall, synthesizing the discussions above, we will inherit the epistemology constructed by Paul Carter and further expand, extend and supplement it in design activities from the viewpoints of sustainable transitions. Here, we proposed a new concept of *Designerly Ways of Material Thinking* in this context, which means designers collaborate with materials to innovate sustainable material outcomes. The concept of 'designerly ways' origins from Nigel Cross in his book < Designerly Ways of Knowing > [15]. In this way, the updating epistemology of *Designerly Ways of Material Thinking* is defined -- 'thinking exchanging with making of the meaningful.'

Remarkably, the concept of 'making' here ('collaborating with materials') has been extended a lot following the development of science and technology. The physical properties of materials have rapidly broadened, e.g., 'Growing' materials [16], 'Interactive-Connected-Smart (ICS)' materials [17], 'Trans' materials [18], 'Morphing' materials [19], etc., which means the tools and methods that can be applied into 'making' are steadily innovated. With more and more interdisciplinary knowledge integrated into design practice, equipment in scientific experiments becomes the tool, and programming turns into the method, bringing more approaches to create sustainable materials and changing the affordances of traditional materials [20].

3   Model Proposal of *Designerly Ways of Material Thinking* Based on Transition Design

3.1   Visions for Transitions: Reflection on Material Interactions with NHSCA

Transition Design was proposed by four academic leaders in Design at Carnegie Mellon University based on the viewpoints proposed by Buckminster Fuller, "You can never change things by fighting the existing reality. If you want to change something, you need to build a new model that makes the existing model obsolete". The first conceptual model is about the position and stage of Transition Design in design progress, which aims to construct future paradigms and systems through incubating and clustering emerging phenomena. Our study is consistent with this stage [21, 22]. The second conceptual model is about the Transition Design framework outlining four mutually reinforcing and co-evolving areas of knowledge, action, and self-reflection: Vision for Transition, New ways of Designing, Posture and Mindset and Theories of change [21]. The third conceptual model is about designers' roles in Transition Design, including 'Questioner', 'Connector', 'Gardener', 'Acupuncture' and 'Maker' [23].

The world is constituted of four systems from the perspective of humankind: Human Being System, Artificial System, Nature System, and Cyber System [24]. After reviewing the current researches on material innovation in design practices, we found a trend about the innovation purpose of the material is transforming from Human Being System to the four systems restricting and balancing each other. For example, the models or methods proposed in the first ten years of the 21st century, such as a Meanings of Materials model [25], a Material Emotion model [26], Expressive-Sensorial atlas [27], etc. were all oriented to enhance user experiences and promote their consumption behaviors. However, more and more approaches like Design Driven Material Innovation(DDMI) method [28], Design Driven Value Chains in the World of Cellulose(DWOC) [29], Material Ecology [30], etc. are emerging.

This trend can be visualized in Fig. 1. On the left, the other three systems are oriented to and serve human beings. Materials are connected with the other three systems through an Artificial System by giving artifacts form and function. The future vision will be turned into weak-Anthropocentrism and new material culture. We discovered a trend that all four systems will treat materials as a medium to balance and restrict each other (see the center model of Fig. 1). More specifically, the right model shows the present overseas and domestic-focused areas and the vision for their new relations in the future from sustainable transitions. This model presents the vision of designers to understand materials from a systematic view and motivates the roles of the designers as 'Questioner' and 'Maker' from the holistic and top-level perspective as proposed in Transition Design.

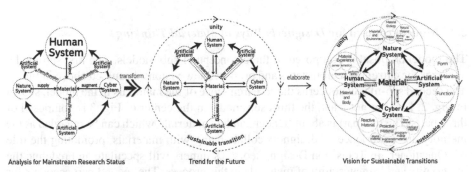

Analysis for Mainstream Research Status   Trend for the Future   Vision for Sustainable Transitions

Fig. 1. Present research status, trend and future visions about interactions between materials and NHCAS system, source: Ye Yang.

3.2 Research Scope of Materials from a Transition Perspective

As shown in Fig. 2, from the perspective of sustainable transitions, the materials for study can be decided from the material-flow circulation, which can be classified into two significant kingdoms: degradable materials and wasted materials. These two kingdoms can be further divided into secondary subclasses through the classification method of DIY materials [31]. In this way, the study will be carried out around degradable materials with the sub-categories of animals, plants and microbes, and wasted materials concerning the sub-categories of surplus materials in the production process, food wastes, and consumption wastes.

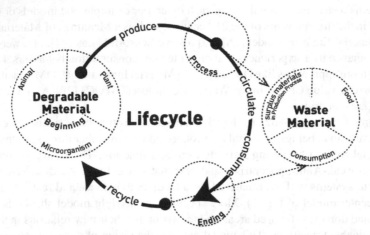

Fig. 2. Research scope and classification of materials based on material-flow circulation, source: Ye Yang

3.3 Model Proposal for *Designerly Ways of Material Thinking*

The model proposal is composed of three conceptual sub-models. The first sub-model analyzes the current research status and proposes new visions discussed above in Fig. 1. The second sub-model concerns the research scope of the materials in the model, shown in Fig. 2. Last but not least, the third sub-model in the center of Fig. 3 is composed of three parts. The first part is about 'Understanding material,' which can be regarded as the memory and experience of designers collaborating with materials, promoting the role of 'Questioner' in Transition Design theory. Designers will speculate and redefine the materiality and immateriality of materials in this process. The second part accounts for 'Tinkering materials', which means designers work deeply with materials. During this period, the perception or experience of designers will bump into new phenomena, and designers can act as a 'Maker' from a holistic perspective. The last part aims to create new material culture and meanings. Acting as an 'Acupuncture,' designers critically reflect on the existing material culture to change the nailed systems and create new narratives. These three parts will interact with each other, and new meanings might emerge from any part of the process. When integrating all the three conceptual sub-models, we aim to facilitate the theory revolution to make radical changes and achieve the vision of ecological civilization according to the Transition Design theory. The whole process will iterate back and forth in such a loop.

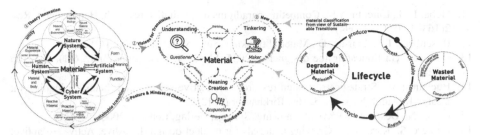

Fig. 3. The proposed model of *Designerly Ways of Material Thinking* from the viewpoints of Sustainable Transitions, source: Ye Yang

4 Conclusion

Nowadays, the traditional mainstream ways designers select physical materials at the end of the design process can't satisfy the objective for sustainability in the post-industrial era. Material-centered or material-driven design activities have been emerging. It is high time we should redefine the relationship between designers and materials in design education. In this paper, we tried to transform the indeterminate situation into the determinate one by inquiring the designers' unique thinking mode to collaborate with materials from the viewpoints of sustainable transitions. We proposed a new concept of *Designerly ways of Material Thinking* based on the concept of *Material Thinking* claimed by Paul Carter. We explained the nature of the new concept from the philosophical base and proposed a constructing model framework on the basis of Transition Design. However, the model proposed in this paper is a preliminary framework. We plan to test and estimate it in our future work, and we will improve the details of the model simultaneously.

References

1. Buchanan, R.: Strategies of design research: productive science and rhetorical inquiry. In: Design Research Now, pp. 55–66. Birkhäuser, Boston (2007)
2. Buchanan, R.: Thinking about design: an historical perspective. In Philosophy of Technology and Engineering Sciences, pp. 414–417. Elsevier, North Holland (2009)
3. Zhao, J.H.: Design and design approach research within 40 years. Decoration, **185**(09), 44–47(2008)
4. Wang, M.: Ulm's design concepts under the influence of value-free thoughts. Hundred Schools Arts **30**(06), 189–193 (2014)
5. Moholy-Nagy, L.: The New Vision, 1928. Schultz Press, Wittenborn (1947)
6. Itten, J.: Design and Form: The Basic Course at the Bauhaus (1963)
7. Dewey, J.: Logic: The Theory of Inquiry (1938)
8. Yang, Y., Zhou, H.T.: Material-oriented active making: a promising approach for sustainable transitions. In: Proceedings of HCI International 2022. Part I, LNCS 13311, IBSN: 978–3–031–06037–3(in press). Springer, Cham (2022). https://doi.org/10.1007/978-3-031-06038-0_19
9. Carter, P.: Material Thinking: the theory and practice of creative research. Melbourne University Press (2004)
10. Tonkinwise, C.: Knowing by Being-There Making: Explicating the Tacit Post-Subject in Use (2008). http://www.materialthinking.org. Accessed 10 Oct 2021

11. Guba, E.G., Lincoln, Y.S.: Competing paradigms in qualitative research. Handb. Qual. Res. **2**(163–194), 105 (1994)
12. Rosenberg, T.E., Fairfax, D.: Material thinking. Stud. Mater. Thinking **1**(2) (2008)
13. Swanson, G.: Educating the designer of 2025. She Ji: J. Des. Econ. Innov. **6**(1), 101–105 (2020)
14. Buchanan, R.: Strategies of design research: productive science and rhetorical inquiry. In: Design Research Now, pp. 55–66. Birkhäuser (2012)
15. Cross, N.: Designerly Ways of Knowing. Springer Verlag, London (2006)
16. Camere, S., Karana, E.: Growing materials for product design. In: Alive. Active. Adaptive: Proceedings of International Conference on Experiential Knowledge and Emerging Materials (EKSIG 2017), pp.101–115 (2017)
17. Ferrara, M., Rognoli, V., Arquilla, V., Parisi, S.: Interactive, connected, smart materials: ICS materiality. In International Conference on Intelligent Human Systems Integration (pp. 763–769). Springer, Cham (2018). https://doi.org/10.1007/978-3-319-73888-8_118
18. Brownell, B.: Transmaterial Next: A Catalog of Materials that Redefine Our Future. Chronicle Books (2017)
19. Qamar, I.P., Groh, R., Holman, D., Roudaut, A.: HCI meets material science: A literature review of morphing materials for the design of shape-changing interfaces. In: Proceedings of the 2018 CHI Conference on Human Factors in Computing Systems, pp. 1–23. (2018)
20. Barati, B., Karana, E.: Affordances as materials potential: what design can do for materials development. Int. J. Des. **13**(3), 105–123 (2019)
21. Irwin, T., Kossoff, G., Tonkinwise, C.: Transition design provocation. Des. Philos. Pap. **13**(1), 3–11 (2015)
22. Irwin, T., Tonkinwise, C., Kossoff, G.: Transition design: an educational framework for advancing the study and design of sustainable. Ensayos **105**, 31–65 (2020)
23. Narberhaus, M.: A practical guide for the Great Transition. https://seed.uw.edu/wp-content/uploads/narberhaus-reimaging-2015.pdf. Accessed 10 Oct 2021
24. Lou, Y.Q.: Human-computer interaction, sustainability and design in the view of NHCAS. Decoration **285**(01), 66–70 (2017)
25. Karana, E.: Meanings of Materials (PhD dissertation). Delft University of Technology, Delft (2009)
26. Desmet, P.M.A.: A multilayered model of product emotions. Des. J. **6**, 4–13 (2013)
27. Rognoli, V.: The Expressive-Sensorial Characterization of Materials for Design (PhD dissertation). Politecnica de Milano, Milan, Italy (2004)
28. Tubito, C., et al.: APPLIED DDMI: A white paper on how Design-Driven Material Innovation methodology was applied in the Trash-2-Cash project (2019)
29. Somervuori, M., et al.: Design Driven Value Chains in the World of Cellulose DWoC 2013–2015 (2015)
30. Ingold, T.: Toward an ecology of materials. Annu. Rev. Anthropol. **41**, 427–442 (2012)
31. Rognoli, V., Ayala-Garcia, C.: Defining the DIY-materials approach. In: Materials Experience 2, pp. 227–258. Butterworth-Heinemann (2021)

Tactile Cognition and Art Product Design for the Blind Based on Emotional Interaction

Xiaotong Zhang⑩, Jingwen Tian⑩, Tanhao Gao⑩, Dingwei Zhang⑩, and Hongtao Zhou(✉)⑩

College of Design and Innovation, Tongji University, Shanghai, China
xiaotongzhangwood@qq.com, lifeisfurniture@gmail.com

Abstract. As one of the most important cognitive modalities for blind people, meeting and ensuring efficient tactile cognitive learning for blind people is socially essential. This study aims to investigate the design of digital art products for the blind based on the perspective of emotional interaction and to improve the tactile, emotional cognition of the blind. Based on the theory of "emotional interaction" in cognitive psychology and the research method of design psychology, we introduced art and design to develop tactile cognitive art product design for the blind. Through 3D printing technology, we transformed two-dimensional flat information into different three-dimensional recognizable cognitive learning interface styles and used different blind reading and exhibition methods to improve the tactile cognition and art appreciation of blind people. The results show that 3D printing technology is innovative and sustainable in improving the emotional cognition of blind people and broadening the design style of artworks. Based on the modern technology development of a new tactile cognitive art interface for blind people, it serves the new era of cultural learning for blind people and provides design ideas and empirical references for developing artworks for blind people.

Keywords: Haptic cognition · Emotional interaction · Blindness · Art · Product design · 3D printing

1 Introduction

In the second decade of the 21st century, China has comprehensively implemented the cause of protecting people with disabilities. In the early 20th century, China vigorously developed urban public culture, and the essential life of the blind and low-vision people was ensured. Still, the cultural and artistic products provided for them are largely missing [1]. However, there is a lack of cultural and creative products for them, and to a large extent, they are still at the stage of simply helping them to "identify objects," and cognitive learning tools for blind people are not popular. This study aims to enrich the cultural and artistic products for blind people's learning life and create art products that are more suitable for cognitive learning and emotional communication among blind and low vision groups.

As of May 2020, there are 82.96 million people with disabilities in China, accounting for 7% of the total population. About 12.33 million people with visual disabilities and nearly 5 million blind people [2]. The country has one of the highest numbers of blind people globally, with 450,000 new blind people each year, and this number is growing [3]. However, essential public facilities and cognitive teaching apparatus are minimal, and cultural and artistic products and entertainment products are lacking. The mental design products serving the daily lives of blind people in China are in a severe backward state. The majority of blind people have a single life and social activity, and the number of occupations they can engage in and choose from is even more limited. In addition to improving education for the blind and expanding employment opportunities for the blind, the blind need more spiritual comfort and a medium that can create an image and atmosphere to reflect real life. Art, as a form of expression that can be understood and transmitted by all, expresses emotions, sets up the environment, portrays mental activities, conveys the spirit, and can engage in cognition, learning, and emotional interaction with objective and subjective objects through emotion and analysis, integration and application, and capture and excavation, and get feedback through feelings (visual, auditory, and tactile). Blind people have the same aspirations for independence, freedom of thought, knowledge, and culture as ordinary people. They are even more sensitive to information and more eager to learn. With the rapid economic and educational development in China in recent years, more and more attention is being paid to particular people to improve people's living environment and meet people's expectations for a better life.

1.1 Art Involved in Tactile Cognition

Cognition is a human perception in which a person perceives, learns, and thinks about information [4]. *Aristotle* divided senses into five types: sight, hearing, touch, taste, and smell in his Treatise *On the Soul*, and he believed that touch is the primary form of human sensory perception and is the basis for other sensory perceptions and that humans can accurately judge the intensity and strength of touch as a form of sensory perception above that of animals [5, 6]. *James Gibson* provided a useful framework for perception research and introduced the concepts of distal objects, information media, proximal stimuli, and perceptual objects [7]. The sensory perception of blind and low-vision people is primarily through touch, the two-dimensional flat objects and books with Braille that they usually touch in their daily lives, and the three-dimensional objects transmitted to the brain image through touch. This way of acquiring information is often only possible by touching a simple textual introduction in Braille or by someone else relaying the appearance of the two-dimensional image in terms of form, spatial structure, and object color. The text and individual imagination are transformed into a three-dimensional image in the mind through language. This cognitive way of converting words into three-dimensional images, or the way to obtain adequate information, has excellent limitations and uncertainties and lacks sure normality and homogeneity.

1.2 Emotional Interaction and Blind Cognition

According to Professor *Arlie Russell Hochschild* of the University of California, Berkeley, "*Emotion is something individuals perceive and reveal only in situational norms and broad cultural conceptions.*" [8] Emotional interactions all have specific limiting effects that reflect the vibrant culture and emotional ideas required for the interaction. She also explained that the so-called emotional functioning mechanisms, including body work, surface acting, deep acting, and cognitive work, are limited by the fact. Blind people are afraid to interact with ordinary people for physiological reasons, which can improve the quality of life of the group and the feedback of the experience of the supporting life and work products. Based on the combination of emotional interaction theory and the concept of "empathy" in Design Thinking, we explore the value of tactile cognition in design and its role in human-centered design and design for the advantages of blind people's sense of touch and tactile design products for blind people from theoretical and practical perspectives. In addition to developing and improving existing learning tools, products, and artworks, we will also redesign the tactile space for the blind based on the above design process.

2 Artistic Interventions to Reconfigure Tactile Cognitive Products for the Visually Impaired Groups

2.1 Tactile Symbol Recognition Teaching Aids Design

Touchable three-dimensional objects are indispensable tools for blind people to form object concepts and spatial forms in creating their minds. 3D printing technology can quickly convey object information to blind people for cognitive learning, especially for objects that are not accessible daily, such as 3D scanned objects to aid cognition. In addition, pictures in Braille books can be converted from flat to semi-stereoscopic touchable books using 3D graphic conversion technology and 3D printing technology to enhance cognitive education for the blind. The author's team developed a series of cognitive learning products for the blind based on their cognitive research to improve existing aids to learning and popularize design and art, working with schools for blind children, special education, and institutions with Braille art educational aspirations. The design uses 3D printing resin, nylon, ABS, PLA, silicone, and acrylic to create realized products in a variety of materials (Fig. 1 and Fig. 2). The materials are explored and practiced in stages to generate efficient, low-cost, and sustainable learning and cognitive tools to serve the blind. It also allows more design forces to understand the lives of blind people and promotes the development and dissemination of cognitive products for blind people.

Fig. 1. D printing, PLA red material (Color figure online)

Fig. 2. D printing nylon material

2.2 Touch Products Adapted to the Education of Blind People in China

Based on in-depth research on the habits, learning styles, and cognitive characteristics of blind people, we developed a touch cognitive learning tool suitable for age-appropriate blind children Braille Touch Literacy (Fig. 3). The work selected the classical Chinese enlightenment textbook *"Hundred Family Surnames"* to develop the touch literacy series. Since Chinese characters are the oldest pictographs, it is difficult for many blind people to recognize their surnames. Through the design of touch symbols and the rapid transformation of 3D printing technology, blind people can quickly recognize and learn text graphics, assist teachers in dictating the content of lectures, facilitate memory and stimulate curiosity and exploration of blind children, and intervene in the mental health of blind people to a certain extent. It is suitable for the visually impaired to learn to read and write, especially in blind schools and special education schools. First, the use of 3D printing rapid prototyping, the use of existing design sharing platforms, and the promotion of popularization of low-difficulty schools and educational institutions can be made according to their use characteristics. Secondly, the product is safe and sustainable, using biodegradable materials. Compared with traditional paper, Braille paper durability is higher, not easy to damage, more minor, and easy to carry.

Fig. 3. Braille touch literacy Hundred Family Surnames

2.3 Artistic Design of Touch Art Products

Based on the development of 3D Braille teaching products, the team strives to explore the artwork that blind people can read, enhance and enrich the aesthetic level of art for blind people, and focus on the emotional world of blind people. In the form of retaining the basic version of the touched text of *"Hundred Family Surnames"*. The team has made artistic designs for the Chinese names of blind people, which can be integrated into the characteristics of the topographical form of the name person's hometown and create a 3D art exhibit with local sentiment and their exclusive names together with blind people.

Blind people can share the 3D printed artistic cognitive interface with their peers by touching it, deciphering their names, and depicting their hometowns in their minds. In addition, in order to let the blind understand the development of cities around the world, the author's team developed a tactile cognitive art interface for the blind (Fig. 4), which is based on the blueprint of coastal cities around the world, and designed to focus on the undulating patterns of urban architecture. The interface is designed to show the urban landscape and human history in different languages and to show the global urban development for the blind and low vision people so that the blind can understand the joy of the development of our human world in a new way and enhance the emotional awareness of the blind. There are two main versions of the tactile cognitive art interface for the blind. One is a text visualization version with multi-country text and text building high and low for the sighted and visually impaired. The other version is suitable for people who use Braille to read. Touching the Braille dotted high and low falls can be fed back to get visual images to feel the distribution of urban planning and geographic terrain patterns.

Fig. 4. Touch of urban artistry works

2.4 Artistic Expression of Traditional Chinese Culture

As a unique form of tactile cognitive art expression, the team explores its more profound connotation of traditional cultural expression. Using the new tactile art form as a carrier of traditional culture, the Touch Culture series: the Chinese character "五谷豐登" with auspicious symbolic meaning is used in an idyllic landscape of mountains and hills to express people's good wishes for good wind and rain, and good harvest (Fig. 5). The classical poems from the classic Chinese literature "*Tang Poetry*" and "*Song Lyrics*" are selected and transformed into readable and appreciable 3D traditional cultural artworks. The creative transformation of design ideas through 3D printing and molding technology has become an important way for the blind community to inherit and develop traditional Chinese culture.

Fig. 5. Folk Culture - "五谷豐登"

3 Conclusion

For people with visual disabilities, using tactile cognition to understand the world is not just about words but also 3D tactile art. For blind and low-vision people to better "see" the world, it is not only necessary to start from existing tactile cognitive product design but also to pay attention to the psychological needs of the visually impaired. By introducing art and design into the product design of tactile cognitive art for the blind, developing super-scale cognitive interfaces for the blind, tactile symbolic cognitive interfaces, and cognitive learning aids, as well as continuing to study the exhibition space of tactile cognitive art for the blind, we will enhance the enjoyment of art and a better spiritual and cultural life for the blind and low-vision people. Based on the current results, the team will continue to develop other blind tactile cognitive 3D printing art products and blind tactile cognitive art product designs based on the "emotional interaction" theory, which will be used to guide the construction of blind tactile cognitive product design system and develop blind tactile cognitive art derivative products. The research can get the attention of more researchers and designers to design and produce more suitable products for blind and low-vision people to perceive the world more accurately, which is also an indispensable part of the whole society towards shared prosperity.

References

1. Liu, C.: Exploring the language life of speech disabled groups – a review of Pan Shisong, dun zuchun and Wang JinFang on the prevention and Countermeasures of speech disability. Journal of Jianghan University: humanities edition, pp. 73–75 (2012)
2. CDPF.: Annual overview of the development and social progress of the disabled in China. Qiuzhen Press, Beijing (2020)
3. Chai, L., Wang, X., Du, B., Wang, Y., Zhang, H., Wang, G.: Research on the design of blind simulation navigation system based on AR technology. Bus. Inf. **37**, 164 (2019)
4. Sternberg, R., Sternberg, K.: Cognitive Psychology. China Light Industry Press, Beijing (2017)
5. Aristotle, A.: On The Soul. Alex Catalogue (2000)
6. Sorabji, R.: Aristotle on demarcating the five senses. Philos. Rev. **80**(1), 55–79 (1971)
7. Gibson, J.: The perception of visual surfaces. Am. J. Psychol. **63**(3), 367–384 (1950)
8. Hochschild, A.R.: Emotion work, feeling rules, and social structure. Am. J. Sociol. **85**(3), 551–575 (1979)

HCI Research and Design Across Cultures

Comparison of Online Transportation Policy Problems Between Major Cities in Indonesia

Pahmi Amri[1,2]($\boxtimes$), Dyah Mutiarin[1], and Achmad Nurmandi[1]

[1] Universitas Muhammadiyah Yogyakarta, Bantul, Indonesia
[2] Universitas Islam Riau, Pekanbaru, Indonesia
Pahmi.amri@soc.uir.ac.id

Abstract. His study aims to explain the problems of online transportation in big cities such as Jakarta, Medan, and Surabaya in Indonesia. The method used in this research is qualitative analysis. Furthermore, this study uses Nvivo-12 Plus Software to analyze qualitative data and present cross-tabulation and Visual analysis. There are five stages in using the Nvivo application in this study: data collection, data coding, data classification, and data presentation. The data that has been processed with Nvivo-12 Plus is then carried out with qualitative analysis. The data sources in this study were from well-known local media websites. The findings in this study indicate that the highest level of problems for online transportation is DKI Jakarta, with seven problems: congestion problems, fictional orders, violence, tariff problems, licensing, quotas, and zoning, Ranked second in Surabaya with problems of thought order, tariffs, permits, quotas, zones, and permits, Then the third rank is Medan City, with licensing problems, quota problems, and the controversy over the Minister of Transportation Regulation No. 108 of 2017. This study only analyzes the problems that arise due to online transportation by comparing them in three big cities. Further research is needed regarding the government's response in providing solutions to the problems caused by the arrival of online transportation.

Keywords: Sharing economy · Online transportation · Innovation disruptive

1 Introduction

Technological developments can help humans to carry out various kinds of activities. Efficient facilities are needed in their activities. One of the facilities referred to in supporting community mobility is the mode of transportation. Each available mode of transportation has its advantages. In the transportation sector, converting transportation services from traditional/conventional to modern is a technological advancement [1].

In the era of technology-based transportation, effectiveness and efficiency are factors that everyone needs. The name of online transportation has realized Internet-based transportation sector innovation. This type of transportation can connect directly with the applications available on smartphones. Online transportation has its advantages when compared to the previous transportation system. Some of the advantages of online transportation include accessibility, transparency, and cost-efficiency [2]. Another advantage of online transportation is that it can provide the speed of time, convenience, security, and is environmentally friendly, all of which are connected to one system platform [3]. The following online mode of transportation also offers other conveniences such as goods delivery services, cash, and food ordering [2].

The presence of online transportation in Indonesia since 2015 began with PT. Gojek. Online transportation was present in Indonesia at a time when the government did not well organize the transportation system. Some Indonesians think that online transportation is a solution to support their activities, but some people who depend on conventional transportation think online transportation is a new problem. Along with the development of transportation, online transportation has triggered social jealousy for conventional transportation such as motorcycle taxis, taxis, buses, etc. In California, online transportation is considered a company that creates unfair competition in the transportation sector because it charges lower prices and drivers who do not have professional driver's licenses [4].

Several previous studies on the problems that arise due to the presence of new entrants in the transportation sector. Have an impact on the socio-economic conditions of conventional transportation, namely a decrease in the income of conventional transportation drivers caused by tariff problems, the shift in passenger interest [5]. Online transportation has succeeded in driving social change at three levels: the individual level, the inter-individual level, and the community level [6]. The reduction in the income of conventional transportation drivers, up to 70%, makes the social conflict between stakeholders of transportation services unavoidable [7].

This study is different from previous research. This study analyzes several problems caused by online transportation in three major cities in Indonesia. A comparative study was conducted to see which cities had the highest problems caused by disruptive innovations. Furthermore, the data used is sourced from a collection of reputable online media news narratives in the form of a spreadsheet.

2 Literature Review

2.1 Sharing Economy Online Transportation Sector

Literature on online transportation is increasingly in demand to observe application technology development that can change behavior when choosing travel transportation (Pawlak et al. 2019). The utilization of application-based information and communication technology in the online transportation sector is commonly referred to as the online transportation sector sharing economy [8–10].

The sharing economy as a new business model is trending in the transportation sector. Slowly, the sharing economy has changed people's travel patterns and significantly impacts work and social relations [11]. The sharing economy of the online transportation sector is a concept often used by carpooling and vanpooling [12].

This type of online transportation is to make it easier to connect passengers and taxi drivers. Anyone easily accesses online transportation through an application on a smartphone [13]. Online transportation can be used by individuals who previously did not know each other using online platforms. Online transportation is more dominated by students or groups who do not have private vehicles [14]. Furthermore, online transportation can support the mobility of low-income groups of workers, singles, and women [15].

Online transportation benefits from the convenience and security sector, supports the mobility of households without a vehicle and people with physical limitations and provides very efficient rides [16]. Another positive impact is minimizing the use of car parkland [17, 18].

2.2 Disruptive Technology in the Transportation Sector

Disruptive innovation, such as the online transportation business, is a leap of innovation in services triggered by chaos in competition law [19]. Disruptive innovations emerge outside previously established corporate networks [20]. Innovations that disrupt the transportation sector arise not through formal competition, such as promotions through billboards or door-to-door promotions. These new entrants are present in the market through information technology (IT), providing the same service products in different ways [21].

The disruptive innovation of the transportation sector has changed the conventional business model to a modern one equipped with internet-based applications. It is causing competition between existing business actors and new business actors in the same market. Innovations that disrupt the transportation sector have created radical changes in the transportation industry, marked by the emergence of new products and services [22].

One innovation that disrupts the transportation sector is the online platform-based Uber company [23]. Furthermore, online transportation companies born in Indonesia, such as Grab and Gojek, have also caused problems in urban transportation governance. Disruptive innovation has resulted in competition using an online platform model that is very different from the previous model. Fundamentally disruptive innovations can influence the behavior of privately owned assets into shared consumption so that such a pattern can challenge existing traditions and social patterns [24]. Disruptive innovations can affect people's travel behavior patterns and have also influenced the government in implementing regulations on the new business model [19]. Competition problems, changes in people's travel behavior patterns, and disruption of existing policies have caused social chaos in several countries such as the Philippines, Taiwan, the United States, the European Union, Japan, and others [19].

3 Methods

This research uses qualitative methods; then, this research uses a content analysis approach sourced from searches on Google using the keywords online transportation problems. News related to online transportation issues for the next coding stage using the Nvivo 12 plus software. The stages in using nvivo 12 Plus include data collection, data import, data coding, data classification, and data visualization. Data was obtained from nvivo 12 Plus for further qualitative analysis.

4   Results and Discussion

Online transportation is a new technology service rife in big cities in Indonesia, such as DKI Jakarta, Surabaya, and Medan. However, behind the success of online transportation, it also has a significant impact on the community environment and the taxi industry. The three sub-discussions below discuss the problems in the three big cities.

4.1   Online Transportation Issues in Jakarta

Online transportation has entered DKI Jakarta since 2015. From 2015 to 2022, several problems have also emerged, specifically for DKI Jakarta. Here you can see a list of online transportation problems by year (Fig. 1);

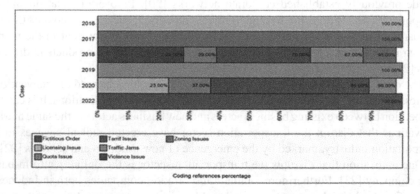

Fig. 1. Online transportation issue in DKI Jakarta

   Online transportation entered DKI Jakarta in 2015; in 2016, the first problem related to licensing was a percentage of 100%. In 2016 the narrative related to the issue of operating permits was not yet straightforward. The government at that time still did not have the proper permits to regulate online transportation. In 2017 the problem of online transportation arose regarding zoning or regions with a percentage of 100%. In that year, the online transportation space sector was problematic in several public places, including airports. In 2016, they only allowed online transportation to operate in the airport area. In 2018, more complex problems emerged, including the problem of fictitious orders, which accounted for 28% of all orders. Unscrupulous online transportation drivers carry out fictitious orders to make fraudulent attempts to obtain daily bonuses offered by the application. Next is the problem of online vehicle quotas with 39%. The number of online vehicles in DKI Jakarta is increasing, making the government take quick steps to limit the potential for new problems that will arise. The next problem is the tariff or cost per kilometer set by the application with 70%. The low rate set by the application company makes online transportation drivers take action to the streets, demanding that the government also provide solutions for setting low rates. The congestion problem is also part of the online transportation problem in DKI Jakarta, with 87%. The congestion problem is unavoidable in DKI Jakarta, which comes from unscrupulous online transportation drivers who eat the shoulder of the road. The last problem in 2018 was the problem of the prohibition zone for taking passengers with a percentage of 98%. The problem arose due to the government's prohibition against shutting down applications at specific points of prohibition, receiving a response from online transportation drivers who protested. It was judged that the policy did not provide a good solution for online transportation.

In 2019, online transportation also created a congestion problem with a percentage of 100%. Congestion occurs due to unscrupulous online transportation drivers who are not orderly in waiting for orders on the shoulder of the road and in front of public facilities such as terminals and busway stops. In 2020 there are legality or permit issues with 23%. The problem of clarity on the professional status of online transportation drivers requested by online transportation drivers to application companies and the government is related to their rights and obligations as application partners. The next problem is related to the quota with a percentage of 89%. Online transportation drivers protest against application companies limiting the acceptance of new drivers because the number of drivers is not proportional to the number of passengers. The last problem in 2020 is related to congestion with 98%. Congestion occurs due to unscrupulous transportation drivers who are again disorganized in waiting for orders at road shoulders and busway stops.

In 2022 online transportation problems arise about the tariffs set by the application companies no longer by the provisions in the regulations. So online transportation drivers protest and demand the DKI Jakarta government provide the best tariff problem solution.

4.2 Online Transportation Issues in Surabaya

Online transportation has been in Surabaya since 2015. From 2015 to 2022, several problems have also emerged, specifically for the city of Medan. Here you can see a list of online transportation problems by year (Fig. 2);

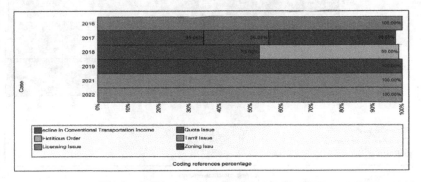

Fig. 2. Online transportation issue in Surabaya

Online transportation entered the city of Surabaya in 2015 as an application company that challenges incumbents. The dynamics of the entry of online transportation in that year have begun to be felt. As the diagram data above shows, in 2016, there were licensing problems with a percentage of 100%. The polemic about licensing occurred because, in 2016, the Surabaya city government temporarily had not issued an online transportation permit to operate. This step was taken to prevent new problems in the community, especially the competition in the urban transportation sector.

Furthermore, the online transportation problem that emerged in 2017 was associated with a 35% decline in the income of traditional transportation drivers due to the emergence of newcomers. The second problem arises regarding the quota with a percentage of 56%. The high growth rate of online transportation in Surabaya made the government respond to online transportation companies to provide accurate data to the government to record the ratio of Surabaya urban vehicles. The third problem is related to the operational area of online transportation with a percentage of 98%. The prohibition against online transportation in transporting passengers in certain areas has become a polemic between the government and online transportation drivers.

In 2018, the problem caused by online transportation was linked to a 53 percent decrease in the income of conventional transportation drivers. In 2018, there was another increase in competition between new transportation companies and incumbents. In 2019 problems arose regarding the online transportation operation zone, and the prohibition of picking up passengers at some point was carried out again. In 2021 and 2022, the same problems arise regarding tariffs. The low rate set by the applicator has made several online transportation drivers take action against it.

4.3   Online Transportation Issues in Medan

Online transportation has been in Medan since 2015. From 2015 to 2022, several problems have also emerged, specifically for the City of Medan. Here you can see a list of online transportation problems by year (Fig. 3);

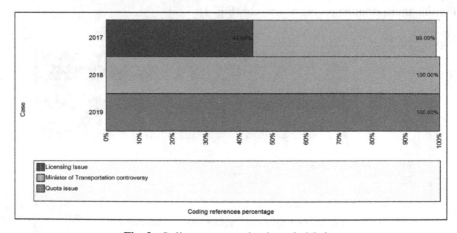

Fig. 3. Online transportation issue in Medan

Medan city is a part of the city that the arrival of online transportation companies. The presence of online transportation in the field also reaps several similarities, including; in 2017, licensing problems emerged with a percentage of 44%. The rejection of online transportation emerged from groups of conventional transportation drivers, asking the government not to permit online transportation to operate. In 2018 there was a problem with the Minister of Transportation Regulation No. 108 of 2017; protests against several points in the Minister of Transportation's regulation occurred from online transportation drivers, such as refusing to give unique labels to online vehicles. The polemic of protest against the regulation of the minister of transportation continued in 2018. Finally, in 2019 problems arose regarding online transportation quotas. The increase in driver partnerships with online transportation companies continues to increase, so online transportation drivers provide input to companies so as not to limit quotas.

5 Conclusion

The presence of online transportation in the three major cities studied in DKI Jakarta, Surabaya, and Medan presents new problems in the transportation sector. DKI Jakarta is the highest-ranking city with transportation problems among the other two cities. Found seven problems that arise: licensing problems, congestion problems, quota problems, fictitious order problems, violence problems, tariff problems, and zoning problems. Next, the city of Surabaya is ranked second with problems that arise, such as the problem of decreasing the income of conventional transportation drivers, congestion problems, quota problems, tariff problems, licensing problems, and zoning problems. Finally, the city of Medan has the fewest problems, including licensing issues, transportation ministerial regulations issues, and quota issues. This study cannot only analyze the problems that arise due to the presence of online transportation by comparing them in three big cities. It is necessary to do further research related to the government's response in providing solutions to problems caused by the arrival of online transportation.

References

1. Anwar, A.A.: Online Vs Konvensional: Keunggulan dan konflik antar moda transportasi di Kota Makassar. ETNOSIA J. Etnogr. Indonesia **2**, 220–246 (2017)
2. Alamsyah, A., Rachmadiansyah, I.: Mapping online transportation service quality and multiclass classification problem solving priorities. J. Phys: Conf. Ser. **971**(1), 12021 (2018)
3. Wijayanto, I., Sasami, I., Nugroho, R., Suharto, D.: 34. Conflict resolution of online transportation vs conventional transportation. In: 5th International Conference on Social and Political Sciences (IcoSaPS 2018), pp. 168–173 (2018)
4. Di Amato, A.: Uber and the sharing economy. Ital. LJ **2**, 177 (2016)
5. Al Mukaromah, M., Yuliari, K., Arifin, M.: Dampak Keberadaan Transportasi On Line Terhadap Kondisi Sosial Ekonomi Transportasi Konvesional Di Kota Kediri. JIMEK J. Ilmuah Mhs. Ekon. Kediri **2**(2), 168–181 (2019)
6. Widiyatmoko, F.: Dinamika Kebijakan Transportasi Online. J. Urban Sociol. **1**(2), 55–68 (2018)
7. Istianto, B., Maulamin, T.: Kebijakan Transportasi Online dan Konflik Sosial. J. Ilmu Adm. Negara ASIAN (Asosiasi Ilmuwan Adm. Negara) **5**(2), 99–136 (2017)
8. Gössling, S., Michael Hall, C.: Sharing versus collaborative economy: how to align ICT developments and the SDGs in tourism?. J. Sustain. Tour. **27**(1), 74–96 (2019). https://doi.org/10.1080/09669582.2018.1560455

9. Levinson, D.M., Krizek, K.J.: The end of traffic and the future of access: a roadmap to the new transport landscape (2017)

10. Lyons, G.: Getting smart about urban mobility–aligning the paradigms of smart and sustainable. Transp. Res. Part A Policy Pract. **115**, 4–14 (2018)

11. Zhou, Y., Wang, X.C.: Explore the relationship between online shopping and shopping trips: an analysis with the 2009 NHTS data. Transp. Res. Part A Policy Pract. **70**, 1–9 (2014)

12. Shaheen, S., Cohen, A.: Shared micromoblity policy toolkit: Docked and dockless bike and scooter sharing (2019)

13. Ferrero, F., Perboli, G., Rosano, M., Vesco, A.: Car-sharing services: an annotated review. Sustain. Cities Soc. **37**, 501–518 (2018)

14. Rotaris, L., Danielis, R.: The role for carsharing in medium to small-sized towns and in less-densely populated rural areas. Transp. Res. Part A Policy Pract. **115**, 49–62 (2018)

15. Shaheen, S., Cohen, A.: Shared ride services in North America: definitions, impacts, and the future of pooling. Transp. Rev. **39**(4), 427–442 (2019)

16. Tirachini, A.: Ride-hailing, travel behaviour and sustainable mobility: an international review. Transportation **47**(4), 2011–2047 (2019). https://doi.org/10.1007/s11116-019-10070-2

17. Henao, A., Marshall, W.E.: The impact of ride hailing on parking (and vice versa). J. Transp. Land Use **12**(1), 127–147 (2019)

18. Hernández, A.T., Antoniou, C.: The economics of automated public transport: Effects on operator cost, travel time, fare and subsidy (2020)

19. Fajar, M.: Disruptive innovation on competition law: regulation issues of online transportation in Indonesia (2021)

20. De Streel, A., Larouche, P.: Disruptive innovation and competition policy enforcement (2015)

21. Kasali, R.: The great shifting series on disruption (2018)

22. Wei, H.-F.: Does disruptive innovation 'Disrupt' competition law enforcement? the review and reflection (2016)

23. de Streel, A., Larouche, P.: Disruptive innovation and competition law enforcement. SSRN Electron. J. (2015)

24. Sahlman, E.: Sharing economy as disruptive innovation: consumer viewpoint (2018)

The Cross-Cultural Acceptance of Japanese Animation, Analysis of Social Media

Riza Ardyarama[✉], Fajar Junaedi, and Filosa Gita Sukmono

Department of Communication, Universitas Muhammadiyah Yogyakarta,
Bantul Regency, Indonesia
riza.a.isip18@mail.umy.ac.id, {fajarjun,filosa}@umy.ac.id

Abstract. The development and spread of foreign culture are not only limited to offline distribution through events or other offline movements. This study aims to analyze *the social media* movement through *#anime* on social media Twitter to find out the spread of Japanese culture in Indonesia through the hashtag #anime. Scientific literature data is taken from hashtags on Twitter social media focusing on the #anime community. The keywords used in this research are social media movements and Anime. Data analysis uses the Social Network Analysis method to identify and map social movements and explain the position of SNA nodes active in campaigning for these issues. In analyzing data, researchers used netray—id web software. The results of data analysis answered that there are many hashtags from #anime which are hashtags in general; in this hashtag, there are hashtags that lead to the title of the anime series #onepiece, #aot, #jujutsunokaisen. Twitter social media platform through #anime discusses information about Anime, character cosplay, next upcoming anime season. Then have a discussion related to the prediction of the storyline episode. This study found a cross-culture in social media related to Anime. With the phenomenon of #anime promotion on Twitter social media through communities in the development of Japanese culture in Indonesia, fans are starting to get a lot, and people understand Japanese culture in Indonesia.

Keywords: Anime · Japanese culture · Social media

1 Introduction

Japanese Anime's interest and consumption have increased exponentially in the last ten years [1]. Currently, the relationship between Western countries and Japan is also significantly related to pop culture [2]. Over the past few decades, Japanese popular culture products have been exported, traded, and consumed mainly throughout East and Southeast Asia, such as Taiwan, Hong Kong, Singapore, Thailand, Vietnam, Korea, and Indonesia [3]. In terms of introducing culture in a modern way like this, it can be categorized as Japan creating Anime as an instrument of cultural diplomacy, thereby attracting attention from various circles in the world.

Japan's strategy in carrying out and maximizing its cultural values in a diplomatic relationship is entirely appropriate. The Japan Foundation holds the JakJapan Matsuri as an annual routine, which utilizes pop culture as an attraction and means of Japanese cultural diplomacy [3]. Japanese culture has become a natural thing for young people in Indonesia, especially the existence of Japanese animation or Anime. The presence of Anime becomes the realm of education for the audience, where they begin to know the Japanese language and become interested in the Japanese language to the point of wanting to learn it [4]. Many schools have started to include Japanese as one of the elective subjects that students can choose from. Therefore, the existing popular culture also makes significant changes in social values in society [5].

There is still little research on social media that discusses this issue in cultural research on social media. Only a few studies have specifically examined the possible effects of culture on social media [6]. Few studies to date have looked explicitly at the micro-level relationship between culture and the diffusion of information technology [7]. The rise of social media has made it easier for teachers and students from various cultures to meet and work together [8]; with the development of the era, teachers also began to teach intercultural communication to their students through social media.

In its success in carrying out diplomacy positively, Japanese culture can be used as an example for countries in intercultural diplomacy. It is interesting for researchers to conduct research on Japanese culture in Indonesia through social media. The difference in this study is that researchers discuss cultural developments through the media. In contrast, many studies have raised this issue based on previous journals, not on social media or the field. So that this research is interesting to discuss based on the journal above, and this research will fill the void of previous studies. So the purpose of this study will be to discuss how social media can affect the development of Japanese culture in Indonesia.

2   Literature Review

The formation of a social movement begins with establishing a virtual community based on shared interests and goals. The potential of this mixed media is very high to replace other conventional media because it provides easy access to information [9]. According to a 2009 survey by DigiActive, social networking sites (SNS) are the most common gateway to online activism, even though SNSs are not created with activism [10]. The main problem of social movements is how to get enough motivated people to start mobilizing and attract more participants, but with social networking sites, all it takes is a click of the mouse for participants. Social media users in various countries have their cultural behavior and criteria for receiving information on social media [11]. Some social mechanism connects enough people with appropriate interests and resources so that they can act.

In the early 1980s, several anime shows with subtitles were broadcast via cable T.V. in Japan. An anime fan community began to form, and popular demand for Anime rose steadily to the mainstream [12]. With the popularity of Anime and manga around the world, Japan can use Anime and manga as *soft power* in spreading and introducing Japanese culture in various countries, one of which is Indonesia. Based on data from

The Japan Foundation, as of 2012, 872,411 people in Indonesia studied Japanese [13]. This is evident in Anime, an educational area for the audience, where they begin to know the Japanese language and become interested in the Japanese language to the point of wanting to learn it [14]. Of the 40 people surveyed (28%) expressed interest in Japanese culture and language and several reasons for being interested in Anime, manga, and drama [13]. In this case, popular culture has formed an order in the famous world in the form of a community and a fan culture that supports disseminating information and technology and the development of popular culture in society [5].

3 Method

In this research, the researcher uses a qualitative research type by using a research method that is considered relevant to the research to be carried out, namely the case study method. In this study, researchers used social media analysis techniques. SNA is an analytical method often used to measure a relationship and describe some information. SNA is an analytical approach that can identify social structures and explain the position of key stakeholders or what can be called key actors [15]. This method can also be used to analyze a social media activity. In this case, SNA will be used to analyze the activities contained on Twitter social media related to interactions between individuals in discussing the same topic (Fig. 1).

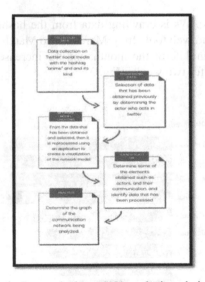

Fig. 1. Research phase (SNA analysis techniques)

4 Results and Discussions

The development of Japanese culture in Indonesia occurs through #Anime and the like on Twitter social media resulting in data crawling, assisted by using the Netray.id web tools with a vulnerable time of data collection on 1 March-31 March 2022. The hashtag #anime is a general hashtag from various hashtags that include anime titles on Twitter that contain everything from discussions to learning. The hashtag #anime on social media is still active as long as there is an anime released in each season, and an example of the data can be seen below (Fig. 2).

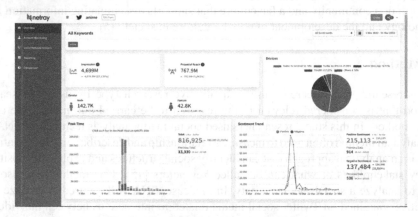

Fig. 2. Visualization of data from Netray.id

The image above displays is crawling data from the hashtag #anime, which was carried out using Netray.id web tools from March 1 – to March 31, 2022. The keyword used is "Anime" in the middle of the month, and the increase in statistics made this hashtag trend on Twitter for two weeks (Fig. 3).

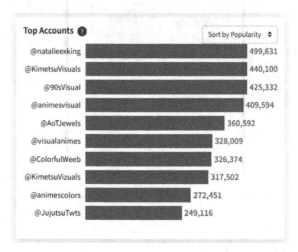

Fig. 3. Top accounts statistics

There are accounts in the communication network in the #anime hashtag, which is considered the main account with the highest popularity in spreading #anime. Based on the data obtained, @natalieexking has the first position in the role of the account in spreading the #anime hashtag with the highest number of posts related to #anime.

Extraction Knowledge extraction is some information that has been extracted in #Anime on Twitter social media or related to #Anime by identifying tweets spread by several actors that influence its distribution in Indonesia. These Twitter accounts represent several companies, influencers, and creators who take Japanese pop culture in Indonesia as their market for doing business and creating.

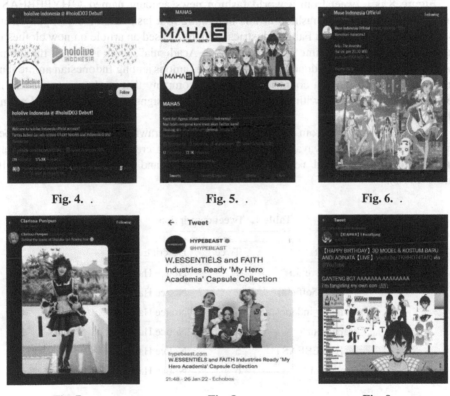

Fig. 4. .   Fig. 5. .   Fig. 6. .

Fig. 7. .   Fig. 8. .   Fig. 9. .

Figure 4 is a Twitter account from Hololive Indonesia, a subsidiary of an international virtual Youtuber named Hololive from Japan, one of the pop culture companies in Japan that are eyeing the Indonesian market to develop its company outside of Japan.

Figure 5 is the Twitter account of Maha5, which is a "modification" of a virtual YouTuber company founded in Indonesia to meet the Japanese pop culture market in Indonesia and participate in spreading pop culture in the form of virtual YouTubers with talents, staff, and creators from Indonesia with avatar elements—mixed with Indonesian cultures such as clothes, stories, or characters from Indonesian folklore.

Figure 6 is a Twitter account from muse Indonesia, one of the official Anime streaming companies in Indonesia which is constantly updated every season and participates in spreading Japanese pop culture in the form of Anime in Indonesia through free Anime watching services on the Youtube platform as the broadcast media.

Figure 7 is a tweet from a cosplayer from Indonesia who is always active in cosplaying various anime characters. Clarisa Punipun is a professional cosplayer who often becomes a judge or guest at cosplay festivals held in Indonesia; apart from being a cosplayer, she also ventures into entertainment as a brand ambassador and influencer host, and many more. Punipun is also still active for cosplay and always updates every week on cosplaying characters and participating in spreading cosplay pop culture in Indonesia.

Figure 8 is a tweet from a world fashion news account named @HYPEBEAST that tweeted about a new fashion article belonging to a fashion anime company from Bandung Indonesia named Faith Industries, which released an article on new clothes in collaboration. With an anime called "My Hero Academia". Faith is one of the anime brands originating from Indonesia, which is quite famous among Indonesian anime fans and other Southeast Asian countries. Faith is a company that is always consistent in releasing fashion articles with Japanese pop culture designs such as games and anime characters.

Figure 9 is a tweet from one of the creators or drawings of a virtual Youtuber in Indonesia named @xeyaya, who is always active in creating content and actively drawing for several virtual YouTubers from Indonesia and outside Indonesia (Fig. 10 and Table 1).

Table 1. Tweet description

Account	Tweet	Description
@hololive_id	1	Notice Hashtag
@maha5official	2	Notice Hashtag
@muse_indonesia	3	Notice Hashtag
@punipun7	4	Notice Hashtag
@HYPEBEAST	5	Notice Hashtag
@xeyaya	6	Notice Hashtag

The key actor in Indonesia is an account that influences the spread of the #anime hashtag in Indonesia, which often exchanges information on the #anime hashtag. The key actors here are company accounts that also impact the spread of Anime in Indonesia, such as Netflix, @BandwagonAsia, @muse_indonesia, and Youtube. Indonesia itself is the top organization, a keyword associated with #anime.

Social media users in various countries have their cultural behavior and criteria for receiving information on social media [11]. In this case, social media can influence cultural exchange movements, especially Japanese culture in Indonesia and the world. Twitter is a good service in communication, especially for mass communication, because it can provide information to many people without limiting people in receiving what

Top Organizations ⑦

Indonesia	2,937
@discotekmedia	1,451
Netflix	1,240
@BandwagonAsia	1,177
@muse_indonesia	877
YouTube	706
china	443
Jepang	437

Fig. 10. Data top organizations

information is there [9]. The influence of the mass media Twitter is very influential on the spread of Japanese culture in Indonesia in this is based on the data obtained, the Japanese culture market in Indonesia has experienced much interest with the presence of content providers who take Japanese culture into it, such as the @hololive_id account which is one of the pop culture companies in Japan that are interested in the Japanese culture enthusiast market in Indonesia, until An anime fashion company from Indonesia Faith Industries that can go international by carrying the theme of Japanese culture in their fashion designs. Due to the existence of popular culture, it can form order in the popular world in the form of a community and also a fan culture that supports the dissemination of information and technology as well as the development of popular culture in society [5], in this case, many Twitter social media accounts that affect the movement of exchanges. Japanese culture in Indonesia. The potential of this mixed media is very high to replace other conventional media because it provides easy access to information [9]. This can be seen in the hashtag movement statistics from #anime which have increased in certain weeks with discussion factors that can affect the movement of the discussion.

5 Conclusion

In conclusion, cultural exchange through social media is a phenomenon that can provide a new market for anime enthusiasts in Indonesia. With the existence of cultural exchanges through social media, many creators, influencers, and even Japanese pop culture companies are looking to Indonesia as their market for doing business. Moreover, many companies, creators, and influencers from Indonesia look to the Japanese pop culture market as their selling power in their work or business because of the significant interest in Japanese pop culture in Indonesian society. Indonesia is also one of the countries that gets much attention from Japan because Japanese pop culture enthusiasts in Indonesia are one of the biggest fans. With this phenomenon, Indonesian people who like Japanese culture can easily find information, entertainment, work, and even education through the #anime media; with a large number of anime markets in Indonesia, anime lovers and anime creators from Indonesia and abroad make Indonesia as a promising market for them.

References

1. Leonard, S.: Progress against the law anime and fandom, with the key to the globalization of culture. Int. J. Cult. Stud. **8**(3), 281–305 (2005). https://doi.org/10.1177/1367877905055679
2. Lamerichs, N.: The cultural dynamic of doujinshi and cosplay : local anime fandom in Japan, USA and Europe, vol. 10, no. 1, pp. 154–176 (2013)
3. Kartikasari, W.: The role of anime and manga in Indonesia-Japan Cultural Diplomacy.
4. Diyan, R., Putri, C., Yogyakarta, U.M.: Anime Menjadi Diplomasi Budaya yang Diambil Jepang dalam Menarik Kesan Positif dalam Soft Powernya," no. October (2021)
5. Lubis, M.I.S.: Komodifikasi Anime sebagai Budaya Populer Pada Komunitas Anime One Piece Di Kota Medan. J. Interak. J. Ilmu Komun. **3**(2), 129–141 (2019). https://doi.org/10.30596/interaksi.v3i2.3351
6. Straub, D., Keil, M., Brenner, W.: Testing the technology acceptance model across cultures: a three country study. Inf. Manag. **33**(1), 1–11 (1997). https://doi.org/10.1016/S0378-7206(97)00026-8
7. Straub, D.W.: The effect of culture on IT diffusion: E-mail and FAX in Japan and the U.S. Inf. Syst. Res. **5**(1), 23–47 (1994). https://doi.org/10.1287/isre.5.1.23
8. Tuzel, S., Hobbs, R.: El uso de las redes sociales y la cultura popular para una mejor comprensión intercultural. Comunicar **25**(51), 63–72 (2017)
9. Abraham, F.Z.: Pemanfaatan Twitter sebagai media komunikasi massa: Twitter utilization as mass communication media. J. Penelit. Pers dan Komun. Pembang.**18**, 1–30 (2014). http://jurnal-p2kp.id/index.php/jp2kp/article/view/11/16
10. Harlow, S.: Social media and social movements: Facebook and an online Guatemalan justice movement that moved offline. New Media Soc. **14**(2), 225–243 (2012). https://doi.org/10.1177/1461444811410408
11. Ratikan, A., Shikida, M.: A study of cross-culture for a suitable information feeding in online social networks. In: Rau, P.L.P. (ed.) CCD 2013. LNCS, vol. 8024, pp. 458–467. Springer, Heidelberg (2013). https://doi.org/10.1007/978-3-642-39137-8_51
12. Whatley, E.: Sources: understanding manga and anime. Ref. User Serv. Q. **47**(3), 301 (2008). https://doi.org/10.5860/rusq.47n3.301
13. Jaohari, A.L., Nurul, D.: The effectiveness of Japanese learning through anime (study on student of Japanese language department Widyatama University). Rev. Int. Geogr. Educ. Online **11**(6), 311–315 (2021). https://doi.org/10.48047/rigeo.11.06.37
14. Safariani, P.: Penyebaran Pop Culture Jepang Oleh Anime Festival Asia (Afa) Di Indonesia Tahun 2012–2016. eJournal Ilmu Hub. Int. **5**(3), 729–744 (2017). http://ejournal.hi.fisip-unmul.ac.id/site/wp-content/uploads/2017/08/Ejournal Putri Safariani (08-08-17-07-14-28).pdf
15. Guerrero, A.M., et al.: Key considerations and challenges in the application of social-network research for environmental decision making. Conserv. Biol. **34**(3), 733–742 (2020). https://doi.org/10.1111/cobi.13461

Character Evaluation and Derivative Product Design of "Hetalia" Based on Kansei Image

Wenqian Hu[✉]

East China University of Science and Technology, Shanghai, China
819778429@qq.com

Abstract. The cartoon characters with unique charm and excellent design not only have tremendous artistic value, but also contain huge market profits.In order to reduce the cognition difference of designers and consumers to the animation character image. This paper adopts the evaluation method of animation character image design based on kansei image, in order to find out what users thought of the characters in "Hetalia", so as to better design its derivative products. The results show that some characters have seemingly unfavorable characteristics and are still loved by the audience. There are certain differences in kansei evaluation between character design and product design. When designing a character, a character designer does not only give the character rich advantages to attract the audience, but also needs to consider the audience's cultural and geographical background and combine the audience's preferences to design a charming character.

Keywords: Kansei engineering · Anime characters · Derivative product design · Principal component analysis

1 Introduction

Whether an animation or cartoon can be attractive or successful is closely related to the character image of the work. The role is the main character of cartoon and caricature works, is its most basic constituent element. With the further development of the animation industry chain, the value of the animation character image has been promoted to the height of commercial operation; the animation character with unique personality charm not only has far−reaching artistic value, and it's a huge market and a huge profit. "Heitalya" is a Japanese comic book, which has also been adapted into an animation. It incarnates each country in the second world war into a specific character image, the dialogue between the characters vividly shows the strength and foreign policy of each country at that time, recreating the boring and bloody history of the Second World War [1]. The preference of the user is often different from the design idea of the role designer to some extent, and the ideal role image in the eyes of the role designer may be difficult to arouse the resonance of the user, even more difficult to excavate its commercial value. In order to make up for the cognitive differences between designers and consumers, this paper adopts the evaluation method of animation character design based on perceptual image, to gain insight into the user experience of the characters in Heitalya in order to better design its derivatives.

2   Establish a Research Process

The derivative product design of Heitalya is mainly based on the research of the role image and the evaluation of the role image to meet the expectations of the users. The process of product modeling innovation design is shown in Fig. 1, and is improved according to reference [2].

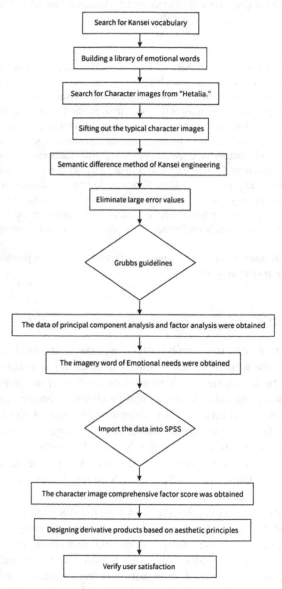

Fig. 1. Design study flow

3   Construction of Perceptual Semantic Space and Selection of Representative Role Images

3.1   Construction of Perceptual Semantic Space

The semantic space of Kansei engineering is based on the acquisition of a large number of kansei words, which are generally adjectives, such as simple, elegant, etc. User's perception of a role is often diverse, when the introduction of appropriate perceptual vocabulary, help designers better understand user thinking.

This paper refers to the perceptual words in paper [3], in this paper, by acquiring the original viewer's perceptual image, extracting the attractive items from the original perceptual image, evaluating the attractive items with the perceptual method of linguistic difference, using factor analysis to refine and reduce the dimension of the items, defining the attractive dimension, and testing the credibility of the perceptual evaluation system, finally, a knowledge base of evaluation factors including six dimensions is established, which is composed of a number of perceptual words.

This paper will be collected from the above—mentioned papers of the perceptual vocabulary questionnaire, provided to the participants to choose perceptual vocabulary, here the participants asked for "Hetalia" has a considerable love, and the main reason for choosing college students and graduate students as subjects is that this group has a higher level of knowledge, in the cultural level, consumption concept and aesthetic aspects have more rich than other groups of commonness and personality differences. After 100 questionnaires were sent out and 97 valid questionnaires were collected, 25 groups of Kansei words with the highest frequency were obtained. Finally, two role designers and five derivatives designers were consulted, and 14 perceptual image phrases with the highest frequency were selected by KJ method and expert discussion method according to their experience and professional knowledge, used to ask users to rate the character design in heitalya, as shown in Table 1.

Table 1. The perceptual image vocabulary of the character image after screening

Evaluation dimension	Perceptual image vocabulary group		
Overall feeling	Rustic—Handsome	Rigid—Vivid	
Ability Trait	Ordinary—Extraordinary	Stupid—Smart	
Personality charm	Discreet—Enthusiastic	Rational—Funny	Evil—Kindhearted
Design elements	Old—fashioned—Modern	Nondescript—Distinctive	
In a situation like this	Ungeographically attractive—Geographically attractive	Not culturally attractive—Culturally attractive	
Image design	Unattractive hair—Attractive hair	Unattractive finery—Attractive finery	Unattractive props—Attractive props

3.2 Selection of Representative Role Images

Role image is an important factor that affects the evaluation and data of perceptual vocabulary groups. Considering the influence of many factors, such as the difference of popularity, the difference of appearance frequency and the difference of audience, this study adopts the method of questionnaire, FOCUS Group and expert evaluation [4], finally, 5 characters with high popularity and relatively high frequency of appearance will be retained, and a unified animation character setting chart will be adopted to avoid misjudging the design caused by different style of character presentation, the final character image selected is shown in Fig. 2. Role 1 is List of Hetalia: Axis Powers characters, representing China; role 2 is Alfred the Great Jonnes, representing the United States; role 3 is Ivan Braginskiy, representing Russia; Character 4 is Kirkland, representing the country as England; character 5 is Francis, representing the country as France.

Fig. 2. Representative role image

4 Analysis of Character's Whole Perceptual Data and Modeling Element Data

4.1 Perceptual Data Analysis of Representative Style

The above−mentioned 5 characters were combined with 14 perceptual words, and the perceptual evaluation was made in the form of questionnaire. The questionnaire was scored by Likert scale, and the scores were 3, 2, 1, 0, −1, −2, −3. Among them, 3 indicates that the intention words fit the role design perfectly; 0 indicates that the participants have no feelings toward the role design; And −3 indicates that the intention words don't fit the role design at all. A total of 52 questionnaires were distributed and 52 valid questionnaires were recovered. By numbering all valid questionnaires, the following perceptual intention matrix can be obtained:

$$A = \begin{bmatrix} A_{11}^k & A_{12}^k & \cdots & A_{1j}^k \\ A_{21}^k & A_{22}^k & \cdots & A_{2j}^K \\ A_{31}^k & A_{32}^k & \cdots & A_{3j}^k \\ \cdots & \cdots & \cdots & \cdots \\ A_{i1}^k & A_{i2}^k & \cdots & A_{ij}^k \end{bmatrix} \tag{1}$$

In the formula: A_{ij}^k represents the participants of the K Questionnaire's evaluation of the J perceptual intention of the I role, $1 \le k \le 52$, $1 \le i \le 5$, $1 \le j \le 14$.

Considering that the questionnaire data may have some random deviation, it is necessary to screen and judge the data systematically. By using Grubbs test method to check the data, the abnormal value of the data is eliminated. Because each valid questionnaire is independent, the perceptual image value of each character image is unique for each subject ($1 \le j \le 5$), that is, K subjects correspond to K image values, among them, the value of J perceptual image is also independent, and the value of each type of J perceptual image is normal distribution, which satisfies the premise of Grubbs criterion.

According to Grabs's Grubbs rule, to determine whether there are outliers in A_{ij}^k, you need to list all of the 52 perceptual image measurements and rank them from small to large, using $O_1, O_2,.., O_{52}$ is expressed as a permutation of the image measurements. According to reference [5], it is necessary to determine whether the maximum and minimum values are outliers. The steps are as follows:

(1) Selective significance level β, and Reliability $P = 1-\beta$.
(2) According to Formulas (2) and (3), the mean value and standard deviation of each perceptual image phrase in perceptual image matrix A are calculated.

$$\overline{A}_{ij} = \frac{A_{ij}^1 + A_{ij}^2 + A_{ij}^3 + \ldots + A_{ij}^k}{k} = \frac{1}{k}\sum_{k=1}^{52} A_{ij}^k \tag{2}$$

$$\beta = \sqrt{\sum_{k=1}^{52} \left(A_{ij}^k - A_{ij}\right)^2 / (K-1)} \tag{3}$$

In the formula: K represents the number of valid questionnaires.
(3) The ratio of the calculated residual to the standard deviation G. if the minimum O_1 is suspected to be an outlier, it can be calculated according to formula (4), and if the maximum O_{52} is suspected to be an outlier, it can be calculated according to Formula (5).

$$G_1 = |\overline{A}_{ij} - O_1|/\beta \tag{4}$$

$$G_{52} = |O_{52} - \overline{A}_{ij}|/\beta \tag{5}$$

(4) Based on Grabs Checklist for Valid Questionnaire K and the Critical value $G_P(K)$ of β.
(5) If $G > G_P(K)$, the value is outlier and can be rejected.

(6) Then the other 51 perceptual image measurement value according to the above steps to determine whether the abnormal value. The test uses Python code to test, a total of 18 outliers are eliminated, and the filtered and determined values are rearranged and imported into SPSS to calculate the average values, as shown in Table 2.

Table 2. The average value of perceptual evaluation of representative character image

Perceptual image vocabulary group	Character ID				
	1	2	3	4	5
Rustic−Handsome	1.538	1.961	1.827	1.865	2.173
Rigid−Vivid	1.500	2.510	1.577	1.481	2.340
Ordinary−Extraordinary	2.451	2.192	2.346	2.137	2.231
Stupid−Smart	2.346	1.173	1.904	1.922	2.020
Discreet−Enthusiastic	−0.577	2.596	−0.538	−0.692	0.192
Rational−Funny	−0.692	2.000	−0.538	−0.481	0.615
Evil−Kindhearted	1.308	0.019	−0.635	0.288	0.596
Old−fashioned−Modern	0.173	1.135	0.788	0.942	2.019
Ungeographically attractive	2.078	2.212	2.346	2.192	2.481
Ungeographically attractive−Geographically attractive	2.346	1.863	2.212	1.788	2.173
Not culturally attractive−Culturally attractive	2.519	1.231	2.173	2.160	2.385
Unattractive hair−Attractive hair	1.885	1.481	1.058	1.096	2.346
Unattractive finery−Attractive finery	1.077	1.308	1.538	1.519	2.200
Unattractive props−Attractive props	1.961	1.647	2.231	2.078	1.827

4.2 Analysis of Perceptual Measurement of Character Image

Because of the possible correlation between the data, the analysis becomes complicated, so we can understand the correlation structure by means of principal component analysis and factor analysis. The mean value of Kansei evaluation in Table 2 was introduced into SPSS for lithographic analysis. The results showed that 14 kansei words were suitable for factor analysis.

According to SPSS analysis, the characteristic values of common factors 1, 2, 3 and 4 are all greater than 1, which indicates that the influence index is larger. As can be seen from Table 3, the variance contribution of the four principal components were 47.328%, 25.279%, 18.658% and 8.734% respectively. After the rotating load, the variance contribution of the four principal components did not change. The total contribution rate of cumulative variance is 100.00%, which is higher than the standard index of 85%. The importance of each perceptual word to the design of character image was calculated, and the component matrix of 4 common factors for perceptual image words was obtained, the principal components 1, 2, 3 and 4 are set to E1, E2, E3 and E4 respectively. The scores of each perceptual phrase of the four principal components are shown in Table 4.

Table 3. Principal component extraction

Principal component	Initial eigenvalue			Square sum of rotating loads		
	Total	Contribution to variance%	Accumulates%	Total	Contribution to variance%	Accumulates%
1	6.626	47.328	47.328	6.626	47.328	47.328
2	3.539	25.279	72.607	3.539	25.279	72.607
3	2.612	18.658	91.266	2.612	18.658	91.266
4	1.223	8.734	100.000	1.223	8.734	100.000

Table 4. Constituent scoring factor array

Image phrase	Coefficient of component score			
	E1	E2	E3	E4
Rustic−Handsome	0.109	0.188	−0.059	−0.094
Rigid−Vivid	0.135	0.023	0.147	0.186
Ordinary−Extraordinary	−0.083	0.036	0.128	0.618
Stupid−Smart	−0.133	0.112	0.081	−0.115
Discreet−Enthusiastic	0.133	−0.086	0.117	0.166
Rational−Funny	0.139	−0.053	0.114	0.147
Evil−Kindhearted	−0.054	0.002	0.310	−0.381
Old−fashioned−Modern	0.112	0.187	0.006	−0.094
Ungeographically attractive	0.079	0.216	−0.119	0.165
Ungeographically attractive−Geographically attractive	−0.106	0.128	−0.140	0.336
Not culturally attractive−Culturally attractive	−0.114	0.174	0.072	−0.089
Unattractive hair−Attractive hair	0.018	0.148	0.323	−0.050
Unattractive finery−Attractive finery	0.064	0.248	−0.071	−0.098
Unattractive props−Attractive props	−0.096	0.104	−0.254	0.126

The factor scores of E1, E2, E3 and E4 in each style are calculated in S P S software, and are expressed in B1, B2, B3 and B4. The composite factor scores are calculated by combining the component coefficient scores in formula (6) and Table 4, and are expressed in B as shown in Table 5.

Table 5. Sample comprehensive factor score

Character ID	b1	b2	b3	b4	B
1	−1.30217	−0.46652	1.13430	−0.00831	−0.52331
2	1.29378	−1.09961	0.33106	0.45542	0.43590
3	−0.50212	0.30517	−1.14711	1.24052	−0.26618
4	−0.09692	−0.28742	−0.94566	−1.48786	−0.42492
5	−0.60743	1.54838	0.62741	−0.19976	0.20355

$$B = (47.328\% / 100.000\%) \times b1 + (25.279\% / 100.000\%) \\ \times b2 + (18.658\% / 100.000\%) \times b3 + (8.734\% / 100.000\%) \times b4 \tag{6}$$

B1 is the style factor 1 score, B2 is the style factor 2 score, B3 is the style factor 3 score, and B4 is the style factor 4 score.

According to the compositional matrix after the moment of rotation, the main compositional coefficients of attractive, vivid, fashionable, funny, warm−blooded and handsome Kansei words are higher, which shows that they meet the Kansei needs of users.

Table 5 shows that a character with numbers 2 and 5 is more acceptable to the audience, especially when the design of character 5 is stylish, vivid, handsome and distinctive, which meets the audience's expectations. The composite scores of 1 and 4 characters were lower, which indicated that the design features were not the perfect and attractive type that users expected.

5 Design and Verification of Character Image Derivatives in Heitalia Based on Aesthetic Principles

The aesthetic principle involves the elements of formal beauty: color, shape, sound, quality and taste [6, 7], take, for example, a clay brooch. The final design for each character's character features using a different expression design to show the characteristics of the temperament and charm of the role.

The above clay brooches will be available for sale at the Comicup exhibition on June 12, 2021 at a price of 50 yuan per pin, as shown in Table 6.

Table 6. Sales volume of clay Brooch

Character ID	1	2	3	4	5
Sales volume	7	2	4	4	1

6 Conclusion

Cartoon, animation works as an important entertainment and creation of one of the carrier, its role image design contains great artistic value and commercial value. With the development of society, the users' preference for the role image presents the trend of diversification and high standard, and the design of its derivatives should also pay attention to the improvement of users' satisfaction.

Therefore, based on Kansei engineering theory, a representative character image and Kansei vocabulary are selected, and a kansei evaluation of character image is made by using the semantic difference method, use the Grabs criterion to judge the measurement value and eliminate the abnormal value. Then, the principal component analysis and factor coefficient quantitative analysis are carried out on the Kansei evaluation data by applying the software of S P S, and the main kansei image words that affect the role design are obtained, then, according to the aesthetic principle, the color, shape and quality of the clay brooch are optimized.

To find out how satisfied users were with the design, clay brooches were sold at comicup, and it turned out that some of the characters were still loved by the audience for their seemingly undesirable features. There are some differences between role design and product design in terms of perceptual evaluation. Generally, products with commendatory evaluation are more popular with consumers, such as fashion, easy to use, steady and so on, while those with non−commendatory evaluation are more popular, but will also be liked, has the high popularity. For example, character 1 has been relatively widely described as rustic, rigid, cautious and rational, but is very popular among Chinese audiences because of its cultural and geographic appeal, its popularity among Chinese audiences is also unusually high among other characters, so sales of its clay brooch are significantly higher than those of several other characters. This has certain enlightenment significance to the later role design and the derivative design, the rich, the multi−faceted role design is more attractive than the simple pile up the merit role. In addition, the cultural attraction of a character is also one of the important factors that determine its audience.

References

1. Yang, S.: Heitalya and the teaching of Chinese reading in middle school. Asia Pac. Educ. **2015**(16), 60 (2015)
2. Hu, S., Fu, K., Jiang, X., Jia, Q., Luo, Y.: Wardrobe design based on Kansei engineering. J. For. Eng. **6**(04), 176–183 (2021)
3. Fu, Y., Luo, S., Zhou, Y.: Animation character evaluation based on perceptual image. J. Zhejiang Univ. **45**(09), 1544–1552+1570 (2011)
4. Wang, N., Wang, J.: Research on the modeling design of Home Service Robots for emotional needs. Mech. Des. **35**(11), 111–116 (2018)
5. Fu, Y., Yang, L., Yu, F.B.: Microsoft Excel application in Environmental monitoring data processing. Sichuan Environ. **23**(6), 107–109 (2004)
6. Uxillin. Aesthetic principle. Beijing Higher Education Press (2017)
7. Rudolf, A.: Art and Visual Perception. Hunan Fine Arts Publishing House, Changsha (2008)
8. Zhou, C., Leng, C., Zhan, X., et al.: Color quantitative analysis of customized wardrobe based on HVC. Forest Ind. **57**(9), 37–40 (2020)

9. Zhou, Z.: Animation Character Design. Southwest Normal University Press, Chongqing (2008)
10. Luo, S., Pan, Y.-H.: Review of theory, key techno logies and its application of perceptual image in product design. Chin. J. Mech. Eng. **43**(3), 8–13 (2007)
11. Zhou, M.: Sensibility Design. Science and Technology Press, Shanghai (2011)

Understanding Agendas of Unmanned Stores: The Case of South Korea

Yongseok Lee[1], Xu Li[2], and Hyesun Hwang[3]($\boxtimes$)

[1] Convergence Program for Social Innovation, Sungkyunkwan University, Seoul, South Korea
[2] Department of Consumer Science, Sungkyunkwan University, Seoul, South Korea
[3] Department of Consumer Science, Convergence Program for Social Innovation,
Sungkyunkwan University, Seoul, South Korea
h.hwang@skku.edu

Abstract. This study aimed to find the overall issues of unmanned stores from the media in South Korea. For analysis, 5,261 online news articles published between 2018 to 2021 were collected. As an overview, we analyzed the annual word frequency. The results showed emerging terms related to the COVID-19 after 2020. Then, latent dirichlet allocation (LDA) topic modeling analysis was conducted to explore the agendas of unmanned stores, and as a result, 12 topics were derived. The results showed that most topics focused on the various types of unmanned stores including specific franchise brand names. In addition, as a structural aspect of the unmanned store field, agendas such as business prospects, major countries, and leading companies in unmanned stores were derived. Furthermore, social issues such as the spread of COVID-19 and crime cases were found. The results of this study provide an understanding of the various agendas related to unmanned stores.

Keywords: Unmanned store · Topic modeling · Text analysis

1 Introduction

The rapid development of information communication technology has led to the transformation of new types of industries. As advanced information communication technologies, such as the Internet of Things (IoT) and big data, are widely applied to customer services, these technologies accelerate the transformation in distribution. As technologies apply to offline stores, services produced by offline store workers are being replaced by technologies, and their importance is diminishing. In retail and other markets, contact-free services are becoming familiar to consumers [1]. Since the appearance of Amazon Go, there are now "unmanned stores" where there are no service workers there for consumers [2]. In unmanned stores, the method varies by store; consumers purchase goods by themselves using kiosks, touch screens, mobiles, and other tools without the interaction of cashiers and workers. After Amazon Go was first introduced in Seattle, other countries, such as China, Russia, Japan, and South Korea, adopted such business strategies and developed their business models [3].

C. Stephanidis et al. (Eds.): HCII 2022, CCIS 1654, pp. 267–274, 2022.
https://doi.org/10.1007/978-3-031-19679-9_33

With its strength in information technology, South Korea has rapidly adopted such business models and established various types of unmanned stores. It has been argued that South Korea's rapid transition to a contact-free era due to an aging population, a decrease in the labor force, and the digitalization of services is a natural progression [4]. In this vein, the term "untact" marketing, a combination of the prefix "un" and the word "contact," spread like a fashion and applied to various industries. However, the field of unmanned stores is still in the development stage despite their potential and competitiveness, and continuous improvement must be established as a sufficiently mature distribution method [5]. Therefore, we examine the issues related to unmanned stores, spreading as a new distribution strategy in South Korea. To this end, we aimed to discover the agendas of unmanned stores in the media. The present study analyzes online news articles on unmanned stores using a text-mining approach.

2 Literature Review

2.1 Unmanned Store

Since the unmanned store gained attention recently, related literature has emerged to discuss corresponding topics fruitfully in academic fields. Considering the importance of technology in unmanned stores, the major focus of the literature is on specific technologies that enable the structural operation of unmanned businesses. Zhang et al. focused on a convolutional neural network (CNN)-based object detection algorithm of a recognition model for security and claimed that it could efficiently identify theft and non-theft behaviors [6]. Kim et al. examined CNN-based real-time cabinet object detection (RCOD) to suggest an effective detection model for tracking purchasing behaviors [7]. Hamidi et al. focused on the existing apps of franchise stores and compared the technologies used for each application [8]. Lee, S. H. and Lee, D.W. also focused on the leading technologies of information and communication technology of unmanned retail stores in China and the US, which are the leading unmanned stores [9]. Guo et al. focused on 5G and IoT technologies used in retail stores in China [10].

In addition to the technological approach to unmanned stores, efforts have been made to focus on their social aspects. Denuwara et al. evaluated the impact of unmanned stores in terms of sustainability [5]. They examined the supply chain, pricing strategy, and overall business model compared to traditional models to test the sustainability of unmanned businesses [5]. Kwak and Cho focused on obstacles to unmanned store usage [3]. Highlighting the digital divide and the challenges consumers may face, they claimed the need for change in legislation and applications of unmanned stores in their study [3]. There are academic efforts to understand and develop the concept of "unmanned store," besides these efforts, we aim to add more value to such fields with our study.

2.2 Text Analysis

We focused on a text analysis approach to navigate the media portrait of unmanned stores. Numerous exploratory methods and methods exist for text analysis. Among these methods, we chose to apply a topic modeling approach. Topic modeling is a method frequently used in social science to identify important contexts within a corpus of documents [11]. Specifically, the latent dirichlet allocation (LDA) model is one of the most popular strategies owing to its explicit representation and document flexibility. It is a powerful tool for discovering topics in documents without keywords or labels [12]. Given these strengths of text analysis, we utilized the LDA topic modeling method to discover crucial contexts within the media portrait.

3   Methods

3.1   Data Collection

We collected data related to unmanned stores from newspapers in Korea. We used a website named "BigKinds," which provides collective news articles from different media in Korea. Considering the emerging period of unmanned stores in Korean society, we collected all articles published from January 2018 to November 2021. After removing duplicate and irrelevant articles, 5261 articles were included in our study.

According to the timeline, the number of articles collected for our study showed a recognizable difference. In Fig. 1, the amount of collected data has dramatically increased since February 2020. While the official numbers of unmanned stores were unobtainable, this could explain how the unmanned industry has expanded recently.

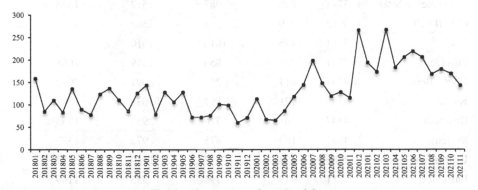

Fig. 1. The number of news articles.

3.2   Analysis Procedure

Our main research method focused on text analysis to overview the media portrait of unmanned stores, especially using the LDA topic modeling model. Pre-processing and cleaning procedures were performed before analysis. We removed all the emails and special characters using Python for the collected data. In addition, the number of words listed as stop words was used to remove irrelevant characters. After cleaning, we first conducted an annual word frequency analysis to view the sketch of media portraits and then staged LDA topic modeling to understand the details.

4 Results

4.1 Annual Word Frequency

As we aim to examine the overall media portrait of unmanned stores, we first conducted an annual frequency analysis of words. We analyzed the word frequencies for each year and listed them as a combined total set in Table 1.

Table 1. Annual word frequency.

Word	Total	2018 Freq.	2019 Freq.	2020 Freq.	2021 Freq.
Store	14387	3028	2655	3518	5186
Corporation	9381	2695	1781	2028	2877
Service	9029	1683	1859	2748	2739
Customer	7874	1765	1308	2215	2586
Payment	7366	1539	2210	1595	2022
Operate	7180	1564	1168	1992	2456
Technology	6436	1420	1377	1541	2098
Industry	5809	1677	1035	1346	1751
Convenience Store	5741	1698	983	1512	1548
COVID-19	4913	0	3	2562	2348
Use	4911	945	1016	1310	1640
Provide	4791	934	850	1319	1688
Contactless	4591	217	255	2097	2022
Korea	4490	1171	894	1038	1387
Business	4347	901	770	957	1733
System	4591	1109	875	976	1387
Utilization	3885	774	677	1147	1287
Introduce	3811	933	796	933	1149
Security	3505	959	542	574	1430
Product	3478	978	671	965	864
Kiosk	3406	666	772	763	1205
Variety	3376	654	697	946	1079
Amazon	3316	1660	731	533	392
Time	3242	784	529	789	1140
Expand	3241	758	599	951	933

We could find a few interesting points about unmanned stores portrayed by the Korean media from the dataset. First, through the analysis of total frequency, it was observed that the Korean media focused on related keywords such as "Corporation," "Store," "Service," and "Customer." The keywords of "Service," "Convenience Store," and "Security" directly represent specific business fields. By comparing the yearly frequency, we found a shift in media focuses on unmanned stores. The leading corporation of the unmanned store, "Amazon," appeared as the top keyword in 2018 and yet continuously lost its attention after. This could be interpreted as an implication that the Korean economy first focused on Amazon as a role model for this field and later neglected its focus by focusing on local development. The pandemic-related terms "COVID" and "Contactless" have appeared as the top keywords since 2020. Considering that these keywords were not significantly mentioned in 2018 and 2019, their frequency seems remarkable. Lastly, "Technology," "Business," and "Security" showed a dramatic increase in 2021, which projects the latest focus of media portrait.

4.2 Topic Modeling

In this study, LDA topic modeling was performed to recognize the latest agendas of unmanned stores in the Korean media. Twelve topics, which were chosen considering appropriateness and relevance, were labeled and listed with corresponding words in Table 2.

Table 2. Unmanned stores topics from LDA modeling.

Topic	Label	Terms
1	Management	Job, Minimum Wage, Government, Increase, Employment, Aged, Issue, Decrease, COVID-19, Aged, Social, Economy, Regulation, Self-employed, Policy, Metropolitan, Society, Worker, Wage, Spread
2	Automated city	Automobile, Region, Blockchain, Build, Operate, Resident, Installation, Place, Use, Variety, Provide, Citizen, City, Smart, Parking lot, Process, Business, Eco-friendly, Promote, Busan*
3	Crime	Crime, Cash, Police, Ice cream, Order machine, Occur, Teenager, Male, Suspicion, Vault, Seoul*, Business owner, Incident, Prevention, Time, Confirm, Holiday, Whole Area, Arrest, Imprison
4	Unmanned convenience store	Store, Payment, Convenience Store, Operate, Customer, Introduce, Product, E-Mart**, System, Seven Eleven**, Self, Kiosk, Use, Item, Installation, Counter, Employer, Card, CU**, Industry

(continued)

Table 2. (*continued*)

Topic	Label	Terms
5	Policies	Support, Small business owner, Choice, Ministry of SMEs and Startups, Smart mart, Business, Smart, Operate, Promote, Plan, Mart, Kakao**, COVID-19, Assignment, Government, Minister, Contactless, Schedule, Seongnam-Si*, Kospi
6	Shopping places	Department store, Gas station, Lotte**, Place, The Hyundai, Seoul, Shinsegae**, Store, Library, Shopping, Lotte Shopping, Size, Lotte group, Group, Underground, S-Oil**, Commerce, Brand, Caltex**, Nature
7	Unmanned mobile stores & banks	Customer, Store, Service, Bank, Use, Smartphone, Digital, Contactless, Kiosk, Provide, Employer, Task, Operate, Mobile, Branch, U Plus**, Telecom, Purchase, Finance, Handle
8	Unmanned café & restaurants	Robot, Café, Order, Coffee, Delivery, Beverage, Food, Time, Menu, Restaurant, b;eat**, Laundromat, Ministop**, Table, JD**, Laundry, Operate, Barista, Machine, Recommendation
9	Unmanned Industry	Corporation, Industry, Korea, USA, Brand, Market, Franchise, Goods, China, Start a Business, Consumer, Sale, Japan, Turnover, Time, Price, Start, Store, Operate, Variety
10	Market environment	Corporation, Business, CEO, Representative, Field, Global, Korea, China, Startup, Growth, Innovation, Digital, Future, Market, Strategy, Industrial Revolution, World, Promote, Enter, Investment
11	Technology	Technology, Service, Amazon, Security, Corporation, Artificial Intelligence, Development, Provide, Utilization, Solution, Distribution, System, Industry, Data, Apply, Platform, Korea, Shopping, Offline, Variety
12	COVID -19	COVID-19, Contactless, Online, Turnover, Increase, Industry, Prospect, Expand, Consume, Spread, Record, Market, Profit, Decrease, Growth, New, Contactless, Researcher, Service, Offline

Notes. * Korean cities ** Name of corporates

Topic 1 consisted of keywords related to the management of unmanned stores. Keywords such as "Minimum wage," "Employment," "Job," and "Workers" were extracted. Topic 2 represents automation of the city, with extracted keywords of "City," "Smart," "Parking lot," and "Resident." Our study suggested these keywords as the role of partners of unmanned stores in media portraits. Considering that they often mentioned automated cities with unmanned stores as an ongoing process of futuristic expectations for our society, such keywords seem to be extracted within Topic 2. Topic 3 shows keywords related to crime issues in unmanned stores. Keywords such as "Crime," "Cash," and "Police" directly show criminal acts, while "Ice cream" and "Holiday" refer to specific cases. Topic 4 consists of extracted keywords related to unmanned convenience stores. Names of specific convenience stores such as "CU," "E-Mart," and "Seven-Eleven" were included in the topic. As convenience stores are one of the main fields in the unmanned industry, specific technology-related terms of "Card," "Self," and "Kiosk" were remarkable.

The listed keywords in Topic 5 were policy-related terms such as "Support," "Ministry of SMEs and Startups," and "Government." A brief sketch of government intervention in unmanned stores could be seen. Topic 6 showed the names of popular department stores in Korea, such as "Lotte," "Hyundai," and "Shinsegae" as well as other shopping places where unmanned stores are located. The keywords in Topics 7 and 8 show how the Korean economy focuses on various fields of unmanned stores. Presentation of "Café," "Restaurant," "Coffee machine," "Bank," and "Telecom" and corresponding franchise brand names of "U Plus" and "b; eat" implicates the development of unmanned industries in detail. Topics 9, 10, and 11 demonstrate unmanned stores' overall technologies and business terms. An interesting point could be detected in Topic 9. In contrast, leading countries in such fields as "Korea," "USA," "China," and "Japan" are listed along with the terms "Corporation," "Brand," and "Franchise." Topics 10 and 11 provide more specific terms for the unmanned store, such as business terms of "Start-up," "Investment," and "CEO," and technological terms of "Artificial Intelligence," "Data," and "Security." The last topic shows pandemic-related terms of "COVID-19," "expanding," "contactless," "offline," and "online." Although the importance of the pandemic in the period was recognizable, that given terms appeared along with our research keyword, and media seemed to connect these topics.

5 Conclusion

This study analyzed the agenda for unmanned stores, focusing on the case of South Korea with advanced information and communication technology infrastructure. We conducted text analysis focusing on topic modeling method to understand the social issues of unmanned stores by analyzing online news articles. This study shows various interests and the latest agenda for unmanned stores, ranging from general characteristics of unmanned stores to related policies, technologies, industries, and environmental issues. Issues related to COVID-19 were also identified. The results contribute to the literature on unmanned stores as a new retail method by providing a general sketch that can be extended to other research topics in this field. Nevertheless, our study had some limitations. Since the field of unmanned stores has recently emerged, the data available for analysis have not been massively accumulated. Further studies should be conducted when more data are available. In addition, future research should consider the different unmanned stores and analyze how different issues may emerge. In future research, it is necessary to analyze data that can deal with various aspects such as industry-specific characteristics and sales trends of unmanned stores to develop more detailed business strategies.

References

1. Kang, J.W., Namkung, Y.: Classifying quality attributes of self-service kiosk in the restaurant industry using Kano Model. Korean J. Hospitality Tourism **27**(8), 263–279 (2018)
2. Seo, S.: The effects of shopping value on the usage intention of unmanned fashion stores -application of technology acceptance model-. J. Fashion Bus. **23**(2), 140–155 (2019)
3. Kwak, Y.A., Cho, Y.S.: Unmanned store, retail tech and digital divide in South Korea. J. Distrib. Sci. **17**(9), 47–56 (2019)
4. Lee, Y.: The South Koreans left behind in a contact-free society, https://www.bbc.com/ worklife/article/20200803-south-korea-contact-free-untact-society-after-coronavirus. Accessed 27 May 2022
5. Denuwara, N., Maijala, J., Hakovirta, M.: The impact of unmanned stores' business models on sustainability. SN Bus. Econ. **1**(10), 1–27 (2021). https://doi.org/10.1007/s43546-021-001 36-8
6. Zhang, Y., et al.: A new intelligent supermarket security system. Neural Netw. World **30**(2), 113–131 (2020)
7. Kim, D.H., Lee, S., Jeon, J., Song, B.C.: Real-time purchase behavior recognition system based on deep learning-based object detection and tracking for an unmanned product cabinet. Expert Syst. Appl. **143**, 1–10 (2019)
8. Hamidi, S.R., Yusof, M.A.M., Shuhidan, S.M., Kadir, S.A.: IR4.0: unmanned store apps. Indonesian J. Electr. Eng. Comput. Sci. **17**(3), 1540 (2020)
9. Lee, S.H., Lee, D.W.: A study on ICT technology leading change of unmanned store. J. Convergence Inf. Technol. **8**(4), 109–114 (2018)
10. Guo, B., Wang, Z., Wang, P., Xin, T., Zhang, T., Yu, Z.: DeepStore: understanding customer behaviors in unmanned stores. IT Prof. **22**, 55–63 (2020)
11. Asmussen, C.B., Møller, C.: Smart literature review: a practical topic modelling approach to exploratory literature review. J. Big Data **6**(1), 1–18 (2019). https://doi.org/10.1186/s40537-019-0255-7
12. Liu, Y., Du, F., Sun, J., Jiang, Y.: iLDA: an interactive latent Dirichlet allocation model to improve topic quality. J. Inf. Sci. **46**(1), 23–40 (2020)

Cultural Discourse on Keyboards: The Selection of Alphabets

Chunyan Wang[1(⊠)], Xiaojun Yuan[2], and Xiaoxin Xiao[3]

[1] Xiangqingmei Co., Ltd., Hangzhou 31000, Zhejiang, China
ahwangchunyan@126.com
[2] University at Albany, State University of New York, Albany, NY 12222, USA
xyuan@albany.edu
[3] Longcheng High School, Shenzhen 518100, Guangdong, China

Abstract. By investigating into the alphabets of the Apple keyboard in 16 languages, we have arrived at two findings. First, language marks, special letters with marks and alphabets are chosen and listed on keyboards in all languages except simplified Chinese; Second, influenced by the English-oriented design form, English language places every letter on a single key within letter areas, other languages prefer scattering, squeezing, or cropping their letters within the existing letter, number, or punctuation areas, which we call as the phenomenon of language gravity. We therefore propose that Chinese pinyin—23 initials, 24 finals, and 5 tones—should be fully displayed on a keyboard, that self-contained keyboards should be developed to meet the increasing demands of non-English keyboard market.

Keywords: Keyboard · Alphabets · Cultural Discourse · Language gravity

1 Introduction

Back in the early 1980s, in order to sell PCs to non-technical users in non-English speaking areas [1], the IT companies of the United States began the localization process by "adapting their hardware or software to a specific locale" [2]. Different countries (e.g., China) or regions tried to set technical standards, even laws to recommend or regulate the official language usage in information processing [3]. However, in China, nearly alphabets of all computer keyboards sold are of English rather than Chinese pinyin letters or Wubi symbols in China.

We collected information on JD.COM [4]—a Chinese e-commerce giant, like Alibaba, but famous for quality products—to learn the status quo of simplified Chinese keyboard on March 24th, 2020. The results (see Fig 1) show that (a) with "键盘" (keyboard) as a keyword to search, there are no Chinese characters on the keyboard excluding their Chinese brand names on all the top 15 brands out of the 6, 300 pieces of items; (b) with "中文键盘"(Chinese keyboard) as a keyword, the only Chinese key is Apple's "中/英(Chinese/English)" among top 10 brands in 5,075 items; (c) after manually checking by picture for a long time, we have found that only 4 Chinese keyboards are among (b), and one of them, POLIGU, is traditional Chinese; (d) The highest comments of (a) is Rapoo, 960, 000+, while that of (c) is 精晟, with 40+.

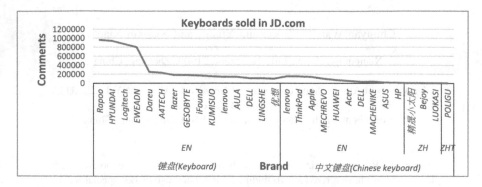

Fig. 1. Keyboards sold in JD.com (As of 2020/3/24)

From the data, we can see that almost all alphabets of keyboards available for potential buyers in China are English ones, which seems to violate the requirements of localization.

To redesign the keyboard, we first focus on the alphabet area, simply because it constitutes the main part of a computer keyboard.

2 Apple Magic as a Case Study

To investigate the alphabets on a keyboard, we use elements of discourse content, discourse form, the relationships between different discourses in the frame of Cultural Discourse Studies [5] to choose and organize the body of this paper.

Apple Magic [6] was chosen because Apple is famous for its design in IT hardware industry. Magic keyboard has 16-language versions. To make the analysis neat, here we combine ISO 639-1 [7] language identifiers with common names to refer to these languages: Arabic (AR), British English(BRE), Chinese (Pinyin) (ZH), Chinese (Zhuyin) (ZHT), Danish (DA), French (FR), German (DE), Italian (IT), Japanese yi (JA), Korean (KO), Portuguese (PT), Russian (RU), Spanish (ES), Spanish (Latin American) (LES), Swiss (CH) and US English (EN).

Though we didn't cover all the languages in the world, the sample languages we selected include 6 official languages of the UN [8] and top 10 most popular languages in the non-English speaking world in language service industry [9].Without live preview of keys of Magic keyboard, common users can access Windows keyboard layouts [10] to get and check the name of every key except KO, JA and ZHT.

The letters on keyboards, mainly alphabets, are the discourse content we studied in this paper. Alphabets in Writing Systems [11] help us quickly find all the alphabets in the world and Language Families in Languages [11] tell us the relationships between languages. The pronunciation marks, however, are usually learned from the Unicode Standard [12].

In this paper, we focus on the alphabets displayed on the keyboards and divide them into two groups – Latin-only languages and Latin+ (local) languages—according to their similarities with English based on their language families and letter spellings. The first category is: BRE, DA, FR, DE, IT, PT, ES, LES, CH and EN; the second encloses the rest: AR, ZH, ZHT, JA, KO, and RU.

The places of keys are the form of discourse to display. The comparison of English position and non-English ones is discussed to disclose the influence of English on other languages.

3   Latin-only languages

All Latin languages have at least 26 Latin (we ignore their different pronunciations, meanings, but concentrate on the same writing forms) letters on the keyboards.

3.1   Written Content – Besides 26 Latin Letters

Additional Letters from Alphabets. DA, DE, ES and LES add additional Latin letters from their alphabets. On the DA keyboard, there are "Æ" (combination of AE), "Ø"(O with stroke), and "Å"(A with ring above). On the DE keyboard, 3 letters ("Ä", "Ö", and "Ü") with diaeresis (as in English naïve), and "ß" (a small sharp S) are added.

ES and LES letter "Ñ" showed how the typical national culture survived in the information technology. Faced with keyboards without "Ñ" under the promotion of European Union, Spanish government issued BOE-A-1993-10532, which required that "All mechanical, electrical or electronic operating devices used for writing, recording, printing, retransmission of information and data transmission, and that are sold in Spain, must include the letter <ñ>…" [13] in accordance with the Treaty of the European Union, which proclaims the "flourishing of the cultures of the Member States" [14].

Latin Marks. Besides letters in alphabets, there are accent, spelling, and grammar marks and letters with marks (see Table 1). They are often above or besides the 26 letters on the right.

Table 1. Language marks and Letters with marks

Type	Feature	Unicode name	Mark	Type	Feature	Unicode name	Letter
Language marks	Accent	Acute	´	Letters with marks	Accent	With Acute	é
		Grave	`			With Grave	è/ à/ ù/ ì/ ò
		Circumflex	^			With Diaeresis	ü/ ö/ ä
		Diaeresis	¨			With Cedilla	ç/ Ç
	Spelling	Tilde	~				
	Grammar	Masculine Ordinal Indicator	o̲				
		Feminine Ordinal Indicator	a̲				

Acute, grave, circumflex, and diaeresis are placed above a vowel to show the pronunciation quality. Take FR as an example, acute mainly indicates that the vowel is stressed, as in café, or the vowel is close or tense, as in été. Grave shows that the vowel is secondarily stressed, or the vowel is open or lax. Circumflex is the marker of a long vowel. Diaeresis separates the second vowel from its adjacent first vowel.

Tilde is placed over "n" only in ES to indicate a palatal nasal sound or over a vowel in PT to indicate nasalization.

In ES and PT, all ordinal indicators have masculine and feminine forms to follow masculine or feminine nouns respectively. For instance, the first car is "o carro primeiro" and the first house is "a casa primeira."

Cedilla is under one letter "c" in FR, IT, CH, PT and ES. It indicates that the letter sounds "s" instead of "k." So "ç" in FR, IT and CH, or "Ç" in PT and ES are listed on keyboard other than the mark itself.

3.2 Discourse Form

As to the 26 letters, most letters follow the practice of English, ignoring the usage frequency of letters in their own languages. Only FR, DE and CH keyboards modify several keys' places.

DE, CH and EN belong to Germanic languages, but the frequency of Y and Z are different. FR, a branch of Romance languages under Indo-European languages, exchanges letter "A", "Q", "Z", "W", and "M" places with their English counterparts.

Table 2. Different places of 26+ letters

EN	`	2	4	7	9	0	-	=	[		]	;	`	\
Others	o/aˊ	é	ç	è	ç	à	ß	ì /ˊ/ˋ	Å/Ü/é/ è /o/ a/ü/ˊ/ˋ/ˊ	ˊ/ˊ/ˋ	Æ/Ö/Ç/Ñ/ç/ò /é/ö	Ø/Ã/ù/à/ä/ˊ/ˋ/ˊ/~	Ç/ù/ˊ

While some small letters with mark scatter on the number keys or the right punctuation keys (see Table 2), all capitals are on the right of P and L, such as "[", ";", "", and "\" (see Table 2). The number of Latin keys is the same. Specifically, all adopting European "Return", they exchange the position of English "Return" and "\."

4   Latin+ (Local) Languages

The Latin+ keyboards seem more crowded than Latin ones, because two systems of alphabets other than one, the local and English, displayed except ZH. Russian, with no special letters or marks, is easy to list its 33 letters besides the 26 English letters and the right punctuations. ZH will be discussed in Sect. 5. The other 4 languages, AR, ZHT, JA and KO are more complex and will be discussed separately.

4.1   Latin and Local Alphabetical Systems

Arabic Marks and Letters with Marks. Arabic has complex pronunciation marks besides 28 consonants plus hamza in the alphabet. Arabic Tashkil [12] is a phonetic guide to help people pronounce the words correctly. Arabic vowels do not appear in common written documents but for Al Quran, children's books, or textbooks to teach beginners. There are 3 short vowels (fatha "ó", kasra "ọ", damma "ó"), 3 long vowels (fathatan "ó", kasratan "ọ", dammatan "ó"), one absence of a vowel (sukun "ó"), and one consonant gemination mark (shadda "ó") on the keyboard. Moreover, there are combined marks: hamza's combined marks "إ ,ؤ ,أ,ئ", Alef with marks "آ", two special endings "ى ,ة", and an extension mark "ـ" as part of Arabic keyboard.

CJK Special Letters and Marks. CJK refers to Chinese (Pinyin and Zhuyin), Japanese, Korean in localization industry and Unicode standard [12].

KO is the only one in 16 languages that selects 33 out of its 40 letters in the alphabet on the keyboard. The rest seven are two single vowels ("ㅚ, ㅟ") and 5 combined vowels ("ㅘ, ㅝ, ㅙ, ㅞ, ㅢ").

The Japanese language has two native writing systems, hiragana and katakana, besides kanji. On the keyboard, there are 26 English letters, 46 basic hiragana syllables and more marks to write. Japanese Industrial Standards Committee has established a series of standards involving the inputs and conversions of Kana and Kanji, the display of every key on the keyboard. One of them is JISX4064: 2002 Basic functions of Kana-Kanji conversion systems [15]. Small letters of hiragana and some special marks are also part of Japanese written language. Small letters include five vowels ("ぁ,ぃ,ぅ,ぇ,ぉ") to transcribe foreign words or indicate a long vowel sound, the small tsu (sokuon "っ") to indicate a stop, and three small yōon characters ("ゃya,ゅyu,ょyo") to replace an "i" sound with the "ya, yu, yo" sound respectively. Another two marks (dakuten "゛" and han-dakuten "゜") are used to distinguish the voiced or semi-voiced sounds. One katakana mark "ー" is also on the keyboard, indicating prolonged sound mark.

Chinese features for its tones. ZHT and ZH are two systems of one language pronunciation. While ZHT adopts Chinese graphs, ZH turns to employ Latin letters. As a result, ZHT has 37 letters plus 3 (万v, 兀ng, 广gn) dialect-only letters. There are 14 more letters and 4 tones than ZH on the keyboard, of which the first tone is defaulted (Table 3).

Table 3. More vowels on ZHT keyboard

Mean-ing	Consonants			Vowels								Vowels	Special vowels			Tones			
ZHT	ㄓ	ㄔ	ㄕ	ㄞ	ㄟ	ㄠ	ㄡ	ㄢ	ㄣ	ㄤ	ㄥ	ㄦ	ㄝ	ㄩ	ˇ	ˋ	´	·
ZH	zh	ch	sh	ai	ei	ao	ou	an	en	ang	eng	er	ê	ü				

Most of these letters are spelled as two or three letters in ZH. They might look like compound consonants or vowels, but they are indeed just one consonant or vowel. It is more obvious to see in ZHT which uses one sign to represent the pronunciation.

4.2   The Places of AR, ZHT, KO, and JA

While Every English letter and its similar 26 Latin letter stands alone comfortably in the middle of every key, Asians choose to divide the key into four parts and share half of places with their English counterparts (see Table 4). AR and JA are on the right side and KO and ZHT on the left.

Table 4. Key parts

Lan	AR	JA	KO	ZHT
Key parts				
Comment	The blue squares are English letters, the red squares are locals.			

The diagonal positions of English capitals are local main letters. The opposite of them are local special letters and marks. In Table 4, the diagonal place of "Q" is "ض" in AR, "た" in JA, "ㅂ" in KO, and "夕" in ZHT.

KO puts the similar letters together and splits the keyboard into consonant and vowel areas. ZHT and JA extend their letters on the number keys, and JA even cuts the long space bar into three to realize the conversion of complex Japanese letters.

5   Pinyin

The content of Pinyin is prescribed in the "Scheme for the Chinese Phonetic Alphabet" [16]. Apart from the Pinyin Alphabet (26-English-form-letter), there are another four parts: Initials, Finals, Tones, and Apostrophes. Chinese Pinyin is composed of 23 initials, 24 finals, and 5 tones. In practice, either in language learning or in typing, initials, finals, and tones should be mastered.

The usage of Pinyin Alphabet has been debated since its appearance. To be short, it lays down the form, name, and order of pinyin [17]. Grade 1 students of the elementary school were required to recite the Pinyin Alphabet [18], especially the order of letters, before they are to learn to use Chinese dictionary. On the current ZH keyboard, 3 initials, "zh, ch, sh", are not presented. As to the finals, 18 out of 23 are neglected. Chinese tones should be inserted as symbols. If we have a real pinyin keyboard, we can type most Chinese characters with an initial, a final, and/or a tone. Usually, two or three keys are enough before we choose the needed character. English letters, included in pinyin, will not be necessary to list aside.

6   Language Gravity—Influence of English Language

As the computer keyboard originated from typewriter, which was patented and improved by American inventor Christopher Latham Sholes [19], the letter area was designed in size and numbers according to the English letters. In a complete localization process, theoretically, all the other languages are expected to replace the content and form of English with their native ones in the letter area, in this case, to enlarge or narrow the existing English letter area based on the number of their native letters. In practice, however, as we can see from the above analysis that the other languages choose only to modify their versions of a keyboard by appending their letters to the English ones. Therefore, while English enjoys the concise unity of form and content of letter area, the others are generally given to scatter their letters first to the right punctuation area, and second to the above number area and even to the below space bar, or to squeeze their letters at a corner of a key, or crop theirs to adjust the existing English form. In short, the forms of local language versions are unfit for their contents. We call this phenomenon of disunity of content and form of versions of other language keyboard as they are under the influence of English language gravity, just like the planets are forced to change their expected perfect circle orbits to ovals under the attraction of the sun.

As gravity is determined by quality, a language gravity, is determined mainly by a nation's military strength and economical power [20]. Therefore, languages are not equal in strength [21], but with different gravity. The stronger influences the weaker and changes the latter's normal form. Nowadays, English is the global lingua franca [21], standing on the top of the first level with around 1.5 billion people in the early 2000s [21], other Latin languages second, and Asians follow behind, based on combination of numbers and territories of language users [22].

In localization practice, this phenomenon is confirmed by language priority order. Most computer products were written directly in English or translated first into English no matter what the inventor's native language was. FIGS (FR, IT, DE, ES) were localized second, the third, CKJ and other Asian languages. The order is not fixed, but changes with a nation's economic status. While the Asian economy became stronger, more and more Asian languages were among the to-be localized language list [9].

Moreover, keyboard is more than a common product. Unlike a fruit, which is to be consumed once and for all by users, keyboard is also a language medium to communicate between the national and international markets. In this way, localization is not a one-stop solution, but a process with many stages.

In the first stage, an English keyboard is convenient for professionals, most of whom are users who are using computers or practicing English. For such users, English or computer English is not an obstacle, on the contrary, it is a necessity to write codes or letters. At this time, localization is second to internationalization. The present ZH keyboard, in English clothes, is simply a reflection of Chinese export-oriented economy.

When the local language market is big enough, often the consumers are non-professional users, either the international companies or the local producers will come up with more localized products. Until then, the local languages will enjoy more suitable forms to accommodate their contents.

7   Conclusion

Our study shows that all languages except for ZH display their language marks on the keyboard by traditions, laws or industrial standards. We point out that the importance of all the languages is not the same in that the other languages, attracted by English gravity, tend to exchange information through English. The localization process is, as a result, often consistent with each nation's economic status.

Next, we will plan to investigate the rules of layouts of keys in different languages, analyze the frequency of Pinyin letters, and then provide advice to design a real ZH keyboard to replace the current English-clothed Pinyin keyboard.

References

1. Translation Royale A Brief History of IT Localization. https://www.translationroyale.com/history-of-it-localization/. Accessed 17 Feb 2022
2. Gala: What is localization? https://www.gala-global.org/knowledge-center/about-the-industry/language-services. Accessed 17 Feb 2022
3. State Administration for Market Regulation: Chinese Information Processing–Vocabulary–Part 02: Chinese and Chinese Character. GB/T 12200.2-1994. http://c.gb688.cn/bzgk/gb/showGb?type=online&hcno=267C1B057CA270BBF28AFBE756213D84. Accessed 17 Feb 2022
4. Jingdong.com. https://www.jd.com/. Accessed 24 Mar 2020
5. Shi-xu: Communication of Contemporary China: Studies in a cultural discourse studies perspective. Peking University Press, Beijing (2010)
6. Apple Magic: Accessories. https://www.apple.com.cn/shop/product/MQ052CH/A. Accessed 23 Apr 2021
7. ISO 639-1: 2002. Codes for the representation of names of languages — Part 1: Alpha-2 code. https://www.iso.org/standard/22109.html. Accessed 17 Feb 2022
8. Official Languages. https://www.un.org/en/our-work/official-languages. Accessed 13 Oct 2021
9. Localizedirect: The most popular languages for game translation and LQA 2021. https://www.localizedirect.com/ebook/report. Accessed 13 Oct 2021
10. Microsoft: Windows keyboard layouts. https://docs.microsoft.com/en-us/globalization/windows-keyboard-layouts. Accessed 23 Feb 2022
11. Omniglot. https://www.omniglot.com/index.htm. Accessed 24 Feb 2022
12. The Unicode Consortium: The Unicode® Standard Version 14.0 – Core Specification. https://www.unicode.org/versions/Unicode14.0.0/. Accessed 22 Feb 2022
13. Agencia Estatal Boletín Oficial del Estado: Real Decreto 564/1993, de 16 de abril, sobre presencia de la letra «Ñ» y demás caracteres específicos del idioma castellano en los teclados de determinados aparatos de funcionamiento mecánico, eléctrico o electrónico que se utilicen para la escritura. https://www.boe.es/eli/es/rd/1993/04/16/564. Accessed 24 Feb 2022
14. EU: Treaty on European Union (Maastricht, 7 February 1992) — Consolidated version 2007. https://www.cvce.eu/content/publication/2010/5/3/e92737d6-7557-4ea1-9ca5-123368a7fb88/publishable_en.pdf. Accessed 24 Feb 2022
15. Japanese Industrial Standards Committee: JISX4064: 2002 Basic functions of Kana-Kanji conversion systems. Japanese Standard Association, Tokyo (2002)

16. Scheme for the Chinese Phonetic Alphabet (《汉语拼音方案》) (1958). http://www.moe. gov.cn/jyb_sjzl/ziliao/A19/195802/t19580201_186000.html. Accessed 23 Apr 2021
17. Li, P.: Functions of alphabet in scheme for the chinese phonetic alphabet. Mod. Chin. **1**, 20–21 (2005)
18. Wen, R.M.: Chinese (Grade 1, Part II). People's Education Press, Beijing (2020)
19. Britannica: Christopher Latham Sholes. https://www.britannica.com/biography/Christopher-Latham-Sholes. Accessed 23 Mar 2022
20. Ostler, N.: Empires of the Word: A Language History of the World (Reprint edition), p7. Harper Perennial, New York (2006)
21. Crystal, D.: English as a Global Language (Second edition), p6, p9-10, p60-71. Cambridge University Press, Cambridge (2003)
22. Zhou, Y.G.: Collections of Zhou Youguang, Volume IV: History of World Words, p31. Central Compilation & Translation Press, Beijing (2013)

Research on Visual Design of Tibetan Medicine Mud Mask Based on HTML5 Technology -- Taking Tibetan Medicine Mud Mask as an Example

Jie Zhou[✉] and Ziyi Kong

School of Art Design and Media, East China University of Science and Technology,
Shanghai, People's Republic of China
wy_zj2009@163.com

Abstract. The rapidly developing new media technology and revolutionary communication technology have provided more effective communication methods for inheriting and protecting intangible cultural heritage. HTML5 technology is widely favored for its portability and strong interaction. The intangible cultural heritage spread by words and deeds in the past has made a new breakthrough in this era of digital informatization.

The Tibetan medicine mud mask is used as the research object in this paper. It is a kind of intangible cultural heritage originated from the era of Songzan Ganbu and Princess Wencheng more than 1,300 years ago. It is a Buddha statue made of clay together with precious raw materials such as Tibetan medicine, spices and gemstones. It has been regarded as a sacred object because of its beautiful wishes and its own medical effects. As an outstanding representative of Tibetan culture, Tibetan folk arts and crafts, religious culture and Tibetan medicine culture, it reflects the moral concept, philosophical thought, aesthetic psychology, rich imagination and creativity of this nation, but it is facing difficulties in protection and dissemination. In this paper, the Tibetan medicine mud mask is reproduced, displayed and promoted in the form of HTML5 interactive page through a series of processes such as investigation, text combing, content mining and design, and transformed from oral, text to image as well as from static to dynamic. Hence, this paper is helpful for the protection and dissemination of Tibetan medicine mud mask, and of far-reaching significance for the promotion of national culture and the expansion of cultural diversity.

The article is divided into the following three parts: 1. From the perspective of cultural heritage protection Tibetan medicine mud mask; This paper is structured into three parts. 1) Tibetan medicine mud mask from the perspective of cultural heritage protection; 2) The path and typical case analysis and logical structure of intangible cultural heritage digital communication, including basic information, product function, use driving force, advantages, characteristics, disadvantages, etc.; 3) Mud mask design based on HTML5, including positioning, aesthetic characteristics, interaction design, etc.

Keywords: HTML5 · Tibetan medicine mud mask · Visual design

© The Author(s), under exclusive license to Springer Nature Switzerland AG 2022
C. Stephanidis et al. (Eds.): HCII 2022, CCIS 1654, pp. 284–291, 2022.
https://doi.org/10.1007/978-3-031-19679-9_35

1 Tibetan Medicine Mud Mask from the Perspective of Cultural Heritage Protection

Originated from the era of Songzan Ganbu and Princess Wencheng [3] more than 1,300 years ago, Tibetan medicine mud mask is a Buddha statue shaped by mud mixed with Tibetan medicine, spices, gemstones and other precious raw materials. It is regarded as a sacred object because it embodies the Tibetan people's wishes for peace, dharma protection and exorcism, and it itself has the effect of sterilization, anti-fatigue, intelligence and health.

The making process of Tibetan medicine mud mask is mysterious and complex, which generally involves at least ten processes including water and soil collection, mud fermentation, sculpture, coloring, etc. As recorded in *Introduction to Wise Man*, medicinal mud needs to be mixed with more than 80 kinds of religious relics such as relic and manna pills, more than 60 kinds of precious Tibetan medicines such as pearl 70 pills, more than 60 kinds of Chinese herbal medicines such as Rhodiola, more than 80 kinds of precious stones such as agate, and 25 kinds of fragrant medicines such as grass and fruit. Finally, minerals are the raw material for coloring [1].

The medicine mud mask of Silong Jiangze family in Xinlong County, Ganzi Prefecture has become the representative of Tibetan medicine mud mask because of its ancient, rigorous and comprehensive production process. Due to complex production skills and strict requirements for trainees, few people can practice patiently. The popularity of cloth and paper masks has affected the status of medicine mud mask, making it gradually disappear.

Tibetan medicine mud mask is an outstanding representative of Tibetan national culture, Tibetan folk arts and crafts, religious culture and Tibetan medical culture. Combined with the regional characteristics of Tibetan ethnic minorities, intangible cultural heritage has a very important reference value for the study of the spiritual life, religious beliefs and customs of ethnic minorities. Therefore, the spread and popularization of Tibetan medicine mud mask is of far-reaching significance to the expansion of civilization diversity.

Tibetan medicine mud mask is currently a national intangible cultural heritage. This paper discusses the inheritance and protection of Tibetan medicine mud mask in the era of new media, aiming to provide a possible beneficial exploration for the transmission path of similar intangible cultural heritage in the endangered state. At present, the protection and research status of this topic is: 1) Only in the hands of a few heirs; 2) Relevant written records are not systematic; 3) The protection and dissemination of digitization need to be strengthened.

2 The Path of Intangible Cultural Heritage Digitization

2.1 Main Path of Intangible Cultural Heritage Digitization

With the iterative upgrading of technology and information processing, digital media, as the main form of media expression and expansion, provides a more diverse technical support and display platform for protecting intangible cultural heritage [2]. The digitization of intangible cultural heritage can be reflected in all links of heritage protection and dissemination [3], especially in the three levels of preservation and management, restoration and reproduction, display and dissemination, which are the main paths of intangible cultural heritage digitization. In the process of cultural heritage protection, digital media art reduces the distance from cultural inheritance to historical interpretation, and continuously enhances the public's feeling and cognition of tangible cultural heritage. Meanwhile, other technologies and hardware and software facilities centered on digital media technology have to some extent spawned the development of digital industry and projects, which not only effectively preserves tangible cultural heritage, but also expands and extends the heritage with the assistance of various forms of digital media in the process of communication and exchange, thereby achieving the multiple inheritance of social, historical and artistic values of intangible cultural heritage.

The digitization of intangible cultural heritage mainly involves the following processes: digital collection, recording, sorting and display, mainly in the form of images, pictures and audio, digital media technology and art, such as 3D scanning, virtual reality, augmented reality, motion capture, human-computer interaction, AI synthesis, etc., which provide important technical support for the production, preservation and display of intangible cultural heritage. Online museum exhibition and game animation with different carriers can be used for exhibition. In today's mobile phone as an important interactive terminal, the digital display and dissemination of intangible cultural heritage by using H5 games with the help of mobile phone network not only intensifies interest and convenience but also gives full play to application scenarios.

2.2 Advantages and Disadvantages of HTML5

HTML5 has obvious advantages. H5 web pages are usually opened on mobile devices. People's focus on small screens will enable them to pay more attention to information transmission. HTML5 can be opened on any platform without downloading, and it belongs to external chain, allowing for finer and more flexible actions. Data connection is not limited to mobile terminals. Instead, more scenarios are available. Pages can be interspersed with animation, interaction, games, etc. Increased interactivity reduces the distance between culture and people. At the same time, with the help of H5 pages of WeChat, microblog and other terminals, rapid online loading and dissemination can be achieved, thus effectively enlarging the scope and improving the means of disseminating cultural heritage. The interactivity of HTML5 technology enables two-way communication mode of input and output, and makes the communication effect get twice the result with half the effort. For example, HTML5 is relatively weak in fine and sticky data opening, without obvious disadvantages. The intangible cultural heritage is intentionally promoted, mainly aiming at a wider range of audiences, which can be achieved by H5.

3 Typical Case of Intangible Cultural Heritage Digitization Based on H5

3.1 Connection Between Creative Expression and User Emotion

Visual interaction "digital supporter" is a "King's glory x digital supporter plan" jointly produced and launched by Tencent and Dunhuang Research Institute to protect and spread Dunhuang culture. The whole H5 lasts about three minutes. The key to its success is the close connection between the expression form of creativity and user's emotion. In order to keep users from feeling bored during the experience, designers have made great efforts in visual and auditory performance. First of all, in terms of creativity, users can get a creative sense of accomplishment in the experience and experience the beauty of Dunhuang murals firsthand by clicking on the color to color lost murals. In terms of expression, it adopts slow and simple tone. The visual design mainly follows the characteristics of gravel texture and traditional color matching of murals. Secondly, bells and flutes are used for acoustic design to greatly enhance the realism and beauty of H5 as well as users' sense of substitution and experience.

3.2 Entertainment and Interaction

HTML5 interactive game fingertips "March 3: playing Hydrangea Xiaole" is one of a series of HTML5 games designed and produced by Guangxi Museum to help its local Zhuang nationality spread and promote national culture. Among the 14 HTML5 Games launched, three about March 3, the traditional Festival of the Zhuang people were released, namely "March 3 National guess", "national help March 3" and "Hydrangea Xiaole" [4]. Compared with the first two answer types of H5 games, "fingertip March 3: playing Hydrangea Xiaole" is more entertaining by integrating the typical elements of March 3 such as Hydrangea into Xiaole, a popular game category. In the gaming process, players can not only obtain a sense of achievement by passing different levels, but also feel spiritually satisfied with learning. And after making breakthroughs level by level, players will have the opportunity to win exquisite cultural and creative products presented by the museum, which intends to attract more users.

The "March 3" Video Game Museum of Guangxi combines "March 3" video game resources with "HTML5" video game resources unique to Guangxi Zhuang nationality. The operation rules are simple and easy to understand, which attract players of different ages, thus contributing to the rapid promotion of the game and promoting Guangxi ethnic culture in a short time. Unique national cultural elements such as Guangxi's 12 ancient ethnic costumes, five-color glutinous rice and Hydrangea have been skillfully integrated into the game in the process of design, enabling players to better understand Guangxi ethnic culture in the gaming process, which is in line with what game design originally intends for.

4 Design of Mud Mask Based on HTML5

4.1 Design Positioning

This design aims to promote Tibetan medicine mud mask by means of HTML5, which is to make it more popular among people and win their understanding and respect on multiculturalism. Firstly, the expression content and method of H5 were studied. The author found that Tibetan people's spirits, such as diligence, simplicity, piety and kindness, are portrayed in the complex and fine fabrication process of medicine mud mask, which endowed impetuous and restless young people in modern life with an opportunity for reflection alone. Therefore, H5 project mainly focuses on the production process of medicine mud mask, which can most intuitively reflect the essence of Tibetan medicine mud mask.

H5 displays major contents using manually painted linear illustration. Thangka is a unique painting art form in Tibetan culture, and line drawing is the key to Thangka painting. The linear illustration draws on the characteristics of Thangka painting line drawing to a certain extent to prevent it from being too divorced from theme background or making it as harmonious as expected. Secondly, the picture depicted by line drawing and illustration is clear, which is in line with modern people's aesthetic habits and is more easily accepted.

HTML5 technology provides rich and diverse media expression forms. Considering that static illustration is relatively single in expression, the author added dynamic effects to make it more vivid, and designed interaction points to make H5 more expressive and interesting.

After identifying basic style, the author began to work out basic framework by taking the H5 project as a whole. The origin and production process of Tibetan medicine mud mask were introduced. The production process was indicated by scenarios. Considering cultural differences and other factors, many users may be exposed to Tibetan culture for the first time and lack basic cognition and understanding of Tibetan culture. As a result, they have a vague feeling when watching H5 and do not know what to show, thus affecting communication effect. Therefore, it is important to design copywriting and narration in this project. Each scenario is equipped with a simple and general narration not only to facilitate users' understanding but also to make all the scenarios more coherently connected, thus improving user experience.

4.2 Extraction of Aesthetic Elements

The author summarizes that Tibetan medicine mud mask has the following visual characteristics: The image of Tibetan medicine mud mask mainly comes from the Buddha and Bodhisattva or Dharma protector in Tibetan Buddhism, featuring exaggerated shape and exquisite expression. In terms of color expression, colors with strong contrast and high saturation are often used to highlight massy mask image. Among them, common colors are red, orange, yellow, blue, green, black and other pure and bright colors rich in Tibetan regional characteristics, which basically maintain the artistic style of ancient India and Tibetan Buddhism. Gold has been endowed with special significance in Tibetan Buddhism. It is also used in mask making as an ornament to highlight the sanctity and inviolability of god.

Tibetan medicine mud mask brings visual impact and shock in shape and color, enabling people to appreciate cultural diversity. In the H5 project, the author continues the realistic and exaggerated modeling and color matching characteristics of medicine mud mask (Fig. 1), truly and intuitively reflecting medicine mud mask and endowing the picture with more artistic expression and decoration.

The author decided to display main content in the form of manually painted illustration, and add creative ideas and thoughts to scenario design. For example, Princess Wencheng in the sky looked kindly at the people on the grass (Fig. 2), which is to demonstrate her worship of Buddha using mud mask rather than incense or fire, thus making mud mask recognized, favored and worshiped by Tibetan people. On the contrary, she also watches over the faithful in the darkness. Thus, the image is more artistic and content is more touching to users.

Fig. 1. The modeling and color characteristics of medicine mud mask in illustration by Ziyi Kong

Fig. 2. Creative illustration performance by Ziyi Kong

In addition, some Tibetan elements, such as Sutra turning barrel and prayer flags, are used to add distinct regional features to the picture. From medicine mud mask to Tibetan culture, this H5 project is not only limited to the popularization of a Tibetan skill, but also an opportunity to promote Tibetan culture. At the same time, these elements also make scenarios more coherent and smoother.

In terms of color matching, major content is expressed by traditional bright and exaggerated color matching of Tibetan style to highlight main body, distinguish primary and secondary colors, and avoid the adverse experience of visual fatigue arising from long-term appreciation of colors with high saturation. The H5 background is composed of dark colors such as black, navy blue and red brown, and appropriate materials such as gold lines used for contour points and lines to enrich the picture, prevent the background from being too monotonous and boring and enhance the texture of the whole H5.

4.3 Interaction Design

With the development of digital media technology, people are no longer satisfied with the visual impact brought by static pictures. The dynamic effect can add interest to H5 and improve the overall viewing experience of users. In this H5 project, dynamic effect is designed to revolve around scenarios. In the process of drawing materials in scenarios, the author considered how to best fit the picture while thinking about and conceiving dynamic effect.

It takes a certain amount of time to load materials, so a number of cyclic transformation of medicine mud masks were set for different scenarios on the loading page to not only attract users' attention but also enables users to have a good first impression on medicine mud mask, thus laying a solid foundation for developing what follows. The dynamic effect of main content mostly serves the whole, highlighting the focus of the picture and making it more vivid. Therefore, when drawing scenario materials in the early stage, many manifold and streamer lines (Figs. 3 and 4) were added to express smell, sound and feeling so that H5 is more expressive.

Fig. 3. Smell and wind represented by manifold lines by Ziyi Kong

Fig. 4. Bell sound represented by manifold lines by Ziyi Kong

In addition, the dithering effect of some important elements is designed in the scenarios to make them more interesting. The medicine mud statue is the most concentrated part of the whole H5 interaction. Users interact by clicking and moving "Daiwan", and the process of medicine mud from a mass of soil to a god mask will be displayed on the screen. The overall quality of H5 is improved by combining dynamic effect and interaction.

H5 design and creation mainly focus on vision, hearing and touch, among which vision and hearing are the most easily achieved on digital screens. The acoustic effect of H5 mainly involves background and auxiliary sounds. Background sound effect is an important element to establish the emotional tone and atmosphere of the whole H5. It should be theme targeted and conforms to the principle of audio-visual consistency in the selection of background sound. Auxiliary sound effect is a detailed design added according to the needs of content, which plays a role in setting off content description and bringing users an all-round audio-visual experience.

Considering that the medicine mud mask is the product bred under the influence of Tibetan culture, mask making process is a way to calm down one's mind despite its tediousness. Therefore, the author selected gentle light music as background music. In addition to tonal key sound effect, auxiliary sound effect also adds a narrator to tell the origin and spiritual and cultural connotation of the mask. The addition of two kinds of sound effects enables users to be appealed by music and enjoy a more immersive experience when enjoying the exquisite and simple cultural heritage.

5 Publicity and Marketing Approaches

H5 can be combined with WeChat official account and short video so that users feel it initiative and convenient in browsing. It is also advisable to make full use of jumping HTML5, attach more importance to online and offline links and work with local museums to better develop cultural and creative products and establish cultural brands. It can also be linked to e-commerce mini programs to expand sales channels and promote regional economic development [5].

At present, trendy cards and trendy toys are deeply loved by young people. Cross-border cooperation and co-branding in the field of intangible cultural heritage and culture is an effective means to rapidly promote ancient culture among young groups, and the form of H5 is also very consistent with the "trend" concept of these brands. Therefore, it can be used as a means to promote products and make audiences' consumption behaviors accompanied with cultural communication.

References

1. Fan, W.: Model text religious connotation and aesthetic intention of Tibetan mask. Sichuan Drama, **2005**(05), 51–52 (2005)
2. Jie, Z.: The role of digital media art in the protection of material cultural heritage. Grand View Art **04**, 137–138 (2021)
3. Guan, Z.: Digital rescue protection of representative inheritors of intangible cultural heritage in the information age. J. Phys.: Conf. Ser. **1744**(4) (2021)
4. Jie, L.: HTML5 games help spread the national culture of "Zhuang March 3" – Taking the development and application of "Zhuang March 3" series HTML5 games of Guangxi Museum as an example. Ind. Technol. Forum **18**(24), 99–100 (2019)
5. Du, X.: On the role of H5 in the publicity of intangible cultural heritage. Art Technol. **31**(06), 93 (2018)

Self-organized Structure in Theory and Production: Contemporary Origami as Mathematical, Mechanical and Cultural System

Rongrong Zhou[✉]

Peking University, Haidian District, Beijing, China
rongrongzhou2018@163.com

Abstract. Origami is an extensively discussed subject in art, design and mechanism, but new discipline to study with the perspective of inter disciplinary science and cultural history. This paper assumes basic awareness of the artistic and design concept of the audience. It further investigates origami, together with history of math, as a clue of cross cultural study and technology development of the 20th century. Also, it discusses how its self-organization structure is formed artistically, scientifically and industrially, with its special role in art modernization. The paper referee to theories by R. L. Wilder and Thomas. S. Kuhn. Based on the volumetric examples of origami usage, it introduces the topics of science communication and generative design history marked by software development. It tries to construct a multi-aspect view of cultural history through technology, and manifests the perspective of art and humanities in it.

Keywords: History of math · Computing art · Design history

1 Introduction

Origami is an old subject in art, design and mechanism, but new discipline to study with the perspective of inter disciplinary science and cultural history. In art and mechanics, origami manifests the universality of mathematics across generations, industries, media, cultures, aesthetics and functions. Its construction as an art subject, a mathematical field, and an engineering subdivision has involved the spontaneous participation of interdisciplinary scholars, and there are particular origami associations in the United States and Japan, with a elaborate system of software, monographs, and papers, reflecting origami's efficient self-organizing ability as a production method in theory and practice. Volumes of existing research and applications in engineering, mathematics and arts leaves little need for case enumerating, but a more in-depth cross-cultural and history of technology study is the next step, providing a valid paradigm for the possibility of integrating computer-based technological work into cultural and artistic production.

C. Stephanidis et al. (Eds.): HCII 2022, CCIS 1654, pp. 292–296, 2022.
https://doi.org/10.1007/978-3-031-19679-9_36

2   Origami as Cross-Cultural Subject and Inter-disciplinary Clue of 20th Century History of Science and Technology

The development of origami as a cross-disciplinary practice is often vaguely attributed to the borrowings of Japanese artistic tradition by computing technology, as if there were a simple chronological and causal relationship between the two. But this may only be a speculation that is taken for granted. Origami is a technological tradition closely related to the the distribution of mathematical centers of pre-modern human society. It originated in various civilizations around the globe in different forms and on similar principles, similar to the case of printmaking. Referring to the theoretical insights of R. L. Wilder, who combined the history of mathematics and anthropology, origami could be an important clue to the cultural tradition of mathematics and a cutting tool for cross-cultural comparison [1]. The appearance of Japanese origami in the Heian dynasty began with the introduction of Chinese paper. The corresponding term of Papiroflexia in Spanish, introduced in 12th century from Arabian society, is consistent with the pattern of mathematical knowledge producing and transmission in East Asia and Europe [2]. Yoshizawa's overseas exhibition was first held at the Amsterdam City Museum in 1955, and according to the history summarized by Erik and Martin Demain, Josef Albers began the modern European and American origami art stream from the Bauhaus and Black Mountain Institute in the 1920s, which is clearly not in the same vein as the Japanese craft tradition represented by Yoshizawa [3].

Origami as a technical discipline is a clue of 20th century history associating craftsmanship and generative design, which exemplifies the importance of introducing artistic and cultural perspective as viewing the history of technology. It also reveals the diverse relationship that has occurred between the history of mathematics and modern art, a relationship that has yet to be studied in greater depth. The model designed by Duks Koschitz of the Bauhaus is already very close to the parametric design in form, which shows a priori of how craftsmanship extends in the history of computing technology. The priori was clearly identified by the artists like Erik Demain in the Computer Science department in MIT, whose thesis focused on waterproof structures, but his origami creations carried on the legacy of Albers and Koschitz, among others [3]. Meanwhile, the origami sculptures of Paul Jackson and others are closer to the minimalist art of the 1960s onwards [4]. Considering the constructivism movement initiated by Bourbaki School in abstract math in the same century, whose influence in art was waning at the time [5]. Origami is thus part of the whole reaction of visual creation on science in the century. Meanwhile, Process Art (also known as "systems art") and Cybernetic Art emerged in Europe and the United States, with artists in residence at the Department of Mathematics and Physics at the University of Bristol. Simon Thomas has used the language of mathematics to produce a great deal of public art, such as PLANE LINER, a work in residence at Bristol University's Physics Department [2]. It shares the methodology of origami, and is composed by a three dimensional mathematical function, where the sculptural shape is theoretically infinitely extensible, but the apex is always empty.

3 Self-organized Scientific Paradigm and Science Communication

3.1 Mathematical Structure in Geometry and Numerical Analysis

The self-organizing feature allows and deserves origami to be examined more critically as what Thomas. S. Kuhn calls a scientific paradigm [6]. The mathematical structure determines the academic architecture itself. Different research orientations determine the choice of mathematical models. Each particular model determines an scholarly branch. Industries and sectors could collaborate with separate branches with minimized communication cost with the language of mathematics. "Self-organizing" here has multiple indications in the context. It, at least, includes: the universality of the mathematical language that allows origami to effectively surpasses the barriers of different cultural systems; mathematical principles functions as meta-model of design and public art, with production procedures clearly drawn; mathematical forms eliminates the boundaries between art and industrial applications, virtual and physical worlds, allowing the same set of theoretical language to be applied across a wide range of media, but with a different emphasis between the geometric formal induction of the former and numerical analysis of the latter. Unlike digital art and general origami works, the vast amount of origami research in architecture, mechanics, and dynamical systems is based on structural affordances and realistic feasibility. DNA origami, on the other hand, is more informational than geometric, except that its idea of modularity is connected to origami in three dimensions. It is a metaphor for the rapid growth of knowledge and the expansion of the scientific paradigm [7].

An easily overlooked fact is that origami itself involves a relatively wide range of branches of mathematics, which underlies the reason why mathematicians and physicists actively maintain the self-organizing community: in the process of making, presenting, and writing on origami, the extremely complex and divided contemporary mathematics is communicated at low cost among peers. The underlying logic expand to differential equations and group theory as the folding complicates. The action of "folding a trace on a piece of paper" in real space is mathematically equivalent to "drawing a straight line on a plane in three-dimensional space and folding the plane along this line". "planning the action steps of folding traces" is the process of "deducing geometric and algebraic transformations of a plane along a straight line", which results in the writing and deduction of analogous algorithms.

Abstract math related to origami are discussed in detail by three European professors in *"The Art of Mathematics"*, edited by Yau Shing-Tung, who relate its principles to partial differential equations [8]. Drawing a crease diagram on a piece of paper, once the folding action takes place, is equivalent to a smooth plane undergoing a transformation leading to some position discontinuity, so the crease diagram is reduced to a discontinuous point set. The relationship between origami and more complex mathematics is established in the repetition and organization of such simple actions, such as performing the Fujimoto approximation of N-equivalence folding in a way that can be taught in connection with number theory and discrete dynamics, and Hull's classroom lecture notes that include homomorphic algebra, and origami demonstrations of Gaussian curvature.

3.2 Software Development in History of Technology

Due to its feature of unifying visual presentation and shape analysis, origami in industrial design exemplifies the history of computing technology marked with software development. Kawasaki and Maekawa's theories are extensively elaborated in every topic defined by a single geometric case. Cases divide by rigid and non-rigid folding. The rigid folding surface is always a rigid plane, and the crease is regarded as a rotating axis. Non-rigid folding does not have this assumption, that can occur within the folding surface twisting, bending and other deformation, can produce deformation [9]. Force tolerance and shape sustainability are calculated through softwares like Adams (Automatic Dynamic Analysis of Mechanical System) [10].

In terms studying computing art, architecture and public art in forms, the approach of history of technology marks their innate relation in the bottom, which origami makes explicit. Dating back to 1960, Denavit and Hartenberg in Northwestern University were awarded the first National Science Foundation research grant in the U.S. in kinematics to develop a numerical analysis tool for digital computers, which later was upgraded to Adams by their students. 1961, Northwestern University acquired an IBM 709 digital computer based on FORTRAN IV from the Boeing airplane, which was not powerful as hand calculator today [11]. In the same era, in 1960, Thomas Banchoff began using software to simulate the projection of high-dimensional objects in two dimensions, and his collaborator, Davide Cervone, created a new work in 2002. In the 1970s, mathematicians at IBM developed fractal geometry [2]. After 2000s, Roland Snooks, one of the practitioners of "Swarm Intelligence" (the intelligent behavior of many low-intelligence individuals through simple cooperation with each other), has created architecture and public art that includes algorithm-led self-similar geometries, with surfaces that can be left to robotic arms and robots [12].

In addition, specialized origami softwares that still serves paper-folding, such as Geogebra and Geometer, provide a category that drive complicate math theory illustrations (i.e. differential equations) closer to computing language. Repetition of several folds can be calculated to approximate a parabola is summarized in Geogebra as a direct Lotus instruction; the result of solving cubic equations by the Lill method of paper folding is a reenactment of the 19th century Austrian engineer Eduard Lill's construction and the discoveries of the 20th century mathematician Margherita Bolech. Systematic treatises that combine mathematics and art include *The Secrets of Origami - Mathematical Methods in Ancient Art* by R. Lang, *The Secrets of Origami Design* by Thomas Hull, etc., and works of many Japanese scholars [13, 14].

References

1. Wilder, R.L.: Mathematics as a Cultural System. Elsevier (1981)
2. Gamwell, L.: Mathematics and Art: A Cultural History. Princeton University Press (2016)
3. Demain, E.: http://erikdemaine.org/curved/history/. Accessed 25 May 2022
4. Jackson, P.: http://foldtogether.org. Accessed 25 May 2022
5. Aczel, A.D.: The Artist and the Mathematician: The Story of Nicholas Bourbaki, the Genius Mathematician Who Never Existed. Thunder's Mouth Press (2006)
6. Kuhn, T.S.: The Structure of Scientific Revolutions. University of Chicago (2012)

7. Wang, J., Zhang, P., Xia, Q., Wei, Y., Chen, W., et al.: DNA origami in nanobiotechnology. J. Southern Med. Univ. **41**(06), 960–964 (2021)

8. Yau, S.-T. (丘成桐), et al. (ed.): The Art of Mathematics (数学的艺术). Higher Education Press (2015)

9. Zhang, R., Zhang, F., Zhuang, Y., Zhang, Y., Wang, F.: Analysis of rigid origami degrees of freedom for multi-vertex triangles. J. Chongqing Technol. Bus. (Nat. Sci.) **38**(05), 23–28 (2021). https://doi.org/10.16055/j.issn.1672-058X.2021.0005.004

10. Hexagon. https://www.mscsoftware.com/product/adams. Accessed 25 May 2022

11. Snooks, R.: http://www.rolandsnooks.com. Accessed 25 May 2022

12. Uicker, J.J.: History of multibody dynamics in the U.S. ASME. J. Comput. Nonlinear Dynam. **11**(6), 060302 (2016). https://doi.org/10.1115/1.4034308

13. Lang, R.: Origami Design Secrets: Mathematical Methods for an Ancient Art. Taylor & Francis (2011)

14. Hull, T.: Project Origami: Activities for Exploring Mathematics. A K PETERS (2006)

Cultural Heritage Experience Design

A Deep Learning Approach to the Artwork of Art Museums Utilizing Instagram Hashtags

Minyoung Chung(✉) ⓘ

Yonsei University, Yonsei-ro 50, Seodaemun-gu, Seoul, Republic of Korea
minyoungch@yonsei.ac.kr

Abstract. This study is conducted to examine the potential of hashtag (#) images to classify artwork. This study has two aims, Firstly, an attempt to find the reliability of using shareholders' Instagram images. Secondly, as an approach to predict the style of the art museum with a degree of validity. CNNs (Convolutional Neural Networks) are used for image classification from hashtags that can determine image style from the Instagram hashtag. For data sets, top-rated hashtags from Instagram - #Cute, #Fashion, #Nature, #Food - are firstly processed in the frequency domain to artwork images which can be treated as a hashtag classification. 1,000 painting artwork posts from each art museum – MoMA (Museum of Modern Art) and the Getty (J. Paul Getty Museum) - were collected for test data. As for the artwork image cluster, 8,000 images from hashtags are inputted into CNNs. The output data resulting from the deep learning process is evaluated using a Tensor board. Images of #Cute, #Fashionable, #Food, #Natural trained in a minute. Each label consists of 2,000 Instagram images with over 80% accuracy in the reliability of using hashtag images. This data proves that it works to classify artwork images. #Fashion predicted as MoMA and #Natural predicted as the Getty with a high score of consistency. Finally, compared to MoMA, the Getty has more consistency with the 4 hashtags listed above. Therefore, this study has concluded that hashtags are expected to help shareholders search for artwork and art museums.

Keywords: Hashtag · Shareholder · Artwork · Image · Deep learning

1 Introduction

To support shareholder experience for Art, museums share their enormous data [1, 2] and explore the tools developed [2, 3]. Here, we should explore how shareholders' images are possibly related mutually to the art museum. Given that mutual interaction of Instagram emerged [4], art museums have Instagram accounts to interact with visitors for marketing [5]. The hashtag has determined curatorial aspects [5, 6]. However, visual culture studies show that art museum visitors have difficulty meeting their needs to consume the visual culture of Art [6–8]. Thus, visitors are provided with selectable criteria to search for artwork as an accessible, marketable, and educational experience in art museums. Hashtags can be a solution for limitations approaching images of Art. The subjectivity of selection is the critical point to the experience of Art [8, 9]. Therefore,

© The Author(s), under exclusive license to Springer Nature Switzerland AG 2022
C. Stephanidis et al. (Eds.): HCII 2022, CCIS 1654, pp. 299–305, 2022.
https://doi.org/10.1007/978-3-031-19679-9_37

this study suggests that hashtags will enhance the search images of art museums. For this reason, shareholders' image archives from Instagram are important to support finding art images of their style, check if usual types of images are not overfitting data [10], and improved searching for visual perception. Accuracy and usability from hashtags images can support curating and searching [3], this study verifies the validation and consistency while training and testing deep learning.

2 Methodology

2.1 Data Setup

For training, 1) hashtags were selected, 2) hashtag image data was collected, and 3) hashtag images were pre-processed. Selecting standard is distinctive images for their keyword. #Cute (Top10 ranked of frequency), #Fashion (Top3), #Food (Top 27), and #Nature (Top 14) [12] are selected. 8,000 images from hashtags were pre-processed: deleting images of advertisements and selfies. For the test, 1) Art Museum selected, 2) images collected, and 3) pre-processed. The art museum is where history is made rather than collected history in the Museum. Therefore, MoMA is a critical place as the exhibition and curatorial discourse for Modern Art. Moreover, the Getty is a comparison cluster that is well-known as a Getty image, a great archive and research place. Each Art Museum's images of paintings were focused on this paper other than the place, sculpture, or picture of performances. All image data were collected from Instagram in April 2015. Images until March 2022 images were collected.

2.2 CNN Models Transit Learning

To present mutual network images of Art and shareholder, this study explores the usability of hashtag images from Instagram and analyzes the accuracy of image Deep learning convolutional neural networks (CNNs) of pre-trained Inception V3 [11] from Tensor-Flow authors. AlexNet (DNN) is also used for image deep learning, however, CNNs outperform all other computational methods for classifying paintings by artist, style, or genre [9, 11]. The CNNs model's ability to automatically identify meaningful patterns has proven useful for learning complex image attributes [11]. CNNs could implement the mutual interaction of images based on Hashtag and the Art Museum on Instagram with these aims. First, it examines hashtags images that can classify Art images, and second, the classification of Art museums with specific styles from people's data.

2.3 Procedure

The experimental procedures are presented twofold. Displayed Left-side Fig. 1 part will be determined by training accuracy, and on the Right-side Fig. 1 part will be determined by test validation. This study explores the relation of different image predictions. The training dataset was tested during training to validate the classification model and transit bottleneck computation as a final stage of training. Given input images, rating, and attribute assignments are proved by 4 hashtag layers and then their weights are regularized during training. Each attribute layer employed to output a prediction score layer can be a feature extractor of the predicted hashtag score. The artwork is classified by hashtag images in the stage displayed in Fig. 1. After validating the model as fitting data, in the next stage to support the style utilization, the art museum will be classified on hashtag style.

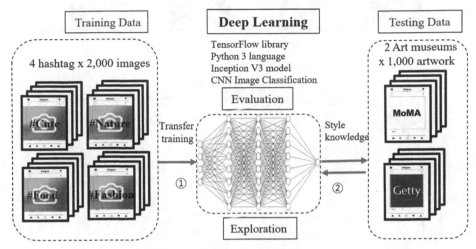

Fig. 1. Constitution style from Instagram Hashtag images to artworks

3 Results

3.1 Training Accuracy

To be considered a reliable training model, an Accuracy result of over 80% is needed while a small gap between training and validation might require to be adjusted to other data [13]. It is trained by using 8,000 hashtag images in Table 1. It is collected 4 hashtags as below. The Tensor board displayed the images used for classification Fig. 2. Displayed the images of training accuracy.

To support that hashtag recognition and classifying art images posted on Instagram were tested. Instagram data training is over 80% accurate. The little gap between train and validation [13] makes classified images of Fig. 2. Proven.

Looking at the training result it can be considered that this retrained model is enabled in the investigation related to the art style.

Table 1. Training data categories and Images from the hashtag on Instagram

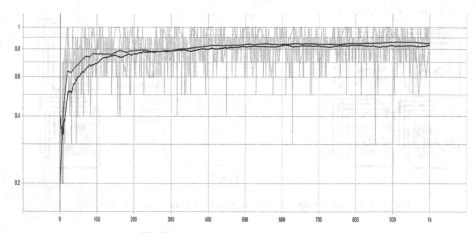

#Cute	#Fashion	#Food	#Nature

Fig. 2. Accuracy: Training and Validation

3.2 Test Validation

To validate the result, a consistency score is key to the analysis. Thus, Table 2. Displayed artwork classification.

The scores present the value of the similarity of the hashtag to artwork. The result shows the consistency of over 90%, #Cute matched 128 works of art that consisted of 30 in MoMA & 98 in the Getty. Meanwhile, #Fashion matched 13 works of art, 8 in MoMA and 5 in the Getty. #Food matched 8 works of art in the Getty. Finally, #Nature matched 69 works of art, 5 in MoMA and 64 in the Getty.

218 Artworks spread over 2,000 works were proven classified by hashtag for feature attributes. Here, there was an examined consistency of over 90%. Artworks can be classified as hashtags. The hashtag could conduct in art museum style. The test classified each style with a hashtag in Table 1. This retrained model found similarities in visual features.

Table 2. Hashtag classifying Artwork above 90% consistency score

	#Cute	#Fashion	#Food	#Nature
The Getty Image [14,15,16,17]				
Consistency Score	0.98319	0.96636	0.98505	0.99306
Sub 175	98	5	8	64
MoMA Image [18,19,20]				
Consistency Score	0.97146	0.91881		0.97024
Sub 43	30	8	0	5
Total 218	128	13	8	69

3.3 Finding and Discussion

Very little was found in the literature on #cute of Art in Museum. People who do not visit museums would not expect cuteness much. This study set out with the aim of assessing the importance of hashtag image data in Instagram. One interesting finding is #Cute in both Art museums, shown in Table 2. Limited in hashtags - Cute, Fashion, Food, Nature. Hashtag implemented a high score. As displayed in Fig. 3. In this study, comparing MoMA with the Getty showed that the mean over 90% consistency of hashtag. It is somewhat surprising that little #Nature and was noted in MOMA. The Getty has more images of nature in high scores. However, the number of art image classification is not enough that is more #Fashion in MoMA than the Getty. Art museums have less tendency for # food than Instagram. This finding broadly supports the work of other studies in this area linking Instagram images with artificial interagency marketing.

While image style classification correlate feature [21] little corelate keyword. Hashtags are an important way to get more reach. This result supports evidence from previous study. It's been proven posts that include hashtags get over 12% more interaction [22], a possible explanation for hashtag may be easy way to boost art engagement. Furthermore, with this result, Art images are positioned in the hashtag style, in the context of art museums, as well as a shareholder gets the displayed tendency. Perhaps Deep learning could be used in other styles and genres of images for classification.

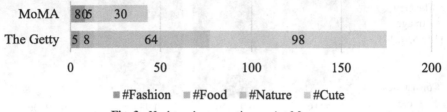

Fig. 3. Hashtags' perspective on Art Museums

4   Conclusion

This study examined the feasibility of using hashtags as a cluster of images to find artworks in art museums. The results have shown the possibility that shareholders find artwork with their usual image style through a keyword. The result of study suggests the capability of hashtags in determining Art Museum style. When using hashtags for accessibility, it is supposed that the active use of Image Deep learning will improve both finding Art and Museum cognitive appraisal. In addition, hashtags broaden searches and can be effective for those with difficulties in searching with their standard. The technology's effectiveness still needs to be validated in the art world because this study only focused on limited hashtags and museums. Since the study is only concerned with Instagramable images from hashtag, the generalizability of these results is subject to certain limitation. However, the Instagramable aspect, and can offer accessibility to Art. This is because this limited way can be a visual perspective on Art who may have little knowledge about artists, styles, or genres based on curatorial theory and history. Each user has their own image for hashtag too. For instance, hashtags provide alternative accessibility for art. This would be a fruitful area for further work. Each style of user's data access that the way we consume visual culture has transformed to be a mutual communication and a place to meet Art. Understanding the network could make it possible to understand the requirements. Deep learning images network utilizing hashtags is a need in diagnosing today's Art and finding ways for future visitors to study better.

Acknowledgements. This paper was supported by the BK21 FOUR funded by the Ministry of Education in Korea.

References

1. Martinez, J.L.: The Musée du Louvre launches online collection database and new website (2021). https://presse.louvre.fr/le-musee-du-louvre-met-en-ligne-ses-collections-et-dev oile-son-nouveau-site-internet-3/. Accessed 17 July 2022

2. Google Art Project. https://artsandculture.google.com/. Accessed 11 May 2022
3. Curator group. https://curator.io/blog/8-tips-for-choosing-the-right-hashtags-for-your-hashtag-aggregator-tool. Accessed 11 May 2022
4. Budge, B., Burness, A.: Museum objects and Instagram: agency and communication in digital engagement. Continuum **32**(2), 137–150 (2018)
5. Dornan, R.: Reflecting the Museum: how Instagram brings back seeing originally. Museum-iD Mag. **18** (2016). https://museum-id.com/reflecting-the-museum-how-instagram-brings-back-seeing-by-russell-dornan/. Accessed 11 May 2022
6. Benoit, E., III., Eveleigh, A.: Participatory Archives: Theory and Practice. Facet, London (2019)
7. Walker, J., Chaplin, S.: Visual Culture an Introduction. Manchester University Press (1997)
8. Kanter, B., Fine, A.: The Networked Nonprofit. Jossey-Bass (2010)
9. Simon, N.: The Participatory Museum, Museum 2.0. Santa Cruz (2010)
10. Cetinic, E., et al.: A deep learning perspective on beauty, sentiment, and remembrance of art. IEEE Access **7**, 773694–73710 (2009)
11. Messina, P., et al.: Exploring content-based artwork recommendation with metadata and visual features. arXiv:1706.05786v3 [cs.IR] (2017)
12. Newberry, C.: Instagram Hashtags 2022: The Ultimate Guide. Instagram hashtags can make or break your Instagram strategy (2021). https://blog.hootsuite.com/instagram-hashtags/. Accessed 16 May 2022
13. Raschka, S., Mirjalili, V.: Python Machine Learning, 2nd edn. Packt Publishing, Birmingham (2017)
14. The Getty #Cute, The Temperate and the Intemperate: Miniature from Valerius Maximus, Facta et dicta memorabilia (detail), Tempera colors and ink on parchment about (1475–1480). https://www.instagram.com/p/B0T4RdCnamS/. Accessed 19 May 2022
15. The Getty #Fasion, Millet, J. portrait of Feuardent (1841). https://www.instagram.com/p/CIB5hrWHNIN/. Accessed 19 May 2022
16. The Getty #Food, Monet, C. Flower, and Fruit (1869). https://www.instagram.com/p/B-kjPx4nDUP/. Accessed 19 May 2022
17. The Getty #Natual.Wenglein, W. Detail of River Landscape, Charcoal. (Late 19th/early 20th century). https://www.instagram.com/p/CEsNRban3AF/. Accessed 19 May 2022
18. MoMA #Cute. Yoshitomo Nara. Pup King Plush (2020). https://www.instagram.com/p/CFiQj29hVni/. Accessed 19 May 2022
19. MoMA #Fashion. Weems, C. "From Here I Saw What Happened, and I Cried" (detail). Chromogenic color prints with sand-blasted text on glass. (1995–96). Photo by Powel, G. https://www.instagram.com/p/CLFs__vHVWK/. Accessed 19 May 2022
20. MoMA #Natural, Miller, D. Untitled. Acrylic and ink on paper (2016). https://www.instagram.com/p/BiM8K2aFPpz/. Accessed 19 May 2022
21. Chu, W.-T., Wu, Y.-L.: Image style classification based on learnt deep correlation features. IEEE Trans. Multimed. **20**(9), 2491–2502 (2018). https://doi.org/10.1109/TMM.2018.2801718
22. Nicholson, C.: https://www.huffpost.com/entry/5-ways-to-organically-boost-engagement-on-instagram_b_59642097e4b0deab7c646b41. Accessed 27 May 2022

Valuation and Communication of Heritage Through Design: Creation of a Graphic Brand from Cultural Heritage Elements Intrinsic to a Place

Cristina Pires dos Santos[1,2(✉)] [iD]

[1] CIAUD, Research Centre for Architecture, Urbanism and Design, Lisbon School of Architecture, Universidade de Lisboa, Rua Sá Nogueira, Polo Universitário do Alto da Ajuda, 1349-063 Lisbon, Portugal
[2] Polytechnic Institute of Beja, Rua Pedro Soares, Apartado 6155, 7800-295 Beja, Portugal
cristina.santos@ipbeja.pt

Abstract. Dissemination of heritage necessarily includes the graphic definition of the materials where the information is presented and, consequently, the definition of the graphic brand associated with these communicational materials. By associating identity and graphic brand with a place or city, the designer's intervention is fundamental in establishing a visual identity program that dignifies the symbols of the city, as well as the spirit of the place, and that is what promotes cultural differentiation and enrichment.

In this sense, the present study proposes a methodology based on a literature review and application of a practical project to a group of students. This project consisted of the development of a graphic identity for a future project entitled *"BEJA VISUAL"*, which would aim to communicate in a graphic and visual way, the tangible and intangible cultural heritage of the city of Beja, located in the *"Baixo Alentejo"* region in southern Portugal.

It was intended to demonstrate the importance of local symbols and graphics in the construction of a graphic brand to promote these same heritage values. The learning of Design stands out in the search for these symbols, codes, and local expressions, and from them, in presenting a solution full of meaning and of symbolic and formal connection with what it communicates and represents, creating a more emotional connection with the user.

Keywords: Visual identity · City brand · Cultural heritage

1 Introduction

A brand of a region/place is composed of its cultural identity and must convey the concept of the product, its attributes, and its benefits [1]. According to López [2], the brand has implicit the idea of distinction in the sense of differentiating one thing from another, and the public, when seeing or hearing of a brand, associates it with a certain meaning – for the public, the brand means something.

C. Stephanidis et al. (Eds.): HCII 2022, CCIS 1654, pp. 306–314, 2022.
https://doi.org/10.1007/978-3-031-19679-9_38

In terms of brand positioning, there will have to be a careful analysis of the message, amplitude, and value of the cultures that are being promoted. The images and phrases used should stimulate the tourist's imagination, motivating him to travel - the promotion of a destination needs, however, to reflect the reality of the region, preventing culture from becoming just a commercial spectacle devoid of sense and meaning [1]. By associating identity and graphic brand with a place or city, Fragoso [3] states that the designer's intervention is fundamental in establishing a visual identity program that dignifies the symbols of the city, as well as the spirit of the place, and that is what promotes cultural differentiation and enrichment.

In this sense, the objectives of this article are: i) to highlight the existing and "visible" cultural heritage aspects in a specific place or city through design; ii) to highlight the need to graphically interpret existing cultural heritage aspects for the construction of a graphic brand that is motivating for the tourist or resident; iii) to build a graphic brand from shapes and graphics that already exist in the cultural heritage of a city and that reflect pre-defined concepts and values, and iv) to create a more emotional connection between the user and the communication materials designed, stimulating greater interaction with the graphic identity and the results of its application, based on the study of shapes of pre-existing graphic heritage elements.

The problem presented here leads us to the question: how can Design value and communicate the heritage of a place? The present study proposes a methodology based on literature review and application of a practical project to a group of students of the bachelor's degree course in Audiovisual and Multimedia, of the Polytechnic Institute of Beja, within the curricular unit of Graphic Design (between the years 2020 and 2022, that is, the project was applied to two different classes over two academic years). This project consisted of the development of a visual identity for a future project entitled "*BEJA VISUAL*", which would aim to communicate graphically and visually, the tangible and intangible cultural heritage of the city of Beja, located in the "*Baixo Alentejo*" region in southern Portugal. In the first part, we will present some reflections of some reference authors, then present the development of the referred project and, finally, the analysis and conclusions of the obtained results.

2   Visual Identity and Brand - Some Considerations

The "necessary" connection with the user is highlighted by Olins [4] who states that the possible differentiation and representation of the values associated with an organization, made possible by the visual identity, is only achieved if there is a connection with the user, because the way in which the identity is interpreted, it is directly associated with the success of the organization. Even today, the graphic brand is often the most important expression of a corporate identity or a product, and for that reason, it is important to clarify some terms that are related. Budelmann, Wozniak, & Kim [5] state that the logo is a graphic representation of a brand. Morgan [6] states that the logo can be typographic, figurative, abstract or a combination of these and it is one of the basic elements in a business or brand identity. Budelmann et al. [5] state that a logo is essentially an image that represents the set of experiences that form a perception in the minds of individuals concerning an organization. The same authors point out that identity is often confused (mistakenly) with the logo and claim that the identity of an organization goes far beyond its logo – the organization's name, the color of the envelopes, or even the music that customers listen to when they are on hold on the phone; they are all examples of elements of organization's identity. They also reinforce that most of the logos we admire are often part of a well-designed system. The same idea is shared by Gomez-Palacio & Vit [7] who also state that the identity or graphic brand goes far beyond the definition of the logo and can be manifested in business cards, uniforms, marketing materials, and other promotional/ communication materials. They reinforce that identity design is the process of identifying a product, service, or organization, through a concise and consistent set of distinct elements - colors, typography, and other visual cues in harmony with a logo. The authors also claim that designers create a visual system that makes a product, service or organization easily identifiable, generating tangible manifestations of its intangible values. Regarding the term *branding* or *brand*, Gomez-Palacio, & Vit [7] add that its objective is to form a general perception of any product, service, or organization, in the consumer's mind, by various means and is typically related to products consumption and services (although the same principles are applied to companies, businesses, and even personalities). Generally, branding results from the collaboration between graphic designers, strategists, researchers, and writers, where all disciplines (web design, advertising, public relations, identity design) come together in a cohesive way to position and present the aspirations, values and benefits of the product, service, or organization. Brand success must create positive associations and establish consistent expectations for the consumer, as well as generate revenue. Wheeler [8] highlights some ideals that she considers essential in a brand's identity, such as vision, meaning, authenticity, differentiation, durability, coherence, flexibility, commitment, and value, considering them fundamental for a responsible creative process. Some of the ideals mentioned by Wheeler [8] stand out, such as *meaning*, which the author says boosts the creativity of designers, by being transmitted through unique visual shapes and expressions, so that it can be understood, communicated, and approved. The author also states that the entire brand identity system must have a meaningful and logical structure. Another of the ideals to be highlighted is *differentiation* and the author states that it is not enough to be different. Brands need to demonstrate their difference and make it easy for customers to understand that difference. Finally, it's important to highlight *value* (*to create value*), which the author considers to be an indisputable objective for most organizations. Regarding this ideal, Wheeler [8] emphasizes that the search for sustainability has expanded the importance of value in the interaction with consumers. Being socially responsible, environmentally conscious, and profitable is the new business model for all brands. A brand is intangible - the brand identity, which includes all tangible expression from packaging to websites, underpins that value.

2.1 Graphic Brand of a Place or City

Associating the identity and graphic brand with a place or city, Fragoso [3] says that the designer's intervention is fundamental in the establishment of a visual identity program that dignifies the city's symbols, and the *spirit of the place*, and that promotes cultural differentiation and enrichment. According to Raposo [9], current brands strive to be more coherent and used in a systematic way but also try to create a symbolic and emotional relationship with the public. The brand seems increasingly to belong to the public and less to the company, being also "a social phenomenon". Anholt [10] states that currently, cities need their brands materialized and organized by a representative visual identity, in a scenario of strong comparison between places - with new technologies and greater ease of mobility, the distances between places narrowed. Ribeiro et al. [11] argue that competition between cities, motivated by globalization, should not engage in strategies that do not address the essential and special characteristics of cities. The authors reinforce that choosing unique elements of a certain place requires certain guidelines and procedures that favor the creation of a promising brand. Therefore, they present the case of the city of São Luís, in Brazil, inscribed as a Cultural Heritage of Humanity, by UNESCO, and provide research carried out at a preliminary stage, on people's perception of the city's image, concerning its cultural heritage. The objective was to develop a model composed of guidelines for place branding projects aimed at Cultural Heritage Cities of Humanity. The emotional connection between the public and the brand is also highlighted by Landa [12], who states that this relationship must be sustained around a set of values and through a well-crafted communication, both visually and verbally and that what defines the user's relationship with a given identity is what he/she thinks of it and the way he/she reacts to it. This emotional connection is further reinforced by Wheeler [8] who says that the brand's differentiation and added value are mainly focused on the search for a connection with the user and on the way it is interpreted. Heskett [13] says that graphic designers use a common vocabulary of signs, symbols, typography, colors and motifs to create messages and structure information, giving the example of the brand created for New York City "I love New York", one of the best-known graphic shapes by Milton Glaser. Berger [14] emphasizes that if the information presented to the visitor in the communication materials is simple, clear and consistent, he will understand the place in a true and welcoming way. Gibson [15] reaffirms the importance of the brand in promoting a place, extending this importance to the moment before arriving at the place and reinforces the relevance of defining an identity that is integrative of all communicational materials: *"Anything visitors experience or encounter should express their brand. For instance, a website is a particularly important branding tool because it helps people form an impression about a place before they actually visit it. When they approach the site, graphic prompts and other signals can confirm that they've actually arrived. Coordinated symbols, colors, names, signage, architecture, and landscaping together reinforce the institutional identity and express a specific sense of place, of being somewhere in particular"*. Yázigi [16, 17] highlights the need to consider the existence of the soul of the place, stating that soul would be what is best in a place and that, therefore, transcends time. The same author points to an interaction of people who have feelings for their place of experience, demonstrating that there is a soul when people are passionate about the place. Still on this subject, it is inevitable to cite Norberg-Schulz [18]. The author states that the term *place* is much more than a location: *"In general, nature forms an extended comprehensive totality, a "place", which according to local circumstances has a particular identity"*. The author refers to the *spirit of the place* and the term *Genius Loci* as a Roman concept, in which according to the ancient belief, every "independent" being has its own genius, its own guardian spirit; this spirit gives life to people and places.

3 Case Study: Project "BEJA VISUAL" (Valuation and Communication of Heritage Through Design)

As already mentioned, it was proposed, within the scope of the Graphic Design curricular unit, the development of a graphic identity for the project entitled "BEJA VISUAL", a project to be carried out in the future and which will aim to communicate in a graphic and visual way, the tangible and intangible cultural heritage of the city of Beja and the region of "*Baixo Alentejo*". In order to define this graphic brand, the students would have to do a thematic graphic research in the city of Beja (walking through the city streets and registering elements through photographs or sketches), which would influence and define the graphic identity for the project (1st phase of the project, see Fig. 1). This project had as its main objectives (in addition to the essential learning objectives of the fundamentals of Graphic Design), the visual research on existing and "visible" cultural heritage aspects in the city of Beja; the graphic interpretation of living cultural heritage aspects, and their reinterpretation; the construction of a graphic identity from shapes and graphics that already exist in the cultural heritage of the city that reflects pre-defined concepts and values; The graphic brand could be developed according to the following optional themes: 1 - Beja's architectural iconography; 2 - Handicrafts or archaeological pieces from the city of Beja; 3 - Tilework in Beja; 4 - "Graphic culture" of the City of Beja (places, graphics or urban art).

Fig. 1. (*left*) Photographic research for the city of Beja under the theme *Tilework in Beja*. Students: Beatriz Ferreira and Luis Gois (2021). (*center*) Photographic research for the city of Beja under the theme *Architectural iconography of Beja*. Students: Filipe Malveiro, José Calhau, Ricardo Santos (2021). (*right*) Photographic research for the city of Beja under the theme *Graphic Culture* of the City of Beja (places, urban graphics). Students: José Fábio Serrão, Inês Costa, Inês Viriato, João Bico and Leonardo Bexiga.

After the photographic research through the city streets, students would have to create the graphic identity and its graphics standards manual for the project (2nd phase) through the following steps: 1. Study/schematization of graphic shapes: visual interpretation and reconstruction (see Fig. 2); 2. Experimental typography; construction of letters, symbols, and icons (see Fig. 2); 3. Creation of the graphic brand and its graphics standards manual for correct use (see Fig. 3).

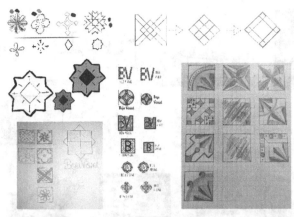

Fig. 2. Study and schematization of shapes from the photographic research carried out in the 1st phase. Students (*from left to right and top to bottom*): Beatriz Reis (2022); João Caetano (2022); Laura Lameira (2021); Bárbara Casimiro (2021) and Margarida Castanheira (2021).

Fig. 3. Selection of some final logos. Students (*from left to right and top to bottom*): Gonçalo Francisco (2022), Joana Costa (2021), Ana Viegas (2021), João Caetano (2022), Sofia Filipe (2021), Luis Góis (2022), Filipe Malveiro (2022), Leonardo Bexiga (2022), José Calhau (2022), Margarida Castanheira (2021), João Bico (2022).

Finally, in the 3rd phase of the project, students would have to apply the defined graphic brand to various communication materials (see Fig. 4). This phase consisted of the following steps: 1. Creation of an editorial graphic object (an 8-page promotional brochure for the city); 2. Creation of various communicational graphic objects to promote the project (poster, packaging, gifts, website, and app); 3. Creation of a written document describing all phases of the project.

Fig. 4. Several applications of graphic identities created. Students: Filipe Malveiro (2022), Leonardo Bexiga (2022), João Caetano (2022), Sofia Filipe (2021), João Bico (2022), Joana Costa (2021), Luís Góis (2022), Raquel Cruz (2021).

4   Analysis of Results and Conclusions

Through an academic project for the construction of a graphic brand applied to a specific city with a vast cultural heritage, it was intended to demonstrate the importance of local symbols and graphics in the construction of a graphic brand to promote these same heritage values. It was also intended that in the learning of Design, the importance of "looking" at the city would be emphasized, more critically, with the specific objective of extracting shapes, ideas, and symbols, later giving them a reinterpretation. It is also worth mentioning one of Wheeler's ideals [8], *the meaning*, which according to the author, boosts the creativity of designers, by being conveyed through unique visual shapes and expressions, so that it can be understood, communicated, and approved.

With this work, it was pretended to make the students "look" at the city of Beja differently, looking at details that are part of the city's landscape, but that often go unnoticed or are unknown by the younger generations. It is considered that all these procedures also have deepened the concepts and knowledge of structuring elements and hierarchy of content in graphic and digital materials, such as layout, grid, typography, or color, as well as the understanding of the technical requirements for the elaboration of all print and digital materials. The definition of the identity and graphic brand of a place (touristic or not) is a fundamental aspect to consider in its communication, differentiating it from the competition and conveying concepts, attributes, and benefits of the place in question. The brand must reflect the cultural personality of the region and create a close connection with the user and must make an emotional appeal by conveying the unique particularities of the places, in addition to contributing to the presentation of information about the destination. The graphic identity of a place must contain social, associative, identity and differentiation values, etc., dignifying the symbols and the spirit of the place, having a communicative function to fulfill, and having to be socially useful and meaningful concerning its environment or context. It must also be unique and convey the concepts and characteristics that are intrinsic to it, so that it is not confused with the identity of any other site; in turn, the place must also reflect the relationship between individuals and their identity, so that their place brand can be defined more concisely, as the brand absorbs content, images, ephemeral sensations, reinforcing the emotional connection between the public and the brand and, consequently, the public and the place. If all these aspects are considered when creating a graphic identity for a city or place and, consequently, in its application to various communication materials (from the most traditional to the most used today, such as websites and apps), all these materials will stimulate/ motivate user interaction with the information presented, enriching the user experience in the "physical" or digital handling of these same materials, through a symbolic charge that contains the spirit and heritage elements specific to the places and that makes the information about them more appealing and exclusive.

Acknowledgments. This work is financed by national funds through FCT - Fundação para a Ciência e a Tecnologia, I.P., under the Strategic Project with the references UIDB/04008/2020 and UIDP/04008/2020.

References

1. Brizolla, T. (ed.): Turismo Cultural- orientações básicas [Cultural Tourism – basic guidelines]. Ministério do Turismo do Brasil, Brasilia (2006)
2. López, A.: Manual de Marketing General y de Servicios Turísticos [Manual of General Marketing and Tourist Services]. Editorial Sintesis, Madrid (1992)
3. Fragoso, M.: A leitura da cidade pelos seus símbolos gráficos [The reading of the city through its graphic symbols]. Convergences - Journal of Research and Arts Education **2**(3) (2009). http://convergencias.esart.ipcb.pt/?p=article&id=45. Accessed 25 May 2022
4. Olins, W.: Wally Ollins: The Brand Book. Verbo, Lisbon (2010)
5. Budelmann, K., Wozniak, C., Kim, Y.: Brand Identity Essentials: 100 Principles for Designing Logos and Building Brands. Rockport Publishers, Beverly (2010)
6. Morgan, C.L.: Logos - Logo, Identidade, Marca, Cultura [Logos - Logo, Identity, Brand, Culture]. Destarte, Lisbon (1999)
7. Gomez-Palacio, B., Vit, A.: Graphic Design, Referenced: A Visual Guide to the Language, Applications, and History of Graphic Design. Rockport Publishers, Beverly (2009)
8. Wheeler, A.: Designing Brand Identity: An Essential Guide for the Whole Branding Team. Wiley, Hoboken (2009)
9. Raposo, D.: Da marca gráfica aos sistemas de identidade visual corporativa [From graphic branding to corporate visual identity systems]. Convergences – J. Res. Arts Educ. (3) (2009). http://hdl.handle.net/10400.11/1726. Accessed 26 May 2022
10. Anholt, S.: Some Important Distinctions in Place Branding. Place Branding and Public Diplomacy. Palgrave Macmillan, New York (2010)
11. Ribeiro, E., Raposo, D., Menezes, M.: Entre a imagem e a identidade de uma Cidade Património Cultural [Between the image and the identity of a Cultural Heritage City]. Convergences – J. Res. Arts Educ. **11**(21) (2018). http://convergencias.esart.ipcb.pt/?p=article&id=289. Accessed 26 May 2022

12. Landa, R.: Designing Brand Experiences. Thomson, Delamr Learning, EUA (2006)
13. Heskett, J.: Toothpicks and Logos: Design in Everyday Life. Oxford University Press, New York (2002)
14. Berger, C.M.: Wayfinding – Designing and Implementing Graphic Navigational Systems. RotoVision, Hove (2009)
15. Gibson, D.: The Wayfinding Handbook- Information Design for Public Places, p. 73. Princeton Architectural Press, New York (2009)
16. Yázigi, E.: A Alma do Lugar. Turismo, Planejamento e Cotidiano [The Soul of the Place. Tourism, Planning and Daily Life]. Contexto, São Paulo (2001)
17. Alves, K.: O Turismo Pedagógico como Indutor de Lugares Identitários para Reconhecer, Interpretar e Reservar [Pedagogical tourism as inductor of identity places to recognize, interpret and reserve]. Revista Turismo & Desenvolvimento [Tourism Dev. Mag.] 4(21/22), 483–491 (2014)
18. Norberg-Schulz, C.: Genius Loci – Towards a Phenomenology of Architecture. Rizzoli, New York (1979)

Computer Reshaping the View of Objects-The Operational Aesthetics of Generative Art

Yue Gu(✉)

Tsinghua University, Beijing, China
387772164@qq.com

Abstract. **Purpose** generation art design redefines the creation method and output form of the art design. The blending of aesthetics and calculation realizes the fusion of "art" and "science", liberating the artist's mind, giving him more forms of creative display, and encouraging them to express new world views and conceive future designs.

Method is based on the digital coding of the computer, and the artistic creation of storing and processing different format information in the form of binary code, such as text, image, and sound, to construct a more rigorous and intelligent form, movement, interaction, etc.

Conclusion. The definition of beauty is contained in the harmony of numbers. Digital information has given birth to new cultural forms and modes of communication. Computers have imperceptibly changed people's clothing, food, housing and transportation. Computers have reshaped the traditional concept of creation. Computer "creation" seems to break the barrier of "instrument" and embody the way of design in virtuality, immateriality and mobility. Generative Art has the characteristics of openness, randomness and interaction, which brings infinite possibilities for design creation.

Keywords: Computer · Generative art · Design · Computational aesthetics

1 Introduction

A large number of geometric figures and mathematical formulas were drawn in the manuscripts of Leonardo da Vinci, a great scientist, artist and mathematician in the Renaissance(15th century BC).The ancient Greek philosopher Pythagorean School used the harmony of numbers to explain the beauty of the universe and put forward that the essence of beauty is numbers(sixth century BC). Dutch artist Escher's scientific thinking is fully displayed in his works, which vividly depicts the concepts of contradictory space, paradox, cycle, polyhedron, curved surface geometry and so on. Over time the boundary enclosing art can be stretched to include new forms that seem to share a "family resemblance" to currently accepted art (Carroll 1999). After the 20th century, the establishment of "Bauhaus design institute" has achieved a large number of avant-garde artists in the new era. Marx bill, a former Bauhaus top student, introduced mathematical models into artistic creation. Bill believes that mathematics is a necessary aid way for

© The Author(s), under exclusive license to Springer Nature Switzerland AG 2022
C. Stephanidis et al. (Eds.): HCII 2022, CCIS 1654, pp. 315–322, 2022.
https://doi.org/10.1007/978-3-031-19679-9_39

art, and the artist's mental world needs to obtain the corresponding formal coat through mathematical laws. With the emergence of computers, "number" is ubiquitous and silent, which invisibly changes our clothing, food, housing and transportation. It can copy, cycle, iterate and upgrade infinitely. Generative Art, parametric design and artificial intelligence design emerge as the times require, creating unlimited possibilities in the information world. The development of computer technology and media constantly promotes and changes the production mode of art. Computer generated art closely connects aesthetics, design, mathematics, computer science, cognitive science and philosophy to create strong visual expression and interactive dynamic art works. After investigating 2500 designers and industry experts in 2015, American Association of professional designers AIGA and adobe pointed out that designers need to understand and make use of tools and technology, and the training of design talents in the future should develop to intersection, integration and diversity. The establishment of creative engineering designers and digital experience designers in Alibaba cloud design requires designers to have both design aesthetic knowledge and algorithm knowledge.

2   Natural Creation, Artificial Creation and Computer Creation

2.1   "Law" and "Beauty" of Natural Creation

Nature is the mother of human beings. The changes of the earth, the operation of the universe, the evolution of ecology, from biological genes to mechanical physics, and even human consciousness, behavior, spirit and society are all part of nature. Nature has existed long before human existence. Natural creation is an objective existence, and natural things will continue to change iteratively with time. People gradually found a large number of mathematical and aesthetic laws from nature. Johannes Kepler pointed out the existence of Fibonacci number series in nature and used it to explain the number of petals of some flowers [1]. The book named growth and form, which describes the spiral growth of animal horns and mollusk shells through simple equations, and the mathematical relationship of plant growth also explains the sequence law contained in nature (Darcy Wentworth Thompson 1917) [2]. The spiral leaf sequence of plants was often expressed in clockwise and counterclockwise golden ratio series (Charles Bonnet 1754). In addition to plants in nature, the formation of many natural landscapes has formal beauty, as shown in Fig. 1. For example, crescent shaped and dome shaped sand dunes formed by wind; A polygonal honeycomb built by bees for daily life and storing nectar; The aesthetic order of fish and reptiles is the source of the beautiful inspiration of human beings.

Fig. 1. Patterns in nature

2.2 The Evolution of Artifacts and the Deepening of "Number"

Human beings' transformation of the material world comes from the process of exploring, mining and using nature. At first, in order to make a living, people's transformation of the material world began with manufacturing tools. There are also a large number of records of creation activities in Chinese traditional literature. At the beginning of kaogong Ji, "heaven and earth have Qi, materials have beauty and workmanship", it is written that creation is based on nature and in harmony with heaven and earth. In the late Ming Dynasty, song Yingxing's "natural work opens things" gradually built the initial cognitive framework of man for nature and laws. The "work" has the meaning of "skill", "artificial" and "science and technology", which also reflects the thought of Ecological Science in China's traditional view of creation. In the Northern Song Dynasty, Li Jie organized and compiled the book "construction method", which highly integrates engineering, technology, art and scientific thinking, and shows the ancient Chinese architectural technology through the analysis of style, structure, functional style and mechanics. Mr. Liang Sicheng, in his notes to the "construction method", regarded the "construction method" as the manual of architectural design specifications, which has a rigorous calculation formula on the balance of building proportion. Thus, it shows the continuous deepening of people's technology and scientific thought in the creation activities in ancient China.

Since ancient times, religion and art have been closely related. As a special ideology, religion is people's consensus and respect for a system. It is one of the earliest forms of human consciousness. Religious belief is defined as a supernatural existence used to resist the unknown forces of the outside world. Since ancient times, in Europe, religion has provided spiritual source and belief support for man-made things. Religion has provided a large number of themes and contents for artistic creation and creation activities, and promoted and disseminated them through art. Therefore, most of the early man-made things activities were carried out around the dissemination of Theology and religion. Taking ancient Greece as an example, the emergence of Plato, Socrates and Euclid in the sixth century BC inspired the Greeks' enthusiasm for philosophy, mathematics, science and art. People began to explore the existence and value of beauty in science and rationality. Greek religion dates back to the worship of gods. The protoss of Olympus mixed the spirituality and naturalness in ancient Greek mythology into divinity. Hegel defined "God" as something created by people in his book "phenomenology of spirit", which is the image of God that poets, sculptors and painters hope to convey to the Greek people [4]. In the "aesthetic Lecture Notes", it is written that architecture is the first attempt of mankind. It gives an entity outside God. Among the Greek temples, Parthenon temple is one of the world-famous perfect buildings. Its overall shape or the spacing between doors and windows is almost close to the golden ratio of 0.618, which makes the whole building contain harmonious beauty and geometric tension, as shown in Fig. 2. The aesthetic value of ancient Greek architecture largely stems from the rigorous design principles: integrate the derived mathematical formula into the formulation of design specifications, and measure and divide the space as a whole through strict proportional constraints.

Fig. 2. Parthenon temple

With the development of agricultural civilization to industrial civilization, large-scale machine production replaced manual workshops. Human creation activities began to focus on mechanized and mass production, created a large number of unprecedented inventions, and brought huge economic growth and scientific progress. However, the high efficiency and standardization emphasized by industrialization ensure the normal and orderly development of social economy, but also lead to the homogenization of product production, waste of resources and energy, etc. After the 20th century, western countries have entered the post industrial era, new thoughts have emerged in the field of natural science, the importance of scientific and technological talents in the field of science and technology has been increasing, and "information" is closely related to human life. American scholar Danny bell wrote in the coming of post industrial society: an exploration of social prediction: "industrial society is a technological society, information society and economic society. In this society, manufacturing gives way to scientific research, machine production gives way to intellectual creation, and the scale economy model in the industrial era has been significantly weakened." With innovation as the main driving force, society has experienced the transformation from production paradigm to service paradigm. Human creation activities are also more diversified. The development of Internet technology makes creation activities no longer stay at the entity level. Network construction and digital information have become an important part of today's society. Digital information has given birth to new cultural forms. Multimedia, new media and we media have brought more information acquisition and communication channels to the public. At the same time, it also emphasizes the integration of culture and science and technology.

2.3 Computer Reshapes the View of "Creation"

In the history of computer, Alan Turing and von Neumann, the two founders of science, are called the father of computer. Modern computer principles were proposed, it verified the machine can calculate the instructions stored on the tape by reading the code language, and had programmability, improved the computer model, and put forward the concept of "Turing machine", which laid a theoretical model for modern computer (Alan Turing 1936).

The main logic circuit of the electronic computer in the "scheme of general electronic computer with stored program", and proposed the use of binary algorithm in the operation of the electronic computer (von Neumann 1945). Modern computer encodes human readable code and assembly language data and instructions into binary numbers or bit sequences, and allows internal storage of instructions. It is the founder of theoretical and technological science and game theory. Generally speaking, the principle of computer "creation" is the operation of numbers. The arithmetic unit processes data by performing various arithmetic and logical operations, and presents the results through the output device. Compared with the traditional view of creation, see Table 1, computer creation is not limited by time, place, carrier and even space, and its form is no longer fixed and static, which is different from the solid and figurative nature of creation in the industrial era.

Table 1. Comparison of characteristics between traditional creation products and digital information products

Traditional products	Digital products
Tangible	Invisible
Static	Dynamic
Eternal	Continuously changing
Exclusive	Open

It can be seen that in the information society, computer science combines technology and art, virtual and reality, seems to break the barrier of "device", and embodies the way of design in virtuality, immateriality and mobility. The traditional concept of "unity of heaven and man" emphasizes the connection between "instrument" and "Tao", which carries Tao to convey ideas and emotions. At present, online products, which rely on the support of Internet and computer technology, break through the limitation of time and space and facilitate our life to a great extent. At the same time, the code art, parametric design and artificial intelligence design that came into being in the information society also bring infinite possibilities for design creation.

3 Generated Art References

3.1 Principles and Aesthetic Value of Generated Art

The American mathematician George D. Birkhoff first proposed the concept of computational aesthetics in his book aesthetic measure. Computational aesthetics aims to study modern technology to assist art creation, generate new art forms, and explore the role and mode of art and aesthetics in the field of computer science. (Birkhoff 1933) [5] In the book, birkhof proposed that the aesthetic value is the ratio of the number of order to the total number of image elements, that is, order o and complexity C, and the aesthetic value m = O/C. This formula specifically discusses the factors affecting beauty and how to measure the works from the perspective of number.

Since the mid-1960s, engineers and computer scientists began to try to generate images by writing computer code. In August 1968, the London Academy of Arts hosted the "cybernetic serendipity", which talked about the randomness behind the generation of computer art, used the concepts of mathematics and natural science, regarded aesthetic expression as the analysis and display of the law of information, and tried to establish a general language beyond art and technology. The word "contingency" describes the random characteristics of computer-generated art, which brings uniqueness and unexpected surprises to artistic creation. In the exhibition, artists and scientists created a large number of graphics, animation and music through computer language and controlled machines [6]. From the principle and structure of computer generated art, generated art advocates orderly arrangement and harmony and unity in complexity. As Gombrich put it: "aesthetic pleasure comes from the appreciation of a pattern between boring and messy. Monotonous patterns are difficult to attract people's attention, while too complex patterns will aggravate people's perceptual system and stop viewing it." Generative Art generates forms through scientific calculation formulas and algorithms. The structure is complex but not chaotic, complex and orderly, and has a strong aesthetic feeling of form and structure.

In 2003, Philip Galanter of New York University presented his paper "what is Generative Art?" It is pointed out that Generative Art is an art work independently generated by artists who hand over the right of art generation to systems, such as a set of natural language instructions, computer programs, biological or chemical processes, machines or other program equipment [7]. The principle of Generative Art refers to the artistic creation based on computer digital coding, which stores and processes different format information in the form of binary code, such as text, image and sound.

Code is a universal language in the world and the main raw material in the information society. Through programming language, more rigorous and intelligent forms, movements, interactions and so on can be constructed. As a result, great changes have taken place in the creative materials and carriers of artists in computer-generated art.

Generative Art is different from the creative process of traditional art. It can organically combine imitation, reproduction, creation and fiction. It has the characteristics of openness, randomness and interactivity, and has specific aesthetic value.

(a) Openness

Generative Art is realized through code language. In 2001, MIT Media Laboratory designed and developed processing programming language, hoping to help non programmers carry out data visual processing and visual and interactive art creation through simplified programming language and humanized design.

Processing is an open source programming language and a branch of Java language. It simplifies a large number of algorithms, enables designers and artists to realize the cross domain expression between art and science, and enriches the forms of electronic art and visual interaction. Designers can learn and call the existing code in GitHub library, and then modify and adjust it according to their own needs, which shortens the cycle and cost of artistic creation. Open source programming language can enable us to stand on the shoulders of giants in artistic creation, recombine and optimize the program modules written by predecessors, and create excellent works with artistic value by conceiving design schemes, drawing on excellent code and integrating multi-media advantages (such as music, light effect, etc.). At the same time, the open network code also provides a convenient technical communication platform for designers, artists and programmers.

(b) Randomness

Randomness is one of the important characteristics of Generative Art. Designers and artists conceive the rules and logic of program language, and the generation results are often unpredictable, uncontrollable, random and accidental. The generation of this uncertainty itself also constitutes artistic creation. Philip Galanter said: "artists can produce relatively self-controlled works of art directly or indirectly through computer programs, language rules, machines and other inventions. This process itself is art." [9] Like the "random" function in the programming language, the works are given a numerical range in the design. The images generated by each program run are different. For the author, it is a creative process full of longing and expectation.

(c) Interactivity

As the product of the combination of computer technology and art, generative art works often appear in public and commercial spaces such as art galleries and exhibition halls. It is necessary to use comprehensive media for technical creation. The interactive characteristics of Generative Art mainly come from two aspects: on the one hand, the flexibility of the code, the audience can change some parameters to participate in the design of the work, so that the artistic creation no longer belongs to a few artists, and the audience's participation in the interaction itself also constitutes the artistic creation; On the other hand, the output of Generative Art is usually combined with various sensors and controllers. For example, works generated through processing language can interact through Arduino (open source platform), or connect external sensors such as Kinect (somatosensory device launched by Microsoft) to interact with the audience. For example, in the exhibition *Immaterial/Rematerial* that a brief history of computer art of UCCA, the work *insect man* by Laurent miniono and Christa zomerel shows the relationship between man and nature through computer art. When the audience stands in front of the screen device, they can see the outline of their body appear on the screen, and then the artificial insects will gather, With the changing body movements of the audience, the outline patterns of insects perched on the image of the audience are also changing, deriving different forms.

The interactivity of Generative Art drives the interaction between the virtual world and people and things in the real world through physical media. There are various forms of interaction: hearing, vision, touch, smell, brain wave, stream of consciousness, etc. can directly communicate and interact with works [10].

4   Conclusion

This paper compares and analyzes natural creation, artificial creation and computer creation, summarizes that the information digital products produced by computer creation have the characteristics of invisibility, dynamics, continuous change and openness, opens a new journey of "creation", and reshapes the concept of creation: mathematics, natural science, aesthetics and art have been closely linked since ancient times. Today's creation is different from the traditional aesthetic meditation. Great changes have taken place in art form and creation paradigm. Generative Art Design redefines the creation mode and output form of art design. It has the characteristics of openness, randomness and interactivity. The integration of aesthetics and computing realizes the integration of "art" and "science". The two permeate each other and promote information, culture Benign interaction between science and technology industry. However, the development of generated art does not mean that the "creative power" of computer can replace human creativity. The key to generated art lies in design algorithms and rules. After all, it is the crystallization of human wisdom. The automatic generation ability of design is only to assist artists and designers to better achieve their goals, express their connotation and improve efficiency.

References

1. The Golden Ratio: The Story of Phi, the World's Most Astonishing Number (First trade paperback ed.), p. 110. Broadway Books, New York (2002)
2. Von Neumann, J.: The Mathematician. Newman J. R. The World of Mathematics, pp. 2053–2063. Simon & Schuster, New York (1956)
3. About D'Arcy. D' Arcy 150. University of Dundee and the University of St Andrews. Accessed 16 Oct 2012
4. Zhang, Y.: Religion and art in ancient Greece – Hegel's religious and philosophical interpretation of Greek spirit. Mod. Philos. 4(01), 105–110 (2017)
5. Author, F., Author, S.: Title of a proceedings paper. In: Editor, F., Editor, S. (eds.) Conference 2016. LNCS, vol. 9999, pp. 1–13. Springer, Heidelberg (2016)
6. Author, F., Author, S., Author, T.: Book title. 2nd edn. Publisher, Location (1999)
7. Author, F.: Contribution title. In: 9th International Proceedings on Proceedings, pp. 1–2. Publisher, Location (2010)
8. LNCS. http://www.springer.com/lncs. Accessed 21 Nov 2016
9. Galanter, P.: Towards Ethical Relationships with Machines That Make Art. Artnodes 2020(26)
10. Zhou, W., Chen, Y.: Research on Network Aesthetics. China Social Sciences Press (2018)

Digital Chuimsae: Evolution of Korean Traditional Performing Arts

Yang Kyu Lim[(⊠)]

IT Media Engineering, Duksung Women's University, 33, Samyang-ro 144-gil, Dobong-gu, Seoul, Republic of Korea
trumpetyk09@duksung.ac.kr

Abstract. A traditional Korean performance is completed through the participation of the audience called 'Chuimsae'. The audience and performers are not separated like Western-style performances, but become one and communicate with each other periodically. During the performance, the audience naturally sings, shouts, and cheers for the characters. 'Chuimsae', which has been passed down for hundreds of years as a performance culture, also affects the way Korean pop music is performed, which is now represented by the genre of K-pop.

The corona pandemic is causing enormous damage to the domestic and international performance industry. In particular, Korean traditional performances have many limitations because they are freely performed at close and physically close distances without any distinction between performers and audiences. In our study, text emotion analysis technology that combines smartphone messenger and machine learning technology is used as a tool for audience communication (Digital Chuimsae). During the performance, the audience simply writes any word or sentence they want to say, and the AI technology analyzes it and displays it as a numerical value of emotion. This will directly or indirectly affect various materials that will be used as background images or elements of composition during performances. For example, if a performer's mood falls into the category of 'enjoyable', it operates on a form that can change the number and size of particles according to the degree. Audiences will be able to digitally implement 'Chuimsae' in real time while watching the performance in a safe place from the coronavirus. We conducted a test drive using this system, and each performance showed the result of being transformed into a different form by the audience. It is expected that there will be continuous development as a new performance platform in the traditional Korean performance industry, which is currently suspended due to the corona pandemic.

Keywords: Chuimsae · Machine learning · Interaction

1 Introduction

A traditional Korean performance is completed through the participation of the audience called 'Chuimsae'. The audience and performers are not separated like Western-style performances, but become one and communicate with each other periodically. During

C. Stephanidis et al. (Eds.): HCII 2022, CCIS 1654, pp. 323–328, 2022.
https://doi.org/10.1007/978-3-031-19679-9_40

the performance, the audience naturally sings, shouts, and cheers for the characters. This is closely related to the traditional Korean performance format where there is no stage. The customs of Kim Heung-do, designated as Korea's Treasure No. 527, have a good description of Korean performances in the late 18th century. In Fig. 1, two men are wrestling on the same line as the audience.

Fig. 1. Wrestling, one of the paintings in "Kim Heung-do's Customs and Paintings," is famous for its detailed depiction of Korean culture in the late 18th century.

Participation is the most important thing in our culture that enjoys culture intertwined with each other without boundaries between performers and audiences. With the influx of Western culture, we have been living ignoring our participatory culture for a while. Ironically, with the development of internet media, our traditional culture began to focus on making it more popular. In particular, many foreign performers who come to Korea are often surprised by the unique Korean-style participatory culture. Excessive audience participation risks damaging the content of the performance. But conversely, being able to enjoy together is a basic mechanism of culture.

The coronavirus pandemic, which started in 2019, is expected to caused enormous damage to the performance market worldwide. Through this, various classes using Internet messenger and Internet media began to grow. Performances were also carried out in various ways, but limited cultural activities were continued through real-time performances and recorded performances using media such as YouTube. Performance's online have exploded with the coronavirus pandemic. In particular, in Korea, where the Internet quality is excellent, people across the country are using the streaming service without any restrictions. Based on the ideas that emerged from environmental and cultural factors, we wanted to launch an online performance service. What is especially important in this service is the way in which the audience participates in the performance.

2 Design and Implementation

In the case of performances with audience participation, restrictions may occur. However, if it is a method that considers the participation of the audience from the design stage of the performance, this is a different story. We have been thinking about how the audience should participate in online performances. Our problems can be solved through a messenger service using the smartphone that everyone has.

2.1 Design

Audience participation is very simple. Using the smartphone messenger that anyone is using, the audience chats with another audience or performance person. Although this is a situation where it may be against the etiquette, as long as the restrictions are lifted, the performance can be enjoyable enough. Many Korean TV programs have already introduced the simple concept of viewer voting to induce audience participation in real time. Not only did the singer I choose win the title, but also in programs such as dramas, audience participation is actively taking place by reflecting viewers' opinions and changing the story.

In this study, emotion analysis technology was used as the core technology of the audience participation method. Through a chat program created by the audience, the audience writes down various opinions during the performance. Opinions written in this way are summarized once with morphological analysis technology. Based on the organized data, we can understand the author's current mood.

Most of these techniques are done through Natural Language Processing using Google's Tensorflow.

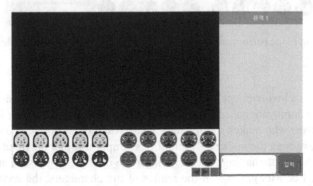

Fig. 2. Basic scene of performance platform using messenger and streaming service

The designed program is implemented as shown in Fig. 2. The black box on the left is the part where the video of the performance is played. The video of the performance is output and various effects are output. The light blue part on the right is the part where chatting takes place and confirmation. When the audience enters what they are thinking, it is expressed. Lastly, the emoticons at the bottom are in the shape of a traditional Korean mask to express joy and sorrow. In particular, the intensity of the emotions can be adjusted by dividing the intensity into 5 stages. It was produced to provide convenience for the audience who do not prefer chatting in order to focus more on the performance. It is also a way to intuitively express my feelings.

2.2 Implementation

The audience's text and emoticons input during the performance are converted into scores and used. Five colors have traditionally been used in various fields in Korea. The five colors represent east-blue, west-white, south-red, north-black, and central-yellow. Also, blue represents Jupiter, white represents Venus, red represents Mars, black represents Mercury, and finally yellow represents Saturn. In addition, various interpretations are possible, and we created particles by mixing these colors with emotional data. Even if there is no input, the simpler particles set by the performance team to basically appear as shown in Fig. 3. A small amount of particles is used as a device to express the dramatic part of the performance more firmly in consultation with the performer in advance.

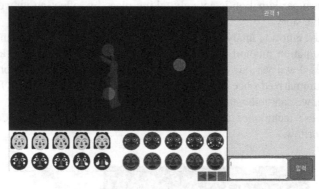

Fig. 3. For the fun of the performance, we basically set a small amount of particles. (Color figure online)

The audience's involvement is shown through energetic particles as shown in Fig. 4. A scene from 'Chunhyangga', the most famous traditional performance in Korea. It is the story of a lover who makes passionate love. If you look at Fig. 4, you can see that it is a form of expressing the audience's intentions simply through the input of emoticons in addition to the input chatting. The content of the chat message is, in order, the first, 'Chunhyang & Lee Mongryong' in the names of the characters, the second, "Is this a happy ending?" The third message after the emoticon is "strange". The black emoticon represents the lowest degree of love.

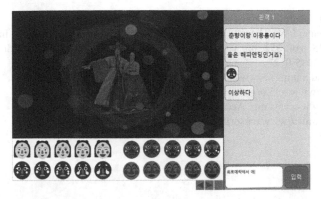

Fig. 4. A video of a performance responding with various particles after a message is input

3 Evaluation and Conclusion

The platform we built was supported by the Korean government as a performance-related project. And we are promoting collaboration with two different traditional performances. Solutions using artificial intelligence in the field of performing arts are no longer a story of the distant future. Various artists from home and abroad have already performed or are planning to perform, and these performances can serve as an example of showing the value of new art to the audience. The level of artificial intelligence technology, we are researching and developing is still insufficient, and it may be difficult to utilize it in the art field. It is a time when good technicians and artists meet more important than anything else.

In the West, which has a long history of performance, the part of audience participation tends to be perceived as an obstacle to performance. However, in the traditional performance culture of Korea, audience participation is recognized as a natural process and a part of the performance under the name of 'Chuimsae'. At this moment when Korean culture is expanding along with the development of digital technology, we recognized not only our performances but also the culture of performance viewing as an important part, and created an audience participation platform using AI emotion analysis technology to implement.

In particular, in order to overcome the various limitations of live performances caused by the current corona pandemic, the performance viewing and audience participation platform using artificial intelligence technology does not simply recognize particles or images flying around, but communicates with the audience. It is expected that the competitiveness of korean traditional performance with digital 'Chuimsae' through internet, which is one step advanced from the existing performance format, will be strengthened.

References

1. Kanber, B.: Hands-On Machine Learning with Javascript. Packt, Birmingham (2018)
2. Sasaki, K.: Hands-On Machine Learning with TensorFlow.js. Packt, Birmingham (2019)
3. Shiffman, D.: Nature of Code. Magicbook Project (2012)

4. Shiffman, D.: Learning Processing. Elsevier, Amsterdam (2015)
5. Lim, Y.K., Park, J.W.: The way to preserve korean intangible cultural assets. In: Stephanidis, C. (ed.) CCIS, vol. 852, pp. 192–195 (2018). Springer, Heidelberg. https://doi.org/10.1007/978-3-319-92285-0_27
6. Nature of Code. https://www.natureofcode.com. Accessed 08 Feb 2022
7. ML5. https://www.ml5.org. Accessed 08 Feb 2022
8. P5Js. https://www.p5js.org. Accessed 08 Feb 2022
9. Tensorflow. https://www.tensorflow.org. Accessed 08 Feb 2022

Metaverse-Driven Interactive Performing Arts Content Development

Jin Young Park[1(✉)] and Yang Kyu Lim[2]

[1] Department of Dance, Hanyang University, Seoul, Republic of Korea
`digna@hanyang.ac.kr`
[2] IT Media Engineering, Duksung Women's University, Seoul, Republic of Korea
`trumpetyk09@duksung.ac.kr`

Abstract. The ongoing COVID-19 pandemic necessitated platform diversification and the revitalization of interactive performance (the metaverse), a new paradigm for the performing arts. In 2019, the authors implemented an online, audience-participatory, interactive dance performance content using AI. This study analyzed the effect of the metaverse on performance content in terms of performer–audience interaction, examining the distinction between face-to-face performances using AI-based Korean dance content on the metaverse platform. Interactive metaverse performances break free from the unidirectional limitations of traditional face-to-face performances, which can only be viewed, and enables audiences guide the performance by expressing emotions through VR avatars during the performance and expressing opinions through chats. This study sought to derive a meaningful application plan after confirming the usefulness and limitations of metaverse convergence with the performing arts by focusing on an interactive Korean dance performance. The findings should enhance performing arts content development and academic and industrial values.

Keywords: Metaverse · Performance · VR · Machine learning

1 Study Purpose

The Fourth Industrial Revolution (Industry 4.0) refers to rapid technological changes, increasing connectivity, and smart automation. Industry 4.0 technologies like artificial intelligence are also revolutionizing art and technology, driving a return to *techne* that has inspired innovative developments that meld performance with technology as never before. One such development is the metaverse, a three-dimensional virtual world mimicking the real world's social, economic, and cultural activities. Although the metaverse concept emerged more than a decade ago, it has gained momentum since 2020 because of the COVID-19 pandemic and the need for social distancing to prevent the spread of the contagious virus (Figs. 1 and 2).

Emergen Research forecasted that the global metaverse market will grow from US$47.7 billion in 2020 to US$829 billion in 2028 at a compound annual rate of 42.9% [2]. Thus, the metaverse has become a hot prospect in various fields such as the gaming

C. Stephanidis et al. (Eds.): HCII 2022, CCIS 1654, pp. 329–335, 2022.
https://doi.org/10.1007/978-3-031-19679-9_41

Fig. 1. In the work "Seven Square," a virtual performer appeared using machine learning through a specific audience's movement.

Metaverse market size forecast

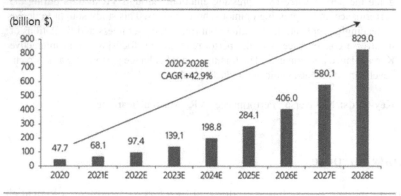

Source: Emergen Research, Samsung Securities

Fig. 2. Metaverse market size forecast [1]

industry, art, and education. For that reason, the authors previously studied AI-based convergence interactive dance performance content design and implementation [3]. They created AI-based content in which an audience directly participated in a performance to confirm their positive response to a technology-based interactive dance performance through an audience survey and interviews. The current study builds on this to confirm the significance and utility of extended reality (XR) performing arts metacontent.

When the ongoing pandemic led to stagnation in the performing arts industry, technology convergence became an essential tool for revitalizing public performances. The metaverse platform enables real-time performer–audience interaction far beyond what is possible in face-to-face performances, creating a new paradigm for the performing arts. This study analyzed the distinction between real-time audience-participation dance performance in the meta-verse and the limited interactivity of face-to-face performances, focusing on the effects of the meta-verse on performing arts content. In addition, this study confirms the diverse practical value of XR performing arts in the extension of artistic boundaries in the period of meta-verse.

2 Differences Between Metaverse and Face-to-Face Performance Content

Metaverse and face-to-face performances typically have different levels of accessibility and physical restriction. These were clearly revealed when the pandemic shifted many parts of everyday life (e.g., meetings, social interactions, education, etc.) onto virtual-space platforms. While traditional live performances were curtailed for health reasons, they thrived in the virtual world. Technology enabled performers and audiences alike to experience new content that reflected modern sensibilities and social changes, breaking the "fourth wall" as never before. Furthermore, it helped develop new approaches for the performing arts industry that have changed both online and offline experiences.

We analyzed the following distinctions between metaverse performance content and face-to-face performance.

2.1 Expansion of the Platform and Interaction with the Audience

Currently, the ongoing pandemic has caused physical space restrictions or face-to-face performances. Content based on a metaverse platform is free from these temporal and spatial limitations and restrictions on audience accommodation. The enabled easy viewing and smooth audience interactions with the performers (Fig. 3).

Fig. 3. View of a metaverse performance

Content based on a metaverse platform is free from these temporal and spatial limitations and restrictions on audience accommodation. The enabled easy viewing and smooth audience interactions with the performers.

Traditionally, the performing arts have predominantly relied on a one-way process in which performers deliver a message (words, music, dance, etc.) to a passively receptive audience. In a metaverse, the audience become part of the performance by becoming 3D avatars who can express feelings about the work and communicate with the perfumers and other audience members. This interactive makes every performance unique. Research is even under way that will soon enable these 3D avatars to be realistic portrayals of audience members [4]. These virtual doppelgängers will further add to the sense of reality. Even the current 3D avatars increase the understanding and in-depth appreciation of the work through question-and-answer sessions on the intention of choreography and the production process after.

2.2 Realistic Experience Through XR Contents

The XR concept includes mixed reality (MR) technology that encompasses VR and augmented reality (AR) [5]. Immersive XR content (e.g., 3D holograms) is a higher concept of AR, VR, and MR that maximizes the sense of being part of a scene. Immersive XR content shared online enables a seemingly real experience without the need to be physically present [6].

In interactive performances, the planned XR content expands into new content by incorporating the interactions of the avatar-audience and their emotional expressions. Metaphorically, this goes beyond the performers walking off the stage and into the audience; it allows the audience to become quasi-performers. This concept revitalizes the performing arts by providing the audience with an immersive experience that increases their interest and emotional connection. The graphic conversion process (avatar manipulation) enables the audience to express emotions as they view the work, and visual effects are added in response to those emotions. Thus, the XR content lets the audience directly participate in a multisensory experience, and their effect on the performance content allows them to share in the satisfaction of artistic creation.

The content can provide sense of welcoming by overlapping the real stage space and with the virtual scene and added visual effects (Figs. 4 and 5).

Fig. 4. Image of original video

Fig. 5. Example of graphic change according to a real-time audience reaction

3 Effect of the Metaverse on Dance Performance

The metaverse platform is affecting various industries, and the performing arts. With the transition of the platform, access to performances has become easier, and opportunities to enjoy culture and art have expanded. This implies that the utility value in terms of marketing is high. Diversified performing arts not only affects the quality of performances, but also the artistic and technical aspects. This suggest the necessity of adapting and utilizing emerging technological platform. Thus, the performing art community should pay attention to the endless possibilities of metaverse platform. The effects of metaverse on dance performance is as follows.

3.1 Enhancing the Uniqueness of Korean Dance Content

Metaverse XR content is not a blind application of technology; the artistry of the essential performance content is important. Korean culture and arts have reached a new turning point with the expansion of the virtual platform base and the global spread of Hallyu content such as the BTS and K-Pop. This suggests the possibility that Korean dance could be established as a core element of K-culture. Thus, there is a need to produce high-quality global content and build an appropriate system. The production of Korean dance content through which the audience can experience and enjoy art could re-emphasize the high value of traditional Korean culture and art and its own historical significance. It enhances the uniqueness and excellence of K-culture and strengthens its status as global content. In this context, we added traditional Korean dance elements into metavers XR platform. In general, ancestors of Korean are known for their complex emotional expressions of 'Heung' (joy) and 'Han' (grief). Social atmosphere of precedent Korean dynasty eras were quite similar to those dark middle-age of Europe. Thus these suppressed emotions of Korean ancestors were often expressed by the form of dance. For instance, 'Salpuri Chum', a famous traditional Korean dance form, contains the plot in which the feeling of grief transcend into joy through the course of narrating the story. This remarks traditional Korean dance as distinguishable K-Culture content.

3.2 Popularization of the Performing Arts

Although technology has expanded the opportunities for enjoying the performing arts, there are still culturally marginalized groups whose lack of access to or understanding of the performing arts have hindered its broader popularization. Especially during the pandemic, not every can travel to a concert hall or arts center to enjoy a live performances content. The shift toward virtual social interactions allows more people to enjoy performances any time without leaving their homes. This has had a positive effect on attracting audiences and increased the marketing potential since larger online audiences can be linked to face-to-face audiences and performances.

The performing arts have always changed with the times, from the morality plays of ancient Greece and the passion plays of ancient Egypt to radio, television, and films. Now they have expanded to the virtual space, too. Online performance content can be enjoyed repeatedly at any time, free from the tethers of specific stages and showtimes—perishable creations that evaporate the moment they are performed. This new paradigm in the performing arts has developed various formats that reflecting the needs of today's audiences. Technology-infused performances are one way to popularize the performing arts online and offline by providing convenience, accessibility, and new levels of immersion.

During the performance, the emotional expression and experience provide the positive feedback to the audience which can bring the potential customer. For this reason, metaverse platform can be used to appeal to the broader audiences.

4   Conclusion

The expected effects of performance contents using the metaverse are summarized as follows. First, for the metaverse content, we expect scalability in the platform and freedom from the constraints of time and space. Performances can flow in an interactive two-way format rather than a one-way message-delivery method. Unlike in traditional face-to-face performances, audiences experiencing metaverse performances can express their feelings mid-performance as 3D avatars, communicating with the performers and each other smoothly.

Second, the production of realistic Korean dance content where audiences experience and enjoy art provides an opportunity to re-examine the value of dance art that contains the overall art prototype. XR content that reflects the emotional reactions of the audience goes beyond passive viewing to provide an immersive experience that feels real. This can increase interest and connection while enhancing the creative artistry and spontaneity in the performing arts.

Third, it promotes the vitalization of the performing arts and establishes a foundation as online performing arts contents through interactive content that reflects the emotional changes and opinions of the audience in real time during the performance. In the Industry 4.0 era, metaverse platform performances are free from physical limitations and can communicate with the audience and create infinite forms of performing arts content.

Fourth, performance content that can be enjoyed without temporal or spatial restrictions has a high utility value from the perspective of performing arts marketing. A positive effect can also be expected in terms of attracting audiences. Online audiences can be linked to face-to-face audiences, promoting the popularization of performing arts. By facilitating the accessibility of performances, performance contents using the metaverse revitalize the performing arts world stagnated by the pandemic.

Fifth, performance content using the metaverse helps develop art and technology convergence research with the synergistic effect of interdisciplinary research by developing content according to the progress of convergence research. The convergence and interrelationship between science and technology and art have been discussed since ancient times. The development of convergence content is meaningful in the interdisciplinary aspect of science and art and in the derivation of new creative research.

This work demonstrates exploitation of metaverse contents for designing the performing art, explores the potential and advantages offered by such an emerging technology platform, and suggests how to utilize audience interactive to gain the public popularity. If consistent analyses and researches on metaverse based content development are progressed, this methodology can be used to establish next-generation performing art.

According to the rapid development of new technology, the metaverse is entering the commercialization stage and is newly evolving as it is integrated in the performing arts field. This study represents the basic stage of research to plan and implement metaverse-based performing arts content. If the development potential and utility value of metaverse performance content are examined and continuous research of exploring the benefits of interacting with an audience and developing various contents are carried out, it is expected that the competitiveness of metaverse performance content, which is one step advanced from the existing performance format, will be strengthened.

References

1. Samsung Securities. https://www.samsungpop.com/common.do?cmd=down&saveKey=res earch.pdf&fileName=2020/20220203083315241K_02_01.pdf&contentType=application/pdf. Accessed 01 Mar 2022
2. Emergen Research. https://www.emergenresearch.com/industry-report/metaverse-market. Accessed 04 Mar 2022
3. Jinyoung, P.: Design and implementation of artificial intelligence (AI) technology driven interactive fusion dance performance. General Graduate School. Hanyang University, Hanyang University PhD thesis, (2021)
4. Zhang, X.-G., Kim, H.-M., Seo, B.-G., Park, J.: 3D photorealistic avatar creation technology for immersive remote meeting. Korea Broadcast. Media Eng. Soc.: Korea Soc. Broadcast Eng. Maga. **26**(3) (2021)
5. Korea Information and Communication Technology Association. http://terms.tta.or.kr/dictio nary/dictionaryView.do?word_seq=177597-1. Accessed 15 Mar 2022
6. Oh, E., Oh, S.: Characteristics of Seoul's smart media industry and direction of activation. Seoul Institute, Policy Report, no. 274, p. 4 (2019)

Cultural Heritage Through Educational Robots: Using a Ukrainian Folk Tale with a Programmable Robot in Early Childhood Education

Robin Samuelsson(✉)

Uppsala University, Uppsala, Sweden
robin.o.samuelsson@nordiska.uu.se

Abstract. Programmable robots are increasingly used to introduce computational thinking and programming to young children. However, how to practically introduce this is still being developed, where storytelling and project-based methods have been promoted as possible ways to achieve this. This paper presents a study from a preschool featuring 4–5 year-olds working with a Ukrainian folk tale, The Mitten, while introducing programming through a programmable floor robot, The Blue-Bot. The paper presents the iterative cycles during a design-based study of merging the folk tale with the Blue-Bot during the project. The paper further examines the educational affordances of a programming board created during the project, showing how the folk tale provided a fitting structure for the board and pedagogical scaffold during the activities. The paper discusses how older forms of cultural heritage can be merged with new technologies and the added importance of the particular case of Ukrainian cultural heritage following the outbreak of the war in Ukraine.

Keywords: Childhood education · Robots · Programming

1 Introduction

There is an ongoing educational movement of teaching computational thinking and programming in early childhood [1], where programmable robots have been used to introduce such skills to young children [2]. An educational goal has been to introduce robotics, programming and computational thinking for increased and diversified participation and, also, for younger children [1, 3].

One proposed way to introduce programming for children has been to use programmable robots and storytelling in projects and activities [4]. This has been shown to create inclusive participation with younger children [3] However, a remaining challenge has been to practically design learning to sustain children's interest [5] and teach programming in playful and engaging ways that are appropriately adopted for young children [6]. Programming for children now has an educational history that goes back to Papert [7], which is becoming more commonplace today as programmable robots, such

C. Stephanidis et al. (Eds.): HCII 2022, CCIS 1654, pp. 336–343, 2022.
https://doi.org/10.1007/978-3-031-19679-9_42

as the Blue-Bot featured in this study, are now making their way into early educational practices [8].

The early childhood education space is often less-structured by subjects, and educational activities are often part of projects, as in the case featured in this study. Project-based methods for education have long been examined as part of children's learning of programming [4, 9], showing educational potential by fostering peer collaboration among children when working on projects related to programming [9].

1.1 The Current Study

The paper examines the work with 4–5-year-old children using the Ukrainian folk tale *Rukavitjka* (*The Mitten*). This paper examined the educational design of combining the folk tale with programming in this early childhood space and presents the affordances of an educational programming board created as part of this project.

2 Methodology and Materials

2.1 Setting

The paper examines parts of a larger design-based study [10] of implementing the programmable robot (the Blue-Bot) at a preschool in Stockholm, Sweden. The study used video-ethnography [11] as a primary methodological approach to data collection and formative interviews with focus groups of teachers during iterative cycles of the educational design.

This study examines the design and educational affordances of the project phases where the preschool merged work with the folk tale to programmable educational materials for the Blue-Bot.

2.2 Participants and Data Collection

The project featured 22 4–5-year-old children and three teachers in a preschool in Stockholm, Sweden. The study followed the preschool for six months, from the first phases of implementing the Blue-Bot until the end of the next project semester. The current paper draws from the overall ethnography and the 10,5 h of recorded programming activities to examine the use of the folk tale in programming activities.

2.3 The Blue-Bot

The Blue-Bot, pictured in Fig. 1, is a programmable floor robot for children. It is programmed through four navigational buttons on top (forward, backward, turn-left, turn-right), an erase, a pause and a "go" button that sets the Blue-Bot into the programmed sequence of commands.

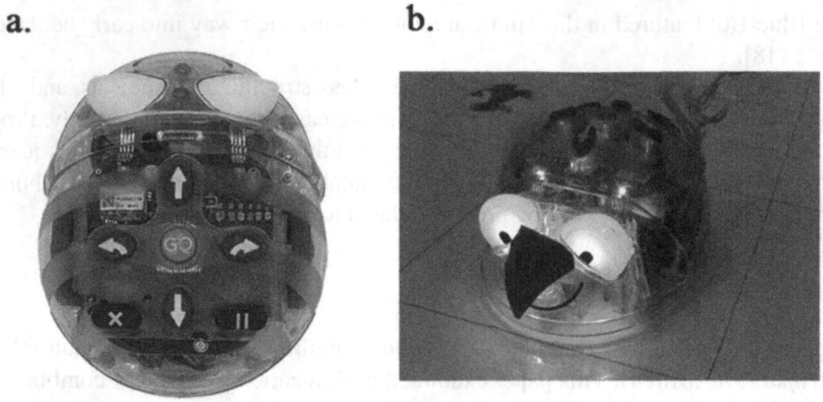

a.   b.

Fig. 1. The Blue-Bot. **a.** Displays the navigational buttons as viewed from the top. **b.** The Blue-Bot in action from the project, here dressed as an owl flying around the wood from the folk tale during the project. (Color figure online)

2.4   The Ukrainian Folk Tale – *The Mitten*

The Mitten (ukr. *Rukavitjka*) is a Ukrainian folk tale, also available as an illustrated children's book and through oral storytelling and as a rhymed tale. There are various variants of the tale with different endings. The story's basic structure featured in this group is a child out in the wood collecting wood that drops his mitten. Various animals come to inhabit the mitten through the tale – a frog, a mouse, a fox, a hare, a boar, and a bear. The repetitive structure of the tale also makes it ideal for rhyming, and the preschool group has worked with a rhymed version of the tale that the children have got to know well.

2.5   Analytical Procedure

The paper first presents descriptions of two major phases from the ethnography of the project, highlighting how the folk tale was combined with the Blue-Bot during the project's design phases.

From this material, around 2 h of video data from work with a programming board created during the project has been examined using multimodal analysis [12] and qualitatively coded [13] for the key educational affordances provided by the board. In the paper, the key educational insights are presented.

2.6   Ethical Considerations

Full documented ethical considerations have been documented, and ethical approval has been granted by the Swedish Ethical Review Authority [2021-05725-01].

3   Findings

The two following sub-sections describe two main phases related to the work with the folk tale and Blue-Bot.

Phase 1: Learning About the Folk Tale the Mitten and the Blue-Bot
When the preschool first introduced the Blue-Bot the group were already working with the Mitten for two months. When the Blue-Bot was first introduced, the teachers showed children the main functions of the Blue-Bot – how it worked and how children could press to program it etc.

As the children had found great enjoyment in the tale, the preschool wanted to find a way to combine these projects. An idea developed through iterated formative focus-group interviews where the researcher talked with the teachers about the research on storytelling as a way of motivating programming in early childhood, and the research supporting this. From these talks, the teachers came up with the idea of creating a programming board for the Blue-Bot based on the tale, which became the material for the educational programming activities in the next phase of the project.

Phase 2: Using the Mitten for a Programming Board
The teachers created a programming board with the different animals from *The Mitten* to implement this idea. While various pre-made boards are sold for the Blue-Bot, they are also reasonably easy to create, by drawing a grid structure of 15x15cm boxes, as this is the length of one Blue-Bot move. This can either be done in straight consecutive boxes (for example, for use with younger children when introducing programming forward and backward), but here the grid matrix was used, which means that children have to use rotate to have the Blue-Bot move around the board.

Fig. 2. The programming board created during the project. The children start at the man (upper left), have to move to the mitten, rotate down one level to the frog, then the mouse, and so on as the teacher reads a rhyme for each of the animals.

The teachers used a left-over cardboard material from a food delivery, printed labels of the animals from the tale, tapered these to the boards' grid and used a translucent plastic film on top (see Fig. 2).

With the board, the teachers could arrange an activity with 'readings' of the tale where children have to walk the Blue-Bot (now dressed as an owl from the wood in the tale). Children's knowledge of the tale and their interest in it could be merged with the programming activities. The key educational affordances of activities using the board are presented next.

3.1 Key Educational Affordances of the Board

The designed board carried educational affordances that, while specific for this case, can provide important insights for programming projects in early childhood either to use the Mitten specifically or to work with children's stories and programming more in any other way using the design elements from this project. Two key features of this educational design were found, one based on the structure and common ground for programming activities that the board provided. The other concerns the multimodal space for interaction afforded by using the board.

Providing a Common Structure and Goal for Activities

As the children were familiar with the story, it provided a structure that could be educationally used in the activity with the programming board. In that the children were familiar with the tale and the order of animals inhabiting the mitten, children could tutor each other and collaborate toward the common goal of 'telling the tale' through programming the robot's movement. This led to that children would perform 'debugging' together, either by correcting each other's or collaboratively figuring out why the Blue-Bot did not reach the intended animal (e.g. 'oh I think you should have pressed that two times, not three').

The focus of the educational activity in these sessions could then be directed to the common goal of going through the story (usually read/rhymed along by the teacher as the children would program the Blue-Bot from animal to animal in the story). The board thus provided a design feature that provided scaffolding structure for the educational activities. We next look at the types of scaffolding that this multimodal material provided during the project.

Providing Multimodal Scaffolding

Using the Blue-Bot together with the board also provided an interactional space appropriate for the 4–5-year-old children in the study. Within this interactional space, children communicate with each other and having the Blue-Bot within reach also allowed teachers and children to use deictic gesturing (e.g. pointing) toward buttons, or helping each other jointly press during the activities. In addition, the design feature using the tale and the educational activities promoted peer talk and tutoring among the children. For example, children world correct, aid and show each other using pointing, pressing and talk as they knew the next step in the activity following the tale (see Fig. 3).

Fig. 3. Image from an activity with the board. The teacher lets the children solve the tale while reading the rhymed tale. The children talk, point and help each other press to make it to the next animal in the tale.

The children in Fig. 3 and other sessions help each other to have the Blue-Bot make it to the end of the story. For example, if the Blue-Bot became misaligned and risked falling off, a child would sometimes 'save' it from falling from the board, giving it a slight push, and realigning it to the storyboard. This show how the common goal provided by the story and the multimodal material created was used for successful educational interaction.

4 Discussion

The paper examined how a design-based cycle using children's interest in a tale could be used to support programming activities in early childhood. This study corroborates the research showing how stories can be used in programming activities for younger children [2, 4], and adds a new territory to this line of research through a folk tale. Projects such as this may have the pedagogical potential to enhance children's understanding of the story structure and simultaneously provide a scaffold for understanding children's programming.

The design-phases show how written and oral stories can be used to create educational tools where older tales and new technology can merge. In this study, a programming board was examined where the story structure was used for multimodal scaffolds that underpinned educational interaction between teachers, children, and their peers. This shows how project work [9] for children's programming can combine a range of materials to be creatively designed into activities affording programming opportunities for children.

The paper promotes a crucial underlying phenomenon in that stories are built on structures, structures that can be used in educational designs and, in this case, for the activities promoting programming skills for young children. In the case of the Ukrainian folk tale, which builds on a repetitive structure, this becomes illustratively clear. Other research and educational technological designs can use this phenomenon.

The project found new relevance following the war in Ukraine, adding an additional dimension to the use of Ukrainian cultural heritage. During the second phase described, the project found a completely unpredicted relevance with the outbreak of the war.

As the project was ongoing, reports of the destruction of Ukrainian culture put a new light on the project's use of cultural heritage material and how it can be designed with new educational technology can offer a new space for future educational designs. The relevance of keeping cultural heritage through new technological forms is heightened relevance in a time of active cultural destruction. A future area can be examining various ways that culture can be transmitted throughout generations, media and technological forms.

5 Conclusion

The study has documented and examined how the novel use of a Ukrainian folk tale, The Mitten, was used when introducing programming for children. As programming skills are now more broadly being implemented into early childhood classrooms worldwide, it has shown an illustrative case of how older cultural forms can be used to create an exciting project merging the folk tale with activities featuring a programmable educational robot, the Blue-Bot. Educational robots and programming activities are still relatively novel in early childhood. Following this study, other researchers and educators can look into merging past cultural knowledge with novel technological equipment in educational designs that takes past culture into the future, promoting understanding of cultural heritages while learning new technological skills. This is a promising educational area for the contemporary age.

References

1. Wing, J.M.: Computational thinking and thinking about computing. Phil. Trans. R. Soc. A. **366**, 3717–3725 (2008). https://doi.org/10.1098/rsta.2008.0118
2. Sullivan, A., Bers, M.U.: Robotics in the early childhood classroom: learning outcomes from an 8-week robotics curriculum in pre-kindergarten through second grade. Int. J. Technol. Des. Educ. **26**(1), 3–20 (2015). https://doi.org/10.1007/s10798-015-9304-5
3. Rusk, N., Resnick, M., Berg, R., Pezalla-Granlund, M.: New pathways into robotics: strategies for broadening participation. J Sci Educ Technol. **17**, 59–69 (2008). https://doi.org/10.1007/s10956-007-9082-2
4. Bers, M.U.: Blocks to Robots: Learning with Technology in the Early Childhood Classroom. Teachers College Press, New York (2008)
5. Bati, K.: A systematic literature review regarding computational thinking and programming in early childhood education. Educ. Inf. Technol. **27**(2), 2059–2082 (2021). https://doi.org/10.1007/s10639-021-10700-2
6. Bers, M.U.: Designing Digital Experiences for Positive Youth Development: From Playpen to Playground. Oxford University Press, Cambridge (2012). https://doi.org/10.1093/acprof:oso/9780199757022.001.0001
7. Papert, S.: Mindstorms: Children, Computers, and Powerful Ideas. Basic Books, New York (1980)
8. Heikkilä, M., Mannila, L.: Debugging in programming as a multimodal practice in early childhood education settings. Multimodal Technol. Interact. **2** (2018). https://doi.org/10.3390/mti2030042
9. Resnick, M.: Lifelong kindergarten: cultivating creativity through projects, passion, peers, and play (2017). https://doi.org/10.7551/mitpress/11017.001.0001

10. Bakker, A.: Design Research in Education: A Practical Guide for Early Career Researchers. Routledge, Abingdon (2018)
11. Heath, C., Hindmarsh, J., Luff, P.: Video in Qualitative Research: Analysing Social Interaction in Everyday Life. SAGE Publications, Inc., London (2010). https://doi.org/10.4135/978152 6435385
12. Samuelsson, R., Price, S., Jewitt, C.: How pedagogical relations in early years settings are reconfigured by interactive touchscreens. Br. J. Edu. Technol. **53**, 58–76 (2022). https://doi.org/10.1111/bjet.13152
13. Braun, V., Clarke, V.: Using thematic analysis in psychology. Qual. Res. Psychol. **3**, 77–101 (2006). https://doi.org/10.1191/1478088706qp063oa

Research on Data Storytelling Strategies for Cultural Heritage Transmission and Dissemination

Xurong Shan[1], Dawei Wang[1(✉)], and Jiaxiang Li[2]

[1] Shanghai University, Jing'an District, Shanghai 200040, China
daweiba118@126.com
[2] Tsinghua University, Haidian District, Beijing 100084, China

Abstract. Cultural heritage is non-renewable and irreplaceable, which needs to be preserved and passed on. In the digital age, cultural heritage can be brought to life through data storytelling, a communication tool that effectively blends science and technology with humanistic structures, empowering cultural heritage and promoting the transmission and dissemination of culture. The research begins with developing and studying data storytelling in the digital age. The concept and development of data storytelling are reviewed through literature research, and its theoretical basis and three essential elements are analysed: data science, visualisation, and narratology. The design objectives, data framework, and visualisation process of data storytelling in cultural heritage are analysed through desktop research and theoretical studies of the project and literature. Finally, the design strategy of data storytelling in cultural heritage is proposed, conducive to promoting digital humanities research, popularising cultural data information and value dissemination, and telling cultural stories.

Keywords: Cultural heritage · Data storytelling · Visualisation

1 Introduction

In terms of existence, cultural heritage is divided into tangible and intangible cultural heritage. They bear witness to the development and evolution of human civilisation and are the embodiment of the wisdom of working people, as well as a manifestation of the convergence and collision of different civilisations. However, there are still many challenges to the transmission and dissemination of cultural heritage, including the imperfection of traditional protection models, the destruction of geographical and climatic environments, loss or damage during transportation, and the loss of skills due to the loss of inheritors, which require our joint protection and transmission.

In the age of DT (Data Processing Technology), along with the growth of people's spiritual and cultural needs and the development of technological humanism and dataism, cultural heritage is increasingly being disseminated in a variety of forms, including digital composite publishing [1], digital collections, e-museums and others. It gradually forms a more systematic and holistic network of data perception and humanism. Traditional forms and models of preservation have proven to be limited and unable to meet the current needs of cultural heritage transmission and dissemination, and it is urgent to preserve cultural heritage and promote dissemination through digital technology [2]. As a tool for information exchange and dissemination that combines technical and humanistic frameworks, data storytelling, in contrast to traditional graphic narratives, use non-linear narratives to deconstruct traditional cultural and artistic forms, weave magnificent networks of values and culture, and enrich aesthetic, cultural experiences [3]. Given the diversity and complexity of cultural heritage information and the differences in perception and understanding among different people, research needs to clarify design goals and processes of data storytelling in cultural heritage and explore data narrative strategies for cultural heritage. The study of data storytelling is necessary and feasible to help promote the living heritage of cultural heritage [4].

For example, in the case of museums, the initial communication strategy was to attract new visitors by organising temporary and permanent exhibitions and updating the collections. However, this traditional approach not only consumed human and financial resources, but also had a limited impact on communication. Since the beginning of the 21st century, museums have been engaged in a digital movement for more than a decade, introducing new technologies such as social media and digital technology to enhance interest in collections and user experience and engagement in the field. Museums have focused on innovative information and communication technologies (ICT), including websites, mobile apps, interactive media devices and other forms of promoting and interpreting cultural heritage through data visualisation [5]. Data storytelling are lightweight, adaptable to various devices and scenarios, flexible, efficient and less costly to produce.

2 Background

The systematic theoretical study of data storytelling in academia and the formation of an academic community in the field can be traced back to 2001. Between 2001 and 2007, the open-ended challenges of digital narrative were explored by two European conferences of groups of researchers and developers (the International Conference on Virtual Narrative and the International Conference on Interactive Digital Narrative and Entertainment), which also facilitated exchanges and collaborations between scholars and developers across disciplines and fields. These two conferences were merged in 2008 to form the International Conference on Digital Narrative, with research findings covering multiple perspectives on digital narrative theory, technology, and practice [2].

The first forms of "data narratives" were Digital Storytelling or Virtual Storytelling, Interactive Storytelling, which focused on real-time and non-linear output and restructuring of storytelling forms through virtual reality technology; they have evolved into several other different conceptual representations, including Visual Storytelling [6], Data-driven Storytelling, and Analytical Narrative. It has evolved into several other different conceptual formulations, such as Visual Storytelling, Data-driven Storytelling, Analytical Storytelling, Storytelling with data [7]. Although digital storytelling are different from data storytelling in terms of their conceptual origins and development paths, there is still a great deal of overlap in their use in academic circles. Data storytelling have more diverse connotations than digital storytelling in terms of conceptual extension.

Data has gradually been integrated into people's daily lives and has become an integral part of information access. More and more content creators, guided by data science, are collecting, organising and processing complex raw data and information through data storytelling, in the form of charts and interactive interfaces that allow users to access and understand and remember critical information more intuitively and transparently. These digital forms are better than raw data tables and large amounts of textual information for effective communication, cultural and conceptual resonance and value realisation. Therefore, data storytelling require three essential elements: theoretical support from data science, visualisation tools, and narrative realisation channels [8]. 1) Data science originated in the 1960s with research related to data analysis, and in 1974 P. Naur defined the concept of "data science as a science-based on data processing", which encompasses various fields such as statistics, data analysis and scientific methods, aiming to treat data as an object of study and uncover its value. In the technical system of digital humanities, the reconstruction of knowledge, the reconstruction of scenarios, the description and representation of digital humanities, must be guided by theory and data [9]. 2) Visualisation is often used to represent the relationships between data. Rather than a single representation of local facts, data visualisation analyses, compares and maps a collection of multidimensional data to resolve connections, improve the audience's perception of information and show how the nature of the object of study is related to the phenomenon. The choice of visualisation strategy has a significant impact on the public's understanding of the information [10]. 3) Narrative is the fundamental way in which humans make sense of the world. It is a technique for telling facts, expressing opinions and clarifying ideas through stories. An overview of the data is presented by visual charts and graphs, while the narrative adds the specific context in which things happen. The two work together to enhance the appeal of cultural heritage to the public, increase the user's understanding of complex facts and data, and improve the efficiency of sharing and reception.

3 Research Methods

Compared to traditional textual narratives, data storytelling are more compelling in presenting the cultural connotations of cultural heritage, the current state of research and development, and the degree of intrinsic logical connection and relevance to audiences. The research begins with the dilemma of cultural heritage in today's digital age and is divided into three steps. Firstly, the research and analysis of literature on the preservation and development of cultural heritage in the digital humanities and interviews with researchers and relevant practitioners on the digitisation of cultural heritage were conducted to filter valid information and analyse the design objectives of the cultural heritage data narrative. Secondly, the data frame structure of cultural heritage is constructed, which is mainly explained in terms of data collection and data classification. Finally, based on the theoretical model of previous data visualisation processes, a visualisation process suitable for cultural heritage is proposed based on the inherent properties of cultural heritage [11].

3.1 Design Objectives for Data Storytelling in Cultural Heritage

Cultural heritage is an integral part of the development of human spiritual civilisation and can fully inspire national identity and pride and promote cross-cultural exchange and dissemination. Cultural heritage data narrative refers to preserving cultural heritage by digitally capturing, processing, displaying, storing and disseminating it by techno-logical means. Through the integration and reproduction of data, cultural heritage is turned into a digital form that can be shared and regenerated, and the needs are fully explored, interpreted and preserved in a new perspective and innovative way. Therefore, the design objectives of the cultural heritage data narrative can be divided into three areas. 1) Data is one of the manifestations of information and reflects things' objective and essential properties. People can quickly obtain information from the processed data. The use of computer technology and information technology to collect data on cul-tural heritage scientifically can support the conservation of cultural heritage. Traditional forms of summarising cultural heritage often require manual recording and filming by professionals, and teaching by word of mouth and other forms of transmission between inheritors, which is less efficient. Digitally extracting and integrating data related to cul-tural heritage and presenting it as a digital narrative can balance the depth and breadth of information with visual presentation, enhancing the efficiency of reading and under-standing for audiences and promoting the standardised preservation and dissemination of cultural heritage archives. 2) The themes of data storytelling should be clear, simple and original, and set in the context of the needs of the times and development trends to stimulate people's curiosity and desire for exploration. Data storytelling are a way to promote the transformation of cultural heritage from the "intangible" to the "tangible" [12], and to educate and disseminate cultural heritage on both a technical and spiritual level. For example, in the transmission of intangible cultural heritage, the main subject should be the performance and production process of the inheritors, which is also the core content of display and dissemination. Data storytelling for this type of cultural her-itage should not be limited to static and passive local displays. However, they should be more comprehensive and holistic, incorporating dynamic data displays and interactive experiences, and dedicated to enabling people to understand and experience ICH skills holistically. 3) The data narrative should focus on the narrative logic of cultural heritage, with a rational planning of the data framework of cultural heritage and corresponding data classification according to the specific types of cultural heritage. Categorising data with common attributes according to the attributes of the data objects will also enhance the use of data information and integration efficiency. The researchers have been able to organise and summarise the data information in a way that helps people to access, understand and remember cultural heritage information more efficiently.

3.2 Data Framework for Cultural Heritage

Data Collection for Cultural Heritage. Data acquisition refers to the collection and colla-tion of text, images, audio and video, motion capture, 3D modelling and virtual reenact-ment of cultural heritage through digital technology and equipment, and is a fundamental part of data narrative. In order to better accommodate diverse data types and formats, the way of data collection has become more diversified from the traditional observation and recording method with the advancement and development of digital technology. This increase in methods and approaches has facilitated data acquisition, storage, and transmission and has dramatically enhanced research efficiency. One of the mainstream data collection methods is to collect and identify data at the data source, and the other is to use electronic devices to collect data, with common data collection software including Splunk, Flume and Nutch.

Cultural heritage data are collected and recorded for the following. 1) Data transformation and storage of documents, pictures, images and other physical materials such as cultural heritage items and related inheritors. 2) Digital recording and storage of cultural heritage field and related practice sites, products, utensils and so on. 3) For intangible cultural heritage, the dynamic process of intangible heritage practices needs to be recorded thoroughly to better pass on the skills. For example, in the case of image capture of embroidery techniques, the three-camera simultaneous filming method is usually used. One camera is used as a fixed distance camera to capture the overall scene of the embroidery, the second camera is used as a medium and close up camera to record the movements, posture and embroidery process of the inheritors, and the third camera is used to take close-ups of the hands to record the specific stitching process.

Data Classification of Cultural Heritage. Data refers to the basic information obtained by people in their productive lives, using various tools and means to perceive the objective world. Data is not numbers in the narrow sense, but also includes meaningful words, symbols, images and audio and video and so on. It is a wide variety and quantity, and therefore needs to be classified before doing visualisation. Data can be classified as quantitative, qualitative and temporal. 1) Quantitative data: Usually used to indicate the quantitative characteristics of things, including location, number, length and width. The places of origin and transmission routes of cultural heritage are quantitative data, as this geographical information can be expressed by latitude and longitude. The type, size, quantity and area of cultural heritage are quantitative data. 2) Qualitative data: Textual data, such as the cultural attributes and categories of things, usually indicate the symbolic meaning conveyed by cultural heritage motifs. In the case of intangible cultural heritage, the skills are closely linked to the bearer's limbs, emotions, physical abilities, and mental state. Variations in these factors lead to the differentiation and individualisation of skills, so it is crucial to collect qualitative data on the bearer, including brain activity, eye movements, muscle movements, limbs, and body posture. 3) Temporal data: Usually used to show the temporal attributes of things, such as dates, duration, years of inheritance, development chronology.

3.3 Visualisation Processes for Cultural Heritage

In Visualising Data, Ben Fry divides the process of data visualisation into seven steps: acquisition, analysis, filtering, mining, representation, modification and interaction [13]. In his book The Beauty of Data: Learning Visual Design in One Book, Nathan Yau suggests four questions for data visualisation. 1) What data do you have? 2) What information do you want to extract from the data? 3) Which visualisation method should be adopted? 4) What do you see? Does it make sense? The four questions interact with each other [14]. Having analysed the type of data and how it is obtained, it is then time to consider what information to get from a large amount of data.

What information one wants to obtain depends mainly on the research topic and the purpose of the research, which needs to be further subdivided and clarified according to the actual situation. Then the corresponding data visualisation mapping is selected according to the purpose of the research. Based on the theoretical research of the two scholars, the design process for the visual narrative process of cultural heritage can be divided into five main steps: data collection, data processing, visualisation mapping, narrative mode and visualisation. When the research focuses on cultural heritage transmission and dissemination, the presentation of massive amounts of data in a single way should be avoided, and the focus should be on representing the stories and connotations behind the data. Choose an appropriate visualisation mapping method according to the audience's needs and design narrative logic and narrative modes in an innovative way to form an emotional connection with the audience. Data storytelling give a storytelling narrative based on visuals that are easy to perceive, understand and remember, and are conducive to making cultural heritage more accessible.

4 Discussion

The exploration and development of data storytelling in different languages and cultures have always revolved around the technical laws of data perception and value discovery and the humanistic framework or paradigm of the narrative discourse system, which constantly iterates and upgrades. Data storytelling, with data science as a platform, information visualisation as a product or service form, and narratology as a channel for value realisation, will be beneficial in promoting the living heritage and dissemination of cultural heritage, becoming an essential tool for integrating data resources and even spreading Chinese culture and Chinese stories.

4.1 Balancing the Professionalism and Communication of Data Storytelling

There is some highly specialised and technical content in the data and information on cultural heritage, which poses an obstacle to the access and interpretation of information by non-specialists. Excessive use of jargon can easily create an impression of being difficult to understand and discourage people from learning and understanding. The overly colloquial and colloquial expressions, on the other hand, tend to lose the depth of popular science and fail to honestly and effectively disseminate information on cultural heritage data, so a balance needs to be found between the two, and some measures can be taken as follows. 1) Reduce the use of jargon. If it is necessary to use it, explain its meaning in layman's terms so that it can be easily understood. 2) Identify who the audience is and their literacy levels and characteristics, and adapt the presentation of data and information to better suit their needs. 3) Develop a style guide in advance to standardise the language style of the narrative and ensure that the tone of the storyteller's language does not deviate from preconceptions. 4) Experimental or playful storytelling formats are used, while ensuring the professionalism and authenticity of the content.

The British Museum in London, for example, hosted an episode of the Royal Ur Game. The museum invited YouTube educational presenter Tom Scott to play against curator Owen Finkel, introducing the rules of the ancient board game in the form of a game that gained widespread attention and had a good impact on communication.

4.2   Use of Descriptive Language and Multisensory Interaction

In order to have a better effect on the transmission and dissemination of data storytelling in cultural heritage, descriptive, fascinating or poetic language should be used, based on respect for historical facts and objective laws. The use of images, audio, video and other sensory stimuli makes the data narrative more fleshed out and interesting. NYC has designed an interactive map where historical images of New York City from the 1980s are superimposed on a map. People can explore different neighbourhoods in a simulated way. Clicking on any point in a neighbourhood reveals more relevant real-life images and information. What is more, it tells people "you are here". (see Fig.1).

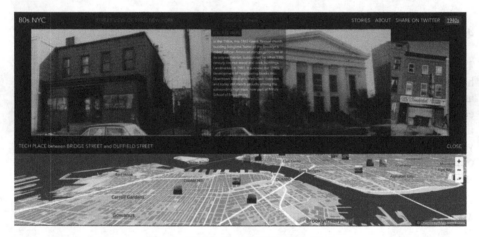

Fig. 1.   Street view of 1980s New York

For the Faint Signals project, the British Library collected data on the sounds of York-shire, including wildlife, weather and nature sounds, as well as some extinct species, and created a digital sound forest environment for people to explore. People can move around the landscape by moving their mouse and hearing nature's corresponding sounds, with thousands of combinations to explore. The project reflects Yorkshire's natural ecol-ogy's complexity and diversity and evokes a sense of reflection and yearning for natural heritage. (see Fig. 2).

Fig. 2. Faint signals (British Library, London)

4.3 Focus on Personal and Historical Connections

Data storytelling can help people glimpse a snapshot of the times in cultural heritage. Incorporating personal stories into the cultural heritage story can make it more vivid and vibrant, with a warmth and human touch that triggers people's emotional resonance. In addition, the introduction of personal stories and historical experiences into the data narrative helps people focus and understand the characteristics of the era in which the cultural heritage is located. Data storytelling should shed light on the human significance of objects and heritage, who designed them and in what contexts, and who used them, all of which help increase awareness, understanding and empathy for cultural heritage.

Deconstructing Tibetan, a data visualisation created by students and teachers of Shanghai Academy of Fine Arts, uses a variety of data visualisations to deconstruct Tibetan, deconstruct writing and visualise the text of a Tibetan poetry collection in a work that is both fun and professional. It spotlights a Tibetan calligrapher, Gajang Nyima, as a data visualisation of a day in the research institution, including how he practices Tibetan calligraphy and learns about other things. In addition, the research team collected brainwave data and electromyographic data from his Tibetan writing to compare the content of the same poem with that of a Chinese calligrapher. Then they presented the results of the comparison in a graphic visualisation. A bridge between Tibetan and Chinese cultures was established by deconstructing Tibetan writing. (see Fig. 3).

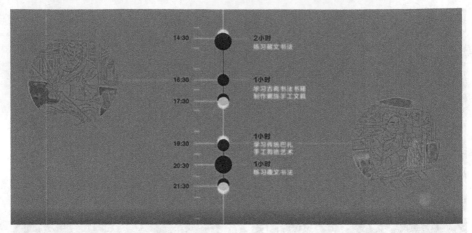

Fig. 3. Deconstructing Tibetan (Shanghai University, China)

5 Conclusion

As one of the practical tools for interdisciplinary collaboration, data narrative deeply integrates humanistic concerns and modern technologies. In cultural heritage, it can be an effective tool for communicating the rational truth, emotional goodness and intellectual beauty of cultural heritage, helping people solve the cognitive challenge of the complexity of information access, and has an excellent cognitive driving value. This paper compares the changes and development of the connotation of data narrative, and analyses the essential components of data narrative from three aspects: data science, visualisation and narratology. Through desktop research and user interviews, the research process of data storytelling in cultural heritage is explored, i.e. identifying design goals, building data architecture and analysing visualisation processes. The design strategies for data storytelling in cultural heritage are analysed and refined from project examples. The data narrative changes the traditional one-way output-based narrative to the audience, enhances the user experience through visualisation and interesting interaction, gives new life to cultural heritage with technology, and allows the cultural lineage to continue and the spirit of civilisation to spread widely.

References

1. Ding, J., Tang, X.: Research on data storytelling and its application from the perspective of digital humanities. Guizhou Ethnic Stud. **45**(02), 121–128 (2022)
2. Madhavan, J., Balakrishnan, S., Hurley, K., et al.: Big data storytelling through interactive maps. IEEE Data(base) Eng. Bull., 46–54 (2012)
3. Segel, E., Heer, J.: Narrative visualization: telling stories with data. IEEE Trans. Vis. Comput. Graph. **16**(6), 1139–1148 (2011)
4. Stone, H., Sports T.: The push and pull of digital humanities: topic modeling the—what is digital humanities. Genre **14**(1) (2020)
5. Lee, B., Riche, N.H., Isenberg, P., et al.: More than telling a story: transforming data into visually shared stories. IEEE Comput. Graphics Appl. **35**(5), 84–90 (2015)

6. Springer. ICIDS [EB/OL]. Accessed 01 Aug 2020. https://link.springer.com/conference/icids
7. Segel, E., Heer, J.: Narrative visualization: telling stories with data. IEEE Trans. Vis. Comput. Graph. **16**(6), 1139–1148 (2010)
8. Echeverria, V., Martinez-Maldonado, R., Granda, R., et al.: Driving data storytelling from learning design. In: Proceedings of the 8th International Conference on Learning Analytics and Knowledge, pp. 131–140 (2018)
9. Unsworth, J.: Scholarly primitives: what methods do humanities researchers have in common, and how might our tools reflect this. In: Symposium on Humanities Computing: Formal Methods, Experimental Practice. King's College, London (2000)
10. Arnav Jhala, R., Young, M.: Comparing effects of different cinematic visualization strategies on viewer comprehension. In: Iurgel, I.A., Zagalo, N., Petta, Paolo (eds.) ICIDS 2009. LNCS, vol. 5915, pp. 26–37. Springer, Heidelberg (2009). https://doi.org/10.1007/978-3-642-106 43-9_6
11. Zhang, W.: Research on Data Visualization Design of Embroidery Craft——Take Tu Embroidery as an Example. Shanghai University, China (2021)
12. Xiao, Y.: A study on the visualization of red history and culture: from data narrative to meaning-making. Design **34**(08), 134–137 (2021)
13. Fry, B.: Visualizing Data. O'Reilly Media, Sebastopol (2008)
14. Yau, N.: The Beauty of Data: Learn Visual Design in One Book, 2nd edn. People's University of China Press, China (2018)

A Study of Visitor Interaction with Virtual Museum

Yanyan Sun[✉] and Yuechan Zheng

Zhejiang Agricultural Business College, No. 770, Century East Street, Shaoxing, China
sunyanyan1988@163.com

Abstract. The development and opening of Virtual Museums have accelerated with the rapid development of human computer interaction and virtual reality technology. The paradigm of interaction between visitor and museum has shown changes. New technologies have significantly transformed the museum visitor experience and the meaning-making process of museum collections. It is proposed that "the interaction behavior of Virtual Museums and visitors is a whole process and space interaction behavior" and "Virtual Museum narrative is a collaborative narrative". This paper summarizes the current status of Virtual Museum research and the four main research directions through literature review; studies the interaction behavior between Virtual Museum and visitors, analyzes the museum interaction object and museum narrative process; deeply explores the similarities and differences between Virtual Museum visitor interaction and traditional museum visitor interaction, and proposes the essential changes brought by virtual reality technology to museum visitors. It is a good indication to improve the visitor experience in Virtual Museums.

Keywords: Virtual museum · Visitor interaction · Museum narrative

1 Introduction

1.1 Background

The development and promotion of high technology and the active use of museums have made us feel first-hand the radical changes that technology has brought to museums. Virtual reality technology has grown significantly in recent years.[1] It is found that the research hotspots on exhibition technology have gradually tended to more virtual technologies such as VR in the past few years. ([2],Fig. 1) The current state of the global epidemic has accelerated the process of opening and developing Virtual Museums. At the same time, the virtual format has its own unique advantages.

Virtual Museum (VM) systems are a very effective solution for the communication of cultural contents, thanks to their playful and educational approach. [3] In fact, their usefulness and value have been demonstrated around the world. Works that are inaccessible or invisible can be exhibited through virtual exhibitions. It is possible to view digitized artworks and explore reconstructed historical sites through VM-hosted facilities. [4].

C. Stephanidis et al. (Eds.): HCII 2022, CCIS 1654, pp. 354–358, 2022.
https://doi.org/10.1007/978-3-031-19679-9_44

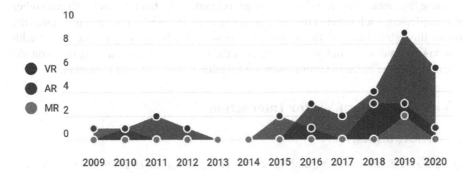

Fig. 1. Graph of the number of relevant studies [2]

1.2 Previous Studies

The current academic research on Virtual Museums is divided into four main areas.

Research on the Virtual Museum as a Tool to Study its Communication Role, Educational Functions, etc. Museum are important communication media. An important goal of museums is to communicate cultural knowledge to visitors. D. Aiello et al. [4] consider Virtual Museum as a means for promotion and enhancement of cultural heritage. For the museum institutions VR and ICT are a valuable tool that allows them to perform different cultural tasks, addressing the public in a much more effective way than has previously been possible.

Research in the Direction of Virtual Technology for Virtual Museums, Study of its Digital Technology Applications, Technology Development for Virtual Displays, etc. Juan A. Botí [5] explores the diverse technologies incorporated in Virtual Museums and the impact of technology on visitors' perceived presence, investigated the technological conditions under which a Virtual Museum enhances the visitors' experience of presence.

Virtual Museum User Research, Study of its User Interface, Visitor Experience, etc. With the advent of the experience economy and the popularization of the human-centered concept, the visitor experience in Virtual Museums is gradually gaining attention. Zou Ning et al. [2] proposed a unique "creation level" experience of VRME. A 'rose model' was proposed to summarize the relationship between display technology, sensory types, LoUX and human-exhibit interaction factors.

A Systematic Evaluation Study of Virtual Museums. Ralf Terlutter et al. [6] analyzed the influence of the environment. Based on empirical evidence of virtual scenes on the Internet, they suggest the use of a 3-dimensional representation to provide various possibilities of interaction and to create a multisensory environment that looks very realistic. Park Namjin [7] explored the relationship between virtual exhibitions and visitors' opinions following the viewing of the virtual exhibit.

These four areas are certainly not studied independently, but intersect with each other and complement each other. Trunfio, Mariapina et al. [8] argue that museums innovate formats through the use of digital and immersive technologies to enhance the breadth of the visiting public, which in turn enhances the visitor experience and satisfaction. At the same time, the cultural communication function of the museum is ensured.

2   Virtual Museum Visitor Interaction

2.1   Virtual Museum

Regarding the definition of Virtual Museums, Normala Rahim et al. [9] consider Virtual Museum is an alternative to a museum in digital form with virtually the same aim as a real museum which is to showcase a museum's collection in turn to provide knowledge to visitors through informal learning.

After reviewing the relevant literature, we have identified two classifications. The first one is the "digital reflection" of the physical museum [10], where the physical space of the museum and the products on display are presented virtually through 3D modeling. The VR Kremer Museum [11], for example, can be accessed remotely by everyone through Viveport to view the artworks. The second type is a virtual exhibition done in a physical museum using new technologies.

This paper develops the first type of Virtual Museum as the research object.

2.2   Interaction Category

Virtual Museum is not just a replica of the traditional museum, but has various innovative forms of interaction through the development of VR and AR. Virtual Museums need to be equipped with platforms or virtual devices to achieve this.

There are two main categories of interaction between visitors and Virtual Museums. One is the interaction with the platform or the virtual device, which is mainly done through the visitor's gestures, touch, sound and other actions. This also includes how to seamlessly link to content interactions. These we can collectively call interface interactions. The other category is the interaction with the content carried by the platform or virtual device, including the visual appeal of the interface, the logic of the interaction, the fun of the interaction, and also how to seamlessly link to the first category of interface interaction and smoothly leave the platform or exit the device. These we collectively call content interaction.

2.3   Interaction Objects

The interaction between visitors and museums in traditional museums is the interaction between visitors and museum exhibits in the process of visiting. In the virtual museum, the interaction is transformed into the whole process of the visitor's visit inside and outside the virtual exhibition hall. The whole process includes the interaction with the platform or equipment before entering the virtual museum, the interaction with the museum content during the visit in general awareness, and the interaction with the platform or equipment after leaving the virtual museum.

In addition, the interaction between visitors and museums in traditional museums is mostly one-way simple interaction with exhibits, while in virtual museums it changes to multi-dimensional interaction with the full space. It includes the interaction with the peripheral space of the platform or equipment, the interaction with the virtual building exterior, the interaction with the virtual building space, the interaction with the virtual exhibition, etc.

3 Museum Narrative

3.1 Museum Narrative

Since the dawn of the new museology, the status of "human" has been on the rise, and museums have placed greater emphasis on the visitor experience. New technological advances have opened up many new possibilities for museums. The creation of virtual museums has once again redefined the relationship between museums, visitors, and each other.

Museum narratives are stories that museums tell to visitors. Museum narratives generally include architectural narratives, exhibition narratives, exhibit narratives, and landscape narratives. In Virtual Museums, the visitor changes from the role of receiving knowledge and education from the museum to the role of dialoguing with the museum and completing the story together, i.e. the visitor also becomes the subject of the narrative.

3.2 Collaborative Narrative

Part of the museum narrative in the Virtual Museum shifts from a static narrative to a dynamic narrative. Dynamic narrative refers to visitors completing the narrative through behavior, action, or even being part of the process of creating the narrative. Besoain Felipe et al. [1] has shown through a virtual reality (VR) usability tests how important it is to make the user part of the creation process. The virtual museum narrative is a synergistic narrative in which static and dynamic narratives work together.

In addition to the change in narrative style, the object of interaction changes from the individual to the group. The virtual museum makes it possible for multiple people to face the same scene together in real time.

4 Conclusion

The creation of Virtual Museums enriched the form of museum presence and redefined the relationship between museums and visitors. The interaction between visitors and the museum in Virtual Museum is a full process and space interaction. The narrative of Virtual Museum is a synergistic narrative where static narrative and dynamic narrative work together.

Museum research related to virtual technology has been hot in recent years. In addition to virtual technology, the research fervor of MR technology is also on the rise. In the future, we should not only focus on the relationship between virtual museums and visitors, but also hybrid museums that combine virtual technology with real environments and real exhibits should be continuously focused.

Acknowledgments. This work was supported by Zhejiang Agricultural Business College, China (Project NO. KY202235).

References

1. Felipe, B., Liza, J., Ismael, G.: Developing a virtual museum: experience from the design and creation process. Information **12**(6), 244–244 (2021)
2. Zou, N., Gong, Q., Zhou, J., Chen, P., Kong, W., Chai, C.: Value-based model of user interaction design for virtual museum. CCF Trans. Perv. Comput. Interact. **3**(2), 112–128 (2021). https://doi.org/10.1007/s42486-021-00061-7
3. Barbieri, L., Bruno, F., Muzzupappa, M.: Virtual museum system evaluation through user studies. J. Cult. Herit. **26**, 101–108 (2017)
4. Aiello, D., Fai, S., Santagati, C.: Virtual Museums As A Means For Promotion And Enhancement Of Cultural Heritage. ISPRS – Int. Arch. Photogram. Remote Sens. Spat. Inf. Sci. **XLII-2/W15**, 33–40 (2019)
5. Botf, J.A., et al.: Exploring the effect of diverse technologies incorporated in virtual museums on visitors' perceived sense of presence. Ambient Intell. Smart Environ. **17**, 493–506 (2013)
6. Terlutter, R., Diehl, S.: Marketing for real and virtual museums: a marketing model to explain visitor behavior in real museums and an outlook on its applicability to virtual museums. J. Glob. Acad. Mark. Sci. **10**(1), 45–70 (2002)
7. Namjin, Z.P.: An Exploration of the relationship between virtual museum exhibitions and visitors' responses. Arch. Des. Res., 181–190 (2006)
8. Trunfio, M., et al.: Innovating the cultural heritage museum service model through virtual reality and augmented reality: the effects on the overall visitor experience and satisfaction. J. Herit. Tour. **17**, 1–19 (2022)
9. Rahim, N., Wook, T.S.M.T., Zin, N.A.M.: Analysis on user interaction in virtual heritage: virtual museum environment. Indian J. Sci. Technol. **10**(48) (2017)
10. Sylaiou, S., et al.: Leveraging mixed reality technologies to enhance museum visitor experiences. In: 9th International Conference on Intelligent Systems (IS). 2018, Funchal, Portugal (2018)
11. http://www.thekremercollection.com/the-kremer-museum/. Accessed 25 May 2022

Exploring the Applications of Computational Thermochromic Embroidery Interfaces

Qi Wang[1], Huasen Zhao[1], Yueyao Zhang[1], Yuan Zeng[1], Zhichao Wang[2],
Lingchuan Zhou[2], Yanchen Shen[2], Yuan Sun[1], Yuxi He[1], Yuxi Mao[1],
and Jiang Wu[2]([✉])

[1] Tongji University, Shanghai, China
{qiwangdesign,zhaohuasen,zhangyueyao,2033676}@tongji.edu.cn
[2] University of Nottingham Ningbo China, Ningbo, China
{biylz14,ssyzw1,ssyys8,Jiang.wu}@nottingham.edu

Abstract. Traditional Chinese embroideries have a long history and take the most important role in the textile Intangible Cultural Heritage (ICH) in China. At the same time, smart textiles have become a dominant trend in textiles development and the thermochromic textile interface resulted in increasing explorations. In order to study how computational thermochromic interface may contribute to the transmission of traditional embroidery craftsmanship, we investigated a novel color-changing embroidery interface and explored various prototypes in multiple scenarios including future cockpit, fitness promotion, and household items.

Keywords: Thermochromic · Smart Textile · Embroidery

1 Introduction

Traditional Chinese embroideries identify unique aesthetics, there are more than 29 kinds of embroideries that represented the local customs and practices in different areas. Embroideries are not unique forms of art but also serve valuable and essential roles in the textile artifacts which are also crucial transmission methods of Intangible Cultural Heritage (ICH). While the challenge in the Digital Era is the lively revitalization and how the younger generation may become better aware of the preciousness and apply them in daily life.

Currently, lots of work have been done for promotion and one promising direction is to activate ICH through the integration of technology and design, for example, fashionable wearables, etc. At the same time, smart textiles have become a dominant trend in textiles development and the thermochromic textile interface resulted in increasing explorations. Previous research proposed various structures and potential applications, for example, sewing the conductive thread through [1] or under [2] the display layer drawn with thermochromic pigment, weaving and crochet techniques based on thermochromic yarn that the conductive threads are coated with thermochromic pigment [3], and contributed to clothing with dynamic textile displays. Relatively, few studies investigated the scenario-oriented applications of thermochromic embroidery interfaces.

C. Stephanidis et al. (Eds.): HCII 2022, CCIS 1654, pp. 359–363, 2022.
https://doi.org/10.1007/978-3-031-19679-9_45

To study how computational thermochromic interface may contribute to the transmission of traditional embroidery craftsmanship, we investigated a novel color-changing embroidery interface and explored various prototypes in multiple scenarios including future cockpit, fitness promotion, and household items.

2   Mechanisms of the Thermochromic Embroidery Interfaces

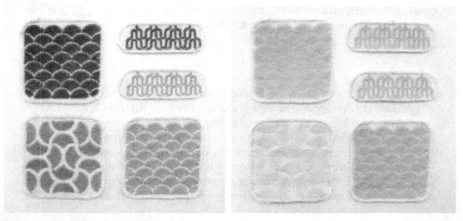

Fig. 1. Embroidery thermochromic interface demos with a plain stitch, a.) initial colors of the embroidery patterns; b.) the conductive threads as the bobbin threads heat up and thermochromic embroidery pattern is activated.

Among the various traditional embroidery techniques and skills, we have strong interests in plain stitch (see Fig. 1) and crossing stitch. The interface consists of three layers, we apply the top thread as the thermochromic thread and the conductive thread as the bottom thread. While the specific unit could be activated in a programmable way by connecting the conductive threads to the micro-controller and heating the specific area as the interactive pattern requested.

3   Investigations of Thermochromic Embroidery Interfaces

WE held a thermochromic embroidery workshop to explore the appropriate means of applying smart textile technology to non-heritage textile art design. The workshop consists of four stages which are the material introduction and demonstration, brainstorming, prototyping, and demo presentation. 15 participants joined the workshop and the brainstorming session focused on 3 topics which are future mobility, health, and ICH. Following are the main concepts as investigations.

3.1   BLOOM, a Textile Interface that Demonstrates the Status of a Smart Cockpit

Autonomous driving is developing rapidly, and shared mobility is one of the future trends. The layout of the intelligent cockpit will shift from a fixed model to a more free-flowing one. Flexible occupant relationships and seat positions in driverless vehicles, therefore, bring more possibilities for in-vehicle interaction. From the perspective of thinking about peripheral interaction, we propose an interface for displaying the layout state of a smart cockpit with seat belts as a carrier. As shown in Fig. 2, considering the various layouts in the future cockpit we proposed a thermochromic textile display as the indication of seat status in real-time, namely, different parts of the embroidery patterns will light up accordingly to the seat status as input data. The Pattern of the flower is divided into 3 circles from inside to outside, corresponding to the relationship of the seat (see Fig. 2). The initial state corresponds to the activation of the middle circle, the activation of the outer circle corresponds to the distant relationship of the seat and the activation of the inner circle corresponds to the proximity of the seat.

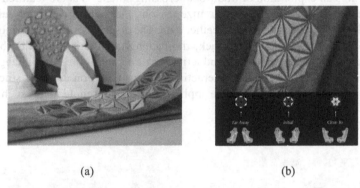

(a)   (b)

Fig. 2. Textile interface for displaying the status of smart cockpit layouts on the seat belt. a) Bloom in the exhibition, b) seat status and corresponding pattern.

3.2   Step-Square, Textile-Based Odometer

Wearable systems play a vital role in promoting people's health behaviors and activities. Previous wearable systems have done a great deal of work in accurate sensing and monitoring, but it is well worth exploring how the data can be better interpreted by the user and how to design more effective and natural feedback to promote behavioral change. Therefore, a concept of a soft odometer on the shoe tongue was brought out to be an interesting part of running shoes. The embroidery patterns consist of thermochromic squares, the number of the light-up squares is according to the number of steps. The white embroidered pattern on the fabric band will turn blue and pop out from the white canvas base. Step-Square is not only a novel way of visualizing step data for proactive health promotion, but also has great potential as personalized decoration and appearance of shoes (Fig. 3).

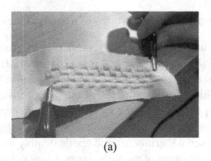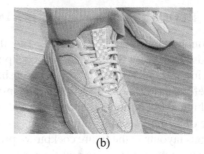

(a)   (b)

Fig. 3. Textile interface for displaying the daily steps. a) demonstrations of part of the squares are activated, b) Step-Square on the shoes.

3.3 Crossing Stitch Household Items Based on Thermochromic Embroidery Interfaces

In general, it is an exploration of traditional crossing stitches that are featured in many ICH textiles projects. Users could customize seasons and weather elements and the patterns could be activated through the weather data. The display layer uses thermochromic yarns to achieve color change feedback, the heating module is controlled by a programmable circuit to energize the conductive yarn to control the color-changing area and time of the display layer. The interactive patterns based on crossing stitches (see Fig. 4) are very decorative and could be applied to textile household items, such as smart curtains, wallpaper, tablecloths, etc.

(a)   (b)

Fig. 4. Household textile interface based on thermochromic patterns. a) patterns are not activated, b) patterns are activated.

3.4 Seeing the Smell, a Textile Interface that Visualizes the Release Process of Perfume

ThiS is an installation that makes the fragrance dissipation accompanied by the process of pattern fading during the test of perfume. It will be used in perfume shops or exhibitions to offer customers a new experience of trying perfume, creating a duet of smell and sight. As smell and sight mutually reinforce, Seeing the Smell aims to enable the customer to perceive the complete perfume test in less than one minute. When a customer sprays the perfume in the shop, Seeing the Smell will warm up the fabric, making the fragrance patterns appear. With the evaporation, the temperature of the fabric decreases so the patterns disappear in sequence (Fig. 5).

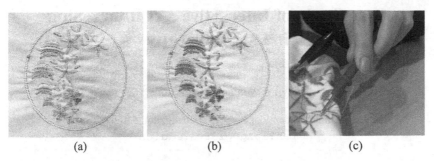

(a)   (b)   (c)

Fig. 5. Household textile interface based on thermochromic patterns. a) patterns are not activated, b) patterns are activated, c) testing of the conductive threads.

In general, in this article, we proposed our explorations of computational thermochromic embroidery interfaces, and we hope our work may motivate more designers and practitioners in the field to create more intersections of interactive technology and embroideries to promote more opportunities for revitalization.

Acknowledgment. This work is supported by the Shanghai Art & Science Planning Project [grant number YB2020F03] and Shanghai Yangfan Youth Talented Program [grant number 20YF1451200].

References

1. UNESCO. Convention for the Safeguarding of the Intangible Cultural Heritage (2003). http://unesdoc.unesco.org/images/0013/001325/132540e.pdf. Accessed 8 June 2021
2. Song, M., Jia, C., Vega, K.: Eunoia: dynamically control thermochromic displays for animating patterns on fabrics. In Proceedings of the 2018 ACM International Joint Conference and 2018 International Symposium on Pervasive and Ubiquitous Computing and Wearable, pp. 255–258. ACM, New York (2018). https://doi.org/10.1145/3267305.3267557
3. Wang, Q., Ye, Y., ten Bhömer, M., Jiang, M., Sun, X.: Seasons: exploring the dynamic thermochromic smart textile applications for intangible cultural heritage revitalization. In: Ardito, C., et al. (eds.) INTERACT 2021. LNCS, vol. 12935, pp. 92–99. Springer, Cham (2021). https://doi.org/10.1007/978-3-030-85610-6_6
4. Devendorf, L.,et al.: I don't want to wear a screen: probing perceptions of and possibilities for dynamic displays on clothing. In: Proceedings of the 2016 CHI Conference on Human Factors in Computing Systems, pp. 6028–6039. ACM, New York (2018). https://doi.org/10.1145/2858036.2858192

Case Study of Interactive Art Intervening in Psychotherapy

Xueying Wen and Liang Tan$^{(\boxtimes)}$ (iD)

Guangzhou Academy of Fine Arts, Guangzhou 510260, China
tanliang@gzarts.edu.cn

Abstract. With the COVID-19 Outbreak leading to the public's the mental stress and psychological burden, many researchers pay attention to mental health problems. Interactive art combines a variety of art forms and has comprehensive advantages, which is conducive to providing new methods for art therapy. By examining related concepts and views, this paper proposes two orientations of interactive art therapy and summarizes specific forms of interactive art intervening in psychotherapy. Based on analyzing a range of cases, this study explores how interactive art can better generate healing effects in psychotherapy.

Keywords: Interactive art · Psychotherapy · Mental health

1 Introduction

The COVID-19 Outbreak can have drastic negative effects on the mental health. According to estimates by the World Health Organization, after natural disasters or major emergencies, 30%–50% of people may have moderate to severe psychological problems. If psychological intervention and social support can be obtained in time, most can be relieved. Studies have shown that art is a tool for enhancing mental health and well-being, and that public participation in art activities and clinical art interventions can help alleviate mental and physical health problems [1]. In the digital age, art therapy has more possibilities and acceptance. Interactive art as a unique art form can create more effective healing effects in psychological interventions.

2 Interactive Art

Interactive art is a dynamic art form that responds to an audience or environment. Interactive art features computers, interfaces, and sensors that respond to motion, heat, weather changes, or other types of input. Jeffrey Shaw, one of the pioneers of interactive digital media art, has described interactive art as a virtual space of images, sound and text. Roy Ascot, a professor at the University of Plymouth in the United Kingdom and a scholar of new media art, explained the characteristics of interactive art: it enables the audience to realize instant interaction through visual, hearing, touch, smell and other sensory means or intelligent art works, so as to achieve whole-body integration, experience, immersion

C. Stephanidis et al. (Eds.): HCII 2022, CCIS 1654, pp. 364–369, 2022.
https://doi.org/10.1007/978-3-031-19679-9_46

and emotional communication. There are many methods and means of healing art, and the art form based on visual art is the most commonly used, while interactive art is different from traditional visual art. Interactive art has the interactive characteristics of multi-sensibility, feedback and immersion. The three-dimensional interactive space is expressed in a more direct and diverse way, allowing the audience to become participants and integrate with art. These characteristics enable interactive artworks to create a natural and multi-directional interactive relationship in terms of psychological intervention. One is the emotional synthesis relationship between the work and the creator; the second is the emotional transmission relationship between the work and the audience; the third is the emotional connection between the creator and the audience relation. Therefore, interactive art can help the people express their inner emotions and vent their negative emotions, induce self-healing, and stimulate the ability of positive transformation.

3   Case Study of Interactive Art Intervening in Psychotherapy

According to the characteristics of interactive art and related art healing practices [2], this paper comprehensively summarizes two methods of applying interactive art to psychotherapy: the first direction is based on the guidance of art works. Based on the knowledge system of healing art, the artist proposes new creative concepts and creative practices, and explores more creative ideas related to humanism and psychology. The purpose is to complete an emotional dialogue in the healing relationship between the artwork and the audience, to heal people's body and mind through the artwork, and to make the audience's behavior tend to "participate" in artistic healing. The second direction is as a psychotherapy aid. With the support of the Department of Psychology, therapists use interactive art creation as an aid in psychotherapy, integrating interactive technology into psychological therapy. This method helps the treatment subject to better create and express, and enhance the thinking expression and emotional verbalization of the treatment subject.

4   Direction 1: Healing of Interactive Art Works

Faced with disaster, many artists will spontaneously create artistic practices that are healing and caring. The interactive art practice in which the artist establishes a direct or indirect interactive way through various creative methods can fully arouse the empathy of the audience and achieve the purpose of closely connecting the common emotions of human beings. Two New York-based artists Candy Chang and James A. Reeves created an interactive installation titled "After the End" [3]. The installation presents visitors with a simple interactive question: describe your loss. Visitors will be invited to share their personal experiences of loss on the scroll, which will be placed on a glowing altar where visitors can read the reflection of the text on the altar, or sit in the apse and watch the ever-changing projected reflection above cycle. This space documents the many ways people have struggled to change their lives during the pandemic. "After the End" provides a refuge, reminding viewers that we are not alone as we mourn the end of one reality and move on to the next. During the pandemic, doctors and nurses have become the groups most vulnerable to job stress and burnout. Staff shortages, increased work-loads and complex work environments are all sources of stress and anxiety. So Inneract Studio has installed an innovative interactive digital art installation called Immersive Healing Art System (IHAS) at Chelsea and Westminster Hospitals in the UK [4]. The installation uses sensors and facial-scanning software to identify audience emotions and capture expressions, and then applies artificial intelligence algorithms to generate a unique, personal piece of visual art, a piece of music and meaningful words associated with emotion. It can make the audience emotionally calm, relax and improve negative psychological problems.

Fig. 1. "After the End" interactive device.

Fig. 2. "Immersive Healing Art System" interactive device.

In terms of public projects, interactive art has been widely used as a means of artistic psychological healing, especially in children's hospitals. In 2018, Disney launched the initiative "Reimagining the Patient Experience at World Children's Hospital —— Creating a Personalized and Engaging Atmosphere that Motivates Young Patients and Relieves the Stress of Hospitalization". In a collaborative project at three children's hospitals in central Florida, digital imaging is used to create interactive artwork including murals, enchanted windows and magic, where children can use devices to scan the artwork and appear Disney characters [5]. According to Elissa Margolis, senior vice president of corporate social responsibility at The Walt Disney Company, the interactive artwork is specifically designed to distract and comfort patients during their most anxious moments. In China, there are similar cases. "No Crying Hospital" proves that interactive art can effectively relieve preoperative anxiety of children and optimize the user experience of the medical environment. The project was created by the design team of Shanghai Institute of Visual Arts and Shanghai Children's Medical Center. With the idea of designing interactive environments for children's healing, the design team integrated functional spaces such as operating rooms and infusion rooms with interactive media to create a comfortable space. The space is immersive, narrative and playful. According to official statistics released by the hospital, within five months of the operation room renovation, the children's cooperation and crying rate improved significantly during the preoperative preparation. The preoperative cooperation rate increased from 63.2% to 89.5%, the incidence of crying decreased from 36.8% to 10.2%, and the patient satisfaction increased from 68.8% to 96.7%.

Fig. 3. Children's AR scanning interactive mural.

Fig. 4. Interactive device of Shanghai children's medical center, by Hongjiang Wang.

5   Direction 2: Interactive Art as an Aid to Psychotherapy

Generally speaking, when using art for psychotherapy, the therapist provides an artistic medium, which enables the subject to express potential psychological information through the creative process and works of art, so as to resolve emotional conflicts, reduce anxiety and depression, and gain insight into psychological problems. Currently commonly used art media include painting, sculpture, collage, clay, etc., while interactive art is still not widely used. To examine how interactive art-making activities can improve quality of life, Texas A&M University conducted a case study of using interactive art to re-energize older adults [6]. For the study, the research team designed an eight-week "Elderly Interactive Art Project" project that included three main activities, namely interactive sound painting, lighting up cards, and interactive soft objects. Participants are free to create their work using interactive techniques. Finally, research finds great potential for interactive art creation to foster collaboration and intergenerational relationships by stimulating creativity and self-expression. This program actively engages seniors and significantly improves their daily lives.

Fig. 5. Participant designs: interactive sound paintings and luminous cards.

Another study at Drexel University in the United States demonstrated the successful use and impact of virtual reality technology in art therapy interventions [7]. The research used HTC VIVE VR headset, remote control and Leap Motion controller, mainly equipped with three kinds of software, one is Google's Tilt Brush software, which allows users to paint in 3D environment. The second is the Kodon virtual sculpture software. The third is Nature Treks software, which creates a relaxing virtual healing environment. Virtual reality technology is a common technology in interactive art, which can help the subject enter an immersive self-world. They can express their emotions and improve their psychological conditions through artistic creation in the virtual space. This discovery will help to broaden the application and development of interactive art in psychotherapy.

6 Conclusion

Compared with traditional art forms, the unique artistic characteristics and performance of interactive art make the relationship between the work and the audience change from passive to active, which determines its potential value in the field of psychotherapy. The innovative application of interactive art in psychotherapy can highlight its connection and interaction. In China, interactive art still has great potential for application in current art psychotherapy practice. With the continuous research in this field, it is believed that in the near future, art healing forms combined with interactive art will gradually appear in the public, contributing to the activation and promotion of social mental health resources.

Acknowledgement. This study is supported by Guangzhou Academy of Fine Arts 2021 Graduate Innovation and Entrepreneurship Training Program Project.

References

1. Jensen, A., Bonde, L.O.: The use of arts interventions for mental health and wellbeing in health settings. Perspect. Public Health **138**(4), 209–214 (2018). https://doi.org/10.1177/175791391 8772602
2. Shen, S.: Non-verbal Communication—— the Intervention of art therapy in psychological reconstruction after disaster. Art Observation, pp. 15–19 (2020). Liu Liyu. New Media and The Reform of Chinese Contemporary Art. Chinese National Academy of Arts (2010)
3. "After The End" interactive device: https://ritualfields.com/work/after-the-end/
4. "immersion treatment system (IHAS) of art" interactive art installation at. https://ddw.nl/en/programme/5742/immersive-healing-art-systemihas
5. Disney Project. https://6abc.com/nemours-childrens-hospital-delaware-disney-artwork-interactive-murals/11225074/
6. Wang, H., Tong, Z.: New trend of spatial interactive public art design in children'shealing environment. Public Art, 62–67 (2019)
7. Seo, J.H., Copeland, B.M., Sungkajun, A., Gonzalez, K.I., Mathews, N.: Re-powering senior citizens with interactive art making: case study with independent older adults. In: Extended Abstracts of the 2018 CHI Conference on Human Factors in Computing Systems (2018)

Analysis of the Attainable Design Paths of Non-heritage Cultural Tourism Immersion Experience - An Example of the Tujia City Living Room Project in Enshi Prefecture

Jinbo Xu[✉] and Yueqing Wei

Wuhan University of Technology, Wuhan, China
3384516630@qq.com

Abstract. Background: with the rise of Generation Z consumer group, the existing forms of tourism experience gradually fail to satisfy the public. The creation of immersive experience can help improve the sensory experience of tourists and their stickiness to the scenic environment, and NRM is undoubtedly a better solution in the construction of cultural tourism immersive experience, but at present, there is a tendency to "emphasize protection, but not development" in NRM projects, and the multi-dimensional development of NRM resources is becoming an issue worth exploring.Meaning: To explore the key factors of new media technology for a more immersive and experiential NRM in China, and the factors of visitors' sense of experience, participation, interactive accessibility and change of cultural tourism model in the space to bring a new experience path for future NRM.Methods & Results: Based on the development of multimedia technology and qualitative research on the participants of the experience, we proposed the design objectives of visualizing the content of NRM, matching multimodal sensory immersion with the scenes of NRM, and personalizing the experience of visitors, using MATD, virtual reality development engine Unity 3D and augmented reality development toolkit Vuforia SDK. Using MATD, virtual reality development engine Unity 3D and augmented reality development toolkit Vuforia SDK, combined with LBS technology, the design path of "content + scene + sensory + business model" is proposed to build an immersive interactive experience system for cultural tourism of non-heritage.Conclusions: The above design paths help increase the immersiveness and interactive accessibility of the experience system of NRM, and provide new perspectives and solutions for design interventions in topics such as NRM conservation and tourism scenarios.

1 Introduction

Tourism industry and cultural industry are increasingly becoming the backbone of China's economic and cultural integration development. At present, China's cultural tourism industry, cultural resources in tourism development only play an instrumental supporting role, capital investment focus on scenic spots, tourism facilities and other "hard assets", the development of the whole area of tourism and tourism experience

C. Stephanidis et al. (Eds.): HCII 2022, CCIS 1654, pp. 370–377, 2022.
https://doi.org/10.1007/978-3-031-19679-9_47

upgrade to be strengthened. In China, there are only a dozen of intangible cultural heritage tourism, the heritage and protection of intangible cultural heritage is important to maintain cultural diversity and continuity, and its value and vulnerability determine the need to protect it, especially like traditional festivals such as intangible cultural heritage with economic and social value. With the rapid development of new technologies such as mobile Internet+, extended reality (XR), ubiquitous intelligence, big data, 5G, holography and sensing, human beings have entered the "third media era" where information is highly intelligent, networked and pan-mediated [1], and immersive experiences have been increasingly valued and applied. Especially in the field of cultural tourism, the characteristics of immersive experience such as borderless, interactivity, pleasantness, and selfhood have created a more high-quality experience space. The immersive experience is composed of three mechanisms: content, technology, and interaction, and the commercial promotion of the implicit field interventions, which together constitute the scene and sensory sensation of "realm-body-integration" and enable the high-quality and sustainable development of China's cultural tourism industry.

2 Research on the Transformation Path of China's Non-traditional Cultural Tourism Industry

China's cultural heritage includes both tangible and intangible cultural heritage. Unlike tangible cultural heritage, which is "tangible" and "physical", intangible cultural heritage generally lacks physical carriers, and its manifestations are often in the form of traditional oral literature, music and dance, acrobatics, festivals and customs, etc. It is often expressed in the form of traditional oral literature, music and dance, Chinese opera and acrobatics, festive customs, and so on. Under certain conditions, the combination of intangible cultural heritage and tourism industry will produce valuable tourism industry results. The cultural value and connotation of intangible cultural heritage items can meet people's high-level spiritual and cultural needs, and are tourism resources with strong development value. However, in terms of the current form and policy of cultural development in China, although intangible cultural heritage items are valued by the state and protected by corresponding policies, it is not enough to rely on government funding alone, as tourism is a kind of spatial consumption, an economy formed through spatial transformation [2]. Therefore, Chinese intangible cultural heritage projects should actively cultivate "self-blooding capacity" and the ability to adapt to media changes in order to maintain their own development in the protection and inheritance.

The ecological media is changing under the empowerment of technology. The media form is shifting from human-led to everything is media; the media field is shifting from active and explicit to "passive and implicit"; the speed, frequency and adaptability of switching the role of everything media are greatly enhanced by 5G technology and artificial intelligence technology; the relationship of elements is shifting from interactive communication to interactive construction. The change of media ecology is based on the development of new media technology, and Heidegger said that what kind of tools are used means what kind of world is presented [3]. The visualization is a new way of experience. In the intangible cultural heritage of the Tujia family in Enshizhou studied by the author, the boundaries of cultural space and time, such as Tujia's horn, hand dance and Xilankalp, will be broken, and the experience environment and experience mode will become a borderless immersive experience space where virtual and reality, digital and physical are integrated. In this space, visitors can interact with the scenes as they wish, fully experience the fun of interacting with the immersive environment, stimulate interest in non-heritage culture and deepen their understanding and application of non-heritage culture.

3   Analysis of the Immersive Experience Path of Enshu Tujia City Living Room Project

In his book "The Laws of Design", William Lidwell explains "immersion" as "flow of mind" [4]. In his book "The Laws of Design", William Lidwell explains "immersion" as "flow of mind" [4], which means that an individual is immersed in a certain activity with all his energy flowing mindfully, ignoring the presence of the outside world, in order to achieve a state of forgetfulness. In the project of the Tujia City Living Room in Enshi, Hubei Province, Enshi Nuo Opera, Tujia Hand Dance, and Xilan Kapu as cultural tourism elements infiltration is an important cultural source to attract visitors' continuous participation and interaction. This "high fidelity" cultural scenario restoration is not only reflected in the natural landscape and human characteristics of the full range of restoration, but also in the presentation of landscape details, ecological consistency and three-dimensional visual presentation of the real sense of creation. The biggest breakthrough of this project is the use of 3D motion capture to establish the virtual time and space of "sprinkling lotus leaves", which is the first in China to combine intangible cultural heritage with motion capture system (Fig. 1). The "Xuanen Peach Blossom Jellyfish" immersion trail is designed in the city living room square, and the peach blossom jellyfish is designed by taking the unique creature of Xuanen, the peach blossom jellyfish, and the West Lancapian hand dance as elements, as shown in Fig. 2 and Fig. 3 below. "The peach jellyfish as a design element is put into the urban space, converting the first soft modeling characteristics of the peach jellyfish itself into color patchwork texture. It makes the jellyfish more spiritual, highlighting its own natural state and creating a sense of immersion experience on the periphery of the square. The author analyzes the immersive experience design of Enshi City Living Room project from two aspects: intangible culture and regional tourism, as shown in Fig. 4.

Fig. 1. Tujia "Sa Ye Er Ho" three-dimensional action collection

Fig. 2. Peach jellyfish motif lamp   **Fig. 3.** Tujia hand swing dance

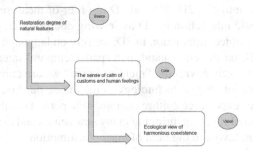

Fig. 4. A framework for the integration of cultural and tourism elements

Based on the research sequence, the design of an immersive experience in the urban living room of Enshu Tujia consists of six main stages of design process:

1. Identify relevant people: general tourists and intangible heritage enthusiasts, and conduct user research using quantitative research, user interviews and user probe kits to gain insight into their experience requirements in intangible cultural heritage tourism spaces; 2. Identify design objects: extract cultural elements from local intangible cultural heritage and visualize the content in three dimensions; 3. Explore design pain points: through preliminary insight 3. Identify the design pain points: through the case study of "immersive" experience for cultural tourism and related research, three pain points are summarized: the accurate extraction and presentation of intangible cultural heritage content, how to enhance the perception of immersive space, and how to improve

the mind-flow in intangible cultural experience; 4. Design interventions to solve the problem: the integrated application of immersive interaction design methods, collaborative user design methods, mind-flow experience design methods, realistic 3D design methods, etc., focusing on the four aspects of "scenario - perception - mind-flow - immersion"; 5. Design proposal construction direction: Based on the logical relationship between content and design, interaction methods and driving technologies in ICH tourism, the "information-experience-situation-intangible culture" system will be constructed at multiple levels, such as immersion and pleasure in space, personalisation of interaction modes and three-dimensional scenario reproduction system.

4   Non-foreign Heritage Cultural Tourism Immersive Experience System Construction

4.1   System Build Path Analysis

The "immersive" experience combines virtual and reality, digital twin, MATD and other technologies, and its unique experience is combined with the cultural tourism space to form a very contemporary "immersive" product, bringing new life to the dissemination of intangible cultural heritage. In the process of building intangible cultural tourism system, I believe that the situation of interactive experience system is like early movies, although we have not yet designed the most mature language mechanism for the development of immersive experience system, but we can classify the experience mechanism of interactive system into 1D, 2D, 3D and 4D in order of measurement [5]. From the act of lexical-linguistic interaction in 1D to drawing and printing, diagrammatic symbols in 2D, to human-object interaction in 3D, we rely on language and objects that we can actually feel. 4D, on the other hand, is a spatio-temporal interaction mechanism, which has some convergence with the "meta-universe" we are currently studying, that is, through immersive interaction technology to maximize our human sensory perception. The "immersive" experience culture combines the perfect combination of technical means and innovation of thinking, bringing many new senses and experiences to people, thus winning frequent favors in the field of mass consumption.

4.2   Field

The field mechanism, with the gradual refinement, reintegration and optimisation of the immersive technology and experience, has led to a quality presentation and iteration of immersive content and interaction [6]. With the integration of smart technologies, the development of ubiquitous smart immersive experiences has become inevitable. While ubiquitous intelligence supports content and interaction, it constructs an immersive field mechanism consisting of technology, content and interaction.

4.3   Mechanisms for the Realization of Immersive Experiences

Content of the Immersive Experience. At the level of content construction, technologies such as virtual and realistic, digital twins and MATD have overturned the traditional visual presentation [7]. Through the use of computer technology for image construction and three-dimensional space, the 'boundaries' of content and information no longer exist. With the addition of IP design, the player has to accept the worldview setting, plot experience and quest exploration in the immersive narrative, gradually begin to substitute for the character or plot, develop emotions and empathy, and finally lose their sense of time and self-consciousness subjectively, and interact according to instinctive intuition, thus reaching the highest level of total immersion and forgetfulness. In current film and television productions, the director controls the camera angle, the subject, the editing, and the editing technique to shape the language of the camera in order to express the content of the story and build meaning.

Driving Technologies for Immersive Experiences. Firstly, in terms of global interaction, the pursuit of individual experience, group socialization and a sense of belonging has stimulated research in related cognitive fields and stimulated the potential market for immersive experiences. In the immersive space, the interaction form of participants gradually changes from "passive acceptance" to "active participation" and even instant "co-creation". The use of VR, holography and other technologies can realize virtual interaction in three-dimensional space, and can even use gestures, voice, ideas, brain waves and other forms of interaction, providing participants with a multi-sensory, multi-dimensional, multi-level immersive interactive experience.

Second, in terms of technological reinvention, digital twin (DT) technology can map the virtual digital space based on objective physical reality and update the virtual space in real time according to the changes in the physical space, creating a dynamic and more realistic immersive space. In addition, emotion and spatial computing are constantly added to the immersive experience to intelligently push the appropriate content to meet the actual needs of the participants by recognizing their emotional changes [8].

Third, in terms of dynamic intelligence, AI processing technology is moving from the "cloud" to the "edge" and advancing the evolution of the IoT to the IoT, with the low-latency nature of edge cloud + 5G allowing for high-capacity information processing. This device-side data processing and rapid response capability can be used to coordinate and configure relevant and scalable smart devices in a timely manner, with the added benefits of privacy protection and personalized services. The dynamic and intelligent wireless edge architecture has broad adaptability, relying on increasingly powerful computational support to complete real-time algorithms and rapidly integrate resources, providing a more flexible and intelligent system solution for immersive experiences.

Fourth, in terms of image building, AI, 5G, holographic and other technologies can optimize the presentation of immersive scenes, improve the visual quality of images, and perform dynamic processing such as geometric transformation of images to improve image fidelity and high definition. For example, with the help of ray tracing and real-time rendering technologies of high-end "30 series" graphics cards, it is possible to simulate the tracing of light paths and to provide a more realistic element to the scene by using algorithms to handle the visual phenomena generated by the optical properties of the camera and the human eye, such as simulated lens flare, depth of field or motion blur [9].

In a nutshell, global interaction, technology reshaping, dynamic intelligence, and mimetic building technologies have become key drivers for the upgrade of immersive experiences. Together, they are changing the way people learn, live and experience, as well as the way people collaborate and interact. While the technology is gradually improving, the content and interaction forms are naturally facing innovation and rethinking.

Interaction Mode of Immersive Experience. The body, as part of the medium, is an important factor in the coupling of technological and social configurations, and no medium can be separated from the direct participation of the body with subjectivity. The scholar Peng Lan defines the scene as not only a spatial and temporal location, but also a "behavioral and psychological environment", i.e., virtual reality superimposes the physical and mental experience of the subject on top of time and space [10].

First, visual tracking. The virtual immersion environment is different from the traditional interface fixed perspective state, when the participants enter the three-dimensional space, they can get a 360-degree free perspective. Intangible cultural heritage contains the essence of China's five thousand years of culture, and if the viewer's interest in this field is not captured in time, the first interest of the viewer in this field will be lost. Eye Tracking technology solves this problem by identifying the position of the eyes or the movement of the eyes relative to the head to achieve dynamic tracking of vision; it also collects more accurate visual dynamic data from the participants for project feedback and analysis to optimize and improve the content of the immersive experience.

Second, gestural interaction. As a natural interaction method, gesture has a decisive advantage in designing immersive experiences. This will greatly enhance the viewer's interest in experiencing intangible culture and prompt him or her to quickly enter a state of immersion.

Third, acoustic feedback. Sound has a great impact on immersion, as it helps participants notice objects beyond their sight and encourages them to view the entire 360-degree space, stimulating their curiosity and desire to explore, and prompting them to actively explore and enter the immersion state.

Fourth, voice interaction by voice pattern. In the area of voice interaction, in addition to speech command recognition, the use of voice recognition technology to analyze changes in voice intonation and trigger interaction is also another scenario application in the field of natural language interaction. Voice recognition enables intelligent devices to naturally and quickly identify participants and sense the essential source of their needs to achieve a personalized experience in an immersive field.

Fifth, haptic feedback. The role of haptic feedback to enhance immersion is very obvious. The human sense of touch is generated through a large number of receptors (e.g., pressure, vibration receptors, thermoreceptors, and pain) distributed throughout the body at different densities with the nervous system in order to perceive and process spatio-temporal perception of external stimuli in a timely manner (Fig. 5).

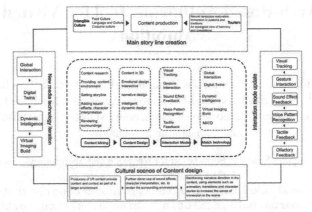

Fig. 5. Intangible cultural tourism experience pathway framework

5 Concluding Remarks

In the process of building immersive fields and optimizing immersive experiences, the core imperative is to develop a library of quality content and expressions to enhance the retention rate of participants. In turn, participants' tendency to consume the experience can contribute to the continuous updating of technology applications. Technology continues to drive and support the upgrading of all elements of content and interaction to create a more credible, realistic, and enjoyable immersive experience, presenting a more refined and exciting immersive field, and ultimately driving a virtuous cycle of immersive industries and applications.

References

1. Li, Q.: Immersion. Communication: A Communication Paradigm in the Third Media Era. Tsinghua University Press, Beijing (2013)
2. Zhang, H., Yue, Y.: Rational thinking of territorial tourism. J. Tourism **31**(09) (2016)
3. Guosheng, W.: Heidegger's thought of technology. J. Seeking Knowl. 33–40 (2004)
4. Ridwell, Horton, Butler.: The Laws of Design. Liaoning Science and Technology Press, Shenyang (2010)
5. Mogridge, B.: Critical Design Report - Changing the Past to Influence the Future of Interaction Design. In: Xu, Y.: Translation. CITIC Press, Beijing (2011)
6. Xu, R., Chen, W.: The construction, realization mechanism and educational application of immersive experience: a new field of AI+immersive learning. J. Distance Educ. **39**(01) (2021)
7. Song, K., Yang, C.: Interactive immersive experience: the constructive law of virtual reality space. J. Chinese Radio Telev. (2020)
8. Biocca F, Delaney, B.: Immersive virtual reality technology. In: Proceedings of Communication in the Age of Virtual Reality (1995)

Web-Based Authoring Tool for Virtual Exhibitions

Emmanouil Zidianakis[1(✉)], Nikolaos Partarakis[1], Eirini Kontaki[1], Stella Kopidaki[1], Aldo Xhako[1], Zacharias Pervolarakis[1], Antonis Agapakis[1], Michalis Foukarakis[1], Stavroula Ntoa[1], Ioanna Barbounaki[1], Emmanouil Ntafotis[1], Anastasia Ntagianta[1], and Constantine Stephanidis[1,2]

[1] Institute of Computer Science, Foundation for Research and Technology—Hellas (FORTH), 70013 Heraklion, Crete, Greece
{zidian,partarak,ekontaki,skopidaki,aldo,zackper,agantos,foukas, stant,barbounaki,ntafotis,dagianta,cs}@ics.forth.gr
[2] Computer Science Department, School of Sciences and Engineering, University of Crete, 70013 Heraklion, Crete, Greece

Abstract. This work presents a web-based authoring tool that enables museum curators and individuals to make digital collections of exhibits accessible and explorable via the Web. It allows users to create interactive and immersive virtual 3D/VR exhibitions using a unified collaborative authoring environment based on a Human-Centered Design approach with the active participation of museum curators and end-users. Main contributions are pertinent to the fields of (a) user-designed dynamic virtual exhibitions, (b) exhibition tours, (c) visualization in web-based 3D/VR technologies, and (d) immersive navigation and interaction.

Keywords: Virtual exhibition · Virtual museum · Web-based 3D/VR exhibitions · Photorealistic renderings

1 Introduction

Virtual Exhibitions (VEs) have become easily available to the public, fostering a more efficient exchange of information and interaction with museum visitors in the virtual display arena [1]. The ever-increasing role of such technological breakthroughs has led to accessible, affordable virtual exhibitions available worldwide, delivered through multiple platforms and technologies, aiming to visually present history, architecture, and or artworks [2]. Web-delivered VEs provide content globally through the Web and are facilitated by a wide variety of 3D viewers aiming to provide 3D interactive applications "embedded" in browsers. However, existing VEs set various obstacles, including lack of a unified platform for the presentation of virtual exhibitions on any device and lack of mechanisms for personalized interaction with knowledge and digital information.

In this context, this research work presents the Web-based authoring tool of VEs that allows users to create interactive exhibitions using a unified collaborative authoring environment. The proposed tool comprises technologies that allow novice and expert

© The Author(s), under exclusive license to Springer Nature Switzerland AG 2022
C. Stephanidis et al. (Eds.): HCII 2022, CCIS 1654, pp. 378–385, 2022.
https://doi.org/10.1007/978-3-031-19679-9_48

users to create original exhibitions in a collaborative fashion. Thus, digital collections of exhibits can be promoted to different target groups to foster knowledge, promote cultural heritage, and enhance education, history, science, or art in a user-friendly and interactive way [3].

The ambition of this research work is to provide a useful and meaningful medium for creating and experiencing cultural content, setting the foundation for a framework with direct benefits for museums, Cultural and Creative Industries, as well as the society.

2 Background and Related Work

The most popular technology for the World Wide Web (WWW) visualization includes Web3D [4], which offers standards and tools that allow numerous functionalities such as (a) animations providing dynamic and continuous 360 views [5], (b) panning and high-quality zooming [6, 7], and (c) hotspots and panoramas interconnection with other files [8]. Additionally, there are tools able to combine both geometry and runtime behavioral descriptions into a single file, incorporating advanced physics functionality such as collision detection and friction (e.g., X3D, COLLADA) [9]. Powerful technologies including open-source multiplatform high-performance 3D graphics toolkits and a variety of 3D game engines have been used in museum environments [10–12].

This work builds upon the aforementioned advancements and introduces technical contributions in the field of (a) user-designed dynamic virtual exhibitions, (b) exhibition tours, (c) visualization in Web-based 3D environments, and (d) immersive navigation and interaction in photorealistic renderings.

3 A Web-Based Authoring Environment

The aim of the tool has been formulated after a thorough user requirements analysis, including (a) structured interviews with curators, (b) co-creation workshops, and (c) use case analysis with user groups that defined its functionality and target groups.

The presented tool aims at facilitating curators to design the virtual exhibitions of their preference. The web-based authoring environment provides predefined spaces based on existing templates or spaces created in the past, as well as virtual spaces to be designed from scratch. Firstly, the surrounding of the environment should be formed in a two-dimensional floorplan. Afterwards, the system automatically generates a 3D representation of the exhibition, allowing users to add details including doors, windows, and decorative elements (e.g., furniture, floor textures, etc.). To add an exhibit in the 3D virtual space, users are able to select the exhibit of their preference in the given formats (i.e., 2D images, 3D models, videos) and position it in the exhibition space as depicted in Fig. 1. Users are allowed to enter exhibits in the platform through an integrated content management system, using standardized semantic web technologies (e.g., Europeana Data Model – EDM [13]).

Moreover, the exhibits can be rotated and scaled properly in all three dimensions. Different types of showcases (i.e., glass, frame, stand, etc.) and lights (i.e., ceiling/floor/wall lighting) with customizable characteristics are provided. Free navigation within the 2D/3D environment is supported through the use of the keyboard and the mouse. Users

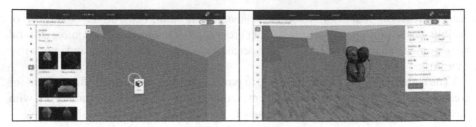

Fig. 1. A 3D design tool for creating virtual museums.

are also able to preview the virtual exhibition tour before finalized and generated into a fully explorable virtual exhibition.

3.1 Co-creation of Virtual Exhibitions

The presented authoring tool facilitates the creation of virtual exhibitions in a collaborative fashion. In detail, the owner of an exhibition is able to invite other registered users as potential co-creators. In case an invited co-creator does not own an account in the platform, they receive an invitation link via email.

Co-creators have editing permissions in exhibitions; however, the owner is responsible to review all the entries, suggestions, and modifications made and eventually decide whether to approve, edit, or discard them. This feature works more as a safety net toward creating consistent and qualitative content in the platform. More specifically, a notification mechanism informs the owner when edits or adjustments have been submitted by co-creators. The platform also allows users to exchange private messages, thus facilitating the collaboration between two or more parties (i.e., museums, organizations, etc.) through integrated communication channels.

3.2 Exhibition Tours

The provided authoring tool supports tour-oriented exhibitions including (a) free tours displaying all the available exhibits, (b) short tours comprising the most popular artifacts of a virtual exhibition, (c) tours oriented to the age group of users, (d) thematic tours, (f) chronological tours, and so on. The platform automatically creates at least one free virtual tour. When creating a new tour, curators need to enter information, such as starting point, language, title, short description, sequence of the exhibits, and other.

3.3 Interaction in VR

Visitors of the platform can navigate in 3D virtual exhibitions and interact with the exhibits using either a web browser or any VR headset consisting of a head-mounted display, stereo sound, and tracking sensors (e.g., Oculus Quest).

Navigation in VR is readily available upon the selection of a virtual tour. By initiating a virtual tour, the Exhibition Viewer, a Web-based 3D/VR application, provides the 3D construction of the exhibition area, giving prominence to the virtual exhibits. Visitors can interact with any exhibit and retrieve related information.

The platform automatically recognizes whether a VR headset is connected to the computer and enables the virtual tour through the VR headset. Otherwise, the virtual exhibition is loaded in the web browser. In case a VR headset is connected to the computer but the visitor wishes to proceed through the web browser, the platform offers the option to enable the VR tour later on. Through a dedicated menu additional information about the virtual tour progress is provided, including total number of available exhibits, elapsed time of the tour, option to switch the current tour to VR headset, settings, and full-screen view option.

The way visitors may interact during a virtual tour depends on the selected navigation method (i.e., web browser or VR headset). In the case of web browser navigation, the interaction can be achieved by clicking on each exhibit. Whereas, VR headsets allow a more immersive interaction with the assistance of their tracking sensors. Keeping track of a user's hand motion in the physical world has as a result the conversion of their movements in the virtual world, allowing the interaction with virtual exhibits and the navigation in the virtual environment.

4   System Implementation

The platform was implemented following the Representational State Transfer (REST) architectural style, exposing the necessary endpoints that any client application (web or mobile) can consume to exchange information with the system and interface with its resources. The back-end API was developed using the NestJS framework, which is an advanced JavaScript back-end framework that combines robust design patterns with best practices offering the fundamental infrastructure capable of building and deploying highly scalable and performant server-side applications. User authentication and authorization services were built upon the OAuth 2.0 industry-standard authorization protocol with the use of JavaScript Web Tokens. At the deployment level, the Web Services are packaged as containerized Docker applications.

The proposed web-based authoring tool is based on MongoDB [14], allowing developers to process data naturally and intuitively, mainly due to its JSON data format. This approach ensures short application development cycles, decreased estimated time for developing new features or tackled potential issues. In this way, the authoring tool is considered flexible to changes and upgrades. The back-end services utilize libraries such as Mongoose, an Object Data Modeling (ODM) library for MongoDB and NestJS, to apply schemas to these entities aiming to provide software constrained resource specifications that prevent data inconsistency or even data loss.

4.1   Employing Web-Based 3D/VR Technologies

The authoring tool is based on the Angular frontend framework that constitutes a scalable web app solution. The Angular framework allows building features quickly with simple and declarative templates [15]. It achieves maximum speed and performance, while at the same time meets huge data requirements. The frontend architecture implementation takes advantage of the Angular module system to create a maintainable code-base. The main modules are derived for the major resources of the platform, namely its Users,

Exhibits, and Exhibitions. However, separate models are used to handle Authentication and User Profiles. Modules implement their business logic in the form of Angular components and their services. These components are reusable by any service via dependency injection, thus minimizing duplicate code. Some of the functions that these services are responsible for are user registration and authentication, exhibit and exhibition creation, and user profile customization. The Web application support responsive design principles by incorporating the Bootstrap front-end framework and uses Sassy CSS (SCSS), an extension to basic CSS, to style and customize its UI components. In that way, user experience on both desktop and mobile devices is equally pleasing and intuitive.

4.2 Photorealistic Renderings

To deliver Web-based 3D/VR experiences, the platform is based on a Web framework named A-Frame [16] supporting all WebXR browsers available for both desktops and standalone VR headsets (e.g., Oculus Quest) [17].

A-Frame [16], the Web framework for building 3D/AR/VR applications based on HTML/Javascript, is useful for multiplatform applications, however performance tests revealed a limitation on the number of light sources a scene, since numerous light sources might affect the performance of the application and aggravate the user experience. A-Frame's rendering engine calculates only direct lighting. However, the absence of indirect lighting disengages users from gaining an immersive experience, simply because a flat-shaded scene falls into the uncanny valley of computer graphics. For that reason, the framework was further explored following different approaches on lighting the scene. After experimenting with the framework, a number of basic guidelines were concluded aiming to enhance the visualization of an exhibition room to look more attractive and at the same time save performance. These include the following: **(i)** the less ambient lighting, the more realistic the scene, **(ii)** windowless interior spaces are preferable, since windows increase the cognitive expectations of lighting, **(iii)** the more point lights or spotlights in combination with ambient lighting the better, and **(iv)** more than 5–6 lights should be avoided, in case of standalone VR headsets, to significantly reduce the performance.

The best possible result has been achieved given the available resources on the real time lighting pipeline of A-Frame (see Fig. 2).

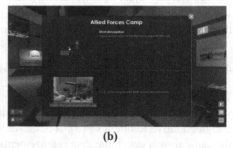

(a)   (b)

Fig. 2. (a) Lighting of virtual exhibition space and 3D exhibits; (b) Displaying exhibits' information.

Taking into consideration that A-Frame does not support baking functionality, the Blender Bakery pipeline was additionally integrated [18]. Its main use in the industry is 3D modeling and animation, however it is also able to perform baking and scripting, making it a perfect match for the specific case. The pipeline is being activated automatically at the time a curator finishes the design of a virtual exhibition space. The virtual exhibition serves real-time, low-quality graphics rendered by A-Frame and saves user-changes continuously on the database. On completion, the Blender Bakery pipeline is triggered. The baking process takes place on Blender, using the ray-tracing rendering engine of Blender called "Cycles", producing as output a.glb file that will be stored back to the database. As a result, when visitors start an exhibition tour, a photorealistic virtual space with great performance will be activated.

5 Evaluation Results

Different evaluation methodologies throughout the development cycle of the proposed tool were applied following a Human-Centered Design approach[1]. Thus, ensuring that the platform will serve user needs in the best possible way and provide an engaging experience both for content creators and content consumers. In particular, the following evaluation iterations were carried out: (a) heuristic evaluation of the designed mockups applied iteratively, (b) group inspection of the final implemented mockups, ensuring that they are usable for the target users, and (c) cognitive walkthrough to assess the intuitiveness of the application at each step of the interaction.

The heuristic evaluation with UX experts took place during the design phase, in which initial mockups were created. Based on the feedback acquired, an extensive set of mockups both for the Web and the VR environment were designed, which were further evaluated by end-users, as well as by domain and UX experts.

During the group usability inspection, comprising three evaluation sessions, mockups of the implemented system were presented and evaluated through group discussions, aiming to assess whether the requirements defined during previous phases were met.

A cognitive walkthrough was conducted with the participation of three UX experts and one domain expert, in separate one-hour sessions, driven by a set of tasks that should be executed, aiming to assess the system actions and responses. A facilitator observed the evaluators and kept notes regarding whether they tried and achieved the desired outcome.

Several conclusions were drawn concerning the design of the tool, addressing to cultural institutions and individual content creators. Overall, evaluators appraised the clear design and the UI consistency, as well as the well-integrated functions into a logical flow. The most severe problems identified referred to the lack of adequate information about the exhibits and of more detailed guidance during a tour. Moreover, the functionality for creating and editing a 3D virtual space can entail difficulties, especially since some functionality appears to be hidden. Finally, some improvements were pointed out concerning the terminology used especially affecting the non-professional content creators.

---

[1] The study was approved by the Ethics Committee of the Foundation for Research and Technology—Hellas (Approval date: 12 April 2019/Reference number: 40/12–4-2019).

Future evaluation efforts will target larger numbers of end-users, including professional and non-professional content creators, as well as museum visitors.

6 Conclusions and Future Work

This work presented a Web-based authoring tool for Virtual Exhibitions that allows users to create interactive and immersive virtual 3D/VR exhibitions using a unified collaborative authoring environment. In summary, the platform offers (a) user-designed dynamic virtual exhibitions, (b) exhibition tours, (c) visualization in Web-based 3D/VR technologies, and (d) immersive navigation and interaction in photorealistic renderings.

The platform differentiates from other similar works in the sense that it is a generic technological framework not paired to a specific real-world museum. Its main ambition is to act as a tool that supports the representation and presentation of virtual exhibitions through Web-based 3D/VR immersive visiting experiences.

With regard to future improvements, emphasis will be placed on the experiential part of the visit focusing on hybrid exhibition tours that combine AR augmentation of physical exhibitions.

Acknowledgment. The authors would like to thank the employees of the Historical Museum of Crete, as well as all end-users who participated in the co-creation and evaluation of the web-based authoring tool, providing valuable feedback and insights.

Funding. This work has been conducted in the context of the Unveiling the Invisible Museum research project (http://invisible-museum.gr), and has been co-financed by the European Union and Greek national funds, under the call RESEARCH–CREATE–INNOVATE (project code: T1EDK-02725).

References

1. Kamariotou, V., Kamariotou, M., Kitsios, F.: Strategic planning for virtual exhibitions and visitors' experience: a multidisciplinary approach for museums in the digital age. Digit. Appl. Archaeol. Cult. Heritage **21**, e00183 (2021)
2. Partarakis, N., et al.: Digital cultural heritage experience in ambient intelligence. In: Ioannides, M., Magnenat-Thalmann, N., Papagiannakis, G. (eds.) Mixed Reality and Gamification for Cultural Heritage. Springer, Cham (2017). https://doi.org/10.1007/978-3-319-49607-8_19
3. Partarakis, N., Antona, M., Zidianakis, E., Stephanidis, C.: Adaptation and content personalization in the context of multi user museum exhibits. In: Proceedings of the International Working Conference on Advanced Visual Interfaces (AVI 2016), Bari, Italy, pp. 7–10 (2016)
4. Web3D Consortium: Open Standards for Real-Time 3D Communication. https://www.web3d.org/. Accessed 21 Dec 2022
5. Hughes, C.E., Stapleton, C.B., Hughes, D.E., Smith, E.M.: Mixed reality in education, entertainment, and training. IEEE Comput. Graph. Appl. **25**(6), 24–30 (2005)
6. Sinclair, P.A., Martinez, K., Millard, D.E., Weal, M.J.: Augmented reality as an interface to adaptive hypermedia systems. New Rev. Hypermedia Multimedia **9**(1), 117–136 (2003)
7. Goodall, S., et al.: Knowledge-based exploration of multimedia museum collections (2004)
8. Museum het Rembrandthuis. https://www.rembrandthuis.nl/. Accessed 27 April 2022

9. Barnes, M., Levy Finch, E.: COLLADA–Digital Asset Schema Release 1.5.0. https://www.khronos.org/files/collada_spec_1_5.pdf. Accessed 27 April 2022
10. OpenSceneGraph-3.6.5 Released. http://www.openscenegraph.org/index.php/8-news/238-openscenegraph-3-6-5-released. Accessed 27 April 2022
11. Technologies, U. Unity Real-Time Development Platform: 3D, 2D VR & AR Engine. https://unity.com/. Accessed 27 April 2022
12. Second Life: Virtual Worlds, Virtual Reality, VR, Avatars, Free 3D Chat. https://www.secondlife.com/. Accessed 27 April 2022
13. Doerr, M., Gradmann, S., Hennicke, S., Isaac, A., Meghini, C., van de Sompel, H.: The europeana data model (EDM). In: Proceedings of the In World Library and Information Congress: 76th IFLA General Conference and Assembly, Gothenburg, Sweden, 10–15 August 2010, pp. 10–15
14. The Most Popular Database for Modern Apps. https://www.mongodb.com. Accessed 27 April 2022
15. Angular. https://angular.io/. Accessed 27 April 2022
16. A-Frame–Make WebVR. https://aframe.io/. Accessed 27 April 2022
17. Immersive Web Developer Home. https://immersiveweb.dev/. Accessed 27 April 2022
18. Foundation, B.: blender.org-Home of the Blender project-Free and Open 3D Creation Software. https://www.blender.org/. Accessed 27 April 2022

HCI for Health and Wellbeing

Detecting Early Warning Indicators of Covid-19 Pandemic in the Context of United States: An Exploratory Data Analysis

Md Morshed Jaman Adnan(✉), Knut Hinkelmann, and Emanuele Laurenzi

University of Applied Sciences and Arts Northwestern, Olten 4600, Switzerland
adnan.cse13@gmail.com

Abstract. This work aims to investigate if social media data, Twitter in particular can be used to detect early warning indicators of COVID-19 pandemic in the United States (US). To demonstrate the viability of this work, English tweets were collected with a hasghtag of COVID-19 related topics ranges from 12th March to end of April 2020. With the help of with N-gram language model and Term Frequency and Inverse Document Frequency (TF-IDF) significant bi-grams such as ("new york"), ("social, distancing"), ("stay, safe"), ("toilet, paper"), ("wash, hand"), ("tested, positive"), (look, like), ("front, line"), ("grocery, store") etc. are extracted. Our analysis shows that, the natures of the bi-grams directly reflect the characteristics of the infection cases and are almost similarly distributed over different clusters. This study also reveals that, the tweets of ("new york") increases with ("stay, home"), ("social, distancing"), ("stay, safe"), ("look, like") and ("tested positive"); and decreases with ("toilet, paper"). Bi-grams with such relationships are recognized as indicators and are validated with the number of infection cases on each day. Results show that, social media data can project the actual scenario of infection curve and able to detect warning indicators once the pandemic is moderately recognized.

Keywords: COVID-19 · Early indicators · Social media mining

1 Introduction

The outbreak of an infectious disease threatens society, especially when it evolves into a pandemic in a short period [1]. Coronavirus Disease (COVID-19), an emerged infectious disease first discovered in Wuhan China in December 2019 [2] and the World Health Organization (WHO) declared the Chinese outbreak of COVID-19 to be a public health emergency on 30th January 2020 [3]. The surveillance of COVID-19 pandemic is carried out through tracking the number of infection cases, as well as using mathematical models of disease spread for predicting the trajectories of the number of cases [4]. Although the standard mathematical models showed promising results in the evaluation of the trajectories of the disease spread, their primary focus remains on the nature of the disease spread after outbreak, which limits the capacity to determine population response towards pandemic risk at the early stages of an outbreak.

C. Stephanidis et al. (Eds.): HCII 2022, CCIS 1654, pp. 389–396, 2022.
https://doi.org/10.1007/978-3-031-19679-9_49

Since quarantine measures have been implemented across most countries around the world, people have been increasingly relying on different social media platforms to receive news and express thoughts. In the past, Twitter communications between users, demonstrated a reliable source of early information. For instance, Twitter data were valuable in revealing public discussions and sentiments to interesting topics, real-time news updates in global pandemics such as H1N1 and Ebola [5]. The objective of this research is to observe user's communication from social media data, Twitter in particular, and draw conclusion of events which can be used to mitigate future crisis of COVID-19 pandemic.

The research questions of this poster are the following:

1. What are the early warning indicators?
2. How can early indicators be identified directly from social media data?

2   Literature Review

A number of mathematical models have been investigated by researchers to describe the interactive dynamics of infectious diseases [6]. For instance, a mathematical model deployed to identify the pattern of local transmission of COVID-19 and predict the epidemic size and the timing of the end of spread in Korea [7]. Similar approach has been studied by [8], where they propose a compartmental mathematical model to predict and control the transmission dynamics of COVID-19 pandemic in India with the epidemic data up to April 30, 2020. Leveraging social media to detect early-warning signals of an upcoming pandemic is indeed a good example of epidemiological monitoring [9, 10]. However, there exist no literature where the focus is concentrated on leveraging public opinion from social media in indicating early warning signals to a pandemic.

3   Research Method

The proposed research method in this study is a case study research embedded with exploratory data analysis. According to the author [11], case study research must satisfy 6 steps linear iterative processes such as plan, design, prepare, collect, analyze and share. It is possible to explain the justification of case study research in the context of this study. This study satisfy the principle of author's [11] single case study, as the study refers to a discrete scenario based on a specified data range. The use of multiple data sources is also ensured in this research according to the author [11]. Furthermore, this study also satisfies the principle of "no control over behavioral elements" [11] as the outcome of an exploratory analysis is not known beforehand. In regards to the use of social media data, the author [11] urges to deal with great caution which is also taken care by incorporating primary visualization techniques.

4 Data Collection and Preparation

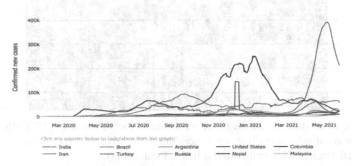

Fig. 1. Daily confirmed new cases [12]

This study is conducted considering the date ranges from 12th March 2020 to 31st April 2020 as the infection cases has already spread to a moderate number. The dataset is collected from Kaggle [13], which comes with filtered tweets in csv format and is scrapped with keywords related to COVID-19 associated keywords. In addition to the Twitter dataset, the number of daily infection cases are also collected from the CDC website [14].

4.1 Pre-processing

A pre-processing function was written in python 3.7, which involves in removing punctuation, tokenization, stopwords removal, lemmatization, removal of HTTPS, removal of single letters and special characters from the filtered tweets (see Fig. 2).

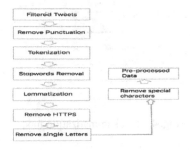

Fig. 2. Text Pre-processing

4.2 Exploratory Data Analysis

Word cloud distribution is illustrated to check the relevancy of the dataset (see Fig. 3).

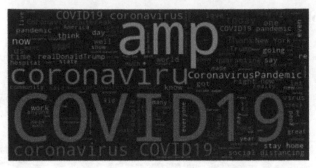

Fig. 3. Word cloud distribution shows the most frequent words such as COVID19, amp, coronavirus, CoronavirusPandemic etc. corresponding to this corpus. The larger a word in the distribution, the more common the word is in the document (s).

It is therefore, possible to state that, the collected dataset is relevant for the analysis aligned with the research goal.

5 Data Analysis Method

The data analysis method involves in summary generation, which is illustrated in the model (see Fig. 4). The proposed model loads pre-processed text as input and calculate N-gram out of text data. The model then calculates Term Frequency and Inverse Document Frequency (TF-IDF) of the N-grams to find relevant terms in the document. Parallel to the calculation of TF-IDF, standardized z score is applied in order to scale the tweets. The result of standard scales of the tweets facilitate summary of the corpus.

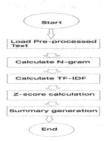

Fig. 4. Text summarization model

In the process of summary generation, the N-grams (N = 2) are sorted based on their TF-IDF score in descending order. TF-IDF assigns higher score to the terms that appear rarely in the document and lower score if a term appears frequently in a document [15]. A total 25 terms were generated and found that the terms (bi-grams) consist of higher TF-IDF score comes with significantly fewer data points. It is therefore, insignificant to interpret some form of relationship based on fewer data points. It is obvious that, tweets related to COVID-19 happen to appear in large scale during the pandemic since it was completely a new infectious disease and spread globally in a short period of time. Therefore, it is possible to sort the list of bi-grams with their corresponding terms in descending order (see Table 1).

Table 1. Weighting measures of bi-grams based on terms

index	token	term	tf	df	tf-idf
0	coronavirus,covid19	16093	0.0769230769230769	15799	0.23346447559142366
1	covid19,coronavirus	14669	0.1	14633	0.3111700534259591
2	new,york	6016	0.0769230769230769	3537	0.34857588669106426
3	stay,home	5214	0.043478260869565216	4431	0.18722596405549768
4	social,distancing	4548	0.0625	4413	0.26939167593043023
5	covid19,pandemic	4229	0.0833333333333333	4196	0.3633898448641646
6	coronavirus,pandemic	3441	0.0555555555555555	3417	0.2536662521126683
7	stay,safe	2689	0.0454545454545454	2650	0.21909596342793367
8	due,covid19	2496	0.0833333333333333	2478	0.4072324635453782
9	toilet,paper	2458	0.1	2213	0.5000247288434984
10	covid19,case	2188	0.0714285714285714	2143	0.35945534853663375
11	covid19,covid19	2025	0.0769230769230769	1938	0.3948365958816088
12	covid19,stayhome	1987	0.0384615384615384	1987	0.1964584236341172
13	covid19,coronaviruspandemic	1848	0.0588235294117647	1845	0.30482511686122166
14	look,like	1805	0.0625	1728	0.32796905725126724
15	due,coronavirus	1781	0.0769230769230769	1775	0.4015911137039577
16	tested,positive	1688	0.043478260869565216	1562	0.2325409161426995
17	wash,hand	1632	0.047619047619047616	1406	0.25969468307567506
18	coronavirus,quarantine	1591	0.034482758620689655	1579	0.1840559750235363
19	covid19,quarantine	1586	0.25	1586	1.3333006702942891
20	spread,covid19	1578	0.1	1572	0.5342063408645268
21	confirmed,case	1562	0.0357142857142857	1370	0.19569670436218756
22	public,health	1562	0.0666666666666666	1430	0.3624449748098077
23	covid19,crisis	1549	0.043478260869565216	1543	0.23307268135299322
24	front,line	1525	0.0588235294117647	1489	0.3174277648684742

Table 2. COVID-19 infection cases retrieved from CDC website

	Dates	Number of Cases		Dates	Number of Cases
1			26	Apr 5, 2020	27327
2	Mar 12, 2020	1148	27	Apr 6, 2020	28563
3	Mar 13, 2020	1348	28	Apr 7, 2020	30112
4	Mar 14, 2020	1823	29	Apr 8, 2020	33579
5	Mar 15, 2020	2881	30	Apr 9, 2020	34888
6	Mar 16, 2020	2921	31	Apr 10, 2020	31998
7	Mar 17, 2020	4031	32	Apr 11, 2020	32509
8	Mar 18, 2020	6096	33	Apr 12, 2020	27550
9	Mar 19, 2020	7199	34	Apr 13, 2020	25177
10	Mar 20, 2020	8287	35	Apr 14, 2020	25438
11	Mar 21, 2020	10044	36	Apr 15, 2020	25758
12	Mar 22, 2020	11631	37	Apr 16, 2020	31600
13	Mar 23, 2020	11400	38	Apr 17, 2020	30394
14	Mar 24, 2020	12266	39	Apr 18, 2020	27706
15	Mar 25, 2020	14839	40	Apr 19, 2020	27968
16	Mar 26, 2020	19434	41	Apr 20, 2020	26247
17	Mar 27, 2020	20705	42	Apr 21, 2020	25040
18	Mar 28, 2020	20820	43	Apr 22, 2020	31353
19	Mar 29, 2020	21389	44	Apr 23, 2020	32513
20	Mar 30, 2020	21729	45	Apr 24, 2020	33970
21	Mar 31, 2020	23146	46	Apr 25, 2020	33454
22	Apr 1, 2020	28664	47	Apr 26, 2020	27947
23	Apr 2, 2020	30157	48	Apr 27, 2020	24202
24	Apr 3, 2020	31728	49	Apr 28, 2020	23595
25	Apr 4, 2020	32524	50	Apr 29, 2020	28877
			51	Apr 30, 2020	32135

The distribution of the bi-grams of the entire period is illustrated with line graph (see Fig. 5) in standardized frequency.

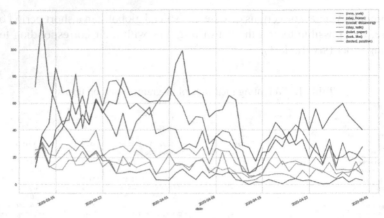

Fig. 5. Line graph of top bi-grams. The graph further shows that, the bi-grams "toilet, paper", "new york", "stay, home" and "social, distancing" were significantly appearing in the user tweets during the period of analysis. The representation of the bi-grams directly reflected in the daily infection cases (see Table 2).

In order to investigate if these bi-grams represent any form of relationship; a correlation matrix is drawn (see Fig. 6).

	('new', 'york')	('stay', 'home')	('social', 'distancing')	('stay', 'safe')	('toilet', 'paper')	('look', 'like')	('tested', 'positive')
('new', 'york')	1.000000	0.576665	0.234518	0.447875	-0.289862	0.115788	0.286081
('stay', 'home')	0.576665	1.000000	0.583136	0.704050	-0.007011	0.405950	0.470456
('social', 'distancing')	0.234518	0.583136	1.000000	0.692495	0.399627	0.519615	0.491683
('stay', 'safe')	0.447875	0.704050	0.692495	1.000000	0.374037	0.680062	0.645623
('toilet', 'paper')	-0.289862	-0.007011	0.399627	0.374037	1.000000	0.612151	0.493341
('look', 'like')	0.115788	0.405950	0.519615	0.680062	0.612151	1.000000	0.516037
('tested', 'positive')	0.286081	0.470456	0.491683	0.645623	0.493341	0.516037	1.000000

Fig. 6. Correlation matrix of top bi-grams.

The correlation matrix shows that, the bi-gram "new york" demonstrates positive correlation with the bi-grams "stay, home", "social, distancing", "stay, safe", "look, like", and "tested, positive". Meaning when the tweets of "new york" has increased, the bigrams of the "stay, home", "social, distancing", "stay, safe", "look, like", and "tested, positive" have also increased to a certain degree in user tweets. Based on the relationship, such bi-grams can be defined as early indicators as they also reflect the real life infection cases.

5.1 Cluster Analysis

The unsupervised cluster analysis with K-Means revealed that, the terms are almost similarly distributed over the clusters (see Fig. 7) and it is insignificant to infer any patterns, as there was no cluster that separates the keywords from the other clusters.

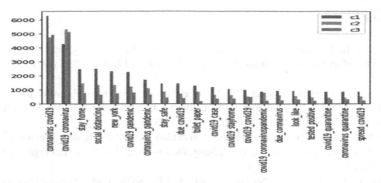

Fig. 7. Distribution of terms in clusters

5.2 Interpretation

In order to validate the claim of early indicators, a correlation matrix is drawn combined with the infection cases to see if they form any relationship (see Fig. 8).

	('new', 'york')	('stay', 'home')	('social', 'distancing')	('stay', 'safe')	('toilet', 'paper')	('look', 'like')	('tested', 'positive')	cases
('new', 'york')	1.000000	0.576665	0.234518	0.447875	-0.289862	0.115788	0.286081	0.189282
('stay', 'home')	0.576665	1.000000	0.583136	0.704050	-0.007011	0.405950	0.470456	-0.367009
('social', 'distancing')	0.234518	0.583136	1.000000	0.692495	0.399627	0.519615	0.491683	-0.673739
('stay', 'safe')	0.447875	0.704050	0.692495	1.000000	0.374037	0.680062	0.645823	-0.520035
('toilet', 'paper')	-0.289862	-0.007011	0.399627	0.374037	1.000000	0.612151	0.493341	-0.776816
('look', 'like')	0.115788	0.405950	0.519615	0.680062	0.612151	1.000000	0.516037	-0.588470
('tested', 'positive')	0.286081	0.470456	0.491683	0.645823	0.493341	0.516037	1.000000	-0.555811
cases	0.189282	-0.367009	-0.673739	-0.520035	-0.776816	-0.588470	-0.555811	1.000000

Fig. 8. Correlation matrix of bi-grams combined with cases

The correlation matrix shows that, only the "new york" has positive correlation with the infection cases. All the other bi-grams showed negative correlation with the infection cases. It is therefore, possible to infer that, once the infection cases were already widely recognized, users in social media tend to discuss these indicators keywords in less volume, as there was nothing new to warn of the disease spread.

5.3 Limitations

This study is limited to the range of time period. Additional studies need to carryout for the validation of the results by spanning the periods with higher and lower infection cases.

6 Conclusions

The study reveals that, the discussion in Twitter directly reflects the real life infection cases in the early stage of the pandemic. The significant terms are defined as early indicators, which demonstrate linear relationship among them. Health authorities can consider using such indicators in the early stage of pandemic and take pre-cautionary measures to mitigate future infection cases.

References

1. Bloom, D.E., Cadarette, D.: Infectious disease threats in the twenty-first century: strengthening the global response. Front. Immunol. **10**, 549 (2019). https://doi.org/10.3389/fimmu.2019.00549
2. Hui, D.S., et al.: The continuing 2019-nCoV epidemic threat of novel coronaviruses to global health — the latest 2019 novel coronavirus outbreak in Wuhan, China. Int. J. Infect. Dis. **91**, 264–266 (2020). https://doi.org/10.1016/j.ijid.2020.01.009
3. Sohrabi, C., et al.: World health organization declares global emergency: a review of the 2019 novel coronavirus (COVID-19). Int. J. Surg. **76**, 71–76 (2020). https://doi.org/10.1016/j.ijsu.2020.02.034
4. Qingchun, L., Zhiyuan, T., Natalie, C., Ali, M.: Detecting Early-Warning Signals in Time Series of Visits to Points of Interest to Examine Population Response to COVID-19 Pandemic, vol. 9, p. 12 (2021). https://doi.org/10.1109/ACCESS.2021.3058568
5. Chew, C., Eysenbach, G.: Pandemics in the age of twitter: content analysis of tweets during the 2009 H1N1 outbreak. PLoS ONE **5**(11), e14118 (2010). https://doi.org/10.1371/journal.pone.0014118
6. Anderson, R.M., May, R.M.: Infectous Diseases of Human. Oxford University Press, Oxford (1991)
7. Kim, S., Seo, Y.B., Jung, E.: Prediction of COVID-19 transmission dynamics using a mathematical model considering behavior changes. Epidemiol Health, e2020026 (2020)
8. Samui, P., Mondal, J., Khajanchi, S.: A mathematical model for COVID-19 transmission dynamics with a case study of India. Chaos, Solitons Fractals **140**, 110173 (2020). https://doi.org/10.1016/j.chaos.2020.110173
9. Fu, K., Zhu, Y.: Did the world overlook the media's early warning of COVID-19? J. Risk Res. **23**(7–8), 1047–1051 (2020). https://doi.org/10.1080/13669877.2020.1756380
10. Mavragani, A.: Tracking COVID-19 in Europe: infodemiology approach. JMIR Public Health Surveill **6**(2), e18941 (2020). https://doi.org/10.2196/18941
11. Yin, R.K.: Case Study Research and Applications: Design and Methods, 6th edn. SAGE, Los Angeles (2018)
12. New COVID-19 Cases Worldwide (2021). https://coronavirus.jhu.edu/data/new-cases
13. Smith, S.: Tweets using hashtags associated with Coronavirus (2020). https://www.kaggle.com/smid80/coronavirus-covid19-tweets/version/12?select=2020-03-12+Coronavirus+Tweets.CSV
14. Trends in Number of COVID-19 Cases and Deaths in the US Reported to CDC, by State/Territory (2021)
15. Jones, K.S.: A statistical interpretation of term specificity and its application in retrieval (1972)

Bringing Innovation to the Medical Sector Through the Role of the Medical Designer: A Study on the Error Factor of Pump-Syringe Devices and a UX/UI Design Proposal

Mario Bisson⬭, Stefania Palmieri⬭, Alessandro Ianniello⬭,
and Margherita Febbrari(✉)

Politecnico di Milano, Milan MI 20158, Italy
{mario.bisson,stefania.palmieri,alessandro.ianniello}@polimi.it,
margherita.febbrari@mail.polimi.it

Abstract. The elements examined in the research concern the theme of the error factor of medical devices, the theme of usability and the theme of the user experience. The results of the research concerns a project proposal that directly addresses the configuration and functionality of the actual device in use by proposing an innovation of the device itself, in terms of functionality, use and interaction, with the ambition to enhance its User Experience, as well as to participate in the discussion regarding the proposal of an improved perception of this device. Furthermore, the present contribution starts by considering and analizing the elements that compose the sanitary scenario, today and in its evolutionary tendencies, evidencing the elements that should be implemented to tackle the construction of an integrated and spendable model. This should be able to bridge both the world of the research and of the technological progress, and the actual design of the innovations in the medical field, formalizing and proposing the verticalization of such elements in the so renamed figure of the "Medical Designer".

Keywords: Design for medical devices · Medication errors with infusion pumps · UX of care

1 Introduction

1.1 Context Delineation

The world reality is showing us an unprecedented population growth [1] and making us living in the period that Brynjolfsson and McAfee [2] call "The Great Transformation" or Schwad "Fourth Industrial Revolution"[3]. Technological growth and societal evolution have resulted in higher standards of quality of life, which combined with the insurable phenomenon of population growth, has brought to an increasing in the number of elderly population [4]. These elements require the concern and the predisposition to face these transformations correctly [5]. In fact, an increment of the elderly population would mean an increment of chronic pathologies and consequently an increment of the demand for

C. Stephanidis et al. (Eds.): HCII 2022, CCIS 1654, pp. 397–405, 2022.
https://doi.org/10.1007/978-3-031-19679-9_50

care [6]. What the Covid-19 pandemic has highlighted is the inability of our current healthcare systems to meet the rising demand for care: for example, it has shown how our healthcare system is "hospital-centric" and not inclined to the "territorialization" of care [7], or, how it is necessary to digitalize part of the medical and/or bureaucratic procedures in order to further streamline the systems that articulate the logistics of care [8]. In addition, technological growth and innovations [9] pose questions about the type of interaction and/or relationship that will be increasingly delineated between man and machine so that it should be configured as an enhancing relationship [10].

The outlined scenario brought us to the definition of the figure of the "medical designer", a designer who can deal with multidisciplinary innovation [11] in the medical sector, looking for areas of application of new technologies, building innovative bridges [12] between the medical system and / or medics and the patient (Fig. 1).

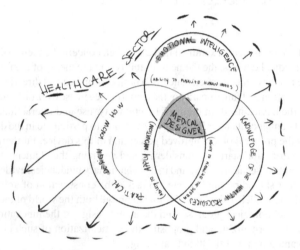

Fig. 1. The role of the the new "medical designer" (draw by Margherita Febbrari)

One of the primary activities of this research was the delving into the medical sector by assessing the state-of-the-art in terms of availability and configuration of products. In particular, the activity focused on the investigation of the medical device market and on the production of a benchmark. The elements examined through the research concerned the theme of the medical devices' error factor, the theme of usability and the theme of the user experience. The study "Medical error-The third leading cause of death in the US" [13] reported more than 250,000 deaths per year caused by medical errors, placing the topic of human factor error, also driven by the bad design of the devices, as the third leading cause of death in America (Fig. 2) .

Among the error rates of this sector, an interesting design opportunity regarding the world of Syringe Infusion Pumps was highlighted. In fact, these infusion devices, starting from the paper published by the FDA, "U.S. Food and Drug Administration. White Paper: Infusion Pump Improvement Initiative" [14] and according to several studies including the study "Risk of Medication Errors With Infusion Pumps - A Study of 1,004

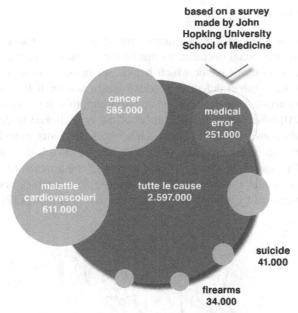

Fig. 2. The impact of medical error by "Medical error-The third leading cause of death in the US" (reworked image)

Events From 132 Hospitals Across Pennsylvania" [15] underscore their profound need for innovation.

The proposed project in this research directly addresses the configuration and functionality of the actual device in use, and proposes an innovation of the device itself, in terms of functionality, use and interaction, with the ambition to enhance its User Experience, as well as to participate in the discussion regarding the proposal of an improved perception of this device.

2   The Issue of Medical Devices

2.1   The Design of Medical Devices

The theme of the de-hospitalisation of care [16], which concerns, among the various aspects to be considered [17], the movement of medical devices towards the patient's home, generates important challenges for the world of design and proposes new spaces for intervention, starting from the consideration of further themes such as the level of safety of medical devices, aspects of usability, accessibility, inclusiveness for the end user.

To corroborate what has been affirmed, various international regulations can be cited, that introduce the theme of usability (new European regulation on Medical Devices, which came into force on 26 May 2021, CEI EN 62366 Medical Devices, or the FDA guidance: Applying Human Factors and Usability Engineering to Medical Devices [18]), as fundamental in the sector of interest; furthermore, that focus attention on the theme of safety, risk and error.

2.2 The Error Factor

The relevance of the phenomenon of human error needs to shift away the 'focus' of the problem from the individual operator, victim of the 'culture of blame', to the clinical practices and the conditions under which healthcare operates in its complexity [19]. Within this topic the issue of defective product design is obviously considered, which does not take into account the needs of the end user and, therefore, requires a paradigm shift. Norman [20] offers an initial definition of the error linked to defective design, arguing that it is the consequence of a mismatch between the mental model of the designer and the mental model of the end user: if the two mental models do not communicate, there is a risk of producing a level of poor usability of the artefact, to the point of the possibility an error could manifest itself. Furthermore, in a complex system, the actual accident is never caused by a single action, but by a series of factors [21] (see Fig. 3).

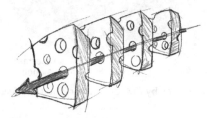

Fig. 3. Accident dynamics illustrated with the Swiss Cheese Model (Image reprocessed by Margherita Febbrari)

In the healthcare sector, the various types of errors do not have a standardised classi-fication [22] for the recognition and definition of adverse states. The medical field, due to various factors, is a context in which accidents can be frequent and very significant.

3 Methodology from Design

The issue of error in medicine requires the design and implementation of strategies to reduce its impact on the system, such as applying an iterative process that moves from macro to micro in a continous cycle, and principles of User Experience design.

3.1 The Iterative Process from Macro to Micro

The iterative process is the design method that considers repeating an indefinite number of cycles in order to achieve desired goals [20]. It consists of four stages in repetition: observation (or design research), ideation (generation of possible solutions), prototyping (from the highlighted solution, development of an initial artifact), verification (that the proposed solution actually solves the problem). The iterative process is set in a context where macro decisions are defined and then move on to micro decisions [23]. What can happen is that by developing project solutions without knowing the user's true needs or, alternatively, by developing aprioristic solutions, problems are generated in the interaction with the end user [24]: people's true needs should be discovered and analysed in detail, i.e. at the micro level; also, the macro decisions that are taken in the preliminary stages of the design process can be subjected to the same iterative review process. The iterative process and the design activity that consider the transition from the macro scenario to the micro scenario differ from the "Waterfall Model" [25], generally more widely used in engineering, which is a design process with linear development, where once decisions have been made there is no turning back, and where the development of the project follows a uniquely top-down path (Fig. 4).

Fig. 4. The iterative model from macro to micro (draw by Margherita Febbrari)

3.2 Usability VS User Experience

The usability of a product is defined on a convergence of the mental schemes of the user and the designer [20]. The designer's role lies in adhering to ergonomic standards and introducing a design component that creates proper communication with the end user. Regarding the requirement of usability, there are general guidelines for the system to be comprehensible and well-designed in terms of efficiency and effectiveness. However, comparing the usability and the User Experience definition, it can be seen that the satisfaction of the user experience is approximated at a first level of the satisfaction within the usability requirements. By comparing the two definitions, contained in ISO 9241–210:2010 and IEC 62366–1:2015, one can come to the conclusion of one fact: through design it is possible to facilitate and control people's actions, reduce the possibility of error and bring about a general aesthetic appreciation. Through design, it is also possible to arouse positive feelings, sensations of 'pleasure', defining what is considered 'the experience' [26] (Fig. 5).

ISO 9241-210:2010 - Definitions	
Usability:	**User Experience:**
The extent to which a system, product, or service can be used by specific users to achieve specific goals with effectiveness, efficiency, and satisfaction in a specific context of use.	The person's perceptions and responses resulting from the use and/or intended use of a product, system, or service. NOTE 1: User experience includes all user emotions, beliefs, preferences, perceptions, physical and psychological responses, behaviors, and realizations that occur before, during, and after use. NOTE 2: User experience is a consequence of the brand image, presentation, functionality, system performance, interactive behavior, and serviceability of the interactive system, the internal and physical state of the user resulting from previous experience, attitudes, skills, and personality, and the context of use. NOTE 3: Usability when interpreted from the perspective of users' personal goals can include the type of perceptual and emotional aspects typically associated with the user experience. Usability criteria can be used to evaluate aspects of the user experience.

Fig. 5. Definitions of Usability and User eXperience from ISO Source.

The term User Experience refers not only to the moment when we actually experience the episode but, also, to memories and emotions, which are at the base of the Emotional Design approach, theorised and described by Donald Norman in the book Emotional Design [27]: the emotional component consists of three levels which are the visceral level, related to appearance and aesthetics; the behavioural level, linked to the pleasure and the effectiveness derived from using a product; and, finally, the reflexive level that revolves around the self-image, the personal satisfaction, and the memories generated by the product. Each level has a different role in communicating with the user, as well as fulfilling different functions in design. Designers not only have to possess and govern transversal knowledge of user-friendliness, practicality, efficiency, usability, inclusivity, [28], marketing methods, materials property, production methods and processes, costs, but they should also be able to add value in terms of emotion and engagement. The term User Experience evokes a more comprehensive and permeating concept for design, because requires the designer to empathize with people's emotions, preferences, perceptions, beliefs, behaviours, responses, and memories, whether they occur before, during or after interaction with a product, service or system.

4 Design of an Innovative Syringe-Pump Device

Despite the extensive application of syringe pumps for drug infusion in the world's major health care settings, as already mentioned, these devices are subject to numerous critics due to their functioning and error rates [14, 15].

To summarize, the possibilities for error in intravenous pump-syringe therapy are essentially of two types, respectively in drug setting and in patients' therapy response.

The product born also from the results of this research innovates the pump-syringe device in terms of usability and perception, through its redesign and the implementation of its functionality. Its innovative features are based on a change of configuration and on the inclusion of an under-used technology in the field: the device automatically monitors the patient's vital parameters and the intravenous drug infusion. Also, the product can recognise the patient's vital state, facilitating the diagnosis, while controlling the correct management of the therapy. From the placement of the device on the patient's arm, non-invasive blood pressure detection, measurement of heart rate, blood oxygenation, and body temperature can be obtained (Fig. 6).

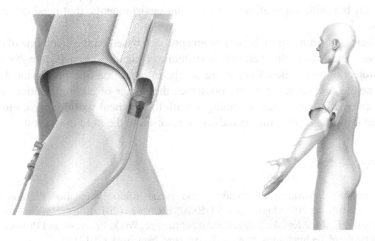

Fig. 6. Explanatory pictures of the new innovative pump-syringe configuration

The applicative scenarios of an intelligent, telemetry-controlled device that considers therapy as a continuum [28] between monitoring vital parameters and drug therapy leads to imagining the device as a catalyser for the technological empowerment of the patients, who can spend their daily life without worrying for the management of their disease. The project upgrades the product's usability, perception and UX, while reducing the possibility of error. This product should bring back the patients' conditions from a pathological state to a physiological state.

5 Conclusions

Beginning with highlighting the general problem, the incisiveness of human error in the medical field, the research found the design of medical devices to be one of the factors causing the aforementioned errors. The analysis further made clear how a gap exists in the area of interest, to be found in the lack of application of User Experience principles, in favor instead of less innovative concepts, such as the usability of a product, which do not conceive important aspects, such as the perception of the product itself, the emotions that its use may arise and the behaviours it could foster or limit. To demonstrate how an approach based on UX can be extremely effective in overcoming the issues highlighted, a designed product is presented to be understood as a case study, which makes explicit the actual need and opportunity that the introduction of UX can bring to the field.

In the case of the presented product, it is important to note how starting from an innovative operation itself (in terms of configuration, in terms of functionality, in terms of UX) a new design space is predisposed. The definition of a new medical product brought out, or affirmed, the new needs of end-users and gave the possibility to imagine future scenarios of application. For example, the pump-syringe product is a device used for situations where high precision of therapeutic infusion is needed. Still, with an "outstanding" product configuration, in terms of portability and optimisation, functionality and aesthetics, fertile ground is prepared for structuring products with similar characteristics but with applications for different environments, that need delocalized approaches.

The research has thus highlighted how an approach based on the discipline of design can contribute significantly to overcoming systemic criticalities, transforming them into potential project opportunities. Even more so, the introduction of a professional figure who is trained as a designer, but who possesses the means of communication and the horizontal knowledge necessary to dialogue with the medical world, appears to be of fundamental importance in bringing radical innovation to the field of interest.

References

1. United nations, department of economic and social affairs, population division: world population prospects 2019: highlights. ST/ESA/SER.A/423 (2019)
2. Brynjolfsson, E., McAfee, A.: The second machine age: Work, Progress, and Prosperity in a Time of Brilliant Technologies. Norton & company, New York (2014)
3. Nankervis, A., Connell, J., Montague, A., Burgess, J. (eds.): The Fourth Industrial Revolution. Springer, Singapore (2021). https://doi.org/10.1007/978-981-16-1614-3
4. OECD. Health at a glance: OECD indicators 2005, OECD Publishing, Paris (2005)
5. UN general assembly, transforming our world: the 2030 agenda for sustainable development, 21 October 2015, A/RES/70/1. (2015). https://www.refworld.org/docid/57b6e3e44.html. 20/05/2021
6. Colombo, F.: Health systems are still not prepared for an ageing population, OECD Insights blog (2015). http://wp.me/p2v6oD-23V
7. Tibaldi, V., Ricauda, N.A., Rocco, M., Bertone, P., Fanton, G., Isaia, G.: "L'innovazione tecnologica e l'ospedalizzazione a domicilio", in Recenti progressi in Medicina 104 (5), pp. 181–188 (2013)
8. EPHA, European Public Health Alliance.: Digital Solutions for Health and Disease Management, Digital Health Discussion Paper. (2017)
9. Saxon, L.A.: Benvenuti nell'era della medicina digitale, in Wired, 84 (spring), pp. 81–85 (2018)
10. Cerati, F.: Perché l'intelligenza artificiale non potrà mai sostituire il medico. Il sole 24 ore: domenica 15 luglio p. 9 (2018)
11. Minder, B., Lassen, A.H.: The designer as facilitator of multidisciplinary innovation projects. Des. J. 21(6), 789–811 (2018). https://doi.org/10.1080/14606925.2018.1527513

12. Demers-Payette, O., Lehoux, P., Daudelin, G.: Responsible research and innovation: a productive model for the future of medical innovation. J. Responsible Innov. **3**(3), 188–208 (2018). https://doi.org/10.1080/23299460.2016.1256659
13. Makary, M.A., Daniel, M.: Medical error, the third leading cause of death in the US. BMJ **353**, i2139 (2016). https://doi.org/10.1136/bmj.i2139(2016)
14. U.S. food and drug administration. white paper: infusion pump improvement initiative (2010)
15. Taylor, M., Jones, R.: Risk of medication errors with infusion pumps, a study of 1,004 events from 132 hospitals across Pennsylvania (2019). https://doi.org/10.33940/biomed/2019.12.7
16. Landers, S.H.: Why healthcare is going home. New Engl. J. Med. **361**(18), 1690–1691 (2010)
17. Committee on the Role of the Hman Factors in Home Health Care. Health care come home: the Human Factors. The National Academies Press, Washington (2011)
18. FDA, U.S. Department of health and human services, food and drugs administration: applying human factors and usability engineering to medical devices (2016)
19. Tartaglia, R., et al.: Adverse events and preventable consequences: retrospective study in five large Italian hospitals. Epidemiol. Prev. **36**(3–4), 151–161 (2016)
20. Norman, D.A.: The Design of Everyday Things, Basic Books, New York.: Norman, p. 2013. Revised and expanded edition by Norman, MIT Press, Cambridge, MA, D.A., The design of everyday Things (1986)
21. Reason, L.: Human Error, Cambridge University Press, Cambridge (1990). second edition, EPC,edito, Rome. (2014)
22. Institute of Medicine (IOM): To err is Human: Building a Safer Health System. National Academic Press, Washington, DC (2000)
23. Resende, A.E., Castro, S.I., Mascia, F.: From micro to macro dimension: an inverted way to think solution in designs. In: Bagnara S. Tartaglia, R., Albolino, S., Alexander, T., Fujita, Y. (eds.) Proceedings of the 20th Congress of the International Ergonomics Association (IEA 2018). IEA 2018. Advances in Intelligent Systems and Computing, vol. 824, pp. 1761–1766 (2019). https://doi.org/10.1007/978-3-319-96071-5_181
24. Tosi, F., Pistolesi, M.: Home care design for Parkinson's disease, FrancoAngeli (2022)
25. Cooper, R.G., Winning at new products: accelerating the process from idea to launch. Basic Books; Perseus, Reading Mass. Great Britain (2001)
26. Pistolesi, M.: Desing & Usabilità in ambito sanitario. FrancoAngeli (2021)
27. Norman, D.A.: Emotional Design - Why We Love (or Hate) Everyday Things. Basic Civitas Books, New York (2004)
28. Bandini Buti, L.: Ergonomia Olistica: il progetto per la variabilità umana, pp. 251–226. FrancoAngeli, Milano (2008)
29. Antonovsky, A.: The salutogenic model as a theory to guide health promotion. Health Promot. Int. **11**(1), 11–18 (1996)

Empathic Smart Conversational Agent for Enhanced Recovery from Abdominal Surgery at Home

Fidel Díez Díaz[1]([⊠]) [iD], Ignacio Pedrosa[1] [iD], Pelayo Quirós Cueto[1] [iD],
and Pedro Álvarez Díaz[2]

[1] CTIC Centro Tecnológico, Gijon, Spain
ctic@ctic.es
[2] TESIS Medical Solutions, Gijon, Spain
palvarez@tesis.es

Abstract. Fast-track Surgery entails the application of perioperative procedure measures and strategies aimed at patients with the purpose of reducing secondary stress, enhanced patient's recovery and decrease complications and mortality.

Although surgical checklists/guidelines have been implemented worldwide, individual compliance is highly variable and dependent on the ways in which it is introduced, its perceived relevance and surgical team engagement. Moreover, existing checklists/guidelines are queried usually on plain text, and without any real-time clinical support. On the other hand, conversational agents are increasing in healthcare applications, although HCI has been relatively timid in embracing this modality as a central research focus. Considering these issues, the perioperative period stands as a great scenario in which a conversational agent can be considered.

An innovative conversational agent with empathic abilities considering both Natural Language Understanding and emotional user recognition and to provide an interactive tool to patients at home to undergo surgery in a user-friendly way is shown.

By designing an anthropomorphic agent, a friendly interaction is promoted on plain text and speech-to-text. Considering user interaction, the agent is able to provide an empathic reply both by plain text or in text-to-speech mode. Moreover, user's emotions are considered while interacting to provide a feedback based on five emotions (happiness, sadness, surprise, anger, worry). Furthermore, interactions such as greeting, looking at the user, waiting and requesting information are also included.

An empathic smart conversational agent has been developed providing an innovative tool to improve perioperative UX, diminish surgery cancelation, and enhance surgical rehabilitation.

Keywords: Artificial Intelligence · Smart conversational agent · Personalized care

1 Introduction

1.1 Smart Solutions Facing Ageing Population and Emerging Challenges

Most developed countries are undergoing a process of population aging, which, according to many projections, will continue and intensify over time [1]. The number of people 60 + is expected to double by 2050 and triple by 2100 [2]. This situation poses demanding social and economic challenges, including healthcare.

Addressing these emerging health and population challenges, the World Health Organisation (WHO), European health care institutions and a large number of professional and scientific organizations have long advocated the need to shift the emphasis of public policies on care towards a major transformation process.

Person-centered approaches to health and care organization can enable citizens to take more responsibility for their health, improve their well-being and quality of care, and contribute to more sustainable health systems. Thus, empowering individuals is an absolute priority and a key prerequisite for sustainable global development and the improvement of the overall quality of life of the population.

In this context, information technologies, and particularly the appearance of so-called intelligent or smart solutions, paved the way for the endowment of tailored services adapted to the needs and expectations of each individual.

Particularly, Artificial Intelligence (AI), became enabler of a varied array of services, devices and applications aimed at radically improving people's lives [3]. Focusing on healthcare, AI implementation is a compelling vision that has the potential in leading to significant improvements for achieving the goals of providing real-time, better personalized and population care in a cost-efficient way [4].

Conversational Agents on Healthcare
Advances in speech recognition, natural language processing (NLP), and AI have led to the increasing availability and use of conversational agents. Over the last two decades, a solid body of evidence has shown the potential benefits of using conversational agents for health-related purposes. However, most of these agents only allowed for constrained user input (e.g. multiple-choice options), not being able to understand natural language input [5]. Advances in machine learning, particularly in neural networks, have endorsed more flexibility and complex dialogue management methods [6]. In light of their expanding capabilities, conversational agents have the potential to play an increasingly important role in healthcare, assisting clinicians during the consultation, supporting users with behavior change challenges, or assisting patients and elderly individuals in their living environments.

Analysis of Facial Information for Healthcare Applications
The ability to effectively communicate emotion is essential for adaptive human function and affective computing, a discipline that develops devices for detecting and responding to user's emotions [7], is a growing research area in HCI [8].

Among all technologies involved, computer vision has reached very high accuracy in the automatic recognition of facial expressions [9]. In particular, healthcare frameworks which include an emotion recognition module, have been introduced to provide suitable solutions for: Ubiquitous healthcare systems, Computational diagnosis and assessment of mental of facial diseases, Machine-Assisted Rehabilitation, and Smart Environments. And, from an overall point of view, computer emotion identification may provide humans with a satisfying human-computer connection interface [8].

Nonetheless, it emerges that face analysis aimed at health applications is still in an embryonic state. There is indeed an untapped potential linked to new methods of computer vision and machine learning that are currently narrowed to academia [10].

1.2   Human-Computer Interaction on Healthcare

Research and design regarding HCI in healthcare domains highlights interaction concepts focused on safety and efficiency [11]. In this sense, most of the analysis focuses on "classic" or "first-wave" HCI theories [12] are not generally applied in healthcare [11], and UX has received limited attention in practice and research [13].

1.3   Fast-Track Surgery as a Rising Demand

Among existing health conditions, those involving some sort of surgery demand an important cooperation between practitioners, but especially prior preparation and adherence to a set of clinical recommendations that allow not only the surgery to be carried out, but also an adequate recovery afterwards. In particular, Multimodal surgical rehabilitation, also known as Fast-track Surgery, is especially interesting since it involves these aspects and there is increasing demand for major surgery in high risk patients.

Fast-track Surgery entails the application of perioperative procedure measures and strategies aimed at patients who are going to undergo a (emergency) surgical procedure to reduce secondary stress caused by the surgical intervention and thus achieve enhanced recovery of the patient and decrease complications and mortality [14, 15].

Bearing in mind all the above, this is a great scenario to introduce innovative solutions also considering specific evidence-based approach per procedure.

1.4   Objective

The approach of this paper is two-fold: 1) to present an innovative conversational agent with empathic abilities considering both Natural Language Understanding and emotional user recognition; 2) and to provide an interactive tool to patients at home to undergo surgery in a user-friendly way empowering citizens through the use of digital tools for self-managed health. Considering this goal:

On the one hand, NLP has been extensively refined in recent years in several sectors. However, in the healthcare context, such tools have been scarcely available to date mainly due to the complexity of handling highly sensitive data.

On the other hand, the emotional analysis of the user while interacting with a conversational agent via facial analysis is also an innovative feature considering the ongoing evolution of these systems in this field. Although the use of computer vision technology for facial recognition in the healthcare sector is beginning to spread, the main interest currently lies in its use for secure patient identification.

Finally, providing a user-friendly tool, suited to the way in which a large part of the population currently interacts and offering continuous support in all the phases of a clinical intervention, is an innovative proposal aimed at strengthening personalized medicine and the implementation of novel tools based on the eHealth approach.

2 Methodology

2.1 Identifying Unmet Clinical Opportunities

Fast-track Surgery implies a new approach to the management and care of surgical patients that aims to ensure that people arrive at the operating theatre in the best possible condition, that they have the finest possible treatment and that their subsequent recovery is as effective as possible by reducing surgical complications and improving the perceived quality of life. However, to date, this protocol was based on guidelines queried in an autonomous way by the user, usually on plain text, and without any real-time clinical support. So, this paper has brought ICTs to offer a tool for continuous and immediate evidence-based support to the patient in a protocolled manner by an innovative conversational agent with empathic abilities. Thus providing an interactive tool to patients at home to undergo surgery in a user-friendly and continuous way aligned with current trends and preferences of the population.

To achieve this goal, healthcare practitioner's involvement was a cornerstone: 1) to provide the expert knowledge to the agent, 2) to understand their performance and the benefit it brings to them and 3) to convey appropriate instructions for use to patients.

2.2 Concept Solution Design

Interaction Interface Module

Structure based on the use of a procedural standardized guide on Fast-track Surgery that allows the system to guide the system according to a set of Q&A designed using expert knowledge. Thus, this guide will consist of a series of consecutive questions with a decision tree structure.

Interaction may take two types on the part of the user: plain text and speech-to-text. The starting point will be the question to be asked to the user by the smart conversational agent. Once the question has been asked, the user proceeds to the spoken answer. This audio is collected and processed by the Speech to Text model and transcribed into text. Finally, this text is used to apply Natural Language Processing (NLP) techniques and the agent is able to provide an empathic reply both by plain text or in text-to-speech mode.

Camera/Face Recognition Module

This module receives as input data the sequence of images captured via webcam and provides a single output data corresponding to the emotion detected at each moment. An intelligent model provides the functionality to the emotion recognition module. For each image or sequence of images, the face is detected and the facial characteristics necessary for the interpretation of the emotional state are extracted.

Smart Conversational Agent

The agent provides a complementary graphical interface for providing friendly feedback to enrich the patient's experience during consultations. A detailed design process was carried out to finally reflect an anthropomorphic character skilled to convey a range of emotions or states according to the appropriate reaction at any given moment.

A 3D design was chosen, as it is more popular among social users, focusing on Low Poly graphic style. The design of the 3D model of the agent involved the definition of its shapes (geometry) in a CAD modelling tool, the addition of rigging structures to define the movements of specific geometric parts to create animations, its texturing and the addition of these elements in a graphic engine that enables interactions with the model to be programmed (see Fig. 1).

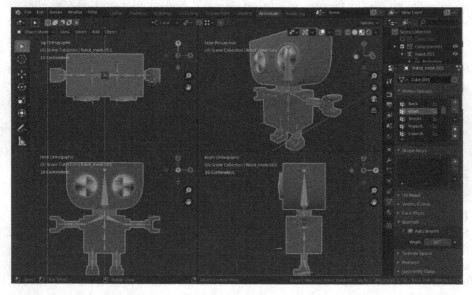

Fig. 1. Agent rigging designed on blender software

A humanoid skeleton was used as a base, to which the different lengths and positions of the bones were adjusted and a series of animation tracks were defined in Blender to depict the emotions. The model was exported to FBX format supported by the Unity framework in its 2019.4.7 version, where the required components were built to code the agent's performance. Finally, different visual feedback was coded to provide a good user experience.

3 Results

Once the different modules were developed and integrated, a smart conversational agent aimed at the intended purpose was obtained, which showed positive results in terms of functionality, thus providing an innovative tool to support patients and clinicians in the perioperative period of Fast-track Surgery.

Regarding HCI, a conversational agent with empathic abilities considering both Natural Language Understanding and emotional user recognition was achieved. The agent shows an anthropomorphic but neutral design to facilitate friendly interaction while avoiding any bias related to particular preferences.

Based on the user's emotional state, the smart conversational agent is able to respond to it based on five emotions (happiness, sadness, surprise, anger, worry). Furthermore, interactions such as greeting, looking at the user, waiting and requesting information are also included (see Fig. 2).

Fig. 2. Emotions implemented in the smart conversational agent (From left to right and from top to bottom: neutral, greeting, joy, sadness, fear, query, anger, surprise, disgust)

Testing and validation of the agent showed positive feedback from both practitioners and potential users, highlighting its ease of use, robustness and usability, thus implying a positive user experience.

4 Discussion

An empathic smart conversational agent has been developed providing an innovative tool to improve perioperative UX on Fast-track Surgery. This proposal represents an innovative continuum of care at home that allows for proactive patient support, empowerment and self-care.

From a technical point of view, it is worth highlighting, on the one hand, its unique approach, as the vast majority of conversational agents are mainly for leisure or companionship purposes and focus on text-to-text. The proposal showcases the ability of technology to establish natural communication, allowing the generation of non-verbal interaction means such as gazes, facial expressions or gestures. These technologies combined with NLP play a major role in improving human-machine interaction, especially with low digitally literate users or users with cognitive or motor disabilities. Therefore, this human-centered approach is deemed to ease its applicability within care-oriented home environments.

In addition, due to its human-centered design and its ability to recognize emotions, it provides additional qualitative information on the emotional state. This is a remarkable feature in comparison with existing solutions, as it provides a comprehensive approach to personal health, being able to provide prompt feedback to enhance both the user's physical state and mood.

Furthermore, it contributes a tool that can offer evidence on the use of Artificial Intelligence to reduce the burden on health services and optimize surgical interventions, improve self-management of health and incorporate tools aimed at digitizing health.

As a result, it is assumed this solution promotes a simple and user-friendly HCI, with high adherence and regular use, proving the great potential of this type of innovation for integrated health care and person-centered care, using technology at its core. In the short term, it is therefore expected that AI solutions and, in particular, conversational agents will experience significant growth in the healthcare sector, improving the quality of life of the population and optimizing healthcare resources.

References

1. Gu, D., Andreev, K., Dupre, M.E.: Major trends in population growth around the world. China CDC Wkly. **3**(28), 604 (2021)
2. United Nations: world population prospects. department of economic and social affairs population division. United Nations, New York (2017)
3. Dwivedi, Y.K., et al.: Artificial Intelligence (AI): multidisciplinary perspectives on emerging challenges, opportunities, and agenda for research, practice and policy. Int. J. Inf. Manage. (2019). https://doi.org/10.1016/j.ijinfomgt.2019.08.002
4. Ahmed, Z., Mohamed, K., Zeeshan, S., Dong, X.: Artificial intelligence with multi-functional machine learning platform development for better healthcare and precision medicine. Database **2020**, 1–35 (2020)
5. Laranjo, L., et al.: Conversational agents in healthcare: a systematic review. J. Am. Med. Inf. Assoc. **25**(9), 1248–1258 (2018). https://doi.org/10.1093/jamia/ocy072
6. Radziwill, N., Benton, M.: Evaluating quality of chatbots and intelligent conversational agents. arXiv Prepr, 1704 (2017)
7. Picard, R.W.: Affective Computing. MIT Press, Cambridge, MA (1997)
8. Ali Alnuaim, A., et al.: Human-computer interaction with detection of speaker emotions using convolution neural networks. Comput. Intell. Neurosci. **2022**, 7463091 (2022). https://doi.org/10.1155/2022/7463091
9. Dong, C.-Z., Catbas, F.N.: A review of computer vision-based structural health monitoring at local and global levels. Struct. Health Monit. **20**(2), 692–743 (2021). https://doi.org/10.1177/1475921720935585

10. Leo, M., Carcagnì, P., Mazzeo, P.L., Spagnolo, P., Cazzato, D., Distante, C.: Analysis of facial information for healthcare applications: a survey on computer vision-based approaches. Information **11**, 128 (2020). https://doi.org/10.3390/info11030128

11. Norros, L.: Developing human factors/ergonomics as a design discipline. Appl. Ergon. **45**, 61–71 (2014). https://doi.org/10.1016/j.apergo.2013.04.024

12. Rogers, Y.: HCI theory: classical, modern, and contemporary. Synth. Lect. Human-centered Inf. **5**(2), 1–129 (2012). https://doi.org/10.2200/S00418ED1V01Y201205HCI014

13. Savioja, P., Liinasuo, M., Koskinen, H.: User experience: does it matter in complex systems? Cogn. Technol. Work **16**(4), 429–449 (2013). https://doi.org/10.1007/s10111-013-0271-x

14. Hajibandeh, S., Hajibandeh, S., Bill, V., Satyadas, T.: Meta-analysis of enhanced recovery after surgery (ERAS) protocols in emergency abdominal surgery. World J. Surg. **44**(5), 1336–1348 (2020). https://doi.org/10.1007/s00268-019-05357-5

15. Cheung, C.K., Adeola, J.O., Beutler, S.S., Urman, R.D.: Postoperative pain management in enhanced recovery pathways. J. Pain Res. **15**, 123 (2022)

Visualization of Parkinson's Disease Tremor for a Telemedicine System

Tingyu Du[1] , Takashi Komuro[2](✉) , and Keiko Ogawa-Ochiai[2]

[1] Graduate School of Science and Engineering, Saitama University, 255 Shimo-Okubo, Sakura-Ku, Saitama City 338-8570, Japan

[2] Department of General Medicine, Hiroshima University Hospital, 1-2-3 Kasumi, Minami-Ku, Hiroshima City 734-8551, Japan

komuro@mail.saitama-u.ac.jp, okeiko22@hiroshima-u.ac.jp

Abstract. In this paper, we propose a method for visualizing Parkinson's disease tremors using augmented reality to support telemedicine. The proposed method utilizes OpenPose to extract body joints and connects the coordinates of every two adjacent joints with straight lines in the video. We made the angular changes of adjacent joints representing tremors, with each angle's latest 64 data points as a set of signals. The color and thickness of the lines are changed by using the frequency of the maximum amplitude and the strength of tremors. We created a prototype system and conducted an experiment to evaluate the proposed method. The experimental results showed significant color and thickness changes in the lines where tremors occurred. Moreover, we sent the video with the visualization results to a doctor, and the doctor found this method to be useful in visualizing the characteristics of tremors.

Keywords: Parkinson's disease · Telemedicine · Augmented reality

1 Introduction

In recent years, countries worldwide have been faced with the issue of aging populations and age-related diseases. Due to limited mobility, older people may not receive a timely diagnosis. Telemedicine makes it possible to facilitate patients and simultaneously improve the efficiency of doctors' diagnoses. Parkinson's disease is a neurological disorder that mainly affects middle-aged and older people, with tremors being a prominent early symptom in over 70% of patients. However, limited transmission speed causes poor video quality, making it difficult for doctors to detect tremors in telemedicine during early consultation.

There have been some studies for diagnosing Parkinson's disease based on hand movement. Some of them require patients to wear acceleration sensors on their hands [1–3]. Another approach is to recognize hand postures using two cameras installed in a fixed environment [4]. There are also some studies based on body motions. Some of them focus on patients' gait, such as the characteristics of the gait speed and stride length [5–8]. There is also a study that extracts the full-body movements from a video using

© The Author(s), under exclusive license to Springer Nature Switzerland AG 2022
C. Stephanidis et al. (Eds.): HCII 2022, CCIS 1654, pp. 414–419, 2022.
https://doi.org/10.1007/978-3-031-19679-9_52

a deep learning-based pose estimation algorithm to detect Parkinson's disease motions [9].

Existing studies are mainly aimed at automated diagnosis. In this paper, we propose a method for visualizing Parkinson's disease tremors using augmented reality to support telemedicine. The proposed method extracts human body poses from a video to visualize tremors in Parkinson's disease. This method is expected to allow a doctor to identify the characteristics of tremors.

2 Method for Visualizing Tremors from Video

Telemedicine is performed via video between a doctor and a patient. To provide maximum convenience, we only use a camera rather than sophisticated devices such as motion sensors. In early clinical consultation, the frequency and amplitude of tremors are important indicators to assess the severity of tremors. Therefore, the proposed method visualizes the frequency and amplitude of tremors in a video.

2.1 Human Skeleton Extraction Using OpenPose

In order to extract body postures, we utilize OpenPose [10], an open-source real-time method for pose estimation. This technology combines computer vision and deep learning to automatically detect and output two-dimensional coordinates of human joints, including the body, foot, hand, and facial key points. An example of OpenPose output is shown in Fig. 1.

Fig. 1. An example of OpenPose output.

Using OpenPose, we can obtain the coordinates of 25 key points of the body. Parkinson's disease tremor symptoms usually begin in the distal part of the upper limb. As the disease progresses, tremors develop in the lower limb of the same side, and tremors in the head or neck also occur. Therefore, we select 14 of the 25 points included in these parts, and the system calculates angles between every two adjacent joints as shown in Fig. 2.

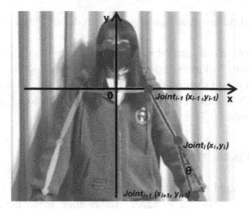

Fig. 2. Calculation of the angle of two adjacent joints.

2.2 Frequency Analysis

The frequency of tremors in Parkinson's disease usually lies in the range of 3–8 Hz. Therefore, the fast Fourier transform is applied to each angle's latest 64 data points as a set of tremor signals, which can be regarded as a short-time stationary signal, to analyze the frequency domain characteristics.

In a band of 3–8 Hz, we obtain frequencies of maximum amplitude. The sum of the squared signal amplitude values at each frequency is calculated, as shown in Eq. 1, where n indicates the number of frequency components.

$$S = \sum_{n=n_{3Hz}}^{n_{8Hz}} |X[n]|^2 \tag{1}$$

As the video is being processed frame by frame, the positions of body joints jump around the actual positions, which causes jitters in the positions. We analyze the amplitude of jitters at each frequency and subtract the average amplitude from the amplitude at each frequency when processing the tremor videos.

2.3 Visualization Using Augmented Reality

We use straight lines to connect the coordinates of the selected adjacent joints extracted by OpenPose. The color of lines indicates the frequency of the maximum amplitude of tremors, and the thickness of lines indicates the strength of tremors.

The data in the 3–8 Hz band are used to change the parameters of the lines to enable visualization. First, the frequencies are normalized so that 3 and 8 Hz are mapped to 0.0 and 1.0, respectively. As shown in Fig. 3, a colormap is used to obtain the color of the frequency with the maximum amplitude.

3 Hertz   ~   8 Hertz

Fig. 3. The color map used to visualize tremor frequencies.

The sum of the squared signal amplitude values at each frequency in a band of 3–8 Hz is used to indicate the strength of tremors. The higher the strength is, the thicker the line is drawn.

3 Experiment

3.1 Experiment on Parkinson's Disease Patients

We created a prototype system and conducted an experiment to evaluate the proposed method. We invited a Parkinson's disease patient to participate in the experiment. As the patient did not show significant tremors, we asked the patient to simulate left upper extremity tremors. With the patient's permission, we captured a video of this patient and used it to generate visualization results.

3.2 Result

Using the left wrist and the left elbow coordinates as examples, we generated a frame sequence waveform of angular and fast Fourier transform results as shown in Fig. 4. Figure 5 shows the visualization results of tremors in the patient. The patient had apparent tremors in the upper extremity on the left side of the body, and the changes in the lines of that parts were evident in the video.

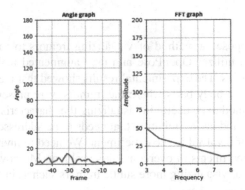

Fig. 4. Frame sequence waveform of angular and fast Fourier transform result.

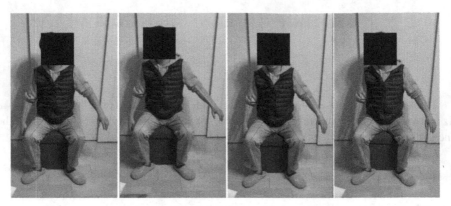

Fig. 5. Visualization results of tremors of a patient.

3.3 Feedback from a Doctor

After the experiment, we sent the visualization results to a doctor and asked her to evaluate the usability and give suggestions from a medical perspective. The doctor's comments are as follows:

- The thickness of the lines on the body skeleton indicating the amplitude of tremors in that part is considered very useful to visualize the characteristics of tremors.
- Since it is difficult to distinguish that only the lines' colors represent the frequency, it might be better if the frequency numbers were also marked next to the lines.
- Early Parkinson's disease development has finer tremors. I hope that this system will be feasible for more subtle tremors such as finger joints in the future.

4   Conclusion

In this paper, we proposed a method of visualizing tremors to support telemedicine. The proposed system utilizes OpenPose and uses augmented reality to visualize the characteristics of tremors. The experimental results showed that the visualization video was able to indicate the body parts where the tremors were present in the video. The doctor found this method to be useful in visualizing the characteristics of tremors.

The proposed method has a limitation that needs to be addressed. We had only one patient and one doctor involved in the experiment. We need to invite more participants and conduct more experiments to overcome this problem. Moreover, we will work on developing a method of visualizing more subtle tremors such as in fingers in the future.

References

1. Bhat, M., Inamdar, S., Kulkarni, D., Kulkarni, G., Shriram, R.: Parkinson's disease prediction based on hand tremor analysis. In: 2017 International Conference on Communication and Signal Processing (ICCSP), pp. 0625–0629 (2017)

2. Kostikis, N., Hristu-Varsakelis, D., Arnaoutoglou, M., Kotsavasiloglou, C.: A smartphone-based tool for assessing Parkinsonian hand tremor. IEEE J. Biomed. Health Inform. **19**(6), 1835–1842 (2015)
3. LeMoyne, R., Mastroianni, T., Cozza, M., Coroian, C., Grundfest, W.: Implementation of an iPhone for characterizing Parkinson's disease tremor through a wireless accelerometer application. In: 2010 Annual International Conference of the IEEE Engineering in Medicine and Biology, pp. 4954–4958 (2010)
4. Pang, Y., et al.: Automatic detection and quantification of hand movements toward development of an objective assessment of tremor and bradykinesia in Parkinson's disease. J. Neurosci. Methods **333**, 108576 (2020)
5. Polat, K.: Freezing of Gait (FoG) detection using logistic regression in parkinson's disease from acceleration signals. In: 2019 Scientific Meeting on Electrical-Electronics and Biomedical Engineering and Computer Science (EBBT), pp. 1–4 (2019)
6. El-Attar, A., Ashour, A.S., Dey, N., Abdelkader, H., Abd El-Naby, M.M., Sherratt, R.S.: Discrete wavelet transform-based freezing of gait detection in Parkinson's disease. J. Exp. Theor. Artif. Intell. **33**(4), 543–559 (2018)
7. Bigy, A. A. M., Banitsas, K., Badii, A., Cosmas, J.: Recognition of postures and freezing of gait in Parkinson's disease patients using Microsoft Kinect sensor. In: 2015 7th International IEEE/EMBS Conference on Neural Engineering (NER), pp. 731–734 (2015)
8. Fleyeh, H., Westin, J.: Extracting body landmarks from videos for Parkinson gait analysis. In: 2019 IEEE 32nd International Symposium on Computer-Based Medical Systems (CBMS), 2019, pp. 379–384 (2019)
9. Li, M.H., Mestre, T.A., Fox, S.H., Taati, B.: Vision-based assessment of Parkinsonism and levodopa-induced dyskinesia with deep learning pose estimation. J. Neuroeng. Rehabil. **15**(1), 1–13 (2017)
10. Cao, Z., Hidalgo, G., Simon, T., Wei, S., Sheikh, Y.: OpenPose: realtime MultiPerson 2D pose estimation using part affinity fields. IEEE Trans. Pattern Anal. Mach. Intell. **43**(1), 172–186 (2021)

Management of Electronic Medical Records. Decision-Making Tool. MINSA Hospital Case – Peru

Danicsa Karina Espino Carrasco[1]([✉]) [iD], Moisés David Reyes Pérez[2] [iD],
Luis Eden Rojas Palacios[1] [iD], Carmen Graciela Arbulú Pérez Vargas[1] [iD],
and Alberto Gómez Fuertes[3] [iD]

[1] Cesar Vallejo University, Pimentel, Peru
despinoc@ucvvirtual.edu.pe
[2] Universidad Privada Norbert Wiener S.A., Lima, Peru
[3] Universidad César Vallejo, Trujillo, Peru

Abstract. In the last decade, Peru has made significant progress in the development and implementation of digital technology policies that allow strengthening health information systems in hospitals, turning them into modern institutions that provide health services throughout the world. Country. The general objective of this article is to manage the implementation of the electronic medical records registry in an integrated information system, in order to improve the efficiency of care processes. Specific objective Design a methodological proposal for the management of the EHR in the public hospitals of the minsa of Peru. The design was non-experimental, descriptive level and qualitative approach. The population was made up of health professionals in the area of clinical record management. The sample was made up of the entire population. The following techniques and instruments were used to collect the information: Documentary analysis Instrument: Interview and educational analytical summary (RAE) which were validated through the expert judgment technique, who evidenced the relationship between the objectives set, the categories, the indicators, the items and the response options considering their coherence, relevance and wording. The results obtained show that in order to strengthen the health system, the registration of electronic medical records should be implemented from the first level of care, with powerful, efficient and timely information technology, it has to do with governance, management, infrastructure, financing and most importantly trained human resources willing to face challenges and achieve changes in management, following guidelines in an orderly manner approved by the Ministry of Health (Planning, organization, direction and control). It is concluded that the electronic medical record is a tool that will allow strengthening medical assistance in a timely manner and that, through the interconnection with the different health institutions of the minsa, will help in decision-making in the care provided to the patient.

Keywords: Medical records · Electronic medical records · Decision making · Hospital

C. Stephanidis et al. (Eds.): HCII 2022, CCIS 1654, pp. 420–426, 2022.
https://doi.org/10.1007/978-3-031-19679-9_53

1 Introduction

1.1 Problematic Reality

The quality of care is the application of science and medical technology that is used in a way that maximizes its health benefits without increasing the risks. Health institutions face great challenges in order to determine the level of satisfaction that patients have. Users regarding the service received and thus identify errors and try to implement improvement plans. (Gavilánez 2020).

In the last fifty years, information and communication technology (ICT) has been developed to benefit the health sector worldwide, in order to improve the quality of life of the community and the well-being of people, The medical record is a unique medical record that needs to be standardized and merged to allow doctors to better understand the real condition of patients.

The standardization of medical records has been taken seriously in some countries, including Spain, which despite its territorial expansion and various difficulties has managed to establish a centralized and efficient system. (Gavilánez 2020). The main information systems in eHealth developed and implemented by the General Office of Statistics and Informatics of the Ministry of Health in Peru, have been the registration of the certificate of live birth online, geominsa, take care of your mobile health, telehealth, medical appointments online and his, these policies and advances in the implementation of technology have made it possible to take an important step, to bring the public services of the Ministry of Health closer in a timely and effective manner, strengthening public health management and decision-making. of decisions. (Curioso, 2014) The Peruvian state approves the Regulation of Law No. 30024, the purpose of said Law is to create the National Registry of Electronic Medical Records and establish its objectives, administration, organization, implementation, confidentiality and accessibility; involving health institutions, public, private or mixed, to digitize the medical record, with the purpose of standardizing data, maintaining the record of electronic medical records, ensuring the availability of the clinical record, where it will allow access to the user or their representative legal and health professionals, obtain information on the care provided, likewise, this system will improve the quality of care in health institutions. (Rojas et al. 2015).

In this regard, the hospitals have a software called Galenhos that was made available by the Ministry of Health to all establishments in the regions free of charge, in order to improve the registration of information and improve hospital management processes, each The health institution will make the decision whether to use the software, since there is no regulation or obligation to use it. It has been shown that this software is being used in other areas, but it has not yet been implemented for electronic medical record information., both for the outpatient, emergency and hospitalization areas (Curioso 2014).

Likewise, in the public hospitals of the Ministry of Health, the electronic medical record has not yet been implemented despite the existence of current laws, policies and regulations, as an automated tool, we have made little progress in determining the management and use of this source of information, at present, manual medical records are still being used where they have to be written and most of the time is spent on it, having to dedicate that time to the people who are cared for and favoring their care, in addition, these clinical history documents are lost and deteriorate due to the lack of space in the file area, likewise, it is observed that for many hours people form queues to be able to access an appointment or care, in this regard, the health sector has a greater demand for people who require care, and many times there is a duplication of medical records for each person served.

1.2 Literature Review

Historically, administration has emerged recently, being a science focused on doctrine in the 20th century. Likewise, it has a history of more than a century, the result of the accumulation and participation of different pioneers, economists, politicians and philosophers, who develop and disseminate their hypotheses and works in the area that have evolved over time. Some historical citations from ancient civilizations such as Egypt, Assyria, and Mesopotamia believe that there are leaders who have the ability to plan and guide thousands of workers in their efforts to complete magnificent projects, and these projects continue to this day. Management by results is one of the methods, created by Peter Druker in a work on management by objectives, he explained that his work is based on his own experience, rather than based on administrative discipline. Being a method for managers and subordinates to determine 20 general goals, and use it as a guide to formulate joint goals, specify joint goals, determine the obligations of all and attribute the expected results to the expected results. Both were evaluated. The results will be compared to the planned plan to determine if you have achieved the expected results.

By analyzing the systematic theories of goal management and the different management models that have emerged in history, it is believed that management continuously achieves goals through planning, organization and direction. The management of the clinical history and the management of objectives is a fundamental link, since at the beginning of each period, the establishment of goals under the intervention of managers and subordinates allows efficient and effective management to be achieved because they analyze the goals to reach Likewise, the theory of the system and the management of medical records, is of equal importance because it will work in an interrelated way to achieve certain objectives.

A deep analysis was carried out in different bibliographic sources that support the study. In this regard, research conducted by (Smaradottir et al. 2020), showed that there is a lack of interoperability between digital systems and limited support for teamwork between organizations, resulting in the need for more manual work to maintain the information flow of coordination and planning tools between organizations, proposed a cloud-based health portal, which has shared workspaces, organizations, teamwork functions between health teams and automatic back-end synchronization of information stored, the main importance of this work lies in the proposed principles, which can be transferred to a variety of clinical settings, in which shared medical information can be temporarily accessed. Importance of making decisions and saving lives.

For their part, Mercedes & Ghiglia (2019), state that the promulgation of the health system analyzed in this article differs by more than 20 years, but the implementation of the EHR is not far behind. In Uruguay, through the HCEN project, each provider advanced in the development of electronic medical records at the national level, integrating information from different levels of care, which helps the continuity of the care process. However, to achieve this objective, in addition to the implementation of the EHR, it is necessary to make cultural changes in an organization where users are the axis of all the activities of the organization, to the extent that these aspects are deepened, the necessary synergy to achieve the task of continuity of care. Soto (2019) also concludes that due to insufficient resources in the national MINSA reference hospitals, they constitute problems that require immediate treatment, supplies, the lack of equipment and medicines endangers user care, Peruvian doctors practice medicine with tools of the last century and the ability to treat serious diseases, especially those that require urgent attention, has produced enormous inequalities, poverty, lack or inequality of health care opportunities and bureaucratic obstacles should not be a reason for death in a country of medium and high resources like Peru in the 21st century. On the other hand, (Alarcon-loayza et al. 2019) analyze that the interoperability model approach only reveals ways to access the patient's medical record from anywhere and it must be understood that for the full implementation of the electronic medical record, address other types of aspects of digitalization of medical procedures in the country's health posts. However, (Curioso et al., 2018) argue that it is essential to establish an e-health government with a departmental information system, where it allows the interconnection of medical and health facilities from the primary level of care with more complex institutions, being necessary to strengthen primary care and continue training basic health professionals, including distance training tools, In this regard, (Kharrazi et al. 2018), examined when US hospitals will adopt more advanced features of EHRs, using HIMSS EMRAM data and Bass diffusion models, based on the adoption of the capabilities of EHRs from a paper-based environment (Stage 0) to an environment in which only electronic information is used to document and direct care delivery (Stage 7), they concluded that in 2006, the first year of observation, they showed peaks of stages 0 and 1, since the adoption of electronic health records predates the HIMSS EMRAM, in 2007 it reached stage 2, in 2011 it reached stage 3, in 2014 it reached its peak of the stage 4, this forecast indicated that stage 5 should peak by 2019 and stage 6 by 2026 and extended until the year 2035, US hospitals, are decades away from fully implementing sophisticated applications of decision support and interoperability functionalities in electronic medical records, as defined in Stage 7 of EMRAM however, a significant number of hospitals will not reach EHR Stage 7 maturity by 2035, given no major policy changes. Likewise, (Yen et al. 2017), they proposed a new method for adaptability in health information technology (HIT), this method refers to the adoption and acceptance approach, in which it consists of modifying the existing conditions for achieving consistency, which involves redesigning workflows, training users, and maintaining technology, this method clarifies the factors that promote or hinder the use of HIT and improve quality of care. On the other hand, (Herrera 2020), concludes that the health workers of the Madre Berenice Hospital have demonstrated an excellent level in the organization and management process, demonstrating the ability to coordinate the resources established for the different departments, as an independent tool. to analyze and prevent problems, and comply with the process with the leader, inspire the team and increase productivity, and earnestly implement the set strategy to achieve the goal by finding smart ways to optimize resources.

Objectives. Manage a model for the implementation of the electronic medical records registry in an integrated information system, in order to improve decision-making in MINSA hospitals, Department of Lam-bayeque, 2021.

Design a methodological proposal for the management of EHR in public hospitals in the Department of Lambayeque, 2021.

2 Method

The present investigation called Management of electronic clinical history: tool for decision-making of the Minsa hospitals in the Department of Lambayeque, 2021, is an investigation, which was framed within the qualitative method, (Guba and Lincón 2015), the same that has a vision in the participants to achieve sustainable development through technological innovation. This position underlies the relevance assumed from the hermeneutic paradigm (Taylor and Bogdan 1990, chap.1) which allows explaining and understanding implicit fundamental aspects in decision making (Hernández et al. 2018).

The collaborators of the Sub Management of Information Technology and Computer Processes formed the population that were 4 servers that participate in the electronic government of this commune; also the workers of the associated areas that were a total of 46 people, the population of 46 workers was equal to the sample, therefore there were no sampling techniques. The inclusion criteria considered were: belonging to the municipal entity and working during the research period. The exclusion criteria were: Not working during the research period, and not belonging to areas related to Electronic Government (Fig. 1).

3 Results

Proposal Design

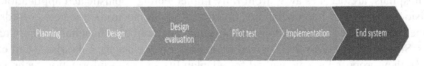

Fig. 1. Phases of the proposal

First Phase: Planning. In this phase, the guidelines for the application of the EHR are established, it is agreed and plans the general structure of its model and the SI requirements. In this phase, the participation of an interdisciplinary group that includes doctors, nurses and professionals of information and documentation systems and engineers of computer systems and programmers. It is important at this stage to establish clear objectives regarding the design and development of the IS, based on relevant requirements to medical care.

Second Stage: Design. Identify the information needs related to the management of the HC, determine guidelines for the organization of clinical information, assess whether the system meets the needs of the entity, develop a risk analysis, development of standards and system applications, determination of guidelines, development of a training plan.

Third Phase: Design Evaluation. Once the prototype of the system has been elaborated, it is implemented. Here are detected problems and are solved to find the final design of the system, likewise, review of the design, detect shortcomings in the system, establish proposals for improvement.

Fourth Phase: Pilot Test. Determine according to the requirements defined in the planning phase the design of the system.

Fifth Phase: Implementation. Implementation of the system is adopted throughout the institution and training is carried out corresponding to all personnel for subsequent handling.

Sixth Phase: Final Design. Present the final design of the system that will allow managing medical records in hospitals in Peru, also, determine the administration of the system, establish which people manage the system, determine the rules and procedures, develop system tools such as controlled languages or thesauri.

4 Conclusions

The present investigation, evidence that it is relevant the adoption of archival processes in the conservation and preservation and management of electronic medical records, in order to regulate the proper use of the information contained therein, since it is verifiedthat the lack of standards that ensure the correct management of the content of clinical records, allows that inconveniences continue to occur, such as information errors in the diagnoses, delays in analyzing information about a patient's care, loss of information, the lack of chronology of the records, the lack of security in the access to confidential information.

The electronic medical record presents problems and it is not fully implemented in all health-providing institutions. The Physicians state that there are some key points to improve in the electronic medical record, among these are finds technical problems as the main ones, such as system crashes, slowness that the system sometimes presents, the redundancy of orders requested by the system, the amount of forms to fill out and the lack of equipment to enter the system.

The implemented proposal has allowed to reduce the waiting time of patients, unify personal information, diagnosis, treatment, medicine and evolution of the disease and the patient.

References

Alarcon-loayza, L., Rubio-ortiz, C., Chumán-soto, M.: Interoperabilidad de Historias Clínicas Electrónicas en el Perú Electronic Health Records interoperability in Peru. **2**(1), 3–14 (2019)

Curious, W., Henriquez-Suarez, M., Espinoza-Portilla, E.: From Alma-Ata to the digital citizen: towards digitized primary health care in Peru. Peruvian Journal of Experimental Medicine and Public Health, **35**(4), 678–683 (2018). https://doi.org/10.17843/rpmesp.2018.354.3710

Gavilanez, N.. *Master's degree in health services management topic: standardization of health clinical records in the city of Guayaquil - 2020*. [Master's Thesis Catholic University of Santiago de Guayaquil] UN Institutional Repository (2020). http://repositorio.ucsg.edu.ec/handle/3317/14221

Guba, E., Lincoln, Y.: Competing paradigms in qualitative research. In: Derman, C., Haro, J., Through the Corners. Anthology of Qualitative Methods in Social Research, pp.113–145 (2015). The Sonora: The Sonora College

Hernández, R., Fernández, C., Baptista, M.: *Metodología de la investigación* (8a ed). México D.F: McGraw-Hill (2018)

Herrera, V., *Administrative management and the quality of medical records in the outpatient clinic of the Madre Berenice Hospital in Guayaquil, 2020* (Master's thesis, César Vallejo University). E-File (2020).https://repositorio.ucv.edu.pe/handle/20.500.12692/7525

Kharrazi, H., Gonzalez, C.P., Lowe, K.B., Huerta, T.R., Ford, E.W.: Forecasting the maturation of electronic health record functions among US hospitals: retrospective analysis and predictive model. J. Med. Internet Res. **20**(8), 1–11 (2018). https://doi.org/10.2196/10458

Mercedes, M., Ghiglia, C.: Electronic clinical history tool for continuity of care. Med. J. Uruguay, **35**(3), 212–217 (2019). https://doi.org/10.29193/rmu.35.3.6

Rojas, L.; Cedamanos, C., Vargas, J.: National registry of electronic health records in Peru I National registry of electronic medical records in Peru. Peruvian J. Exp. Med. Public Health, **32**(2), 395–396 (2015). https://doi.org/10.17843/rpmesp.2015.322.1639

Smaradottir, B., Berntsen, G., Fensli, W.: How to enhance digital support for cross-organisational health care teams? a user-based explorative study. J. Healthc. Eng. 2020 (2020) https://doi.org/10.1155/2020/8824882

Soto, A.: Barriers to effective care in the referral hospitals of Peru's ministry of health: serving patients in the 21st century with 20th century resources. Peruvian J. Exp. Med. Public Health, **36**(2), 304–311 (2019). https://doi.org/10.17843/rpmesp.2019.362.4425

Taylor S. Bogdan, R.: Introduction to qualitative research methods. The Search for Meanings, Mexico: Paidós, 1990, chap. 1 (1990). http://mastor.cl/blog/wp-content/uploads/2011/12/Introduccion-a-metodos-qualitativos-de-investigaci%C3%B3n-Taylor-y-Bogdan.-344-pags-pdf.pdf

Yen, P., McAlearney, S., Sieck, J., Hefner, L., Huerta, R.: Health information technology (HIT) adaptation: refocusing on the journey to successful HIT implementation. JMIR Med. Inform. **5**(3), e28 (2017). https://doi.org/10.2196/medinform.7476

An Integrated Approach to Support Health Monitoring of Older Adults

Michalis Foukarakis[1], Ilia Adami[1(✉)], Stavroula Ntoa[1], George Koutras[2],
Themistoklis Kutsuras[2], Nikolaos Stefanakis[1,3], Nikolaos Partarakis[1],
Danai Ioannidi[1], Xenophon Zabulis[1], and Constantine Stephanidis[1,4]

[1] Foundation for Research and Technology – Hellas (FORTH), Institute of Computer Science,
Vassilika Vouton, N. Plastira 100, GR-70013 Heraklion, Crete, Greece
{foukas,iadami,stant,nstefana,partarak,ioanidi,zabulis,
cs}@ics.forth.gr
[2] OPENIT, Idaiou Androu 9, GR-71202 Heraklion, Crete, Greece
{koutras,kutsuras}@openit.gr
[3] Department of Music Technology and Acoustics, Hellenic Mediterranean University,
GR-71410 Rethymno, Crete, Greece
[4] Department of Computer Science, University of Crete, GR-70013 Heraklion, Crete, Greece

Abstract. The population ageing problem and the need for finding feasible solutions and tools to support elderly people in self-managing their well-being and maintaining their independence and Quality of Life (QoL) have drawn the attention of the research community of multiple disciplines. In particular, mHealth taking advantage of advances in wearables that can track vital signs and smartphone technologies, has shown promising results in this respect in the last decade. Along with the advances in this field, however, a lot of challenges arose, such as safeguarding the elderly persons' privacy and data rights. The proposed system, MyHealthWatcher, is a personalized mHealth system for elderly people which supports wearable sensors and integration with a monitoring platform used by health professionals and caregivers. For the implementation of the system particular emphasis was given to adhering to principles of ethical design, thus allowing users to be in control of their data.

Keywords: mHealth · eHealth · Quality of life · Elderly · Independent living · Monitoring of vital signs

1 Introduction

Population ageing is a well-documented universal phenomenon that has attracted considerable attention from governments, policymakers, and the scientific community around the globe, as the need to come up with innovative solutions that would help ease the socio-economical burdens it can create is more imperative than ever. The number of elderly people has been increasing faster than any other age group globally. The World Health Organisation (WHO) estimates that by 2050, the older adult population will make up 22% of the overall world population [1]. Furthermore, there has been an increase in non-communicable diseases (NCDs), disabilities, and other health disorders among the elderly population around the globe, which has imposed challenges on healthcare systems in both public and private sectors [2]. mHealth, which has been defined by WHO as the "medical and public health practice supported by mobile devices, such as mobile phones, patient monitoring devices, personal digital assistants and other wireless devices" [3], is a field that has produced a significant amount of research on technologies that can support self-care monitoring, chronic disease management, and Quality of Life (QoL) in the past decade. Studies have indicated the effectiveness of the mHealth technology in improving health behaviors, managing chronic conditions of elderly persons, changing their lifestyles and reducing health risks [2]. Also, it has been identified that mHealth has the potential to transform the healthcare system in ageing societies by making healthcare more affordable, accessible, and available [4].

The proposed system, MyHealthWatcher (MHW), is an mHealth system that supports elderly users, as well as their health care professionals and caregivers in monitoring vital signs data captured by wearable devices. The MHW system consists of a mobile application for the elderly, wearable sensors that can be connected to the mobile application, and a Web platform for third persons from the close environment of the elderly, i.e. healthcare professionals, caregivers, and family members. In addition, the system employs a 3D Virtual Character (VC) who acts as an agent for communicating vital signs results and messages from third persons to the elderly.

The system was designed following the User-Centered Design (UCD) principles involving elderly people in all stages of the development process. The results of the user requirements analysis conducted at the earlier stages of the development cycle [15], revealed that there is a wide range of preferences concerning to whom elderly people want to share their health data with and when. Taking into consideration this finding as well as the general principles of ethical design [5] and privacy by design [6], particular attention was given to designing a system in which the decision making on the health parameters to be measured by the system and the people who can have access to these measurements remains in the control of the elderly.

2 Related Work

Nowadays, smartphones are seen as useful and supportive tools for health-related matters, particularly for older adults in assisting them to improve their QoL [7]. They can act as a medium for older users in managing their general well-being and, in a sense, making them more accountable for their own health management [8]. At the same time, mHealth devices such as wearables, utilize embedded sensor technology and self-tracking features to collect, analyze, and present personal health data to the user as a means to support a healthy lifestyle [9]. As a result, through wearables and mHealth smartphone applications, people can perform self-measurements and self-tracking of their health, and maintain their medical records. Due to its increased importance and high potential for sustaining and improving QoL, the domain of mHealth applications has been the subject of much research, however, the focus has not been older adults in most cases.

A major concern, however, with interconnected devices in the Internet of Things (IoT), which has recently received increased attention by the research community, is how to establish interactions that are respectful of user needs and privacy rights [5]. Especially in the context of health-related IoT, the sensitivity of the data stored and exchanged introduces additional concerns and requires careful handling. Key among these concerns is the trade-off between safety and potential violations of personal privacy, which in some cases is seen as a necessary part of aging or managing a chronic illness [10], a compromise, however, that should be avoided to the extent possible. Information privacy and concerns over data control are also common in the case of health IoT, with results from empirical studies highlighting that a balance must be achieved between the desire to control data and enjoying the benefits of services requiring that data [10].

When it comes to older adults, the concern becomes even higher. Older adults feel that privacy threats have a considerable impact on their digital activities, bringing to the foreground the issue of transparency and fear of misuse of private data [11]. In particular with regard to mHealth, older adults often exhibit unwillingness to adopt a solution due to mistrust, perception of high risk, and a strong desire for privacy [12].

In view of the above, MyHealthWatcher aims to leverage modern wearable technologies with a robust mHealth platform for efficient monitoring. At the same time, it adopts a privacy by design approach, putting older adults in control of their data, allowing them to determine which data are collected, if they are shared, and with whom. The adopted approach empowers target users and is expected to alleviate mistrust and foster technology acceptance, thus giving the opportunity to older adults to integrate mHealth technologies into their daily living toward active aging.

3 System Description

The MHW system consists of the following components: 1) a mobile application from which the elderly can view their vital signs measurements captured by the wearable sensors (Fig. 1) and interact with the VC (Fig. 2); 2) wearable sensors that can be connected to the system i.e. the Garmin Vivosmart 4 smartband and the Moodmetric electrodermal activity (EDA) ring (Fig. 3, Fig. 4) [13]; 3) the web-based platform for the healthcare professional that provides the link between the professional and the elderly person whose health is monitored; and 4) a sound-processing subsystem that includes speech recognition and cough detection capabilities [14].

To initialize the MHW mobile application after installation, the user has first to create a personal account and then connect the wearable devices supported by the system. In the personal account setting screen, the user can choose which vital signs he/she wants to activate for monitoring. These options can be changed at any time as necessary. Once the application is initialized and the connection to the wearables is established, the user can then get a continuous flow of the vital signs measurements captured by the sensors of the wearables, i.e. heart rate, blood oxygen, and stress. The user can also choose to activate the coughing detection service, which performs offline acoustic signal processing using recordings captured from the user's mobile device microphone during periods in which the user has allowed the device to record them. Furthermore, screens are provided to allow the user to manually input and store in the application results of other health measurements that cannot be automatically captured by the wearables (e.g. glucose measurements). To enable interaction between the user and a health professional, a caregiver or a relative, the app allows the user to build a contact list of persons with whom they want to share all or a subset of their health data. Users may also receive short messages from their contacts and any personalized advice that health professionals can upload through the MHW Web platform.

Fig. 1. Mobile app main screen

Fig. 2. Mobile app – VC screen

Fig. 3. VivoSmart 4

Fig. 4. Moodmetric ring

In addition to sensor integration, the application offers an ever-present VC, which acts as an assistive agent for the elderly. The elderly can request information from the VC about daily measurements from all the sensors or specific measurements that are of interest and the latest messages from contacts either via verbal commands or via buttons. Speech recognition is processed by the sound-processing component of the system. The information is returned verbally and textually to the user. The VC can be initiated from any screen of the application via a button.

On the other side of the MHW system lies the MHW Web monitoring platform, which allows users with a medical or caregiving background to monitor the vital signs of their contacts (e.g., patients, relatives). The platform accesses a secure time-series database to which the sensors integrated into the mobile application send their measurements. The platform users can easily browse the stored measurements, view information about measurements that have exceeded typical thresholds, view and edit contact information, and send personalized messages to their patients. They can also create health-related content in the form of 'tips' and specify the recipient target group of patients based on ailment category (i.e. patients with cardiovascular disease, patients with diabetes, with high-blood pressure, etc.).

Access to Vital Signs Measurement by a Third Person

As mentioned earlier, one of the main goals of the MHW system is to safeguard the privacy of the elderly users by giving them full authority and control to manage who can have access to their vital signs measurements and when. To achieve this, a two-way linking approach was designed. The first linking approach is initiated by the elderly person via the mobile application (Fig. 5). In this approach, the user sends a monitoring invitation with access privileges to the desired third person (Fig. 6). The invitation is sent as an email. By clicking on the invitation link, the third person is guided to the MHW Web platform to create an account or log in if an account has already been created. Once logged in, the person sees the request for monitoring invitation and can accept it or reject it (Fig. 8). Upon acceptance of the request, the third person is automatically added as a contact in the mobile application of the elderly and can henceforth view the assigned vital signs measurements from the Web platform environment.

Furthermore, recognizing the fact that the well-being status and the health monitoring needs of an elderly person may change over time, it was imperative to provide functionality that allows the user to add or delete a third person or to change the health monitoring access privileges of a specific third person at any moment in time. To do this, the elderly can select the person from the contact list screen and proceed to change the selection of the measurements they have access to or delete their contact altogether (Fig. 7).

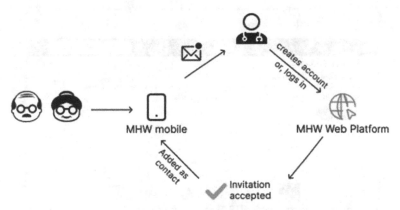

Fig. 5. Mobile user initiates linking to third person workflow

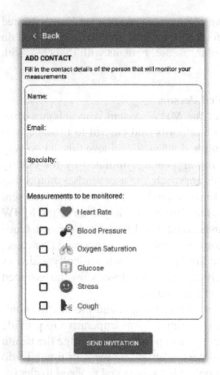 

Fig. 6. Send monitoring invitation to third person – mobile app UI

Fig. 7. Deleting contact or editing access privileges of a third person – mobile app UI

Fig. 8. Received notification of request for health monitoring in the MHW Web platform

The second linking approach is initiated by the third person via the MHW Web platform (Fig. 9). In this case scenario, the third party sends a request for monitoring the vital signs of the elderly person via the platform. The elderly receives the request via an email providing them instructions to download and install the MHW mobile application. In this case scenario, the assumption has been made that the elderly has already been informed about the system and has been provided the wearable devices by his/her doctor. From the mobile application, the elderly can accept the request for monitoring sent by his doctor or caregiver. Upon acceptance of the request, the third person is added to the elderly person's contacts list in the mobile application; accordingly, the elderly is added to the list of persons the doctor or caregiver can monitor in the Web platform. In this case scenario, the elderly can still change the access privileges to the data that the doctor has requested and been given access to through the contact edit screen (Fig. 10).

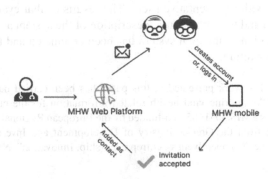

Fig. 9. Third person initiates linking to mobile user workflow

Fig. 10. Send monitoring request to mobile user – Web app UI

4 Conclusion

This paper presented the outcome of MyHealthWatcher, a system which leverages modern advances in wearable sensor technologies and virtual character rendering and animation as well as sound signal processing techniques to develop an integrated monitoring platform for elderly users. Following principles of ethical design, the system has implemented different ways for the elderly to control their data, i.e. initiate sharing of data to third persons, accept/reject access to data requests by third persons, controlling the amount of data third persons have access to at any given moment, and ending access rights previously given to third persons. The system has been iteratively evaluated during the design process with representative users. The results of that evaluation as well as the design approach and the architectural description of the system are reported in [15]. A user-based evaluation of the final system has been conducted and the results will be published in the near future.

Acknowledgments. The work presented in this paper has been carried out in the context of the national project "Monitoring vital health related information for the elderly – MyHealth-Watcher" (grant number MIS 5031685), co-funded by the European Regional Development Fund and national funding from the Greek Ministry of Development and Investments through the Operational Programme "Competitiveness, entrepreneurship, Innovation", NSRF 2014–2020.

References

1. World health organization: world report on ageing and health. World health organization. Retrieved 21 March 2022 (2022). https://apps.who.int/iris/handle/10665/186463
2. Changizi, M., Kaveh, M.H.: Effectiveness of the mHealth technology in improvement of healthy behaviors in an elderly population-a systematic review. mHealth, **3**, 51 (2017). https://doi.org/10.21037/mhealth.2017.08.06
3. WHO Global Observatory for eHealth: mHealth: new horizons for health through mobile technologies: second global survey on eHealth. World Health Organization (2011). Retrieved 22, March 2022 (2022). https://apps.who.int/iris/handle/10665/44607
4. Chiarini, G., Ray, P., Akter, S., Masella, C., Ganz, A.: mHealth Technologies for chronic diseases and elders: a systematic review. IEEE J. Select. Areas Commun. **31**, 6–18 (2013). https://doi.org/10.1109/JSAC.2013.SUP.0513001
5. Baldini, G., Botterman, M., Neisse, R., Tallacchini, M.: Ethical design in the internet of things. Sci. Eng. Ethics **24**(3), 905–925 (2016). https://doi.org/10.1007/s11948-016-9754-5
6. Atlam, H.F., Wills, G.B.: IoT Security, Privacy, Safety and Ethics. In: Farsi, M., Daneshkhah, A., Hosseinian-Far, A., Jahankhani, H. (eds.) Digital Twin Technologies and Smart Cities. IT, pp. 123–149. Springer, Cham (2020). https://doi.org/10.1007/978-3-030-18732-3_8
7. Jeng, M.Y., Yeh, T.M., Pai, F.Y.: A performance evaluation matrix for measuring the life satisfaction of older adults using eHealth wearables. Healthcare, **10**(4), 605 MDPI (2022)
8. Tajudeen, F.P., Bahar, N., Maw Pin, T., Saedon, N.I.: Mobile technologies and healthy ageing: a bibliometric analysis on publication trends and knowledge structure of mHealth research for older adults. Int. J. Human-Comput. Inter. **38**, 118–130 (2022). https://doi.org/10.1080/10447318.2021.1926115
9. Rieder, A., Eseryel, U.Y., Lehrer, C., Jung, R.: Why users comply with wearables: the role of contextual self-efficacy in behavioral change. Int. J. Human-Comput. Inter. **37**, 281–294 (2021). https://doi.org/10.1080/10447318.2020.1819669

10. Mittelstadt, B.: Ethics of the health-related internet of things: a narrative review. Ethics Inf. Technol. **19**(3), 157–175 (2017). https://doi.org/10.1007/s10676-017-9426-4
11. Ray, H., Wolf, F., Kuber, R., Aviv, A.J.: "Woe is me": examining older adults' perceptions of privacy. In: Extended Abstracts of the 2019 CHI Conference on Human Factors in Computing Systems, pp. 1–6. ACM, Glasgow Scotland UK (2019). https://doi.org/10.1145/3290607.331 2770
12. Fox, G., Connolly, R.: Mobile health technology adoption across generations: narrowing the digital divide. Info Syst. J. **28**, 995–1019 (2018). https://doi.org/10.1111/isj.12179
13. Torniainen, J., Cowley, B., Henelius, A., Lukander, K., Pakarinen, S.: Feasibility of an electrodermal activity ring prototype as a research tool. In: 2015 37th Annual International Conference of the IEEE Engineering in Medicine and Biology Society (EMBC), pp. 6433–6436. IEEE (2015)
14. Simou, N., Stefanakis, N., Zervas, P.: A universal system for cough detection in domestic acoustic environments. In: 2020 28th European Signal Processing Conference (EUSIPCO), pp. 111–115. IEEE, Amsterdam, Netherlands (2021). https://doi.org/10.23919/Eusipco47 968.2020.9287659
15. Adami, I., et al.: Monitoring health parameters of elders to support independent living and improve their quality of life. Sensors. **21**, 517 (2021). https://doi.org/10.3390/s21020517

Using Gamified Interactive Experience to Relieve Psychological Pressure in the Post-pandemic Era

Tanhao Gao[ID], Jingwen Tian[ID], Xiaotong Zhang[ID], Dingwei Zhang[ID], and Hongtao Zhou[✉][ID]

College of Design and Innovation, Tongji University, Shanghai, China
7404732@qq.com

Abstract. The COVID-19 Pandemic brought the whole society to a standstill, which has more significant psychological pressure on children and adolescents. Governments, companies, and social groups are trying to confront COVID-19 and social distancing in a gamified way. However, due to fear of the virus and uncertainty about the future, even after the Pandemic is well controlled in physical space, people are still reluctant to stop and play in public areas and are afraid to engage with others because of their internal sense of alienation. From the perspective of urban renewal and environmental design, creating a series of micro-scale design interventions in public spaces to relieve psychological pressure has urgency and relevant significance. This paper analyzes the symbiotic relationship between public art installations and communities. Then discovers the characteristics of public installations based on emotional healing. Furthermore, create two design prototypes to demonstrate more vividly how gamified interactive experience could relieve the mental pressure of the surrounding residents and help them gradually adapt to the new normal life.

Keywords: Gamified interactive experience · Relieve psychological pressure · Playful public installation · Urban micro renewal

1 Sense of Alienation Caused by Covid-19 has More Significant Psychological Impacts on Children and Adolescents

The Covid-19 Pandemic has plunged the world into a physical and psychological public health crisis, forcing people to stay away from friends and maintain social distancing (Farboodi 2021). Worse still, fear of the Pandemic and uncertainty about the future will put heavier psychological pressure on people, especially children and adolescents (Venkatesh 2020). In the early stages of the COVID-19, the government, scientists, and society have not yet figured out the infectious characteristics of the Pandemic. Children were considered less susceptible to COVID-19 (Daniel 2020). However, when more and more infected children are emerging (Phelps 2020). Society has realized that children and adolescent groups are as susceptible to COVID-19 as other populations (Clemens 2020).

As shown in Fig. 1, Dr. Damien Mo's team from Anhui Mental Health Center used the SCARED analysis (The Screen for Child Anxiety Related Emotional Disorders) on February 13–14, 2020, to collect and analyze a total of 5932 students at home isolation by online questionnaire. Including 4928 (91.4%) primary school students aged 7–12 years, and 464 (8.25%) middle school students aged 13–16 years, 2938 (54.5%) males, and 2454 (45.5%) females. SCARED data showed that 1045 students (19.4%) were in a state of psychological anxiety.

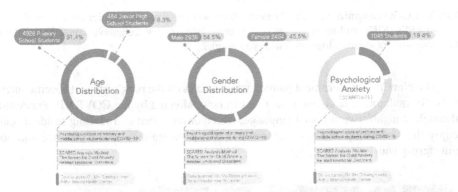

Fig. 1. The SCARED analysis demonstrated the psychological status of primary and middle school students in home isolation. Data source: Dr. Damian Mo's team at Anhui Provincial Mental Health Center. Graphically created by the author.

Due to their immature mental development, children lack the ability to think and recognize independently and have poor tolerance for emergencies (Imran 2020). When a stressful event occurs, excessive stress reactions, such as excessive anxiety and other negative emotions, will seriously affect the psychological state of children (Green 2020). COVID-19 Pandemic and social distancing may not only increase the existing psychological pressure, but even increase the risk of future mental health problems (Wong 2020).

2   Facing the COVID-19 and Social Distancing in a Gamified Way

In this "constant battle" against the entire human immune system, governments, companies, universities, and social groups have spared no effort in finding ways to use game-like methods to convey the seriousness of the Pandemic and the importance of social distancing. In the field of graphic design, Fig. 2 shows the logos of Starbucks, McDonald's, NBA, and other famous companies around the world, which are tailored to the COVID-19 Pandemic and use simple, straightforward, and interesting visualizations to make residents aware of the importance of keeping social distancing.

Fig. 2. LOGO customized for the Pandemic by world-renowned companies such as Starbucks, McDonald's, NBA, and other companies. Source: https://www.designbolts.com/2020/03/24/a-fun-series-of-coronavirus-logos-to-make-you-giggle/.

The New York government painted white circles on the park's grass at specific intervals. By outlining safe social areas that can be unaffected by the COVID-19 Pandemic through straightforward visual language, which ensures that surrounding residents can enjoy the sunbathing and cozy atmosphere while maintaining a safe distance and not interfering with each other (Fig. 3).

Fig. 3. The New York City Government drew the "social distancing" circle on the grass in Domino Park. Source: https://www.designboom.com/design/domino-park-circles-glass-social-distancing-05-19-2020/.

Environmental designers have used playful visualizations to allow residents to enjoy the experience of being outdoors in relative safety. However, due to fear of the Pandemic and uncertainty about the future, even after the Pandemic is well controlled in physical space, people are still reluctant to stop and play in public areas and are afraid to engage with others because of their internal sense of alienation (Zhu 2021). From the perspective of urban renewal and environmental design, creating a series of micro-scale design interventions in public spaces to relieve psychological pressure has urgency and relevant significance (Cheval 2020). Moreover, those interventions could potentially become "urban acupuncture touchpoints" to relieve surrounding residents' psychological pressure (Nassar 2021).

3 Using Gamified Public Art Installations as Touchpoints for Relieving Psychological Pressure

3.1 The Symbiotic Relationship Between Public Art and Urban Communities

Public art and its related fields have a long development history, encompassing architecture's structural logic and thought derivation and combining art's aesthetic and perceptual cognition (Miles 2005). Public art Installations and public spaces are inseparable. Installations need space to show their unique appearance. At the same time, installations can give cultural and artistic connotations and spiritual value in public space (Hall and Robertson 2001). Public space carries a variety of meanings, including conveying meaning, generating meaning, accumulating meaning, spreading meaning, and realizing the perception of people and people, people and society, people and history, people and environment (Suderburg 2000).

3.2 Gamified Public Art Installations Contain the Potential for Relieving Psychological Pressure

The main population for mental pressure relief is the mental sub-healthy residents brought about by the COVID-19 Pandemic, including people of different ages, occupations, and cultural backgrounds. They live in every corner of the city. However, only a few will be willing to go to healing centers or seek help from professional psychologists. Most of them choose to suffer inner alienation alone. Public art installations have some characteristics such as decentralized distribution, repeatability, flexibility, interactivity, and public participation (Cartiere and Willis 2008), which can become emotional healing touchpoints in the community. Allowing residents to interact with the installations and relieve mental pressure in their daily lives, rather than having to make specific trips to a healing center.

Public art installations should seek a delicate balance between "artistry" and "functionality" to empower urban public space. Let public art installations not only have aesthetic considerations but also become a place of communication and understanding between different communities, promoting social innovation.

4 Exploring Design Strategies Through Interdisciplinary Methodologies

This research adopts an iterative process of the analysis-design-prototype-evaluation cycle. This process will be repeated many times to derive more comprehensive and mature research results and design quality. The first step is sorting out and analyzing the literature and practical cases of multiple disciplines such as design, medicine, psychology, and sociology to clarify the reasonable bottleneck and development potential. Then proceed to brainstorming and drafting. After the initial concept process, the design team will produce the first-generation prototype and carry out an internal evaluation. The participants are researchers with a specific disciplinary background. Then, the design team will improve the logic and efficiency of the system according to the evaluation suggestions. After that, a more comprehensive range of people will be invited to partic-ipate in the test again, including different ages, incomes, and educational backgrounds, through questionnaires, observations, and in-depth interviews. This decision-making process will help researchers improve the whole system (Fig. 4).

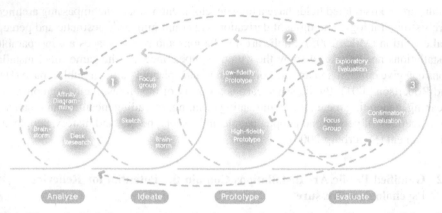

Fig. 4. The analysis-design-prototype-evaluation cycle iterative process. Source: Collaborative course between Tongji University and Aalto University. Graphically created by the author.

5 Design Strategies of Public Art Installations with the Gamified Interactive Experience

5.1 Create Connections with Childhood Memories to Increase Familiarity and Acceptance by Neighborhood Residents

When public art installation is used as touchpoints to relieve the psychological pressure, designers can seek inspiration from traditional culture and combine the original site's cultural, historical, and community characteristics. Furthermore, using innovative design techniques to inherit the community's cultural spirit, which can also bring a sense of familiarity to the residents and evoke their childhood memories to release psychological pressure and heal emotions (Fig. 5).

Fig. 5. "Handshake" emoji in urban villages. Source: https://www.gooood.cn/handshake-emoji-in-urban-villages-china-leaping-creative.htm.

5.2 The Installation Contains Gamified Associativity and Narrativity

The installation with more narrative storytelling makes it more accessible for the residents to understand, accept, and interact with installations more naturally. They pursue integrating urban furniture with places and community atmosphere through narrative techniques, thereby creating an infectious and healing place (Fig. 6).

Fig. 6. Outdoor musical swing installation. Source: https://www.quartierdesspectacles.com/en/about/partnership-productions/work/80/21-balancoires-21-swings-by-daily-tous-les-jours/.

5.3 Simple, Straightforward, and Enjoyable Interactive Experience

Public art installations are scattered irregularly in every corner of the city, and it usually faces passers-by who come and go in a hurry. Therefore, it is unrealistic to require pedestrians to stay for a long time. The interactive experience time should be in several minutes or even several seconds and relieve the psychological pressure of surrounding pedestrians (Fig. 7).

Fig. 7. "Handshake" emoji in urban villages. Source: https://www.gooood.cn/handshake-emoji-in-urban-villages-china-leaping-creative.htm.

6 Design Prototypes for Relieving Psychological Pressure Through Gamified Interactive Experiences

The public art installation intervention site based on relieving mental stress is located on Chifeng Road, Yangpu District, Shanghai. The density of minors and retired elderly groups is denser than in other areas (Fig. 8).

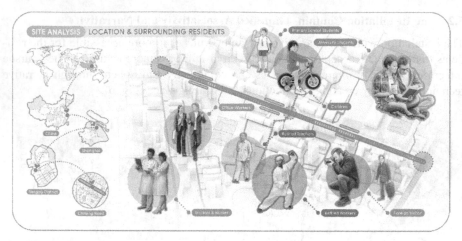

Fig. 8. Analysis of Chifeng Road and community. Graphically created by the author.

The first touchpoint area is located in the first third of Chifeng Road. The thousand paper cranes are a symbol of peace, tranquility, and blessing, originally meant to wish for the speedy recovery of the sick, but later on, they were seen as light objects to convey emotions. The gamified stress relief installation seeks inspiration from cranes and simplifies the structure by beveling the edges or wrapping the spheres around the ends of the cranes to make the installation more suitable for interactive experience and safety. The crane swing allows participants to wrap their hands around the crane's neck or grab the rope on either side of the swing and sway it. The crane swing brings a sense of familiarity to the community, lowering the threshold of understanding while evoking fond memories of their childhood, which is entertaining not only for children but also for adults (Fig. 9).

Fig. 9. The paper crane swing and jumping house installation. Created by the author.

The second contact area is narrow and long, which is suitable as a venue for jumping house games. Jumping house is a popular children's game that carries a generation's fond memories of childhood, arouses positive emotions, and lowers the threshold of understanding. The platform chooses the texture style of linear bricks, which echoes the overall style of the street and the game. The interactive way of jumping house spring installation is to let children jump on it according to the game rules. There are springs at the bottom so that children can get instant interactive feedback when they step on the tablet, adding to the attractiveness of public art installations.

7 Conclusion

Under the impact of the COVID-19 Pandemic, many residents have to suffer from heavy psychological stress. The public art installation with a gamified interactive experience will have the potential to become emotional links between communities and contribute to the cultural cohesion of the surrounding environment, cooperating with various stakeholders to heal and create a better post-pandemic society.

References

Farboodi, M., Jarosch, G., Shimer, R.: Internal and external effects of social distancing in a pandemic. J. Econ. Theory **196**, 105293 (2021)

Venkatesh, A., Edirappuli, S.: Social distancing in COVID-19: what are the mental health implications? Bmj **369**, m1379 (2020)

Daniel, S.J.: Education and the COVID-19 pandemic. Prospects **49**(1–2), 91–96 (2020). https://doi.org/10.1007/s11125-020-09464-3

Phelps, C., Sperry, L.L.: Children and the COVID-19 Pandemic. Psychol. Trauma Theory Res. Pract. Policy **12**(S1), S73 (2020)

Fegert, J.M., Vitiello, B., Plener, P.L., Clemens, V.: Challenges and burden of the Coronavirus 2019 (COVID-19) pandemic for child and adolescent mental health: a narrative review to highlight clinical and research needs in the acute phase and the long return to normality. Child Adolesc. Psychiatry Ment. Health **14**(1), 1–11 (2020)

Imran, N., Zeshan, M., Pervaiz, Z.: Mental health considerations for children & adolescents in COVID-19 pandemic. Pak. J. Med. Sci. **36**(COVID19-S4), S67 (2020)

Green, P.: Risks to children and young people during COVID-19 pandemic. Bmj, **369**, m1669 (2020)

Wong, C.A., Ming, D., Maslow, G., Gifford, E.J.: Mitigating the impacts of the COVID-19 pandemic response on at-risk children. Pediatrics **146**(1) (2020)

Cheval, S., Mihai Adamescu, C., Georgiadis, T., Herrnegger, M., Piticar, A., Legates, D.R.: Observed and potential impacts of the COVID-19 pandemic on the environment. Int. J. Environ. Res. Public Health **17**(11), 4140 (2020)

Nassar, U.A.E.: Urban acupuncture in large cities: filtering framework to select sensitive urban spots in riyadh for effective urban renewal. J. Contemp. Urban Aff. **5**(1), 1–18 (2021)

Miles, M.: Art, Space and the City. Routledge (2005)

Suderburg, E., (ed.): Space, Site, Intervention: Situating Installation Art. U of Minnesota Press (2000)

Cartiere, C., Willis, S. (eds.): The Practice of Public Art. Routledge (2008)

How Service Design Thinking Supports Internal Brand Building Within Organization: A Case Study of Co-design Experiments with Medical Business Domain

Tong Liu and Jun Cai(✉)

Tsinghua University, Beijing, China
t-liu17@mails.tsinghua.edu.cn, caijun@mail.tsinghua.edu.cn

Abstract. This paper aims on the transition of brand awareness in organization through service design thinking. The current local healthcare policy and system are not capable to provide patients with comprehensive service and information. Accordingly, this emerging medical business shows reflection from authorities about brand construction which claims an opportunity to improve service system for user's needs. New methodologies, deriving from service design thinking, are discussed through a long-term case project which demonstrates the progressive actions of implementing an innovative research framework, combined with service design tools and internal branding perspective. The research investigates an exploration of enhancing internal brand building inside organization through empathy and service design thinking, which aims to reach an agreement in manageability with brand communication externally. The discussion focuses on the interaction leading by service designer between employees and decision makers, highlights the form of service design thinking from engaging to rethink empathically. The work concludes that service design thinking is an approach to build brand internally and it will improve efficiency of branding in design research on medical business, as reference to brand strategy, service design or business model innovation.

Keywords: Service design thinking · Internal branding · Co-design workshop · Empathy

1 Introduction

Service design is being developed in various fields with different kinds of deliveries, such as product design, system design and training program design. It shows that service design could be applied to method innovation, product optimization and other aspects [1]. However, one of these capabilities, which is service design thinking, has not been widely discussed in existing research. It has influenced on designers which were contributed to the design process and changed the way of thinking through service design. This study was based on a context that government policies made for service industry which emerged a huge market demand [2]. Since branding is an important topic being talked in different kinds of business field, especially from strategic point of view service corporate is keen to improve brand image through improving service. Service design and brand construction are inseparable nowadays and their relationship has been discussed by some researchers [3]. Some researchers claim that criteria of customers are easily affected by the quality of service that they have already received by the brand [4]. In addition, service design thinking is a new method of cross-interdisciplinary research field which provides a human-centered, holistic, co-creative methodology to develop new services in organization or business [5]. When it comes to the enterprise in early stage, its external brand image is generally not mature enough to support internal branding. This paper investigates an exploration of how internal brand building inside organization could be enhanced through empathy and service design thinking. The study aims to explore the following two questions: 1) How does service design thinking method support internal brand building inside medical enterprises? 2) How could empathy be used to reach a consensus in enterprise? The purpose of this study is to provide a new approach of using service design in practice and to enhance the efficiency of decision-making and internal manageability.

2 Background and Context

Medical business is a particular field compared to FMCG (fast-moving consumer goods) industry because of the higher priority to reliability and security that makes medical branding much more important in the field. The medical industry belongs to the tertiary industry which is service oriented. To highlight the competitiveness, medical enterprises are keen to build strong brand image such as professional and reliable profile. Most of time they are identified as corporate brands [6]. These brand keywords also reveal the medical enterprises are conscious of building relationship rather than only focus on sales motivation. Some researchers claimed that branding is a communicative process among employees, customers and stakeholders. Their interaction is a co-creation of brand experience [7]. Brand building includes two aspects: internal and external (see Table 1). Internal branding has been proven to be a contributing factor in shaping brand value among all the stakeholders of an organization through specific internal procedures [8].

Table 1. An introduction of internal and external branding [9]

Internal branding	Manage the employee's organizational experience
External branding	Deliver a brand consistent message to customer

According to the case study in this article, the traditional theories and skills of internal branding were not sufficient in context, since differentiation and service quality became significantly important. The deep-seated reason for this difficulty was traditional product-dominant logic (P-D logic) is no longer enough to support challenge, but service-dominant logic (S-D logic) provided a new way [10]. It happened with usual and traditional work practice (the magic "4 P's" of marketing) which showed a model of separation would replace by to a model of interaction in the future which S-D logic embraces [10]. Therefore, the value of service design thinking has been proved. Service design could provide a kind of method and tool to understand pain point and balance resources or stakeholders. It shows strong empathic ability whether it comes to user, employee or authority [11].

3 Case Study

In this paper, the case study was focused on a medical business domain. During research process, the main pain point has been found—insufficient internal branding was result in inefficient external branding. Internal and external branding barely formed to a strong brand image. This existing weak brand image was unable to improve brand efficiency due to the deficiency in understanding of brand awareness and communication from employee's point of view.

3.1 Research Process

Service design is an emerging field where provides people with a new way of thinking— service design thinking [12]. It is an innovative approach including human-centered, creative and iterative tools [13]. In service design thinking, the duty of designer is not only to considers user's need, but also to balance stakeholder's benefit and to achieve service sector's purpose [14]. Co-design workshop has explained and proved what the most important steps were for internal brand building—brand ideologies and internal brand communication [9]. In this research, we used service design methodologies mainly to engage both employees and decision makers from medical enterprise in terms of understanding the process of building brand image.

There were three research phases with different purposes including data collection, review and brainstorm (see Table 2). Firstly, 21 groups of users were interviewed to capture their real needs and expectations of brand and service in a variety of scenarios. The 21 groups of users consisted of both patients and doctors who deeply participated in this medical journey. Secondly, after initial analysis of user research and employee research in phase one, the first co-design workshop was held with presence of 18 employees. They were prompted to put their feet into user's shoes and empathize with the pain point by utilizing service design tools called persona and user journey map. At last, the second workshop for senior managers only was held for the theme of co-design as well. The core topic of discussion was specific brand vision and image that they expected to achieve with the help of brand development tools [15], such as "20 Year Roadmap", "The golden circle", "Personality Sliders" and "100 Pic Challenge".

Table 2. Research process and purpose

Research process			Purpose
Data collection	Interview	Observation	
Participator	21 groups of users	Related flow of medical treatment	Understand needs and expectations from different kinds of users
	14 groups of employees	Related working process in different scenarios	
Review	1st workshop	Workshop tools	Empathize with the key users and stakeholders
Participator	18 employees	a) User journey map b) Persona c) Empathy map	
Brainstorm of brand image	2nd workshop	Workshop tools	Discuss specific brand vision and image to engage everyone in the same picture
Participator	7 senior managers	a) 20 Year Roadmap b) The golden circle c) Personality sliders d) 100 Pic Challenge	

3.2 Data Analysis and Evaluation

In research process, we concentrated on empathy during whole medical process rather than one-time action of external branding design. Due to the consistent treatment needs of patients, medical enterprises could benefit from the establishment of stronger external branding which would lead them to a better position in the severe market competition. From the perspective of brand management, the managers were always keen to expand brand value, however, the measures they took may not result in the improvement of brand image that could be perceived by either the users or stakeholders. When we focused on the interior view, it showed that the primary reason was the lack of agreement on brand ideologies, such as brand key words and specific system of brand behavior. This leads to two research questions stated in the introduction part.

Before we answer the research questions, the data revealed three important insights:

1. Brand ideology must achieve consensus. During research process, such as workshop phase, senior managers were not able to arrange an agreement for brand ideology at the beginning of the activity. They have been counting on personal understanding of roughly brand vision to implement marketing and branding. It was easy to overlook the importance of building a guideline.
2. Empathy is a new way to build brand ideology and brand awareness. According to the pain point inside of organization—insufficient internal branding was result in inefficient external branding, external and internal branding were not able to formed. In daily work, employees tended to pay close attention to sales and traditional marketing methods rather than the understanding of users. The loss of perception

in the needs and expectations of users, eventually caused the noticeable issue that they were unable to accurately identify the potential users. Hence, empathy is an important ability leading to practical brand behavior and it also inspires innovation of branding.

3. Internal brand communication is necessary awareness and action inside organization. Through research, we found that most of employees could finish their work but were incapable of spreading the brand culture and image to the external users. Internal brand communication focus on not only regular employees but also senior managers. It is a part of training program as well as a cultural activity to gain sense of belonging and honor for employees [16].

These insights result in the answers of research questions: a) The value of service design thinking in this context was to provide a holistic and empathic perception for the decision-makers. Service design thinking provided a way to assist participators to engage into user's journey. Through different kinds of tools, such as user journey map and persona, participators were able to understand pain point in each medical step and brainstorm solution in each touch-point. Using service design tools was a visualized method to help participators to go through both visible and invisible value. b) Service design thinking helped senior manager or decision maker to reflect and co-work. Reaching a consensus is important but easy to be overlooked by brands, especially in their early development stage. Thus "On the same page" was the only and effective way to expand and improve brand ideology. The co-design workshop is a way to re-build connection [9] with managers and reach an agreement includes brand ideology and brand behavior, so that their motivation can be arranged and achieved. We found the most inspiring part was they were able to share different opinions of brand construction and quickly reach consensus through tools.

4 Conclusion and Future Work

This study intended to propose a new approach of service design to improve internal branding within organization. It was concluded that service design thinking can effectively build brand ideology internally through empathy, thereby potentially affecting organizational decision-making. For enterprises in early stage, it was especially important to put user's shoes on and walk their path. Service design thinking provided the practical co-design tools that helped participators to build a holistic picture of branding, rather than merely focus on the external brand image. Consequently, through service design thinking, there is a possibility to encouraged managers to understand corporate social responsibility and helped them to re-think brand development strategy. This way of thinking is conducive to establishing brand awareness internally. However, service design thinking still needs to be testified through more cases in order to confirm whether it could be effectively applied to other business domains. In the future, by introduction of empathy, service design thinking might be a way to fill up the deficiency of branding research in service corporate (such as medical business domain), as references to brand communication, service design and business model innovation.

References

1. Chowdhury, M.M.H., Quaddus, M.A.: A multi-phased QFD based optimization approach to sustainable service design. Int. J. Prod. Econ. **171**, 165–178 (2016). https://doi.org/10.1016/j.ijpe.2015.09.023
2. Dong-mei, Y.: How to construct the medical enterprise culture. Acad. J. Guangdong Coll. Pharm. **04**, 429–430 (2005)
3. Honglei, L., Jianli, L.: Research on the user experience-based context of business model: toward a value creation & delivery perspective. Foreign Econ. Manag. **42**, 20–37 (2020). https://doi.org/10.16538/j.cnki.fem.20200507.102
4. Kimita, K., Yoshimitsu, Y., Shimomura, Y., Arai, T.: A customers' value model for sustainable service design. In: International Design Engineering Technical Conferences and Computers and Information in Engineering Conference, pp 77–85 (2008)
5. Stickdorn, M., Schneider, J., Andrews, K., Lawrence, A.: This is Service Design Thinking: Basics, Tools, Cases. Wiley, Hoboken (2011)
6. Punjaisri, K., Wilson, A.: Internal branding process: key mechanisms, outcomes and moderating factors. Eur. J. Mark. **45**, 1521–1537 (2011). https://doi.org/10.1108/03090561111151871/FULL/XML
7. Mäläskä, M., Saraniemi, S., Tähtinen, J.: Network actors' participation in B2B SME branding. Ind. Mark. Manag. **40**, 1144–1152 (2011). https://doi.org/10.1016/j.indmarman.2011.09.005
8. Ayrom, S., Tumer, M.: Effects of internal branding and brand-oriented leadership on work-related outcomes. Serv. Ind. J. **41**, 1097–1117 (2021). https://doi.org/10.1080/02642069.2020.1787992
9. Saleem, F.Z., Iglesias, O.: Mapping the domain of the fragmented field of internal branding. J. Prod. Brand Manag. **25**, 43–57 (2016)
10. Helfley, B.: Service Science, Management and Engineering. Springer, New York (2011). https://doi.org/10.1007/978-0-387-76578-5
11. Wetter-Edman, K., Sangiorgi, D., Edvardsson, B., et al.: Design for value co-creation: exploring synergies between design for service and service logic. Serv. Sci. **6**, 106–121 (2014). https://doi.org/10.1287/serv.2014.0068
12. Sun, J., Chu, J.: A new method of product-service system design: product-based, participatory service design method. In: IOP Conference Series: Materials Science and Engineering, p. 12080 (2019)
13. Prestes Joly, M., Teixeira, J.G., Patrício, L., Sangiorgi, D.: Leveraging service design as a multidisciplinary approach to service innovation. J. Serv. Manag. **30**, 681–715 (2019). https://doi.org/10.1108/JOSM-07-2017-0178
14. Patrício, L., Sangiorgi, D., Mahr, D., et al.: Leveraging service design for healthcare transformation: toward people-centered, integrated, and technology-enabled healthcare systems. J. Serv. Manag. **31**, 889–909 (2020). https://doi.org/10.1108/JOSM-11-2019-0332
15. Knapp, J.: The Three-Hour Brand Sprint – GV Library (2017). https://library.gv.com/the-three-hour-brand-sprint-3ccabf4b768a. Accessed 27 Apr 2020
16. Huang, C.Y., Lai, C.H.: Effects of internal branding management in a hospital context. Serv. Ind. J. **41**, 985–1006 (2021). https://doi.org/10.1080/02642069.2018.1491969

Improving User Experience of Assistive Technology Through Codesign and 3D Printing: A Case Study from Cancer Treatments

Alessia Romani[1,2]([✉]) [iD], CarolinaMaria Consonni[1], and Marinella Levi[1] [iD]

[1] Department of Chemistry, Materials and Chemical Engineering "Giulio Natta", Politecnico di Milano, Piazza Leonardo da Vinci 32, 20133 Milano, Italy
[2] Design Department, Politecnico di Milano, Via Durando, 20158 Milano, Italy
alessia.romani@polimi.it

Abstract. Stigmatization negatively affects the quality of life of people living with cancers or chronic diseases. This issue often arises from the use of assistive technology and medical devices during daily activities. These products may create barriers within the social context rather than encourage inclusiveness. This work aims to investigate the role of codesign and digital technologies, i.e., 3D printing, in improving the user experience of assistive technology. The focus is to reduce or eliminate the stigma-related issues and improve the quality of life through codesigned customizable assistive products. A codesign process was carried out within the case study of "B.EAUTYlities", a project focused on the daily life needs of people with cancers or chronic diseases. The design experimentation resulted in the development of two customizable products to manage a central venous catheter for cancer treatments during the user's daily routine, i.e., protecting the catheter during outdoor activities or showers. Two online open-source configurators were developed to allow users to customize their device and manufacture it with low-cost 3D printing processes. Stigma-related issues can be mitigated thanks to the users' active role during the codesign process since their perception and feedback can be considered a key aspect to design new assistive products. Digital technologies and customization can spread accessible assistive technology, as well as open-source principles and distributed manufacturing networks. The user experience may be positively affected not only by the efficacy of these products in fulfilling their primary function but also by their customization, strengthening the emotional attachment to the products.

Keywords: Peripherally Inserted Central Catheter (PICC) · Mass customization · 3D printing · Inclusive design · Open design · Digital fabrication

1 Introduction

Assistive technology represents a powerful way to improve the quality of life of people dealing with impairments and chronic diseases. Its main goal is to enhance the well-being of an individual by increasing the autonomy level within the daily life context.

© The Author(s), under exclusive license to Springer Nature Switzerland AG 2022
C. Stephanidis et al. (Eds.): HCII 2022, CCIS 1654, pp. 450–457, 2022.
https://doi.org/10.1007/978-3-031-19679-9_57

The use of these products is aimed not only to increase a specific functional ability but also to enhance the users' social inclusion [1]. However, the innovation of these products is mainly driven by technology, ergonomics, and their technical feasibility, resulting in a limited users' engagement during the design process. Other key aspects related to the user experience and perception are generally neglected [2, 3]. For instance, the aesthetics of an assistive technology product plays a key role in showing or hiding an impairment and, consequently, in limiting its stigmatization in everyday life. Indeed, an assistive product is often recognizable, threatening the users' daily habits. Its aesthetics acts as a stigmatizing mark that creates social barriers. As a result, these kinds of products are often used for a limited period before their abandonment [4].

Design assumes a crucial role in avoiding the abandonment of assistive devices. Since assistive products can be linked to stereotypes, practitioners have to understand the causes behind the stigmatization in a specific social context, contrasting the abandonment of such assistive devices through stigma-free products [5]. Nevertheless, users' subjectivity and self-perception still represent challenging aspects for inclusiveness. Even if different projects involved the users to design new assistive devices [6–8], only a few works focused on stigma-free solutions [9]. The role of user participation in improving the user experience through the development of stigma-free products has not been adequately defined yet, as well as the contribution of digital tools [8, 10].

This paper explores the role of codesign and digital technologies, especially 3D printing, to foster the inclusiveness of assistive technology products in users' daily habits by improving the user experience. This work shows the results of "B.EAUTYlities", a case study focused on codesign activities for people living with cancers or chronic diseases. First, an overview of the methodology is resumed together with the codesign process. A description of the results is then provided by briefly presenting IF and THEN, the two developed assistive products. Their goal is to help the user to handle a Peripherally Inserted Central Catheter (PICC) for the cancer therapies in everyday life situations. Afterward, the paper discusses the contribution of codesign to reduce the stigmatization and improve the user experience, as well as the role of customization and 3D printing. Thanks to user engagement, codesign may encourage the development of stigma-free solutions by considering aesthetics, user experience, and social acceptance as the main goals. However, the users should be effectively engaged through the design process. Digital technologies can facilitate the use of the products by making them more accessible regardless of the specific disease, widening the perspective. Customization is therefore a key aspect, raising the emotional attachment to the products.

2 Methodology

The activities of "B.EAUTYlities" were carried out in collaboration with "Fondazione Near Onlus", an Italian association of young people with chronic and rare diseases, + LAB, 3D printing lab at Politecnico di Milano, and a medical staff group made by one nurse and two hematologists. This project engaged volunteers from 15 to 35 years old living with cancer or rare diseases in codesign activities for new assistive products.

The principles of codesign, or participatory design, were considered in designing the experimentation. In this work, the researcher took part in the codesign process in first-person as a designer together with the users and the different stakeholders, i.e., the medical staff and the caregivers, since this holistic framework encourages interdisciplinary cooperation and innovation development [11]. Figure 1 depicts the workflow of the overall research. The codesign process was focused not only on the outcome, i.e., the assistive product, but also on the definition of the brief proposals. In detail, the left part of the graph is related to the validation of the briefs for the assistive products, understanding the users' needs, and defining the briefs. The first step corresponds to the detection of those needs, which can be collected during a starting workshop. Further discussion workshops help in understanding the needs, translating them into different briefs. Thanks to further investigations and some specific interviews, the final briefs can be defined and validated. Different stakeholders may be involved in these activities, i.e., the designers, the users, the caregivers, and the medical staff. The right part of the graph focuses on the development of the assistive products for the concept definition and product development phases. After the brief validation, some concepts can be generated and tested through design prototypes and first user trials. Further tests can be done after the concept validation to define the product configuration. Finally, product customization is defined through the development of the corresponding parametric definitions for the product configurators [8]. In this case, the design process is more focused on very specific briefs, hence the codesigners can be limited to the designers and the users, giving to the other stakeholders the role to validate the proposal.

Design prototypes were created by using a fused filament fabrication (FFF) low-cost 3D printer (Prusa i3 MK3S by Prusa Research, Czech Republic) with Polylactic acid (PLA) or Polyethylene terephthalate glycol (PETG) filaments. Flexible silicone was cast into 3D printed molds for water-proof applications. 3D printing gcode files were made with an open-source slicer ("Prusa Slicer" by Prusa Research), and online configurators for customization were designed by using Grasshopper for Rhinoceros (Robert McNeel and Associates, US), and the plugin from ShapeDiver GmbH [12].

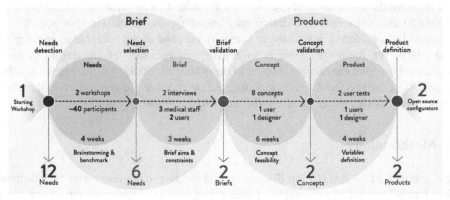

Fig. 1. Main workflow: needs detection from the workshop; needs selection; brief validation; concept validation; product definition; customization. The left part relates to the validation of the brief, whereas the right part deals with the development of the assistive products.

3   Results and Discussion

Different stakeholders were included throughout the codesign process as proper codesigners. They were seen as "experts of their own experiences", providing some expertise that could not be obtained otherwise. Non-hierarchical collaboration between the user and the designer was encouraged in the second part of the workflow to codesign the products. Different activities were used to involve the stakeholders (Figs. 1 and 2).

Workshops were used to detect a set of needs to work on and deepen the debate, and the first screening was done in a non-hierarchical way, according to the participants' feedback. In particular, the request was to think about some needs that the participants may encounter within their user journey. Most of them were related to specific daily habit actions during the cancer treatments (studying during the chemotherapy, managing the intravenous tubes, protecting a central venous catheter during a shower), or the usability of conventional assistive devices (hooking the crutches or transporting them on a bike). Some needs may be felt regardless of a specific disease (transporting a suitcase, opening jars). The desire for stigma-free solutions was shared amongst the participants, and some needs were focused on this aspect (pill organizers or avoiding the stigmatization of cancer treatments during leisure activities). Two additional workshops were then made to narrow down the discussion and discard some needs.

Some interviews were carried out to define and validate the briefs. The users gave some feedback on the perception of alternative existing solutions and their personal experiences related to the issues. Two needs were selected to define the briefs for the next phases: the protection and the stigma mitigation of central venous catheters, especially PICCs. One nurse and two hematologists were interviewed to validate those briefs and collect some critical aspects through two demos, i.e., showing the main parts of a PICC, its dressing, maintenance, use, and side effects from infections or wrong uses.

3D printed prototypes were useful to check the technical feasibility, aesthetics, user experience, and perception. The user and the designer organized short and frequent meetings focused on the definition of the principles and the stigma-related issues. The two concepts were further developed through two simulated user journey tests. This phase was also useful to define the configurator for the customization. The variables were chosen by prototyping some variants through the parametric definition.

Fig. 2. Activities during the codesign workflow of "B.EAUTYlities": (a) needs detection from the workshops, (b) simulation and discussion of the user journey during the interviews, and (c) user tests of the prototypes during the concept development.

Cancer treatments may require mid- and long-term curative therapies administered thanks to intravenous accesses such as Central Venous Catheters (CVCs). Peripherally Inserted Central Catheters (PICCs) represent one of the most used accesses for chemotherapy. PICCs are generally about 50 cm long and can be inserted with local anesthesia into the peripheral veins of the upper arm. Since a PICC ends outside the superior mid-arm through an incision, constant maintenance and dressings are required to avoid complications and failures [13, 14]. The users deal with different issues that may affect their habits. Some activities may be perceived as less comfortable or dangerous and can be restricted by the guidelines provided by the medical staff, i.e., having a shower or a bath. Living with a PICC also represents a challenge for its emotional and psychological impact since it is clearly visible on the arm. Hence, it can generate worry about physical contact and body acceptance, affecting user experience [14, 15].

The two briefs defined in "B.EAUTYlities" resulted in two different products: IF and THEN (Fig. 3). IF helps to handle a PICC during daily life activities (Fig. 3a). It protects the line and its dressing from accidental movements and prevents the removal from its site. Thanks to its holed pattern, humidity can be avoided to limit the infection risks. This product can be 3D printed in PLA with a low-cost small-scale 3D printer. The shape of the 3D printed part can be modified with a standard hair dryer, according to possible drawbacks, i.e., swellings of the arm. The product can be laced as an accessory product rather than an assistive device. THEN aims to protect the PICC during showers and baths (Fig. 3b). It covers the line and its dressing from accidental water during daily hygiene, and it can be adapted thanks to the engraved pattern and its silicone material. The PLA mold of THEN can be customized and 3D printed with a specific online configurator, and a non-toxic silicone can be poured into it. The product can be laced as an accessory. Both products can be customized through an online open-source configurator. The configurator of IF and some variants are visible in Fig. 4.

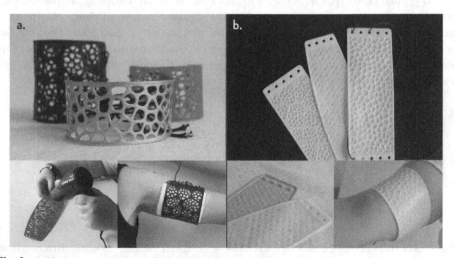

Fig. 3. Assistive products from "B.EAUTYlities": (a) IF (variants, adaptation through a hairdryer and final use); (b) THEN (variants, manufacturing through 3D printed molds and final use).

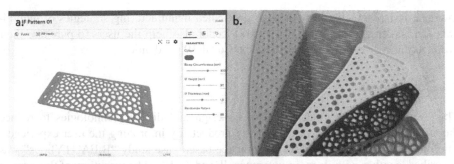

Fig. 4. User customization of IF and THEN: (a) open-source online configurator interface on Shapediver [12] (preview at: https://www.shapediver.com/app/m/if-pattern-01); (b) product variations of IF obtained with low-cost desktop-size 3D printers.

Involving the users in the design process of assistive technology brings several benefits such as designing new products that best fit the specific needs. Even though the acceptance of an assistive product is strongly subjective and depends on different factors, codesign activities can help in reducing the stigmatization thanks to the active role of the users. Considering the user as a codesigner helps in learning from their feedback and expertise. Their contribution can be not only considered for the technical aspects or the usability of a specific product but also the user experience, aesthetics, and perception. Hence, stigma-related issues can be considered at the same level as the technical requirement. In general, users avoid dealing with stigmatizing products, even though their primary functions can be easily accomplished, especially in social contexts. As mentioned before, a product can potentially show or hide a specific impairment [4]. However, some medical devices are difficult to hide. For instance, a PICC cannot be hidden if the user is wearing a t-shirt, causing different behaviors, i.e., wearing a long-sleeved top to cover the PICC despite high temperatures. Designing an assistive product that hides the primary function by highlighting the secondary ones could be a possible way to reduce the stigmatization of those kinds of products by partially associating the user experience of different products. This principle was followed especially for IF. It may be initially recognized as an accessory rather than an assistive device, changing the perception of the product within social contexts. The primary function is hidden by highlighting its secondary functions and moving the focus to the accessory product. Customization could help in increasing the emotional attachment of these kinds of products [7], and this could lead to use IF and similar products for their secondary uses.

The inclusiveness of accessible technology can improve thanks to codesign and digital technology. Codesign processes encourage considering the user perspective during the development of a new assistive product, including the stigma-related issues. Within this project, digital technology contributed to developing customizable products thanks to parametric design. This workflow allowed to create configurators that the users can use to create their variants of IF and THEN. Open Source principles can help in spreading the project to a broader audience of users that can purchase their version on their own [8]. Finally, 3D printing represents the most suitable technology to customize and self-produce these products. Low-cost 3D printers enhance the mass customization of low-tech assistive technology through distributed manufacturing strategies of individuals and maker spaces [16]. This network could also help the users to purchase their products during disruptive events, i.e., the Covid-19 pandemic.

4 Conclusions

This work studied the contribution of codesign and digital technologies to reduce the stigmatization of assistive technology products by improving the user experience. The methodological approach of the practice-based case study "B.EAUTYlities" was described together with its main outcomes, IF and THEN. The workflow of this project allowed to focus on the specific needs, briefs, concepts, and products by involving the users through workshops, interviews, and tests. Thanks to their active contribution, stigma-related issues were considered within the codesign process together with the other requirements. Moreover, the constant and frequent feedback between the user and the designer helped in defining and validating the final products. Their main aim is to support people living with a PICC for cancer treatments during everyday activities. The issues related to social acceptance and stigmatization can be mitigated not only through codesign processes and design strategies, i.e., highlighting the secondary functions, but also thanks to mass customization. Within this framework, open-source principles and digital technologies play a key role in facilitating the spread of accessible and inclusive customized solutions, and low-cost desktop-size 3D printing can pave the way to the distributed manufacturing of assistive products. Customization allows to enlarge the audience of users, i.e., with similar needs and/or impairments, and codesign activities can be carried out by taking this perspective-shifting into account, raising the inclusiveness of the solutions. Although these topics should be further investigated because of users' subjectivity, this work can be considered a pilot study to improve user experience of assistive products through codesign. Future works should: include a broader audience of users, different needs, and social contexts; consider different impairments and/or diseases; refine the methodological workflow by iterating the codesign process.

Acknowledgments. This research received no external funding. The authors would like to thank ShapeDiver GmbH for the support in developing the online configurator, the participants of the workshops, and Valerio Fausti for the participation in the simulated tests.

References

1. McNicholl, A., Desmond, D., Gallagher, P.: Assistive technologies, educational engagement and psychosocial outcomes among students with disabilities in higher education. Disability and Rehabilitation: Assistive Technology, 1–9 (2020). https://doi.org/10.1080/17483107.2020.1854874
2. Fayazi, N., Frankel, L.: Creating emotional attachment with assistive wearables. In: Stephanidis, C., Kurosu, M., Degen, H., Reinerman-Jones, L. (eds.) HCII 2020. LNCS, vol. 12424, pp. 73–88. Springer, Cham (2020). https://doi.org/10.1007/978-3-030-60117-1_6
3. Grieg, J., Keitsch, M.M., Boks, C.: Widening the interpretation of assistive devices – a designer's approach to assistive technology. In: DS 81: Proceedings of NordDesign 2014, Espoo, Finland, 27–29 August 2014, pp. 303–314 (2014)

4. Faucett, H.A., Ringland, K.E., Cullen, A.L.L., Hayes, G.R.: (In)Visibility in disability and assistive technology. ACM Trans. Access. Comput. **10**, 1–17 (2017). https://doi.org/10.1145/3132040
5. Torkildsby, A.B., Vaes, K.: Addressing the issue of stigma-free design through critical design workshops. In: DS 95: Proceedings of the 21st International Conference on Engineering and Product Design Education (E&PDE 2019), University of Strathclyde, Glasgow, 12–13 September 2019. The Design Society (2019). https://doi.org/10.35199/epde2019.11
6. Buehler, E., et al.: Sharing is caring: assistive technology designs on thingiverse. In: Proceedings of the 33rd Annual ACM Conference on Human Factors in Computing Systems, pp. 525–534. Association for Computing Machinery, New York, NY, USA (2015) https://doi.org/10.1145/2702123.2702525
7. Profita, H.P., Stangl, A., Matuszewska, L., Sky, S., Kane, S.K.: Nothing to hide: aesthetic customization of hearing aids and cochlear implants in an online community. In: Proceedings of the 18th International ACM SIGACCESS Conference on Computers and Accessibility, pp. 219–227. ACM, Reno Nevada USA (2016). https://doi.org/10.1145/2982142.2982159
8. Romani, A., Levi, M.: Parametric design for online user customization of 3D printed assistive technology for rheumatic diseases. In: De Paolis, L.T., Bourdot, P. (eds.) AVR 2020. LNCS, vol. 12243, pp. 174–182. Springer, Cham (2020). https://doi.org/10.1007/978-3-030-58468-9_14
9. Romani, A.: Over 5/95: stampa 3D e modellazione parametrica per la personalizzazione di prodotti d'uso quotidiano. Master Degree Thesis in Design & Engineering. Politecnico di Milano (2018)
10. Lee, K.H., Kim, D.K., Cha, Y.H., Kwon, J.Y., Kim, D.H., Kim, S.J.: Personalized assistive device manufactured by 3D modelling and printing techniques. Disabil. Rehabil.: Assistive Technol. 1–6 (2018).https://doi.org/10.1080/17483107.2018.1494217
11. de Couvreur, L., Goossens, R.: Design for (every)one: co-creation as a bridge between universal design and rehabilitation engineering. CoDesign **7**, 107–121 (2011). https://doi.org/10.1080/15710882.2011.609890
12. Shapediver Homepage. https://www.shapediver.com/. Accessed 25 May 2022
13. Bertoglio, S., Faccini, B., Lalli, L., Cafiero, F., Bruzzi, P.: Peripherally inserted central catheters (PICCs) in cancer patients under chemotherapy: a prospective study on the incidence of complications and overall failures: PICC Venous Access for Chemotherapy Delivery. J. Surg. Oncol. **113**, 708–714 (2016). https://doi.org/10.1002/jso.24220
14. Källenius Edström, S., Lindqvist, T., Rosengren, K.: More benefits than problems: a study regarding patients' experiences with a picc-line during cancer treatment. Home Health Care Manag. Pract. **28**, 101–108 (2016). https://doi.org/10.1177/1084822315603678
15. Alpenberg, S., Joelsson, G., Rosengren, K.: Feeling confident in using PICC lines: patients' experiences of living with a PICC line during chemotherapy treatment. Home Health Care Manag. Pract. **27**, 119–125 (2015). https://doi.org/10.1177/1084822314566300
16. Fogliatto, F.S., da Silveira, G.J.C., Borenstein, D.: The mass customization decade: an updated review of the literature. Int. J. Prod. Econ. **138**, 14–25 (2012). https://doi.org/10.1016/j.ijpe.2012.03.002

The Persuasive Impact of Animation in Health Care Sciences Services: A Rhetoric-Based Literature Study

Yi Su[✉]

Tongji University, Siping 1239, Shanghai 200092, China
suyi2018@tongji.edu.cn

Abstract. Animation shows excellent potential for application in the digital era. However, it is shown that many animated videos in the healthcare area are low-quality and do not fulfill the intended function. It indicates that animation's powerful media function is not appropriately used. To investigate the effective use of animation, this paper reviews the literature on animation in the field of Health Care in the Web of Science Core Collection. The study begins by distinguishing animation's persuasive impact from expressive impact and assumes that the persuasive impact has unique nature that affects the reflection of the audience, which is not systematically explored. Next, the article describes the persuasive impact of animation through inducing from the literature. Then, based on rhetoric, the factors of the persuasive impact of animation are analyzed through a framework of Logos, Ethos, and Pathos. The results include: (1) a clarification of animation's persuasive impact and its core audience-centered value, and (2) the nature of the influential factors. The factors include: animation shows the potential to convey knowledge and produce positive emotion, and animation in the healthcare area not only functions as an individual video, but also interacts with other elements, such as other media, participants, and the environment; the trustfulness of content is determined by a group of authors, including the animator, the medical expert, and the audience; and the audience is mentally changed after watching, and they are the important condition to achieve the persuasion, so the development of compelling content requires audience-driven. The study concludes that animation in healthcare is made for a persuasive impact. The effectiveness of persuasive impact is closely related to the audience's condition, requiring the creation concerning related factors. The finding inspires people who make or use animation to understand the purpose and choose an appropriate method clearly.

Keywords: Persuasive impact · Animation · Rhetoric · Logos · Ethos · Pathos · Audience-centered

1 Introduction

The Web of Science database has a continuously increasing sum of literature on animation in the Health Care research area. Unlike animated cinema films and TV serials,

© The Author(s), under exclusive license to Springer Nature Switzerland AG 2022
C. Stephanidis et al. (Eds.): HCII 2022, CCIS 1654, pp. 458–465, 2022.
https://doi.org/10.1007/978-3-031-19679-9_58

animation applied in the health care field is not for entertainment. It is a communication tool between the health caregiver and receiver, such as being used to inform consent (Baris and Ozturkmen 2019). Animation has vivid visual tools for digital communication. But problems follow.

On the one hand, animation has been proved to be capable of playing the role of a health caregiver to educate the patients effectively; on the other hand, paradoxically, many animated videos on video websites on the theme of healthcare education are low-quality. It indicates that the traditional manner of animation filmmaking seems not consistently applied to practical scenarios.

What is the difference between the animation in application scenarios and film art scenarios? What makes animation not applicable to the audience? With these questions, the author browsed the literature from the Web of Science database under the Health Care Sciences Services research area. Although many studies involve impact on the audience, the author noticed essential differences in the connotation of *impact*. One type of impact is *expressive impact*, which refers to the effective communication of information through the effective functioning of the medium. The impact includes an increase in knowledge, understanding, and knowledge-based decision-making. The other category is persuasive impact, which refers to the premise that information is effectively communicated, resulting in a change in the mental status of the audience and subsequently influencing behavior. The latter is essential in health care scenarios where animation is used to intervene in health care receiver's behavior and improve the scientific actions and decisions.

Based on the above, the *persuasive impact* of animation emerges. It is presented in the literature. However, it is not systematically identified in its nature and factor.

Assumes that the vague understanding of the persuasive impact leads to the inappropriate use of animation. This paper will (1) screen the research on animation in the health care area and distinguish animation's persuasive impact from expressive impact. Next, the article describes the persuasive impact of animation through inducing from the literature. Then, based on rhetoric, the factors of the persuasive impact of animation are analyzed through a framework of Logos, Ethos, and Pathos. The inspiration from the results is discussed. The conclusion will help health caregivers and artists eliminate the shackles of past experiences and use animation effectively in the present and future.

2 Method

2.1 Research Strategy

This paper searches the articles with *animation* as the keyword in the Web of Science Core Collection database and limits the research area to Health Care Sciences services. It obtains a total of 643 documents. The following articles were screened out: (1) if animation is not the research object, for example, it is only mentioned in the research of measurement tool (Oh and Song et al. 2021) or measurement tool (Moh and Bangali et al. 2022); (2) if animation is included as the secondary part of the object, for example, as a part of multimedia in the dissemination of medical knowledge (Yeom and Cho 2019; Wynne and Nolte et al. 2022); (3) if the object is animation technology development (Silar and Polak et al. 2019; Stuij and drossaert et al. 2020); (4) if the object is current situation research, such as online health knowledge animation quality research or social health promotion activity research (Silar and Polak et al. 2019; Stuij and Drossaert et al. 2020).

The remaining articles show the impact of animation. According to the above, core articles are defined on persuasive impact. The findings from the other literature are used openly.

2.2 Concept Framework

The conceptual framework of this paper is constructed based on the Rhetoric theory of Aristotle, which is classical in explaining the means of persuasion. Based on Rhetoric, three factors determine persuasion: Logos which refers to 'the logical argument set out in the text,' Ethos, which refers to 'the trustworthy character of the speaker,' and Pathos which refers to 'the emotional effect created by the speaker and text on the audience or reader.' It is pointed out that the three factors apply to all 'speech situations' (Aristotle 2007). Rhetoric has been influential since ancient Greece. It has been used to explore design activities. Logos, Ethos, and Pathos are transformed into the practical, desirable and usable nature of human-made things (Buchanan 2007). Animation is designed with the author's intention of communication to be restricted by the three factors.

The following works are implemented: (1) describe and summarize the performance of the persuasive impact of animation on an audience; (2) discuss the characteristics of Logos, Ethos, and Pathos; (3) integrate and discuss the nature of animation as a persuasive tool and the inspiration.

3 The Nature of the Persuasive Impact of Animation in Health Care Context

3.1 The Expressive Impact and the Persuasive Impact

Some researchers explore whether animation effectively conveys information, such as teaching skills (Ghavami and Samadi et al. 2022) or presenting information with dynamic images in digital tools (Wiemker and Bunova et al. 2022). These findings confirm expressive impacts, which indicate the effectiveness of media expression function. The impact is knowing or understanding some knowledge. Other researches present the mental and behavioral status after watching animation. For example, improving knowledge, skills, and confidence improves self-management after general surgery (Kang and Gillespie et al. 2022). It can be understood as a persuasive impact. Persuasion is achieved when the viewer's behavior and mental status are changed as intended by an argument (Dubov 2015). Persuasive impact relies on successive expressive impact when information is understood. The difference between expressive and persuasive impacts is that persuasive impact involves the audience's mental status and behavior change as intended.

Achieving expressive impact is an important goal of cinema and TV animated film art. Since the late 19th century, the rich experience of artistic animated filmmaking has conceived outstanding works. Expression is author-centered and allows to evoke diverse understanding. Just as E. h. Gombrich said: "There is no such thing as art. There are only artists." (Gombrich 1999) The persuasive impact reflects the audience-centered value and aims to evoke a specific response from the audience. The difference in goals between the two determines the difference in methods. The persuasive impact is essential to the effectiveness of animation in the digital era. If not distinguished with expressive impact, it may lead to animation not being made inappropriately and not applicable to the audience.

Thus, the persuasive impact is based on the information being understood, focusing on the mental status and behavior of the audience. The persuasive impact is audience-centered. What kind of mental status and behavior it will produce is related to the audience's situation. Distinguish the persuasive impact of animation from expressive implications, and understanding its nature is vital to using it efficiently.

3.2 Picturing the Persuasive Impact

When animation is used as a persuasive tool, the authors organize virtual artificial motion pictures into a whole to present an argument. The persuasive impact is reflected in the mental reflection and behavior after the information is accepted. Persuasive impact demonstrates changes in mental status and behavior when the information is well received.

At first, the first manifestation of persuasive impact is that the audience understands what the animation explains. The advantages of animation are that it makes the content catch attention, easy to understand, and comfortable to watch. It produces positive emotions, and Kayler's research confirms that viewers find it comfortable and easy to learn by watching animation, thus helping to relieve anxiety (Kayler 2021), and is feasible in improving knowledge to broad groups of patients on understanding (Kayler 2020). Therefore, animation shows a reasonable degree of inclusiveness compared to text.

Secondly, some mental status is intentionally triggered. This is expressed as the audience thinks based on the visual content being conveyed, forming various psychologies such as attitude, motivation, confidence, trust, fear, etc. The following mental statuses are different for different individuals. In Kayler's study, animation positively impacts decisional self-efficacy (Kang 2022).

Third, the audience is expected to take further action driven by mental status. According to Banerski, Abramczuk, and Biele, Fear triggered by the threat shown in the animation is an important factor that constitutes Self-Protection Motivation (Banerski 2020) since it confirms that the animation-supported education application increases the individuals' knowledge, self-efficacy, and behavior concerning foot care (Dincer 2021).

The above literature proves the existence of Persuasive impact. It contains the relationship between the audience's psychology, behavior, and animated image. This echoes the value of audience-centeredness and indicates that animation can not only convey information but can also be used as a tool to influence the thoughts and behaviors of people. The discovery of the persuasive impact of animation is the basis for a better study and use of it, requiring researchers to readdress the traditional approach of animated filmmaking, expand the goal from author-centered to audience-centered, and explore the factors that influence persuasive impact.

3.3 A Rhetorical Perspective of Persuasive Factors

(1) Logos

According to Aristotle, Logos refers to 'the logical argument set out in the text' (Aristotle 2007); it is presented as a rational structure. Richard Buchanan suggests that Logos relates to the manner of the art of making; it is the nature of usefulness as an artificial product (Buchanan 2007). The Logos of animation is the manner of filmmaking that organizes the visual elements into a visual product.

The symbolic dimension of animation includes the representation of fictional space (image) and timeline (narrative). It can represent both abstract and realistic images in the literature, motion graphics (Kim 2020), and human-liked character (Krieger 2021). Usually, animation is combined with other media, such as sound, text, and static images (Kayler 2021) (Holst 2021).

It is seen from the manner animation is made above that animation is made in different rational thoughts. Animation does not have a standard form like cinema animated films in healthcare. The needs in the scenario determine the manner and form. Sometimes animation functions as an individual video, sometimes as a part of the treatment action or service. It is combined with the environment, the participants, and the other media, making it necessary to consider both the audiovisual language and the interaction with other contents to form the argument.

(2) Ethos

According to Aristotle, Ethos refers to the trustworthy character of the speaker (Aristotle 2007). Richard Buchanan associated it with the quality of an artificial product to be desired (Buchanan 2007). In the context of Health Care, the animation's Ethos refers to the trustfulness of a group, including medical expertise, the animator, and the audience.

The accuracy of professional content is essential for animation in Health Care, closely related to the audience's health and safety, 'ranging from the ineffective to the life-threatening' (Adam 2020). Knowing a patient's dignity and psychological resilience in the face of serious illness (Templeton 2019) is necessary to make the audience feel that their position and interest are concerned and will accept the content.

Thus, the ethos of a healthcare animation is developed through a working group including medical experts, animators, and patients (Kayler 2020). The audience-centered value distinguishes healthcare animation from artistic animation. No artistic expression can alter or distort the claims of professionalism and patients.

(3) Pathos

According to Aristotle, Pathos is 'the emotional effect created by the speaker and text on the audience or reader' (Aristotle 2007), while Richard Buchanan associates it with usable quality (Buchanan 2007). The Pathos of animation in the healthcare area reflects in the appeal and accessibility, which relates to the mental changes and emotions inspired by watching animation. It is decided by the audience's private condition.

On the one hand, animation is accessible. For example, as Baris mentioned in his study, animation increased 'the level of their satisfaction in informed consent' (Baris 2019), is 'eye catching' (Kang 2022), 'easy to watch and understood' and 'comfortable to use to learn' (Kayler 2020). Animated video showed adequate cross-cultural validity (do Nascimento 2021). And animation is preferred. For example, it is 'abstract enough to represent a range of students' (Andraka-Christou 2019).

On the other hand, virtual characters in animation can establish communication with emotions. For example, 'a vertical bar graph that is animated to fill up to be encouraging and emotionally supportive' (Kim 2020); virtual health assistants improve the willingness of participants to talk to their doctor about colorectal cancer screening messages (Krieger 2021).

It is important to note that animation is not naturally effective. Hoetger's study shows that the 'animated model demonstration group performed better than real model group' (Hoetger 2022), while based on Ghavami, 'there was no significant difference between observing animated model and real model' (Ghavami 2022). Another study demonstrates that 3D animation and verbal and leaflet information is relatively equivalent in transferring knowledge (Shqaidef 2021). Moreover, animation can have adverse effects, such as increased cognitive load that hinders deep learning' (Essop 2021). Animation in Health Care needs to be audience-driven (Stoll 2021), iteratively revised, and evaluated (Mills 2017). The audience determines the achievement of persuasion.

3.4 Discussion: The Nature and the Role of Animation as a Tool of Persuasion

The animation used in the healthcare area migrates the experience of animated filmmaking to design, where the core is the change of value from author-centered to audience-centered. It requires concern about the audience in the whole process of making. The audience refers to the healthcare receiver in a healthcare context. By extension, audience refers to users who watch animated videos. Therefore, the nature of animation as a persuasive tool needs to be clarified and concerned in any fields that intend to influence the audience's mind and action. Discuss separately:

1. Having a precise aim of persuasion is the basic to the manner and form. The literature presents animation applied in various forms. No matter used in simply making videos or as a part of a system, animation no longer has a standard category of form. It is necessary to consider the internal and the external structure with the context;
2. The trustful author of healthcare animation is a group that consists of animator, medical expert, and audience. This working model can ensure the professionalism of the content. Therefore, the integrity of the composition of the author group is necessary for animation used in the professional area;
3. Animation can provoke understanding and emotion through visual information, resulting from persuasive impact. The role of the audience reverses from a passive to an active influence. It is an essential difference from traditional filmmaking that one should be aware of. The ignorance of the audience will lead to a failure to persuade.

4 Limitation

Due to time constraints, most of the selected literature originated from the last five years, so more literature reviews are yet to be completed to form a more comprehensive and detailed knowledge.

5   Conclusion

According to the above, animation's intended impact on the audience is different between art and design areas. To impact the audience as intended, the function of animation is no longer an expressive tool but a persuasive tool. To achieve a persuasive impact needs the consciousness of audience-centered value, and an appropriate manner, author group, and audience's active effect are required. The blind use of traditional expressive means may not achieve persuasion and lead to low-quality animated videos. That's what the literature in the healthcare area presents, and it is vital to all areas that use animation to influence the audience.

References

Andraka-Christou, B., Alex, B., Madeira, J.L.: College student preferences for substance use disorder educational videos: a qualitative study. Subst. Use Misuse **54**(8), 1400–1407 (2019)

Aristotle: On Rhetoric: A Theory of Civic Discourse. Oxford University, New York (2007)

Banerski, G., Abramczuk, K., Biele, C.: 3D or not 3D? Evaluation of the effectiveness of 3D-enhanced warning messages for communication in crisis situations. Saf. Sci. **132**, (2020)

Baris, A., Ozturkmen, Y.: The role of advanced technology product animations on informing patients with gonarthrosis preoperatively. Istanbul Med. J. **20**(6), 553–557 (2019)

Buchanan, R.: Strategies of design research: productive science and rhetorical inquiry. In: Design Research Now: Essays and Selected Projects, pp. 55–66 (2007)

Bukkhunthod, P., et al.: Animation as supplementary learning material about carcinogenic liver fluke in classes for primary schoolchildren. J. Cancer Educ. **35**(1), 14–21 (2018). https://doi.org/10.1007/s13187-018-1434-5

Dincer, B., Bahcecik, N.: The effect of a mobile application on the foot care of individuals with type 2 diabetes: a randomised controlled study. Health Educ. J. **80**(4), 425–437 (2021)

do Nascimento, C.D., et al.: Cross-cultural validity of the Animated Activity Questionnaire for patients with hip and knee osteoarthritis: a comparison between the Netherlands and Brazil. Braz. J. Phys. Ther. **25**(6), 767–774 (2021)

Dubov, A.: Ethical persuasion: the rhetoric of communication in critical care. J. Eval. Clin. Pract. **21**(3), 496–502 (2015)

Dubovi, I.: Online computer-based clinical simulations: the role of visualizations. Clin. Simul. Nurs. **33**, 35–41 (2019)

Essop, H., Lubbe, I., Kekana, M.: Bringing literature to life: a digital animation to teach analogue concepts in radiographic imaging during a pandemic - lessons learnt. Afr. J. Health Prof. Educ. **13**(3), 186–188 (2021)

Ghavami, A., et al.: Effects of observing real, animated and combined model on learning cognitive and motor levels of basketball jump shot in children. Biomed. Hum. Kinet. **14**(1), 54–60 (2022)

Hoetger, C., et al.: Content appealing to youth and spend characteristics of electronic cigarette video advertisements. J. Public Health **44**(1), 129–137 (2022)

Holst, C., et al.: Digital health intervention to increase health knowledge related to diseases of high public health concern in Iringa, Tanzania: protocol for a mixed methods study. JMIR Res. Protoc. **10**(4), e25128 (2021)

Kang, E., et al.: Development of a web-based discharge education intervention to improve the postdischarge recovery of general surgical patients. J. Nurs. Scholarsh. **54**(2), 143–151 (2022)

Kayler, L.K., et al.: Development and preliminary evaluation of an animation (simplifyKDPI) to improve kidney transplant candidate understanding of the Kidney Donor Profile Index. Clin. Transp. **34**(3), e13805 (2020)

Kayler, L.K., Dolph, B., Ranahan, M., Keller, M., Cadzow, R., Feeley, T.H.: Kidney transplant evaluation and listing: development and preliminary evaluation of multimedia education for patients. Ann. Transp. **26**, e929839-1 (2021)

Kim, S., et al.: Improving prognosis communication for patients facing complex medical treatment: a user-centered design approach. Int. J. Med. Inform. **141**, 104147 (2020)

Krieger, J.L., et al.: A pilot study examining the efficacy of delivering colorectal cancer screening messages via virtual health assistants. Am. J. Prev. Med. **61**(2), 251–255 (2021)

Majewski, H.: Universities as partners in primary health care innovation. Front. Public Health **9**, 713177 (2021)

Mills, R., et al.: Development and initial assessment of a patient education video about pharmacogenetics. J. Personal. Med. **7**(2), 4 (2017)

Moh, D.R., et al.: Community health workers. Reinforcement of an outreach strategy in rural areas aimed at improving the integration of HIV, tuberculosis and malaria prevention, screening and care into the health systems. "Proxy-sante study". Front. Public Health **10**, 801762 (2022)

Oh, W.-O., et al.: The hospital safety scale for kids: development of a new measurement tool for hospitalized children. J. Child Health Care **25**(1), 146–160 (2021)

Shqaidef, A.J., et al.: A comparative assessment of information recall and comprehension between conventional leaflets and an animated video in adolescent patients undergoing fixed orthodontic treatment: A single-center, randomized controlled trial. Am. J. Orthod. Dentofac. Orthop. **160**(1), 11-+ (2021)

Silar, J., et al.: Development of in-browser simulators for medical education: introduction of a novel software toolchain. J. Med. Internet Res. **21**(7), e14160 (2019)

Stoll, J.A., et al.: Development of video animations to encourage patient-driven deprescribing: a team alice study. Patient Educ. Couns. **104**(11), 2716–2723 (2021)

Stuij, S.M., et al.: Developing a digital training tool to support oncologists in the skill of information-provision: a user-centered approach. BMC Med. Educ. **20**(1), 135 (2020). https://doi.org/10.1186/s12909-020-1985-0

Szmuda, T., et al.: YouTube as a source of information for narcolepsy: a content-quality and optimization analysis. J. Sleep Res. **30**(2), e13053 (2021)

Szmuda, T., ct al.: YouTube as a source of patient information for meningitis: a content-quality and audience engagement analysis. Clin. Neurol. Neurosurg. **202**, 106483 (2021)

Templeton, M., Kelly, C., Lohan, M.: Developing a sexual health promotion intervention with young men in prisons: a rights-based participatory approach. JMIR Res. Protoc. **8**(4), e11829 (2019)

Veldhuijzen, G., et al.: Computer-based patient education is non-inferior to nurse counseling prior to colonoscopy: a multicenter randomized controlled trial. Endoscopy **53**(03), 254–263 (2021)

Wiemker, V., et al.: Pilot study to evaluate usability and acceptability of the 'Animated Alcohol Assessment Tool' in Russian primary healthcare. Digit. Health **8**, 1–11, 20552076211074491 (2022)

Wynne, R., et al.: Effect of an mHealth self-help intervention on readmission after adult cardiac surgery: protocol for a pilot randomized controlled trial. J. Adv. Nurs. **78**(2), 577–586 (2022)

Yeom, M.-Y., Cho, Y.-O.: Nutrition education discouraging sugar intake results in higher nutrient density in diets of pre-school children. Nurs. Res. Pract. **13**(54), 434–443 (2019)

Development of mHealth-Apps for Hearing Aids – Requirements and Assessments of a First Prototype

Verena Wagner-Hartl[✉] [ID], Barbara Schmidtke, Tim Herbst, Janik Rudisile, and Lisa Mix

Faculty Industrial Technologies, Furtwangen University, Campus Tuttlingen, Kronenstraße 16, 78532 Tuttlingen, Germany
verena.wagner-hartl@hs-furtwangen.de

Abstract. An aging of the working population is expected. Consequently, age-related impairments of sensory functions (e.g., hearing impairment) will become more prominent. An increase of people with hearing impairment can already be observed today. In the last years, the importance of digitalization has increased constantly. This was further driven by the COVID19-pandemic. Therefore, the question whether mHealth-apps could be able to improve the first start experience of possible new hearing aid users and how such an app should be designed has continuously become more important. Former research showed that participants rated possible hearing app-functions significantly different. The aim of the presented study was to verify these results and to extend it with additional functions. Furthermore, possible future users should assess first paper-based prototypes. Therefore, an exploratory online study was conducted. Overall, the sample consists of 41 participants (29 female; 19–58 years old). 18 of them were subjectively at least mild hearing impaired. The results of the study show that participants rated possible functions and the different hearing app-prototypes significantly different. Interestingly, effects of hearing impairment and gender can be shown. Overall, the results can improve the development of a new mHealth-app to support new users of hearing aids.

Keywords: Hearing impairment · mHealth-app · Assessment of paper-based prototypes

1 Introduction

An aging of the working population is expected [1]. The number of people with hearing impairment has increased sharply over the recent decades [2] and the number of sold hearing aids has slightly increased from the year 2000 until 2020 [3]. Consequently, age-related impairments of sensory functions like hearing impairment will become more prominent for the future working world [4]. In addition, it was shown in former research [5, 6] that people, who experience first signs of reduced hearing abilities, often report inhibitions to have their hearing tested and, if necessary, purchase and use a hearing aid.

© The Author(s), under exclusive license to Springer Nature Switzerland AG 2022
C. Stephanidis et al. (Eds.): HCII 2022, CCIS 1654, pp. 466–473, 2022.
https://doi.org/10.1007/978-3-031-19679-9_59

In the last years, the importance of digitalization has increased constantly [7]. This was further driven by the COVID19-pandemic [8, 9].

mHealth is the abbreviation for mobile health [10]. That includes the usage of mobile computing and communication advice in health care and public care [11]. They are used to improve the life and health of patients as well as the communication between them and their doctors [12]. Today, mHealth-apps are already being used in the areas of wellness, nutrition, lifestyle, medical conditions and many more [13]. In the future, medical health apps could offer the opportunity for customized diagnoses and therapy and contribute to a better interaction between those involved [14]. Playful and motivating approaches are also positive to address groups that are difficult to reach. When dealing with data, the goal should be to make the relevant data available to medical professionals and patients at the right time.

Due to the mentioned increase of people who suffer from hearing impairments, the question whether mHealth-apps could be able to improve the first start experience of possible new hearing aid users and how such an app should be designed has continuously become more important. Former research [15] has shown that participants rated possible hearing app-functions significantly different. For example, functions like a low battery warning or a search function to locate the hearing aid if it got lost were assessed significantly better than functions to enable a direct connection to an acoustical specialist via the app, connect the app to a PC or smartphone, or listen to music. Significant effects of gender or age cannot be shown regarding the assessment of the different hearing aid-functions.

In general, to ensure product success pre-developmental work is particularly important [16]. Often, prototypes are used for this purpose [17]. They are one of the most effective ways to communicate a concept and can be used to simplify the external communication (e.g., future users, customers) as well as the communication within the development-team.

The aim of the presented study was therefore, (1) to verify the results of the first study [15] and to extend it with additional functions. Additionally, (2) first paper-based prototypes for the development of the app's Home Screen and the possibility to customize features via the Home Screen should be assessed by possible future users. (3) It should be investigated if an app can be seen as an alternative to visiting a hearing care professional. In addition, effects of subjectively perceived hearing impairment and gender were examined.

2 Method

2.1 Participants

Overall, 41 participants aged between 19 and 58 years ($M = 29.05$, $SD = 14.00$) participated in the online study. 29 participants were female, 12 male. To ensure that the participants represent a sample of "new users" only participants who did not use a hearing aid before were included in the sample. 18 of the participants were subjectively at least mild hearing impaired [18, 19; see also 2.2]. The distribution regarding gender and hearing impairment groups does not differ significantly, $\chi^2(1, N = 41) = .03, p = .873$. All participants provided their informed consent at the beginning of the online study.

2.2   Study Design and Materials

The exploratory study was examined with an online survey with a within-subject design. Overall, the participants needed about 15 min to complete the study.

The independent variables (IV) were gender (male, female) and subjectively perceived hearing impairment. The Category Subdivision Scale of Subjective Hearing Impairment (CSS-SHI; [18, 19]) was used for the assessment of the subjectively perceived hearing impairment. The CSS-SHI "(…) is a single item scale where participants rate how much they consider they have difficulties in hearing" ([19] p. 1). The assessment follows a two-step scaling procedure [20]. In a first step, the participants have to scale their subjective hearing impairment in one of five descriptive categories from "not impaired" to "seriously impaired". Afterwards, they have to select one out of ten levels within the descriptive category they selected before (sore: 1–50). Regarding the independent variable subjective perceived hearing impairment, cut-point (a) proposed by Wagner et al. [19] was used to group the participants into two different groups. Cut-point (a) is defined by the authors as follows: CSS-SHI-ratings ≤ 10 – subjectively absolutely not hearing impaired, CSS-SHI-ratings ≥ 11 – subjectively at least very mild hearing impaired. The measurement repetition factor represents five of the six different possible functions of the mHealth-app replicating the study of Wagner-Hartl et al. [15] (search function, if the hearing aid got lost; function to listen to music; low battery warning; possibility to contact an acoustician specialist directly; connection to the smartwatch) and ten "new" functions (search function to find an acoustician specialist; equalizer to customize the sound; remote-function for the acoustician specialist; test-function to prove if hearing aids fit correctly; function to reduce environmental noise; falling alarm e.g., in case of dizziness; acoustic or visual cue when special self-defined stimuli are registered; listening diary; a forum for exchange with other affected persons). Each function was assessed by each participant using a 5-point scale ranging from not useful at all (1) to very useful (5).

To answer the exploratory question regarding the assessment of different paper-based prototypes, the participants were asked to assess different prototypes representing different variants for the development of the app's Home Screen and the possibility to customize features via the Home Screen within three scenarios (see Fig. 1). In Scenario 1 and 3 each paper-based prototype was assessed by each participant using a 5-point scale ranging from very poor (1) to very good (5). The start screen presented in Scenario 2 was assessed regarding its desirability from undesirable (1) to desirable (5).

Furthermore, at the end of the questionnaire, the participants were asked whether they see the app as a useful alternative to visiting a hearing care professional or not [3-point scale: yes (1) – partly (2) – no (3)].

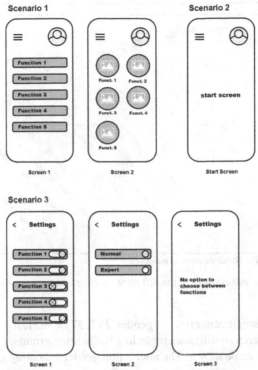

Note. Scenario 1: Display of different functions via the home screen. Scenario 2: Start Screen. Scenario 3: Settings to customize different functions via the Home Screen.

Fig. 1. Paper-based prototypes used in the three different scenarios [21].

2.3 Statistical Analysis

The software IBM SPSS Statistics was used for the statistical analysis. Analyses of variance with repeated measures and univariate analyses of variance were used as statistical procedure. The evaluation was based on a significance level of 5%.

3 Results

3.1 Assessment of the Different Functions of the mHealth-App for New Hearing Aid Users

Following the results of an analyses with variance with repeated measures, significant differences of the perceived usefulness of the different functions of the mHealth-app can be shown, $F(14, 24) = 9.17$, $p \leq .0001$, $\eta^2_{part.} = .842$. The results of the post-hoc analyses (Sidak; $p \leq .050$) are shown in Fig. 2.

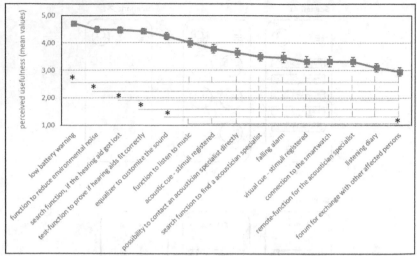

Note. * ... p ≤ .05, I ... Standard error of mean

Fig. 2. Assessment of the different functions of the mHealth-app.

Furthermore, a significant effect of gender, $F(1, 37) = 8.51, p = .006, \eta^2_{part.} = .187$, and a tendency towards significance regarding the hearing groups, $F(1, 37) = 4.08, p = .051, \eta^2_{part.} = .099$, can be shown. The interaction gender × hearing group does not reach the level of significance, $F(1, 37) = .01, p = .926, \eta^2_{part.} \leq .0001$. Overall, women assess the different functions of the app significantly more useful than men. Additionally, at least very mild hearing impaired participants tend to assessed the different functions, more useful than subjectively absolutely not hearing impaired participants.

3.2   Assessment of Different Paper-Based Prototypes

Scenario 1: Display of Different Functions via the Home Screen. The results of an analyses with variance with repeated measures suggest that within Scenario 1, Screen 2 (see Fig. 1; $M = 4.20, SD = .81$) was assessed significantly better than Screen 1 ($M = 3.51, SD = .55$), $F(1, 37) = 12.47, p = .001, \eta^2_{part.} = .252$. No significant effects of gender, $F(1, 37) = 1.53, p = .223, \eta^2_{part.} = .040$, hearing group, $F(1, 37) = .03, p = .864, \eta^2_{part.} = .001$, or the interaction gender x hearing group, $F(1, 37) = .50, p = .485, \eta^2_{part.} = .013$, can be shown.

Scenario 2: Start Screen. The presented start screen (see Fig. 1) was assessed as neutral to rather desirable ($M = 3.27, SD = 1.18$). Following the results of a univariate analyses of variance no significant effects of gender, $F(1, 37) = .85, p = .364, \eta^2_{part.} = .022$, hearing group, $F(1, 37) = .23, p = .638, \eta^2_{part.} = .006$, or the interaction gender x hearing group, $F(1, 37) = .10, p = .749, \eta^2_{part.} = .003$, can be shown.

Scenario 3: Settings to Costumize Different Functions via the Home Screen. The results of an analyses with variance with repeated measures showed a significant inter-action screen x gender, $F(2, 36) = 3.51, p = .041, \eta^2_{part.} = .163$, and a significant effect of screen, $F(2, 37) = 142.31, p < .001, \eta^2_{part.} = .888$ (see Fig. 3). All other effects did not reach the level of significance. Following the results of post-hoc analyses (Sidak, all effect $p \leq .0001$), both, men and women assessed Screen 3 of Scenario 3 (see Fig. 1) significantly poorer than Screen 1 and Screen 2. Furthermore, women assessed Screen 1 significantly better than Screen 2. In addition, regarding Screen 1 women assessed this screen significantly better than men.

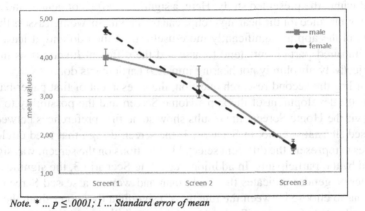

Note. * *... p ≤.0001; I ... Standard error of mean*

Fig. 3. Assessment of the different screens presented within Scenario 3 – gender differences.

3.3 App as Alternative to Visiting a Hearing Care Professional

The results showed, that overall, participants assessed an app as partly useful as alter-native to visiting a hearing care professional ($M = 2.02, SD = .57$). The results of an analyses with variance showed a significant interaction gender x hearing group, $F(1, 37) = 6.93, p = .012, \eta^2_{part.} = .158$. All other effects did not reach the level of significance (gender: $F(1, 37) = .15, p = .704, \eta^2_{part.} = .004$; hearing group: $F(1, 37) = 3.48, p = .070, \eta^2_{part.} = .086$). Post-hoc analyses (Sidak) showed that subjectively absolutely not hearing impaired women ($M = 1.94, SD = .43$) assessed the app as significantly less useful alternative than men of the same hearing group ($M = 2.50, SD = .55; p = .035$). Additionally, subjectively at least mild hearing impaired men ($M = 1.67, SD = .52$) assessed the app as significantly less useful alternative to visiting a professional than subjective absolutely not hearing impaired men ($p = .011$).

4 Discussion

Overall, all different functions that could be implemented in a newly developed mHealth-app to support new hearing aid users were assessed as rather medium to (very) useful.

This is in line with previous research [15]. Even, the significant differences between the originally examined functions (see Sect. 2.2) correspond, with a few exceptions such as the function to listen to music, to those of the first study. Overall, the results show that functions like a low battery warning, a function to reduce environmental noise, a search function if the hearing aid got lost, a test-function to prove the correct fitting of the hearing aids or an equalizer-function to customize the sound were assessed significantly more useful than other functions like a search function to find an acoustic specialist, a connection to the smartwatch, or a forum to exchange with other affected persons (see also Sect. 3.1). In addition, no significant effect of gender can be shown for the six functions used in the first study [15]. This is not valid for the 15 functions analyzed within the presented study: Here, a significant effect of gender and a tendency towards significance for the hearing groups can be shown. So, women assess the different functions of the app as significantly more useful than men do and at least very mild hearing impaired participants tend to assessed the different functions as more useful than subjectively absolutely not hearing impaired participants do.

Regarding the second research question, the assessment of first paper-based prototypes for the development of the app's Home Screen and the possibility to customize features via the Home Screen, the results show some first preferences between the different used alternatives. So, in Scenario 1, the screen design that used circles and not rectangles to represent the different selectable functions on the screen, was significantly preferred by the participants. In addition, regarding Scenario 3, the significant interaction screen × gender indicates that both, men and women assessed Screen 3 (variant "no options to choose between the functions") significantly poorer than, the display of different selectable functions (Screen 1) and the possibility to select between a "normal" and an "expert" mode (Screen 2). Furthermore, women assessed Screen 1 significantly better than Screen 2. Also, women assessed Screen 1 significantly better than men. Furthermore, the presented start screen (Scenario 2) was assessed as neutral to rather desirable.

The results show that the third research question can be answered in a way that overall participants assessed an app as partly useful alternative to a visit to a hearing care professional. Here, subjectively absolutely not hearing impaired women assessed the app as a significantly less useful alternative than men of the same hearing group, and subjectively at least mild hearing impaired men assessed the app as a significantly less useful alternative than subjectively absolutely not hearing impaired men.

Altogether, the results of the presented study can help to improve the development of a mHealth-app for new hearing aid users. In addition, first evaluations of paper-based prototypes will help to improve the information design of mHealth-apps.

References

1. World Health Organization (WHO): Aging, and Working Capacity. World Health Organization, Geneva (1993)
2. Olusanya, B.O., Neumann, K.J., Saunders, J.E.: The global burden of disabling hearing impairment: a call to action. Bull World Health Organ. **92**, 367–373 (2014)
3. Statista: Hörgeräte: Absatz bis 2020 [Hearing aids: Sales until 2020]. Statista (2021)

4. Mathers, C., Smith, A., Concha, M.: Global Burden of Hearing Loss in the Year 2000. Global Burdon of Disease. World Health Organization, Geneva (2000)
5. Hougaard, S., Ruf, S.: EuroTrak I: a consumer survey about hearing aids in Germany, France, and the UK. Hear. Rev. **18**(2), 12–28 (2011)
6. Wagner-Hartl, V.: What are the benefits of newly developed medical devices when the user does not use them? – An investigation of hearing aid use. In: Karwowski, W., Ahram, T. (eds.) Intelligent Human Systems Integration, Advances in Intelligent Systems and Computing 722, pp. 156–162. Springer, Cham (2018). https://doi.org/10.1007/978-3-319-73888-8_26
7. Kravchenko, O., Leshchenko, M., Marushchak, D., Vdovychenko, Y., Boguslavska, S.: The digitalization as a global trend and growth factor of the modern economy. In: SHS Web of Conferences, vol. 65, pp. 1–5 (2019)
8. Mumm, J.-N., Rodler, S., Mumm, M.-L., Bauer, R.M., Stief, C.G.: Digitale Innovation in der Medizin – die COVID-19-Pandemie als Akzelerator von "digital health" [Digital innovation in medicine - theCOVID 19 pandemic as an accclerator of "digital health"]. J. Urol. Urogynäkol. **28**, 1–5 (2020). https://doi.org/10.1007/s41972-020-00126-2
9. Humphreys, G.: Digital health and COVID-19. Bull. WorldHealth Organ. **98**, 731–732 (2020)
10. Matusiewicz, D.: Definition mobile health. Gabler Business Lexicon (2018)
11. Free, C., Phillips, G., Felix, L., Galli, L., Patel, V., Edwards, P.: The effectiveness of M-health technologies for improving health and health services: a systematic review protocol. BMC Res Notes **3**(250), 7 (2010)
12. Zapata, B.C., Fernández-Alemán, J.L., Idri, A., Toval, A.: Empirical studies on usability of mHealth apps: a systematic literature review. J. Med. Syst. **39**(2), 1, 19 (2015)
13. Statista: Weltweite Erwähnungen von Health-Apps in ausgewählten sozialen Medien [Worldwide mentions of health apps in selected social media] (2022)
14. Strotbaum, V., Reiß, B.: Apps im Gesundheitswesen – echter medizinischer Nutzen oder der Weg zum gläsernen Patienten? In: Müller-Mielitz, S., Lux, T. (eds.) E-Health-Ökonomie, pp. 359–382. Springer, Wiesbaden (2017). https://doi.org/10.1007/978-3-658-10788-8_19
15. Wagner-Hartl, V., Saat, S.M., Luther, M., Bauer, A.S.: Requirements for a mHealth-app for hearing aids. In: Kalra, J., Lightner, N.J., Taiar, R. (eds.) AHFE 2021. LNNS, vol. 263, pp. 421–427. Springer, Cham (2021). https://doi.org/10.1007/978-3-030-80744-3_52
16. Cooper, R., Kleinschmidt, E.J.: New products: what separates winners from losers? J. Prod. Innov. Manag. **4**(3), 169–184 (1987)
17. Elverum, C.W., Welo, T.: The role of early prototypes in concept development: insights from the automotive industry. Procedia CIRP **21**, 491–496 (2014)
18. Kallus, K.W., Wagner, V., Rominger, W.: Category Subdivision Scale of Subjective Hearing Impairment (CSS-SHI). Unpublished Questionnaire. University of Graz, Department of Psychology, Austria (2015)
19. Wagner, V., Rominger, W., Kallus, K.W.: The category subdivision scale of subjective hearing impairment – a screening instrument for reduced hearing capacity. J. Ergon. **7**(3), 1000196, 7 (2017)
20. Heller, O.: Listening field audiometry with the method of categorical subdivision (KU). Psychol. Posts **27**, 478–493 (1985)
21. Mix, L.: Scenarios 1–3: paper-based prototypes of the home screen, the start screen and different functions via the home screen. unpublished document. Furtwangen University

Research on Emotional Design of Human Body Temperature Screening Instrument Based on AHP Method

Chenlu Wang(✉), Jie Zhang(✉), Wenqiang Wang, and Wanmeng Tao

East China University of Science and Technology, Xuhui, Shanghai 200237,
People's Republic of China
626683026@qq.com, 339550316@qq.com, 616332476@qq.com

Abstract. In order to better meet the user's needs for the appearance, function and humanized experience of the temperature screening instrument, a design analysis method combining the emotional theory with the analytic hierarchy process and fuzzy evaluation was proposed, and the objectivity and effectiveness of the method in the design process were verified by a practical project. Taking the design practice of the body temperature filter with plate appearance as an example, the user demand index is analyzed by the emotional design theory, and the emotional analysis model of the body temperature filter is established by the analytic hierarchy process (AHP). Qualitative and quantitative analysis were combined to obtain the weight value of the design indicators at each level, and then the comprehensive ranking was carried out. The high weight index items were selected to guide the final design scheme. The fuzzy evaluation method is used to compare and analyze the design scheme with the existing products to verify the validity of the results. In the design practice of the plate temperature screening instrument, the user's recognition degree of the design case influencing experience is significantly higher than that of the existing products, which indicates that this method is effective and provides reference for the design and development of the temperature screening instrument products.

Keywords: Body temperature filter · Emotional design · Analytic hierarchy process · Fuzzy evaluation

1 Introduction

As China has turned into the post-epidemic era, fighting and coordinating against the epidemic has become a daily routine [1]. It is not difficult to find that there are temperature measuring products at the entrances and exits of public places where people go daily or stay, among which the most common one is the temperature screening instrument. Industrial design plays an important role in the research and development practice of many product fields, including the temperature monitoring system [3]. In the past, such products belonged to the medical equipment category, and most enterprises focused their research about product design on technical stability, accurate parameters [2] and low cost. The survey found that the appearance of such products on the market was dull, homogeneity was serious, and the user experience was not good. Emotionalization theory has been widely applied in product design to improve product user experience [4–6]. This paper tries to apply the emotional theory to product innovation, propose design indicators, combine the analytic hierarchy process (AHP) to build an analysis model, quantitatively calculate the weight value of each indicator.

2 Analysis of Temperature Screening Instrument Product

Through online and offline research, there are the following findings:

Based on the relevant research of Baidu Shopping and Amazon shopping, 10 domestic and foreign brands of body temperature screening devices were collected for comparative analysis. The forms of appearance are basically divided into three types, as is shown in Table 1.

Table 1. Samples of existing products from 10 domestic and foreign brands online

外观样式	品牌	产品图片
支架式	健神 优测 欣蒂昊	
板式	甘丹 NYSS TEquipment DERMALOG Viper v1	
门式	中卫 慧云	

Offline interviews were conducted in the form of multi-place surveys. The majority of the 50 visitors found the existing product to be relatively humble in appearance, with female and child users finding it is not cute and approachable enough.

To sum up, domestic users' requirements for the appearance design of temperature screening instrument products are constantly increasing. Domestic products of many brands even appear homogeneous phenomenon. The plate products have good appearance integrity, high recognition of warning, small volume, and good acceptance in terms of technical functions and product experience. The level of product design overseas is slightly higher than domestic.

3 Emotional and Product Design

3.1 Emotional

Donald Norman said in his book Design Psychology that the impact of products on user experience is reflected in three levels: instinct level, behavior level and reflection level [7]. Literature research shows that emotionalization plays a role in a variety of product design neighborhoods. In the design of medical devices and medical-related products [8–11], the three levels of emotional theory are applied to analyze the emotional sustenance of users in the process of using medical products, which can effectively relieve the psychological pressure of patients and improve the experience of users in seeking medical treatment or prevention and treatment. In the design of public goods and furniture in public space [12, 13], the use of emotional concept can effectively discover the functionalism and stiff appearance of traditional products, and improve the satisfaction of people's aesthetic and emotional needs in product design by studying users' needs in aesthetics, use experience and psychological cognition.

Temperature screening instrument products are not only related with health protection products design weaknesses,so using the emotional design in product design can play a certain positive role in aesthetic appearance of the product, interactive way of use and user humanized experiences [10].

3.2 Emotionalization in the Temperature Screening Instrument Product

Temperature screening apparatus has been used in a variety of public places in the post-epidemic era. With the popularity of this product, it is found that the emotional relationship between public users and staff is as follows through literature and research analysis. Instinct layer: The color, material and surface texture without a sense of design will bring aesthetic fatigue to users and create a sense of distance between users and products. Behavior layer: the harsh alarm or harsh red warning light as feedback will increase the possibility of public panic and staff inefficiency. Reflection layer: Most of the temperature screening instruments are rigid in appearance design, rude in interaction mode, and cold in product image.

Therefore, designers need to consider the user experience of product design at all three levels of emotional design, so as to help the product gain user recognition.

4   Emotional Design and Analysis Model of Temperature Screening Instrument Based on Analytic Hierarchy Process

4.1   Analytic Hierarchy Process

Saaty, as a famous American operational research scientist, proposed the analytic hierarchy Process (AHP). Its advantage is to analyze the relationship between different levels more thoroughly, which is easy to understand and apply [14].

In recent years, AHP method has been applied in many different fields, including mechanical structure design [15], product improvement design [16], design scheme analysis [17], education and teaching [18], etc.

4.2   The Application Process of Design Research Methods

The steps of using analytic hierarchy process to excavate design opportunity points are as shown in Fig. 1).

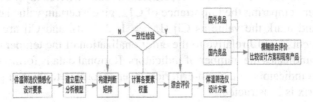

Fig. 1. The process chart of step

4.3   Establishment of AHP Requirements Model

The collected data were classified by using KJ [17] method, and the collected evaluation index elements were supplemented and screened. Taking the design scheme of the emotional temperature screening instrument as a system, the hierarchical analysis structure including target layer.

The first round of 20 sub-criteria elements was obtained through interviews with industry experts, interviews with offline field mobile population and staff, and brainstorming by professional designers. Furthermore, a team composed of 2 industry experts and 5 professional designers was selected for 20 sub-criteria by using KJ method to obtain the 12 preferred secondary evaluation indexes c1-C12.

According to the above content, the analytical hierarchical model is finally obtained, as shown in Fig. 2: The target layer is the optimal design scheme of the temperature screening instrument. Criterion layer is aesthetic X1, ease of use X2, experience X3. Sub-criterion layer is simple shape C1, elegant color C2, material affinity C3 and so on 12 items in turn.

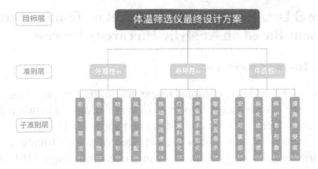

Fig. 2. Design and analysis model of emotional temperature screening instrument

4.4 Construct the Judgment Matrix of Evaluation Index

Through the comparison of evaluation indexes, the importance data is obtained according to the degree, and the judgment matrix of analytic hierarchy process is formed. For the criterion layer evaluation index layer X1, X2, X3, its sub-criterion layer evaluation index C1, C2... After comparing the importance of C12, give a certain value according to the importance, and mark the value as Cij (I, j = 1, 2..., n), and Cij are the important values of elements I and J relative to the emotionalization of the temperature screening instrument; N indicates the number of indicators. Rational data is formed between each two evaluation indicators of the sub-criterion layer according to their importance, and a judgment matrix is constructed:

$$C = (Cij)_{n \times n} = \begin{bmatrix} C_{11} \cdots C_{1n} \\ \vdots \ddots \vdots \\ C_{n1} \cdots C_{nn} \end{bmatrix} \tag{1}$$

In order to quantize the abstract perceptual judgment matrix and facilitate rational processing, the 1–9 scale method is used to verify it and transform it into a numerical judgment matrix.

4.5 Confirm the Weight

According to the above judgment rules, a questionnaire survey was conducted on the existing body temperature screening apparatus according to the elements of each level. A total of 27 people participated in the AHP scoring, including 8 industrial design experts, 8 real product users, 6 security personnel and 5 product industry experts. The Delphi method was used to conduct several rounds of anonymous feedback on the questionnaire survey results, so that the results could be improved and consistent, and the final judgment matrix was formed, as shown in Tables 2, 3, 4 and 5:

Table 2. The final design scheme judgment matrix of the target layer temperature screening instrument

X	X₁	X₂	X₃	Wi
X₁	1.0000	0.5000	0.5000	0.1976
X₂	2.0000	1.0000	0.5000	0.3119
X₃	2.0000	2.0000	2.0000	0.4905

Table 3. Appearance criterion judgment matrix

X₁	C₁	C₂	C₃	C₄	Wi
C₁	1.0000	7.0000	6.0000	1.0000	0.4361
C₂	0.1429	1.0000	2.0000	0.1667	0.0839
C₃	0.1667	0.5000	1.0000	0.1667	0.0612
C₄	1.0000	6.0000	6.0000	1.0000	0.4188

Table 4. Usability criteria judgment matrix

X₂	C₅	C₆	C₇	C₈	Wi
C₅	1.0000	7.0000	8.0000	2.0000	0.5198
C₆	0.1429	1.0000	3.0000	0.1667	0.0897
C₇	0.1250	0.3333	1.0000	0.1429	0.0474
C₈	0.5000	6.0000	7.0000	1.0000	0.3430

Table 5. Experiential criterion judgment matrix

X₃	C₉	C₁₀	C₁₁	C₁₂	Wi
C₉	1.0000	9.0000	8.0000	7.0000	0.7198
C₁₀	0.1111	1.0000	0.5000	1.0000	0.0763
C₁₁	0.1250	2.0000	1.0000	1.0000	0.1099
C₁₂	0.1429	1.0000	1.0000	1.0000	0.0939

4.6 Consistency Test of Judgment Matrix

In order to ensure the reliability of the results, it is necessary to check the consistency of the final judgment matrix. In this study, the sum product method was used to solve the problem, and the maximum characteristic root and consistency index were calculated to obtain the hierarchical single order. The random consistency ratio CR is expressed numerically as the ratio between the consistency index CI and the corresponding RI value of this order. In general, when CR < 0.1, it means that the judgment matrix has passed the consistency test, and the smaller the value is, the better the reliability is; otherwise, the judgment matrix should be reevaluated and modified. The consistency test results of the judgment matrix in this study are shown in Table 6.

Table 6. Consistency test results

	X	X1	X2	X3
CR	0.0517	0.0296	0.0597	0.0213

According to the results in the table, the CR value of each judgment matrix is less than 0.1, indicating that the matrix has consistency and good reliability.

4.7 Analysis and Evaluation

Through the above research, the weight data of each index in the AHP system is obtained (as is shown in Table 7). In the criteria layer of each index, the weight of experience is the largest, followed by ease of use and appearance. In the sub-criteria layer, the sense of safety and reliability > convenient mobile use > intelligent interactive guide > simple form > style adaptation > protector image > improve acceptance > weaken the sense of panic > lighting reminder technology > elegant color > sound prompt soft > material friendly.

Table 7. The weight of sub-criterion layer elements relative to the target layer

	C1	C2	C3	C4	C5	C6
权重	0.0862	0.0166	0.0121	0.0828	0.1621	0.0280
	C7	C8	C9	C10	C11	C12
权重	0.0148	0.1070	0.3531	0.0374	0.0539	0.0461

The weight values of simple form, easy extent to move and use, and sense of safety and reliability are 0.0862, 0.1621 and 0.3531, respectively, which are the most important second-level indexes under each criterion layer. In sub-criterion layer's secondary indexes evaluation factors relative to the sorting of the weight of target layer, according to data visualization bar chart (as is shown in Fig. 3), it can be seen that the sense of safety and reliability, mobile use signage, shape is simple and convenient, intelligent interaction style adapter this 5 is the rule layer relative to other indicators is more outstanding, it is necessary to consider this five requirements in the process of design.

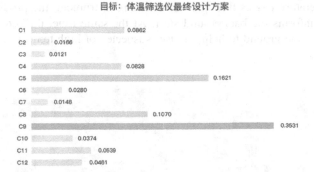

目标：体温筛选仪最终设计方案

C1 　0.0862
C2 　0.0166
C3 　0.0121
C4 　0.0828
C5 　0.1621
C6 　0.0280
C7 　0.0148
C8 　0.1070
C9 　0.3531
C10 　0.0374
C11 　0.0539
C12 　0.0461

Fig. 3. Data visualization bar chart of evaluation index weight ordering

5 Design Practice of Temperature Screening Instrument

In this design practice, the plate temperature screening instrument was selected as the carrier, and the top five indexes were selected as the key design elements through the ranking of the weight value of each index in the sub-criteria layer, forming the final design scheme. As shown in Fig. 4.

Fig. 4. Design renderings of body temperature screening instrument and projection lamp module

5.1 An Instinctive Representation of a Design Proposal

Product appearance design use the form of simple square chamfering design language.The color is suitable for more application scenarios. The product material increases the visual soft touch and psychological acceptance of the product.

5.2 The Behavior Level of the Design Solution

AS shown in Fig. 5. if the user with normal body temperature passes through the screening instrument, the product almost does not have a sense of presence. When a user suspected of high temperature passes through the screening instrument, the product first marks the user and informs the background staff. At the same time, the product projects a guide arrow on the ground to help the user suspected of high temperature to enter the reinspection area.

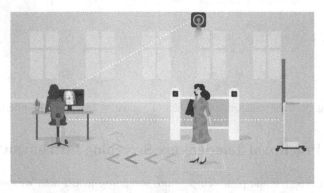

Fig. 5. Operation diagram of intelligent indicator interactive system when suspected high-temperature personnel are detected

5.3 Reflection Layer's Expression of the Design

The simple light prompt and intelligent interactive design of guidance can reduce the panic of users suspected of high temperature and meet the psychological needs of being respected. This use of analytic hierarchy process is based on the emotional design theory analysis and research to obtain the influence of the final design elements of high weight items, and applied in the final design.

6 Design Evaluation

In order to verify the effectiveness of the selection of sub-criteria for product design, the fuzzy evaluation method is adopted to comprehensively compare the output design scheme with the existing products in the market through expert evaluation to verify whether the product design is advanced.

Fuzzy comprehensive evaluation method [20] was used to evaluate and quantitatively calculate the emotionalization elements at all levels of the three products.

To selecte two competing products, and the fuzzy comprehensive evaluation is compared with the final design scheme of this practice, as shown in Fig. 6.

The weight vector of the three criteria in the criterion: America's TEquipment's automated AI temperature screening kiosk scheme scores as: $S = W \times \theta = 67.841$; In this paper, the final design of the temperature screening instrument scored as: $S = W \times \theta = 84.773$. Therefore, it can be judged that the design results of the final design scheme are more prominent in the performance of emotional design at all levels, and the effectiveness of the method has been verified.

a、 Final design scheme b、 TEquipment c、 Gandan

Fig. 6. Fuzzy evaluation of selected products and design schemes

7 Conclusion

In the product design of temperature screening instrument, a design research idea combining emotion theory and analytic hierarchy process is introduced to help designers make more objective decisions, and design results are formed through examples, and the effectiveness of this method is verified.

References

1. Zhang, J.: Normalization of COVID-19 response and economic and social development in the post-epidemic era. Jianghan Forum (08), 15–22 (2020)
2. Zhao, Y.: Industrial design for epidemic prevention. Decoration (02), 16–21 (2020)
3. Wang, H., Bo, C., Wang, J., Yuan, Z., Li, J., Gao, W.: Application of infrared thermometers in COVID-19 response. China Metrol. (05), 17–20 (2020)
4. Zhao, Y.: Emotional design of children's medical devices based on color perception. Mech. Design **36**(02), 142–144 (2019)
5. Yang, A., Wang, Q., Zhu, N., Fu, N.: Research on modeling design of elderly exercise bike based on emotional needs. Mech. Design **34**(11), 123–128 (2017)
6. Zhu, H., Zhang, Y., Xu, B.: Modeling design of children learning companion robot based on emotional design theory. Mech. Design **33**(04), 122–124 (2016)
7. Norman, D.A.: Emotional Design. Citic Publishing House, Beijing (2012)
8. Wang, C.: To explore the emotional design of medical devices. Value Eng. **36**(19), 158–159 (2017)
9. Sun, Y.: Research on trust Design of meridian detector based on emotion. Sci. Technol. Econ. Guide **28**(08), 30–31 (2020)
10. Zhong, Y., Jin, Y.: Research on medical protective clothing based on emotional design. Lit. Artistic Life (Art China) (11), 136–138 (2020)
11. Sun, Y., You, Y.: Discussion on the research of the emotional design of the home children's forehead warm gun. Hebei Agric. Mach. (08), 98+100 (2020)
12. Dai, F.: Emotional design of furniture in public space. Packag. Eng. **33**(04), 110–113 (2012)
13. Rin, Y.: User-centered interactive design for public goods. Art Educ. (01), 175–176 (2018)
14. Saaty, T.L.: Analytic hierarchy process. Math. Models Decis. Support (4), 109–121 (2013)
15. Xu, X., Wang, Z., Li, S.: Analysis and implementation of project design evaluation system for mechanical graduation project. Exp. Technol. Manag. **37**(09), 226–230 (2020)

16. Yang, L., Wang, T., Zhang, R., Rei, J., Ma, Y.: Design evaluation and application of intelligent rice cooker based on fuzzy analytic hierarchy process. Mech. Design **36**(04), 129–133 (2019)
17. Xu, X., Cheng, Y., Chen, G.: Research on rv modeling evaluation method and application based on AHP method. Mech. Design **37**(06), 140–144 (2020)
18. Liu, H., Hu, W., Wu, Y., Xu, X., Fang, D.: Evaluation of special teacher skill training of normal university students in minority areas based on AHP. Mod. Educ. **7**(41), 107–110 (2020)
19. Ye, J.: Study on evaluation method of urban intelligent lighting integrated device form design based on value co-creation perspective. East China University of Science and Technology (2018)
20. Hu, S., Liu, J.: Application of fuzzy comprehensive evaluation method in product design decision. Mech. Design **37**(01), 135–139 (2020)

A Study on Functional Satisfaction with Smart Health Care Air Purification Product in the Post-epidemic Era

LiYan Zhang, JiaLin Han, Qi Jia, LingDa Rong, and Shan Hu

Hubei University of Technology, Wuhan 430000, Hubei, China
hushan@hbut.edu.cn

Abstract. In the context of the COVID-19, respiratory diseases have become the focus of social attention, and the elderly, as a susceptible population, is more significantly affected by the epidemic. In order to fully protect the respiratory system of the elderly and enhance their satisfaction with the function of smart products, this study proposes a design method for smart health care product based on the cognitive behavior of elderly users. Firstly, the user demand gap is explored and determined by using the A-Kano model; secondly, a functional model is created based on the FAST functional theory. After converting the user demand into function, and then the TRIZ theory is applied to choose to use 40 invention principles and 39 general engineering parameters to analyze the problem and get conflict domain solutions, so as to filter out the most ideal solution and innovate its function; Finally, by the design and practice of the smart health care air purification product, its purification range, monitoring data and wearing method will be effectively optimized, and the feasibility of the design solution will be verified by the user interaction satisfaction questionnaire. The study provides new ideas for the design of smart health care products and the solutions of contradictory problems, which would also be a theoretical guidance for relevant designer and researchers.

Keywords: Smart health care product · User satisfaction · A-Kano · TRIZ · Functional innovation

1 Introduction

Since the WHO assessed that the COVID-19 can be characterized as a pandemic, respiratory diseases have gradually become a major social concern. And for the elderly, who are more significantly affected by the epidemic because of their weakened resistance, the cloudy air can lead to lowered immunity and other related diseases. At the same time, cloud technology, intelligence, the Internet of Things and other technologies are gradually becoming mature. The demand for electronic products among the elderly is gradually increasing. Experts and scholars have conducted the following studies on how to explore the problems of elderly users and effectively transform them into innovative

C. Stephanidis et al. (Eds.): HCII 2022, CCIS 1654, pp. 485–494, 2022.
https://doi.org/10.1007/978-3-031-19679-9_61

features to enhance user satisfaction. Wang Wei et al. [1] used the A-Kano (An Analytical Kano) model to research the functional requirements configuration of the WeChat navigation system in SuiTang Luoyang scenic area to improve visitor satisfaction. Chen Chen et al. [2] established the FAST (Functional Analysis System Technology, FAST) functional model to extract its design factors by analyzing the user requirements for waste disposal, and performed functional design to verify the feasibility of the FAST functional model in the development and design of new product. Junwu Ding et al. [3] proposed a requirement analysis of the product internal functions based on TRIZ theory to improve the accuracy and effectiveness of the customer requirement information. Above all, it was found that most of the previous studies had a single research perspective, and existed certain limitations in the testing methods and research models. This study proposes a new method to obtain user pain points more precisely, dig out the key problems that currently exist for elderly users, transform the problems into functional requirements and carry out functional innovations for them, make design more rationalized.

Based on the A-Kano model, FAST functional model and TRIZ innovation theory, this study analyzes the influence of user requirements of smart health care air purification product on functional transformation and determines the importance of functional elements to help designers improve design efficiency, provides the best solution for the design of smart health care air purification product and enhances the transformation rate of requirements to innovative functions.

2   Integrated Innovation Method Construction

The Kano Model solves the problem of positioning of product attributes and meets user demands by classifying different user demands, so as to obtain the relationship between product performance and user satisfaction [4]. A-Kano [5] model extends the traditional Kano model, and is more responsive to users' feelings and more intuitive in converting user satisfaction into functional requirements.

The FAST functional model is based on the invisible demands of users for the product to discover functional points and determine the primary and secondary functions of the product at all levels [6].

TRIZ theory, as one of the most commonly used theories in innovation methods, plays a great role in promoting innovation theory [7]. The classical TRIZ theory does not have tools for analyzing problems, which leads to certain drawbacks in solving practical problems. The A-Kano model, on the other hand, can make up for this drawback of TRIZ theory by analyzing the problem upfront.

This study firstly adopts A-Kano to explore the user demand gap, then applies FAST functional model for functional analysis of user demand, and finally uses TRIZ theory for innovative functional mapping, so as to obtain the functional system of smart health care air purification product. The new model circumvents the blindness in the traditional model and is also more targeted. The innovation process is shown in Fig. 1.

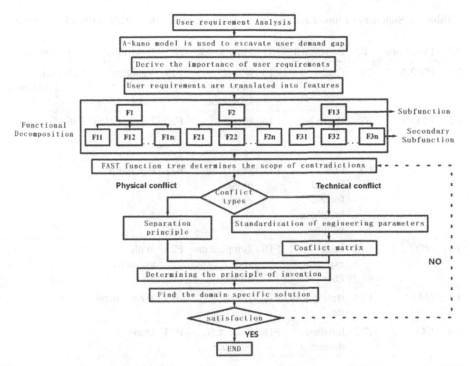

Fig. 1. Design flow chart of integrated innovation method based on A-Kano mod-el, FAST functional model and TRIZ theory

3 Dynamic Equation Solving

3.1 User Requirements Analysis

Product Function Requirement Point Setting. Through the analysis of the target users' research and expert interviews, a total of 26 functional requirements for this product are summarized, which is shown in Table 1.

Questionnaire Research. In order to collect user demands as comprehensively as possible and make the product fit the usage environment. In this study, the questionnaire was set up in a standardized form, with a brief description of the functions and facilities in the table, and a two-way satisfaction evaluation of each function. In the case of monitoring "blood oxygen saturation", the questionnaire in the form is shown in Table 2, using the [0, 1] interval to define the user's assessment of the importance of the function.

Processing of Research Data Results. Let each respondent be j, and the research data results of each function be $\sum_j$, where $j = 1, 2, \ldots, n(n = 100)$, $\sum_j = (x_j, y_j, \omega_j)$, and the values of $\bar{x}$, $\bar{y}$, and $\bar{\omega}$ for each function are derived according to Eqs. (1) and (2), and $\bar{\omega}$ represents the mean value of function weights. The results of the user satisfaction data survey are shown in Table 3

Table 1. Summary of functional requirements for smart health care air purification product

NO	Functional	NO	Functional	NO	Functional	NO	Functional	NO	Functional
F1	PM2.5	F7	CO2	F13	Blood oxygen saturation	F19	Visibility	F25	Sun Protection
F2	PM10	F8	Bacteria	F14	Blood oxygen saturation	F20	Precipitation	F26	Seasonal
F3	SO2	F9	First second forceful breathing volume	F15	Maximum oxygen uptake	F21	UV Index		
F4	NO2	F10	Peak expiratory flow	F16	Temperature and humidity	F22	With umbrella		
F5	O3	F11	Respiratory rate	F17	Wind direction	F23	Wear a mask		
F6	CO	F12	Inhalant dosage	F18	Pneumatic pressure	F24	Dressing		

Table 2. Satisfaction questionnaire for functional facilities of smart health care air purification product

F13: Monitoring of oxygen saturation and data analysis of it					
	Very much like	Right and proper	Doesn't matter	Tolerable	Dislike
With this function	1	0.5	0	-0.25	-0.5
Without this function	-0.5	-0.25	0	0.5	1
How important do you think this feature is.					
Not important at all					Very important
0	0.1	0.2	0.3	0.4	0.5	0.6	0.7	0.8	0.9	1

$$\bar{x} = \frac{1}{\omega} \sum_{j=1}^{n} \omega_j x_j \tag{1}$$

$$\bar{y} = \frac{1}{\omega} \sum_{j=1}^{n} \omega_j y_j \tag{2}$$

where $\bar{x}$ represents the average value of satisfaction when the function is available, $\bar{y}$ represents the average value of dissatisfaction when the function is not available. $\omega = \omega_1 + \omega_2 + \cdots + \omega_j$.

Each functional requirement satisfaction feedback is represented by the vector $S_I = (s_I, \alpha_i)$ in polar coordinate form, α_i is the angle between this function and the $x-$ axis, and representing user satisfaction. s_i is calculated as shown in Eq. (3); according to the score interval of vector S_I shown in Eq. (4), the A-Kano model is drawn and analyzed for functional requirement attributes based on user satisfaction survey data, as shown in Fig. 2.

$$s_i = \sqrt{\bar{x}^2 + \bar{y}^2}, \quad i = 1, 2, \ldots, 26 \tag{3}$$

In Eq. (3), s_i represents the distance value of user satisfaction to the origin for this functional requirement, which represents the importance of the functional requirement.

$$\begin{cases} |s_i| \le 0.5 & \text{No difference demand} \\ 0.5 < |s_i| \le 1 \wedge \alpha \le 25° & \text{Basic demand} \\ 0.5 < |s_i| \le 1 \wedge 25° \le \alpha \le 65° & \text{Expect demand} \\ 0.5 < |s_i| \le 1 \wedge 65° < \alpha \le 90° & \text{Charm demand} \end{cases} \tag{4}$$

Table 3. User satisfaction survey data statistics

Functional	$\bar{\omega}$	$\bar{x}$	y	Functional	$\bar{\omega}$	$\bar{x}$	y
F1	0.52	0.72	0.26	F14	0.63	0.66	0.73
F2	0.61	0.71	0.70	F15	0.62	0.73	0.70
F3	0.62	0.66	0.67	F16	0.66	0.25	0.60
F4	0.64	0.74	0.76	F17	0.68	0.25	0.66
F5	0.58	0.61	0.63	F18	0.44	0.30	0.30
F6	0.61	0.66	0.66	F19	0.66	0.28	0.64
F7	0.50	0.78	0.27	F20	0.66	0.20	0.61
F8	0.51	0.67	0.25	F21	0.67	0.26	0.63
F9	0.59	0.63	0.64	F22	0.68	0.19	0.62
F10	0.56	0.57	0.61	F23	0.50	0.79	0.27
F11	0.50	0.80	0.27	F24	0.43	0.28	0.29
F12	0.65	0.22	0.58	F25	0.45	0.23	0.31
F13	0.50	0.72	0.32	F26	0.47	0.36	0.37

3.2 Function Mapping Structure

In TRIZ theory, both the understanding of problems and the programmed method determine the difficulty of solving the problem. The more thoroughly you understand the problem, the easier it is to find a solution. The FAST functional model defines a clear functional scope, divides the functions according to the results of user satisfaction survey, and searches for the functional scope area in the process of functional decomposition to clarify the contradictory scope, and connects the functions of each element by using

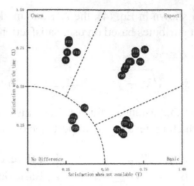

Fig. 2. Analysis of functional requirements by A-Kano model

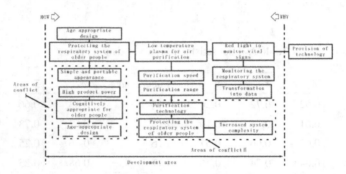

Fig. 3. Function diagram of smart health care air purification product

"how" and "why" as the main guide to draw the functional system diagram of the smart health care air purification product. As shown in Fig. 3.

Problem Description. Through the analysis of the product's own function and the existing situation in the market, it can be found that portable air purification products are not comfortable enough in the process of wearing, it also relatively lacked a lot in function, not in line with the physical characteristics of the elderly, lacked aesthetics and uniqueness of the shape and other deficiencies.

The design purposes are divided into two main categories: one is to add or enhance useful functions; the other is to eliminate or diminish harmful functions. Assuming that the purpose of introducing the design creates a conflict in only one subsystem, this conflict is a physical conflict; if it is created between two subsystems or added its complexity to the system, this conflict will be a technical conflict [8].

3.3   TRIZ Theory Innovation Design

In order to improve the satisfaction of elderly users in using smart health care air purification product and protect their respiratory system, it is necessary to ensure the data accuracy of purification rate and monitoring of body condition during the use of purification technology, and set it as a development target. In this study, two contradictory areas (contradictory area I and contradictory area II) corresponding to the development objectives are identified within the development area by the FAST functional model diagram (e.g., Fig. 3).

Contradiction I corresponds to physical conflict I, if the process of product design eliminated in line with the cognition of the elderly, its design will not conform to the usage habits of elderly users. Combined with the specific description of the conflict 1, the process of product design should choose the separation principle of "separation based on relationship", which have physical contradiction of the opposite needs for different system objects, so that the engineering system has specific characteristics for different objects, so as to meet the corresponding needs, and the problem is solved by combining the inventive principles (No3 Partial quality and No32 Change Color) corresponding to them.

According to the tips of "Partial quality" and "Change Color" principle, different modules of product shape can be used to meet the needs of different functions, and the appearance of product shape and color can be used to meet the pursuit of fashion and comfort of elderly users.

Contradiction II corresponds to technology conflict, where mismatched purification technologies lead to an increase in system complexity. Choosing a suitable purification technology to increase the purification rate and expand the purification range will impose higher requirements on the internal structure of the product, the selection of sensors, and the data transmission configuration, which will significantly increase the difficulty and cost of making structural components.

According to the determination of the conflict, it is known that the parameters to be improved are the purification speed, range of the purifier and the multifunctional combination, which respectively correspond to the action time (NO15) and shape (NO12) of the moving object in 39 engineering parameters, while the parameters to be deteriorated are the consumption of the cartridge in the purifier and the increase in cost caused by the increase in technology and material, which respectively correspond to material loss (NO23) and manufacturing accuracy (NO29). The corresponding contradiction matrix are shown in Table 4. The explanation of the invention principle is shown in Table 5.

Table 4. Archishuler contradiction matrix

Improved parameters	Deteriorating parameters	
	23 Material loss	29 Manufacturing accuracy
12 Shape	35, 29, 3, 5	32, 30, 40
15 Time of action of moving objects	28, 27, 3, 18	3, 27, 16, 40

Innovative Design. The following solutions are proposed based on the hints of the principles of the invention 3, 5, 16 and 32. In the functional innovation, a variety of highly reactive active particles contained in the air are made available through low temperature plasma purification technology to enable simultaneous treatment of a wide range of pollutants. At the same time, the data such as blood oxygen saturation are

Table 5. Archishuler contradiction matrix

Serial number	Principle name	Description of the principle of the invention
3	Local quality	1. Transition from a consistent to an inconsistent structure of the object or external medium (external action) 2. Different parts of the object have different functions 3. Each part of the object has the conditions that are most applicable to its work
5	Combination	1. Spatially, combining similar objects 2. The combination of similar successive operations or functions in time 3. Merge or combine objects with different (or opposite) functions together to achieve new functions
32	Change color	1. Changing the color of objects or external media 2. Change the transparency of the object or external media
16	Insufficient or excess action	If it is difficult to obtain 100% of the required efficacy, a slightly smaller or larger efficacy should be obtained, which will make the problem much simpler

monitored using red light, thus achieving the purpose of monitoring the health of the respiratory system. In the process of design, the physiological and psychological change characteristics of elderly users are taken into account to reduce the cognitive burden of elderly users in using smart products and ensuring the rationality of health care products design. In the innovation of the new program, the combination of new technology and function has increased the design complexity to a certain extent. However, considering the disadvantages of the previous design, the new program is relatively more practical and convenient in terms of wearing method and purification technology, and also more in line with the design concept of age-appropriate design.

Program Design. The smart health care air purification product uses a neck-worn wearing method to make the red light fit the neck to obtain accurate blood oxygen saturation monitoring data, reduces the complexity of operation during the wearing process and matchs the cognitive habits of the elderly. Figure 4 is the structure schematic diagram of the smart health care air purification product: 1. Monitoring bracelet; 2. Red light monitoring; 3. Air inlet; 4. HEPA filter module; 5. Air outlet; 6. Filter module switch; 7. Product switch; 8. Low temperature plasma module; 9. Turbo module, and Fig. 5 is the product effect diagram.

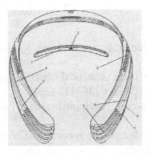

Fig. 4. Structure schematic of smart health care air purification product

Fig. 5. Product effect

3.4 Usability Assessment

After the design was made into a functional prototype, the elderly users of a nursing home in Wuhan were invited to experience the prototype, and the questionnaire for User Interface Satisfaction (QUIS) was used to compare with existing health care air purification product on the market. QUIS divides the evaluation items into five dimensions: overall response, screen, terminology/system information, learning, and system capability. The questionnaire is administered by using a 10-point scale, with the markers subsequently changing depending on the statement sentence. The subjects filled in the questionnaire according to their real experience of using the experimental prototype of air purification products, and a total of 70 questionnaires were distributed and 61 valid questionnaires were collected. The data were imported into SPSS for calculation, and the alpha coefficient of the functional prototype was obtained as 0.89, which indicated that the questionnaire results were credible and the user satisfaction of smart health care air purification product was high.

4   Conclusions

This study proposes an integrated innovation method based on the A-Kano model, FAST functional model and TRIZ innovation theory to solve the problem of difficulties in using smart products by elderly users and the inability of designers to accurately grasp the transformation of user demands to functional needs. It is validated with the example of smart health care air purification product design, and the results showed that the method can effectively determine the importance of functional requirements. The main conclusions of this study are as follows.

1. The study proposes a design method for integrated innovation that can quantitatively analyze the degree of user influence on functional requirements satisfaction, so as to help designers accurately grasp the design elements and guide the design process.
2. The method makes up for the lack of functional transformation in the user demand level of previous research findings and existing recreation products in the market. Comprehensive consideration of the cognitive differences of the elderly and the design factors of health care products has certain guiding significance for helping designers to obtain user demands and then improve the conversion rate of functions.

References

1. Wang, W., Li, Y.: Functional requirements of we chat guide program based on a-Kano model. Packag. Eng. **43**(02), 172–178+185 (2022)
2. Chen, C., Sun, Z., Zhang, L.: Application of FAST method in the conceptial design of domestic intelligent solid organic waste processor. J. Mach. Design **34**(01), 110–113 (2017)
3. Ding, J., Han, Y., Zheng, C.: Research on capturing of customer requirements based on TRIZ. Comput. Integr. Manuf. Syst. (05), 648–653 (2006)
4. Zhang, D., Hou, Z., Huang, L., et al.: Research on the product demands configuration method based on user satisfaction. J. Graph. **41**(04), 649–657 (2020)
5. Xu, Q., Jiao, R.-J., Yang, X., et al.: An analytical Kano model for customer need analysis. Des. Stud. **30**(01), 87–110 (2009)
6. Otto, K.N., Wood, K.L., Qi, C.-P.: Product Design. Electronic Industry Press, Beijing (2007)
7. Sun, Y.-W., Sergei, I.: TRIZ: the Golden Key to Unlocking the Door to Innovation. I. Science Press, Beijing (2015)
8. Chen, N., Luo, Y., Wan, C., et al.: Research and application of TRIZ with FAST method. Coal Mine Mach. **32**(05), 192–195 (2011)

Virtual, Augmented, and Mixed Reality

An XR Optical Camouflage Technology

Nobuki Aizawa[✉], Kazuto Hayashida, and Tatsuya Shibata

Graduate School of System Design and Technology, Tokyo Denki University,
5 Senju Asahi-cho, Adachi-ku, Tokyo 120-8551, Japan
22amd01@ms.dendai.ac.jp

Abstract. In recent years, remarkable progress in science and technology has enabled the realization of many technologies previously imagined in fiction and popular culture. At present, optical camouflage technology designed to render objects transparent and invisible is being studied in various fields. Some optical camouflage methods have been proposed and implemented using special materials and equipment such as projectors. In this study, we developed a system integrating real-world person recognition using augmented reality (AR) and virtual space construction using virtual reality (VR). Our system is designed to recognize a human silhouette and replace it with a background image. The images used to cloak the silhouettes were based on scans of real three-dimensional spaces. Using these technologies, we constructed a system that displays a scene in which a person is rendered transparent using a camera in real time. We then realized optical camouflage as a mobile device application.

Keywords: Optical camouflage · XR · Real-time

1 Introduction

1.1 Research Background

In recent years, science and technology have developed rapidly worldwide. Advances in various fields have enabled cascading advances in others, leading to wide-ranging and dramatic technological progress with a major impact on most people's daily lives. In addition, many technological advances have enabled the realization of previously imaginary or fictional technologies once considered impossible.

Optical camouflage is such a technology. Optical camouflage has appeared as a fictional technology in a wide variety of popular and genre literature in different media. However, recent advances in optical camouflage research have led to some implementations of such systems. As this technology is considered promising, considerable research effort continues to be invested, and future developments are expected. However, optical camouflage is still not widely used or well-known. In this study, we aim to realize optical camouflage as a widely available service by combining it with extended or cross reality (XR) technology. XR is a generic term for augmented reality (AR), virtual reality (VR), and mixed reality (MR). The purpose of this research is to develop technologies to render human forms transparent. Currently, we are mainly considering applications in the two

C. Stephanidis et al. (Eds.): HCII 2022, CCIS 1654, pp. 497–503, 2022.
https://doi.org/10.1007/978-3-031-19679-9_62

fields of entertainment and medical manufacturing. In the entertainment field, we believe that optical camouflage can be applied to show figures as transparent, in interpersonal games, and in children's games. In the medical and manufacturing fields, we expect the system to play a role in clarifying workers' fields of vision by rendering their hands and fingers transparent during detailed work requiring manual dexterity.

1.2 Previous Research

Currently, several methods for realizing optical camouflage are under investigation both in Japan and abroad, and various studies are being conducted. Two main methods for realizing optical camouflage technology have been presented in the relevant literature. A projector or an information device can be used to make an object visually transparent, or an object can be rendered invisible using special materials to modify the path of light itself as it passes through an object. The two techniques differ in terms of their approach to object transparency. Visual camouflage techniques acts on human vision, whereas intrinsic methods focus on light as a natural object. In this study, we address the former.

Retroreflective projection technology (RPT) has been proposed an optical camouflage technology [1]. These methods superimpose a virtual world on the real world using a projector and a half-mirror coated with a special retro-reflective material. The system directs light to an observer's eyes via a half-mirror and an overhead projector. A retroreflective material applied to the display surface enables the observer can see a clear background image. A clear image is projected into the transparent area by a projector. Although this technology requires the use of a head-mounted projector (HMP) and the application of retroreflective material to the object being concealed, it can be used both outdoors and indoors because it is independent of the device.

Diminished reality (DR) technology is similar to optical camouflage [2]. Mori et al. of Ritsumeikan University redefined a technology called diminished reality (DR) and clarified the research issues. DR technology, which we consider in the present work, is designed to render objects invisible by overwriting removal targets that exist in the real world with virtual objects shown instead on a screen. Mori et al. asserted that the goal of DR technology is to achieve high-quality visual removal in a real-world situation so that the viewer does not know that the object has been removed or is not aware of the handling process.

Koizumi et al. developed and implemented a practical system to enable users to see their own image transmitted through a projector, half-mirror, and coating of retroreflective material [3]. The principle of this system is similar to that of the RPT system described above, with the addition of a self-image confirmation system. Koizumi et al. used a ceiling-mounted projector instead of a head-mounted projector, limiting their proposed system to indoor use. They also included the results of an actual museum display that provided many people with the experience of optical camouflage. Similarly, Izumihara et al. cloaked a human figure with transparency using projectors, half-mirrors, and retroreflective material coating [4]. They system also performed optical camouflage using a projector mounted on the ceiling. Their approach designed to photograph a scene and perform geometric and color tone correction to display optical camouflage.

These previous studies used information devices such as projectors and special materials, to create the illusion of visual transparency. In recent years, optical camouflage has increasingly been used as a demonstration to attract interest in technology, science, and other fields by allowing many people to experience transparent cloaking or invisibility effecting a human form.

In this study, we implemented optical camouflage as a smartphone application. In the abovementioned work, the background was projected with a projector or other device using a wall or panel sufficiently large that a single person could not be seen. Other implementations have been achieved using metamaterials, which are special materials that control the propagation of light. These technologies are not readily available for widespread experience.

Based on these studies, the present work contributes an implementation of optical camouflage as a mobile device application to present it in a familiar way that can be easily experienced by many people. Today, a wide variety of applications run on smartphones and are in very widespread usage. By implementing optical camouflage as a smartphone application and enabling more people experience or recognize the technology, we expect this research to lead to further development of such services.

In addition, editing technologies remove people from videos and images. These technologies have been established as services that allow users to edit photos and camera images relatively easily and freely. Software designed to remove people and objects from photographs and images and reconstruct the images without those forms have existed for some time. In recent years, this technology has become available on individual smartphone devices. These technologies eliminate human forms by editing prepared images. In contrast to these technologies, a key element of this study is to render the human body invisible in real time in an optical camouflage program.

2 Method

2.1 System Configuration

In this research, we developed a combination of real-world person recognition using AR and virtual space construction using VR. We used one program to recognize a human silhouette and another to describe the background added as a background image. The silhouette images were based on scans of real three-dimensional space.

The program designed to recognizes human forms using AR technology is shown in Fig. 1 (1). This function automatically recognizes the parts of the human body and displays them as a silhouette. This function must be able to recognize not only individual parts of the body but also the entire body, and must be able to recognize not only one person but also multiple people.

Figure 1 (2) describes the background and uses VR technology to describe the background images. An image of a scene similar to that of an indoor space moves in accordance with the camera's up-down and left-right movements.

The above two programs are combined to realize a program that expresses the optical camouflage in (3).

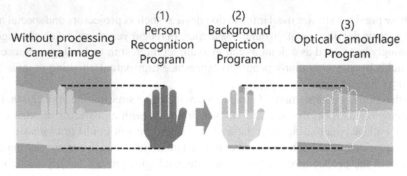

Fig. 1. System configuration diagram

2.2 Development Environment

To develop AR applications, we used Unity [5], a game engine, and AR Foundation [6], which is a framework for AR development. AR Foundation unifies ARKit for iOS applications and ARCore for Android and other applications. In this study, we implemented ARKit for iOS. We did so because the ARKit for iOS includes a human recognition function, which it is not compatible with Android and other devices at this time.

In this study, we used scans of indoor spaces as background images. As the amount of data increases with the size of the environment set up to construct a 3D model, the system developed in this work was designed for use in an indoor space within a certain range of settings. However, improvements in 3D modeling technology may eventually enable the use of the system in external spaces. Because the program in this study required a 3D model of the space to depict the background, we performed scanning to construct a 3D model of the indoor space.

Scanning an interior space requires LiDAR measurements; therefore, we set up an iOS device equipped with LiDAR for this purpose. LiDAR measures the distance and direction of an object by emitting a laser or infrared light and measuring the time required for the light to reflect off the object. The LiDAR function enables the generation of highly accurate 3D models. Hence, we proceeded with development using the iPhone 12 Pro MAX as the necessary device equipped with LiDAR.

2.3 Person Recognition Program

First, we used the People Occlusion function of AR Foundation to recognize human forms. This function uses machine learning to distinguish between human and nonhuman forms in images. It is able to recognize areas that appear as human figures and display them as red silhouettes (Fig. 2).

Fig. 2. Recognition of human body

2.4 Background Depiction Program

Transparent cloaking was achieved by representing the real space as a 3D space and fitting it to the silhouette area. First, an arbitrary interior space was scanned in advance using a terminal equipped with LiDAR to create a 3D space model (Fig. 3). The scanned space was then placed in the VR space, and a smartphone camera was used to provide a 360-degree view of the space, allowing the user to walk around freely. The image projected by the camera was set as the background of the transparent area and matched to the silhouette of the human body to realize optical camouflage.

Fig. 3. 3D model of indoor space

3 Result

As a result, we realized a system to project a background image onto human body parts in real time (Fig. 4). The system operated without problems even with varying positions and viewpoint angles. When the position or angle of the viewpoint changes in real space, the background of the transparent area moves in tandem. The system was also able to transparently cloak multiple people. This research has established the foundation of an optical camouflage system that makes full use of XR technology. The system operates on a smartphone, making it possible for many users to easily experience an optical camouflage effect.

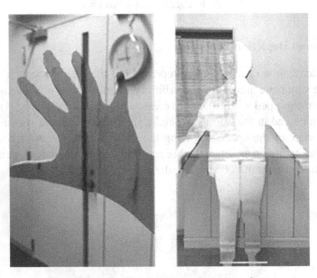

Fig. 4. Transparent cloaking of a human form

4 Discussion

In this study, we performed recognition of people using existing programs. As an extension to this study, the introduction of an object detection program would make it possible to apply transparency to objects other than people.

At present, the program is limited in that the viewpoint position cannot be changed freely after the system is started. The system only operates properly at a specific position. In future work, it should be configured to operate correctly regardless of the position of the user. To solve this problem, a system should be developed to estimate the position in real space based on LiDAR measurements and adapt it to the viewpoint in 3D space.

The 3D scanning method used to create the 3D model in this work can also be used with photogrammetry data. Photogrammetry is commonly used as an information source to create 3D models from multiple images. It can generate highly accurate 3D models by capturing pictures of a subject from various angles and capturing their features as points. Photogrammetry is well-suited to construct 3D models of outdoor landscapes, and can be used to improve the scalability of optical camouflage applications. In the future, as the technology for creating 3D models improves, it may become possible to realize more realistic optical camouflage applications.

5 Conclusion

In this study, we have developed a system that uses XR technology for AR and VR, in contrast to existing lines of research on optical camouflage technology. The actual system that we created succeeded in cloaking a human figure in transparency, establishing a foundation for similar optical camouflage systems. Although the starting position of the system developed in this work is fixed, rendering this position adjustable would enable users to experience optical camouflage while moving freely. As the convenience of optical camouflage improves, this technology is expected to contribute to developments in many fields.

References

1. Tachi, S.: Telexistence and retro-reflective projection technology (RPT). In: Proceedings of the 5th Virtual Reality International Conference (VRIC2003), Laval Virtual 2003, France, 13–18 May 2003, pp. 69/1–69/9 (2003)
2. Mori, S., Lchikari, R., Shibata, F., Kimura, A., Tamura, H.: Framework and technical Issues of diminished reality: a survey of technologies that can visually diminish the objects in the real world by superimposing, replacing, and seeing-through. In: TVRSJ 2011, vol. 16, no. 2, pp. 239–250 (2011)
3. Koizumi, N., Tokiwa, T., Sugimoto, M., Inami, M.: Designing an experience of viewing a self-image that becomes transparent. Acad. J. Virtual Reality Soc. Jpn. 16(2), 149–152 (2011)
4. Izumihara, A., Kawarada, M., Wakisaka, S., Hoshi, T., Inami, M.: Conjugate arrangement of shooting and projection systems in optical camouflage. In: Proceedings of 22nd Virtual Reality Society of Japan Conference (2017)
5. Unity Real-Time Development Platform I 3D, 2D VR & AR Engine. https://unity.com/. Accessed 17 May 2021
6. Unity AR Foundation Framework I Cross platform augmented reality development software I Unity. https://unity.com/ja/unity/features/arfoundation. Accessed 17 May 2021

Reinforcement Learning for Exploring Pedagogical Strategies in Virtual Reality Training

Rifah Sama Aziz[ID] and Bruno Emond[✉][ID]

National Research Council Canada, 1200 Montreal Road, Ottawa, ON, Canada
{rifahsama.aziz,bruno.emond}@nrc-cnrc.gc.ca
http://nrc-cnrc.gc.ca/

Abstract. Pedagogical learning among agents have the power to influence the learning of a new learner in several ways. While such pedagogical approaches of student-teacher interactions are applied on popular games with complex environments, we propose the use of pedagogical learning strategies among autonomous agents on a virtual reality (VR) training application in order to automate the existing tutoring system in the application. Creating four reinforcement learning (RL) agents with Q-Learning algorithm, we experiment the agents with different reward functions to choose the best performer as the tutor. We apply the pedagogical strategy with a budget between the tutor and the learner agent resulting in improvements in the learner's performance.

Keywords: Autonomous agents · Virtual reality · Pedagogical strategies · Reinforcement learning

1 Introduction

Virtual reality (VR) training applications provide a learning environment which can be configured as a mixture of learning by discovery and learning from instructions. When learning by discovery, a person determines what is the best course of action to execute a training task. When learning from instructions, a person is offered a description of what should or could be done. These instructions can be given at the beginning, during a task execution (immediate feedback), or at the end of a task (after action review).

Even on a relatively simple task, the number of possible ways to provide instructions can grow very rapidly, which is a challenge to evidence-based design if the only source of information is human participants' performance and evaluation. Using machine learning, our objective is to reduce the number of design options to be tested later on with human participants. The method consists of comparing different pedagogical strategies and their effects on simulated learners implemented as machine learning algorithms, specifically using reinforcement learning algorithms (RL).

C. Stephanidis et al. (Eds.): HCII 2022, CCIS 1654, pp. 504–511, 2022.
https://doi.org/10.1007/978-3-031-19679-9_63

The domain to which we are applying the method is a virtual reality training environment for first responders learning the initial steps in the management of dangerous goods incidents. The computer simulation consists of a model of the environment (location of the incident, location of the simulated learner, wind direction, time of day), a set of actions the simulated learner can perform (moving left, right, forward, backward, using binoculars, using a phone), and a computerized tutor that can offer advice and feedback to the simulated learner using rewards and recommendations on action choices. The paper will present our results in exploring different pedagogical strategies and their effects on simulated learners.

2   Problem Statement

The pedagogical sequence types listed in Table 1 shows possible variations in providing feedback to a learner. Each of them can be applied to specific knowledge of skill, which can result in a significant number of options to select in the design of a training/learning environment. The determination of which option is more efficient would need to be ultimately supported from empirical data on human performance and learning. However, given the amount of feedback options, the information value derived from an experiment could be overweighted by the cost, effort and duration required to run a data collection study. Beside experiments, other means to collect data to support design decision are available such as relying on expert advice, or conducting ongoing product evaluation with deployed software (A/B testing).

Table 1. Properties related to pedagogical sequences. From Cockburn, Gutwin, Scarr, and Malacria [1].

Property types	Examples
Temporal	Feedback is provided either concurrently, immediately after, or delayed from a learner action
Aggregation	Feedback is provided independently for each discrete action or accumulated or a sequence of actions (after action review)
Modality	Instructions and feedback can be presented as text, speech synthesis, video, or statistics in tabular format
Performance	Feedback is provided in terms of deviation to an ideal sequence with no reference to its outcome or results
Results	Feedback is provided about the outcome of the action such as success or failure in relation to a desired outcome

Our approach consists of using machine learning as a first approximation of the effect of different feedback on learning efficiency. Using machine learning, our objective is to reduce the number of design options to be tested later on with human participants. The method consists of comparing different pedagogical strategies and their effects on simulated learners implemented as machine learning algorithms, specifically using reinforcement learning algorithms.

The following sections review some literature on teacher-student framework in reinforcement learning, and present our preliminary results on applying the method to the design of a virtual reality training environment for first responders who need to learn the initial steps in the management of dangerous goods incidents.

3   Literature Review

The inspiration of tutor-learner agent arises from the work by Torrey and Taylor [7] which uses a teacher-student framework based on reinforcement learning to demonstrate how a teacher agent assists a student agent by proving suggestions on actions to execute. The algorithms used by Torrey and Taylor [7] show how different distribution of the same amount of advice (advice budget) affects significantly the learning process of a student. The variation in advice distribution is determined by teaching algorithms which include early advising, importance advising, mistake correcting and predictive advising. After a teacher agent has learned an effective policy, it teaches student agents by advising them on their course of actions. Early advising is used to benefit the learner at the very early stages of learning. Importance advising prioritize certain states over others, while mistake correcting advice is provided only when the learner makes mistakes. Lastly, in predictive advising the teacher observes the states and actions taken by the student, treating it as data for a Support Vector Machine classifier to estimate future actions of the student [7].

Further improvement of this work is shown in [8] where a principled decision-theoretic setting uses both the teacher and the student as reinforcement learning agents, further proposing a method for the student agent to learn the feedback more productively. Similar work is done by Muslimani et al. [6] with the aim of investigating when the teacher agent should provide feedback to students given a limited feedback budget (i.e., amount of feedback provided). Budgeting the feedback maximizes the student learning performance by creating a controlled environment with restrictions. TAMER is a learning critique algorithm [6] that allows expert agents to learn a way to use the limited number of interactions by relying on the teacher's advice in the reward function to judge over the learner's previous actions. A study by Cruz et al. [2] shows the results of agent-agent interaction focusing on the learning achieved by varying teachers and learners by changing how the advice is taken. A survey by Da Silva et al. [3] on inter-agent teaching methods illustrates the gap between the state-of-the-art reinforcement learning (RL) inter-agent teaching methods and the industry-based applications where the use of RL is not implemented. They further organized the techniques in learner-driven and teacher-driven methods, highlighting the challenges, frameworks, research questions and applications in the stated transfer learning technique [3]. Further work on transfer learning between RL agents under a budget is shown in Fachantidis et al. [5] where they propose a novel RL algorithm, and argue that learning to advise under a budget falls under the generic problem of constrained exploitation in reinforcement learning and experimentally demonstrate that the best performers may not always be the best teacher.

While most of the implementations are carried out on Mountain Car and other available games, we implement a similar student-teacher reinforcement learning approach on a VR application to learn how to initially manage dangerous goods incidents in transportation [4]. The following section describes our work in this area.

4   Computer Simulation Design and Results

Inspired by the pedagogical approach between teaching and learning agents [7], we explored the potential to use a similar approach to design feedback options to be included in a virtual reality (VR) application tutoring system. The VR application involves an incident of a truck leaking corrosive liquids [4] and requires the observer to move to a safe distance that is close enough to determine the substance transported by the vehicle. The virtual reality environment uses levels of dangerous and safe zones which are determined from the distance to the incident. Moving too close to the incident may result in exposing a learner to unnecessary risks. Hence, a tutor system in the application assists the user about the safety knowledge based on the user's location. The current section describes our preliminary work, and exploration of different students and student-tutor interactions during the locomotion to a desired distance from a starting location while avoiding danger zones. A map based on the navigation on the VR environment is created consisting dangerous zones in shades of red and safety zones in shades of green as shown in Fig 1. The red cross represents the location of the truck i.e., the most dangerous location. The goal is to find the best way to move to the green starred location represented as the safest location to observe the incident and identify the dangerous good transported by the truck.

Table 2. Reinforcement learning agents used for the computer simulations.

A_N	Naive	Receives rewards only when reaching the goal or dangerous locations
A_D	Based on Distance to the goal	Receives continuous rewards based on the proximity to the goal. See Eq. 1
A_R	Based on distance to dangerous locations (Risks)	Receives continuous rewards based on the proximity of dangerous locations. See Eq. 2
A_{NT}	Naive with Tutor/Risk	Naive agent (A_N) assisted by and agent that has learned a policy to reach the goal by avoiding risks (A_R)

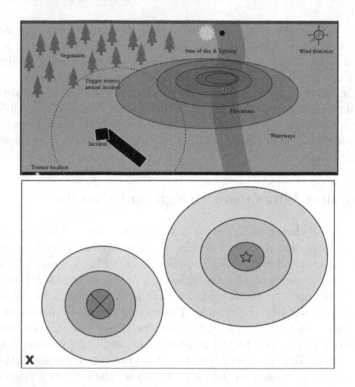

Fig. 1. The map on the VR application (top) and our environment (bottom)

Table 2 lists the agents used for the simulation. The naive agent A_N has the least knowledge about the environment as it is only given information about the goal and danger locations when arriving at them. A reward of positive 1 is given on reaching the goal location and a negative 1 in reaching the dangerous one. The agent possesses no other knowledge about the environment. The second agent A_D is based on how far it is from the goal location. A simple linear increasing and continuous distance function is used to determine the reward based on the distance from the goal. The function is given in Eq. 1. $Dist_{C,G}$ stands for the distance from the current location to the goal location while $Dist_{O,G}$ represents the distance between the origin and the goal location. The reciprocal is squared and subtracted from 1 to keep the reward value normalized and positive. The agent based on the distance has no knowledge of the dangerous locations, hence the rewards increases as it moves closer to the goal. The third agent A_R is only based on the dangerous locations without any knowledge of the goal location. The agent requires crossing several dangerous zones to move to the final goal location. A piece-wise function is used to determine the negative rewards, increasing as the agent moves closer to the truck. The function is given in Eq. 2. In this equation the reward gained is negative as it is considered to be a punishment with d_x and d_y representing the current location in x and y directions. The thresholds m and n are selected based on the location of the truck, creating a boundary till where the risk increases. Once the boundary is crossed, the punishment values decrease continuously. We have intentionally separated the agents focusing on safe and dangerous regions in order to experiment with the importance of prioritizing the goal versus the risks associated to the incident area.

$$reward_{A_N} = 1 - \sqrt{\frac{Dist_{C,G}}{Dist_{O,G}}} \tag{1}$$

$$reward_{A_R} = \begin{cases} -(1 + Dist_{C,O})^2 & \text{if } d_x \le m, d_y \le n \\ -(1 + Dist_{C,G})^2 & otherwise \end{cases} \tag{2}$$

The RL models are based on four actions including movement in forward, backward, left and right directions, and eight states consisting of the three danger zones, three safety zones, the start and the goal position. The three agents (A_N, A_D, A_R) are compared in Fig. 2 and based on the steepness and how fast the stability is reached, the agent with risk information is chosen as the tutor. The agent with risk information depicts steeper learning and faster stability compared to the agent based on distance information and the naive agent.

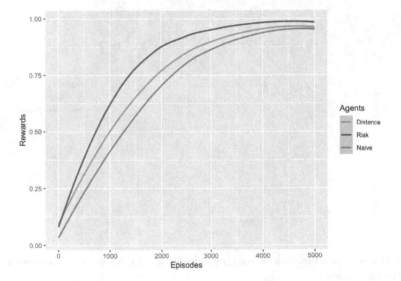

Fig. 2. Rewards as a function of learning episodes for the Naive, Distance and Risk agents.

We tested the different experiences of the reinforcement learning agents based on various knowledge to better understand the importance of the rewards based on the risky regions and safe distances. A simple Q-Learning algorithm is used with 5000 episodes and 200 instances per episode on all four agents to learn about the environment. Initializing the Q-table to zeros, the rewards are calculated differently for each agent. Based on the functions of distance to the goal versus the dangerous positions, the results demonstrate the agent with continuous risk knowledge learns better initially and with fewer variations, leading us to choose this model as the tutor. With the tutor agent possessing the better learning scheme and knowledge, our fourth model is the naive agent acquiring knowledge from the tutor. As the tutor is not meant to share full knowledge to the learner and given that a learner seeks advice only when required, the naive agent only seeks knowledge from the tutor during exploration mode. Using epsilon as 0.5 and a decaying rate of 0.99, the learner initially has 50% chance of exploring and exploiting. Instead of exploring by randomly choosing an action, using the modality pedagogical sequence, the learner seeks knowledge from the tutor's Q-table. In Fig. 3 the performance of the naive agent A_N is compared with the naive agent with the tutor's assistance A_{NT} demonstrating improvement in the initial stages of learning. We have budgeted the lookup to the tutor's Q-table to only the first 200 times for the initial learning to be advised and used epsilon of 0.1 for the experiment in Fig 3. Using an epsilon of 0.1 allows 500 lookup on the tutor's Q-table, and we further limit it to the first 200 lookup.

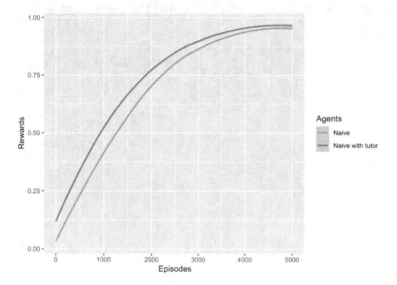

Fig. 3. Rewards as a function of learning episodes for the Naive, and Naive with advice from the tutor agents.

5   Conclusion

The ultimate goal of the application of pedagogical learning among agents for the VR application is to determine which feedback is likely better facilitate student learning. As a first step, we simplified the application map with minimal features. We look forward to augment the complexity of the environment with additional features influencing the risks, such as the wind direction causing additional risk related to the diffusion of corrosive fumes, and the use of binocular to gain knowledge about the incident without moving too close to it. Complicating the environment may also require the use of deep Q-networks. More instances of the model is required to calculate the model variance and the budgeting could be further improved by scattering the number of lookup equally or by focusing on states importance. Moreover, even though we notice improvement in the naive agent using the tutor's advice, the agent is not intended to become as good as the tutor agent as the goal is to improve the initial learning of a naive agent that is completely new to the environment. We aim to assist the naive agent during its exploration through an expert agent's advice. The naive/learner agent (A_N) previously had access to only two information of the map, the specific goal location and the truck's location. The learner-tutor model (A_{NT}) has further information from the tutor's (A_R) Q-table acquiring knowledge of the punishments based on the reward function based on dangerous zones. Therefore, in addition to the rewards based on the map, the agent is given advice as action to perform. To conclude, the future work directs to the creation of a tutor agent possessing sufficient knowledge about the environment's risky and safe locations to guide human players, and eventually replace the manual tutoring system present in the application.

References

1. Cockburn, A., Gutwin, C., Scarr, J., Malacria, S.: Supporting novice to expert transitions in user interfaces. ACM Comput. Surv. **47**(2), 1–36, (2015). ISSN 0360-0300. https://doi.org/10.1145/2659796
2. Cruz, F., Magg, S., Nagai, Y., Wermter, S.: Improving interactive reinforcement learning: what makes a good teacher? Connection Sci. **30**(3), 306–325 (2018). ISSN 0954-0091. https://doi.org/10.1080/09540091.2018.1443318
3. Da Silva, F.L., Warnell, G., Costa, A.H.R., Stone, P.: Agents teaching agents: a survey on inter-agent transfer learning. Auton. Agent. Multi-Agent Syst. **34**(1), 1–17 (2019). https://doi.org/10.1007/s10458-019-09430-0
4. Emond, B., Kinateder, M., Cooper, N., Kondratova, I.: Virtual reality for transportation incident management training of first responders in remote areas. In: Interservice/Industry Training, Simulation, and Education Conference, pp. 1–11, Orlando, FL, (2020). National Training and Simulation Association
5. Taylor, M.E., Torrey, L.: Agents teaching agents in reinforcement learning (nectar abstract). In: Calders, T., Esposito, F., Hüllermeier, E., Meo, R. (eds.) ECML PKDD 2014. LNCS (LNAI), vol. 8726, pp. 524–528. Springer, Heidelberg (2014). https://doi.org/10.1007/978-3-662-44845-8_50
6. Muslimani, C., Johnstonbaugh, K., Taylor, M. E.: Work-in-progress: comparing feedback distributions in limited teacher-student settings (2021)
7. Torrey, L., Taylor, M. E.: Teaching on a budget: agents advising agents in reinforcement learning. In: International Conference on Autonomous Agents and Multiagent Systems (AAMAS). (2013)
8. Zimmer, M., Viappiani, P., Weng, P.: Teacher-Student Framework: A Reinforcement Learning Approach. In: AAMAS Workshop Autonomous Robots and Multirobot Systems, Paris, France (2014)

Measuring Decubitus Wounds Using Augmented Reality Glasses - A User Interface Study

Mathias Bauer[✉] [iD], Nico Leidner, Wladislaw Willhauk, Carina Gansohr[iD], and Stefan Geisler[iD]

Institute of Computer Science and Institute of Positive Computing, Hochschule Ruhr West University of Applied Sciences, Bottrop, Germany
{mathias.bauer,nico.leidner,wladislaw.willhauk}@stud.hs-ruhrwest.de,
{carina.gansohr,stefan.geisler}@hs-ruhrwest.de

Abstract. We present a study on the usability of three different user interfaces for an augmented reality glasses system. The application is intended for use in hospitals by nursing professionals. During wound care, images can be taken with the Microsoft HoloLens 2 and measured directly. The photos must always be taken at the same distance from the wound to follow the healing process. We present and juxtapose three aim assistants to take a picture of the wound and acquire wound data. To gain a first impression about the goodness of usability and the preferred targeting assistant, we conducted a small usability study. Participants were asked to perform wound measuring tasks using our application's varying user interfaces. In this study, we identified strengths and weaknesses for each user interface based on the conducted research and identified approaches for further improvements.

Keywords: User interface study · Usability · Wound measurements · Augmented reality

1 Introduction

Nurses are the backbone of the health and elderly care sector. According to the World Health Statistics report, in stationary hospitals in the United States, one million nurses were additionally needed by the end of 2020 [15]. Furthermore, a quarter of all nurses in the United States are 50 years or older, meaning that the nursing shortage within the next 15 years is expected to be increasing due to retirements [6]. In Germany, employees in health and geriatric care are scarce as well [4]. For this reason the proportion of non-nursing activities like documentation should be kept as low as possible.

Nurses are obliged to document wound assessment, as those nursing records are the main component of quality insurance [14]. Pressure ulcers, like decubitus wounds, might occur in everyday care, although the best efforts by a team of

C. Stephanidis et al. (Eds.): HCII 2022, CCIS 1654, pp. 512–519, 2022.
https://doi.org/10.1007/978-3-031-19679-9_64

specialists are thus no exception to the required documentation for legal reasons [2]. Requirement analysis was performed by contextual inquiries in two affiliate hospitals in Germany. Nurses need to reach sores in uncomfortable positions for both nurses and patients. They use cameras to document the wounds, place meter rulers and labeled foils onto the wound, and hold parts of the patient's body in place.

Our developed system for augmented reality glasses is a tool that aims to provide a simplification for the use case of documenting decubitus wounds, as can be seen in Fig. 1 b) and c). The system can be controlled using gestures, gaze or voice commands, thus leaving the nursing staff's hands-free for wound treatment. Nurses can use this system to take a picture of a pressure wound without using an additional camera device. This is a great advantage in terms of hygiene compliance. These pictures are analyzed automatically to detect the size of the wound and document the wound's properties. In this study, we present three varying user interfaces. The central distinguishing element is the targeting assistant, helping nurses center the image and find the correct distance from the camera to the wound. A focused usability study under laboratory conditions examines the strengths and weaknesses of all three user interfaces. Interviews with the study's participants were conducted, and improvements for future system iterations are presented in detail.

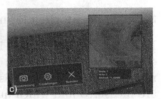

Fig. 1. Overview about the developed system and it's components. a) AR glasses. b) Image acquisition process. c) Wound measurement results.

2 Related Work

Augmented reality glasses are investigated to support nurses in general [10] and also particularly for wound documentation [7,8]. Measuring the size of wounds with digital devices was already achieved by different methods [3,9,16], even if they were not specifically developed for decubitus wounds. However, in order to be able to follow the progress of a wound over several measurement points and to derive the healing process, it is important to always maintain the same distance from the wound. Targeting assistant is a typical task in augmented reality user interfaces. Different methods have been investigated.

Radu et al. compared crosshair targeting systems with classic finger-tapping in an augmented reality scenario. Both input methods did not yield significant differences in tracking losses, the time required to recover tracking and the number of touch errors [13]. Based on Radu et al.'s findings, we decided to implement the first targeting assistant based on a classic crosshairs approach.

A study about robotic-assisted surgery supported by an augmented reality system by Qian et al. showed that they are using other circular approaches for highlighting different parts of patients' bodies [12]. In that study, circular elements were used for different sub-tasks, such as projector-based port placement planning. As this medical study implied, hospital staff might be familiar with circular targeting assistants for various tasks.

Target selection is usually the primary method for selecting virtual objects in an augmented reality application. Asokan et al. tested different targeting assistant techniques, including crosshairs and circles, against classic finger-tapping and found that combining a crosshair and a circle works best in all their tested scenarios [1]. We, therefore, chose to integrate a circle as another variant.

3   Methods

The aim of the research project is to improve the working conditions of nursing staff. Therefore, the nursing professionals were integrated in the design process and a usability evaluation.

3.1   Concept Development and Prototype

In a first step, the most important requirements of nursing staff and wound experts from two German hospitals were collected to ensure professional accuracy. Our partner hospitals provided information on how pressure ulcer wounds are measured and which quality criteria the photo documentation must meet.

Currently, nurses use a sterile paper ruler placed under the wound to measure its size. The depth of the wound is measured with a sterile stick. Both measurements are documented photographically with a camera. Further data are attached to this photo and entered to the hospital information system afterwards.

The underlying idea of automating this task was first mentioned by the nursing staff themselves during participatory design workshops.

After analyzing the activities of the nurses, a rough workflow for a potential digital support with the HoloLens 2 was developed in the design team. The targeting assistant was identified as an important factor with different design solutions from the literature as described in the former section. Therefore, we created a prototype with the approaches from literature research and as an additional alternative, we exploratory developed a rendered line from the camera's point of view to the center of the screen, connecting both the current position and the ideal position for taking a photo of a pressure wound.

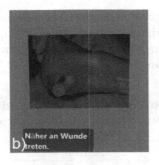

Fig. 2. User interfaces for the targeting assistants. a) Line assistant. b) Circular assistant. c) Crosshairs assistant.

3.2 Usability Study

For a first usability test, we conducted a controlled experiment under laboratory conditions that compares all three aim assistants: One targeting assistant presents a three-dimensional rendered line from the center of the device to the center of the display, the second is a circle displayed in the center of the screen, the third one is a centered crosshairs, as can be seen in Fig. 2. All three assistants appear 70 cm away from the device's camera in augmented reality.

In this study, eight first-semester computer science students with an average age of 22.2 (median = 21) participated. One participant had to be removed from the data set due to suffering from exotropia. This made the participant lose the stereo vision, resulting in two instead of one visual user interface. In addition, only one participant had previous experience using HoloLens 2 augmented reality glasses.

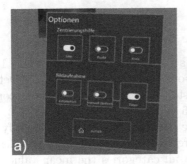
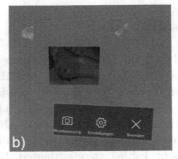

Fig. 3. Application menus. a) Settings. b) Main menu.

After an introduction and informed consent, the participants put on the HoloLens 2 glasses and adjusted them accordingly. The participant's first task was measuring the size of a decubitus wound on a picture on a bulletin board in front of them. There were no detailed explanations on how to proceed with every step. After completing the first task, the next task was to switch to the circular targeting assistant, measuring the wound's size again, using the menus in Fig. 3. Lastly, they were asked to switch to the crosshairs aim assistant, proceeding with the measuring process again.

Table 1. Short usability questionnaire. Items 1 to 4 based on ISO Norm 9241/110 [11]. A 7-point Likert scale was used. The third and fourth Item have been inverted.

Num	Item
1	The application informs you about what it is doing to the extent
2	The application can be operated consistently according to a uniform principle
3	The application requires a lot of time to learn
4	The application requires you to remember many details
5	It's easy to see the controls

Afterwards, a structured interview was conducted. First, participants were asked for their interaction-related technology affinity using the short version of the Affinity for Technology Interaction Short (ATI-S) questionnaire [5]. Next, to gain a first impression about the usability of the user interfaces, we chose four Items from the ISO Norm 9241/110 [11] that can be found in Table 1, as well as another question about the detectability of the user interface elements. Lastly, participants were asked to rate the user interfaces of the three targeting assistants in German school grades from 1 (excellent) to 6 (bad). The study and the interviews were held in German, and both questionnaires were used in the German translation.

4 Results

The results for the ATI-S questionnaire scored in total $M = 4.5, SD = 1.30, \alpha = 0.60$, therewith technology affinity is above the scale average of 3.5. Details can be seen in Table 2. The internal consistency of the ATI-S scale is considered questionable within a range between 0.6 and 0.7.

To gain a first impression about the usability state and to identify general weaknesses within the prototype software system for iterative system design, the five items of Table 1 were evaluated. In all categories the mean value is above the center of the scale 3.5.

The best-rated aim assistant is the crosshairs with an average grade of 2.29 (good), followed by the line assistant (2.43, good) and the circular assistant (2.57, good-mediocre).

The qualitative evaluation revealed that six participants found it difficult to maintain the proper distance from the wound. No targeting assistant fulfilled the requirement of communicating the required length ideally.

Participants expressed problems estimating the distance on the z-axis in space. One participant noted: "It is tough to find the correct distance to the picture on the wall; it takes a lot of time". Furthermore, we observed that participants moved a lot to take a photo of the wound. This is further accompanied by a participant's request to zoom in while finding the correct distance to the wound. Yet, participants stated, finding the center of the pressure wound did not lead to such problems.

The rotation of the line assistant user interface is on occasion displayed incorrectly, as can be seen in Fig. 2 a). One participant was hoping for the line assistant to straighten, as the rotation felt off by a few degrees, irritating the process of finding the center of the wound.

Further, a participant required more information about an targeting assistant before selecting it in the options menu.

Table 2. Results of the system's user interface usability study (1 = worst, 7 = best) and the rating of the targeting assistants a) Line b) Circular c) Crosshairs (1 = best, 6 = worst).

Item	Usability questionnaire					Targeting assistant		
	1	2	3	4	5	a)	b)	c)
Mean	6	5.58	5.58	6.29	5.29	2.43	2.57	2.29
Median	6	6	6	7	5	2	3	2
Std. dev.	1	1.51	1.72	1.11	1.89	1.27	1.27	1.25

5 Discussion and Future Work

The controlled experiment shows that the goodness of usability of the targeting assistant's user interfaces and the system, in general, is in an acceptable state, but further improvements can and need to be addressed.

The average usability results are, overall, rated on the upper end. This indicates that the general usability of this developed system is in a good state but still leaves room for improvements. There is no significant statistical spike, which is further supported by the standard deviation, showing normally distributed values.

According to the subjects, it is difficult to find the appropriate distance to the wound despite the targeting aid. Finding the center of the pressure wound on x- and y-axis was not problematic, but finding the correct distance on the z-axis was more of an issue. For future iterations, it is advised to revisit depth perception for all targeting assistants. Besides the text message prompting users to come closer or to move further away, any additional indicator might yield positive results. A consideration for this feature is additional information in centimeters within the text box and adding a color range to each targeting assistant. Colors might range from green (good/close to a good position) to red (poorly positioned).

Participants themselves suggest a zoom functionality. Moving a lot in a narrow stationary hospital environment might not be possible. Future research might pick up this idea to develop a more subtle solution in which users are less forced to use their whole bodies to zoom in and out.

Subsequently, future iterations should combine the crosshairs and the circular aim assistants and reevaluate the goodness of usability, as Asokan et al. stated that this exact combination worked best in their study [1].

The main limitation of the study is that the systems' usability was tested with a small number of students. As a next step following the technical optimizations, further research needs to be conducted with professional caregivers in a real stationary hospital context. In addition, the participants' request for zoom-in functionality should be evaluated as well.

6   Conclusion

Documentation is a time-consuming task of nursing professionals. For this reason it makes sense to work on automation of this activity. AR glasses like the HoloLens 2 offer a camera and different sensors, which can be used as technical basis. Another important factor is the user interface. We developed three different UI-methods to take a picture for wound documentation and automatic size measurement. The main objective of investigation was the targeting assistant. In our pre-study with students all tested methods turned out to be suitable with a slight preference for a crosshairs approach. The overall feedback was good, but several hints for improvement were given. Especially an indication to support the positioning in the correct distance and a zoom function were requested. In future work an improved version will be tested with nursing professionals.

References

1. Asokan, V., Bateman, S., Tang, A.: Assistance for target selection in mobile augmented reality. In: Proceedings of Graphics Interface 2020, pp. 56–65. GI 2020, Canadian Human-Computer Communications Society (2020). https://doi.org/10.20380/GI2020.07
2. Ayello, E.A., Sibbald, R.G., Delmore, B., Lebovits, S., Saggu, K.: Staging documenting pressure ulcers in the wound care clinic (2014). https://www.hmpgloballearningnetwork.com/site/twc/articles/staging-documenting-pressure-ulcers-wound-care-clinic
3. Bandgar, P.A., Chobe, A.A., Supekar, K., Jawkar, D.: Analyzing and processing of wound detection. Int. J. Eng. Res. 3(3), (2014)
4. Bundesagentur für Arbeit: Tag der Pflege: Mehr Beschäftigte in Pflegeberufen. (2021). https://www.arbeitsagentur.de/presse/2021-19-tag-der-pflege-mehr-beschaeftigte-in-pflegeberufen Accessed Apr 01 2022

5. Franke, T., Attig, C., Wessel, D.: Assessing affinity for technology interaction - the affinity for technology interaction (ATI) scale. scale description - english and german scale version. Tech. rep., Institute for Multimedia and Interactive Systems, Engineering Psychology and Cognitive Ergonomics, University of Lübeck (07 2017). https://doi.org/10.13140/RG.2.2.28679.50081
6. Haddad, L.M., Pavan, A., Toney-Butler, T.J.: Nursing shortage. National Library of Medicine (2022)
7. Janßen, M., Prilla, M.: Investigating the use of head mounted devices for remote cooperation and guidance during the treatment of wounds. In: Proceedings of the ACM on Human-Computer Interaction 6, pp. 1–27 (2022)
8. Klinker, K., Wiesche, M., Krcmar, H.: Digital transformation in health care: augmented reality for hands-free service innovation. Inf. Syst. Front. 22(6), 1419–1431 (2020)
9. Kumar, C.V., Malathy, V.: Image processing based wound assessment system for patients with diabetes using six classification algorithms. In: 2016 International Conference on Electrical, Electronics, and Optimization Techniques (ICEEOT), pp. 744–747. IEEE (2016)
10. Prilla, M., Recken, H., Janßen, M., Schmidt, A.: Die Pflegebrille als Instrument der Digitalisierung in der Pflege: Nutzenpotentiale. In: Assistive Technologien im Sozial-und Gesundheitssektor, pp. 735–752. Springer (2022) https://doi.org/10.1007/978-3-658-34027-8
11. Prümper, J.: Der Benutzungsfragebogen ISONORM 9241/10: Ergebnisse zur Reliabilität und Validität. In: Software-Ergonomie '97, pp. 253–262. B. G. Teubner Stuttgart, 65189 Wiesbaden (01 1997). https://doi.org/10.1007/978-3-322-86782-7_21
12. Qian, L., Wu, J.Y., DiMaio, S.P., Navab, N., Kazanzides, P.: A review of augmented reality in robotic-assisted surgery. IEEE Trans. Med. Robot. Bionics 2(1), 1–16 (2019)
13. Radu, I., MacIntyre, B., Lourenco, S.: Comparing children's crosshair and finger interactions in handheld augmented reality: relationships between usability and child development. In: Proceedings of the The 15th International Conference on Interaction Design and Children, pp. 288–298 (2016)
14. Russell, L.: The importance of wound documentation and classification. British J. Nurs. 8(20), 1342–1354 (1999)
15. Slattery, M.J., Logan, B.L., Mudge, B., Secore, K., von Reyn, L.J., Maue, R.A.: An undergraduate research fellowship program to prepare nursing students for future workforce roles. J. Prof. Nurs. 32(6), 412–420 (2016) 10.1016/j.profnurs.2016.03.008.https://www.sciencedirect.com/science/article/pii/S8755722316000612
16. Wu, W., Yong, K.Y.W., Federico, M.A.J., Gan, S.K.E.: The APD skin monitoring app for wound monitoring: image processing, area plot, and colour histogram. Sci. Phone Apps Mob. Device 5(3) 1–9(2019)

Tiny Hands are Cute: Adaptive Virtual Hands to Accurately Select Nail-Size Arm's Reach Virtual Objects in Dense Immersive VR

Shimmila Bhowmick(✉), Pratul C. Kalita, and Keyur Sorathia

Department of Design, Indian Institute of Technology Guwahati, Guwahati, Assam, India
shimmila.bhowmick@gmail.com

Abstract. Object selection is an essential task in Virtual Reality applications. Current object selection techniques suffer from issues of hand jitter, accuracy, and higher errors in selecting nail-sized objects in a dense virtual environment. We present *tiny hands,* a technique to reduce the size of virtual hands to easily navigate and accurately select nail-sized object in a dense environment. We present 3 gesture based interaction techniques (i) Fisting non-dominant hand (ii) Palm downwards for 2 s and (iii) Pinch-in and Pinch-out non-dominant hand in this paper. Our initial findings indicate that *tiny hands* technique is a versatile approach for selection of small objects in dense VE. Users also found these techniques to be natural, intuitive, easy to use and accurate in selecting small targets in dense VEs.

Keywords: Object selection · Dense virtual environment · Small objects · Virtual reality

1 Introduction

Object selection is an essential task for Virtual Reality (VR) applications. VR applications involving manipulation and locomotion are often preceded by a selection task. However, selection of nail-size objects in a dense Virtual Environment (VE) has challenges of inaccurate selection, higher error rates and increased task completion times [4]. This is mainly due to hand jitters experienced in controllers or controller-less selection in commonly used commercial VR platforms (i.e., Oculus Rift/Quest, HTC Vive etc.). Prior work examined various object selection techniques in dense VEs [1, 5–7], however, the effectiveness of these techniques are limited in the way it is designed, are imprecise and have a significant negative impact on user performance and experience when applied for small object selection in dense VE [1, 2, 4].

A natural form of interaction in VR is the use of virtual hands, enabling direct selection of objects based on analogies from the real world. However, when selecting an object with the virtual hand technique, the user's hand occludes the projection of the object during corrective movements [2], increasing the chance of erroneous selection for nail-size objects. In this work, we explore the possibilities provided by VR technologies of using virtual hands and extend them in ways not possible in real world in order to provide efficient and convenient method for object selection.

© The Author(s), under exclusive license to Springer Nature Switzerland AG 2022
C. Stephanidis et al. (Eds.): HCII 2022, CCIS 1654, pp. 520–527, 2022.
https://doi.org/10.1007/978-3-031-19679-9_65

We propose the *tiny hands* technique that combines the input for 3D interaction in VR (Fig. 1) for selection of nail-size objects within arm's length in dense VEs. It scales down the size of virtual hands for direct selection of small target in dense VE. We propose three interaction techniques of the *tiny hands* concepts. While scaling down the hand size remains same for all the three concepts, the interaction modality changes. In the first technique, the user performs a fist gesture on the non-dominant hand to trigger *tiny hands* that is reflected on the dominant virtual hand for direct selection. In the second technique, the user places the non-dominant hand in front of the user for 2 s to activate *tiny hands* on the dominant virtual hand for direct selection. In the third technique, the user performs a pinch (index finger and thumb) using non-dominant hand on top of the user's dominant hand to trigger *tiny hands* for final selection. We hypothesize that these techniques could prove effective for selection of small targets in dense VEs.

This paper is structured via following section. We explain the design rationale in Sect. 2 with details on each interaction technique presented in Sects. 2.1, 2.2 and 2.3. Section 3 explains the study method, protocol and participants. We discuss the findings in Sect. 4 followed by concluding the paper in Sect. 5.

2   Understanding Tiny Hands

As the name indicates, the concept of tiny hands reduces the size of a dominant virtual hand in immersive VR to easily navigate inside a dense environment and accurately select the desired object. The non-dominant hand performs a gesture (explained based on each different interaction technique) to activate tiny hands in a VE. The size of the virtual hand is reduced to half (a gain factor of 0.5) of the default virtual hand size. The maximum and minimum size of the virtual hand is full (default size 1) and $1/10^{th}$ (a gain factor of 0.1) respectively. The gesture is further manipulated to modify the size of the virtual hand. Users move the physical hand to reflect the same motions for tiny virtual hands in the VE. When the virtual dominant hand reaches to the desired object, user points to select followed by a finger tap to confirm the object selection.

The choice of point and tap for object selection and confirmation respectively is adopted to reduce accidental selection, a commonly experienced challenge in dense VE [3, 4]. The use of point and tap for error-free selection in VR as compared to point is also proven advantageous in previous studies [4].

2.1   Interaction Technique 1: Fisting Non-dominant Hand

Here, fisting the non-dominant hand for 2 s triggers tiny hand. The fist must be palm facing downwards to activate tiny hands. The size of virtual hand reduces to half (a gain factor of 0.5) of the actual size as default. User rotates the wrist in a clockwise and anticlockwise direction to increase and decrease the size of the virtual hand. The fist can be released anytime during user interaction. To deactivate the tiny hands, user fists the non-dominant hand again for 2 s. As described for activation, deactivating tiny hands require the palm to face downward during the fist. Figure 1(a) visually represents the fist-based interaction technique for the concept of tiny hands. When a desired size of the virtual hand is achieved, a user performs point and tap gesture to confirm object selection.

(a)   (b)

Fig. 1. (a) User can see the virtual hands in front of the user (b) user makes a fist gesture on the non-dominant hand to trigger tiny hands. By rotating the fist clockwise/anticlockwise user selects the hand size.

2.2 Interaction Technique 2: Palm Downwards for 2 s

This interaction technique uses the presence of non-dominant hand palm for 2 s to activate tiny hands. The hand palm must be facing downwards to activate tiny hands. Similar to interaction technique 1, the size of the virtual hand reduces to half (a gain factor of 0.5). The vertical movement in upwards and downward direction increases and reduces the hand size respectively. Once the desired virtual hand size is achieved, user performs point and tap to confirm object selection. Tiny hands are deactivated after user places the non-dominant hand again for 2 s. Figure 2(b) showcases the interaction technique 2.

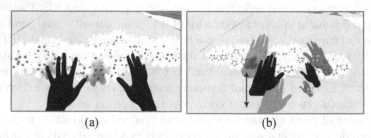

(a)   (b)

Fig. 2. (a) Virtual hands are activated, user places non-dominant hand in the camera view static for 2 s to trigger *tiny hands* (b) Vertical movement of the non-dominant hand up/down increases/decreases the virtual right hand size.

2.3 Interaction Technique 3: Pinch-In and Pinch-Out Non-dominant Hand

Here, pinching (using index finger and thumb) using non-dominant hand for 2 s on dominant hand triggers tiny hands. As described in interaction technique 1 and 2, the dominant hand size reduces to half (a gain factor of 0.5). User further pinches in and out to reduce and increase the size of the virtual hand respectively. The pinch-in and out interactions can be performed without placing on dominant hand after activation. Once the desired virtual hand size is achieved, user performs point and tap to confirm object selection. Tiny hands are deactivated after pinching is performed on dominant hand for 2 s. Figure 3(c) showcases the interaction technique 3.

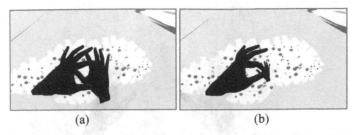

Fig. 3. (a) Pinch-out using index finger and thumb to increase the hand size. (b) Pinch-in using index finger and thumb to decrease the hand size.

3 Usability Evaluation via Think Aloud Technique

We evaluated the usability issues via a think aloud technique with two major objectives. First, we want to understand the challenges and advantages of "tiny hands" concept in selecting small size objects in dense VEs. The second objective was to understand users' perception in terms of naturalness, ease of use and accuracy of the proposed interaction techniques. The interaction techniques were implemented and evaluated with the Wizard-of-Oz technique. The following section describes the VE design, participants, task details and the study procedure.

3.1 Design of Virtual Environment

We developed our prototype using the Unity 3D game engine. The visual stimulus was delivered by the oculus quest HMD with 1440×1600 resolution (per eye) and $115.52°$ diagonal FOV. The headset was connected to a computer (that used i-7 processor, integrated graphics 5500, 16 GB RAM and a Microsoft Windows 10 operating system) using the oculus link cable. We used the mouse scroll to scale the virtual hand (hand prefab provided by the oculus integration kit) during the experiment.

We created a dense molecular structure that composed 1192 spheres. The VE size was $20 \times 15 \times 10$ feet. The structure resembled a design of small-molecule compound used by biologists for molecular modelling (target proteins to determine potential effects on humans). The spheres were colored red as distractor objects and target objects were colored blue. The spheres were static and sized 0.5 mm in diameter for each sphere. The molecular structure was placed at 1-m distance from the participant. Figure 4 shows the VE used for the usability evaluation.

3.2 Participants

A total of 10 non-paid participants (7 males, 3 females) from the age group of 18–35 (Mean = 25.42, SD = 4.07) were recruited for the study. The participants were university students from undergraduate, graduate and PhD programs. The participants were intermediate VR users considering their experience of using different VR platforms (i.e., HTC Vive, Oculus Quest, mobile phone VR) for 2–3 h a week for at least last 6 months.

Fig. 4. A snapshot of the virtual environment and the virtual hands created for the study.

3.3 Study Setup and Apparatus

We used the Oculus Quest for this study. We placed a video camera diagonally to the participant to collect visual evidence and analyze the study findings.

3.4 Task

We conducted an informal evaluation to get insights about the usability of *tiny hands* technique. The objective of the study was to understand the effectiveness of the techniques for selection of small targets in dense VEs. We also wanted to know the naturalness, ease of use, perception of accuracy and fatigue levels of the proposed techniques while selecting the target objects. In this regard the task assigned was to select the blue target that was placed at one location among the molecular structure. Each time the user selects the target, the target colour changed to green to indicate selection and the next target location is indicated. This was repeated for 5 target selection.

3.5 Study Procedure

The study was carried out in a university laboratory by a female moderator. We introduced the concept of tiny hands to the participants followed by introduction and training of 3 interaction techniques for object selection. We assigned the task to select the blue colored target objects using 3 randomly presented techniques. The target objects turned green after their successful selection. The techniques and targets were randomized to eliminate biases. The designed VE was shown to the participants before the task. Participants were asked to verbalize their thoughts at each step during the evaluation. We conducted a semi-structured interview with participants to learn about challenges and advantages of tiny hands, perception of the ease of use, naturalness and accuracy of the interaction techniques. We also asked about their likes and dislikes for the techniques.

The evaluation study was video recorded for post-study analysis. The interview findings and users' thought process were documented via written notes.

4 Study Insights and Findings Discussion

We present the findings in two sections:

(1) Overall concept of tiny hands – whether users find tiny hands technique suitable for selection of small targets in dense VE. What did users like and dislike about tiny hands?

Overall, the findings indicate a positive attitude towards the concept of tiny hands for small object selection in a dense VE. Participants mentioned two primary points that contributed positively for tiny hands, i.e., (i) mapping of making virtual hands small to select a small object and (ii) ease in navigation inside a dense VE due to small virtual hands. Individually, all the three techniques received several positive comments for being natural, intuitive and appropriate for the task at hand. The comments are as follows.

"It is so cool to make the hand small. I can easily select the target." (P1)

"When the virtual hand size is small, the tip of index finger matches with the size of the target which makes selection very easy and precise" (P2)

Three participants pointed out that a visualization could help them understand the current size of the *tiny hands.*

"While rotating the fist, or moving hands vertically there is uncertainty in how much to rotate to make the virtual hands big or small. There could be a visualization (like a meter) showing the current size and how much to rotate the hand clockwise and anticlockwise for desired size." (P4)

Two participant commented,

"Some visualization of a widget maybe provided near the hand for users to understand the hand size currently in use and how much to rotate for increasing/decreasing to the next size." (P5, P7)

Two participants also commented on the asymmetry of the hands (when non-dominant hand is big and right hand is small) while doing the task at hand.

"When the non-dominant hand is big and dominant hand is triggered to tiny hands, it feels a little weird at first, a few times the focus goes to the bigger hand while doing the task. Maybe both the hands could be small".

(2) Findings on proposed 3 interaction techniques – on the perception of ease of use, naturalness and accuracy.

In general, all the three techniques received positive feedback in terms of being intuitive and natural for selection of small objects.

"It was easy to learn the technique, and I quickly became proficient in using it. Using tiny hands makes selection very easy and accurate." (P4)

For the second technique, where users used vertical movement for *tiny hands* participants quoted:

> *"I prefer this technique over the other techniques as the vertical movement up/down to increase/decrease the virtual hand size maps very well. While doing the task, I can remember the vertical hand location and hence the size of the hand selected and can easily chose the next desired size." (P3)*

> *"Controlling the vertical movement becomes demanding when we have to select multiple targets. It caused fatigue by the time I selected the 5th target (P8)*

We also observed that all of the participants did not increase the size of the tiny hands after setting it once to a small value. While asked about it participants said they were able to correctly identify the target size required as the targets were within hands reach. However, a few participants decreased the hand size to its smallest value for selecting the targets. Participants also mentioned that they would prefer the tiny hands size to be of a certain size when tiny hands is triggered and reducing it when only when selection is difficult.

For the third technique, where users used pinch for tiny hands participants quoted:

> *"This is the easiest as I just have to pinch in/out to decrease/increase the virtual hand size. Selecting the targets with the small hands becomes very easy. My index finger tip size matches with the target size which makes it very easy to select." (P9)*

We observed that participants found it easy to use pinch to trigger tiny hands for selection of small objects. A participant suggested the use of multiple finger pinch to increase the size of tiny hands (pinch using index finger and thumb for smallest size, addition of fingers for incremental size increase).

In a dense VE, while the user is in the process of making a selection there might be a situation to make the hand size smaller considering the small size of the target object when the user is closer to the target. Making the hand smaller or bigger at that instance might have an influence in effective selection and could lead to higher error for a dense VE and higher fatigue.

5 Conclusion

The task of selecting a small object in dense VEs is prevalent in immersive VR. When considering the current approaches for object selection in virtual reality, few tackle the problem of selecting small objects dense VEs. In this context, we present the concept of tiny hands for selection of small objects in dense VE. The three interaction techniques of tiny hands in selecting a small target are by fist rotating, palm downwards and vertically up/down movement and pinch-in and pinch-out which trigger tiny hands for final precise selection. We performed a usability study to understand the challenges and advantages of "tiny hands" concept in selecting small size objects in dense VEs and to understand users' perception in terms of naturalness, ease of use and accuracy of the proposed interaction techniques. User evaluation and feedback indicated the technique to be natural, intuitive to use, accurate in selecting small targets in dense VEs. Furthermore, these interactions gave a way towards experiencing something magical otherwise not possible to experience in the real world. As future work, we intend to refine the interaction techniques based on user feedback and conduct a quantitative study to generalize the results for larger context.

References

1. Argelaguet, F., Andujar, C.: Efficient 3D pointing selection in cluttered virtual environments. IEEE Comput. Graph. Appl. **29**(6), 34–43 (2009)
2. Argelaguet, F., Andujar, C.: A survey of 3D object selection techniques for virtual environments. Comput. Graph. **37**(3), 121–136 (2013)
3. Bhowmick, S., Kalita, P., Sorathia, K.: A gesture elicitation study for selection of nail size objects in a dense and occluded dense HMD-VR. In: IndiaHCI 2020: Proceedings of the 11th Indian Conference on Human-Computer Interaction, pp. 12–23 (2020)
4. Bhowmick, S., Panigrahi, A., Borah, P., Kalita, P., Sorathia, K.: Investigating the effectiveness of locked dwell time-based point and tap gesture for selection of nail-sized objects in dense virtual environment. In: Symposium on Spatial User Interaction, pp. 1–2. (2020)
5. Cockburn, A., Firth, A.: Improving the acquisition of small targets. In: O'Neill, E., Palanque, P., Johnson, P. (eds.) People and Computers XVII—Designing for Society, pp. 181–196. Springer, London (2004). https://doi.org/10.1007/978-1-4471-3754-2_11
6. Mendes, D., Medeiros, D., Sousa, M., Cordeiro, E., Ferreira, A., Jorge, J.A.: Design and evaluation of a novel out-of-reach selection technique for VR using iterative refinement. Comput. Graph. **67**, 95–102 (2017)
7. Cashion, J., Wingrave, C., LaViola, J.J., Jr.: Dense and dynamic 3D selection for game-based virtual environments. IEEE Trans. Visual Comput. Graph. **18**(4), 634–642 (2012)

VR for Rehabilitation: The Therapist Interaction and Experience

Ana Ferreira[1,2](✉) , Alena Hanchar[2], Vitória Menezes[2], Bruno Giesteira[3,3] ,
Claudia Quaresma[4,5] , Susana Pestana[6,7] , Andreia Pinto de Sousa[8] ,
Pedro Neves[8] , and Micaela Fonseca[4,8]

[1] Faculty of Medicine, CINTESIS@RISE, MEDCIDS, University of Porto, Porto, Portugal
amlaf@med.up.pt
[2] Faculty of Fine Arts, University of Porto, Porto, Portugal
[3] Faculty of Fine-Arts, Design Department, INESCTEC, HumanISE Human-Centred
Computing, University of Porto, Porto, Portugal
[4] Laboratório de Instrumentação, Engenharia Biomédica e Física da Radiação (LIBPhys-UNL),
Lisbon, Portugal
[5] Departamento de Física, FCT-UNL, Lisbon, Portugal
[6] Departamento de Saúde, Escola Superior de Saúde, Instituto Politécnico de Beja,
Beja, Portugal
[7] Centro de Investigação em Educação, ISPA, Instituto Universitário, Lisbon, Portugal
[8] HEI-Lab, Lusófona University, Lisbon, Portugal

Abstract. Virtual Reality (VR) Serious Games can improve physical, cognitive
and mental rehabilitation by helping patients stay engaged and entertained while
performing rehabilitation exercises. Patients need therapist monitoring and intervention tailored to each patient and to each point in their unique rehabilitation
process. This article reports on a prototype development of a therapist interface
for an occupational therapy rehabilitation VR game, which was guided by user
research and co-creation sessions. Usability testing was carried out with low-
and high-fidelity prototypes. Despite achieving a System Usability Scale score of
93.75, the interface requires further development at the level of game-session creation and parameter personalization. This article showcases relevant challenges in
interaction design for including the therapist in the patient's game-playing while
allowing fast/efficient setup of appropriate game-based therapy, thus balancing
patient outcomes and efficient use of therapist time and effort.

Keywords: User-centered research · VR · Physical rehabilitation · Therapist
interface

1 Introduction

Serious games can improve physical, cognitive and mental rehabilitation processes at
the level of engagement and entertainment [1–3]. Internet of Things (IoT) technologies
allow massive data gathering and personalization [4] which make Virtual Reality (VR)
rehabilitation an attractive option, marrying effectiveness and scalability for both remote

© The Author(s), under exclusive license to Springer Nature Switzerland AG 2022
C. Stephanidis et al. (Eds.): HCII 2022, CCIS 1654, pp. 528–535, 2022.
https://doi.org/10.1007/978-3-031-19679-9_66

therapy and as a supplement to more conventional therapy. VR therapy games need to feature a therapist interface, and this interface needs to be designed to meet therapist requirements as well as fit the diverse range of contexts of therapy sessions [1, 5, 6]. This article reports on prototype development for a therapist interface for the Village Druid VR therapy game [7]. An extensible benefit of this development process is allowing the study of rehabilitation interfaces principles and guidelines for remote therapy [8].

2 Methods

The prototype's development was guided by user research, starting with a literature review followed by interviews with the target population. This was used to define Personas for the prototype's end-users, two use scenarios and associated requirements.

After the first draft of wireflows [10], two co-creation sessions were performed with therapists to obtain their feedback and contributions on information content, structure and interaction flow. These were conducted with an online platform to allow joint-discussion. Thanks to acquiring this understanding of therapist workflow, the low-fidelity prototype was deployed and evaluated in terms of how well VR sessions can be customized for patients, which is the key goal of a VR rehabilitation game and its associated therapeutics. We developed a test plan for the usability tests, which were carried out on an individual basis via an online platform. The participants were given a link for the prototype and were asked to share their screen. At the end of the sessions, some open questions regarding the satisfaction and ease of use were asked to the participants. The same usability test and a System Usability Scale (SUS) questionnaire (Portuguese version [9]) were applied for the high-fidelity prototype. These and the co-creation sessions were video-recorded, with prior permission from the participants.

3 Results

There is a relative lack of published research in this particular subject. Most published research focuses on serious game development and testing and less on therapist interfaces for setting up patient sessions within the game. Common therapist concerns reported in the literature consist of: i) the need to customize game parameters; ii) in a quick/automated way; iii) being able to evaluate and monitor players' performance; as well as iv) intervene during the game to edit parameters, whenever necessary.

We interviewed five participants in April 2022: 2 therapists, 2 physiotherapists and 1 physiatrist; 4 women and 1 man. Three participants had been in clinical practice for more than 10 years, another participant was in practice for more than 5 years and the other was still a student doing her training. The majority worked in private clinics (N = 4) and 2 were active researchers in their specific fields. One worked in a public hospital.

None of the participants used an electronic patient record or online application to register the data from the patient sessions. Commonly, they register session data in paper (pre-formatted or not) and, at the end of the day, they transfer day's session data to an Excel file. This helps them keep up with the history and progress of each patient, and lets them prepare for that patient's coming session. In their clinical practice, all of them would prefer to work on a desktop computer, 4 would use a tablet if that were possible, while 3 also mentioned mobile applications for quicker interactions during the session, but were in agreement that the tablet screen size would be more comfortable.

When asked about desirable characteristics, features and content to keep track of patients' sessions, participants mentioned that such record would need to: retain patient's progress (N = 5); be simple (N = 3); quick (N = 3); a graphical representation would be preferred (N = 2); and allow for the adjustment of variables during a session (N = 2). With these inputs, a Persona, Vanda Sousa, was defined as the typical player for the target population (Fig. 1). Vanda is a therapist and would like to have more time to observe and interact with the patient instead of taking notes to remember what to do for the next session. Doing this in paper format is hard to manage and time-consuming.

Fig. 1. Vanda, the persona representing the target population - rehabilitation therapists.

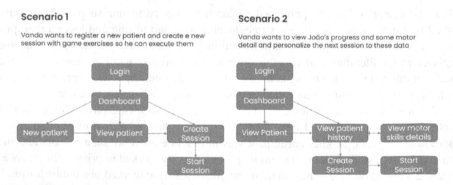

Fig. 2. Main use scenarios. Left: New patient registration and game session creation. Right: View patient's progress and motor skills details and customise patient's next session accordingly.

With these initial data, first draft wireflows were designed so that they could be used as exploratory material within the co-creation sessions. Two co-creation sessions were carried out in early May 2022, with two participants each (the first with two therapists; the second one with one therapist and one psychologist). The main results from the co-creation sessions include: the need for clarification of two contents (e.g., inhibitory category and Z-axis); removing the picture of the patient and inserting their age in all screens; to have a summary diagnosis of the patient but including other data such as hobbies, other interests or specific patient characteristics (e.g., wears glasses); and displaying the name of the professional following the patient.

In the patient session history, more detail on the performance of the sub-category or specific part of the limb to be trained is required; a feature for adding comments for each category (e.g., cognitive or motor) is required. In the session creation screen, a preview of the exercise and more data on the aspects of exercise rehabilitation and how it is performed in the game context are required; search and filters for types of exercises available in the game and the rehabilitation aspects in each exercise are also required.

We took the above suggestions on-board and proceeded to design the low-fidelity prototype (Figs. 3 and 4). This prototype was used in 3 usability tests (2 with physiotherapists and 1 with a physiatrist) in the third week of May. We found that some functionalities were unclear, such as how to access the history screen from the patients' dashboard as well as a feature to manage and search for previously finished sessions. Furthermore, therapists required additional data to be displayed, such as the date of a patient's incident and the date of their medical diagnosis, age (instead of just the date of birth) and the ability to add comments to specific parts of a session.

On the whole, from 1 (very difficult) to 7 (very easy), tasks 1 and 2 (related to scenarios 1 and 2) scored an average of 6; positive test-user remarks include: "very intuitive", "easy", "simple", "clean"; while negative remarks include: "difficult to access patient's history", "none", "need to see more detailed parameters".

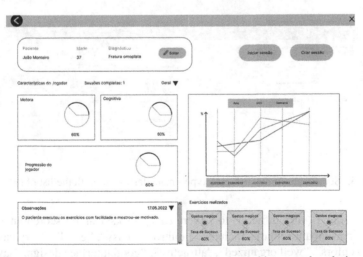

Fig. 3. Screenshot of the low-fi prototype – patient's history and evolution.

The high-fidelity prototype was developed (the main screenshots can be seen in Figs. 5, 6 and 7) taking into account the results of the first round of usability tests. Four usability tests were performed, in the last week of May 2022 for rapid iteration of the high-fidelity prototype. The test-users were the same occupational therapists that had previously participated in the two co-creation sessions.

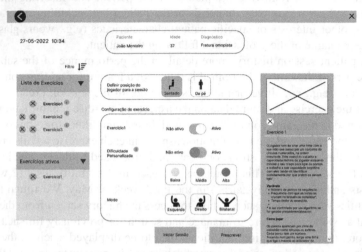

Fig. 4. Screenshot of the low-fi prototype - creating a new patient session.

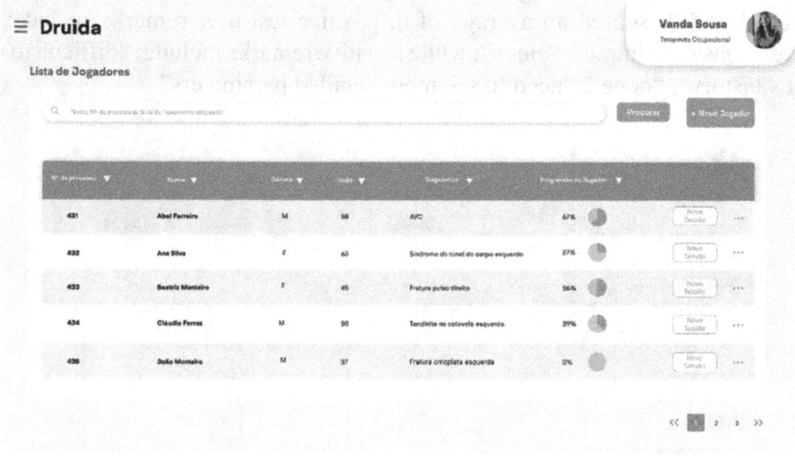

Fig. 5. Screenshot of the hi-fi prototype - main dashboard with the list of patients.

Again, from 1 (very difficult) to 7 (very easy), tasks 1 and 2 scored an average of 6. Positive participant remarks include: "intuitive", "easy", "good", "very easy", "nice layout and colors", "well organized", "attractive", "good interface design, "saves time"; while negative participant remarks include: "difficult to access patient's history", "small letter size", "change Y caption", "not clear the definition of session parameters".

The Systems Usability Score (SUS) score average for the 4 participants was 93.75, suggesting minor improvements in the design are needed. As shown in Fig. 5, this is done by providing easier access to patient history and progress by selecting the three dots on the right, or the whole line for a specific patient (Fig. 5). Other relevant changes were applied in the most "problematic" screen, the one to create a new session (Fig. 6). Since there are different steps and a logic/sequence to configure the various parameters of the game, some doubts arose in how to define session creation. We have altered this screen for improved feedback on the configuration sequence with the next feature being activated each time a step is completed (Figs. 8 and 9).

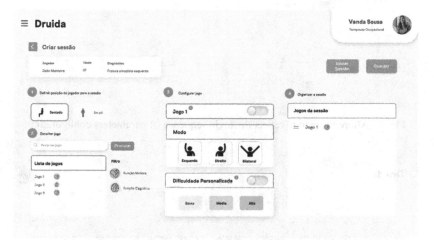

Fig. 6. Hi-fi prototype - personalize session parameters and create a new game session.

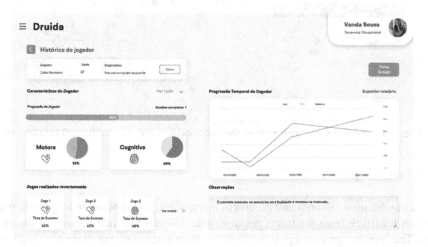

Fig. 7. Screen to visualize patient's progress as well as performed exercises and sessions.

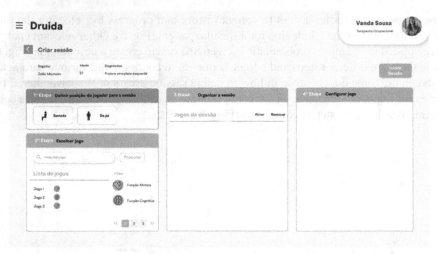

Fig. 8. Altered screen to reflect the logic sequence of parameters configuration.

Fig. 9. Create session screen with all the logic sequence on and configured parameters.

4 Discussion

Thanks to the user research and co-creation activities, it was possible to quickly gather relevant feedback from the target population and iterate the final version of the prototype. This version garnered positive remarks from test-users, but there remained room for improvement in critical aspects, despite a breakthrough in reducing the number of interfaces. These pertain to the screen to configure game sessions and parameters for the patient to execute and the therapist to observe - an essential feature. Improvements were integrated (Figs. 8 and 9) but further tests are needed.

5 Conclusion

This project has demonstrated the relevance of including the therapist in the patient's experience of a VR rehabilitation game, allowing the therapist to easily/quickly setup the most adequate exercises within the game's capabilities.

Future work includes testing and iterating the prototype with a bigger and more varied sample and within the real context of a patient's session while using the VR game to perform rehabilitation exercises.

Acknowledgements. The work was funded by Fundação para a Ciência e Tecnologia (FCT), under HEI-Lab center (UIDB/05380/2020).

The authors would like to thank all participants who helped to shape the final prototype. Ana Ferreira is also supported by project AnyMApp - Anonymous Digital Twin for Human-App Interactions (EXPL/CCI-COM/0052/2021) (FCT – Fundação para a Ciência e Tecnologia).

References

1. Gmez-Portes, C., Lacave, C., Molina, I., Vallejo, D.: Home rehabilitation based on gamification and serious games for young people: a systematic mapping study. Appl. Sci. **10**, 8849 (2020). https://doi.org/10.3390/app10248849
2. González-González, S., Toledo-Delgado, A., Muñoz-Cruz, V., Torres-Carrion, P.V.: Serious games for rehabilitation: gestural interaction in personalized gamified exercises through a recommender system. J. Biomed. Inform. **97**, 103266 (2019)
3. Ogawa, F., You, T., Leveille, G.: Potential benefits of exergaming for cognition and dual-task function in older adults: a systematic review. J. Aging Phys. Act. **24**, 332–336 (2016)
4. Giesteira, B., Silva, J., Sarmento, T., Abreu, P., Restivo, T. Carnival play: ehealth solution to evaluate, rehabilitate, and monitor dexterity and manual strength. In: Alexandre Peixoto de Queirós, R., Marques, A. (eds.), Handbook of Research on Solving Modern Healthcare Challenges with Gamification, pp. 206–242. IGI Global (2021). https://doi.org/10.4018/978-1-7998-7472-0.ch012
5. Hardy, S., Dutz, T., Wiemeyer, J., Göbel, S., Steinmetz, R.: Framework for personalized and adaptive game-based training programs in health sport. Multim. Tools Appl. **74**(14), 5289–5311 (2014). https://doi.org/10.1007/s11042-014-2009-z
6. Tobler, A., et al.: User perspectives on exergames designed to explore the hemineglected space for stroke patients with visuospatial neglect: usability study. JMIR Ser. Games **5**(3), e18 (2017). https://doi.org/10.2196/games.8013
7. PlayersAll: media agency and empowerment. HEI-Lab Center (UIDB/05380/2020) Research Scholarship FCT PeX. Ref. EXPL/COM-OUT/0882/2021 (2022). https://bit.ly/3rXeLb7
8. Giesteira, B., Pereira, E.: hci4d guidelines for interactive content. Emerging trends, techniques, and tools for massive open online course (MOOC). In: Management Advances in Educational Technologies and Instructional Design, pp. 49–77 (2018). https://doi.org/10.4018/978-1-5225-5011-2.ch003
9. Martins, A.I., Rosa, A.F., Queirós, A., Silva, A., Rocha, A.P.: European Portuguese validation of the System Usability Scale (SUS), Procedia Comput. Sci, **67**, 293–300 (2005), ISSN 1877-0509. https://doi.org/10.1016/j.procs.2015.09.273
10. Wireflows: A UX Deliverable for Workflows and Apps. Nielsen Norman Group (2016)

Cruel Parallel: Towards the Designing of a Dynamic Game Adaptation for VR-Based Survival Horror Games

Mike A. Heitzmann[1] and Dvijesh Shastri[2($\boxtimes$)]

[1] Metamoki Inc., San Francisco, CA, USA
[2] University of Houston-Downtown, Houston, TX, USA
shastrid@uhd.edu

Abstract. This study explored the body motion trackers of a virtual reality device in dynamically adjusting game elements for survival horror games. The proposed approach utilizes the hand and head motions to quantify the player's uncanny feelings for updating scary effects, including the game ambiance and the sequence of uncanny events, in a survival horror game. The user study results show that the proposed dynamic game adaptation approach had the intended impact on the players. In particular, the players moderately experienced the correlation between their scary feelings and the change in the sound effect and the monster's behavior. The heartbeat sound got louder, and the monster became more aggressive as the players got more scared. Although some of the issues of this preliminary study remain to be investigated further, it opens a new direction that utilizes body motion measurements for enhancing the user experience for the survival horror game genre.

Keywords: Virtual reality · Video games · Survival horror games · Body motion tracking

1 Introduction

Survival-horror games are among the most popular video games developed for virtual reality (VR) gaming platforms. The games feature the scary ambiance to frighten or arouse uncanny feelings in the players. The immersive environment projected through virtual reality further amplifies the frightening effects. Pallavicini et al. compared emotional induction caused by a survival horror game called Resident Evil 7: Biohazard in virtual reality with that of playing it on the traditional console setup and reported a statistically larger sense of presence (or "be in the game") for the VR environment [1]. Vachiratamporn et al. investigated the impact of the player's affect in adaptively changing fear effects [2]. Later the same group designed a game based on affective adaptation for the survival horror genre [3]. In particular, the timing of horror events was implicitly changed based on the player's affective state.

The approach of adaptively changing game difficulty levels based on the player's affect has already been explored for various other game genres, including the first-person

© The Author(s), under exclusive license to Springer Nature Switzerland AG 2022
C. Stephanidis et al. (Eds.): HCII 2022, CCIS 1654, pp. 536–541, 2022.
https://doi.org/10.1007/978-3-031-19679-9_67

shooter (FPS) games and role-playing games (RPG). In particular, Nenonen et al. used the heartbeats of the players to control the difficulty of a few exercise (or physical) games such as skiing and shooting [4]. Yun et al. proposed the use of the facial thermal signature to adaptively change the game difficulty level to increase the player's game engagement [5]. Xiang et al. explored the facial expressions to dynamically adjust the game difficulty level [6]. However, the affect-based approach for dynamically changing horror effects has only been explored recently [2, 3].

This paper proposes a different approach for dynamically changing the horror effects. Our approach is based on body motion tracking, which capitalizes on the head and hand motion tracking measurements readily available in any off-the-shelf VR devices such as Oculus Quest 2 [7], thus requiring no additional external measurement sensors unlike the affect-based approach.

2 Game Design

In this section, we discuss various aspects of the game design that focus on dynamically changing horror effects to make the survival of the horror game more engaging in the immersive virtual environment. For the proof of concept, we used Oculus Quest 2 [7] as the testing environment and the Unity game engine [8] as the game development environment.

2.1 The Game

The name of our survival horror game is Cruel Parallel. It is developed in Unity – the game development platform [8] and programmed in the C# programming language. The game features a hellish asylum that is constantly evolving. The objective of the game is to face the sequence of uncanny events and survive. Much like the stairs of Hogwarts in J.K. Rowling's Harry Potter series, the asylum shifts and changes at will. This produces a sense of uncanny feeling in the player. As typical with any survival horror game, the game mechanics lets the player realize that s/he is less in control of the situation than observed in any FPS or RPG. This uncanny feeling is further magnified in VR, where the player's mind is far more immersed. The game features a monster that is hunting the player. The monster's entire goal is to generate fear in players. It changes its behavior patterns to scare each player as much as possible.

2.2 Monster Design

Designing of the monster was inspired by the PlayStation 5's Returnal monster designs and the animation process of Housemarque [9]. In particular, the monster was ethereal and Lovecraftian [10]. Its body is made of smoke. Its head is an oily black sphere with tentacle protrusions in constant motion (see Fig. 1a). The tentacles aren't quite attached as if they exist partially within the fourth-dimensional space. The monster was not a premade object, but it was designed from scratch. Specifically, we designed and created a tentacle system in which each tentacle has a reference to its parent node, and it attempts to move with its parent (see Fig. 1b). However, the child node only knows the parent's position in the last frame, so it's always chasing the parent node. This creates an organic, fluid, and biological animation that happens dynamically at runtime [11].

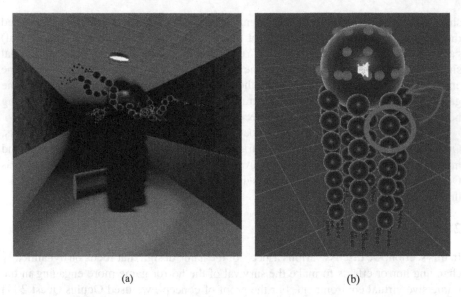

(a)   (b)

Fig. 1. (a) The game monster. (b) Illustration of the tentacle system.

2.3 Sound Design

The game has the Sound Manager – a software entity to manage soundtracks. It randomly selects a track, slightly alters the pitch and volume to create variation, and plays the track. As soon as one track ends, it selects, varies, and plays another to create a seamless soundscape. Each track was selected to be easily played with other tracks, so the soundscape feels consistent without any disjointed. In addition, there are small radios scattered around the rooms within the game. These radios can turn on and off at random to startle the player. They primarily play static sounds, with the occasional sound of a woman crying. The monster also has its own sounds. It generates a garbled demonic whisper when it is near the player. This magnifies the uncanny feeling. The final piece of sound design is the heartbeats. The intensity of the heartbeat sound changes dynamically depending on the player's fear score (Sect. 2.5).

2.4 VR Platform

We used Oculus Quest 2 [3] as the VR testbed. Like the most modern VR technology, Oculus Quest 2 has three main hardware components: two controllers – one for each hand, and the headset (aka Head Mounted Display, HMD). The hand controllers are designed to fit naturally in each hand as if one would hold an everyday object. This provides an immersive experience when interacting with objects in VR. The hand controllers' position and rotation are tracked. HMD typically contains a pair of stereoscopic lenses that project the game world in front of the player's eyes at slightly different positions to create the sensation of depth. The headset's position and rotation are also tracked. Oculus's SDK allows the game customization and access to the position and rotation data.

2.5 Fear Factor

The fear factor is a metric that we designed to compute the player's uncanny feeling. As a proof of concept, it considers the hand and head rotations of the player only. However, it can be modified to consider other factors, including hand and head positions in three-dimensional space. We compute the rate of change of rotation for each of the three controllers every second as shown in Eq. 1 below:

$$R(t) = \sqrt{(R_x(t) - R_x(t-1))^2 + (R_y(t) - R_y(t-1))^2 + (R_z(t) - R_z(t-1))^2} \quad (1)$$

where R_x is rotation in the x-direction (Roll), R_y is rotation in the y-direction (Pitch), and R_z is rotation in the z-direction (Yaw) for each controller, and t is time in second. $R(t)$ for the left-hand controller is represented by $R_{LH}(t)$, $R(t)$ for the right-hand controller is represented by $R_{RH}(t)$, and $R(t)$ for the HMD is represented by $R_{HMD}(t)$. . If the rate of change is higher than a pre-defined threshold (T), the fear factor score is incremented as shown in Eq. 2 below:

$$FearFactor(t) = FearFactor(t-1) + 1, if \begin{cases} R_{LH}(t) > T_{LH} \\ R_{RH}(t) > T_{RH} \\ R_{HMD}(t) > T_{HMD} \end{cases} \quad (2)$$

The thresholds (T_{LH}, T_{RH}, and T_{HMD}) are computed heuristically via experimental trials. An example of the increment in the fear factor score (*FearFactor*) is an abrupt rotation of the head or shaking of hands due to an uncanny event such as a distance sound. The fear score is then fed into the various elements of the game to alter the fear effects dynamically. In particular, as the fear score increases, the heartbeat sound gets louder and faster. This, in turn, makes it very challenging for the player to remain calm. The game also alters the monster's behavior according to the fear score. Specifically, the monster becomes more aggressive as the fear score increases. At lower scores, the monster is elusive, passively relying on the game ambiance to scare the player. Therefore, calmer the player, a more conducive game environment of survival s/he creates.

3 User Study

A total of 5 participants (3 males and 2 females) volunteered in this study. Their ages ranged between 25 and 60 (Average = 38.60, Standard Deviation = 14.89). The participants were given a brief demo of the game at the beginning. Then, they were asked to play the game until the game ended. The game ended either because the participant survived or the monster killed the participant. An average gameplay time was ~13 min. To evaluate how the participants perceived the dynamic adaptation element of the game, they were asked to respond to the following two statements at the end of the game:

S1. I felt that the heartbeat sound got louder and faster as I got more scared.

S2. I felt that the monster was getting more aggressive as I got more scared.

The participants were required to respond to each of these statements on a 5-point scale where 1 being completely disagree and 5 being completely agree. Table 1 summarizes the participants' responses to both questions. The average scores for both statements are above 3, indicating that the participants leaned more towards agreeing with the statements that they experienced loader heartbeats and increased in the monster's aggression as they got more scared.

Table 1. Participants' responses for the dynamic game adaptation element of the game

Participant	S1	S2
P1	3	4
P2	4	4
P3	3	3
P4	3	3
P5	4	4
Average	3.4	3.6

4 Conclusion

In this paper, we propose a dynamic game adaptation approach for a survival horror game in VR. The approach capitalizes on the head and hand motion tracking measurements readily available in any off-the-shelf VR devices such as Oculus Quest 2. The game adaptively changes horror events such as the game sound and the monster's behavior according to the player's body motion. In particular, the game captures the player's abrupt head rotation and hand shaking, and utilizes this information to alter the fear effects in real-time. The results from the user study suggest that the participants moderately experienced the correlation between their scary feeling and the change in the sound effect and the monster's behavior. Specifically, they experienced louder heartbeat sound and increased aggression in the monster as they got more scared.

Our pilot experiment with a limited dataset confirmed the applicability of our approach. One advantage of this approach is that it utilizes the body tracking measurements freely made available by the VR instrument. Hence, it does not rely on external measurement sensors, making the approach practical. Of course, integration of other sensors such as affect measurements can more accurately estimate the player's uncanny feeling, but at the same time, it increases the cost and requires the attachment of multiple physiological sensors to the player's body.

The centerpiece of the proposed approach is the computation of the fear score, which is simplistic for our initial study. In future work, the fear score computation needs to be improved. In particular, the position of the controllers should be incorporated to capture the abrupt motion. The threshold-based score increment approach should be replaced with statistical approaches (e.g., Bayesian classifier) or machine learning approaches (e.g., decision tree or Support Vector Machines).

The current framework is designed for single-player horror games but can be extended to multi-player games which may require integration of body motion data from individual players.

Although the results are promising, their power is limited because the study was conducted on a small sample (n = 5 participants). Given that the results are encouraging, we plan on collecting more data in the near future.

References

1. Pallavicini, F., Ferrari, A., Pepe, A., Garcea, G., Zanacchi, A., Mantovani, F.: Effectiveness of virtual reality survival horror games for the emotional elicitation: Preliminary insights using Resident Evil 7: Biohazard. In: Antona, M., Stephanidis, C. (eds.) UAHCI 2018. LNCS, vol. 10908, pp. 87–101. Springer, Cham (2018). https://doi.org/10.1007/978-3-319-92052-8_8
2. Vachiratamporn, V., Legaspi, R., Moriyama, K., Numao. M.:Towards the design of affective survival horror games: An investigation on player affect. In: 2013 Humaine Association Conference on Affective Computing and Intelligent Interaction, pp. 576–581. IEEE (2013)
3. Vachiratamporn, V., Moriyama, K., Fukui, K., Numao, M.: An implementation of affective adaptation in survival horror games. In: 2014 IEEE Conference on Computational Intelligence and Games, pp. 1–8. IEEE (2014)
4. Nenonen, V., et al.: Using heart rate to control an interactive game. In: Proceedings of the SIGCHI Conference on Human factors in Computing Systems, pp. 853–856 (2007)
5. Yun, C., Shastri, D., Pavlidis, I., Deng. Z.: "O'game, can you feel my frustration? Improving user's gaming experience via stresscam. In: Proceedings of the SIGCHI Conference on Human Factors in Computing Systems, pp. 2195–2204 (2009)
6. Xiang, N., Yang, L., Zhang. M.: Dynamic difficulty adjustment by facial expression. In: Informatics and Management Science, pp. 761–768. Springer, London (2013) https://doi.org/10.1007/978-1-4471-4796-1_97
7. Oculus Quest 2. https://www.oculus.com/quest-2/
8. Unity Game Development Engine. https://unity.com/
9. Housemarque. https://housemarque.com/
10. Lovecraftian horror. https://en.wikipedia.org/wiki/Lovecraftian_horror
11. Jankkila, R.: From Resogun to Returnal: the evolving VFX magic that brought atropos to Life. PlayStation.Blog, https://blog.playstation.com/2021/09/16/from-resogun-to-returnal-the-evolving-vfx-magic-that-brought-atropos-to-life/. Accessed 16 Sept 2021

Using Augmented Reality to Reinforce the Learning of Installation of Electrical Equipment and Machines

Janio Jadán-Guerrero[1,2](✉) [iD], Myrian Zurita-Mena[2], and Juan Murillo-Morera[3] [iD]

[1] Centro de Investigación en Mecatrónica y sistemas Interactivos (MIST), Universidad Tecnológica Indoamérica, Avenue Machala y Sabanilla, Quito, Ecuador
janiojadan@uti.edu.ec
[2] Maestría en Educación, Mención Pedagogía en Entornos Digitales (MEPED), Universidad Tecnológica Indoamérica, Avenue Machala y Sabanilla, Quito, Ecuador
[3] Universidad Nacional de Costa Rica, Avenue 1, Calle 9 Heredia 86, Heredia 40101, Costa Rica
juan.murillo.morera@una.cr

Abstract. The educational level of technical high schools has been affected by the current state of emergency caused by the Covid-19 pandemic, due to the lack of educational resources for subjects that require laboratory practice. The objective of the research is to describe a pedagogical strategy using interactive support material focused on augmented reality for equipment installations and electrical machines learning, in order to supply the lack of laboratories. The research carried out surveys to seven teachers, who teach practical subjects, and evaluations to 60 students who underwent the intervention with the application of augmented reality. The results of the pre-test and post-test were analyzed to verify the stated objectives, demonstrating that there are motivating results with the application of two tools Mywebar and Assemblr in the performance of the classes, affirming that the augmented reality tool impacts and motivates the teaching-learning process in the technical area in the professional figure of installations, equipment and electrical machines in a favorable way.

Keywords: Augmented reality · Electrical equipment · Installation of machines · Virtual laboratory · Mywebar · Assemblr

1 Introduction

The use of technological tools facilitates practicing that lead to understand the theoretical foundations, especially in areas of professional improvement. This research aims to explore the field of augmented reality and propose an interactive material for learning the professional figure of facilities, equipment and electrical machines, aimed at improving educational practice in a virtual environment. The curriculum that is taught has a technical orientation in which modules are taught on interior installations, electrical engineering, training and labor orientation, automation and electrical panels, maintenance of electrical machines, link installations in transformation centers, installations of special services and automated electrical installations. All of them require a practical component that allows students to learn from the visualization, manipulation and repetition of exercises. Given this need in virtual education and later in hybrid education, augmented reality is proposed to replace experimentation in laboratories. Augmented reality is a technology that complements the perception and interaction of elements with the real world by adding additional information generated by a computer, cell phone or tablet, invading new areas of application in education, offering benefits by helping to understand and improve knowledge [1, 2]. In the same way, augmented reality is beginning to be used in professional training in industries or police and military institutions [3].

Currently, augmented reality is a great learning alternative in different areas of knowledge, motivating children, young people and adolescents to develop independent thinking interactively by manipulating 3d objects instead of flat figures, the use of mobile devices allows to have a combination of the real world and the virtual world by implementing new innovation to the classroom [4, 5].

2 Related Work

In a specialized laboratory at Mining University, an augmented reality system was developed for the maintenance of electrical equipment as a control object, the device is used by schneider electric "smart shield", which allows load, distribution and management, technical energy accounting, operational services and power quality monitoring [6]. The contribution of a specialized laboratory helps students to learn and understand components, tools and electrical equipment when developing practices.

Augmented reality learning is fun and interesting, with the help of electric light installation media AR app, students can learn anytime, anywhere, at their fingertips. Electric lighting installation instructors also help teachers improve their study time as in theory subjects, students can describe electrical components, features, functions, and lighting fixtures at home. This lamp installation learning aid provides basic installation knowledge in the form of lighting installation component introduction, feature introduction, component selection for home lighting installation design, adjustment of technical drawings to actual installation methods [7].

There are many advantages of using virtual environments, since they provide didactic materials, being indispensable instruments in academic training, providing information and guiding learning, that is, they provide an important basis for conceptual thinking, contributing to a significant increase in the development and the continuity of thought, allowing learning to last longer and providing a real experience that stimulates the skills and competencies of students; also providing internships that offer a high degree of interest for students; evaluating the knowledge and abilities of the students, the increase of environments for the motivation of the students, and the variety of learning activities.

Augmented reality in the substation work environment is an effective solution to mitigate the risks associated with the activities that take place there. However, two defined limits must be addressed in a future project, such as: the low resolution of the video, which makes it difficult to read the information from a mobile phone; and difficult model identified by the user to represent the electrical panel, market design standards can be recommended and/or the substation implements the technology to make the interface familiar to the user [8]. By using augmented reality, it guarantees the protection of health and safety of students and/or workers against electrical risks; In addition, it is possible to work properly with the equipment and its operation will be controlled periodically, according to the instructions and needs of the manufacturers and installers.

One of the greatest uses that has been found in Augmented Reality for Industry 4.0 is the possibility of using it to facilitate maintenance work. Combining it with other technologies such as Artificial Vision, it is possible to obtain information regarding certain objects such as, for example, the stock number, characteristics of the object, parameters, temperatures, the place where it should be taken for storage, information related to a package. In this way, multiple tasks can be facilitated, since in addition to allowing quick and easy access to information, it also facilitates the way of viewing said information [9].

Currently, in the educational field, certain applications have been incorporated that have improved the performance of students and have increased their participation and interest in the classes taught. Educational applications have become important teaching and learning tools. Due to its diverse nature, there are many possibilities in different branches and 3D elements can be used to broaden research horizons, motivate students and even increase their interest in any subject [10].

Finally, it can also be seen that in the area of education there are educational resources that strengthen emotional learning through audiovisual elements generated by augmented reality. Therefore, it is increasingly accessible to teachers with a basic guide to its implementation. The present investigation is based on the information collected in documentary sources to solve a problem of training in the educational institution, for this in the following section a methodology to follow is proposed.

3   Method

The approach of the present investigation is quatitative, the same one that allows to obtain a collection of numerical data, establishing models of behavior and interest in the students and technical teachers in the teaching-learning process when using the augmented reality in the Professional Figure of Installations, Equipment and Electrical Machines.

For the design of the research, the context of the Educational Unit "Marco Aurelio Subía Martínez-Batalla de Panupali" in the city of Latacunga, in the Tanicuchi parish, was taken into account. As well as the socioeconomic level of the students for the acquisition of electrical tools and equipment. Taking these aspects into account, the research considers a model of pre-test, intervention and post-test.

The type of research used is considered exploratory, since it allows a closeness to the central problem, the same one that is intended to be studied and applied augmented reality to improve the teaching-learning process with the use of technological resources.

Descriptive research involves the use of tools in order to detail the situation of the problem, and explanatory because it specifies the origin of the problem detected. In the research to obtain data, questionnaires applied to students in the technical area and a questionnaire applied to teachers were used as instruments.

3.1 Participants

The study population consisted of 156 students, of which 33 were female and 123 were male, to whom a pre-test was applied as a starting point, and based on the results, a sample of 60 students was taken to whom the intervention with the augmented reality application was carried out. Seven teachers of different subjects also participated in the study.

3.2 Materials

For the elaboration of the didactic material, a laptop, smartphones and applications of the network were used. For the design of the activity, two very easy, fun and interactive tools for students and teachers have been considered, such as Mywebar and Assemblr, these platforms with Augmented Reality (AR) technology, allow teachers to create interactive 3D lessons with photos, videos and texts in a minute.

For data collection, a survey was developed for the teachers of the professional figure, the same one that was structured with the actions, which will be used in the learning guide; and for the students, an evaluation instrument was developed with five questions related to the training modules.

With the analysis of the results of the information collected, the lack of knowledge of teachers in the subject of augmented reality is evident, and especially in the low performance in the evaluations that were made to the students on the subject of electrical elements. Therefore, it can be concluded that the advantage of applying augmented reality in the development of classes will help the teaching process with strategies supported by technology that help build student knowledge.

3.3 Procedure

Through this research, the ADDIE methodology was used for the design and implementation of the technological proposal. This methodology is widely used in the technological field and in the development of digital resources, particularly in the educational field. The methodology consists of the following phases: Analysis, Design, Development, Implementation and Evaluation. Next section describes each of these phases with the development of the proposal.

4   Design of the Technological Proposal Based on Augmented Reality

Specific research, for the realization of interactive support material focused on augmented reality for learning the professional figure of installations, equipment and electrical machines. This material will facilitate the process of communication and assimilation of the subjects of connection facilities and transformation centers collaborating in the teaching-learning of the students.

In MyWebAR and Assemblr support a wide range of devices, including smartphones, tablets and laptops, in addition, it is compatible with old devices and can even run on laptops, making it the most affordable augmented reality solution; AR lessons can be shared directly to Instagram, Facebook, WhatsApp and email in a minute, or export the 3D design as FBX/OBJ files for cross-platform uses like: Facebook posts, PowerPoint presentations, 3D printing, etc.

In order for students to learn in a collaborative environment in problem solving, educational resources with augmented reality have been developed to complement the teaching-learning process. These resources were designed with the MyWebAR platform (https://dashboard.mywebar.com), which has a friendly interface and easy resource construction, a fundamental characteristic for the institution's teachers. Table 1 shows the QR code that is generated by each of the 3D objects.

Table 1. QR code of electrical equipment in MyWebAr

Element	QR Code	Presentation
Electric Tower		

It is possible to generate this type of resources with the Assemblr Studio platform (https://studio.assemblrworld.com), which also has a friendly interface and easy application of augmented reality, it is observed how objects can be designed in 3D and they can be pinned to a bookmark based on QR codes. In this platform, images related to electrical installations were designed according to the study units of the electrical engineering module and connection facilities and transformation centers. Table 2 shows QR code that is generated by each of the 3D objects.

Table 2. QR code of installation electrical equipment in Assemblr

Element	QR Code	Presentation
Electric y Electronic Elements		
Lamppost		

5   Results and Discussion

When obtaining the results, it is seen that the students totally improved their knowledge.

We run an evaluation where 100% passed the evaluation with a grade equal to or greater than 7.5. On the other hand, 68% of the students passed the evaluation with a grade higher than 9.0, while 24% were between 8.0 and 8.5. The mean of the evaluation was 8.75 which gives us a high value. The following Table 3 gives a summary of all test evaluation scores.

Table 3. Test evaluation scores

Score	Number of students	Percentage
7,5	5	8%
8	7	12%
8,5	7	12%
9	17	28%
9,5	15	25%
10	9	15%
Total	**60**	**100%**

Finally we improved their knowledge by 98% and in the metacognitive part by 90%, with which it was possible to show that the proposal of an interactive material based on augmented reality to learn the professional figure of facilities, equipment and electrical machines, is acceptable to all students and can be applied, improving the teaching-learning process and results in terms of content, methodology, usefulness, resources, applicability and scope, being the proposal validated.

6   Conclusions

With the development of this degree work, it has been possible to investigate different tools for generating content with augmented reality such as MyWebAR and Assemblr, being Assemblr a more didactic application with greater reception for students.

Using the Assemblr application, it has been possible to carry out the design and application of an educational strategy that consists of the development of 3D images referring to the Link Installations and Transformation Centers subject from which the QR codes were created so that later they could be scanned by the application and it allows the appreciation of its characteristics.

With the execution of the educational strategy with senior high school students, it can be seen that the results are positive since, when using the application, students have significantly improved their grades both in the technical and metacognitive aspects, in addition it improved their motivation.

References

1. Navas, E., Oleas, J., Zambrano, M.: Augmented reality to facilitate the process of Teaching - Learning in school textbooks. In: 2021 Fifth World Conference on Smart Trends in Systems Security and Sustainability (WorldS4), pp. 316–321 (2021). https://doi.org/10.1109/WorldS 451998.2021.9514007
2. Cóndor-Herrera, O., Acosta-Rodas, P., Ramos-Galarza, C.: Augmented reality teaching resources and its implementation in the teaching-learning process. In: Nazir, S., Ahram, T.Z., Karwowski, W. (eds.) AHFE 2021. LNNS, vol. 269, pp. 149–154. Springer, Cham (2021). https://doi.org/10.1007/978-3-030-80000-0_18
3. Lucero-Urresta, E., Buele, J., Córdova, P., Varela-Aldás, J.: Precision shooting training system using augmented reality. In: Computational Science and Its Applications – ICCSA 2021. ICCSA 2021. LNCS, vol. 12957. Springer, Cham (2021) .https://doi.org/10.1007/978-3-030-87013-3_22
4. Guevara, C., Coronel, D.M.V.: Multisensory Learning system applying augmented reality. In: Nazir, S., Ahram, T., Karwowski, W. (eds.) AHFE 2020. AISC, vol. 1211, pp. 336–342. Springer, Cham (2020). https://doi.org/10.1007/978-3-030-50896-8_48
5. Borja Galeas, C.M., Maldonado, C.G.: Development of editorial models applying augmented reality for children's learning. In: 2019 14th Iberian Conference on Information Systems and Technologies (CISTI), pp. 1–7 (2019). https://doi.org/10.23919/CISTI.2019.8760897
6. Zhukovskiy, L., Koteleva, N.: Electrical equipment maintenance system with elements of augmented reality technology. In: IOP Conference Series: Materials Science and Engineering, p. 643 (2019). https://doi.org/10.1088/1757-899X/643/1/012024

7. Khairudin, M., Iskandar, M., Djatmiko, I., Nashir, I.: Virtual Trainer for Mobile Augmented Reality Based Electrical Lighting Installation. International Association of Online Engineering. Obtenido de (2020). https://www.learntechlib.org/p/216466/
8. Filipe, J., Śmiałek, M., Brodsky, A., Hammoudi, S. (eds.): ICEIS 2020. LNBIP, vol. 417. Springer, Cham (2021). https://doi.org/10.1007/978-3-030-75418-1
9. Damiani, L., Demartini, M., Guizzi, G., Revetria, R., Tonelli, F.: Augmented and virtual reality applications in industrial systems: a qualitative review towards the industry 4.0 era. IFAC-PapersOnLine $51(11)$, 624–630 (2008)
10. Eady, M., Lockyer, L.: Tools for learning: technology and teaching. In: Learning to Teach in the Primary School, pp. 71–89. Cambridge University Press, Cambridge (2013)

Augmented Reality and 3D Balance Learning

Andrés Lara-Calle[1]([⊠]) [iD], Juan Cruz[1] [iD], and Nicolás Mejía[2]

[1] SISAu Research Group, Facultad de Ingeniería y Tecnologías de la Información y la Comunicación, Universidad Tecnológica Indoamérica, Ambato 180103, Ecuador
{andreslara,juancruz}@uti.edu.ec
[2] Facultad de Derecho, Universidad Libre, Pereira 660001, Colombia
nicolasa.mejiag@unilibre.edu.co

Abstract. The augmented reality is presented as an opportunity to help understand students with attention problems. The objective of this research is to determine the incidence of augmented reality with academic performance and the satisfaction of learning 3D (Third dimension) balance in the training project of Vector Mechanics of the Industrial Engineering career at the Indoamerica Technological University. The problem identified in this investigation was the loss of interest in students when solving problems with three-dimensional systems, unfortunately the textbooks present their printed diagrams in two dimensions, which means, the student cannot locate himself correctly in the system, making errors in his analysis and calculations. This research has a quantitative approach with a positivist and socioformative paradigm. The applied methodology obeys to create didactic material of three-dimensional systems with Computer-Aided Design (CAD), and presented in augmented reality with collaborative work of the students. We used the Pearson's correlation analysis to verify the correlation, obtaining a low coefficient of 0.204 between the variables analyzed. As a result, the hypothesis "The use of augmented reality relates academic performance with the satisfaction of learning Equilibrium 3D in students" was verified.

Keywords: Augmented reality · Academic performance · Student · Balance · Learning tools

1 Introduction

Augmented reality (AR) allows the visualization, and interaction of virtual objects merged in real-world space, the appreciation of their characteristics, and the ability to analyze them; simultaneaously [1]. Part of virtual reality (VR) allows users to experiment with a virtual world through glasses and programmed systems, which permits entering a virtual environment [2]. Currently, these technologies are helping in education as they arouse students' interest and understanding [3].

Augmented reality is also used for professional practices such as virtual training camps that use weapons and scenarios that provide a realistic experience for security companies [4]. In medicine, it constitutes a valuable emerging technology through which an adequate response is given to the new forms of learning required by students in the information and knowledge [5].

© The Author(s), under exclusive license to Springer Nature Switzerland AG 2022
C. Stephanidis et al. (Eds.): HCII 2022, CCIS 1654, pp. 550–555, 2022.
https://doi.org/10.1007/978-3-031-19679-9_69

The balance in the third dimension is part of the knowledge students acquire in their third semester of industrial engineering at Indoamerica Technological University through a project regarding Vector Mechanics. The project consists of studying Newton's first law in systems with applications of forces in space, the Varignon principle, and the calculation of torques or moments in third-dimensional reference systems [6]. In addition, it was possible to identify a proposal on augmented reality for the study of statics where the teacher developed a book with (AR) to facilitate student learning [7].

The objective of this research is to use augmented reality as a strategy for learning balance in 3D. It is presented as an innovative educational tool considering that currently, students quickly lose interest in developing learning [8]. The usability of systems in augmented reality is highly important in terms of effectiveness, efficiency, and satisfaction [9]. Furthermore, the use of augmented reality has the potential to improve academic performance in children [10, 11]. The present work seeks to identify the academic performance and the satisfaction of the methodology in university students. This work is presented in four parts, the introduction, methods tools used, results, and conclusions of the research.

2   Materials and Methods

This section presents the materials and methodology used in the development of the research study, first with a description of the materials and tools used and then the definition of methods of the educational process.

2.1   Materials

For the development of this educational proposal, the AutoCAD Computer-Aided Design software has been used to develop the balanced systems that the students design with the support of the teacher; the exercises were taken from the Statics for Engineers book [12]. The developed systems present the information on the distances between the main points of the solids in the third dimension to identify the behavior of the forces in the line of action in the third dimension.

Through the Navisworks Freedom 2019 software, the format of the design file made in CAD with a dwg extension must be changed to FBX, there are versions of AutoCAD prior to 2019 that allow saving directly to FBX format, and this file was uploaded to the Augin application where it was achieved presenting in augmented reality an action that allows students to arouse interest by observing their work and improve understanding. To be able to observe augmented reality was necessary a smartphone with a camera and internet access. The device must have the Augin application installed to generate the geometric representation in AR, as shown in Fig. 1. SPSS Statistics was used to determine Pearson's statistical coefficient.

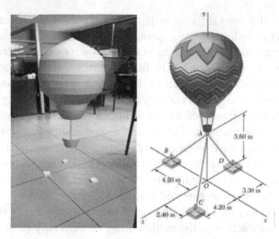

Fig. 1. Representation of systems in equilibrium in AR.

2.2 Methods

The educational proposal was developed in the training project of Vector Mechanics in the academic period (October, 2021–February, 2022), with the 28 third-level students of the industrial engineering career at the Indoamerica Technological University. We considered the current ethics regulations for research and learning at the University; policies of information management, and protection of the identity of the students. In this research was carefully taking in account the health and safety of the students since it is a purely educational analysis and the students consent the development.

It began with the study of basic force systems with literature review and computer-aided design development, where students apply their CAD knowledge. When the designs were ready, they brought to augmented reality.

Then equivalent systems of forces are studied with a calculation of torques with Newton's first law and Varignon's principle. Finally, these designs were presented with the mathematical definitions of the performed processes, allowing the students to observe, to design, and to understand the structure of what was studied to appreciate augment reality.

Learning is generated with the students, allowing collaborative work and the exchange of valuable ideas when developing designs that can serve future generations for the study of balance with designs presented in augmented reality. To evaluate this educational methodological proposal, two variables have been considered: the dependent variable; satisfaction in learning (The information was obtained with a survey of closed questions), and the independent variable; the academic performance of the students in two partial periods. The academic period in which it was studied reflects the results of all academic activities, managing to identify whether this proposal allows the correlation of academic performance with satisfaction in learning.

3 Results

In this section, we present the results obtained from validating the educational methodology. With the data obtained from the study variables, it was possible to make a scatter graph, the horizontal axis shows the academic achievements of the students in the Vector Mechanics training project, and the vertical axis is the coordinate axis provided by the level of satisfaction at the end of the academic period. Figure 2 shows the dispersion of the data of the two variables (obtained with SPSS software).

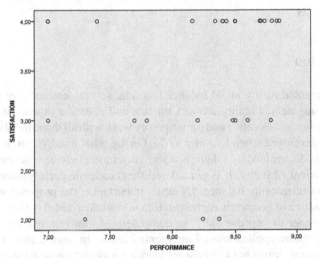

Fig. 2. Performance dispersion with learning satisfaction.

From the foregoing, it can be deduced that the majority of the students of the Vector Mechanics training project consider a degree of satisfaction with a medium-high level and a very high level when using the geometric representation in 3D and augmented reality; however, there are students who consider that their level of satisfaction is Medium, so they are invited to identify any existing problem in their learning.

To test the hypothesis "The use of augmented reality relates academic performance with the satisfaction of learning 3D Balance in students". Pearson's correlation coefficient is applied using the SPSS software between the data obtained from the academic performance of the students and the level of satisfaction with the student's learning, obtaining a 95% confidence interval. Table 1 presents a double-entry table which contains the Pearson coefficient that indicates the level of correlation between the study variables. The bilateral significance reveals the degree of compatibility between the study variables' data and N, which represents the sample size, as presented in Table 1.

A Pearson correlation coefficient of 0.204 is determined; this value indicates that there is a poor correlation between academic performance and learning satisfaction.

Table 1. Correlation de Pearson

		Performance	Satisfaction
PERF	Pearson correlation	1	**0.204**
	Two-sided significance		0.299
	N	28	28
SATIS	Pearson correlation	0.204	1
	Two-sided significance	0.299	
	N	28	28

4 Conclusion

By using augmented reality in 3D balance learning, several lessons have been learned; among them, augmented reality arouses interest and attention in studying balance. In addition, it allows collaborative and participatory work with all those involved, constructivism is also developed when learning to do. On the other hand, through the statistical analysis, it was determined that there is a low correlation between the variables with a Pearson coefficient of 0.204. It is considered that academic performance is related to the satisfaction of learning balance. Of equal importance, the proposal was accompanied by the practice of geometric representation in computer-aided design, which allows the future engineer to improve skills in computerized drawing, use web applications and search for future applications of augmented reality in engineering. However, it is suggested for future work not to consider learning satisfaction as a variable since it is subjective.

References

1. Kaplan, A.D., Cruit, J., Endsley, M., Beers, S.M., Sawyer, B.D., Hancock, P.A.: The effects of virtual reality, augmented reality, and mixed reality as training enhancement methods: a meta-analysis. Hum Fact. **63**, 706–726 (2021). https://doi.org/10.1177/0018720820904229
2. Marin-Diaz, V., Sampedro Requena, B.E., Gea, E.V.: The virtual and augmented reality in secondary education class. Camp/ Virt.. **11**, 225–236 (2022). https://doi.org/10.54988/CV.2022.1.1030
3. Andaluz, V.H., et al.: Multi-user industrial training and education environment. In: De Paolis, L.T., Bourdot, P. (eds.) AVR 2018. LNCS, vol. 10851, pp. 533–546. Springer, Cham (2018). https://doi.org/10.1007/978-3-319-95282-6_38
4. Lucero-Urresta, E., Buele, J., Córdova, P., Varela-Aldás, J.: Precision shooting training system using augmented reality. In: Gervasi, O., et al. (eds.) ICCSA 2021. LNCS, vol. 12957, pp. 283–298. Springer, Cham (2021). https://doi.org/10.1007/978-3-030-87013-3_22
5. Cabero Almenara, J., Barroso Osuna, J., Obrador, M.: Realidad aumentada aplicada a la enseñanza de la medicina. Educación Médica. **18**, 203–208 (2017). https://doi.org/10.1016/J.EDUMED.2016.06.015
6. Museros Romero, P.: Mecanica: estatica y calculo vectorial. Editorial de la Universidad Politecnica de Valencia (2017)

7. Gallego, A.M., Fernández, E., Teresa Garibay, M., Manuel Zapata, J., Zapata, R.: Estática en Realidad Aumentada. Educación en Ciencias y Tecnologí as **56** (2018)
8. De, J., et al.: Entorno de aprendizaje ubicuo con realidad aumentada y tabletas para estimular la comprensión del espacio tridimensional Ubiquitous Learning Environment with Augmented Reality and Tablets to Stimulate Comprehension of the Tridimentional Space Norena Martin-Dorta (2013)
9. Dutta, R., Mantri, A., Singh, G.: Evaluating system usability of mobile augmented reality application for teaching Karnaugh-Maps. Smart Learn. Environ. **9**(1), 1–27 (2022). https://doi.org/10.1186/s40561-022-00189-8
10. Menon, S.S., Holland, C., Farra, S., Wischgoll, T., Stuber, M.: Augmented reality in nursing education – a pilot study. Clin. Simul. Nurs. **65**, 57–61 (2022). https://doi.org/10.1016/J.ECNS.2022.01.007
11. Low, D.Y.S., Poh, P.E., Tang, S.Y.: Assessing the impact of augmented reality application on students' learning motivation in chemical engineering. Educ. Chem. Eng. **39**, 31–43 (2022). https://doi.org/10.1016/J.ECE.2022.02.004
12. Beer, F.P., Russel Johnston, E.: Mecánica vectorial para ingenieros. McGraw Hill, México (2013)

Varying Stressors in a Game with a Purpose Changes Human Stress Levels

Timothy Lee[1,2(✉)], Andrew Chu[1,2], and Tzyy-Ping Jung[1]

[1] Institute for Neural Computation, University of California San Diego,
9500 Gilman Drive, La Jolla, CA 92093, USA
timothytlee56@gmail.com, chu.andrew.h@gmail.com, tpjung@ucsd.edu
[2] Westview High School, 13500 Camino Del Sur, San Diego, CA 92129, USA

Abstract. This study investigated the effect of game stressors, such as time and tasks, on players' stress levels. We collected objective physiological measurements and subjective stress ratings to measure the relationship between changing stressors and players' stress during a game-with-a-purpose (GWAP) in an authentic environment. The GWAP is based on a dyadic virtual-reality game titled *Keep Talking and Nobody Explodes*. It has three difficulty levels, each with a different number of tasks and time constraints. Participants played six pairs of difficulty levels, with a one-minute break between the two difficulty levels in each pair. Subjects rated their stress levels before, during, and after gameplay, in addition to having their heart rate variability (HRV) measured with an electrocardiogram. We computed normative stress ratings by subtracting baseline stress scores from ratings during and after gameplay. Subjective and objective data support the notion that the three difficulty levels of the GWAP are sensitive enough to induce changing levels of stress in an individual. The HRV and stress rating data collected in this study found a positive correlation between the intensity of stressors and subjects' objective and perceived stress levels.

Keywords: Virtual reality · Stress · Heart rate variability · GWAP

1 Introduction

Psychological stress has significant implications on human health. Studies have shown correlations between stress levels and important human functions such as memory recall and immune system activity [4,5,8]. Stress is defined as any type of change that causes physical, mental, or emotional strain. To determine and change levels of stress in people's lives, researchers have relied on manipulating factors in a laboratory-oriented task, such as workload. However, these methods cannot capture human responses in an authentic environment with real-life stressors.

T. Lee and A. Chu—Contributed equally to this work.

© The Author(s), under exclusive license to Springer Nature Switzerland AG 2022
C. Stephanidis et al. (Eds.): HCII 2022, CCIS 1654, pp. 556–563, 2022.
https://doi.org/10.1007/978-3-031-19679-9_70

In contrast, studies can test more authentic situations and human reactions with the same testing standards as a highly controlled facility by creating a controlled virtual-reality (VR) environment. This study uses a controlled VR game that depicts authentic situations close to real-life scenarios; such types of games are called games-with-a-purpose (GWAPs). Greater control can be exerted over the measurement of subjects' performance and stress while performing a variety of tasks, allowing for more accurate findings regarding psychological stress in real life. This study builds on Lee & Jung's work [3] in creating a VR framework to help researchers measure participants' stress and performance.

While Lee & Jung's research focused on objective stress levels induced by time pressure, this study varies the time pressure and task difficulty within a VR GWAP to assess relative changes in the stress levels of human subjects as the intensity of stressors is increased or decreased. Participants' stress levels were assessed by both objective heart rate variability (HRV) data and subjective stress ratings. Additionally, we aim to demonstrate that the stressors in VR games are sensitive enough to cause changes in the participants' stress levels.

2   Methodology

This study used a VR game to explore physiological responses to stress. The VR game allowed researchers to adjust the experimental stressors while maintaining the subject's immersion. Based on electrocardiograms (ECGs) collected during the game, the study calculated the heart rate variability (HRV), a widely used physiological signal. The Lab Streaming Layer (LSL) was used to time-stamp and label in-game events to synchronize ECG data with these events. In addition, subjective stress ratings were collected periodically from the subjects during gameplay.

2.1   VR Game Design

This study's GWAP was based on *Keep Talking and Nobody Explodes* [6], a VR game released by Steel Crate Games in 2015. In this game, two players were tasked with defusing a virtual bomb by solving various puzzles. The Defuser, who wore an HTC Vive Pro virtual reality headset, attempted to defuse the bomb by following the instructions of the second player, the Expert, who could not see the puzzles. The Expert spoke with the Defuser to gain insight into the puzzles, then read from a bomb-defusing manual that included information on each puzzle module before giving the Defuser instructions. The bomb was defused if all puzzle modules were solved before the bomb's time limit expired. The bomb exploded and the players lost if the time limit was reached or the Defuser made too many mistakes while attempting to solve the puzzles. The time pressure, as well as the disparity in information between the Defuser and the Expert, demanded high levels of communication and cooperation between the two players.

A small display at the top of the bomb showed the countdown timer and the number of errors the Defuser had made, with an "X" for each mistake. The bomb exploded when the timer reached zero or when three mistakes were made. Based on the amount of attention, time, and communication required, we classified our puzzle modules into three difficulty levels: easy, medium, and hard.

Our easy modules were: "Wires," "Simon Says," and "Button Press." Easy modules were designed to create a low-stress situation by presenting the players with trivial tasks. In Wires, the Defuser was tasked with cutting one wire from an array of three to six wires based on their coloring and order. In Simon Says, the Defuser had to press colored buttons in a specific order based on flashing colored lights. In Button Press, the Defuser had to hold down a single button and release it at a time specified by the Expert's game manual.

Our medium modules were: "Keypad" and "Vent Gas." Medium games were designed to waste players' time, but also incorporated more difficult mechanics and required more communication. Keypad presented the Defuser with four random combinations of symbols and required the Defuser to press them in a specific order. Vent Gas was a needy module, meaning that the Defuser had to solve the module when prompted, as opposed to other modules that could be solved in any order. Vent Gas prompted the Defuser with a question—"Vent Gas?" or "Detonate?"—and required the Defuser to respond correctly with a "Y" or "N" button.

The hard modules were: "Morse Code" and "Piano Keys." Hard modules were extremely difficult, requiring significant amounts of time to understand and solve. In addition, they required precise physical coordination as the Defuser could easily make a mistake by misclicking a button in these modules. Morse Code required the Defuser to communicate a series of dots and dashes to the Expert, then change a frequency dial on the module to a certain frequency value based on the word that the Expert deciphered from the Morse code. In Piano Keys, the Defuser played a set of musical notes on an in-game piano keyboard when presented with a musical symbol that corresponded to a musical phrase.

Table 1 shows how the three different module levels were used to create three different game difficulty levels for this study. The easy level had four easy modules with a time limit of three minutes to solve all four modules. The medium level included six modules selected from both the easy and medium modules, with two minutes of play time to solve all six modules. The hard level included eight modules selected randomly from the easy, medium, and hard modules, with one minute of play time to solve all eight modules.

Table 1. VR gameplay setup

Difficulty	Play time (mins)	# of Modules presented
Easy	3	4
Medium	2	6
Hard	1	8

2.2 Measuring Changes in Stress

Because this study focused on the effect of varying stressors on the subjects' stress levels, we measured stress at different combinations (pairs) of difficulty levels. We labeled the first difficulty level that the subject played in a given pair as *L1* and the second difficulty level as *L2*. Table 2 shows the six different sequences of difficulty levels that were studied.

Table 2. Combinations of difficulty levels tested

Combination	Sequence of first level (*L1*) and Second level (*L2*)
I	Easy $\longrightarrow$ Medium
II	Easy $\longrightarrow$ Hard
III	Medium $\longrightarrow$ Easy
IV	Medium $\longrightarrow$ Hard
V	Hard $\longrightarrow$ Easy
VI	Hard $\longrightarrow$ Medium

In each of the six combinations, the subjects in the experiment played two different difficulty levels, with a one-minute break in between. For example, for Combination I, we collected ECG and subjective stress rating data while subjects played the easy level for three minutes, then rested for one minute before playing the medium level for two minutes. Each subject played the six combinations three times to ensure that sufficient data were collected. The purpose of using a pairing sequence was to expand on Lee & Jung's work by examining stress levels in relation to one another. We reasoned that the results would be more accurately tailored to an individual's relative stress level.

2.3 Software Tools Used to Develop the VR Game

Various software tools were used to create the virtual reality game for this study, such as Blender, Unity, and VR Toolkit. We used Blender (an open-source 3D computer graphics software) as a 3D-modeling tool to develop and design all the game assets. Game assets included the bomb and all the different modules for the bomb. After these assets were created, we transferred them to Unity, a cross-platform game engine. The behavior and mechanics of the modules were designed and programmed using C#, a language compatible with Unity. From Unity, we applied textures to the game assets to create a sense of realism, and we used Unity's built-in functionality to make the assets manipulable by the player. We used VR Toolkit, a library designed to translate Unity functionality into virtual reality, to make this game compatible with VR.

Next, we needed a method to synchronize our ECG data stream with game events. Lab Streaming Layer (LSL) [7], a scientific data-collection tool used for measurements in time-sensitive situations, to synchronize key events in the game with ECG data. LSL was compatible with both C# and MATLAB, which was essential for this study. LSL markers were inserted in the Unity C# code to mark and record the times of game events. These times indicated an interval of gameplay so that we could calculate HRV over the time interval marked by the LSL.

2.4 Recording Electrocardiogram Data

The Defuser's ECG data were collected to study the physiological responses to changes in game stressors. Heartypatch [1], an open-source, single-lead, ECG-HR, was attached to the Defuser's chest. The recorded ECG data for each gameplay session is described in Sect. 2.2 (the first level of difficulty, a period of rest, then the second difficulty level). Afterward, the ECG data were analyzed to calculate the Defuser's HRV at each difficulty level during gameplay.

2.5 Heart Rate Variability Calculations

Heart rate variability measures the variations in the time interval between heartbeats. As HRV is more or less controlled by the autonomic nervous system for signaling the hypothalamus for flight-or-flight reactions, measuring HRV can serve as a proxy for measuring stress in an individual. HRV provides a noninvasive and simple method to collect quantitative data on these reactions. Lee & Jung (2020) previously established, using a VR GWAP, that time-stress intensity and HRV values are inversely correlated.

Our use of HRV in this study is justified by past research. Kim HG et al. [2] conducted a meta-analysis to establish a rationale for using HRV as a psychological stress indicator. They concluded that HRV changed in response to low parasympathetic activity and that these changes could be linked to cortical regions involved in stress analysis.

To calculate HRV, we first used MATLAB's Signal Processing Toolbox to find the R waves in ECG. Then, we calculated the RR interval, the time between two successive R waves of a QRS complex of a heartbeat. After that, we calculated the differences between successive RR intervals. By taking the root mean square of the successive differences, we could calculate the HRV values for a given time interval of ECG data during gameplay.

2.6 Subjective Stress Evaluations

We collected subjective data in conjunction with objective HRV data in order to better gauge changes in the subjects' stress. We implemented a subjective stress scale measurement in which the Defuser rated their stress on a scale of 1–10, with 1 being minimal stress. The subject was asked to rate their stress four times per gameplay session (a pair of difficulty levels), as summarized in Table 3: before starting the first difficulty level, after finishing the first level, after the one-minute resting period, and after finishing the second level. We used the stress ratings after finishing the first and the second level to establish the level of stress

Table 3. Timings of stress ratings

Rating	Time
1	Before $L1$
2	After $L1$ and Before Resting Period
3	After Resting Period and Before $L2$
4	After $L2$

that a difficulty level induced in the subject. To keep stress ratings consistent between different subjects, we normalized the stress ratings by subtracting the baseline rating before starting the first level from the subject's ratings during gameplay. For example, if the baseline was 2, and the subject's $L1$ stress rating was 4 and the $L2$ rating was 5, the data would be normalized to 2 for $L1$ and 3 for $L2$.

3   Experimental Results

We analyzed HRV and subjective stress data to investigate whether varying stressors in our GWAP led to changes in the subjects' stress levels. Our null hypothesis was that, as the intensity of experimental stressors increases or decreases, there is no statistically significant difference in the subject's HRV and stress ratings. Our alternative hypothesis is that as the intensity of environmental stressors varies, there is a significant change in the subject's HRV and stress ratings.

A p-value of less than 0.05 is typically used to prove statistical significance and reject a null hypothesis. We used one-tailed statistical testing with a significance level of 0.05. For both the HRV and the stress rating data, we used the methods described in Lee & Jung's study to compute the p-values for each pair of difficulty levels.

3.1   Analyzing Heart Rate Variability Data

Table 4. Effect of difficulty level combinations on HRV

Combination ($L1$ and $L2$)	$L1$ Mean HRV	$L2$ Mean HRV	HRV p-value	% Change
I (Easy → Medium)	45.731	34.538	0.00045	−24.47
II (Easy → Hard)	48.349	41.317	0.02854	−14.54
III (Medium → Easy)	41.018	49.742	0.01490	21.27
IV (Medium → Hard)	47.610	39.874	0.01500	−16.25
V (Hard → Easy)	53.341	65.953	0.00286	23.65
VI (Hard → Medium)	36.633	50.034	0.00077	36.58

Table 4 compares the mean HRV values between $L1$ and $L2$ for each of the six difficulty level combinations. For all six combinations, we found that the p-values were less than the significance level of 0.05, indicating a statistically significant difference in HRV values between two successive difficulty levels.

We found a negative percent change in HRV levels for Combinations I, II, and IV, in which the $L2$ is more difficult than $L1$. In addition, we found a positive percent change in HRV levels for Combinations III, V, and VI, in which the $L2$ is less difficult than $L1$. The greatest magnitude of change in HRV occurred in Combination VI, where the mean HRV between the hard difficulty level and the easy difficulty level increased by 36.58%.

Because HRV is inversely correlated with psychological stress levels, our HRV results show that increasing time pressure and task difficulty (i.e. game difficulty level) increases subjects' stress levels.

3.2   Analyzing Subjective Stress Rating Data

Table 5. Effect of difficulty level combinations on subjective stress ratings

Combination ($L1$ and $L2$)	$L1$ Mean rating	$L2$ Mean rating	Stress rating p-value	% Change
I (Easy → Medium)	0.67	1.83	0.04179	175.00
II (Easy → Hard)	0.83	2.67	0.00230	220.00
III (Medium → Easy)	2.00	0.67	0.02181	−66.67
IV (Medium → Hard)	1.50	2.67	0.03446	77.78
V (Hard → Easy)	3.33	1.17	0.00270	−65.00
VI (Hard → Medium)	3.00	1.17	0.01097	−61.11

We compared the mean subjective stress ratings in $L1$ and $L2$ for each of the six difficulty level combinations, as shown in Table 5. The p-values for all six combinations were less than the significance level of 0.05, indicating the difference in stress rating values between two difficulty levels is statistically significant.

We found a positive percent change in stress ratings for Combinations I, II, and IV, in which the $L2$ is more difficult than $L1$. In addition, we found a negative percent change in stress ratings for Combinations III, V, and VI, in which the $L2$ is less difficult than $L1$. Combination II had the greatest magnitude of change in stress rating, with a 220.00% increase in mean stress rating between easy and hard difficulty levels.

Thus, our subjective ratings show that increasing time pressure and task difficulty increases subjects' subjective stress levels, in addition to objective stress measurements.

3.3   Findings

Our data demonstrate that the three difficulty levels of the GWAP are sensitive enough to induce changing levels of stress within an individual. We found a positive correlation between the intensity of stressors and subjects' objective and subjective stress levels. Therefore, we can reject the null hypothesis and accept the alternative.

4   Conclusion

We studied the effect of stressors, such as time pressure and task difficulty, on a human subject's objective and subjective stress levels. Building on Lee & Jung's (2020) work, we used a VR GWAP to investigate changes in a subject's stress levels in a more immersive environment than a typical laboratory setting. The combination of our HRV data and subjective stress rating data showed a positive relationship between the intensity of stressors and the participant's stress levels.

Furthermore, the results of the study revealed that the proposed VR GWAP is sufficiently sensitive to elicit measurable changes in participants' stress levels. We believe that the use of VR GWAPs as a tool to discover connections between mental states and physiological signals can be expanded to a larger group of scientists. Virtual simulations, we hope, will be used to accomplish what would be difficult or impossible in a traditional laboratory setting, broadening the scope of future cognitive neuroscience research.

Acknowledgments. This work was supported in part by grants from the US National Science Foundation (CBET-1935860, NCS-1734883, IP-1719130, and SMA-1540943), as well as contracts from the US Army Research Lab STRONG Program and Microsoft Corp to TPJ. The authors thank Daniel Lee for his assistance with the Unity game code.

References

1. HeartyPatch: ProtoCentral HeartyPatch (2022). https://heartypatch.protocentral. com/
2. Kim, H.G., Cheon, E.J., Bai, D.S., Lee, Y.H., Koo, B.H.: Stress and heart rate variability: ad meta-analysis and review of the literature. Psychiatry Investig. **15**, (2018). https://www.ncbi.nlm.nih.gov/pmc/articles/PMC5900369/
3. Lee, D.H., Jung, T.P.: A virtual reality game as a tool to assess physiological correlations of stress (2020). https://arxiv.org/abs/2009.14421
4. Neupert, S., Spiro, A., Mroczek, D., Almeida, D.: Daily stressors and memory failures in a naturalistic setting: findings from the VA normative aging study. Psychol. Aging **21**, 424–429 (2006). https://pubmed.ncbi.nlm.nih.gov/16768588/
5. Stawski, R.S., Mogle, J., Sliwinski, M.J.: Intraindividual coupling of daily stressors and cognitive interference in old age **66 Suppl 1**, i121-9 (2011). https://academic. oup.com/psychsocgerontology/article/66B/suppl_1/i121/551124
6. Steel Crate Games: (2022). https://keeptalkinggame.com/
7. Swartz Center for Computational Neuroscience: Lab Streaming Layer (2022). https://github.com/sccn/labstreaminglayer
8. Zhang, H.Y., Stevenson, C., Jung, T.P., Ko, L.W.: Stress-induced effects in resting EEG spectra predict the performance of SSVEP-based BCI (2020). https:// ieeexplore.ieee.org/document/9127967

Using Virtual Reality to Investigate the Emergence of Gaze Conventions in Interpersonal Coordination

Gregory Mills[1,2]([⊠]) [iD] and Remko Boschker[1]

[1] Centre for Language and Cognition, University of Groningen, Oude Kijk in 't Jatstraat 26, 9712 EK Groningen, Netherlands
g.j.mills@rug.nl
[2] Dep. Computer Science, Kingston University, London, England

Abstract. Gaze plays a central role in regulating turn-taking, but it is currently unclear whether the turn-taking signals of eye gaze are static and fixed, or whether they can be negotiated by participants during interaction. To address this question, participants play a novel collaborative task, in virtual reality. The task is played by 3 participants, and is inspired by games such as Guitar hero, Rock Band, Beat Saber, and Dance-Dance Revolution. Crucially, the participants are not allowed to use natural language – they may only communicate by looking at each other. Solving the task requires that participants bootstrap a communication system, solely through using their gaze patterns. The results show that participants rapidly conventionalise idiosyncratic routines for coordinating the timing and sequencing of their gaze patterns. This suggests that the turn-taking function of eye-gaze can be flexibly negotiated by interlocutors during interaction.

Keywords: Dialogue · Transformed social interaction · Eye-gaze · Turn-taking

1 Introduction

When people speak with each other, they dynamically adapt their language to that of their conversational partner (Pickering and Garrod 2004; Clark 1996; Gregoromichelaki et al. 2020; Nölle et al. 2018). A central finding in dialogue research is that the meanings of words and phrases used are negotiated ad hoc by participants. Thus, one recurring feature of dialogue is that participants develop novel, idiosyncratic referring expressions. For example, experiments that set participants the task of describing abstract shapes to each other have shown that, when referring repeatedly to a particular novel shape, one pair of participants might conventionalise a referring expression such as "ice-skater", whereas another pair of participants might conventionalise an entirely different referring expression ("the ballerina") to refer to exactly the same shape (Clark and Wilkes-Gibbs 1986; Clark and Bangerter 2004).

In addition to natural language expressions, face-to-face conversation is underpinned by myriad non-verbal signals (see e.g. Eijk et al., 2022), which are used, inter-alia, to

C. Stephanidis et al. (Eds.): HCII 2022, CCIS 1654, pp. 564–571, 2022.
https://doi.org/10.1007/978-3-031-19679-9_71

Fig. 1. The virtual environment in which participants play the task

regulate procedural coordination in the interaction. For example, speakers tend to look away from their addressee when starting to speak, and then re-establish eye-contact at the end of their turn in order to yield the floor or signal the next speaker (Kendon 1967; Degutyte and Astell 2021). Although research has shown clear cultural differences in such gaze-behaviour (Rossano et al. 2009), it is currently unclear whether the communicative meaning of eye-gaze is static and fixed, or whether, like natural language, it might be dynamically negotiated by participants during interaction.

To address this question, participants play a novel collaborative task within a virtual reality environment which allows for testing whether and how idiosyncratic eye-gaze signals might emerge.

2   Methods

2.1   The Task

Groups of 3 participants play a collaborative task[1], in virtual reality, using Oculus Go headsets. Participants, who are rendered as "eye-ball" avatars, are placed equidistantly and facing each other in a virtual environment (see Fig. 1, above). The task is inspired by games such as Guitar Hero, Rock Band, and Dance-Dance Revolution. The three key differences are:

1. Instead of performing target sequences of musical notes or dance moves, each triad needs to perform, together, sequences of gaze events. The possible gaze events are (a) looking at a specific participant or (b) looking at oneself in a mirror that is positioned on the right of each participant. For example, a typical target sequence might be: *"Person B must look at Person C. Then Person C must look at Person A. Then, while Person C continues looking at Person A, Person A and Person B must look at*

---

[1] The source-code is available at https://github.com/gjmills/VRLookingGame.

each other. Then, Person 3 must look at themselves in their mirror". Crucially, if any participant makes a mistake, the triad needs to restart the sequence. On each round, the target sequences are generated randomly by the server. The difficulty (i.e., length) of the target sequence is set dynamically by the server: Initially, triads are presented with simple target sequences. On successfully completing a target sequence, participants are presented with more complex (i.e., longer) target sequences. Conversely if a triad fails to solve a sequence within 90 s (i.e., a "timeout" occurs), the next sequence is less complex.

2. On each trial, only one participant (the Director) sees the target sequence. This means that in order for the group to complete the target sequence, the Director has to instruct the others, while also themselves participating in completing the target sequence (see Fig. 2, below).

3. Crucially, the participants are not allowed to use natural language to communicate – they may only communicate by looking at each other.

This task presents triads with the recurrent procedural coordination problem of communicating and then performing sequences of actions (i.e. "look events") in the correct order and with the correct timing. Solving the task, therefore, requires that triads bootstrap an ad hoc communication system (see, e.g., Scott-Phillips et al. 2009; Nölle and Galantucci 2022; Stevens and Roberts 2019) for instructing and taking turns, solely using their gaze patterns (See https://youtu.be/ctXXtFBr6Cc for a video of participants playing the game).

2.2 Manipulation

In order to test whether participants develop idiosyncratic signals for coordinating procedurally, the experiment used a technique similar to that used by Healey (2008) and Mills (2011), namely, using *transformed social interaction* (Bailenson et al. 2004; McVeigh Schultz and Isbister 2021; Cheng et al. 2017) to artificially manipulate the participants' communicative behaviour.

The experiment was divided into a 25 min "training phase" followed by a 5 min "test phase". During the training phase, triads complete the task as described above. At the start of the test-phase, the identities of the participants were swapped in the following manner: Each participant continues to see the other two avatars in the same locations. However, the participants controlling those avatars are swapped: In Participant A's headset, Participant B's physical head movements are mapped onto Participant C's avatar, while Participant C's physical head movements are mapped onto B's avatar. Similarly, in B's headset, B now sees A's head movements animating C's avatar and sees C's head movements animating A's avatar. Also in C's headset, C sees A's physical head movements animating B's avatar, and vice versa.

While the training phase tests whether participants are able to bootstrap a communication system, this later manipulation[2] in the test-phase investigates whether participants

---

[2] We originally intended to use 3 groups of triads in order to create triads in the test-phase that comprise participants who were members of different triads in the training phase, similarly to the setup in Healey (2008). However, due to technical difficulties with networking 9 headsets we used the approach of 3 triads.

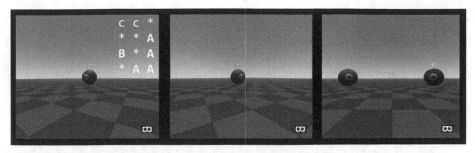

Fig. 2. The view from each of the three participants' headsets (From left to right: Participants A, B, C). Participants are rendered as virtual eye-balls that are anchored at a particular location in the sky. Each participant's ID (e.g., A, B, C) is displayed above their heads. In this example, Participant A is assigned the role of Director, this why the target sequence is displayed in the first screen, i.e., A's view. The target sequence of "look events" is displayed as a three-column table in the top-right hand corner of A's display. The table is read from top to bottom. The left-most column cells represent the actions to be performed by Participant A. The middle column represents the actions to be performed by Participant B, and the right-most column represents the actions to be performed by Participant C. Each row describes a gaze configuration that must be achieved simultaneously by the triad. An asterisk means that the participant corresponding to that cell does not need to perform any action. For example, the target sequence displayed in Participant A's window represents the following sequence of actions: "*First A and B both need to look at C.* (row 1) *Then C needs to look at A.* (row 2). *Then while C looks at A, B needs to look at A.* (row 3). *Then B needs to look at A* (row 4)". The task of the Director is to get the triad to perform this sequence of look events, which requires that the Director communicates this sequence to the other participants. On successful completion of a look event, the corresponding letter in the Director's window changes to lower-case. Crucially, if any participant produces the wrong look event, the triad needs to restart the sequence, i.e., all letters return to upper-case. Figure 2 then shows the configuration of A, B, C after successfully completing the first row: The left-most screen shows, from A's perspective, A looking at C; the middle-screen shows, from B's perspective, that B is looking at C; the right-most screen shows, from C's perspective, both A and B looking at C.s

within the triads develop a different communication system with each partner: participants are unaware that the identities of their partners are swapped, so if they haveindeed established different systems, then, on entering the test phase, they will attempt to reuse a convention with the same partner (who is actually the other partner). Under the effect of the manipulation of identity swapping, this should lead to more errors and less efficient communication.

2.3 Hypotheses

The experiment tested two hypotheses:

1. During the training phase, participants will establish a communication system with each other that will allow them to collaboratively solve the target sequences.
2. In the test phase, the manipulation will cause participants to inadvertently use the wrong signals with each other, causing disruption to task performance.

3 Results

69 triads took part in the experiment.

3.1 Training Phase

During the 25-min training phase, triads completed a mean of 20.5 sets (S.D. = 3.45). The most successful triad completed 27 sets. By the end of the training phase, triads were solving sets with a mean of 5.5 target items (S.D. = 1.2). The most successful triad completed sets containing 8 targets (see, e.g., Fig. 2 which shows a target set containing 7 "look events").

3.2 Test Phase

To test the effect of the intervention, we compared participants' performance in the 5 min preceding the swap with their performance during the 5 min test phase. We used two measures of disruption to task performance.

The first measure, task success, was modelled with a mixed binary logistic regression, using the lme4 package (Bates et al. 2014), which showed that triads solved significantly fewer games in the test phase ($b = -0.49$, S.E. $= 0.193$, $z = -2.54$), $p = 0.0111$). The model predicts that triads successfully solve 66% [95%CI: 0.60, 0.72] of target sets in the training phase and 54% [95%CI: 0.48, 0.61] of target sets in the test phase.

The second measure recorded the number of "look events" per game, i.e., the number of times a participant selected a target. All things being equal, if participants are encountering more difficulties coordinating with each other, this will lead to them having to make more selections, i.e., expend more effort, to solve a set. A linear mixed model using the lme4 package showed that triads produced significantly more look events in the 5-min test phase than in the last 5 min of the training phase ($b = 10.4$, S.E. $= 2.98$, $t = 3.5$, $p < 0.001$). The model predicts 40 [95%CI: 36.2, 43.8] look events per game in the training phase, and 50.4 [95% CI: 45.5, 55.4] look events in the test phase.

4 Discussion

The results provide support for both hypotheses. The average sequence length at the end of the training phase suggests that the participants were solving the sets by communicating with each other, as opposed to solving via individual trial and error. During piloting, we observed participants attempting to solve the sequences without attempting to establish a communication system with each other – these triads almost never managed to solve sequences longer than length 2.

Moreover, the increased number of timeouts and look events in the test phase suggest that the manipulation disrupted participants' coordination. A plausible explanation for this pattern is that many participants communicated differently with each partner. This was confirmed by the participants themselves. On debriefing, we asked participants about the communication system they had developed. Some participants explicitly stated that they noticed that their partners communicated differently (e.g., using different signals for the same actions, or communicated faster/slower), which they had attempted to accommodate.

Given that participants develop idiosyncratic signalling systems with each of their co-players simultaneously, it is clear that they demonstrate ability to discriminate and adapt dynamically to different participants at the same time during a single task. It is an open question how this form of audience design compares with how participants take each other's perspective into account when they adapt their language to the interlocutor, e.g., when producing referring expressions (Fischer 2016; Yoon and Brown-Schmidt 2019; Healey and Mills 2006) or when associating expressions' meanings with particular sequential positions in the unfolding interaction (Mills and Gregoromichelaki 2010; Gregoromichelaki et al. 2011; Mills 2014).

These findings are subject to a couple of important caveats concerning the ecological validity of the experimental setup: First, the participants' movements are severely constrained. The Oculus Go headsets only capture rotations around the x,y,z axes, but do not capture any change in location: throughout the experiment, the avatars are anchored at a fixed location. Second, the setup conflates "head gaze" and "eye gaze", as participants' head-movements are mapped onto their virtual eye-ball (see, e.g., Špakov et al. 2019).

Nonetheless, these findings suggest that the interactive signals that participants use to attract and direct another's visual attention can be flexibly negotiated during an interaction. In addition, the restriction of movement to rotations around the x, y, z axes makes the findings all the more surprising, as they show that participants are still able to bootstrap a communication system within these quite severe constraints.

To conclude, these findings are of central importance for theories of Human-Computer Interaction. Research on dialogue has shown that in order for systems to converse naturalistically with humans, they must be able to dynamically adapt their vocabularies, ontologies, and emotional signals to their conversational partner during the interaction (Healey 2021; Mills et al. 2021; Larsson 2007; Cooper, forthcoming). The findings from the current experiment suggest that, in addition, technologies such as avatars, dialogue systems, as well as self-driving cars when communicating with pedestrians (Habibovic et al. 2018), need to be able to flexibly adapt their non-verbal and turn-taking signals to those of the user.

References

Argyle, M.: Bodily Communication, 2nd edn. Methuen, London (1988)

Bailenson, J.N., Beall, A.C., Loomis, J., Blascovich, J., Turk, M.: Transformed social interaction: decoupling representation from behavior and form in collaborative virtual environments. Presence Teleoperat. Vir. Environ. **13**(4), 428–441 (2004)

Bates, D., Mächler, M., Bolker, B., Walker, S.: Fitting linear mixed-effects models using lme4. arXiv preprint arXiv:1406.5823 (2014)

Cheng, L.P., Marwecki, S., Baudisch, P.: Mutual human actuation. In: Proceedings of the 30th Annual ACM Symposium on User Interface Software and Technology, pp. 797–805 (2017)

Clark, H.: Using language. Cambridge University Press, Cambridge (1996)

Clark, H., Bangerter, A.: Changing ideas about reference. In: Experimental Pragmatics, pp. 25–49. Palgrave Macmillan, London (2004)

Clark, H., Wilkes-Gibbs, D.: Referring as a collaborative process. Cognition **22**(1), 1–39 (1986).

Cooper, R.: From Perception to Communication: An Analysis of Meaning and Action Using a Theory of Types With Records (TTR). CUP (Forthcomimg)

Degutyte, Z., Astell, A.: The role of eye gaze in regulating turn taking in conversations: a systematized review of methods and findings. Front. Psychol. 12 (2012)

Eijk, L., et al.: The CABB dataset: A multimodal corpus of communicative interactions for behavioural and neural analyses. NeuroImage, 119734 (2022)

Fischer, K.: Designing speech for a recipient: the roles of partner modeling, alignment and feedback in so-called 'simplified registers, pp. 1–337 (2016)

Gregoromichelaki, E., et al.: Incrementality and intention-recognition in utterance processing. Dial. Discourse **2**(1), 199–233 (2011)

Gregoromichelaki, E., et al.: Completability vs (In) completeness. Acta Linguistica Hafniensia **52**(2), 260–284 (2020)

Habibovic, A., et al.: Communicating intent of automated vehicles to pedestrians. Front. Psychol. **1336** (2018)

Healey, P., Mills, G.: Participation, precedence and co-ordination in dialogue. In: Proceedings of the 28th Annual Conference of the Cognitive Science Society, vol. 320. Cognitive Science Society, Vancouver (2006)

Healey, P.: Interactive misalignment: the role of repair in the development of group sub-languages. In: Language in Flux, p. 212. College Publications (2008)

Healey, P.: Human-Like Communication. Oxford University Press, Oxford (2021)

Kendon, A.: Some functions of gaze-direction in social interaction. Acta Physiol. (Oxf) **26**, 22–63 (1967)

Larsson, S.: A general framework for semantic plasticity and negotiation. In: Proceedings of the Seventh International Workshop on Computational Semantics (IWCS-7) (2007)

McVeigh-Schultz, J., Isbister, K.: The case for "weird social" in VR/XR: a vision of social superpowers beyond meatspace. In: Extended Abstracts of the 2021 CHI Conference on Human Factors in Computing Systems, pp. 1–10 (2021)

Mills, G.: The emergence of procedural conventions in dialogue. In: Proceedings of the Annual Meeting of the Cognitive Science Society, vol. 33 (2011)

Mills, G.J.: Dialogue in joint activity: Complementarity, convergence and conventionalization. New Ideas Psychol. **32**, 158–173 (2014)

Mills, G., Gregoromichelaki, E.: Establishing coherence in dialogue: sequentiality, intentions and negotiation. In: Proceedings of SemDial (PozDial) (2010)

Mills, G., Gregoromichelaki, E., Howes, C., Maraev, V.: Influencing laughter with AI-mediated communication. Interact. Stud. **22**(3), 416–463 (2021)

Nölle, J., Staib, M., Fusaroli, R., Tylén, K.: The emergence of systematicity: how environmental and communicative factors shape a novel communication system. Cognition **181**, 93–104 (2018)

Nölle, J. & Galantucci, B.: Experimental Semiotics: past, present and future. In: Garcia, Ibanez (eds.) Handbook of Neurosemiotics. Routledge (to appear)

Pickering, M.J., Garrod, S.: Toward a mechanistic psychology of dialogue. Behav. Brain Sci. **27**(2), 169–190 (2004)

Rossano, F., Brown, P., Levinson, S.C.: Gaze, questioning and culture. Convers. Anal. **27**, 187–249 (2009). https://doi.org/10.1017/CBO9780511635670.008

Scott-Phillips, T.C., Kirby, S., Ritchie, G.R.: Signalling signalhood and the emergence of communication. Cognition **113**(2), 226–233 (2009)

Špakov, O., Istance, H., Räihä, K.J., Viitanen, T., Siirtola, H.: Eye gaze and head gaze in collaborative games. In: Proceedings of the 11th ACM Symposium on Eye Tracking Research & Applications, pp. 1–9, June 2019

Stevens, J.S., Roberts, G.: Noise, economy, and the emergence of information structure in a laboratory language. Cogn. Sci. **43**(2), e12717 (2019)

Yoon, S.O., Brown-Schmidt, S.: Audience design in multiparty conversation. Cogn. Sci. **43**(8), e12774 (2019)

Mixed Reality for Mechanical Design and Assembly Planning

Emran Poh[1], Kyrin Liong[2], and Jeannie S. A. Lee[1(✉)]

[1] Infocomm Technology, Singapore Institute of Technology, Singapore, Singapore
{emran.poh,jeannie.lee}@singaporetech.edu.sg
[2] Engineering, Singapore Institute of Technology, Singapore, Singapore
kyrin.liong@singaporetech.edu.sg

Abstract. Design for Manufacturing and Assembly (DFMA) is a crucial design stage within the heavy vehicle manufacturing process that
involves optimising the order and feasibility of the parts assembly process to reduce manufacturing complexity and overall cost. Existing work
has focused on conducting DFMA within virtual environments to reduce
manufacturing costs, but users are less able to relate and compare physical characteristics of a virtual component with real physical objects.
Therefore, a Mixed Reality (MR) application is developed for engineers
to visualise and manipulate assembly parts virtually, conduct and plan
out an assembly within its intended physical environment. Two pilot
evaluations were conducted with both engineering professionals and non-
engineers to assess effectiveness of the software for assembly planning.
Usability results suggest that the application is overall usable (M=56.1,
SD=7.89), and participants felt a sense of involvement in the activity
(M=13.1, SD=3.3). Engineering professionals see the application as a
useful and cost-effective tool for optimising their mechanical assembly
designs.

Keywords: Assembly planning · Mixed reality · Gesture · 3D user
interface · Digital twin

1 Introduction

The ability to realistically visualise and intuitively manipulate an engineering
assembly is key to an efficient design process [6]. When presented with a large
assembly with heavy components, it is vital to cost-optimise its design and
assembly process to mitigate prototyping costs. This 'optimisation' is known
as DFMA, and improves upon areas such as material selection, machining tol-
erances, and most importantly the order of assembly of complex components to
lower manufacturing and assembly overheads.

Existing work has explored conducting DFMA in virtual environments to
reduce physical prototyping, however users are less able to do spatial correlation
[6–8]. Spatial correlation refers to the ability to visualise, relate, and compare

physical characteristics of a virtual object with real physical objects or environment. Within the context of virtual DFMA, the capability of visualising a virtual assembly within its intended environment is vital for assembly planning. Augmented Reality (AR) has also been utilised to allow virtual assemblies to be overlaid onto physical environments for visualisation, although with limited interaction [10,13]. Mixed Reality (MR) presents a useful platform where engineers will be able to intuitively interact, conduct design reviews without prototyping, and visualise their virtual Computer-Aided Design (CAD) assemblies within their intended physical environment.

Understanding the requirements of conducting an assembly within a mixed reality environment through a requirements gathering session, the goal is to develop an intuitive and effective MR application for conducting assembly planning. Two pilot studies were conducted to quantitatively and qualitatively evaluate the usability of the proposed application and gather useful insight into its effectiveness and learnability.

2 Related Work

Existing virtual assembly planning systems allow users to be able to visualise and evaluate the assembly of their mechanical systems in various virtual environments with different tools. External controllers such as a mouse [5] or a haptic device [4] provide a physical object for the user to interact with the virtual environment, however will incur cost for setting up the tracking system for each device. VR-based systems [2,6,11,12] provide a useful platform for simulating different environments, however it is limited in its ability to replicate dynamic and realistic environments. AR systems [10] addresses the lack of spatial correlation through overlaying useful information onto physical surfaces, however the virtual objects do not interact with the physical world. While conducting engineering design reviews in a virtual environment shortens the product development life-cycle and lowers manufacturing overheads [7,9], these systems lack the spatial awareness needed to conduct feasibility tests of comparing the virtual models within a real physical environment. Mixed reality presents a platform in which virtual objects could interact with the physical world through spatial mapping and gesture interaction. Through conducting assembly planning within MR, the user will be able to visualise and iterate on their designs quickly, intuitively interact with their virtual models, and reduce manufacturing and prototyping overheads.

3 Assembly Planning Features

The goal of this work is to utilise MR as a platform to conduct engineering design reviews. A list of assembly planning features were obtained through a requirement gathering session with professional design engineers. Within the list, three primary categories of features were identified: *Component Manipulation, Assembly Guidance, Spatial Awareness*.

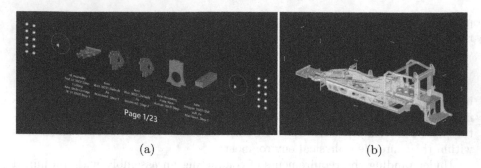

(a)   (b)

Fig. 1. Assembly planning features. (a) Component browsing interface, (b) 'Bounds' interface for anchoring

Component Manipulation. Being able to manipulate assembly component parts is critical in testing and planning out possible manoeuvres for assembly. A 3D browsing interface (Fig. 1a) enables the user to spawn and hide component objects to allow the user to bring parts into the assembly area when the user requires of it. A toggle button from the 'Hand Menu', the user will be able to toggle between freehand bi-manual manipulation and single-axis rotation.

Spatial Awareness. Spatial awareness is critical in developing a useful MR application, especially within the context of an engineering design review. Spatial anchoring was added such that the virtual assembly model would be able to adhere to a specific location in the real physical environment to improve transfer of knowledge and correlation. This anchoring also helps in visualising the 1:1 scale of the model in real life. To provide a frame of reference for assembly orientation, the Orientation Indicator rotates along with the user in relation to the anchored assembly. Upon spawning a component, an arrow will appear

Table 1. List of assembly planning features

Category	Feature
Component manipulation	Assembly Component Spawning
	Assembly Component Browsing
	Manipulation (Single-Axis Rotation, Translation)
Spatial awareness	Spatial Anchoring
	Orientation Indicator
	Directional Indicator
Assembly guidance	Component Positioning Guidance
	Audio Feedback
	Component-to-Component Collision

around the component pointing towards the direction of its position within the anchored assembly.

Assembly Guidance. To provide assembly guidance, a list of visual and audio prompts were introduced to assist during assembly planning. Upon manipulation of an assembly component, a translucent copy of the same component appears in the position of where the component should be within the anchored assembly. Component-To-Component collision is an effective tool to definitively validate assembly manoeuvres. To simulate this interaction, the components change colour from a base colour of white (indicating no collision) to blue (indicating collision). Audio feedback emphasises any application events such as button presses, component collisions, and manipulation.

4 Implementation

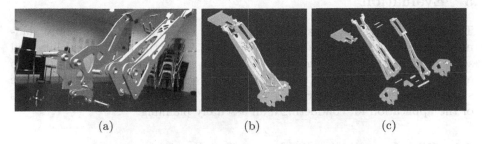

| (a) | (b) | (c) |

Fig. 2. Vehicular heavy lifter with 13 parts (13 parts). (a) View of assembly components with orientation indicator within MR view, (b) shows a completed view of the assembly, (c) shows an exploded view of the assembly

All assembly planning features and interactions were built using gestures and interaction components within Microsoft's Mixed Reality Toolkit (MRTK). The application was developed using Unity Engine and deployed and tested on Microsoft Hololens 2. For the CAD models, the assembly model used were designed and tested through SolidWorks and converted into a Unity-compatible format using Blender. The subject (Fig. 2) is a large assembly of a vehicular heavy lifter (Dimensions: 3.5 m × 1.5 m × 2 m, Actual Physical Assembly Weight: 4 tons).

The user is able to carry out several basic interactions for manipulation and rotation through the attachment of *ManipulationHandler* script for input detection and handling. For single axis rotation, the *Bounds* component provides a visible interface which users could interact with to pivot the model along its axes. To simulate collision, a non-convex collider is generated and attached to each assembly component upon spawning. Upon contact between components, a collision event will be triggered which will modify the colour of the material of each colliding components. To avoid false collisions caused by overlapping and jagged colliders, a user-defined parameter was introduced to define a margin of error that the colliders could overlap before triggering a collision event Fig. 3.

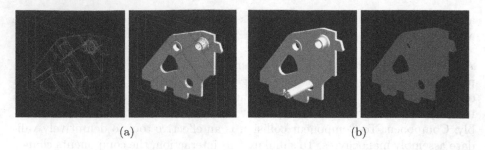

(a)   (b)

Fig. 3. Component collision collider implementation. (b) (From Left to Right) Box collider and the generated non-convex collider. Base component with box collider. (b) (From Left to Right) Two solid assembly components in varying levels of collision (No collision, colliding)

5   Evaluation

To evaluate the effectiveness of the application as a platform for assembly planning, two preliminary studies were conducted. First, the relative usability and sense of flow of the application was assessed by a group of users with little to no existing expertise through a pilot quantitative study. Second, a pilot qualitative study was conducted on a group of senior engineers to evaluate the effectiveness of the application for conducting a an assembly planning.

5.1   Pilot Quantitative Study and Results

In this study, participants (n=7, Age: 20–45) who have no prior experience in mixed reality and engineering are required to assemble the vehicular lifter through the use of all available assembly guidance. At the end of the assembly session, the relative usability [1] and perceived flow [3] of the application were recorded.

The usability results from the experiment in Table 2 suggest that the interface is empirically usable (M=56.07, SD=7.89). Given the lack of prior experience in engineering or mixed reality, this could suggest that more visual instruction may be necessary for first-time users to navigate the application. Findings also show in Table 3 that the participants felt that they were clear about their goals (M=12.29, SD=1.60), had a sense of control when experiencing the application (M=11.57, SD=1.51), and their thoughts ran somewhat smoothly with minor difficulty in concentrating (M=17.00, SD=2.16). However, the participants felt that there was too much challenge in understanding the interface and that they feel that they were somewhat competent (M=13.1, SD=3.3). Despite this, most participants reported they enjoyed the experience (M=6.57, SD=1.13).

5.2   Pilot Qualitative Study and Results

A pilot think-aloud was conducted on senior design engineers (n=3, Age: 35–50) to assess the feasibility of the features developed in the application. The participants had 8 to 10 years of experience in coordinating assembly planning and conducting design reviews. The participants were required to assemble the heavy vehicular loader. A thematic analysis was conducted upon the think-aloud and semi-structured feedback by the participants.

During the walkthrough, participants mentioned that finger-pointing and pinch-tap as a tool for basic manipulation 'feels' natural however compromises on accuracy that is needed for more complex manoeuvres. While there were visible assembly guidance prompts, participants suggested that more guidance is needed when conducting an assembly in a mixed environment. While collision exists in real life, other physical information such as assembly tolerance and sub-assembly information could be useful. Overall, participants mentioned the suitability of the application for macro-structure assembly planning and highlighted its potential for visualising and validating possible sub-assembly interactions involved without the need for physical prototyping.

Table 2. System usability scale scores (n=7)

No.	Question	Mean	SD
1	I think I would like to use this interface frequently	4.29	0.76
2	I found the interface unnecessarily complex	3.86	0.38
3	I thought the interface was easy to use	4.29	0.49
4	I think that I would need the support of a technical person to be able to use this interface	2.86	1.21
5	I found the various functions in this interface were well-integrated	4.57	0.53
6	I thought there was too much inconsistency in this interface	3.86	0.90
7	I would imagine that most people would learn to use this interface very quickly	3.71	0.49
8	I found the interface very cumbersome to use	4.29	0.49
9	I felt very confident using the interface	4.00	0.58
10	I needed to learn a lot of things before I could get going with this interface	3.57	1.40
Usability score		56.07	7.89

5.3   Evaluation Summary

Quantitative results show that while the interface can be initially challenging, users were eventually able to find enjoyment and a sense of control when navigating. For engineering professionals, this could hint at a steeper learning curve when first introduced to concepts that require specialised knowledge in an unfamiliar environment. Qualitative results suggest that engineering professionals find part collisions and superposition of virtual assembly parts within a physical context as a useful and cost-effective tool for conducting an assembly design

Table 3. Flow state scale scores (n=7)

No.	Question	Mean	SD
1	I was not confused about my objectives	6.29	0.76
2	I knew what I had to do each step of the way	6.00	1.15
3	My thoughts/activities ran fluidly and smoothly	5.14	1.57
4	I had no difficulty concentrating	5.43	1.40
5	I was totally absorbed in what I was doing	6.43	0.53
6	I feel just the right amount of challenge	3.57	1.51
7	I felt that I must not make any mistakes	4.43	1.72
8	I think that my competence in this area was	5.14	1.21
9	The right thoughts/movements occurred of their own accord	5.71	0.49
10	I felt that I had everything under control	5.86	1.21
11	I enjoyed the experience	6.57	1.13
Subscale 1: Clear Goals (Qns 1, 2)		12.29	1.60
Subscale 2: Action-Awareness Merging (Qns 3, 4, 5)		17.00	2.16
Subscale 3: Challenge Skill Balance (Qns 6, 7, 8)		13.14	3.34
Subscale 4: Sense of Control (Qns 9, 10)		11.57	1.51
Subscale 5: Autotelic Experience (Qn 11)		6.57	1.13

review. A further study could be conducted on a larger population of engineering experts which would yield greater accuracy in understanding the effectiveness of the application.

6   Conclusion

The developed application is designed to enhance the efficiency of mechanical design engineers when conducting DFMA. MR presents a compelling platform for testing and visualising complex virtual assembly models and component interactions onto physical space without the need for prototyping. Results from the preliminary studies reveal that the application is usable and accessible despite a learning curve. Feedback from design engineers highlights that they foresee a potential for using MR in improving their DFMA process. Future work could involve exploring a multi-user experience for assembly planning to correlate better with the nature of assembly planning in a group.

Acknowledgements. The authors of this paper wish to acknowledge the contributions provided by the technical staff of HelloHolo and Hope Technik Pte Ltd Singapore. This research was supported by the Singapore Institute of Technology Ignition Grant (R-MOE-E103-G001).

References

1. Brooke, J.: System usability scale (SUS): A quick-and-dirty method of system evaluation user information. digital equipment co ltd. Reading, UK, pp. 1–7 (1986)
2. Chen, Q., et al.: Immersive virtual reality training of bioreactor operations. In: 2020 IEEE International Conference on Teaching, Assessment, and Learning for Engineering (TALE), pp. 873–878 (2020). https://doi.org/10.1109/TALE48869.2020.9368468
3. Csikszentmihalyi, M., Abuhamdeh, S., Nakamura, J., et al.: Flow (1990)
4. Gallegos-Nieto, E., Medellín-Castillo, H.I., González-Badillo, G., Lim, T., Ritchie, J.: The analysis and evaluation of the influence of haptic-enabled virtual assembly training on real assembly performance. Int. J. Adv. Manufact. Technol. **89**(1), 581–598 (2017)
5. Ganier, F., Hoareau, C., Tisseau, J.: Evaluation of procedural learning transfer from a virtual environment to a real situation: a case study on tank maintenance training. Ergonomics **57**(6), 828–843 (2014)
6. Jayaram, S., Connacher, H.I., Lyons, K.W.: Virtual assembly using virtual reality techniques. Comput. Aided Des. **29**(8), 575–584 (1997)
7. Jayaram, S., Jayaram, U., Wang, Y., Tirumali, H., Lyons, K., Hart, P.: Vade: a virtual assembly design environment. IEEE Comput. Graphics Appl. **19**(6), 44–50 (1999)
8. Kim, C.E., Vance, J.M.: Using VPS (voxmap pointshell) as the basis for interaction in a virtual assembly environment. In: International Design Engineering Technical Conferences and Computers and Information in Engineering Conference. vol. 36991, pp. 1153–1161 (2003)
9. Poh, E., Liong, K., Lee, J.S.A.: Mixed reality interface for load application in finite element analysis. In: Meiselwitz, G. (ed.) Social Computing and Social Media: Experience Design and Social Network Analysis, pp. 470–483. Springer International Publishing, Cham (2021)
10. Poupyrev, I., Tan, D.S., Billinghurst, M., Kato, H., Regenbrecht, H., Tetsutani, N.: Tiles: a mixed reality authoring interface. In: Interact. vol. 1, pp. 334–341. Citeseer (2001)
11. Seth, A., Vance, J.M., Oliver, J.H.: Virtual reality for assembly methods prototyping: a review. Virt. Real. **15**(1), 5–20 (2011)
12. Wolfartsberger, J.: Analyzing the potential of virtual reality for engineering design review. Autom. Constr. **104**, 27–37 (2019)
13. Zauner, J., Haller, M., Brandl, A., Hartman, W.: Authoring of a mixed reality assembly instructor for hierarchical structures. In: The Second IEEE and ACM International Symposium on Mixed and Augmented Reality, 2003. Proceedings, pp. 237–246. IEEE (2003)

A Study on Software Proposals for Optimization of Augmented Reality Glasses

Bo Kwang Shim, Ju Yeon Seo, Kyeong Yun Na, Da Young Lee, Min Hye Moon,
and Yang Kyu Lim[✉]

IT Media Engineering, Duksung Women's University, Seoul, Republic of Korea
trumpetyk09@duksung.ac.kr

Abstract. The advent of Google Glass was expected to bring about a big change in the AR industry, but it was difficult to popularize it due to various technical limitations. Microsoft HoloLens, which was later revised and fine-tuned in many parts, was also dismissed by the public. Although it is known on the surface that the reason is a lack of content and services, according to investigations, the actual cause is discomfort that is not optimized for human vision.

Recently, with the advent of the metaverse, AR glasses equipped with various services are being released again, but as explained earlier, it is having a lot of difficulty in popularizing it. It could be concluded that there would be many difficulties in marketing until the limitations and problems of their angle of vision and image reproduction were resolved.

We presented a guideline to solve the fundamental technical limitations of hard-ware such as the viewing angle problem that would occur when manufacturing a navigation program using AR glasses, and produced a prototype suitable for it and tested it with various people. In particular, the most common and universal AR app such as a wayfinding service was implemented, and the guidelines for solving the discomfort felt in the distance and the solution to the discomfort were presented and tested as much as possible with the software method without any hardware improvement.

If this experiment is improved through more types of programs so that it can be applied to various services and assist human physical limitations in the future, it is expected that it will be a starting point that can have a good influence on the industry.

Keywords: AR glasses · Optimization · Wayfinder

1 Introduction

With the advent of Google Glass, it was expected that a big change would come to the AR industry, but it failed to popularize due to various limitations. Microsoft's Holo Lens, which was released as a successor, also did not overcome the technical limitations. Although it is known on the surface as a lack of content and services, the actual cause is discomfort that is not optimized for human viewing angles Recently, with the advent

C. Stephanidis et al. (Eds.): HCII 2022, CCIS 1654, pp. 580–586, 2022.
https://doi.org/10.1007/978-3-031-19679-9_73

of the metaverse, AR glasses equipped with various services are being released again. Unless it solves the problem of human viewing angle, it is difficult to become popular.

This study aims to solve the fundamental technical limitations of hardware such as the viewing angle problem that will occur when creating a navigation program using AR glasses. Then, it provides guidelines for problem solving and produces proto-types that fit it. In addition, implementing the most common and universal AR apps such as a wayfinding service, and providing guidelines for solving the discomfort felt there and how to solve the discomfort with only the software method without im-proving the hardware as much as possible.

2 Background

In order to make navigation for AR glasses, the existing AR navigation UI is searched in advance. Commonly seen UIs can often be seen in AR navigation for smartphones similar to Fig. 1 below.

First, by referring to AR navigation for smartphones, problems arising from application to AR glasses are analyzed. By understanding the differences between AR for smartphones and AR glasses, it can be concluded that there is a basis for presenting an optimized UI for AR glasses.

Fig. 1. Examples of smartphone AR navigation UI

2.1 Main Viewing Angle

One of the differences between AR for smartphones and AR glasses is the viewing angle.

As shown in Fig. 2, when AR is used with a smartphone, there is a tendency to raise the smartphone to a height similar to the real environment, but we instinctively move the height and angle of the smartphone with our hands when walking on the street.

This action helps to refer to information from the smartphone without interfering with the main viewing angle. Plus, it doesn't interfere with the main viewing angle. However, it is impossible to control the viewing angle using the hands while wearing the AR glasses. In other words, all UIs are placed in the main viewing angle.

Let's explain the act of viewing a smartphone navigation system. People quickly look at the guidance UI on the screen with minimal movement and turn their eyes back to see the way they were going. Small actions that only move the eyes rather than moving

Fig. 2. When using AR with a smartphone, raise the smartphone to a height similar to the real environment

the head are the main ones. In conclusion, any size or color of the UI in the smartphone does not act as a big factor. The UI, which is large enough to cover the entire road, and the color dark enough to not recognize the material at all, has nothing to do with smartphone AR. This is because if the UI blocks the main viewing angle or makes the eyes uncomfortable, we can naturally change the position of the smartphone to view it in a better way.

As a result, viewing the navigation using smartphone AR means that the reality and the screen are placed in front of you, as shown in Fig. 2, and alternate viewing as needed. Smartphone AR has the advantage of being able to quickly switch while viewing the screen and reality at the same time using your hands.

2.2 Smartphone vs Glasses

Fig. 3. The UI in the screen will cover the projected image that is real

If the real world vision becomes like Fig. 3, we will have vision problems. People first analyze the difference between a road and a sidewalk visually in order to judge whether the place they are currently in is safe or not. People find the characteristics of the sidewalk through texture, find the boundary with the road, and analyze the material of the road to determine whether it is slipping or not. A person makes a momentary decision whether to slowly touch the ground as much as possible with the entire foot, or as usual from the heel (this part may depend on your usual walking habits), or whether to shorten or lengthen the stride length. At the same time, the person analyzes the height angle of the road, and analyzes whether the height angle is different in a certain section, such as stairs, or the height angle is irregularly different. In addition to this, people quickly calculate for many situations in an instant. In other words, when a UI of a size that completely blocks the road is placed right in front of the main viewing angle, we cannot see ahead.

2.3 UI Creation for AR Glasses

The optimal condition is to cover all viewing angles of a person, but the size of the display mounted on the AR glass is small. Therefore, the number and size of UIs that can be exposed at once are limited. Information should be sufficiently exposed in a size and number that does not block the field of view.

You have to turn your entire head to see information on a specific location with AR class. The display size is also small, which can cause significant physical fatigue and confusion to find UI or information.

Fig. 4. UI that tells you the direction

For example, you may need a UI that informs the direction as shown in Fig. 4 below. In this case, when using a smartphone, even if the height of the UI is located just above the ground, it does not feel much inconvenience. The reason is that the screen of the smartphone is used only for information reference, and it is possible to change the view quickly at any time. And you can see the screen just by moving your eyes. Conversely, in the case of AR glasses, you have to lower your head to see the UI on the floor. Fatigue increases as you move your head to see the UI.

In the case of a navigation app, the perspective expression should be sufficient. As shown in Fig. 5, the UI that informs the point where the rotation is required may not be important in the city center or on the pavement. This is because we can understand the need for rotation at that location by looking at the bending angle of the sidewalk or the continuity of the road, which are the characteristics of the part where the UI is located.

Fig. 5. UI to indicate where rotation is required

However, it is difficult to know where to turn on an unpaved road as shown in Fig. 6. The project was an AR glass navigation project for the Jeju Olle Trail, and the Jeju Olle Trail has several unpaved roads and hard-to-recognize forked roads. In this case, if there is no clear sense of principal expression, we will know only past the location where the UI is entered.

Fig. 6. AR glass navigation project for Jeju Olle Trail

3 Implementation

There are several ways to express perspective. Among them, due to the characteristics of AR, the methods that can be expressed are the perspective method and the overlapping perspective method. The famous line perspective among perspective perspectives was inspired by train tracks. If the entire road is colored, it can be inconvenient to walk because it is difficult to distinguish the material and height of the road. However, if only both ends of the road are expressed as shown in Fig. 7, the direction and degree of bend of the road can be expressed only with small objects.

Fig. 7. If the creator expresses both ends of the road, small objects can express the direction of the road and the degree of bend.

In the case of a UI that exposes rotation information, if it is output from a fixed position, the difference in size versus distance cannot be understood. In this case, it is easy to express perspective by applying a simple animation that moves the image created in front of the user by the corresponding distance to express the size difference compared to the distance.

4 Conclusion

When the user is looking in a direction in which the navigation UI is not displayed, it is set to always indicate which direction to rotate without blocking the view,, shiwn in Fig. 8.

Fig. 8. UI that indicates which direction to rotate in

In Fig. 9, the direction of the road is indicated by a dotted line at both ends of the road. As a result, it was possible to understand the material and height of the road easily without obstructing the line of sight, and the obstruction of view disappeared. We drew an arrow UI at the position where rotation is required and applied a simple animation to move to that point. Three additional arrows are generated towards the direction the rotation is required to indicate how far away and in which direction to rotate.

Fig. 9. Three additional arrows are created towards the direction the rotation is required to indicate how far away and in which direction to rotate.

5 Future Works

Geometry information and object recognition functions will be combined to expose more accurate information. Currently, it is not possible to accurately express the width, height, and degree of bends of the road, but it is expected that the accurate width of the road can be expressed if geometric information and object recognition become possible in the future. In particular, it is predicted that it will be possible to express from where it is to the road or whether it is out of the sidewalk block.

References

1. Zhao, B.C., Ahmad, A.N., Jang, C.H., Lee, K.S., Jo, G.S.: A mobile landmarks guide: outdoor augmented reality based on LOD and contextual device, J. Intell. Inf. Syst. **18**(1), 1–21 (2012)
2. Kang, D.E., Kim, D.E., Lee, Y M.: User interface design for tourism route guidance based on augmented reality utilizing smart glass, In: Proceedings of Korea Geospatial Information Society Joint Fall Conference, pp. 173–175 (2016)
3. Park, J.S., Lee, J.G., Park, J.: Urban environment location estimation method for outdoor AR games. In: 2017 24 Encontro Português de Computação Gráfica e Interação (EPCGI), vol. 27, pp.167–173 (2017)
4. Jung, S.H., Ryu, S.H.: Interaction-based mobile UI design utilizing smart media augmented reality. Digit. Conver. Res. **17**(7), 311–316 (2019)
5. Jeon, S.J., Hwang, J.: The experiential value of mobile augmented reality (MAR) travel and its impact on satisfaction. Percep. Disab. Soc. Serv. Manag. **22**(4), 98–122 (2021)
6. NRSDK User Guide. https://nrealsdkdoc.readthedocs.io/en/v1.6.0/index.html.
7. Unity Manual. https://docs.unity3d.com/Manual/XR.html. Accessed 8 Feb 2022
8. Unity AR+GPS Location Docs (v3.6.0). https://docs.unity-ar-gps-location.com/. Accessed 8 Feb 2022
9. Kakao Maps API. https://apis.map.kakao.com/android/documentation/. Accessed 8 Feb 2022

Augmented Reality System with a 3DCG Character Running on a Spinning Analog Record

Nanami Yoshikawa, Yousuke Kinoshita, and Kazuhisa Yanaka(✉)

Kanagawa Institute of Technology, Atsugi-Shi, Kanagawa-Ken 243-0292, Japan
s1923087@cco.kanagawa-it.ac.jp, yanaka@ic.kanagawa-it.ac.jp

Abstract. A new type of augmented reality (AR) using smartphones has been developed that uses a label attached to the center of a real spinning analog record as a marker. The Vuforia Augmented Reality SDK and the Unity game engine are used to develop applications for smartphones. The smartphone screen shows an animation of a 3D character running on a real record, which can be enjoyed visually and aurally. With the use of a Unity script to rotate the 3D character in the opposite direction of the record, the 3D character can be displayed as if it were running on a treadmill and always in the same place on the screen.

Keywords: AR · Vuforia · Record · Rotating marker

1 Introduction

Today, music is commonly enjoyed through compact discs, portable music players, and online distribution. However, before the advent of these devices, people used to enjoy music through analog records. Theoretically, digital media should be superior to analog media in terms of frequency response and signal-to-noise ratio. Nevertheless, even in today's digital age, some people still love analog records. This may be because analog records contain memories of the good old days, which stirs up nostalgia. Merely watching a record spinning leads them into a dream world. In recent years, vinyl records have shown signs of revival in the U.S.

This study aims to introduce augmented reality (AR), with which an animation of a character running on a spinning record is displayed on the screen of a smartphone, thus evoking new sentiments and enhancing the amusement value.

For this purpose, this study uses vision-based AR, a type of AR technology that analyzes AR markers acquired from a camera and displays related digital information.

Generally, a label is attached to the center of an analog record. By using this label as an AR marker as it is, we can save the time and effort to create and attach a new marker. Furthermore, because music titles and other information can be identified by markers, displaying different animations for various discs is possible in principle.

C. Stephanidis et al. (Eds.): HCII 2022, CCIS 1654, pp. 587–591, 2022.
https://doi.org/10.1007/978-3-031-19679-9_74

2 Method

This system is basically a marker-based AR system that uses smartphones. In normal AR, markers are usually considered stationary. However, in our method, the marker rotates at the same speed as an analog record.

Therefore, AR systems, which require high-speed processing, must recognize markers even when they are rotating. Therefore, we verified that AR markers can be tracked regardless of the speed at which they rotate. In the experiment, among three types of standard analog records, the markers were recognized in time for LP (33 1/3 rpm), but sometimes, the markers were not processed in time for EP (45 rpm) and were not recognized at all for SP (78 rpm). Our system was developed using the game engine Unity [1] and the AR development library Vuforia [2]. Unity-chan [3] with animation was used as the 3DCG character. Unity-chan is an original character for developers that is provided by Unity Technologies Japan.

3 Experiment

3.1 Development Environment

We developed an application for Android smartphones by using the Google Pixel 3a smartphone. The application is developed using Unity (2019.4.24f1), a popular game engine that runs on a Windows 10 PC. The PC and smartphone are connected via a USB cable. Our application needs the ability to make any image a marker. Vuforia, an augmented reality software development kit (SDK) for smartphones and other devices, is suitable for creating our AR application. Therefore, we installed Vuforia in Unity.

3.2 Registration of an AR Marker

The label attached to the center of the record is photographed with a digital camera, and the image data, trimmed to a circular shape only at the label part by a PC, are uploaded to a Vuforia server. The uploaded marker image is subjected to feature point analysis on the server and registered as a marker. Next, a Unity package that includes the feature point file created on the server is downloaded (Fig. 1).

Before trimming   After trimming

Fig. 1. Labels for records before and after trimming

3.3 Image Marker and Character Settings in Unity

The Unity engine with Vuforia installed has a game object called an image target. If an image marker is set on the image target, it will look like the setup shown in Fig. 2. When a 3D character is placed on the image target, it will look like the setup shown in Fig. 3.

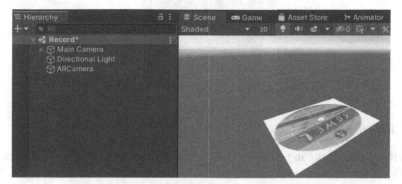

Fig. 2. Image target with a marker set

Fig. 3. Image target on which Unity-chan was placed (© UTJ/UCL).

3.4 Animation of a Character Running

To show a running character, we will use the running motion (Fig. 4) that comes with Unity-chan.

Unity-chan comes with a variety of motions other than running, such as jumping. Therefore, changing this motion allows motions other than running to be used.

Fig. 4. Running motion (© UTJ/UCL)

3.5 Character Position

When the system is run in this state, Unity-chan also rotates as the record rotates.

When a person runs using a treadmill, the person appears to stay in one place. To use a record as a treadmill, Unity-chan must rotate backward at the same speed as the record. To do so, a script similar to that shown in Fig. 5 must be added to the game object. In this figure, the property Time.deltaTime [4] provides the time between the current and previous frame in seconds. The number 203 represents the rotation speed, and the unit is degrees/second. The minus sign means that Unity-chan rotates in the opposite direction of the record disc. Since an LP record rotates 33 1/3 times per minute, one minute is 60 s, and one rotation is 360°, an LP record rotates 200 degrees per second.

We chose 203 instead of 200 because we thought it would look better if Unity-chan moved slowly rather than staying in exactly the same position.

```
1    using System.Collections;
2    using System.Collections.Generic;
3    using UnityEngine;
4
5    public class NewBehaviourScript : MonoBehaviour
6    {
7        // Start is called before the first frame update
8        void Start()
9        {
10
11       }
12
13       // Update is called once per frame
14       void Update()
15       {
16           transform.Rotate(new Vector3(0, -203, 0) * Time.deltaTime);
17       }
18   }
```
Add one line

Fig. 5. Script added to Unity-chan

3.6 Character Position

When the completed system was executed, the animation of Unity-chan running on a real record disc was displayed on the smartphone screen, as shown in Fig. 6.

Fig. 6. Completed system (© UTJ/UCL)

4 Conclusion

We proposed a new AR system that can present a 3DCG character as if it were running on an analog record. With the use of the record's label as a marker, the character can be made to run or stay in one place as if it is running on a treadmill. In most conventional AR, a marker does not move, but in this system, the marker rotates. As long as the rotation speed is 33 1/3 rpm or less, the AR system can track the marker. This system allows us to propose a new way to enjoy analog records not only aurally but also visually.

References

1. Unity. https://unity.com/. Accessed 27 May 2022
2. Vuforia. https://www.ptc.com/en/products/vuforia. Accessed 27 May 2022
3. Unity-chan!. https://assetstore.unity.com/publishers/7659. Accessed 27 May 2022
4. Time-deltaTime.   https://docs.unity3d.com/ja/2019.4/ScriptReference/Time-deltaTime.html. Accessed 27 May 2022

Design Case Studies

ColorTable: Manipulating Tasting Experiences, Impact of Light Color on Food Flavor Perception

Patrick Burkert[1]([✉]), Benjamin Schaufler[1], and Jan-Niklas Voigt-Antons[1,2,3] [iD]

[1] Quality and Usability Lab, Technische Universität Berlin, Berlin, Germany
patrick@weareognc.com
[2] German Research Center for Artificial Intelligence (DFKI), Berlin, Germany
[3] Immersive Reality Lab, Hamm-Lippstadt University of Applied Sciences, Hamm, Germany

Abstract. Multi-sensory perception of taste and flavour is one of the more complex perceptional experiences. The taste itself in food can be perceived differently by its presentation and therefore, flavor perception can be manipulated. ColorTable is a dining table with a lighting system based on Philips Hue Wireless Lighting System. The table can illuminate dishes with thousands of various colors. In this paper, we examine if different light colors of ColorTable influence the perception of taste and the visual appearance of food. We show that food experience and taste perception is changed by different colors emitted by ColorTable. As food items, we choose sweet and salted popcorn and more complex flavored industrial produced Black Forest Cake. Based on a qualitative pretest with participants, we selected the light colors for the food items. Participants selected the best and worse matching light colors for both items to be used. As a result, the cake was illuminated in the experiment with pink and orange light color and sweet and salty popcorn with white and blue light color in a neutral light lab environment. The overall flavor of the cake was significantly higher with pink light color than with orange light color. A similar result was persistent for sweet popcorn, which was rated better when consumed with blue light color than with white light color. We conclude that the perceived taste and visual appeal of food can be altered with ColorTable. Objectively same quality food can be served tastier and improve the food experience, not only through the taste and smell of food itself but also by its presentation and representation. This approach can enhance the tasting experience and on the long run probably also enable a better understanding sense of smell and taste for food experiences.

Keywords: Human computer interaction · Experience design · Taste perception · Visual appearance

1   Introduction

Most meals are served with an objective high food quality. Due to the fact that more and more restaurants offer high food quality, the experience e.g. fun and presentation of a meal is getting an important selling point. Food experience is concerned with hedonic and sensory perception of flavor and visual stimuli of food affected by color, materials and environment (e.g. office or restaurant). Food experience research aims to enhance the overall perceptual flavor experience while drinking and eating, which can be supported by the use of technology. Since 1990 the research field is growing constantly [1]. Especially in the last years food experience became a focused research area in which influences of visual cues like color of plates on taste perception, liking and emotion were examined. Flavor perception involves multiple senses: olfaction (smelling), gustation (taste), tactile sense (touch) and oralsoma sensation (thermic sensation of food on the mouth surface). These senses are all contributing to the stimulation of final flavor experience called for instance strawberry, cherry, rosemary, spice and so on. Before the actual food consumption takes place, these receptors are getting triggered by visual clues like the food color of each food item. Further cross modal effects on flavor and taste identification is related to the attention level, cognitive expectancy and bottom-up multi-sensory integration. Not least, taste is a subjective sensation and e.g. differs between people of different age and culture because of more heightened or different palates experience.

2   Related Work

Recent studies investigated the surroundings in which food is presented and consumed. For example [3–5] measured the influences of different tablecloth colors, ambient light, plate and cup colors on the perception of food. Furthermore [7] found out that the appearance of beverages or the food itself is more important for expectation of flavor than e.g. cutlery and ambient lightning. Spence at al. tested the influence of different colored bowls and plates on desserts like strawberry mousse and popcorn [1]. The results show that sweet popcorn was e.g. saltier when eaten out of blue bowls than out of white bowls. Spence et al. examined strawberry mousse and found the effect that it tasted sweeter, more intense and more liked from a white plate than when it is served on a black plate [6]. Fernandez-Vzquez examined the influence of different colors of orange juice on expected flavor and showed that orange juice with a green dye was perceived significantly more sour [2].

2.1   Color Symbolic

Referring to Wierzbicka, every color has a connotation and triggers a flavor expectation because food coloring plays a natural role in human cognition and therefor as well as in perception of food identity [8,9]. Color is used by our sensory perception for e.g. cognition of healthy food. For example, the specific blue or green color of mold on food is a signage for inedibility food. Furthermore, color triggers emotions and brings humans in specific moods, e.g. blue stands for harmony and relaxing, red symbolizes luck, energy and heat and yellow implicates joy and happiness [9].

2.2 Preview

In this paper we examine the impact of different light color settings on flavor and expectations of taste. In an experiment, cake was illuminated with pink and orange light color as well as sweet and salty popcorn with white and blue light color in a neutral light lab environment. ColorTable can influence the visual appearance and how appetizing food will be perceived without changing any physical items just by using different light colors.

3 Methods

3.1 Prototype

The setting consisted mainly of ColorTable, a dinner table with a milk glass pane for four participants and the Philips Hue Connected Bulb LED-System that includes a router and four WLAN-connected light color bulbs. Each Bulb is mounted under the milk glass pane with a prototypical implemented appliance. Each participant seated at ColorTable has one light color bulb available for the plate (see Fig. 1).

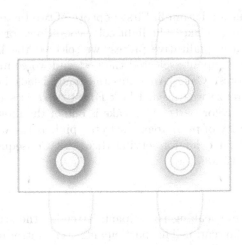

Fig. 1. ColorTable from areal perspective looking on four different colored plates, milk glass pane and four seats.

3.2   Controller

ColorTable bulbs are controlled over a wireless connection by a prototype smart-phone application based on Philips Hue SDK for Android OS. Different visual user interface hot keys can adjust all bulbs separately with a predefined color setting or all bulbs with one color setting at once (see Fig. 2 for exemplary light colors). All dishes in the performed studies were served on similar white dessert plates. The experiments took place in an empty and silent office room. The only natural source for ambient light was given by daylight from a window front. The experiment took place between 1:30 and 6:15 pm with neutral daylight conditions. Fluctuations in the brightness of the daylight were compensated by the fact that a repeated measure analysis was used.

Fig. 2. Food stimuli donuts, pudding and croissant on light color stimuli white, green and yellow. (Color figure online)

3.3   Stimuli

We used two different food stimuli. First popcorn of two tastes (salty and sweet) and second Black Forest Cake. The light color conditions for popcorn were blue and white. Based on a qualitative pretest we selected the light colors for the cake. Twenty-two participants selected the best and worse matching light color for serving Black Forest Cake. An industrial made Black Forest Cake by the brand Confiserie Firenze was used. Black Forest Cake is a complex food with black, red and white color parts. This cake is one of the most popular cakes in Germany. The majority of participants selected pink as the worst and orange as the best matching light color for serving this cake. Consequently we used this light colors as light stimuli.

3.4   Participants

Twenty-eight German-speaking participants attended the study (14 female, 14 male, mean age = 26 years). The participants were introduced with a short-description and had to fill in a socio-demographic questionnaire. The participants were informed about the experiment beforehand, and they agreed to it by signing the informed consent sheet. The study abides by the standards specified in the Declaration of Helsinki, by the ethics committee of the Faculty IV of Technical University Berlin and the Guideline of the German Research Foundation.

3.5   Procedure

The participants had to attend on two different days at the same time of the day to avoid influences due to daylight condition. Every participant rated all possible food/light color combinations: cake served with pink (1) and orange (2) light color, sweet popcorn served with white (3) and blue (4) light color and salty popcorn served with white (5) and blue (6) light color. The order in which the food and light colors were presented was randomized. Between one and up to four persons sat on the table, where they halted not to talk with each other.

3.6   Questionnaire

Questionnaire: The questions asked for each served food/light color condition were based on [1] and were: 1) How appetizing is the dessert?, 2) How much do you like the appearance of the dish overall?, 3) How intense is the color of the dessert?, 4) How intense is the flavor of the food?, 5) How intense is the sweetness of the food?, 6) How intense is the saltiness of the food?, 7) How intense is the bitterness of the food?, 8) How intense is the sourness of the food? and 9)How much did you like the food (gustatory)?. In addition the participants had to rate their general liking of cake. All scales had to be rated on 9-Point-Likert-Scales.

4   Results

The data analysis was done for separately for the three dishes.

4.1   Results Cake

For the cake a repeated-measure analysis of covariance (ANCOVA) with color as independent variable and liking of overall taste, intensity of overall taste, sour intensity, bitter intensity, salty intensity, sweet intensity, intensity appearance, overall appearance as dependent variables were used. Using the co-variate general linking of cake we were able to determine the influence of the light color on the taste and all the sub-scales without keeping individual differences due to the subjective general liking of cake. For the cake we found the following significant results. The color had a significant effect on the overall linking of the cake $(F(1,26) = 7.38, p ¡ .05, 2 = 0.22)$. As can be seen in Fig. 3 the overall taste of the cake is perceived as significant better with pink light (7,3) as with orange light (7,0). In addition we found a significant effect of the color on the perceived bitterness of the cake $(F(1,26) = 5.43, p ¡ .05, 2 = 0.19)$. As can be seen in Fig. 4 the perception of bitterness.

4.2   Results Sweet Popcorn

For the two different sorts of popcorn we calculated a repeated measure analysis of variance (ANOVA) with color as independent variable and liking of overall

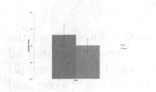

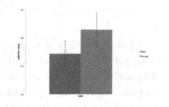

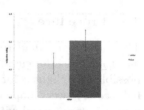

Fig. 3. Mean overall liking of the cake for pink and orange light color. (Color figure online)

Fig. 4. Mean bitterness intensity of the cake for pink and orange light color (Color figure online)

Fig. 5. Mean overall liking of sweet popcorn for white and blue light color. (Color figure online)

taste, intensity of overall taste, sour intensity, bitter intensity, salty intensity, sweet intensity, intensity appearance, overall appearance as dependent variables. As the general liking of popcorn strongly depends on the preference of the salty or sweet variant we have not asked this question. For the sweet popcorn we found the following significant results. The color had a significant effect on the overall linking of sweet popcorn ($F(1,27) = 4.39$, p ¡ .05, 2 = 0.14). As can be seen in Fig. 5 the overall linking of sweet popcorn is much higher with blue light color (5,0) as compared with white light color (4,2). In addition we found a significant effect of the color on the perceived sweetness of the sweet popcorn ($F(1,27) = 9.96$, p ¡ .01, 2 = 0.27) and the perceived intensity of the overall taste ($F(1,27) = 14.14$, p ¡ .01, 2 = 0.34). Sweet popcorn is perceived as sweeter with blue light color (5,6) compared to white light color (4,2). The intensity of sweet popcorns was higher with blue light color (5,4) compared to white light color (4,0). Figures for the latter two effects were omitted for brevity.

5   Discussion and Conclusion

In general the reported results showed that using different light color of ColorTable can influence the perception of liking, tasting and the intensity of food. Therefor we showed that the change of light colored tabletops can be manipulated to improve or lower the overall food experience. For the judgment of the cake we found, that the participants liked it more, when the plate was illuminated in the light color pink. This was surprising as the average selection of the qualitative pretest suggested that the orange would be the best matching light color for this food item. We conclude that after the multi-sensory integration, the first selection of the purely visual appealing light color was overruled. This result is in-line with the fact that the bitterness intensity was rated higher for the orange light color condition, as bitterness is in many cases not positively associated with sweet desserts. For the sweet popcorn it was evident that the blue light had a positive effect on the food experience. The overall liking, the intensity of sweetness and the intensity of the overall taste was higher for the blue light condition. The non-existent effect of the light color conditions on the salty popcorn was maybe caused by the fact that in each session sweet and salty stimuli were consumed. Salty taste had an outstanding position that probably had a stronger impact on the ratings than the light color conditions. ColorTable allows to manipulate food experiences through the use of technology and opens up the potential of creating complete new food experiences, through technology-driven and holistic experience design in first place for instance. Imagining, that ColorTable could transform its visualization from one second to the other, regarding to the course and food on the table served or even through tracked behaviour of participants in real-time. It will be interesting to investigate the influence of adaptive and interactive responses of ColorTable for automation in switching light colors based on eating behavior of a participant, such as type of food item, mood or even physical conditions.

References

1. Spence, C., Harrar, V., Piqueras-Fiszman, B.: Assessing the impact of the tableware and other contextual variables on multisensory flavour perception. Int. J. Hum. Comput. Interact. **26**(8), 741–785 (2010). https://doi.org/10.1080/10447311003781409
2. Fernández-Vázquez, R., et al.: Colour influences sensory perception and liking of orange juice. Flavour **3**(1), 1–8 (2014)
3. Guéguen, N.: The effect of glass colour on the evaluation of a beverage's thirst-quenching quality. Curr. Psychol. Lett. Behav. Brain Cogn. **2**(11) (2003)
4. Harrar, V., Piqueras-Fiszman, B., Spence, C.: There's more to taste in a coloured bowl. Perception **40**(7), 880–882 (2011)
5. Oberfeld, D., Hecht, H., Allendorf, U., Wickelmaier, F.: Ambient lighting modifies the flavor of wine. J. Sens. Stud. **24**(6), 797–832 (2009)
6. Piqueras-Fiszman, B., Giboreau, A., Spence, C.: Assessing the influence of the color of the plate on the perception of a complex food in a restaurant setting. Flavour **2**(1), 1–11 (2013)
7. Shankar, M.U., Levitan, C.A., Spence, C.: Grape expectations: the role of cognitive influences in color-flavor interactions. Conscious. Cogn. **19**(1), 380–390 (2010)
8. Spence, C., Levitan, C.A., Shankar, M.U., Zampini, M.: Does food color influence taste and flavor perception in humans? Chemosens. Percept. **3**(1), 68–84 (2010)
9. Wierzbicka, A.: The meaning of color terms: semantics, culture, and cognition (1990)

Desktop Calculator for Multiple Analysis of Environmental Risk

Lorena Cáceres[1]([⊠]) [iD], Eduardo Teneda[1] [iD], and Guillermo Palacios-Navarro[2] [iD]

[1] SISAu Research Group, Facultad de Ingeniería y Tecnologías de la Información y la Comunicación, Universidad Tecnológica Indoamérica, Ambato 180103, Ecuador
lorenacaceres@uti.edu.ec

[2] Department of Electronic Engineering and Communications, University of Zaragoza, 44003 Zaragoza, Spain
guillermo.palacios@unizar.es

Abstract. Anthropic activities have a significant influence on the environment, from the extraction of raw materials to the environmental impact generated by the processes developed and products manufactured. For this reason, rigorous control of the exploitation of resources must be introduced and industrial processes optimized to achieve efficiency in using raw materials and energy consumption through evaluating environmental risks with a life cycle approach. This work aims to design an application that allows assessing the environmental risks generated by a productive activity. The advantages of this proposal are the reduction of costs based on the quantification of resources used and the comparative analysis of the results with reference limits cited in national and international regulations, which allow decision-making to minimize environmental impact. As a result of this research, a calculator was obtained, which is executed from a user interface allowing the calculation of the most significant environmental risks in terms of CO_2 emissions, wastewater, and waste generation associated with production processes under regular conditions, warning conditions, and in emergency situations. Finally, to validate its operation, real data from an industry dedicated to the production of dairy products were applied, obtaining a risk analysis in terms of CO_2 emissions and wastewater generation.

Keywords: Calculator applications · CO_2 emissions · Environmental risk · Production process · Environmental impact

1 Introduction

In the last 50 years, the ecological footprint generated by human activities has increased by 190%, which shows the imbalance in the man-environment relationship [1], as well as the ability of human beings to live within the biological limits of the planet [2]. These data require a significant rethinking of how resources are produced and distributed for a change in consumption habits, which implies responsibility and awareness that are prerequisites for sustainable behavior [3].

C. Stephanidis et al. (Eds.): HCII 2022, CCIS 1654, pp. 602–611, 2022.
https://doi.org/10.1007/978-3-031-19679-9_76

Humans can be aware of the pollution generated from the consumption of resources [4]. Various types of calculators allow for determining the environmental impact produced by anthropic activities [5]. According to [6], many organizations have created online carbon footprint calculators with a large number of input categories and user customization to communicate both the causes of climate change and the opportunities to reduce the emission of greenhouse gases. In his work, the nitrogen footprint (NF), which quantifies the use of nitrogen in the environment, he has used the N calculator tool to determine the food nitrogen footprint, which is the most representative in the provinces of China from 2000 to 2018 using exploratory data to analyze spatial correlation and changes in it [7].

According to [8] the demand of tools for quickly assessing the environmental impacts produced by the emission of greenhouse gases in the agricultural sector has prompted the development of "GHG (Greenhouse Gases) calculators", which use a combination of emission factors and empirical models to calculate Greenhouse Gases emissions with minimal data entry.

As it is well known that greenhouse gas emissions, wastewater discharge, and noise generation pose a high environmental risk, which is determined based on different methodologies proposed the Interpretive Structural Modeling (ISM) methodology [9], which uses the priority number and risk mitigation number to prioritize risk mitigation strategy decisions for the industry. Another way of determining environmental risks and the most common is based on the probability of occurrence and the severity of the consequences valued in the natural, human and socioeconomic environments [10].

Due to the above and considering that computer applications are a key element in assessing environmental risks. This work aims to design an application that assesses the environmental risks that productive activity generates with a life cycle approach. The advantages of this proposal are cost reduction based on the quantification of resources used, comparative analysis with reference limits cited in national and international regulations, reliability of the information, and generation of reports in a simple way. The document has been distributed as follows: 1.- Introduction, where the use of calculator-type tools for the analysis of pollution sources is analyzed; 2.- Methodology, where the method used for the design of the application and the assessment of environmental risks is shown; 3.- Results where the operation of the application is disclosed through the spreadsheet and the results of the environmental risks obtained from the case study company; 4.- Conclusions, where the conclusions obtained regarding the use of the application and the assessment made of the risks of a company dedicated to the production of dairy products are established.

2   Methodology

2.1   Design of the Application for Environmental Risk Assessment

To design the application was used the MS-Excel application, in which the spreadsheets were generated with the basic information divided in hyperlinks to facilitate de information management. The options are detailed below:

• *Home*: An interface is presented where options are given to enter the different segments of the application.

• *Diagram of Inputs and Outputs.* This section presents the scheme for entering the processes stages to be evaluated with the outputs generated from the environmental perspective.

• *Data entry normal/abnormal conditions.* The determined outputs are entered based on the process stages indicated in the diagram (Fig. 3), and the corresponding assessment scales.

• *Environmental Risk Assessment under regular/warning conditions.* The application calculates the risk levels depending on the scales used.

• *Data entry Emergency Situations.* The data corresponding to scenarios is entered for evaluation based on the productive activity.

• *Environmental Risk Assessment in emergency situations.* The risk values are obtained automatically in the three environments evaluated, which allows the generation of a report; tools to help the decision-making.

2.2   Components of Environmental Risk Assessment

For the evaluation of environmental risks was necessary to define the environmental aspects of a production process. For this propose we used the methodology presented by [11], which refers to the steps indicated in Fig. 1.

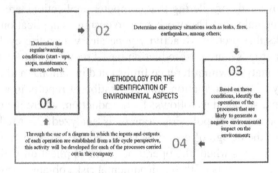

Fig. 1. Methodology for the identification of environmental aspects.

The environmental aspects are determined based on the production process and the scenarios established in the company. It is evaluated according to the methodology proposed by [12] where we considered two conditions: regular/warning conditions and emergency situations. To assess the risk based on these conditions was used the Eq. 1 [13].

$$Rcn/a = M + 2(AL) \tag{1}$$

where: Rcn/a is the environmental risk under regular/warning conditions of the process; M is the magnitude that determines whether the value of the environmental aspect increases or decreases concerning an initial or reference value; AL is the approach to the limit indicates how close the value of the environmental aspect measured is concerning the permissible reference limits in the current legal regulations. The environmental risk assessment scale under regular/warning conditions is given by the elements shown in Table 1.

Table 1. Environmental risk assessment scale under regular/warning conditions.

Magnitude (M)		
Qualitative scale	Quantitative scale	Description
High	50	More than 15% compared to the previous year
Half	25	15 to 10% higher or lower than the previous year
Low	1	Less than 9% compared to the previous year
Approach to Limit (AL)		
Qualitative scale	Quantitative scale	Description
High	50	Between 90%-100% of the reference limit
Half	25	Between 50%-89% of the reference limit
Low	1	Less than 49% of the reference limit

The results obtained based on the application of the scales in Table 1, a colorimetric scale was used, as shown in Table 2.

Table 2. Colorimetric scale for environmental hazards under regular/warning conditions

Qualitative Scale	Quantitative Scale	Colorimetry
Significant	150 - 125	
Moderate	124 - 75	
Tolerable	74 - 3	

To assess environmental risks in emergency situations was used the Eq. (2)

$$Rse = P * GC \tag{2}$$

where: Rse is the environmental risk in emergency situations; GC is the Severity of the consequences evaluated in three environments (Natural, Human, and Socioeconomic). To determine the probability value, the scale shown in Table 3 was used.

Table 3. Probability assessment scale in emergency situations

Probability of occurrence	Assigned value
Highly probable	5
Quite likely	4
Likely	3
Unlikely	2
Very improbable	1

To determine the GC, the parameters observed in Table 4 were used, and with these elements, the variables in Eqs. (3), (4), and (5) are replaced with the values from the quantitative scale.

Table 4. Consequence severity assessment scale

Quantity (C)			Hazard (P)		
Qualitative scale	Quantitative scale	Description	Qualitative scale	Quantitative scale	Description
Very high	4	> 100	Very dangerous	4	Toxic, Causes short-term irreversible effects
High	3	50–99	Dangerous	3	Explosive, corrosive, flammable
Low	2	5–49	little dangerous	2	fuels
Very low	1	< 5	nothing dangerous	1	Causes mild and reversible damage
Extension (E)			Receivers (R)		
Qualitative scale	Quantitative scale	Description	Qualitative scale	Quantitative scale	Description
Very extensive	4	> 1 km	Very high	4	More than 50 people
extensive	3	< 1 km	high	3	Between 30 and 49 people
little extensive	2	company surroundings	Low	2	Between 15 and 29 people

(*continued*)

Table 4. (*continued*)

Quantity (C)			Hazard (P)		
Qualitative scale	Quantitative scale	Description	Qualitative scale	Quantitative scale	Description
Punctual	1	place where it happens	Very low	1	Less than 14 people
Affected natural environment (MNA)			Socioeconomic impact of the damage (ISD)		
Qualitative scale	Quantitative scale	Description	Qualitative scale	Quantitative scale	Description
Very extensive	4	> 1 km	Very high	4	> 200000 $
extensive	3	< 1 km	high	3	Between 200000 and 100000 $
little extensive	2	company surroundings	Low	2	Between 99000 and 20000 $
Punctual	1	place where it happens	Very low	1	< 20000 $

$$Gravity\ on\ the\ natural\ environment = C + 2P + E + MNA \qquad (3)$$

$$Gravity\ on\ the\ human\ environment = C + 2P + E + R \qquad (4)$$

$$Gravity\ on\ the\ socioeconomic\ environment = C + 2P + E + ISD \qquad (5)$$

where: C: Quantity; P: Hazard; E: Extension; MNA: Affected Natural Environment; A: Receivers; ISD: Socioeconomic Impact of Damage. To evaluate the results were applied the Eqs. (3), (4), and (5), the criteria established in Table 5.

Table 5. Scale for assigning values to the severity of the consequences

Qualitative scale	Quantitative scale	Colorimetry	Value assigned to gravity
Very serious	20 - 16		5
Serious	15 - 12		4
Moderate	11 - 9		3
Slight	8 - 6		2
Not relevant	5 - 1		1

To estimate the environmental risk associated with the different scenarios, the scale shown in Table 6 was used.

Table 6. Scale for risk assessment in emergency situations

Qualitative scale	Quantitative scale	Colorimetry
Very high risk	25 - 21	
High risk	20 - 15	
Moderate risk	14 - 10	
Low risk	09 -05	
Very low risk	04 - 01	

3 Results

3.1 Application for Environmental Risk Assessment

Figure 2 shows the application's main interface developed using the spreadsheet where five options were added, where is enter the information corresponding Companys' name, Name of the Evaluator. The input and output data has to be entered in the diagram, the scales for risk assessment in normal conditions, and the scales for scenarios in emergency situations.

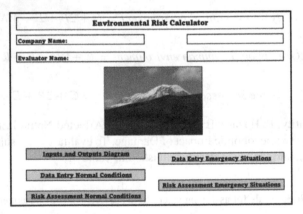

Fig. 2. Application main interface for environmental risk assessment with the principal options

3.2 Assessment of Environmental Risks

In Fig. 3 the production stages were established with their respective inputs and outputs diagram. For emergency situations in the data entry section, five scenarios were determined for risk assessment, which can be seen in Fig. 4.

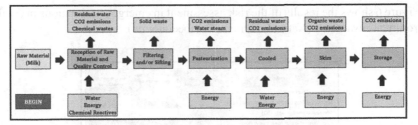

Fig. 3. Inputs and outputs diagram for data input.

Scenarios Emergency Situations	
Incident Area	**Scenarios (Environmental Aspects)**
Accidents	Accidental fuel spill (E1)
	Accidental spill of chemical reagents (E2)
	Accidental sewage spill (E3)
Fires	Fires Generation of toxic gases (E4)
	Generation of particulate matter (E5)
BEGIN	

Fig. 4. Entry of scenarios for emergency situations

In Fig. 5 are show the results generated by the application for regular/warning conditions, where it is evident that in the process of receiving raw material and quality control. The generation of wastewater presents a significant risk, as in the pasteurization process, CO_2 emissions. In reference to skimming, the generation of organic waste and CO_2 emissions present a Moderate level of risk; In the cooling process, CO_2 emissions and wastewater generation present a tolerable risk.

Process	Environmental Aspect	Environmental Risk	Description
Reception of Raw Material and Quality Control	Residual water	150	Significant
	CO2 emissions	75	Moderate
	Chemical wastes	100	Moderate
Filtering and/or Sifting	Solid waste	51	Tolerable
Pasteurization	CO2 emissions	150	Significant
	Water steam	52	Tolerable
Cooled	Residual water	52	Tolerable
	CO2 emissions	27	Tolerable
Skim	Organic waste	100	Moderate
	CO2 emissions	100	Moderate
Storage	CO2 emissions	27	Tolerable
BEGIN			

Fig. 5. Results of the environmental risk assessment under regular/warning conditions

Figure 6 shows the results of the risk assessment in emergency situations in the three environments evaluated (Natural, Human, Socioeconomic).

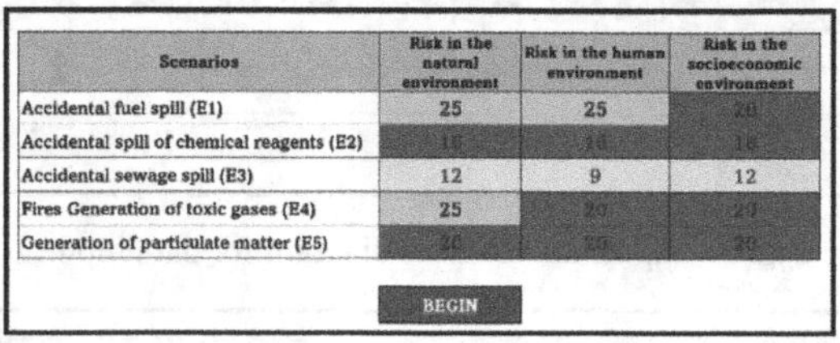

Scenarios	Risk in the natural environment	Risk in the human environment	Risk in the socioeconomic environment
Accidental fuel spill (E1)	25	25	20
Accidental spill of chemical reagents (E2)	16	16	16
Accidental sewage spill (E3)	12	9	12
Fires Generation of toxic gases (E4)	25	20	20
Generation of particulate matter (E5)	20	20	20

BEGIN

Fig. 6. Results evaluation of environmental risks in emergency situations

3.3 Discussion

According to the results obtained for the risk level based on the data entered from the case study, it is verified that the application is useful for obtaining results that lead the fast decision-making. It is important that before entering the information on the application, the user fully knows the process to be evaluated and give accurate information. Mulrow concludes that the use of calculators allows the user to understand the impact that their activity generates on the environment [6]. For data entry, the user must know the data that must be entered to obtain reliable results and that they allow them to educate themselves about their consumption habits so that they can improve them [3].

4   Conclusions

The use of this calculator applications is considered a good option to assess environmental risks and improve the organization's environmental performance. In addition, knowing the environmental behavior leads to reducing costs, improving the corporate image, optimizing the use of resources such as water, energy, and therefore the reduction of the environmental impact.

The developed application allows to determine the corresponding stages of a production process or service giving numerical scales to evaluate the environmental risk, considering the regular/warning conditions operating conditions and the emergency situations that arise in the activity of a company.

References

1. Collins, A., Galli, A., Hipwood, T., Murthy, A.: Living within a one planet reality: the contribution of personal footprint calculators. Environ. Res. Lett. **15**, 025008 (2020). https://doi.org/10.1088/1748-9326/ab5f96
2. Zald, H.S.J., Spies, T.A., Harmon, M.E., Twery, M.J.: Forest carbon calculators: a review for managers, policymakers, and educators. J. For. **114**, 134–143 (2016). https://doi.org/10.5849/jof.15-019

3. Collins, A., Galli, A., Patrizi, N., Pulselli, F.M.: Learning and teaching sustainability: the contribution of ecological footprint calculators. J. Clean. Prod. **174**, 1000–1010 (2018). https://doi.org/10.1016/j.jclepro.2017.11.024
4. Salo, M., Mattinen-Yuryev, M.K., Nissinen, A.: Opportunities and limitations of carbon footprint calculators to steer sustainable household consumption – analysis of Nordic calculator features. J. Clean. Prod. **207**, 658–666 (2019). https://doi.org/10.1016/j.jclepro.2018.10.035
5. Kok, A.L., Barendregt, W.: Understanding the adoption, use, and effects of ecological footprint calculators among Dutch citizens. J. Clean. Prod. **326**, 129341 (2021). https://doi.org/10.1016/j.jclepro.2021.129341
6. Mulrow, J., Machaj, K., Deanes, J., Derrible, S.: The state of carbon footprint calculators: an evaluation of calculator design and user interaction features. Sustain. Prod. Consum. **18**, 33–40 (2019). https://doi.org/10.1016/j.spc.2018.12.001
7. Liu, C., Nie, G.: Spatial effects and impact factors of food nitrogen footprint in China based on spatial durbin panel model. Environ. Res. **204**, 112046 (2022). https://doi.org/10.1016/j.envres.2021.112046
8. Richards, M., et al.: Limits of agricultural greenhouse gas calculators to predict soil N2O and CH4 fluxes in tropical agriculture. Sci. Rep. **6**, 1–8 (2016). https://doi.org/10.1038/srep26279
9. Prakash, S., Soni, G., Rathore, A.P.S., Singh, S.: Risk analysis and mitigation for perishable food supply chain: a case of dairy industry. Benchmarking An Int. J. **24**, 2–23 (2017). https://doi.org/10.1108/BIJ-07-2015-0070
10. Durango-Cordero, J., et al.: Risk assessment of unlined oil pits leaking into groundwater in the Ecuadorian Amazon: a modified GIS-DRASTIC approach. Appl. Geogr. **139**, 102628 (2022). https://doi.org/10.1016/j.apgeog.2021.102628
11. Carretero-Peña, A.: Aspectos ambientales: Identificación y Evaluación, Génova (2018)
12. Carretero, A.: Norma UNE 150008:2008 Análisis y evaluación del riesgo ambiental. Aenor, 1–46 (2008)
13. Caja-Molina, A.V., Iannacone, J.: Evaluación del riesgo ambiental por petróleo crudo en las especies acuáticas Lemna minor, Daphnia magna y Danio rerio. Rev. la Acad. Colomb. Ciencias Exactas, Físicas y Nat. **45**, 777–794 (2021). https://doi.org/10.18257/raccefyn.1398

A Study of Moba Game APP Design Methods Based on Design Psychology

Xilin Chen[1] and Tao Xi[2(✉)]

[1] School of Design, Shanghai Jiao Tong University, Shanghai 201100, China
[2] School of Media and Communication, Shanghai Jiao Tong University,
Shanghai 201100, China
torchx@sjtu.edu.cn

Abstract. With the progress of society and the popularity of smartphones, more and more people are becoming mobile game players. Most of them are willing to invest time and money in mobile games. Game design as an emerging discipline is gradually emerging. It is more cross-cutting than other traditional design disciplines, with psychology being an important part of it. The goal of designing a game product is to create a better gaming experience that people can have fun with. Therefore, studying the psychology of the player is central to our mastery of the gaming experience. This paper will use design psychology as a basis to explore how game apps can meet the psychological needs of players. Take the current popular MOBA mobile game product "Honor of Kings" as an example. The impact of its excellent game product design elements on players' psychology is studied. The paper not only examines and summarizes the principles and methods of game product design from a theoretical level but also focuses on the exploration of the technical aspects of the game. The conclusions help to understand the behavior of game users and their patterns, and provide some reference value for the development of future game products.

Keywords: Design psychology · Game design · Product design · Mobile games · Moba games · Honor of Kings

1 Introduction

The core of games is to create a human-computer interaction between the player and the game. A great game product must be emotionally engaging and memorable. The most important part of the gaming experience is play and challenge. A successful game needs to stimulate curiosity, surprise, and delight the player in the process. Artificial constraints and choices such as time limits, scarce resources, and competition between players make it more difficult to complete tasks which adds to the excitement of the game and enhances the experience. Therefore, there is a demand for content that is intense and rich enough to stimulate the player and create an emotional impact. Research shows that rewarding players for completing a task are more engaging than punishing them for failure. The internal logic of games is that players overcome challenges, achieve

© The Author(s), under exclusive license to Springer Nature Switzerland AG 2022
C. Stephanidis et al. (Eds.): HCII 2022, CCIS 1654, pp. 612–619, 2022.
https://doi.org/10.1007/978-3-031-19679-9_77

goals and receive rewards and rewards [1]. A game that is all tension and excitement and no relaxation will quickly become mentally fatiguing. In this respect, designers must anticipate players' psychology from multiple perspectives. The paper focuses on individual and group psychology to analyze the function systems of "Honor of Kings", listing their main functions and corresponding user behavior. In addition, the reasons behind the user behavior are analyzed using the KANO model, the Censydiam model, and the hook model of fairness and norms. It also draws insights into the use of psychological principles of the "Honor of Kings" App.

2 Psychological Motivations for the Functional Design of Game Products

Design psychology differs from traditional design and psychology in that designers need to be able to study and understand human psychology and behaviour in a way that is oriented towards human demands. The psychological responses generated by people are reflected in the design. This chapter analyses the main functions and corresponding user behaviours based on the functional systems design of the "Honor of Kings" App. The principles of individual psychology and group psychology behind the behaviours are explored.

2.1 Individual Sychology

Adler was the founder of individual psychology. The basic theoretical perspective of individual psychology emphasizes the cognitive factor of the subject and the subjective initiative of the person. It is not innate factors but acquired efforts that determine one's destiny [2]. The cognitive factor is a factor that is not inherent in a person's destiny, but rather in his or her efforts. The key psychological principles are applied as below:

The refusal to surrender function - Exchange Theory. Exchange theory means that people always believe that a certain amount of effort needs to be rewarded in return. In the design of "Honor of Kings", one person in a match initiates a surrender, and four people in a team of five have to agree to complete the surrender. Teammates can simply choose to refuse to surrender. This satisfies some players who do not want to give up the time and effort they have invested. They feel that they should achieve victory in return and are reluctant to surrender. Also in the system settings, it can be set to always refuse to surrender, directly clarifying the psychology of some groups who are convinced of the exchange theory and are unwilling to surrender.

First charge - the Threshold Effect. The game "Honor of Kings" features the first charge. First-time spenders can get access to beautiful hero skins for only 6 RMB. This feature is an accurate use of the threshold effect in individual psychology, starting with lower demands and gradually making higher demands, which are often also more acceptable. A lower consumption requirement can increase the user's acceptance of game consumption while promoting more consumption in the future.

Character experience card - Birdcage Effect. Some of the characters for sale in "Honor of Kings" can be obtained by using a character experience card for 3 days in addition to buying them. This reflects the birdcage effect, which means after owning the birdcage, one is more likely to buy the bird. This is reflected in the character experience card, which means that after experiencing the use of a character, one is more likely to buy the character, prompting the user's desire to buy it.

Recovering the rank - Sunk Cost. The "Honor of Kings" consumption module has a noble rank to measure the user's consumption and grant the corresponding privileges. The noble rank will increase as consumption accumulates. However, no consumption in a month will result in a drop in the noble rank. This will satisfy some users who are reluctant to give up their previously held noble rank. In this case, the game has a prompt to restore your rank, so that you can regain your rank by spending any $1. This reflects the principle of individual psychology: the sunk cost, which means that people tend to place too much value on things they own and feel bad about throwing them away.

2.2 Group Psychology

Group psychology is an important part of social psychology, which studies the social psychology and behavior of people living in group settings and the impact of this psychology and behavior on the group [3]. The key psychological principles are applied as below:

(1) The 5v5 match mode - Rule of 150. According to the principles of Dunbar's number, high trust and intimacy in group size will only occur in social networks of around 5 people. The most core matchmaking mode in the "Honor of Kings" matchmaking system is 5v5 matchmaking, forming a 5-player team matchmaking mode. Users can gain high trust and intimacy with their teammates within a 5-player group game, enhancing the teamwork nature of the game.

(2) The in-game-like function - the Aronson Effect. In the game "Honor of Kings", users want to receive praise from others for their game performance. This reflects the Aronson effect in group psychology, whereby people prefer people or things that reward and praise them more and more; and dislike people or things that diminish and punish them more and more. In games that motivate groups to keep moving forward and gain a stronger sense of achievement in the game, the Aronson effect, the need for praise, is something that must be met. In addition to the function of in-between game likes, the in-between game broadcast, the match display page likes, and the personal homepage like all highlight "Honor of Kings" consideration of the need for appreciation. It also highlights the incentives in the hook model as well as the focus effect. This satisfies the user's need to receive praise and attention, which in turn drives their continued hook to the game.

(3) Incentives - the Free-rider Effect. The hitchhiking effect refers to the efforts made by a member within a group with the same interests for the benefit of the group, a practice that potentially benefits everyone in the group but at no cost to the other members. To reduce the possibility of hitchhiking by team members and to improve the overall fairness of the game. "Honor of Kings" rewards different team members with different levels of game effort during and after the match. Individual contributions are highlighted, enhancing the player's sense of access to the game.

(4) Leaderboards - catfish effect. The game leaderboard, a major component of the game "Honor of Kings", is set in an important position on the left side of the game

lobby. It contains 21 forms of leaderboards, such as peak, ladder, glory, and heroes, as well as information on the ranking of friends and the whole region. The use of rankings is a function that is set up in most APPs and its importance is reflected in the group psychological principle: the reaction of the catfish effect.

3 Methods of Using Design Psychology to Increase User Viscosity in Game Products

Psychological mechanisms are often used in games to increase the attractiveness of the game to the player. Based on the analysis of the various psychological principles above, this chapter summarises and draws out three psychological models. Psychological models are often constructed from fragmented facts, with only a superficial understanding of the context, and are based on psychology to form a perspective on the causes, mechanisms, and interrelationships of things [4]. These three psychological models encompass the design priorities of "Honor of Kings" in terms of user motivation, user purpose needs, and increasing user stickiness, respectively. The KANO model is used to identify the attributes of user needs. The hook model is designed to address the core mechanics of the overall game process.

3.1 The Censydiam Model

The Censydiam model is a model of user motivation developed from the personality theories of Freud, Jung, and Adler. It was first developed by Synovate in the field of market research [5]. It has since been widely used in the field of consumer research.

It has been widely used to analyze user motivation. In the coordinate system of the Censydiam model, the horizontal axis describes people's strategies for addressing needs on a social level, assessing the balance between belonging to a group or being an independent self. The left-hand side of the axis represents the need for self-expression and identity, while the right-hand side represents the need for group affiliation and security. The vertical axis describes the user's strategy for addressing needs on an individual level, assessing whether people tend to suppress or release their desires. The upper part of the vertical axis represents the tendency toward release, towards sensuality. The lower side represents the tendency towards repression, the rational direction [6]. The Censydiam model is used to analyze user information, uncover new emotional needs, construct user needs content, achieve precise positioning, and guide product design practice. The Censydiam model is a prerequisite for the smooth implementation of design practice, in which the user needs are precisely positioned according to the user needs and the target audience and scope of the design.

Through the user psychological model and related behaviors of King's Glory, we have analyzed, filtered, generalized, and summarised a series of user behaviors with clear purpose and psychological factors (see Fig. 1). From the model, it can be seen that achievement-oriented players are more inclined toward power, vitality, and enjoyment. The social player prefers security, belonging, and sharing. Casual players are more oriented towards enjoyment.

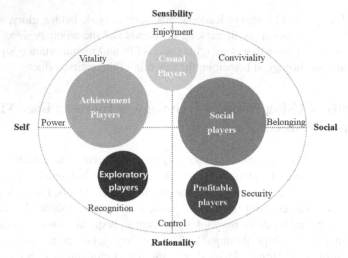

Fig. 1. The purposeful behaviors were positioned on the coordinates of the Censydiam model through post-it notes.

3.2   The KANO Model

The KANO model was developed by Noriaki Kano, a professor at the Tokyo Institute of Technology, for classifying and ranking requirements. The KANO model is based on an analysis of the impact of user requirements on user satisfaction and represents the non-linear relationship between product performance and user satisfaction. The KANO model is used to qualitatively and quantitatively analyze the product quality requirements collected, derive the quality attributes of the requirements, obtain the user's demand tendencies, and increase the economic value and sales of the product while improving user satisfaction [7]. The KANO model divides requirements into five categories: essential requirements, desired requirements, attractive requirements, undifferentiated requirements, and reverse requirements.

A must-have attribute is a feature that the product must have, without which the user's satisfaction will decrease; while adding this feature will not increase the user's satisfaction. Desired attributes are features that the user would like to have, adding the feature will increase user satisfaction, and not adding the feature will decrease user satisfaction. The Attraction attribute is a feature that does not decrease user satisfaction without the feature but increases user satisfaction significantly with the feature. The no-difference attribute is that user satisfaction does not increase or decrease with or without the feature; this attribute is not felt by the user. The reversed attribute is that with the feature, user satisfaction will be greatly reduced; without the feature, user satisfaction remains unchanged.

The design of the assessment of the purpose requirements. The questionnaire divides the dimensions into two: satisfaction when provided, and satisfaction when not provided. And the level of satisfaction is divided into 5 levels (very satisfied, satisfied, average, dissatisfied, and very dissatisfied) [8]. This is because human satisfaction tends to change gradually rather than abruptly. This study modifies the text of satisfaction levels flexibly to suit the actual problem. A more visual description of (very much like, deserved, indifferent, barely accept, very much dislike) was used (see Fig. 2). The product functional orientation was mapped out according to the above questionnaire design, internally assessed by the group members, and recorded and collated (see Fig. 2).

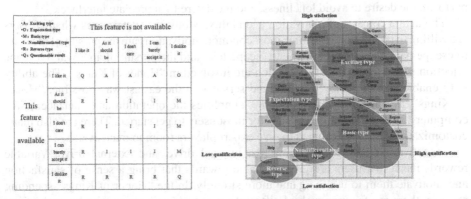

Fig. 2. A summary of the requirements was made and the five categories of requirements were derived as contained in the KANO model.

3.3 The Hook Model

The hook model (see Fig. 1) consists of four components and forms a virtuous cycle: triggers, actions, incentives, and inputs [9] (Fig. 3).

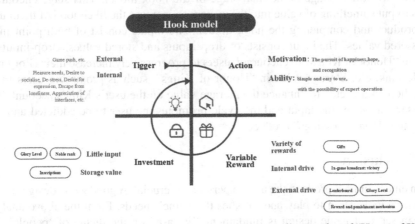

Fig. 3. The hook model is an important mechanism for the overall gameplay of "Honor of Kings"

Triggers consist of external and internal triggers. External triggers, where the user is cued by a call to action, are the first step in creating a habit-forming technique. At the same time, external triggers communicate the next action step to the user. Mobile push notifications are the most important external trigger in the app. The game push involves activities, tasks, station orders, etc., which entice users to open the software by rewarding them for completing it. The internal trigger is mainly the internal emotional trigger. In the King's Quest game, users are often driven by emotional needs such as the need for pleasure, the desire to socialize, the desire to dispatch pressure, the desire to perform, the desire to avoid loneliness, and the desire to appreciate interface.

The action consists of motivation and ability. Motivation determines whether users are willing to take action. The three most common motivations are the pursuit of pleasure to escape pain, the pursuit of hope to escape fear, and the pursuit of approval to escape rejection. All three forms of motivation are involved in "Honor of Kings". The ability is to enable users to enjoy products and services in the easiest way possible. "Honor of Kings", as a MOBA handheld game, simplifies the operation and interface of the computer-based game, making it easy for most users to get started. There are also many customization features designed to give expert players room to maneuver.

Incentives include variable rewards, internal drive, and external drive. Variable rewards mean that users are given variable rewards that bring a sense of satisfaction and motivate them to use the game more strongly. In the "Honor of Kings" spending module, there are features such as gift packs and treasure hunting, similar to the form of a lottery. Uncertainty gives users a variable chip reward type of incentive, prompting constant anticipation and purchase. The internal drive is the inner factor that drives a person to inner satisfaction and pleasure. In "Honor of Kings", winning the game is the core internal drive. To highlight the effect of internal drive, "Honor of Kings" sets off the joy of winning through exaggerated interface design and in-game broadcast of wins. External drives are external factors that drive behavioral change, such as receiving rewards like bonuses and fame. Many forms of rewards exist in "Honor of Kings" such as leaderboards, glory levels, mission rewards, game badges, etc.

The investment stage is the final stage of the hook model. This stage encourages users to put something of value into the system to increase the likelihood of them using the product and completing the hook model. The inputs consist of both point inputs and stored values. The input consists of drop-inputs and stored values. Drop-inputs are used in "Honor of Kings" to encourage users to progressively increase their Glory rank, Noble rank, etc. Storage value in "Honor of Kings", such as prompting users to buy some hero skins, etc., to enhance the storage value on the user's King's account. Thus the user completes the input and the cycle promotes the user to be addicted and keep using the "Honor of Kings" product.

4   Conclusion

As an entertainment product, the user experience is crucial. A good game design triggers the user's motivation to play and satisfies the game's needs. From the above analysis, we can see that game design is fundamentally based on the theme of 'people'. It is necessary to consider the emotional and psychological aspects of the human being and to analyze these factors to put them into the design of the game. This paper focuses on the psychological needs of people and how to meet them in game design from the perspective of design psychology. The conclusions are obtained as below:

(1) From a psychological perspective, it is analyzed that excellent game products meet the psychological and emotional needs of individual players and groups.
(2) It summarizes the psychological models that enhance the player experience and increase the stickiness of the game.
(3) Game products should make use of the Censydiam model, the KANO model, and the hook model to explore innovative points in game design. We should design products that are more interesting and experience-friendly.

References

1. Anderson, S.P.: Throbbing - A Guide to Emotional Interaction Design. People's Post and Telecommunications Publishing House, Beijing (2012)
2. Liu, G., Ge, L.: The historical influence and contemporary response of individual psychological thought. J. Yinshan Stud. (3), 85–912+2 (2018)
3. Zhixia, C.: Social Psychology. People's Post and Telecommunications Publishing House, Beijing (2016)
4. Dai, L.: Design Psychology. China Forestry Press, Beijing (2014)
5. Adler, A.: Beyond Inferiority Complex, pp. 88–96. Economic Daily Press, Beijing (1997)
6. Yilei, Z.: The application of Censydiam model theory in character construction. Design **11**, 133–134 (2013)
7. Meng, W., Han, Y.Q., He, L.: A fuzzy kano model-based approach to customer service demand classification. Technol. Econ. **33**(06), 54–58 (2014)
8. Yu, F., Xu, L., Ye, Z., et al.: Research on personalized demand based on fuzzy Kano model. Sci. Ind. **22**(2), 185–190 (2022). https://doi.org/10.3969/j.issn.1671-1807.2022.02.029
9. Schell, J.: The Art of Game Design, 2nd edn. Electronic Industry Press, Beijing (2016)

Computational Simulation of Stress - Deformation Analysis in Machinery Related to the Food Industry

Juan Cruz[1]([✉]), Andrés Lara-Calle[1] [ID], Leonardo Cuenca[1] [ID], and Aida Viera[2] [ID]

[1] SISAu Research Group, Facultad de Ingeniería y Tecnologías de la Información y la Comunicación, Universidad Tecnológica Indoamérica, Ambato 180103, Ecuador
{juancruz,andreslara,leonardocuenca}@uti.edu.ec
[2] Facultad de Seguridad y Defensa, Unidad Académica Especial ETFA, Universidad de las Fuerzas Armadas ESPE, Latacunga 050103, Ecuador
apviera1@espe.edu.ec

Abstract. The food industry in Ecuador occupies a high position in financial products, especially in the Tisaleo town, where their main activity is the production of strawberry and blackberry wine, which is becoming the principal activities associated with the sector. However, the vulnerability of the area means that most of its producers develop the wine with manual processes. On the other hand, virtual simulation based on FEM tools, serve to develop products in an accurately way. Thus, in this work was carried out the computational simulation of stress and strain applied to a fruit pulping machine necessary for the production of wine. Through this approach the user can understand the magnitudes that serve to identify mechanical stresses and being possible to used as a teaching-learning tool. For the development, the CAD tool was used, and for the computational simulation of the machine, the finite element method (FEM) was applied, all this to have the best option according to the required mechanical characteristics. The simulation realeases a maximum stress of 4910.1 psi. In this proccess In this proccess was applied a fastening int the shear levers, and maximum deformation of 0.0387 mm at the end of shear levers. On the other hand, in the mathematical relationship was determined a safety factor of 6.10 in the critical points of the proposed model. With this parameters, the results were favorable since the values obtained allow them to be optimized to reduce their costs according to the needs without affecting their regular operation.

Keywords: Finite element theory · Mechanical design · Fruit pulper · Food machine

1 Introduction

Currently in different cities of the world and especially in Ecuador, have been developed policies, and programs that encourage the industrialization of the country. These regulations are described in the Change of Productive Matrix project elaborated by the

C. Stephanidis et al. (Eds.): HCII 2022, CCIS 1654, pp. 620–627, 2022.
https://doi.org/10.1007/978-3-031-19679-9_78

National Secretary of Planning and Developing [1]. These policies allow the creation of entrepreneurship or businesses that give job opportunities to people in the sector, contributing to the area's development and strengthening its economy [2]. The Tisaleo town of the Tungurahua Province in Ecuador is the main reference in the production of fresh blackberries and strawberries of the highest quality in the country, so it is ready to receive the entire population so that they can acquire and savor the best blackberries and strawberries with Tungurahuense brand [3]. Diferents products are produced with strawberries and blackberries, such as the production of artisanal wine [4]. It is also observed that the producers of the sector do not have the complete machinery to carry out the production process, so on certain occasions, they ask the municipality for a loan and thus carry out their daily activity [5]. On the other hand, it is identified that the inhabitants of the sector make wine, generating their product in various ways, primari by hand, and in the best of cases they use a manual machine tool [6].

This manual production method does not provide greater profitability, since it not only generates an excess of downtime but also generates a large amount of waste in the raw material, causing the quality of the wine to decrease, because it increases the acidity, decreasing the degree of alcohol and increasing the reddish tone of the wine [7] However, with the use of modern industrial machinery that is within the reach of wine producers, they could not only save time but also reduce water consumption in the process of fruit pulping, and manual work and additional resources. Therefore, his machinery would be the ideal component to optimize the production process [8]. The purchase of a pulping machine is presented as a firsst option to solve the present problems; however, the costs of the machines are high and vary according to the brand, size, and quality [9]. It has been identified in other studies how equipment costs can be reduced based on an FEM analysis, allowing attacking only the important points that help reduce costs [10], For this reason, the simulation of mechanical stresses in computational packages has been taken into account, and applied to the design of a fruit pulping machine, to make it economical so that it can later be replicated by other entities dedicated to wine production process [11] This document, in particular, describes the computational simulation of stress and strain applied to a fruit pulping machine, using the computerized FEM methodology [12], in which the behavior of the materials that make up the machine can be measured, reaching the maximum and minimum mechanical stresses in its entire structure, as well as the values regarding the deformations that can be applied in each of its components [13]. All this is to identify its maximum mechanical resistance and how much the material and geometry can be optimized to reduce its costs [14]. The safety factor presented in the design proposal, supported by the design theory, is also analyzed. The acceptance or rejection design criteria during the simulation of mechanical stresses are based on the finite element theory [15]. Which says that a continuous element is divided into a finite number of parts, whose behavior is specified by a determined number of parameters, associated with certain characteristic points called nodes, being thus that the behavior of each element is defined using the interpolation function of said nodes [16].

This document is divided into 4 sections, including the introduction in Sect. 1, then the materials and methods are shown in Sect. 2, and after Sect. 3 the tests and experimental results are displayed. And finally the conclusions in Sect. 4.

2 Materials and Methods

2.1 Formulation

For the wine producers of Tisaleo town, having an low-cost pulping machine of medium size and with industrial characteristics, would be the beginning of the development of a productive chain in the manufacture of wine, since it will allow producing wine in greater quantity and in the right way, profitable, safe, and hygienic. For this propose, a deep investigation has been carried out, applying the computational simulation to the proposed model, with this simulation it was possible to select the components with greater mechanical efficiency and at the same time apply the theory of finite elements through a computer. It is also known that the simulator allows shaping the machine's components in three dimensions. With the measurements, it is also possible to apply colors and textures just as they appear in reality, allowing greater clarity of the product in all its context. To optimize the proposed design through computational simulation allowing to choice the best materials that meet the performance but at the same time reduce manufacturing costs. Solving the problem of the high prices that a team of this nature can reach in the market. Figure 1 shows the methodology applied to the process of simulating and optimizing the product, first the requirements that the equipment to be manufactured will have been described, then the data will be presented through its different variables, The product was shaped using 3D digital tools, and finally, the FEM simulator will be used to calculate the maximum efforts in the product, this tool will be the key to optimize the final product.

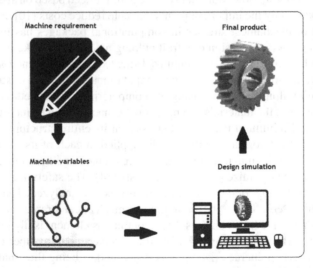

Fig. 1. Methodology applied to the product simulation and optimization process.

2.2 Mechanical Simulation

To carry out the computational simulation in our study, we have chosen a machine, which is a fundamental part of the wine obtention process (pulping machine), this device contains mechanical elements, electrical conditions, and geometries that make a piece of equipment has industrial characteristics, in the Fig. 2A has been detailed the different components of the the prototype, the digital CAD model can be visualized that will serve to carry out the computational simulation in its different components or machine elements. The proposed component consists of a solid exterior structure, the main work axis, arms with couplings for blades, and a conical auger screw, which will serve to move the fruit to the cutting area. All these components are coupled to a drive shaft attached to a pulley coupled to an electric motor. Figure 2B shows the internal mechanisms contained in the fruit de-pulping machine; it contains an axis to couple the circular bases of the drum, the blades and the upper casing. Figure 2C shows the placement of loads before performing the analysis. Figure 2D shows the triangular meshing;the fundamental basis for generating the matrix of internal equations that allows the calculation of its final results. The distribution of the mesh applied to the entire machine shows the embedment points detailed in green, and the applied forces in purple color. After finishing the pulping machine's meshing, we applied the computer simulation.

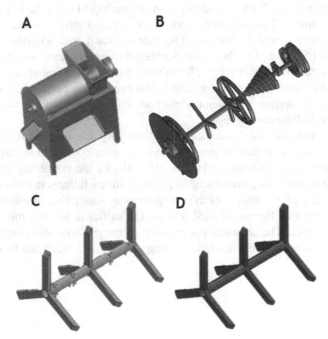

Fig. 2. Digital model. **A**. 3d machine. **B** Equipment internal mechanisms. **C** Placement of forces. **D** Meshing before equipment design

To understand the simulation regarding the stresses and deformations that a material can present when loads or workforces are applied, the Von Mises theory was used in all its mathematical analysis. The effective Von Mises stress (σ') was defined as the uniaxial tensile stress that would create the same distortion energy as the actual combination of applied stresses. The σ' is defined by the Eq. (1).

$$\sigma' = \sqrt{\sigma_1 2 + \sigma_2 2 - \sigma_{1*}\sigma_2} \tag{1}$$

The Von Misses failure theory is the best option since this analysis is applied to metallic materials with ductile properties. The simulator generates a triangular mesh, which is configured by the user. The mesh has the criterion designer and, and has a influence of time analysis. The smaller mesh involve y more time process, including the determination of its resistance and maximum deformation.

3 Resulted

Figure 3A shows the simulation of mechanical stresses. The maximum efforts and deformations that our components can have been identified. The color bar indicates exactly where a greater or lesser effort can be generated, and the dark tones, especially the blue parts, detail the minor efforts in pounds per square inch (PSI), and the tendency to light colors as an example. The color red, is where the greatest efforts that the material can withstand can be observed. In this case, it is observed that there is a maximum resistance effort of 4910 PSI related to the union between the cutting lever and the main drive shaft. On the other hand, in the Fig. 3B the maximum and minimum deformations are observed, in the same way, the color strip is observed and especially the red and blue tones respectively, finding a maximum deformation of 0.0387 mm and which is related to the upper end of the cutting lever.

The computational simulation allowed identifying the maximum and minimum efforts and deformations that an industrial system or component that can reach when they are subjected to different workforces. That allows the possibility of repowering the equipment before being manufactured avoiding future failures in critical equipment areas. However, with the results of the computational simulation of efforts and deformation, it is clear that the use of AISI 304 steel is sufficient to meet the requirements regarding resistance; The chemical composition of the material also contributes to the issue of corrosion because the machine is going to work with fluids and food in general.

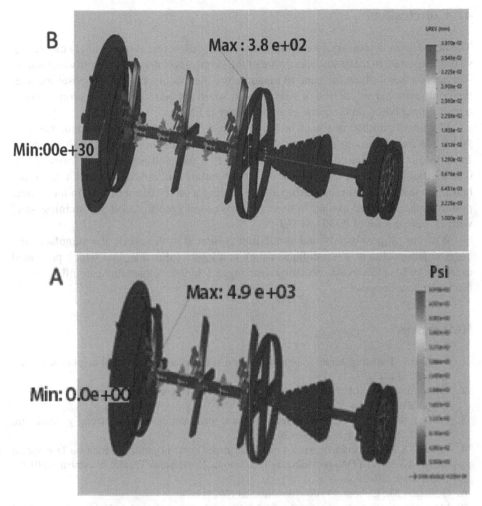

Fig. 3. Cutting mechanism; A. Maximum efforts; B. Maximum deformation

3.1 Manufacturing Costs

Manufacturing costs are analyzed based on materials, equipment size, solid components (Frame, pulleys, shafts, blades), and flexible components (Bands), as well as electrical components such as the motor, contractors, etc. Regarding the construction process, direct labor, indirect costs, and engineering costs are considered, reaching a value of 1790 dollars. In the study of Messrs. Edison Defaz and Fernando Tuzaindicate that the construction costs of a pulping machine reach 2,838.4 dollars [17]. In the thesis of Mr. Julio Espinoza, he indicates that the construction of a machine to pulp fruit reaches a value of 4978.71 dollars [18].

4 Conclusions

The acquisition of industrial machinery for vulnerable sectors is increasingly expensive, so it is important to make students aware of the simple tools that help simplify mathematical approaches without the need to manufacture the machinery. This proposal includes the computational simulation of stress versus strain applied to the main components of a fruit pulper based on the finite element theory (FEM).

The stress simulation found in the proposed model reaches a minimum stress of 409.2 psi and maximum stress of 4910.1 psi and focuses directly on the shear levers. In addition, a minimum deformation of 3.225 E^{-3} mm and maximum deformation of 0.0387 mm can also be observed at the upper end of said cutting levers. On the other hand, the mathematical relationship allows finding a safety factor of 6.10 in the critical points of the proposed model. In this case, it was analyzed for AISI 304 stainless steel with an elastic limit of 29994.81 Psi.

With the proposal study and simulation presented in this work, the manufacturing costs reach a value of 1790 dollars, which is a lower value than that which presented in other studies ($2838.40), reaching a savings of 36.9%. Values that can influence the final purchase decision.

References

1. Senplades. Transformación de la matriz productiva. Secretaria Nacional de planificacion y desarrollo (2012)
2. Garces Jímenez, K.C.: Ecosistema emprendedor y emprendimiento en la provincia de Tungurahua (2017)
3. Paulina Sanchez, F.S.J.A.: Proyecto integral para agricultores de fresa y mora. In: VÍNCULOS-ESP, Caso, Tisaleo (2019)
4. Poveda, S.: Producción de vino a partir de desecho de la pulpa de fruta en la empresa (INALPEV CIA LTDA) provincia de Tungurahua. Universidad Técnica de Ambato (2018)
5. Gad Tisaleo (2012)
6. Gonzalez, M.: Elaboracion de vino artesanal (2021)
7. Martinez, R.: Caracterización física y química de vinos tintos producidos. Universidad Autónoma de Querétaro (2012)
8. Espinoza, L., Alberto, J.: Estudio de factibilidad para la implementación de una máquina despulpadora de naranjilla para la empresa Mr. Freeze (2016)
9. Saquinga, B.A.B.: Diseño y construcción de una máquina despulpadora de frutas con una capacidad de 500 kg/h para la empresa productos suiza dajed cia. ltda. de la ciudad de ambato (2019)
10. Varela-Aldás, J., Buele, J., Cruz, J.: Construction of a low-cost semi-automatic machine for tensile testing. In: Botto-Tobar, M., Montes León, S., Camacho, O., Chávez, D., Torres-Carrión, P., Zambrano Vizuete, M. (eds.) ICAT 2020. CCIS, vol. 1388, pp. 225–235. Springer, Cham (2021). https://doi.org/10.1007/978-3-030-71503-8_17
11. Lardies, J.: Criterio de Diseño mecánico en tecnologías industrials. Prensa de la Universidad de Zaragoza (2015)
12. Avilés, C.A.: Teoría de falla bajo carga estática (2005)
13. Kästner, M., Müller, S., Ulbricht, V.: XFEM modelling of inelastic material behaviour and interface failure in textile-reinforced composites. Elsevier (2013)

14. Reydezel, T.M.: Aplicación y análisis comparativo de los criterios de diseño mecánico por resistencia a esfuerzos, rigidez y modos de vibración. Científica (2012)
15. Szabó, B., Babuška, I.: Finite Element Analysis. Method, Verification and Validation (2021)
16. Granizo, E., Escudero, F., Pachacama, R., Aquino, M., Lozano, E.: Optoacoustic effect analysis by FEM. In: AIP Conference Proceedings (2018)
17. Defaz Pallasco, E.M.: Diseño y construcción de una despulpadora de frutas horizontal con una capacidad de producción de 250 Kg/h (2011)
18. Julio Espinoza, A.L.: Diseño y construcción de una despulpadora de frutas horizontal con una capacidad de producción de 250 kg/h. Universidad Tecnológica Equinoccial (2016)

SonoUno Web: An Innovative User Centred Web Interface

Gonzalo De La Vega[1,2,3], Leonardo Martin Exequiel Dominguez[1,2,3], Johanna Casado[1,2(✉)] (iD), and Beatriz García[1,3]

[1] Instituto en Tecnologías de Detección y Astropartículas (CNEA,CONICET, UNSAM), Mendoza, Argentina
[2] Instituto de Bioingeniería, Facultad de Ingeniería, Universidad de Mendoza, Mendoza, Argentina
johanna.casado@um.edu.ar
[3] Universidad Tecnológica Nacional, Buenos Aires, Argentina
http://www.sonouno.org.ar

Abstract. Sonification as a complement of visualization is been under research for decades as a new ways of data deployment. ICAD conferences, gather together specialists from different disciplines to discuss about sonification. Different tools as sonoUno, starSound and Web Sandbox are attempt to reach a tool to open astronomical data sets and sonify it in conjunction to visualization. In this contribution, the sonoUno web version is presented, this version allows user to explore data sets without any installation. The data can be uploaded or a pre-loaded file can be opened, the sonification and the visual characteristics of the plot can be customized on the same window. The plot, sound and marks can be saved. The web interface were tested with the main used screen readers in order to confirm their good performance.

Keywords: Sonification · Graphic user interface · Human centred design

1 Introduction

The need to explore data sets beyond the visual field has led the community to study new ways to represent it, this is the case of sonification. In this sense, since 1992 the ICAD conferences [1] has existed bringing together scientists from different fields to discuss sonification, how people perceive it and how it can be used. Related to sonification Phillips and Cabrera [2] present a sonification workstation; and related to astronomy Shafer et al. [3] and García Riber [4] develop specific projects to sonify solar harmonics and light curves.

During the past years some sonification programs were created as tools to make possible the multimodal exploration of visual and audio graphs, this is

Supported by the Project REINFORCE (GA 872859) with the support of the EC Research Innovation Action under the H2020 Programme SwafS-2019–1the REINFORCE (www.reinforceeu.eu).

the case of xSonify [5], Sonification Sandbox [6], Sonipy [7,8], StarSound [9] and SonoUno [10]. All are standard alone software that requires you to download a package and install it. Related to the possibility of analyze data with sonification, Díaz-Merced [11] in her thesis, using the standard alone sonification software xSonify, concluded that sonification as a complement to visual display augments the detection of features in the data sets under analysis.

Given the complexity to use the available standard alone software and to avoid errors and problems during the software installation, the idea of a sonification software working through the web began to make sense. TwoTone [12], TimeWorkers [13], Sonification Blocks [14] and Web Sandbox [15] are different attempts to make it real, but none of them allow the end user to explore, make choices about the configuration and how they want to display the data and functionalities. In this sense, we present in this contribution a graphic user interface available in the web that presents the same user centred framework and almost same functionalities of sonoUno [16] desktop software.

The sonoUno software, in its web and desktop versions, is a public tool to display, sonify and apply mathematical functions to any data set. The actual original application of the software is to astronomical data, but it can be used with any type of data presented in two or more columns (csv or txt) files. SonoUno presents a user centred approach from the beginning, first with a theoretical framework, second with focus group sessions and then with a community of people that kindly test the software and send the feedback to the developers [17].

The sonoUno web interface was tested in different operative system and with different screen readers. This work was partially financiated by the Project REINFORCE (GA 872859) with the support of the EC Research Innovation Action under the H2020 Programme SwafS-2019–1 the REINFORCE www. reinforceeu.eu.

2   Methodology

Taking in mind that the end user must have the ability to choose, configure and decide how they want to explore their data sets, this project requires the use of HTML, JavaScript, CSS and ARIA (Accessible Rich Internet Applications) tools and protocols to make it possible. It is a novel approach, because it is not common that web interfaces allows users to make decisions and to configure the display during the interaction. Concerning that, collapsible panel were used, maintaining the principal framework with few functionalities and giving the user the power to decide what they want to display and use.

In consideration of how people with visual impairments handling the digital interface, and how screen reader read the graphic user interface, sonoUno web design use the ARIA standard. Not only the ARIA-labels were indicated, but also an specific order to generate a good workflow thought functionalities and ensuring that the screen reader describe the things just as the visual display indicates. Moreover, the unnecessary elements of the visual display are not read by the screen reader, for example, the plot are not read as plot, instead the button play allows to sonify the data plotted.

Another big challenge for this development was to ensure the synchronization between the audio and visual graph, bearing in mind the asynchronous nature of JavaScript. Events with timer were used to guarantee the correct relationship during the reproduction of the data set. Furthermore, during the last tests using large data sets a new problem arise, in the web version and with all this functionalities to plot and sonify large data sets is very difficult, take a lot of time and produce errors in some cases. To solve this issue a decimating filter is being tested.

2.1   Graphic User Interface Design

In order to maintain the web display as similar as possible to the desktop deployment, a menu was constructed at the top containing: input (allows to open csv/txt data sets, sound and marks that could be done in a data set pointing to parts of interest in the data); output (allows to save the sound, png plot and marks); sample data (this menu item contain pre-loaded data sets that can be displayed on the tool); help (open the complete manual of the tool); and quickstart (open a summary of what to expect and how to use the principal functions).

The reproduction buttons are always displayed and under the plot, these buttons are: play/pause, stop, mark point, delete mark, reset plot, the command text entry and the two sliders to indicate the x position and the tempo. On the other hand, math functionalities and the configurations are located on collapsible panels, this allows to maintain an organized display and few elements that have to be read by the screen reader (helps to reduce memory overload).

The sound and graphic display can be customized by the end user as their desire. About the sound the maximum and minimum frequency can be set, the volume, the sound type (sine, flute, piano and celesta), choose between continuous and logarithmic scale, and the envelope of the sound. Secondly, the plot configuration allows to set the titles, the grid, the line, the markers, and to flip the x and y axis.

3   Results

A screenshot of the interface was shown in Fig. 1. This web tool allows users to see and hear data sets opened from csv or txt files, also end users can load data sets from 'Data Sample' menu item, for example the gravitational wave glitch showed in Fig. 1 was selected from that menu item. At the bottom, the text entry box, allows to write the functionalities available on the interface (this feature allows to use the web interface from there avoiding the use of the mouse).

The plot section allows to zoom it directly on the same plot with the mouse. The abscissa position slider (see Fig. 2 at the top) allows to move the cursor through the data set and to begin the reproduction from there. The tempo slider allows to speed up and down the reproduction time. Figure 2 also shows opened

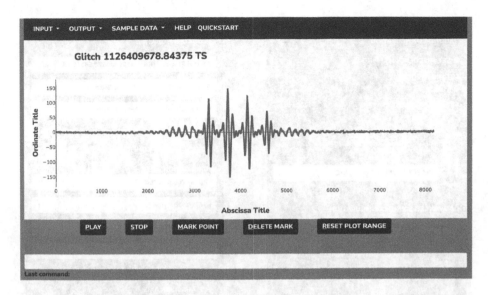

Fig. 1. A sonoUno web interface screenshot, it include the menu, plot, reproduction buttons and the command line text box. The plot shows a gravitational wave glitch, detected by EGO [18] and part of the open data provided by the REINFORCE project

the math function panel, where at the moment there are four functions ready to use: peak finder (in this case a new window allows to select the percentage of sensitivity and if you want to clean or mark the peaks); logarithmic; quadratic; and smooth. At bottom of Fig. 2 the configuration panels collapsed are shown. Figure 3 shows the configuration panels opened with all it functions.

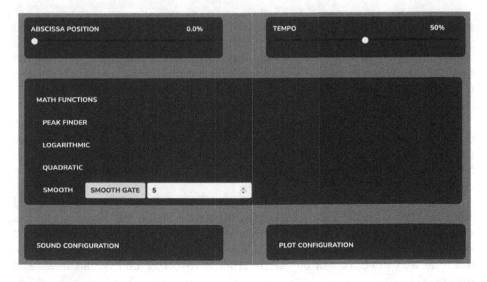

Fig. 2. A screenshot with the x position and tempo sliders at the top, the math function panel opened and the sound and plot configurations collapsed.

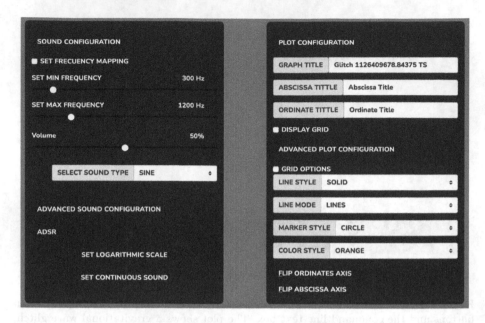

Fig. 3. A screenshot of sound and plot configurations panels opened.

The SonoUno web interface was tested in different platforms with different screen readers (NVDA on Windows, Voice Over on MAC and Orca on Ubuntu). All the elements are enunciated by the screen reader, the elements on the panels are only recognizable when the panel is opened (this is very important to maintain the relation between the visual and auditory display).

4 Conclusion

A web interface of sonoUno software was developed, maintaining the original functionalities distribution as same as possible, continuing the user center design from the beginning of the tool. This web interface allows the user to explore the data set, making decisions about what the want to display and how.

Concerning the use of screen readers, the elements of the interface present descriptions and the order of the audible display was carefully design, to ensure the adequate correlation between visual and audible deployment. The principal free screen reader of each operative system was tested, and the results show a good performance.

This innovative approach seeks to continue growing, removing barriers and offering more accessible tools to analyse data sets. Since the beginning of the year, this web interface is being used by a professor at Spain with visual impaired students. This experience will let us know some features to enhance and if the sonoUno web interface can be use by student to better understand math and science.

As future works, the web interface is adapting to be used from any mobile device, and the axis limits of the plot will be set indicating the specific number to cut. New user tests and focus group will be performed to maintain and assure the user centred design philosophy of sonoUno and all the associated tools.

References

1. ICAD Conferences page. https://icad.org/conferences/ Accessed 15 Mar 2022
2. Phillips, S., Cabrera, A.: Sonification Workstation. In: the 25th International Conference on Auditory Display (ICAD 2019). Northumbria University (2019). https://doi.org/10.21785/icad2019.056
3. Shafer, S., Larson, T., diFalco, E.: The Sonification of Solar Harmonics (SoSH) PROJECT. In: the 25th International Conference on Auditory Display (ICAD 2019). Northumbria University (2019). https://doi.org/10.21785/icad2019.011
4. García Riber, A.: SonifigrapheR. Sonified Light Curve SynthesizeR. In: the 25th International Conference on Auditory Display (ICAD 2019). Northumbria University (2019). https://doi.org/10.21785/icad2019.016
5. Diaz-Merced, W.L., et al.: Sonification of astronomical data. In: Proceedings of the International Astronomical Union, vol. 7(S285), pp. 133–136. (2011)
6. Davison, B.K., Walker, B.N.: Sonification Sandbox reconstruction: software standard for auditory graphs. Georgia institute of technology (2007)
7. Worrall, D., Bylstra, M., Barrass, S., Dean, R.: SoniPy: the design of an extendable software framework for sonification research and auditory display. In: Proceedings of the 13th International Conference on Auditory Display, Montréal, Canada (2007)
8. Sonipy GitHub repository. https://github.com/lockepatton/sonipy Accessed 17 Mar 2022
9. Cooke, J., Díaz-Merced, W., Foran, G., Hannam, J., Garcia, B.: Exploring data sonification to enable, enhance, and accelerate the analysis of big, noisy, and multidimensional data: workshop 9. In: Proceedings of the International Astronomical Union, vol. 14(S339), pp. 251–256 (2017)
10. SonoUno GitHub repository. https://github.com/sonoUnoTeam/sonoUno Accessed 17 Mar 2022
11. Díaz-Merced, W.: Sound for the exploration of space physics data. Doctoral dissertation, University of Glasgow (2013)
12. Welcome to TwoTone - A free web app to turn data into sound and music. https://twotone.io/ Accessed 17 Mar 2022
13. Chafe, C.: Browser-Based Sonification. In: Proceedings of the 17th Linux Audio Conference (LAC-19), CCRMA, Stanford University, USA (2019)
14. Sonification Blocks - Stanford University. https://ccrma.stanford.edu/~lja/sonification/ Accessed 17 Mar 2022
15. Kondak, Z., Liang, K., Tomlinson, B., Walker, B.N.: Web Sonification Sandbox - an Easy-to-Use Web Application for Sonifying Data and Equations. In: Web Audio Conference WAC-2017, pp. 21–23, 2017, London, UK (2017)
16. Casado, J., García, B., Diaz-Merced, W.L.: Analysis of astronomical data through sonification: reaching more inclusion for visual disable scientists. In: Proceedings of the International Astronomical Union, (S358) (2019)
17. Casado, J., De La Vega, G., Diaz-Merced, W.L., Gandhi, P., García, B.: SonoUno: a user-centred approach to sonification. In: Proceedings of the International Astronomical Union Symposium No. 367, (2020)
18. Gravity Spy. https://www.zooniverse.org/projects/zooniverse/gravity-spy/classify Accessed 17 Mar 2022

Design and Development of a Searchable Database of Veterinary Curriculum

Serhat Demir and Aliye Karabulut-Ilgu[✉]

Iowa State University, Ames, IA 50020, USA
`aliye@iastate.edu`

Abstract. Curriculum maps visually present all components of a curriculum by providing a broad overview of what is taught, in what order, and how it is taught. As an analytical tool for organizing, managing, and evaluating curriculum, a curriculum map, therefore, is a powerful tool in identifying gaps and redundancies in a curriculum. Common approach used in curriculum mapping is to map learning objectives whether at the course or lecture level to program outcomes or competencies. This process is extremely laborious and time consuming, and fails to provide a comprehensive visual representation of the curriculum. Further, it may not reflect the realities of classroom teaching as it relies on intended learning objectives. In this study, we argue that machine learning and text mining techniques could be utilized to create a comprehensive overview of the curriculum using real classroom data. This work-in-progress tool will have three distinct components 1) searchable curriculum, 2) network modeling of the curriculum, and 3) outcome mapping. This paper reports the processes we followed to create a searchable database of the veterinary medicine curriculum.

Keywords: Curriculum analysis · Curriculum mapping

1 Background

Preparing well-rounded veterinarians equipped with the required skill sets is essential for our society as they play a critical role in the health of animals, environmental protection, research, food safety, and public health [1]. Veterinary medicine students go through a comprehensive curriculum that combines basic sciences with clinical practices. Such a curriculum requires a great harmony across courses for students to be able to skillfully create mental models of the knowledge and skills they gain over the course of their veterinary education and graduate as practice-ready professionals. Even though such harmony is desired in all curricula, it is easy to fall short of the ideal due to the number of people and disciplines involved in enacting a complex curriculum. One approach adopted by many veterinary and medical schools to continuously check and assess the coverage is curriculum mapping, which is an analytical tool for organizing, managing, and evaluating curriculum. Curriculum maps help stakeholders identify gaps and redundancies in a curriculum as they visually present a broad overview of what is taught, in what order, and

C. Stephanidis et al. (Eds.): HCII 2022, CCIS 1654, pp. 634–638, 2022.
https://doi.org/10.1007/978-3-031-19679-9_80

how it is taught. The most common approach used in curriculum mapping is to manually map course or lecture level learning objectives to program outcomes or competencies. This process is extremely laborious, time consuming, and resource-intensive [2] and it fails to reflect the realities of classroom teaching as it relies on intended learning objectives. Furthermore, program objectives and outcomes are usually very broad and may not capture granular details about the curriculum. Therefore, there is a critical need for an automated, sustainable system to map all components of a curriculum that relies on real classroom data to enhance the quality of instruction in veterinary sciences.

2 Design and Development Process

We are following the human-centered design (HCD) principles recommended by Abras, Maloney-Krichmar and Preece [3] which has four parts; preparing and manipulating transcript text for JSON data, installation and testing development environments, creating and testing the first template and API methods, implementing and testing view sets (Fig. 1). We initiated our design process by identifying the context for implementation and potential users. Informal conversations with faculty members as well as findings from focus groups conducted for curriculum review indicated that many faculty members highlighted how little they knew what courses were required in the curriculum, who was teaching the courses, and what content they covered in various courses. They expressed a need for a system that would provide them all this information and facilitate the communication amongst faculty members teaching related courses. They also mentioned how students lacked the skill of integrating knowledge they gained in compartmentalized courses. Such a system that displays the relationship across courses to assist students with the integration skills was perceived as a critical need. Based on these expressed needs, we designed the first prototype of the searchable database described in the next section. In order to prepare JSON data, we needed to change transcript text line by line. After that, we tested the data in the ElasticSearch development environment. Then we completed all environment installation and moved forward to the first template design. We kept the first template design as simple as possible so we could test API methods as soon as possible. We are currently at the stage of the search result page design, which is the first component of the last part.

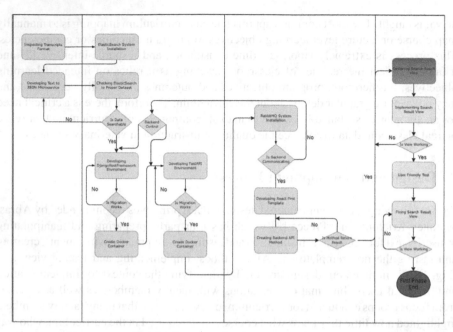

Fig. 1. Prototype development process.

3   Prototype Development and Systems Used

The College of Veterinary Medicine at Iowa State University, like many other peer institutions, has been video recording all the core course lectures using a lecture capture technology since 2007 [4]. We decided to use the transcripts of these lecture recordings to create a database of lecture content that can be tied back to actual recordings. Users, then, can search for a keyword and see in which courses that keyword was mentioned. Potential users for this component are students, faculty, and curriculum administrators.

While determining the system components, we tried to choose them as flexibly as possible to meet our needs. The main decision point was handling most of the task in backend development and create dashboard and mapping features in frontend development. In this context, we preferred to React for frontend development. It enables us to create interfaces easily with React installation, and it enables us to make these interfaces in the most logical, easiest, most cost-effective, and most performance way. In the backend, we used two separate Python frameworks. These are Django and FastAPI. By modeling the system with Django, we enabled to organize of the frontend within a certain pattern. It gives simplicity because it also enables rapid development. By making ElasticSearch talk with FastAPI, which is the fastest among Python rest frameworks, we aimed to make get respond at maximum speed with these two robust systems. Since the course transcripts are kept in the veterinary system by naming them in folders, firstly we read the information such as the year and course code of the courses with a help of microservice that we implement and put them in the relevant fields in the JSON data that we will upload to ElasticSearch. Before uploading it to the ElasticSearch database, we assigned the remaining bag of words to the summary field in the generated JSON by cleaning unnecessary words and stemming in the transcript in order to increase the matching. In order to ensure the match, the words searched on FastAPI were also cleaned with unnecessary words and stemming. Afterward, these bags of words are searched in the index associated with ElasticSearch RestfulAPI, and the returned results are transmitted to React via FastAPI, and the list information is transmitted in which courses and in which years the user passed the matched words. On the other hand, we will enable FastAPI and Django to send requests to each other without delay and processing problems with the help of RabbitMQ. In this way, a fast communication cycle will be provided for each component. This architecture gives us great flexibility to do what we need but creates complications and compatibility problems. The backend and frontend were created on the Docker container to solve this issue. Also, we supported it with docker architecture in order to make the components scalable and controllable. In this way, deployments will be faster and safer. In addition, when there is a need to increase the service in the coming periods, the problem will be solved by simply increasing the number of components instead of re-installing (Fig. 2).

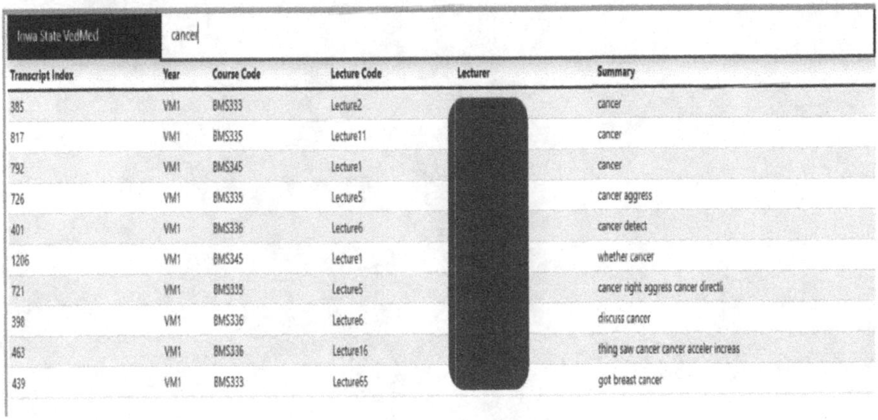

Fig. 2. Screenshot of the first prototype.

4 Conclusion and Future Work

After all the technology and design analyses we made, we decided to keep the design very simple so that users could access information as quickly as possible. In this way, waiting times on the system and intelligibility will increase. While constructing the system, we took great care to provide this flexibility at every stage. In future stages, we will create a 3-layered search result page and start the usability tests. After the usability tests, we will make changes in our design with the same flexibility and provide the most efficient experience to the users.

References

1. AVMA: Veterinarians: protecting he health of animals and people. https://www.avma.org/resources/pet-owners/yourvet/veterinarians-protecting-health-animals-and-people (2022). Accessed 18 Mar 2022
2. Bell, C.E., Ellaway, R.H., Rhind, S.M.: Getting started with curriculum mapping in a veterinary degree program. J. Vet. Med. Educ. **36**(1), 100–106 (2009)
3. Abras, C., Maloney-Krichmar, D., Preece, J.: User-centered design. In: Bainbridge, W. (ed.) Encyclopedia of Human-Computer Interaction, vol. 37, issue 4, pp. 445–456. Sage Publications, Thousand Oaks (2004)
4. Danielson, J., Preast, V., Bender, H., Hassall, L.: Is the effectiveness of lecture capture related to teaching approach or content type? Comput. Educ. **72**, 121–131 (2014)

Development of Interactive Story Tales Using MIT App Inventor

Janio Jadán-Guerrero[1]([✉]), Ana Pérez-Cazares[2], and Marcos Chacón-Castro[3]

[1] Centro de Investigación en Mecatrónica y Sistemas Interactivos (MIST), Universidad Tecnológica Indoamérica, Av. Machala y Sabanilla, Quito, Ecuador
`janiojadan@uti.edu.ec`
[2] Maestría en Educación, Mención Pedagogía en Entorno Digitales (MEPED), Universidad Tecnológica Indoamérica, Av. Machala y Sabanilla, Quito, Ecuador
[3] Fundación Universitaria Internacional de la Rioja, Bogotá, Colombia
`marcos.chacon@unir.net`

Abstract. Today mobile technologies have become essential in people's lives. The use of smartphones and tablets has increased in times of pandemic due to their low cost, ease of use, ubiquity, portability, communication, and interactivity. Reading habits have changed significantly in favor of the digital format. This article describes a study to identify the way children from 8 to 12 years of age read on smartphones. The study was carried out in three phases: the first where an instrumented inquiry was carried out, collecting and analyzing data by applying a diagnostic test to 20 students; as well as a survey of 20 parents and 4 teachers in the language area. In the second stage, with the information collected, mobile educational resources were designed based on unpublished stories and activities focused on four language skills (reading, speaking, listening and writing). In a third stage, an intervention was carried out using the Thinking Aloud technique. The students were separated into two groups, 10 of them participated in a virtual session and 10 in a face-to-face session. In both cases, the results showed some reading habits as well as interest, motivation when there are interactive resources.

Keywords: Mobile resources · Reading habits · m-learning · Thinking Aloud · MIT App Inventor

1 Introduction

Reading is an essential act for human beings, because through it each individual knows better who he or she is and where he or she comes from. Through reading we can transform the real and imaginary world, awaken curiosity, stimulate the imagination, help develop creativity, so the promotion of reading has to be a priority in education to provide a cultured society. However, developing countries such as Ecuador still have problems of illiteracy, which is one of the greatest challenges for the education system. Ecuador has a literacy rate of 92.83% and is ranked 81st in the literacy ranking [1]. According to the latest data published by UNESCO, 26.2% of Ecuadorians do not dedicate time to reading, of which 56.8% do not do so due to lack of interest and 31.7% due to lack of time

© The Author(s), under exclusive license to Springer Nature Switzerland AG 2022
C. Stephanidis et al. (Eds.): HCII 2022, CCIS 1654, pp. 639–645, 2022.
https://doi.org/10.1007/978-3-031-19679-9_81

[2]. These statistics are the result of a problem that starts at an early age with the lack of reading habits and continues in many cases until adulthood. The lack of reading habits in Ecuadorian students is reflected in the results of evaluations by various organizations such as The Programme for International Student Assessment (PISA), a worldwide test developed by the Organisation for Economic Co-operation and Development (OECD) [3].

In relation to this problem, a study proposes that it is necessary to develop a new pedagogy for the development of reading competence, taking into account the current technological challenges [4]. These challenges constitute an opportunity to develop some skills with the use of technology. For example, one study investigated how to expand linguistic vocabulary through reading electronic stories. The authors start from the premise that children have a limited vocabulary due to low reading motivation, therefore, the objective was to propose the intervention of electronic stories, applying a random sampling design with pre- and post-tests, obtaining as results the lexical development and comprehension of literary texts [5].

In the same way, a study analyzed the use of cell phones and their impact on reading habits. To this end, the authors conducted data collection through interviews to identify the real problems of the reading process. The authors determined that reading spaces are often boring, and therefore assume that the development of a digital reading may be more advantageous [6].

Other authors were able to determine the application of cognitive strategies for the development of reading comprehension skills through stories, through the implementation of cognitive strategies. The methodological approach emerged through the analysis of perceptions by means of the diagnostic evaluation of various linguistic criteria. The results show that an adequate cognitive process strengthens reading processes [7].

In relation to the teaching of reading at early ages, one study explored the initiative of a reading instruction time policy and discussed how it was developed and secured in early grade classes. Reading, as a cognitive process, is considered to require effective time allocation. The researchers were able to determine the importance of instruction in improving performance standards and achievement in reading skills [8].

Teachers use storytelling as a powerful literacy tool that engages children in making connections between academic content and pedagogy. This strategy is also useful for integrating classroom diversity. Increasing or varying the types of materials available to children is another way to make the classroom more inclusive [9].

All these studies highlight the importance of motivating reading processes, gradually responding to technological challenges and seeking new ways to link learning and reading. Reading motivation through mobile educational resources becomes important, since it goes beyond conventional reading methods, and new ways of motivating and innovating linguistic skills development in reading are sought. The following section describes the research process to carry out this study.

2 Method

The research is of a descriptive level, under a mixed approach with a sequential design in two stages; the first stage with a quantitative approach, where an instrumented inquiry is carried out, collecting and analyzing data using instruments; In the second stage, a qualitative approach is applied, it is oriented to the design of the strategy as a proposal to the problem, where the use of empirical methods is applied, for the processing and collection of data, carrying out an analysis and interpretation of results.

2.1 Participants

The population of this research study consisted of 4 teachers from a regular education school in the province of Imbabura in Ecuador and 20 students between eight and nine years of age, in the fourth and fifth grades of general basic education. On the other hand, the participation of 20 parents was considered.

2.2 Materials

The research process was supported by the use of different materials and instruments, among the material resources were the computer, cell phone with internet, web 2.0 resources. While among the instruments in the study were: a survey to teachers, with a structure of two open questions and eight closed questions with Likert scale. Also a survey, with a structure of two open questions and eight closed questions with Likert scale for parents. Finally, an observation guide made to students, with a structure of 10 questions with a Likert scale. The execution of the instruments is applied through the digital tool Google Forms. The data collection instruments applied to the study population were subjected to validation through Cronbach's Alpha, this validation process ensured the reliability of the internal consistency of the instruments.

2.3 Procedure

The research applied a survey to teachers, in order to identify their digital skills through the use of mobile educational resources, as well as to determine the motivation methods and reading processes that they apply with the students. Next, a classroom observation was carried out on the students to determine their levels of motivation to read, based on the educational processes applied by the teachers. In addition, a survey was applied to parents, in order to validate their satisfaction in the teaching-learning process of their children, and their openness to the implementation of mobile educational resources in the reading training processes. Finally, the Thinking aloud technique was used to evaluate the prototype of the mobile educational resource.

3 Development of the Mobile Educational Resource

The implementation of the design and programming of the mobile application "Fantastic Mobile Legends of Milo and Anilu", was developed in different stages:

In the first stage, the linguistic macro-skills needed to develop literacy skills were identified, including reading, writing, listening and speaking. In the second phase, different activities and mobile educational resources were analyzed, through four captions, which were integrated into the development of the mobile application with MIT App

Skill	Digital Tools	Activities	Prototyping
Reading		The mysterious lady The duenditas. The golden chicks. The Virgin of Peace	
Writing	UIZIZZ	Guess, guess What legend am I?	
Listening	Wordwall H5P	Interactive video. Image game. Maze game. Alphabet soup.	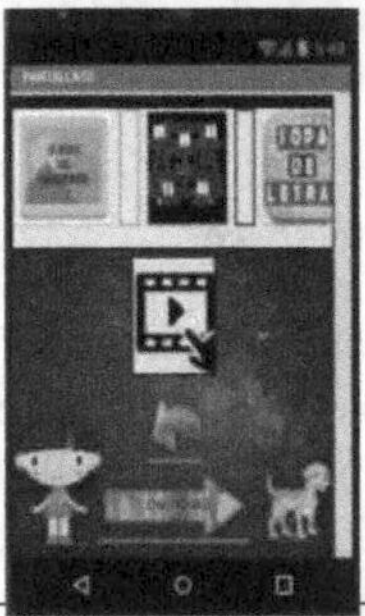
Speaking	padlet	What am I left with?	

Fig. 1. Activities and digital tools for macro-skills.

Inventor. Playful activities were integrated such as: image games, maze, word search, videos; through digital tools such as: Quizz, Kahoot, Padlet, H5P. Figure 1 shows a summary of the activities for each skill and the web 2.0 tools used.

In the third stage, the App Inventor platform was used for developing the App, which allowed integrating the four macro-skills (reading, writing, listening, speaking), through web 2.0 educational resources. The Fig. 2 shows a screenshot of the App.

Fig. 2. The main and menu screens of the App.

The interface has four buttons that were programmed so that each one directs to the screen where the captions are located. When a legend is selected, the text is presented and buttons at the bottom to select the activities.

Following a design thinking methodology proposed by Jadán-Guerrero for the development of hybrid interfaces and educational resources for children, educational resources developed in other web 2.0 platforms were embedded and activities were integrated with hybrid educational resources such as reading QR codes [10].

In the four stage, the implementation of the proposal, the students had two modalities, one virtual and one face-to-face. In the virtual modality, students used smartphones, tablets and other mobile devices at home with the help of their parents. While in the face-to-face modality, worksheets were used with the help of a teacher. In both cases the educational resource developed was evaluated with the Thinking Aloud technique, which allowed improving the interface of the developed prototype.

4   Results

Based on the results obtained, it is evident that teachers use conventional educational resources, which have been used frequently, producing a disinterest in the student in the learning process, specifically in reading; Therefore, this research is feasible, since there is a lack of knowledge of the great variety of digital tools to induce spontaneous reading, it is important to motivate reading through mobile educational resources, enabling young students to function in an educational setting, more dynamic and interactive reading, strengthening the four linguistic macro-skills (reading, writing, listening, speaking).

As mentioned by [11] the importance of motivating reading and strengthening linguistic skills, through the use of digital narrations, which facilitates learning and expansion of vocabulary, as well as assertive expression, all of this will be supported by the effective use of learning environments, as a means to motivate reading processes. Likewise [12], they explored the incidence of online readings, for the motivation to read, promoting active participation by students, who are part of a new reading experience in the educational setting. Once the analysis of the research results has been carried out and complemented with contributions from specialists, Fig. 3 highlights the most relevant results.

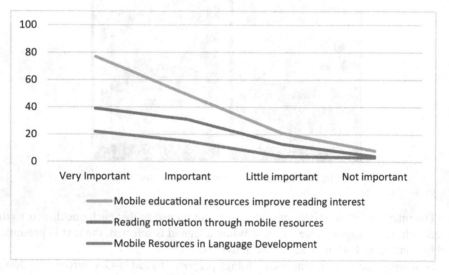

Fig. 3. Relevant results.

5 Conclusions

The students, once the mobile educational resources were applied interactively, had motivating reactions in the learning process, where they expressed their thoughts, referring to the fact that the application interface is very friendly, which is why there is greater attention and interest in the innovative proposal in the reading learning process development in its four macro-skills.

The execution of the mobile application proposal "Fantastic Mobile Legends of Milo and Anilu", was very useful, by offering a variety of dynamic and interactive activities and easy access, the students felt extremely familiar, generating reading emotions.

The reading motivation processes used by teachers are based on classical methods that are not very dynamic and attractive, since it is usually the teacher who fulfills the role of generator of new knowledge and not the student, for which the teacher is the one who must promote educational resources that generate motivation.

References

1. UNESCO: Ecuador—Tasa de alfabetización 2017 (2017). https://datosmacro.expansion.com/demografia/tasa-alfabetizacion/ecuador
2. INEC: Resultados de la búsqueda. Instituto Nacional de Estadística y Censos (2019). https://www.ecuadorencifras.gob.ec
3. PISA-D: Ecuador participó en PISA-D en 2017 – Ministerio de Educación (2017). https://educacion.gob.ec/ecuador-participo-en-pisa-d-en-2017/
4. Hempel-Jorgensen, A., Cremin, T., Harris, D., Chamberlain, L.: Pedagogy for reading for pleasure in low socio-economic primary schools: beyond 'pedagogy of poverty'? Literacy **52**(2), 86–94 (2018). https://doi.org/10.1111/lit.12157
5. Klop, D., Marais, L., Msindwana, A., De Wet, F.: Learning new words from an interactive electronic storybook intervention. S. Afr. J. Commun. Disord. **65**(1), 1–8 (2018). https://doi.org/10.4102/sajcd.v65i1.601
6. Levratto, V., Šuminas, A., Schilhab, T., Esbensen, G.: Smartphones: reading habits and overuse. A qualitative study in Denmark, Lithuania and Spain. Educación XX1 **24**(2), 167–188 (2021)
7. Sua, M.R.: Cognitive strategies for developing students' reading comprehension skills using short stories. REXE-Revista de Estudios y Experiencias en Educación **20**(44), 233–253 (2021)
8. ur Rehman, A.: The impact of reading instructional time in the classroom: early grade reading time policy initiative in Pakistan. Sisyphus: J. Educ. **9**(3), 88–107 (2021)
9. Jadán-Guerrero, J., Sanchez-Gordon, S., Acosta-Vargas, P., Alvites-Huamaní, C.G., Nunes, I.L.: Interactive storytelling books for fostering inclusion of children with special needs. In: Nunes, I.L. (ed.) AHFE 2020. AISC, vol. 1207, pp. 222–228. Springer, Cham (2020). https://doi.org/10.1007/978-3-030-51369-6_30
10. Jadán-Guerrero, J., et al.: Building hybrid interfaces to increase interaction with young children and children with special needs. In: Nunes, I.L. (ed.) AHFE 2019. AISC, vol. 959, pp. 306–314. Springer, Cham (2020). https://doi.org/10.1007/978-3-030-20040-4_28
11. Hava, K.: Exploring the role of digital storytelling in student motivation and satisfaction in EFL education. Comput. Assist. Lang. Learn. **34**(7), 958–978 (2021). https://doi.org/10.1080/09588221.2019.1650071
12. Schreuder, M.C., Savitz, R.S.: Exploring adolescent motivation to read with an online YA book club. Lit. Res. Instr. **59**(3), 260–275 (2020). https://doi.org/10.1080/19388071.2020.1752860

Building an Escape Room to Raise Awareness of Bullying and Cyberbullying

Janio Jadán-Guerrero[1]([✉]), Marcos Chacón-Castro[2], Lourdes Illescas[3], and José Chacón[4]

[1] Centro de Investigación en Mecatrónica y Sistemas Interactivos (MIST), Universidad Tecnológica Indoamérica, Bolívar 2035 y Guayaquil, Ambato, Ecuador
`janiojadan@uti.edu.ec`
[2] Fundación Universitaria Internacional de la Rioja, Bogotá, Colombia
`marcos.chacon@unir.net`
[3] Universidad de Cuenca, Cuenca, Ecuador
`lourdes.illescasp@ucuenca.edu.ec`
[4] Grupo de Investigación GIIDAC, Universidad de Pamplona, Pamplona, Colombia
`jose.chacon@unipamplona.edu.co`

Abstract. Aggressive conflicts are part of the natural social behavior of students in schools, which can lead to bullying when there is a form of discrimination or abuse of power, either because of their characteristics or their way of life (sexual orientation, gender identity, nationality, immigration status, ethnicity, sex, socioeconomic status, health, disability, religious beliefs, pregnancy, among others). In the face-to-face mode, the aggressors could be identified and in some way the conflicts were mediated by teachers or authorities of the institution. However, since education changed to a virtual modality caused by the global coronavirus pandemic, new forms of aggressive behavior have emerged with cyberbullying. In this new scenario teachers, parents and law enforcement should take an active role in raising awareness about bullying and cyberbullying. The main objective of this paper is to describe a proposal based on gamification strategy to prevent and raise awareness of aggressive behaviors among students in a virtual environment. The study focuses on three objectives: a) to study the use of visual methods based on microlearning and the techniques to engage students; b) to identify game scenarios and strategies to design an interactive Escape Room; and c) to evaluate the design and content with three experts in psychology. The results indicate that the Escape Room is a different alternative to understand the problems derived from Bullying and cyberbullying. In the future, we are planning to carry out an intervention with students from Ecuador and Colombia to evaluate the impact.

Keywords: Microlearning · Awareness · Cyberbullying · Social media platforms · Messaging platforms · Gaming platforms · Escape Room · Breakout · Gamification

1 Introduction

A new form of aggressive behavior is cyberbullying, which shares characteristics with traditional bullying, but is characterized by the fact that it takes place on social media

C. Stephanidis et al. (Eds.): HCII 2022, CCIS 1654, pp. 646–653, 2022.
https://doi.org/10.1007/978-3-031-19679-9_82

platforms such as Facebook, Instagram, Snapchat or Tik Tok; as well as instant messaging platforms such as WhatsApp, Messenger or Telegram. Unlike traditional bullying, bullies can be anonymous and are physically absent, which can make it difficult to confront them [1].

Emotional intelligence is the capacity and ability of people to manage their emotions and empathize with those of others. In relation to this, it is necessary for schools to work on "emotional education, attention to diversity and cooperative learning and work" [2]. Some researchers designed programs with gamification elements, leading to active participation and collaborative work [3, 4]. With this experience arises the idea of creating a Digital Scape Room that helps the development of skills that teach self-regulation, emotion management, problem solving, communication skills and friend-ship skills to aim at the decrease of bullying and cyberbullying.

The Escape Room is defined as a closed scenario in which one or a group of students solve riddles in a given time in order to get out [5]. An educational lesson can be created through playful teaching methods and processes, such as narratives that teach children how to cope with certain situations and develop bullying awareness. These methods and the choice of topics make it possible to interrelate various educational content and subjects [6].

The aim of this paper is to propose the use of a Digital Escape Room as immersive game in which participants are locked in a room and must solve a series of puzzles to escape. In virtuality these types of games have also increased interest in the educational field as a learning tool to transform students from passive spectators to active participants. Immersive learning allows students to learn about a topic while practicing teamwork and communication [7, 8].

The main objective of this paper is to describe a proposal based on an Escape Room strategy to prevent and raise awareness of aggressive behaviors among students in a virtual environment and that can also contribute in the return to face-to-face.

The design begins with the creation of a storyboard of a series of scenarios that present real experiences of students. Each scenario contains a short creative video and activities are created based on its content to raise awareness about cyberbullying, its effects and how we can all help prevent it.

2 Background

Cyberbullying can take place on messaging platforms, social networks or gaming platforms. For example, posting embarrassing photos or videos of someone on social networks, sending hurtful lies or spreading abusive or threatening messages, images or videos through messaging platforms. Typically, offenders impersonate someone and send malicious messages to others in their name or through fake accounts [9].

One way to prevent these practices is by creating awareness on the same social and messaging platforms through the use of short videos based on the principles of microlearning. Which is understood as a learning perspective oriented to the fragmentation of didactic contents, of short duration, to be visualized at any time and place [10].

These didactic contents that are used virtually can be disseminated through educational capsules, which are tools that provide information on a specific topic using multimedia resources of very limited duration (images, text, voice, video) [11].

These types of tools seek to change the paradigm in the learning process, since a structured message with clear objectives is transmitted at specific times and in specific situations, allowing meaningful learning that generates an imprint in the collective ideology of a society [12].

But it is not enough to simply post them on social networks and wait for them to be seen, it is necessary to articulate these educational capsules with some other learning activity and that is why in this research we propose the design of an Escape Room in which these resources are integrated with other activities that leave a memory or emotional impact [13, 14].

3   Method

This research has an exploratory approach in order to design and validate an Escape Room to raise awareness about bullying and cyberbullying to students between 10 and 15 years old. The research activities were conducted in two Latin American countries, Ecuador and Colombia. The participants, instruments and the process that was carried out are detailed below.

3.1   Participants

We recruited 12 students studying digital design and multimedia at the Universidad Tecnológica Indoamérica, who developed the storyboards and videos. Three psychologists also participated and validated the microlearning content of the videos. Finally, three Gamification experts, two from Colombia and one from Ecuador, contributed with the design of the activities and the integration of all the elements in the Escape Room.

3.2   Materials and Instruments

Two types of resources were used in the research, the first oriented to collect information for the design of the storyboard of videos and one form to validate the microlearning content. The second resources were used in the implementation of the Escape Room, between them, Genially, video editors and interactive technological tools.

3.3   Procedure

The research was carried out in the following four phases: State of the art, design of educational resources, implementation of the Escape room and expert validation. In the first phase, a search for campaigns based on microlearning and technological tools to help prevent bullying and cyberbullying was carried out.

In the second phase, some ideas and inputs were taken to create the educational capsules, for which three working sessions were organized with a psychologist, an expert in audiovisual design and the 12 students of the Digital Design and Multimedia career to coordinate the construction of 6 educational capsules. The microlearning content of these videos was validated by psychologists before being used. Table 1 gives an example of the storyboard of the video.

Table 1. Example of the storyboard of videos.

No.	Scenery	Video	Audio	Text
1	**Place**: school playground **Time**: mid-morning **Atmosphere**: sunny **Attire**: P1-offender (leader of group of 8-year-olds in school uniforms) P2-victim (8-year-old girl, with intellectual disability, attends regular school with an educational inclusion program; she is with school heater)	**P1** in challenging position in the center of the playground together with the team of partners, forming a circle **P2** in the center of the circle, the girl is subdued	**P1** if you take off your shirt I'll give you a pacifier **P2** I don't want to, I can't **P1** you can't because you're dumb **P2** I can	The video will have the subtitles with the text of the audios
2	Place: Same place	**P1** claps her hands and makes her victim sweep, defiant behavior and mocking laughter **P2** the girl feels challenged and starts doing what her peers tell her to do	**P1** you are going to take off your T-shirt and shorts I bet you can't either **P2** I can do everything **P1** do you want the pacifier? **P2** I do **P1** Then hurry up and take off all your clothes **P2** yes I'm coming and give me the pacifier	

In the third phase, the three experts in Gamification designed the storytelling, activities and challenges for the Digital Escape Room. The audience considered in the design was the aggressor, the victim and the observer. That is, the content of the capsules and activities leave a message for the three types of roles that could be had in the Escape Room.

In the fourth phase, a form was used to comprehensively validate the Escape Room by three psychologists. The following section shows the results of the design and validation.

4   Results

As part of the search carried out in the first phase, several resources and campaigns were found that use microlearning to build educational capsules to prevent cyberbulling [15]. For example, leading short-form mobile video platform TikTok, launched #CreateKindness[1], a global campaign that reinforces TikTok's commitment to eliminating online bullying and harassment and building a welcoming and supportive community. This campaign kicks off the delivery of a series of creative videos, featuring real and personal experiences from TikTok creators and animators, to raise awareness about cyberbullying, its effects and how we can all help prevent it.

Educational resources based on microlearnig and gamification were also found, among them: Stop Bullying[2] a portable Escape Room for schools, where students learn to fight against child bullying in an original and fun way. The resource can adapt the difficulty of the activities according to the age of the students, who through team play are made aware of the importance of eradicating child bullying.

A resource was found on Genially with the Spanish name "El acoso escolar, un enemigo silencioso (Bullying, a silent enemy)"[3], designed by Xiomara Pedreros. The educational resource integrates short videos that explain the meaning of bullying and the difference with pranks. It contains scenarios of a school, and each scenario has a video, a playful activity and a reflective message.

Taking these ideas and the Genially template, a narrative was adapted based on the story of Carito, an intellectually disabled and visually impaired girl who lost her glasses and who is being bullied at school. The narrative takes place in a school that has six scenarios, where each scenario has a video and challenges. The challenges are based on helping Carito find her glasses with clues hidden in the lockers, the playground, basketball court, classroom and and at home by means of cellular phone messages. Exploration, logic and deduction come into play so that participants can help her. The activities in the designed scenes are detailed below. The Fig. 1 shows the Escape Room main scene and the school corridor where the story begins.

The Fig. 2 shows the staging of the storyboard of Table 1 in which Carito is harassed by a group of children. In addition, a scene is presented on a basketball court in which children who have physical or visual difficulties in exercising are mocked.

The privileged scenario in which bullying dynamics take place corresponds to the educational space, mainly classrooms, during class hours, in some cases with the presence of teachers but without adequate interventions. In other cases, it occurs without the presence of the teacher or when they are alone using mobile devices. The Fig. 3 shows these two scenarios.

---

[1] https://newsroom.tiktok.com/es-es/tiktok-lanza-createkindness-fomentar-la-solidaridad-onl ine-luchar-contra-cyberbullying.

[2] https://www.playduca.com/stop-bullying.

[3] https://view.genial.ly/5f590bd51835080da96a0217/game-breakout-el-acoso-escolar-un-ene migo-silencioso.

Fig. 1. Escape Room main scene and the school corridor where the story begins.

Fig. 2. Scenes at the playground and basketball court

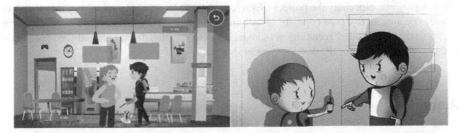

Fig. 3. Scenes of bulling at classroom and cyberbullying by mobile devices

The validation of the Escape Room was carried out by three psychologists through a form containing questions related to the narratives, the videos presented and the activities. The three experts agree that the Escape room will help to generate greater awareness than just watching videos, since by playing they live a digital experience. In relation to the narrative, they consider that by telling the story of a girl with an intellectual disability, a very complex and little studied issue is addressed.

Finally, they agree that the design of the scenarios are in line with the target age group. The selected template has colorful and attractive graphics; as well as the musical backgrounds and sounds of the Escape Room allow to generate that emotional impact.

5   Conclusions

An Escape Room was designed with a narrative to raise awareness about bullying and cyberbullying through experience and emotions. As a tool, it focused on developing challenges and activities to help education professionals increase interactivity and emotional engagement in their classrooms. Through the Escape Room game, it is intended to raise awareness among students between the ages of 10 to 15 about the importance of eradicating bullying and cyberbullying.

The results of the experts indicate that the Escape Room is a different alternative to understand the problems derived from bullying and cyberbullying. Teaching the basic concepts and scenarios in a school leads to the analysis of a complex circle of school violence among peers. The violation of other rights and the possibility that the same individual goes from aggressor to victim, or vice versa, are manifestations of this problem that involves different situations, spaces, actors and perspectives.

The main forms of harassment of which students are victims, especially those with disabilities, correspond to those of a verbal and psychological nature, expressed through insults and offensive nicknames, the spreading of rumors or the disclosure of secrets, in addition to the sending of threatening or insulting messages, especially through social networks. Along with these, there are cases of theft of belongings, mainly school supplies or personal objects.

In the future, we plan to carry out an intervention with students from Ecuador and Colombia to evaluate the impact left by the Escape Room.

Acknowledgments. The authors would like to thank the Coorporación Ecuatoriana para el Desarrollo de la Investigación y Academia- CEDIA for their contribution in innovation, through the CEPRA projects, especially the project CEPRA-XVI-2022-04, "Implementación y despliegue de cápsulas de aprendizaje para combatir el bullying y el ciberbullying en niños, niñas y adolescentes"; also the Universidad Tecnológica Indoamérica, Universidad de Cuenca and Universidad del Azuay for the support for the development of this work.

References

1. Collins, T.A., Dart, E.H., Arora, P.G.: Addressing the internalizing behavior of students in schools: applications of the MTSS model. Sch. Ment. Heal. **11**(2), 191–193 (2019). https://doi.org/10.1007/s12310-018-09307-9
2. Epelde-Larrañaga, A., Oñederra Ramírez, J.A., Estrada-Vidal, L.I.: Music as a resource against bullying and cyberbullying: intervention in two centers in Spain. Sustainability **12**, 2057 (2020). https://doi.org/10.3390/su12052057
3. Chacón-Castro, M., Aimacaña-Espinosa, L., Jadán-Guerrero, J.: Escape rooms: mathematical challenges available to educators. In: Mesquita, A., Abreu, A., Carvalho, J.V. (eds.) Perspectives and Trends in Education and Technology. SIST, vol. 256, pp. 195–205. Springer, Singapore (2022). https://doi.org/10.1007/978-981-16-5063-5_16
4. Adams, V., et al.: Can you escape? Creating an escape room to facilitate active learning. J. Nurses Prof. Dev. **34**(2), 1–5 (2018)
5. Veldkamp, A., et al.: Escape education: a systematic review on escape rooms in education. Educ. Res. Rev. **31**, 100364 (2020)
6. Nicholson, S.: Peeking behind the locked door: a survey of escape room facilities. White Paper (2015). http://scottnicholson.com/pubs/erfacwhite.pdf
7. Sowell, M.: Incorporating curriculum content into educational escape games for middle school students. Clearing House: J. Educ. Strat. Issues Ideas **94**(2), 47–52 (2021)

8. Ambrožová, P., Kaliba M.: Online escape games as an educational tool (2021). https://doi.org/10.21125/iceri.2021.1353
9. Edwards, A., Demoll, D., Edwards, L.: Detecting cyberbullying activity across platforms. In: Latifi, S. (ed.) 17th International Conference on Information Technology–New Generations (ITNG 2020). AISC, vol. 1134, pp. 45–50. Springer, Cham (2020). https://doi.org/10.1007/978-3-030-43020-7_7
10. Khlaif, Z.N., Salha, S.: Using TikTok in education: a form of micro-learning or nano-learning? Interdiscip. J. Virtual learn. Med. Sci. **12**(3), 213–218 (2021)
11. Jameel Aburizaizah, S., Abdulaziz Albaiz, T.: Review of the use and impact of nano-learning in education. In: Proceedings of the 4th International Conference on Research in Education, pp. 17–19 (2021)
12. Gómez, D., Bermeo, A., Prado, D., Cedillo, P.: Microlearning method to building learning capsules for older adults: a case study for COVID-19 prevention at home. In: 2021 IEEE Fifth Ecuador Technical Chapters Meeting (ETCM), pp. 1–6. IEEE (2021). https://doi.org/10.1109/ETCM53643.2021.9590793
13. Marcial, D.E., dela Peña, L., Montemayor, J., Dy, J.: The design of a gamified responsible use of social media. Front. Educ. **6**, 635278 (2021). https://doi.org/10.3389/feduc.2021.635278
14. Navas, E., Armedariz, S.: Interactive application with motion comics in the school bullying awareness process. Perspectives and Trends in Education and Technology, International Conference in Information Technology & Education (ICITED 2022) (2023)
15. Jadán-Guerrero, J., Bermeo, A., Cedillo, P., Nunes, I.: Helping kids and teens deal with Cyberbullying through informative learning capsule. In: 13th International Conference on Applied Human Factors and Ergonomics (AHFE 2022), Human Factors and Systems Interaction, AHFE Open Acces (2022). https://doi.org/10.54941/ahfe1002176

A Study of a System that Reduces the Burden of Expressing Opinions by Gradually Changing the Face of the Dialogue Partner

Yuichi Morioka[✉], Kenro Go, Kazunori Kojima, and Masato Furuno

SoftBank Corp., Tokyo, Japan
`yuichi.morioka@g.softbank.co.jp`

Abstract. When the relationship between users is shallow, it is considered to be a mental burden to deny the opinions of the other party or to express one's requests. In order to reduce this burden, systems such as anonymous messaging systems can be used. However, it is likely to remain difficult to express opinions in situations where these systems cannot be used. In order to solve this problem, we make a hypothesis that characteristics in which users are able to feel intimacy for interlocutor enable users to express their opinions to the interlocutor. Based on this hypothesis, we propose a system that reduces the burden of expressing one's opinion by replacing the user identification information such as a face with other information, then gradually restoring it according to the depth of the relationship. In this system, the user feels familiar replaces it with a part of the information for user identification among the information of the dialogue partners. This system is expected to enable users to express their opinions to a certain extent even to those with whom users have a relatively short relationship. In this paper, as an initial study of this research, we report on the construction of a chat system that focuses on faces, synthesizes the faces of the other party and the user, and restores the original information to the other party's face step by step as the user communicates with each other.

1 Introduction

In order to increase employee motivation and improve trust among employees the activation of internal communication is recommended. It is considered that communication between users is important to prevent solitary deaths, not only in the company but also in private life. However, the burden of expressing opinions depends on the relationship between users. It is particularly difficult to express opinions to the user whose relationship is shallow. For Example, it is difficult to propose a new idea to a superior in a section to which you have just been assigned.

It is also difficult to point out inconsistencies to new colleagues during the meeting with their new colleagues whom users have just gotten to know. Communication deepens the relationship between users. However, it became difficult due to the spread of the coronavirus.

© The Author(s), under exclusive license to Springer Nature Switzerland AG 2022
C. Stephanidis et al. (Eds.): HCII 2022, CCIS 1654, pp. 654–661, 2022.
https://doi.org/10.1007/978-3-031-19679-9_83

2 Related Work

There are many studies to support communication between users whose relationship is shallow, due to the first meet or different position. Marshmallow [1] is one of the systems which allows to anonymously express an opinion to the user. In this method, users do not directly communicate with each other. The user who receives a message replies to the received message during the video streaming or on their own SNS. Taga et al. [2] proposed a system that allows to anonymously express opinions of positive/negative during the meeting by making a gesture with their feet wearing the slippers. This proposed method is effective for increasing the number of positive/negative opinions expressed. Abe et al. [3] proposed a web application system that enables anonymously express the opinion of agreement/disagreement/opinions during the Meeting. This system is effective in decreasing the time of silence and facilitating communication among participants during a meeting. These systems allow opinions to be expressed anonymously. Therefore it facilitates expressing one's own opinion even to those with whose the relationship is shallow.

3 Research Goal

It seems that existing research facilitates the expression of their own opinions. However, there are some problems. First, there are restrictions on what can be expressed. In the methods of Taga et al. [2] and Abe et al. [3], the participants can only express their approval or disapproval of the opinions of others, and it is difficult to express specific opinions such as reasons for their approval. Second, even if the continuous use of the system increases the number of communications between users, there is a danger that communication may become impossible without the system. In the existing studies, the use of the system enables the participants to express their opinions to some extent during ad hoc communication. However, it is difficult to encourage all communicators to use the system in each communication, therefore it is difficult that users will be able to express their opinions in situations where the system is not available. Based on the above, we propose the construction of a system for expressing opinions that satisfies the following requirements.

1. Enable users to express their opinions.
2. Enable users to express their opinions without the system finally.

4 Proposed Method

In order to accomplish the research problem described in Sect. 2, we hypothesized that users would be more likely to express their opinions to some extent if users can find characteristics that make users feel familiar even with people with whom users do not have a deep relationship. Based on this hypothesis, we propose a system that reduces the burden on users when users express their opinions by replacing the information for user identification with something else and restoring it step by step according to the depth of the relationship. This system replaces some of the user identification information, such as face and voice, with information that is more familiar to the person expressing the opinion and restores the replaced information to the original information like the relationship between the users deepens. This system is expected to enable users to express their opinions to some extent, even to those with whom users have a shallow relationship. Finally, it is possible to communicate with a person without the system. This is because the interlocutor in the system will have a similar identification same as the original user. Although this system is still in the conceptual stage, we have focused on the fact that people are likely to feel a familiarity with people who look like themselves [4]. In Fig. 1, when users communicate with each other for the first time, the chat face of the interlocutor is replaced with a composite of the faces of the person expressing the opinion and the person with whom the user is communicating. The more the relationship between the users deepens, the closer the substituted face becomes to the face of the interlocutor. Finally, it is restored to the original face of the interlocutor.

This system is intended to be installed in SNS and videoconferencing systems where people can express their opinions anonymously or non-anonymously. As described above, we assume that the information to be substituted by the Interlocutor is a face of the part or whole of the face, or the voice, etc. As characteristics that we synthesize to the interlocutor, we assumed a person who expresses an opinion, a third person, a robot, an animated character, etc.

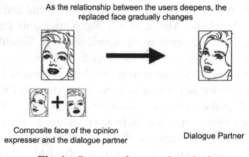

As the relationship between the users deepens, the
replaced face gradually changes

Composite face of the opinion
expresser and the dialogue partner

Dialogue Partner

Fig. 1. Concept of proposal method

5   Implementation

Figure 2 shows a diagram of the implemented system. We implemented the proposed chat system as a mobile application. The user registers their photos as a profile image on the system. We will clarify the best appropriate by constructing a prototype system. We assigned an individual User ID to each user. After registering a photo of the user, we register the user IDs of users other than the user themselves on the system (hereinafter referred to as "friend registration"), thereby linking users together.

In this chat system, the name and the profile image of the chat partner are different for the receiver and the sender of the chat. In order to ensure the anonymity of the sender, we change the name and profile picture of the sender to fictitious ones, therefore the recipient of the chat cannot identify the sender (Fig. 3). On the other hand, the sender side of the chat displays the name of the chat partner and the profile image generated by the proposed method. We use a profile image of the own user and the profile image of the target user who registered as a friend, then the composite images are displayed using Style-GAN [5] (Fig. 4). It is necessary to verify whether this value is appropriate for reducing the burden of communication with the other user. On the side of the sender, the displayed profile image of the chat partner changes with each chat exchange. For each message sent by the user in the chat, the percentage of the composite image of the user is gradually decreased, while the percentage of the composite image of the interaction partner is gradually increased. The final result is 0% for the user and 100% for the interlocutor (Fig. 5).

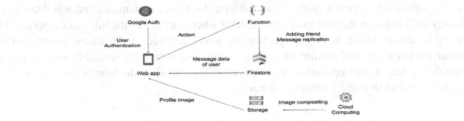

Fig. 2. System configuration

Fig. 3. Screen of receiver.   **Fig. 4.** Screen of sender.

Fig. 5. The transition of restoring the composited face by over and over communication

6 Experiment

In order to verify the effectiveness of the proposed method, it is necessary to verify whether the proposed method enables to reduce the psychological burden of communicating opinion to a person with whom the user does not feel familiar and whether there is any difference in the impression of the user when the face of the interaction partner is combined with that of the original partner, even when the face of the interaction partner is returned to the original partner. In this paper, as a first step of the research, we examined the difference in the impression of each synthesis ratio when the face of the own user is synthesized to that of a conversation partner.

6.1 Experimental Conditions

The experimental participants in this research are 3 males. In the experiment, the figures in Fig. 6 is the composite ingredient of the face of the participants. We use Style-Gan [5] for generating the Fig. 6. We combined the faces of the person in Fig. 6 with the face of the experiment collaborator at 10% intervals from 0–100%. Hereafter we referred to Man 1–0 to Man 1–10 and Female 2–0 to Female 2–10.

Fig. 6. Composite ingredient of the face of the participants.

6.2 Experimental Procedure

We asked the participants to identify Man 1–0 to Man 1–10 and Female 2–0 to Female 2–10. Each time participants check it once, we asked for a response to the questionnaire shown in Table A on a 5-point Likert scale (5: I feel very much to 1: I don't feel at all). It was random to cancel out the order effect, the order in which we asked the participants to identify Man 1–0 to Man 1–10 and Female 2–0 to Female 2–10. After having the participants check all of Man 1–0 to Man 1–10 and Female 2–0 to Female 2–10 and answer for Q1–Q4, ask participants to recheck Man 1–0 to Man 1–10 and Female 2–0 to Female 2–10 again.

Q1: Did you feel familiar with the person in the photo?
Q2: Did you feel that you would like to engage in a dialogue with the person in the photo?
Q3: Did you feel comfortable with the person in the photo?
Q4: Did you feel you could trust the person in the photo?
Q5: Please indicate the person with whom you feel most familiar.
Q6: Please indicate the person with whom you would most like to have a dialogue.
Q7: Please indicate the person with whom you felt most comfortable.
Q8: Please indicate the person you felt most trustworthy.

6.3 Experimental Result and Consideration

For Q1–Q4, the median responses for Male 1–0 to Male 1–10 and Female 2–0 to Female 2–10 are shown in Figs. 7, 8, 9 and 10. In terms of Q1, the score of the Likert scale of Male 1–3, Male 1–7, and Male 1–8 was high when compositing left of Fig. 6 with the face of participants, and the score was equivalent except Female 2–8 when compositing right of Fig. 6 with the face of participants. In terms of Q2, the score of Male 1–3, Male 1–8, and Male 1–10 was high when compositing left of Fig. 6 with the face of participants, and the score was equivalent except Female 2–4, Female 2–8, and Female 2–10 when compositing right of Fig. 6 with the face of participants. In terms of Q3, the score of Male 1–3, Male 1–7, Male 1–9, and Male 1–10 was high when compositing left of Fig. 6 with the face of participants, and the score of Female 2–2, and Female 2–7 was high when compositing right of Fig. 6 with the face of participants. In terms of Q4, the score of Male 1–6 to Male 1–10 was high when compositing left of Fig. 6 with the face of participants, and all score was equivalent when compositing right of Fig. 6 with the face of participants. From the experiment results, the score of Male 1–7 to Male 1–10 were high when compositing the face of the participants with the male in terms of Q1 to Q4. Therefore the result suggests the possibility that users feel more familiar when compositing the element of the face of the participant with the face of the other person. In terms of Q1 to Q4, the score of Female 2–7 to Female 2–8 was a high score when compositing with the face of females. Therefore, same as the males the result suggests the possibility that users feel more familiar when compositing the element of the face of the participant with the face of the other person. In terms of Q5 to Q8, participants selected Male 1–6 and Female 2–7. Therefore it is possibly effective to composite more elements of the face of the other person than the face of the user. We conduct an interview with the experiment participant in order to consider the reason. Experiment participants answered that when compositing the higher ratio of the face of the user than the other person, participants felt strange due to users regarded the composited face as themselves. On the other hand, experiment participants answered that when compositing the lower ratio of the face of the user than the other user, participants regarded the composited face as trustful. This is because participants recognized the composited face as another person, then participants felt familiar from the common elements of the composited face. From the above, we suggest the possibility to reduce the burden of expressing one's opinion even against the first meet or different position, using the system which replaces the face of the interlocutor to the composited face with user and interlocutor, whose compositing ratio restores from which user unable to regard as own face to original.

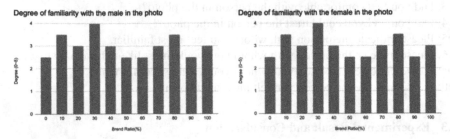

Fig. 7. The results of Q1 (N = 3).

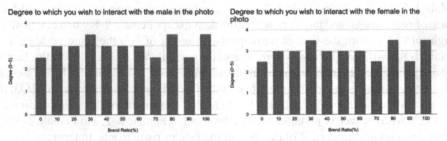

Fig. 8. The results of Q2 (N = 3).

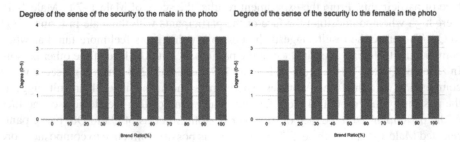

Fig. 9. The results of Q3 (N = 3).

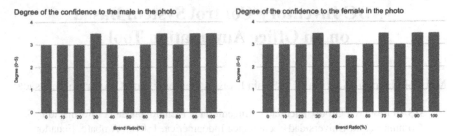

Fig. 10. The results of Q4 (N = 3).

7 Conclusion

Conclusion In this research, we suggested a system that gradually restores the face of the interlocutor from the face that is composited with the user, depending on the relationship progression, in order to reduce the psychological burden to express one's opinion to the first meeting and people whom the user is bad at dealing with. In this paper, we examined how much blending ratio is appropriate when our proposal system composes the user face to the interlocutor at the first stage. The result suggests the possibility of willingness to talk by composing the user face to the interlocutor, and the composition ratio of the face of the user was from 30 to 40%. In the future, based on this experiment, we are going to implement a communication system, then examine the usefulness of the proposed method in the dialogue.

References

1. Marshmallow. https://marshmallow-qa.com. Last visited 04 Oct 2021
2. Taga, R., Go, K., Tominaga, S., Miyata, A.: A study of anonymous feedback system using slippers. In: Proceedings of the DICOMO 2018, vol. 2018, pp. 427–431 (2018)
3. Abe, K., Tsukidate, T., Kuwamiya, Y., Kobayashi, M.: Proposal for a button to visualize feelings to support meeting facilitation. In: Proceedings of the DICOMO 2021, pp. 774–783 (2021)
4. Laeng, B., Vermeer, O., Sulutvedt, U.: Is beauty in the face of the beholder? PLoS ONE **8**, 774–783 (2013)
5. Karras, T., Laine, S., Aila, T.: A style-based generator architecture for generative adversarial networks. In: Proceedings of the IEEE Conference on Computer Vision and Pattern Recognition, pp. 4401–4410 (2019)

ABC Inventory Control System Based on an Office Automation Tool

Marisol Naranjo-Mantilla[1]([✉]), Sònia Llorens Cervera[2], and Guillermo Tenesaca[1]

[1] SISAu Research Group, Facultad de Ingeniería y Tecnologías de la Información y la Comunicación, Universidad Tecnológica Indoamérica, 180103 Ambato, Ecuador
onaranjo@indoamerica.edu.ec

[2] Fundació Tecnocampus Mataró-Maresme, Universitat Pompeu Fabra, Barcelona, España

Abstract. Inventory management concerns most companies, whatever their size and the sector of their activity. This concern is mainly due to avoiding delays in deliveries. Therefore, inventories must be well managed with an automated system to define the goods to be ordered. The ABC inventory classification method comes from the Pareto rule. This is used to segment and organize products in a warehouse based on unit cost, inventory value, turnover, and value. In this work, an inventory control system is carried out to adequately determine the stock of merchandise for a distributor of automotive parts using an office automation tool. An application-type methodology was modified. The techniques used were data collection in situ, information classification, and processing through functions. The application of this method is based on an office automation tool focused on spreadsheets that allow creating data tables and performing operations in an orderly manner for the ABC classification method. The inventory control system is managed through a user interface made up of hyperlinks in the form of buttons. In the results, the segmentation of products was obtained according to the established criteria, unit cost, and the annual volume demanded. Where the items with rotation A reach 20% of the inventories, but they are the ones that experience the most rotation and, therefore, have a strategic importance, since they generate 80% of the income, being a priority to avoid out of stock. Items with turnover B represent 22% of inventories and are renewed less quickly. The set of articles with rotation C, represents 58% of the stored references; however, they are the least demanded by customers. With the application of the ABC inventory system, the correct classification and distribution of merchandise in the warehouse was modified, rationally managing its inventories, and identifying those with the highest demand, therefore, higher turnover.

Keywords: Office automation tool · ABC method of inventory management · Control system · Stocks

1 Introduction

The ABC inventory control method, also called the 80/20 rule or Pareto is a tool that allows the company to visualize and determine the best-selling items [3].

C. Stephanidis et al. (Eds.): HCII 2022, CCIS 1654, pp. 662–666, 2022.
https://doi.org/10.1007/978-3-031-19679-9_84

The tool groups the materials into three categories: a, where are the articles that represent 80% of the analysis variable; B, in which 15% is found; and C, which includes the less important articles, concentrating on them only 5% [5]. In many cases, the data can be stochastic [10]. The ABC inventory analysis methodology takes general steps in operational or financial management: information processing, ordering of information, finding percentages of demand, and finding items type A, B, C [1].

The multi-criteria ABC inventory, differs between the classification criteria but is common between the inventory items and follows a predetermined scheme of descending order with respect to the relative importance of classification criteria [7]. All stock management is based on the most real knowledge possible of the demand [2]. The ABC inventory classification in which the inventory is classified based on the objective of cost minimization [8]. This method can make maintenance work more efficient by focusing on the most critical components and can reduce administrative costs for companies [6]. The availability of good quality stock, in the right quantity, at the right place, at the right time, and at the right cost is the essence of inventory control [9].

The proposed model can be easily adapted to the industrial requirement of inventory classification by target cost, as well as other measures of inventory management performance [8]. The data is compiled in Excel and subsequently processed by statistical methods [4]. One of the common methods for classifying inventory items is the ABC classification approach.

2 Materials and Methods

In this section, the materials and methodology used in the development of the research study are presented. The materials and tools used are listed, and then the methods of the inventory system are stated.

2.1 Materials

For the development of this inventory control system proposal, an office automation tool, Microsoft Excel software is used, where the information is transferred. Data tables are created to carry out the operations in an orderly manner. A user interface is designed consisting of hyperlinks in the form of buttons on the cover of the Excel workbook.

2.2 Method

The research method used is based on a case study. The analysis unit is a trading company whose line of business is the marketing of automotive parts.

The first stage consisted of the deductive part, where the pertinent literature on the dynamics of inventory management systems and inventory models was reviewed, as well as the relationship between them.

The second stage was dedicated to obtaining information; unstructured interviews were carried out, with the participation of managers, warehouse managers, and operational sales personnel of the organization, whose work activities were directly related to inventory management within the organization of the company. This activity made it possible to determine the groups of items to be categorized in the inventory system.

The third stage refers to the initial survey of the inventory taking data and information of the articles that are kept in the company, and the count was carried out to establish the number of units on hangers, warehouse, and warehouse shelves. The data was recorded on sheets calculation.

The fourth stage was rooted in data verification, contrasting the information collected with documents such as item records, item requisition, and validation with those responsible for inventory management.

The fifth stage was aimed at classifying the information and processing the data using Excel functions to design the ABC inventory control model, where the classification was made by unit cost, the total value of the inventory, and use and value.

And finally, in the sixth stage, a user interface made up of hyperlinks in the form of buttons was created, and shortcuts were created that allow jumping from one location to another in the Excel workbook or the document stored on a network server, an intranet, is opened or internet.

3 Results

This section presents the results obtained from the validated inventory of the automotive distribution company, the list of items was made with the name of each item, the cost per half-yearly average unit, the half-yearly average units sold, and the value of sales per semester, which according to the inventory model is known as use and value. From these data, the classification by categories A, B, C was obtained.

In the classification of the ABC inventory model, by use and value, the following data was reached. These are included in Table 1.

Table 1. Classification of the ABC inventory model, by use and value.

ABC Classification				
Category	N° Items	% Category	Costs USD.	% Costs
A	14	20.00%	$ 9,808.12	79.27%
B	15	21.43%	$ 2,085.31	15.58%
C	41	58.57%	$ 641.80	5.15%
Total	70	100%	$ 12,535.22	100%

Figure 1 shows the percentage of use and value, fulfilling the Pareto rule where 20% of the articles classified in category A correspond to 80% by use and value.

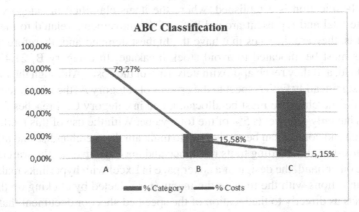

Fig. 1. Pareto analysis with the ABC category and the costs by use and value.

The interface on the front page of the Excel workbook was designed with hyperlinked interface buttons to make it easy to find the items available in the store (Fig. 2).

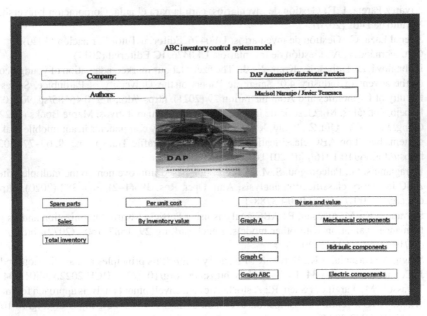

Fig. 2. Front page of the interface in Excel with hyperlinks

4 Conclusions

When carrying out the design of the inventory control system for the trading company, an ABC classification is established, where the items classified in category A, reach 20% of the total and represent around 80% of the movements related to the products costs, that is, they are the ones that have the highest demand and, therefore, resources and efforts must be allocated to avoid stock breakage. In category B, 21.43% of the items are held, and they reach approximately 16% of the costs. Although the importance decreases significantly with respect to the articles of category A, the investment required to supply the merchandise must be allocated, and in category C, it reaches 59% of the references but only represents 5% of the total value. With the use of this method, better organization and control can be carried out to maintain the merchandise and allocate the required investment according to its relevance and the objectives of the warehouse.

On the other hand, the design of a cover page in Excel with hyperlinks makes it easy to carry out actions with the links in the menu, it is selected by clicking on the button, and it directs us directly to the location of the specified sheet or document that we want to consult or update, this allows you to work in a non-sequential way on the electronic document.

References

1. Álvarez Pareja, L.F.: Gestión de inventarios: cartilla para el aula. Corporación Universitaria Minuto de Dios (2020)
2. Arenal Laza, C.: Gestión de inventarios: UF0476. Editorial Tutor Formación (2020)
3. Cruz Fernández, A.: Gestión de inventarios. UF0476. IC Editorial (2017)
4. Dohnalová, Z., Dobeš, K., Kramoliš, J.: The czech labour market: adaptation of young people to the advent of industry 4.0. Scientific Papers of the University of Pardubice, Series D: Faculty of Economics and Administration 29 (2021). https://doi.org/10.46585/sp29021062
5. Espejo González, M.: Gestión de inventarios: métodos cuantitativos. Marge Books (2022)
6. Gong, J., Luo, Y., Qiu, Z., Wang, X.: Determination of key components in automobile braking systems based on ABC classification and FMECA. J. Traffic Transp. Eng. **9**, 69–77 (2022). https://doi.org/10.1016/j.jtte.2019.01.008
7. Karagiannis, G., Paleologou, S.M.: A regression-based improvement to the multiple criteria ABC inventory classification analysis. Ann. Oper. Res. **306**(1–2), 369–382 (2020). https://doi.org/10.1007/s10479-020-03788-1
8. Selvaraju, K., Murugesan, P.: ABC analysis using Particle Swarm Optimization and its performance evaluation with other models. Benchmarking **29**, 1587–1605 (2022). https://doi.org/10.1108/BIJ-11-2020-0594
9. Singh, A., Rasania, S.K., Barua, K.: Inventory control: its principles and application. Indian J. Community Health **34**, 14–19 (2022). https://doi.org/10.47203/IJCH.2022.v34i01.004
10. Tavassoli, M., Farzipoor Saen, R.: A stochastic data envelopment analysis approach for multi-criteria ABC inventory classification. J. Ind. Prod. Eng. 1–15 (2022). https://doi.org/10.1080/21681015.2022.2037761

Applying the Shinayakana Systems Approach to the Design of Software in a Sustainability Context

Nicolás Martín Obesio, Mariana Lilley(iD), and Andrew Pyper(✉)

Department of Computer Science, University of Hertfordshire, Hertfordshire AL10 9AB, UK
a.r.pyper@herts.ac.uk

Abstract. There is a burgeoning interest in supporting Small and Medium Enterprises (SMEs) in reducing their total emissions through accounting, reporting, and target setting. As part of the work reported here, a software prototype named Klima that provides greenhouse gas emissions accounting, reporting, and target setting capabilities was designed, implemented and evaluated. An important aspect of the design and development work involved selecting a model to support users in completing the target setting task. The Shinayakana Systems Approach [5, 7, 8] was applied to the design of the prototype's Decision-Support System (DSS).

The prototype was evaluated by six usability experts. The usability evaluation of the software prototype employed a combination of qualitative (think-aloud) and quantitative (after-scenario questionnaire) methods. Findings from the evaluation were positive overall, and taken to indicate that the Shinayakana Systems Approach is a suitable framework for tackling complex problems such as setting emission reduction targets.

Keywords: Usability study · Shinayakana Systems Approach

1 Introduction

Klima is a software prototype aimed at supporting Small and Medium Enterprises (SMEs) in reducing their total emissions through accounting, reporting, and target setting. Klima's functional requirements were derived from two guides on greenhouse gases measuring and reporting published by the Department for Environment, Food and Rural Affairs [2, 3]. The main functional requirements identified were:

1. Allow users to identify emissions-releasing activities inside their organization;
2. Allow users to periodically upload activity data for their organization;
3. Allow users to generate yearly emissions report for their organization;
4. Allow users to generate absolute emissions reduction targets for their organization.

Klima aims to provide a visual and interactive Decision Support System (DSS) to facilitate target setting (functional requirement 4, above). The Shinayakana Systems Approach [5, 7, 8] was applied to the design of the prototype's Decision-Support System (DSS).

C. Stephanidis et al. (Eds.): HCII 2022, CCIS 1654, pp. 667–674, 2022.
https://doi.org/10.1007/978-3-031-19679-9_85

2 Shinayakana Systems Approach

Traditional systemic approaches often seek to describe and solve real life problems using mathematical models and methods. However, one of the limitations of such approaches is that they often fail to capture the entire complexity of reality [8].

The Shinayakana Systems Approach is a soft systems approach that attempts to integrate human judgment with the ability of computers [8]. The approach prioritises human intervention at every step of the problem-solving process. The approach advocates for the use of mathematical models and methods as tools to facilitate decision making, not dictate it.

The Shinayakana Systems Approach aims to marry human perception, judgement, and intuition with mathematical models and methods. Additionally, the Shinayakana Systems Approach holds that problem solving and decision making can be enhanced using mathematical models and methods. It proposes that models should be built interactively by analysts, domain experts, and decision makers [8].

Klima incorporates this notion by seeing SMEs' business owners as both domain experts and decision makers. Therefore, the users' perceptions and expertise are considered at every step of the target setting process as supported via its Decision Support System.

3 Decision Support System Design (DSS)

Although the Shinayakana Systems Approach was first applied to the creation of a "(…) support system to predict environmental problems in the early 21st century in Japan and to find effective policy alternatives" [8], the application of this approach to the design of Decision Support Systems (DSS) in the context of sustainability appears to be under-represented in the literature.

Notwithstanding this, the Shinayakana Systems Approach was identified as a suitable approach for the prototype's Decision Support System (DSS), and key elements of this systemic approach were incorporated in the design of the Klima's DSS for target setting.

As can be seen in Fig. 1, the user is entirely responsible for deciding what target to set. The use of mathematical models and methods is limited to enhancing the user's understanding of the problem. The user's perception and intuition of the problem at hand are highly valued by the DSS.

To help the user decide on an appropriate target, the system provides feedback in the units of measurement that are more understandable to the user. For example, when selecting the desired percentual reduction for vehicle use, Klima provides the absolute reduction in km or miles. By doing this, the intention is to better equip the user in assessing their targets' feasibility. The system also reflects the percentual reduction on the overall emissions output. The aim is to enable the user to extract useful insights about the problem, such as the influence of each activity on the overall emissions, as captured in [8]: "[t]he interaction is essential at the decision stage as well, and it should be dynamical. We quote its reason from Lewandowski and Wierzbicki (1988) that human decision makers typically learn when using a decision support system, and we cannot assume that a decision maker comes to the system with fixed preferences" [8 p. 113].

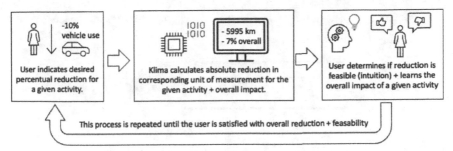

Fig. 1. Klima's Decision Support System Pipeline

From the initial wireframes, the DSS was implemented in the prototype as illustrated in Fig. 2 and 3 below.

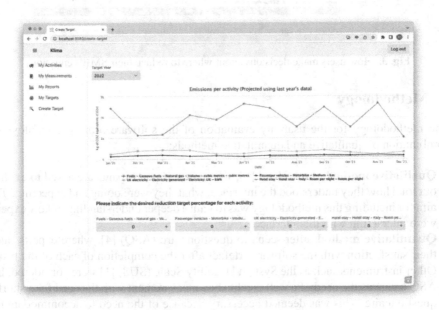

Fig. 2. The DSS chart showing projected emissions for a given year

The prototype provides functionality for SMEs to create their own activities, to log measurements of emissions caused by that activity and generate reports (as specified in functional requirements 1–3). The main point of interest however is in how users may be supported in making decisions about reducing their emissions (functional requirement 4).

Figure 2 and 3 combine to provide a dynamically updated chart view of the changes to projected emissions given the changes that users make. This provides fidelity in what users may change and also insights into the scale of the changes needed. They can then generate the targets for each of the activities that apply to their SME.

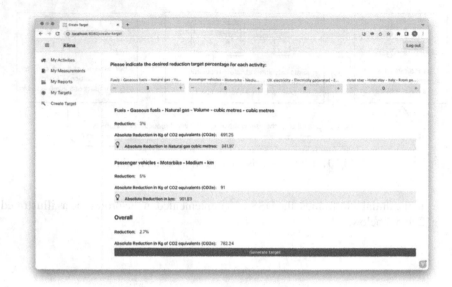

Fig. 3. How users make decisions about where to reduce their SME's emissions

4 Methodology

The methodology for the usability evaluation of the software prototype employed a combination of qualitative and quantitative methods:

- **Qualitative method**: think-aloud [6], where expert participants are asked to explain out loud how they understood the interface, what they were doing and expecting. The aim for including this methodology was to gain a deeper understanding of how experts were interacting with the interface.
- **Quantitative method**: after-scenario questionnaire (ASQ) [4], where experts rated their satisfaction with the software artefact after the completion of each of the tasks. Other instruments such as the System Usability Scale (SUS) [1] were considered, but ASQ balances the need of a well-established measurement with the need for a shorter questionnaire. This was deemed necessary because of the need to accommodate the think-aloud element.

Klima was evaluated by a group of six usability experts. As part of the usability evaluation, each expert was assigned a 45-min slot. All sessions were conducted remotely using Zoom and recorded for later analysis. Experts were asked to engage with four pre-defined tasks using Klima, and complete an ASQ after each task. Tasks and results for each of the tasks are presented next.

5 Results

In this section, a description of each of the four tasks and their results are presented. The combination of the After-Scenario Questionnaire (ASQ) [3] and the think-aloud protocol [6] provided the authors with useful insights. The ASQ provided an efficient and effective way to gauge the system's overall usability by focusing on three aspects: ease of use, time required to complete tasks, and level of support information. The think-aloud protocol provided more in-depth, qualitative insights. These insights informed the analysis of the results from the ASQ.

5.1 Task 1

The description of Task 1 is:

Imagine you are a business owner, and you want to use Klima to track your business's greenhouse gases emissions. The first step is identifying the different emissions-releasing activities conducted in your business. Your task is trying to add 2 or 3 activities.

The ASQ results for Task 1 are presented in Table 1. Statement 2 presented the highest level of satisfaction.

Table 1. ASQ results for Task 1, where 1 = strongly disagree and 7 = strongly agree

Statement	1	2	3	4	5	6	7	Mode	Mean
Overall, I am satisfied with the ease of completing the task in this scenario	0	1	0	1	2	1	1	5	4.8
Overall, I am satisfied with the amount of time it took to complete the task in this scenario	0	0	0	2	1	3	0	6	5.2
Overall, I am satisfied with the support information when completing the task	0	1	1	0	2	1	1	5	4.7

Analysis of the qualitative (think-aloud) data suggest that the lower scores for statements 1 and 2 relate to some participants finding the list of activities to be too long, that activity names are too similar and that multiple attempts are required to find activities using the text filter. It should be noted that the list of activities was based on [2] and [3].

The mode and mean for amount of time required (statement 2) was higher than ease of use (statement 1) and level of support information (statement 3). A potential explanation could be found by looking at the group of participants recruited. All participants are usability experts and, therefore, it is possible they are projecting concerns of an average user (even though these concerns might not be applicable to them).

5.2 Task 2

The description of Task 2 is:

After you identified the different emissions-releasing activities conducted in your business, you would like to upload relevant activity data to help Klima measure your emissions output. For example, if your business consumes electricity out of

the grid, you should periodically upload your electricity consumption in kWh in Klima. In Klima, these are called data measurements. Your task is adding 2 or 3 different measurements to your business's activities.

The ASQ results for Task 2 are presented in Table 2. Most participants agreed with all three statements concerning ease of use, amount of time, and level of support information (mode = 6).

Table 2. ASQ results for Task 2, where 1 = strongly disagree and 7 = strongly agree

Statement	1	2	3	4	5	6	7	Mode	Mean
Overall, I am satisfied with the ease of completing the task in this scenario	0	0	1	0	1	3	1	6	5.5
Overall, I am satisfied with the amount of time it took to complete the task in this scenario	0	0	1	0	0	3	2	6	5.8
Overall, I am satisfied with the support information when completing the task	0	0	1	1	1	2	1	6	5.2

5.3 Task 3

The description of Task 3 is:

After using Klima for a full year, you would like to generate a report describing your total greenhouse emissions for that year. Your task is generating a report for the last year.

The ASQ results for Task 3 are presented in Table 3. This task presented the highest level of participants' satisfaction on ease of use, time required, and amount of information for this task, out of all tasks included in the study (mode = 7 for all statements). Findings from the qualitative (think-aloud) analysis indicate that participants found the graph feature useful and engaging.

Table 3. ASQ results for Task 3, where 1 = strongly disagree and 7 = strongly agree

Statement	1	2	3	4	5	6	7	Mode	Mean
Overall, I am satisfied with the ease of completing the task in this scenario	0	0	0	0	0	1	5	7	6.8
Overall, I am satisfied with the amount of time it took to complete the task in this scenario	0	0	0	0	0	1	5	7	6.8
Overall, I am satisfied with the support information when completing the task	0	0	1	0	1	1	3	7	5.8

5.4 Task 4

The description of Task 4 is:

After using Klima for a full year, you would like to reduce your greenhouse gases emissions by setting a target. Klima aims to facilitate target setting, by providing business owners with an interactive decision support system. Your task is to define a 5% reduction target and obtain some insights on how to achieve it.

Table 4 above summarises the ASQ results for Task 4. Analysis of think-aloud data provide insights into the reasons for the lower scores for statement 1 (some participants expected to find 'Create Target' button inside 'My Targets' page) and statement 3 (some participants wished the overall impact was presented closer to the controls). Notwithstanding this, participants reported that they obtained relevant insights about target setting.

Table 4. ASQ results for Task 4, where 1 = strongly disagree and 7 = strongly agree

Statement	1	2	3	4	5	6	7	Mode	Mean
Overall, I am satisfied with the ease of completing the task in this scenario	0	0	0	2	2	1	1	4	5.2
Overall, I am satisfied with the amount of time it took to complete the task in this scenario	0	0	0	0	4	1	1	5	5.5
Overall, I am satisfied with the support information when completing the task	0	0	1	1	3	0	1	5	4.8

6 Conclusion and Future Work

The work reported here represents an initial study into the use of the Shinayakana Systems Approach within a prototype that aims to support SMEs in understanding their environmental impact, and making decisions about where it can be reduced.

Results from the empirical usability were taken to indicate that expert participants were generally satisfied with the usability of the system. No major usability issues were uncovered during the usability test sessions.

The Decision-Support System (DSS) user interface has room for improvement. Participants were less satisfied with the level of support information provided, as well as the order in which some of the information was presented. Overall, participants were satisfied with the level of interactivity. Importantly, participants reported that they gained useful insights about the problem when using the DSS. This is an important finding, and was taken to indicate that the Shinayakana Systems Approach is a suitable framework for tackling complex problems such as setting emission reduction targets and thus merits further work.

It is planned that the next iteration of work would be a study with participants recruited from SMEs. Involving representative users would provide a basis to investigate the efficacy of the DSS and to better understand the extent to which the Shinayakana Systems Approach improves decision making.

References

1. Brooke, J.: SUS: a retrospective. J. Usability Stud. **8**(2), 29–40 (2013)
2. Department of Environment, Food and Rural Affairs (DEFRA). 2009. Guidelines on how to measure and Report Your Greenhouse Gas Emissions, London: DEFRA, https://www.gov.uk/government/publications/guidance-on-how-to-measure-and-report-your-greenhouse-gas-emissions. Accessed 26 May 2022
3. Department of Environment, Food and Rural Affairs (DEFRA). 2012. Small business user guide: Guidance on how to measure and report your greenhouse gas emissions, London: DEFRA. https://www.gov.uk/government/publications/small-business-user-guide-guidance-on-how-to-measure-and-report-your-greenhouse-gas-emissions. Accessed 26 May 2022
4. Lewis, J.R.: Psychometric evaluation of an after-scenario questionnaire for computer usability studies: the ASQ. ACM Sigchi Bulletin **23**(1), 78–81 (1991)
5. Nakamori, Y., Sawaragi, Y.: Complex systems analysis and environmental modeling. Eur. J. Oper. Res. **122**(2), 178–189 (2000)
6. Nørgaard, M., Hornbæk, K.: What do usability evaluators do in practice? An explorative study of think-aloud testing. In: Proceedings of the 6th Conference on Designing Interactive Systems, pp. 209–218 (2006)
7. Sawaragi, Y., Nakamori, Y.: Shinayakana Systems Approach in Developing an Urban Environment Simulator (1989)
8. Sawaragi, Y., Nakamori, Y.: An interactive system for modeling and decision support–Shinayakana system approach. In: Advances in Methodology and Applications of Decision Support Systems, Collaborative Paper CP-91–17, International Institute for Applied Systems Analysis, Laxenburg, Austria (1991)

Control System Test Platform for a DC Motor

Fernando Saá-Tapia[1]([⊠]) [iD], Luis Mayorga-Miranda[1] [iD], Manuel Ayala-Chauvin[1] [iD],
and Carles Domènech-Mestres[2] [iD]

[1] SISAu Research Group, Facultad de Ingeniería y Tecnologías de la Información y la Comunicación, Universidad Tecnológica Indoamérica, Ambato 180103, Ecuador
{fsaa,lmayorga4,mayala5}@indoamerica.edu.ec
[2] Centro de Diseño de Equipos Industriales, Universitat Politècnica de Catalunya-Barcelona Tech, 08034 Barcelona, Spain
domenech@cdei.upc.edu

Abstract. Currently, control systems are used to improve the behavior of actuators that are part of an equipment or process. However, to enhance their performance, it is necessary to perform tests to evaluate the responses of its operation depending on the type of controller. In this sense, a test platform was developed to compare and optimize the speed control of a DC motor with three types of controllers: Predictive Model Control (MPC), Proportional Integral Derivative (PID) and Fuzzy Logic. Data acquisition was performed using the Arduino MEGA board and LabVIEW software. The mathematical model of the three controllers was developed, taking into account the electrical and physical properties of the DC motor. Through MATLAB IDENT, the state space (SS) and transfer function F(S) equations were generated for the MPC and PID controller, respectively; on the other hand, input/output ranges for the Fuzzy Logic controller were input/output ranges defined by assigning belonging functions and linguistic variables. Experimental tests were carried out with these models under no-load and load. Tests performed in vacuum show that performance index with the motor at 100 rpm results in a PID of 0.2245, a Fuzzy Logic of 0.3212 and an MPC of 0.3576. On the other hand, with load at 100 rpm, a PID of 0.2343, a Fuzzy Logic of 0.3871 and an MPC of 0.3104 were obtained. It was determined that the Fuzzy Logic controller presents a higher over impulse; the PID and MPC have a faster stabilization time and with negligible over impulses. Finally, the MPC controller presents a better performance index analysis according to the Integral Square Error criterion (ISE).

Keywords: Fuzzy Logic · MPC · Modelization · DC motor · PID

1 Introduction

In the last decade, a challenge for researchers in DC motor control has been to implement more efficient and complex algorithms [1], ensuring a dynamic response in industry applications [2].

Many industrial production processes require speed [3] and torque or position control systems [4]. Therefore, DC motors must have high dynamic performance and efficiency

C. Stephanidis et al. (Eds.): HCII 2022, CCIS 1654, pp. 675–682, 2022.
https://doi.org/10.1007/978-3-031-19679-9_86

[5]. In addition, the DC motor control strategy using sensors has gained importance due to the reduction in cost, complexity and maintenance [6].

Test platforms for DC motor control allow experimentally testing the theory of algorithms and comparing different control systems [7]. Some commercial platforms are generally expensive [8], and, in general, industries leave development and innovation to academia. Several alternatives to commercial platforms in the literature, such as Simulink [9] or LabVIEW, are suitable tools for testing control systems [10].

The test platforms for DC motor control allow testing control algorithms to make comparisons that allow understanding their operation and deciding the optimal type according to the industrial problem to be solved. For example, by using the MPC controller, a faster and more accurate response is obtained compared to a PID controller [11], On the other hand, the Fuzzy Logic controller is simpler to implement and does not need high hardware performance [12], obtaining a favorable response to the system, but it is not fast as the MPCs [13].

Our objective was to compare and optimize the speed control of a DC motor with three types of controllers: The Predictive Model Control (MPC), the Proportional Integral Derivative (PID) and the Fuzzy Logic.

An introduction in Sect. 1; Sect. 2 indicates the method; in Sect. 3, the results and finally, in Sect. 4, the study's conclusion.

2   Method

The design method applied for the development of this prototype is based on the definition and characterization of the software and hardware specifications and proceeded to the materialization. For the implementation of the MPC, PID, and Fuzzy Logic controllers, a DC POLOLU motor with a 30:1 speed reducer and a quadrature incremental encoder (CPR) integrated into the motor shaft, which provides a resolution of 64 and 1920 counts per revolution at the input and output of the reducer respectively. Figure 1 indicates the method used to control the DC motor.

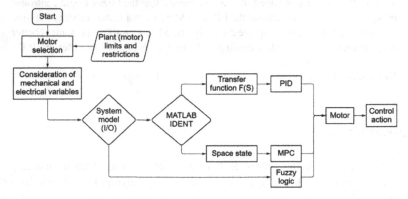

Fig. 1. Methods used to control the DC motor.

The connections between the electronic elements and the mechanical parts were coupled in the materialization phase, obtaining a functional prototype. Then the first tests with data acquisition were carried out, which served as the basis for developing the mathematical model of the plant (DC POLOLU motor). In the first test, the motor speed was controlled manually by employing a PWM, and the minimum and maximum limits of encoder operation were determined. The data obtained was analyzed and adjusted to make the modelling approach reality.

In a LabVIEW virtual instrument (VI), the Human Machine Interface (HMI) and the programming were developed to acquire the different tests' data. Generally, when data acquisition is performed in tests, erroneous data are produced when initiating/terminating the communication between the Arduino MEGA 2560 board and the PC and in the reading of the encoder. These test measurements are exported to an Excel file, where the values outside the operating ranges are filtered out.

2.1 Modeling in MATLAB

The modeling of the DC motor is done in the MATLAB Workspace by applying the MATLAB IDENT toolbox. The refined data of the first test and the DC motor is entered into the IDENT identification system, and the transfer function is obtained, which is used for the PID controller.

The transfer function is validated with the output of the plant. Figure 2 shows the final transfer function.

```
Process model with transfer function:
                 Kp
       G(s) = ----------
               1+Tp1*s

       Kp = 3.4141
       Tp1 = 0.35455
```

Fig. 2. Motor transfer function (DC POLOLU).

Then, the POLOLU DC motor model is obtained in state spaces using the MPC controller and validation is carried out. Figure 3 shows the final model in state spaces.

```
Discrete-time identified state-space model:
    x(t+Ts) = A x(t) + B u(t) + K e(t)
      y(t) = C x(t) + D u(t) + e(t)
A =
          x1      x2
    x1  0.7027  -0.187
    x2  0.6573  0.2576
B =
          [PWM]
    x1  -0.001455
    x2   0.01343
C =
          x1      x2
    [RPM] -376.5 -59.47
D =
          [PWM]
    [RPM]    0
```

Fig. 3. State space model of the motor (DC POLOLU).

2.2 Controller Implementation

A project was created in LabVIEW software to implement the comparative platform between MPC, PID and Fuzzy Logic controllers. This system allows communication between the Arduino MEGA board and the computer and will also process the different algorithms of the controllers. It presents an interface between the computer and the user.

Figure 4 shows the constructed prototype called the algorithm testing platform, which aims to test algorithms and obtain the best behavior of the DC motor according to the control theory applied in each case.

Fig. 4. Algorithm test platform for the control of a DC motor.

3 Results

This section presents the analysis and comparative study of PID, Fuzzy Logic and MPC controllers. Motor controllers (DC POLOLU) are tested at no and under load.

Next, the different motor controllers were tested in the lab with regulation at 100 rpm, with and without load.

Figure 5 shows the response of the system with PID control, the set point in blue, the rpm in red and the control action in green. Figure 5 (a) shows the system's response with the motor without load, which reaches the set point and stabilizes after a small oscillation observed in the control action. Figure 5 (b) shows the system's response with the motor with a load on the shaft, in which the load causes the motor to make a more significant effort to reach its set point. Therefore, the action of control has a faster action. The control action in both cases is overdamped.

Figure 6 shows the response of the system with Fuzzy Logic Control, the set point in blue, the rpm in red and the control action in green. In Fig. 6 (a), the system's response with the motor without load is observed, where the speed passes the set point value and then decreases until it stabilizes at the set point value. The control action shows that it is underdamped, and after a while, it reaches its stabilization. In Fig. 6 (b), the system's response shows the motor with a load on the shaft. The control action remains underdamped. The overshoot produced by the control action at speed is slightly more significant than in the first case, arriving after a time to stabilize at the value of the set point.

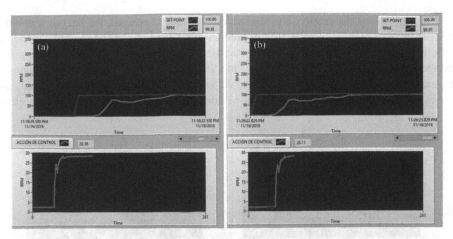

Fig. 5. System response with PID control at 100 rpm. (a) no load (b) loaded.

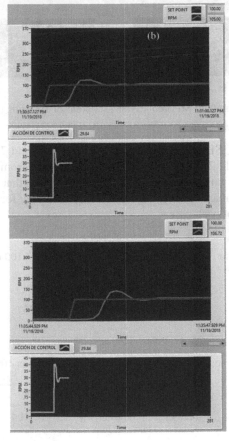

Fig. 6. System response with FUZZY control at 100 rpm. (a) no load (b) loaded.

Figure 7 shows the response of the system with MPC control, the set point in blue, the rpm in red and the control action in green. Figure 7 (a) shows the system's response with the motor without load. The control action, in this case, has critical damping given the speed with which the controller acts, and the speed stabilizes immediately. Figure 7 (b) indicates the response system with load, which is similar to the previous analysis; however, the difference in load causes the motor speed to take slightly longer to stabilize.

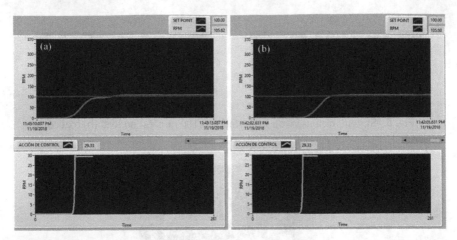

Fig. 7. System response with MPC control at a set point of 100 rpm. (a) no load (b) loaded.

Table 1 shows the ISE indices obtained from Fig. 5, 6 and 7 with the motor shaft without load, and Table 2, shows the ISE indices obtained from Fig. 5, 6 and 7 with the load on the motor shaft. The performance index indicates that a system is optimal if it can minimize this value; thereby, the calculation was made for the three controllers, obtaining the values for each case.

Table 1. Comparison of performance index for a set point of 100 rpm without load.

	PID	Fuzzy Logic	MPC
ISE	0.2245	0.3212	0.3576

Table 2. Comparison of the performance index for a set point 100 rpm with load.

	PID	Fuzzy Logic	MPC
ISE	0.2343	0.3871	0.3104

4 Conclusions

In this project, we infer that the three controllers are within an optimal performance range, according to the results of this particular study with DC motors, so the type of control to be used would be the decision of the operator or designer. Also, it would depend on the specific application in which it is going to be implemented depending on the environment variables that could directly or indirectly affect the performance of each controller.

The performance index analysis uses the ISE expression, which tells us that if a system is optimal, the lower this value is, knowing that the control varies according to the setting of each controller and the conditions of the DC motor. It allows concluded that the PID control presents a better performance index according to the ISE for a set point of 100 rpm, followed by the MPC and the Fuzzy Logic.

The overdrive shown in the Fuzzy Logic control does not exceed 5%. Hence, its performance is good, and it can be applied like the other controllers, taking into account the environment variables and the equipment used for the implementation.

References

1. Fang, G., Pinarello Scalcon, F., Xiao, D., Vieira, R., Grundling, H., Emadi, A.: Advanced Control of Switched Reluctance Motors (SRMs): a review on current regulation, torque control and vibration suppression. IEEE Open J. Ind. Electron. Soc. **2**, 280–301 (2021). https://doi.org/10.1109/OJIES.2021.3076807
2. Dantas, A.D.O.D.S., Dantas, A.F.O.D.A., Campos, J.T.L.S., De Almeida Neto, D.L., Dórea, C.E.T.: PID control for electric vehicles subject to control and speed signal constraints. J. Control Sci. Eng. **2018** (2018). https://doi.org/10.1155/2018/6259049
3. Guzey, H.M., Dumlu, A., Guzey, N., Alpay, A.: Optimal synchronizing speed control of multiple DC motors. In: Proceedings of the 2018 International Conference on Optimization Application. ICOA 2018, vol. 0, no. 2, pp. 1–5 (2018). https://doi.org/10.1109/ICOA.2018.8370508
4. Buele, J., Varela-Aldás, J., Santamaría, M., Soria, A., Espinoza, J.: Comparison between fuzzy control and MPC algorithms implemented in low-cost embedded devices. In: Rocha, Á., Ferrás, C., Montenegro Marin, C.E., Medina García, V.H. (eds.) ICITS 2020. AISC, vol. 1137, pp. 429–438. Springer, Cham (2020). https://doi.org/10.1007/978-3-030-40690-5_42
5. Welsch, M., Fichter, W.: Control of large multicopters with rate-limited electric motors. In: AIAA Scitech 2020 Forum, vol. 1 PartF, no. January, pp. 1–12 (2020). https://doi.org/10.2514/6.2020-1832
6. Aguila Mejía, O., Tapia Olvera, R., Rivas Cambero, I., Minor Popocatl, H.: Adaptive speed controller for a permanent magnet synchronous motor, pp. 142–170 (2019)
7. Qu, L., Qiao, W., Qu, L.: An enhanced linear active disturbance rejection rotor position sensorless control for permanent magnet synchronous motors. IEEE Trans. Power Electron. **35**(6), 6175–6184 (2020). https://doi.org/10.1109/TPEL.2019.2953162
8. Kryukov, O.V., Blagodarov, D.A., Dulnev, N.N., Safonov, Y.M., Fedortsov, N.N., Kostin, A.A.: Intelligent control of electric machine drive systems. In: 2018 10th International Conference on Electrical Power Drive System ICEPDS 2018 – Conference on Proceedings, pp. 1–4 (2018). https://doi.org/10.1109/ICEPDS.2018.8571670
9. Djuric, A., Jovanovic, V.M., Yaprak, E., Chen, W.: Learning module on electric motors modeling, control, and testing (LMEMMCT). In: ASEE Annual Conference Export Conference on Proceedings, vol. 2017-June (2017). https://doi.org/10.18260/1-2--28613

10. Saad, M., Amhedb, A.H., Al Sharqawi, M.: Real time DC motor position control using PID controller in LabVIEW. J. Robot. Control **2**(5), 342–348 (2021). https://doi.org/10.18196/jrc. 25104
11. Alkurawy, L.E.J., Khamas, N.: Model predictive control for DC motors. In: 1st International Science Conference on Engineering Science - 3rd Science Conference on Engineering Science ISCES 2018 - Proceedings, vol. 2018-Janua, pp. 56–61 (2018). https://doi.org/10.1109/ ISCES.2018.8340528
12. Saá, F., Gordón, A., Mendoza Chipantasi, D., Espejo Velasco, P., Velasco, E.N.: Test system for control algorithms on a DC motor. In: Botto-Tobar, M., León-Acurio, J., Díaz Cadena, A., Montiel Díaz, P. (eds.) ICAETT 2019. AISC, vol. 1067, pp. 154–163. Springer, Cham (2020). https://doi.org/10.1007/978-3-030-32033-1_15
13. Lotfy, A., Kaveh, M., Mosavi, M.R., Rahmati, A.R.: An enhanced fuzzy controller based on improved genetic algorithm for speed control of DC motors. Analog Integr. Circ. Sig. Process **105**(2), 141–155 (2020). https://doi.org/10.1007/s10470-020-01599-9

Reputation, Risk, and Trust on User Adoption of Internet Search Engines: The Case of DuckDuckGo

Antonios Saravanos[✉] [iD], Stavros Zervoudakis, Dongnanzi Zheng, Amarpreet Nanda, Georgios Shaheen, Charles Hornat, Jeremiah Konde Chaettle, Alassane Yoda, Hyeree Park, and Will Ang

New York University, New York, NY, USA

{saravanos,zervoudakis,dz40,an83,gs3777,cfh1,jk7231,ay2193, hp2240,xa250}@nyu.edu

Abstract. This paper investigates the determinants of end-user adoption of the DuckDuckGo search engine coupling the standard UTAUT model with factors to reflect reputation, risk, and trust. An experimental approach was taken to validate our model, where participants were exposed to the DuckDuckGo product using a vignette. Subsequently, answering questions on their perception of the technology. The data was analyzed using the partial least squares-structural equation modeling (PLS-SEM) approach. From the nine distinct factors studied, we found that 'Performance Expectancy' played the greatest role in user decisions on adoption, followed by 'Firm Reputation', 'Initial Trust in Technology', 'Social Influence', and an individual's 'Disposition to Trust'. We conclude by exploring how these findings can explain DuckDuckGo's rising prominence as a search engine.

Keywords: End-user adoption · DuckDuckGo · Privacy-conscious search engine · Trust · Risk

1 Introduction

In this paper, we seek to identify the determinants of end-user adoption of the privacy-conscious search engine DuckDuckGo – for those who "are put off by the thought of their every query being tracked and logged" – where there is "absolutely zero user tracking" [5]. We saw the emergence of DuckDuckGo in 2008, recognized as "the first privacy-focused search engine" [9]. The product is designed to cater to a growing number of technology users who value their privacy. The popularity of DuckDuckGo is evident from simply looking at its usage statistics. The company has experienced remarkable growth, going from an annual total of 16,413,461 search queries in 2010, to an annual total of 35,304,278,270 search queries in 2021 [4]. The solution serves as an alternative to the traditional search engines, such as Google, Yahoo, and Bing. While, to the naïve, these search engines may appear to be free, they contain within them a hidden cost: the personal information one imparts to these companies. Certainly, user skepticism regarding the gathering, retaining, and sharing of information by organizations such

© The Author(s), under exclusive license to Springer Nature Switzerland AG 2022
C. Stephanidis et al. (Eds.): HCII 2022, CCIS 1654, pp. 683–691, 2022.
https://doi.org/10.1007/978-3-031-19679-9_87

as Bing and Google "may lead searchers to seek other search engines as alternatives" [3]. Indeed, "just as a car buyer might choose a Volvo over a Ford because the Volvo is said to have better crash impact protection than the Ford, so too might a search engine user choose DuckDuckGo over Google because of the privacy DuckDuckGo offers" [12]. Increasingly we find that there is a newfound awareness amongst users with respect to the tradeoff introduced by search engines: "users are waking up, and search privacy is making its way to the mainstream" [9]. Given DuckDuckGo's rising standing and widespread adoption, there is value in identifying the main determinants of user behavioral intention as well as identifying their respective magnitude.

2   Materials and Methods

In this section, we describe the development of the model and hypotheses that were used to investigate user adoption of the DuckDuckGo search engine. We then go on to outline the experimental approach that was taken to evaluate that model, present the data collection process and, lastly, describe the sample demographics.

2.1   Model and Hypothesis Development

Correspondingly, a model was developed for the specific technology we are evaluating – a privacy-conscious search engine – which can be seen in Fig. 1. Our model was based on the work of Venkatesh et al. [16] and their Unified Theory of Acceptance and Use of Technology (hereafter UTAUT), which is one of the contemporary models designed to provide insight into user technology adoption decisions. Correspondingly, we generate the following hypotheses:

H1: 'Performance Expectancy' positively influences 'Behavioral Intention'.
H2: 'Effort Expectancy' positively influences 'Behavioral Intention'.
H3: 'Social Influence' positively influences 'Behavioral Intention'.
H4: 'Facilitating Conditions' positively influence 'Behavioral Intention'.

To this foundation we seek to incorporate into our model the concept of risk. We look to the work of Miltgen et al. [10] and, accordingly, incorporate their construct of "Perceived Risks", concurrently proposing the following hypothesis:

H5: 'Perceived Risks' positively influence 'Behavioral Intention'.

We also seek to incorporate trust and, to that end, look to Kim et al.'s [8] initial trust model, where the authors propose a construct to reflect initial consumer trust in a technology as well as the antecedents of that, which include a firm's reputation and an individual consumer's personal propensity to trust. As a strategy of how to integrate this construct into our model, we take the approach of Oliveira et al. [11] and subsequently offer the following hypotheses:

H6: 'Initial Trust' positively influences 'Behavioral Intention'.

H7: 'Firm Reputation' positively influences 'Initial Trust'.
H8: 'Firm Reputation' positively influences 'Behavioral Intention'.

Next, we seek to connect trust and risk into our model and look to the work of Miltgen et al. [10] as precedence, which also links trust to an individual's perceived ease of use and usefulness of the technology. Fittingly, proposing the following hypotheses:

H9: 'Initial Trust' positively influences 'Perceived Risks'.
H10: 'Initial Trust' positively influences 'Performance Expectancy'.
H11: 'Initial Trust' positively influences 'Effort Expectancy'.

Finally, we seek to incorporate how trust of the government may influence the perception of risk, as described by Bélanger and Carter [2]. Accordingly, we propose the following hypotheses:

H12: 'Trust of the Government' positively influences 'Perceived Risks'.
H13: 'Disposition to Trust' positively influences 'Trust of the Government'.
H14: 'Disposition to Trust' positively influences 'Initial Trust'.

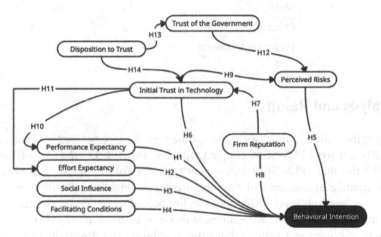

Fig. 1. Illustration of our proposed theoretical framework based on the work of Venkatesh et al. [16], Lancelot-Miltgen et al. [10], Kim et al. [8], and Bélanger and Carter [2].

2.2 Data Collection and Sample Demographics

An experimental approach was taken. Correspondingly, a questionnaire was developed based on the items provided by the respective authors of the respective constructs to measure user perception of the DuckDuckGo search engine. The questionnaire also included questions to capture participant demographics and ascertain both prior experience using search technology and participant attention to the experiment. Following the obtaining of informed consent, participants were presented with a vignette and animated gif illustrating DuckDuckGo. Subsequently, participants were asked to complete the above-mentioned questionnaire. A total of 322 participants were solicited using Amazon Mechanical Turk. Of those, 81 were removed as they failed the attention checks; this left a total of 241 participations relevant to this study (following the approach of Saravanos et al. [14]). The participant characteristics are outlined in Table 1.

Table 1. Participant demographics.

Characteristic	Category	N	Percentage
Age	18–25	9	3.73%
	26–30	31	12.86%
	31–35	40	16.60%
	36–45	68	28.22%
	46–55	46	19.09%
	56 or older	44	18.26%
	Prefer not to answer	3	1.24%
Gender	Female	100	41.49%
	Male	134	55.60%
	Other	2	0.83%
	Prefer not to answer	5	2.07%

3   Analysis and Results

To analyze the collected data, we followed the technique prescribed by Hair et al. [4]; specifically, we used PLS-SEM coupled with the SmartPLS3.3.2 [13] software. Hair et al. [7] write that "PLS-SEM assessment typically follows a two-step process that involves separate assessments of the measurement models and the structural model". Initially, one "measures' reliability and validity according to certain criteria associated with formative and reflective measurement model specification" [7]. This involved the assessment of convergent validity, construct reliability, and discriminant validity. The first of these, convergent validity, saw us examine the factor loadings followed by the average variance extracted (AVE) and the removal of any manifest variables that had values that were lower than 0.7 with respect to both of these. Following the removal of those items, those remaining were statically significant with a p-value of less than 0.05 after bootstrapping with 7000 subsamples. Construct validity was established by ensuring that both composite reliability (CR) and Cronbach's Alpha were above 0.7. Satisfactory discriminant validity was found through the use of cross-loadings and the Fornell-Larcker criterion.

Subsequently, we examined the structural model (see Table 2). The respective R^2 values (see Table 2) show that our model explains: 'Behavioral Intention', 'Effort Expectancy', 'Initial Trust', 'Perceived Risks', 'Performance Expectancy', and 'Trust of the Government' (per the criteria noted by Falk and Miller [6]). We find that the 'Performance Expectancy' ($\beta = 0.4302$; $p < 0.01$) and 'Social Influence' ($\beta = 0.1345$; $p < 0.05$) constructs were statistically significant and played the greatest and fourth-greatest roles in determining user adoption respectively. In other words, the quality of the search results (i.e., 'Performance Expectancy') was the primary determinant of user adoption, and 'peer pressure' (i.e., 'Social Influence') was the fourth greatest. Interestingly, the 'Effort Expectancy' and 'Facilitating Conditions' constructs were not statistically significant. Furthermore, the results revealed that DuckDuckGo's reputation ($\beta = 0.4134$; $p < 0.01$) was the second most important factor (i.e., 'Firm Reputation') with respect to user adoption decisions and, in relative magnitude, almost equal to 'Performance Expectancy'. In other words, DuckDuckGo's perceived reputation was almost as important to users as the quality of the search results yielded using this tool. Trust in the

Table 2. Results for the structural model.

Path	(Direct) β	(Total) β	(Direct) t-Value	(Total) t-Value
Behavioral Intention ($R^2 = 55.05\%$)				
Disposition to Trust	–	0.0279*	–	2.1081
Effort Expectancy	0.0033	0.0033	0.0554	0.0554
Facilitating Conditions	0.0397	0.0397	0.6634	0.6634
Firm Reputation	0.2146*	0.4134**	2.2019	6.6875
Initial Trust	0.0801	0.2580**	1.0020	2.8875
Performance Expectancy	0.4302**	0.4302**	6.9456	6.9456
Perceived Risks	−0.0151	−0.0151	0.2479	0.2479
Social Influence	0.1345*	0.1345*	2.1680	2.1680
Trust of the Government	–	0.0007	–	0.1732
Effort Expectancy ($R^2 = 18.75\%$)				
Disposition to Trust	–	0.0462*	–	2.4671
Firm Reputation	–	0.3337**	–	5.9424
Initial Trust	0.4331**	0.4331**	6.8418	6.8418
Initial Trust ($R^2 = 65.07\%$)				
Disposition to Trust	0.1068*	0.1068*	2.5109	2.5109
Firm Reputation	0.7705**	0.7705**	24.6209	24.6209
Perceived Risks ($R^2 = 44.80\%$)				
Disposition to Trust		−0.0948**	–	2.6064
Firm Reputation		−0.5030**	–	9.3417
Initial Trust	−0.6529**	−0.6529**	11.7024	11.7024
Trust of the Government	−0.0492	−0.0492	0.9938	0.9938
Performance Expectancy ($R^2 = 15.00\%$)				
Disposition to Trust	–	0.0414*	–	2.2815
Firm Reputation	–	0.2984**	–	5.5853
Initial Trust	0.3873**	0.3873**	6.2601	6.2601
Trust of the Government ($R^2 = 25.89\%$)				
Disposition to Trust	0.5088**	0.5088**	9.7178	9.7178

* $p < 0.05$; ** $p < 0.01$.

technology, reflected through the 'Initial Trust' ($\beta = 0.2580$; $p < 0.01$) construct, played the third-greatest role, and 'Disposition to Trust' ($\beta = 0.0279$; $p < 0.05$) the fifth-greatest role.

4 Discussion and Conclusions

In this study we hypothesized that nine distinct factors would impact user behavioral intention for privacy-focused search engine technology adoption (see Table 3). Of these, four factors were found to have zero impact with respect to user adoption. The first two – the amount of effort needed to use the technology (i.e., 'Effort Expectancy') and the availability of (technical) support (i.e., 'Facilitating Conditions') – were not surprising findings. Certainly, we can attribute this result to the technology we study being very simple to use, and to the fact that all major search engines offer a similar interface. Given that almost all participants (98.3%) reported that they used search engines daily, it is reasonable to conclude that they would perceive the use of DuckDuckGo as effortless and one that they would not require third-party support. What was surprising was that their perception of risk (i.e., 'Perceived Risks') with respect to the technology did not play a role in user decisions to adopt. We attribute the lack of significance in the strength played by the firm's reputation (which was found to be the second most significant factor in determining user adoption). Lastly, we look at individual trust in the government (i.e., 'Trust of the Government'). This can be perhaps explained by the (United States) government having no (substantial) history of monitoring individual search activities. Therefore, this makes it not a significant concern on the part of users.

Five factors were found to have a statistically significant effect on user behavioral intention with respect to adoption: 'Performance Expectancy' was found to have the greatest effect on consumer behavioral intention, followed by 'Firm Reputation', 'Initial Trust', 'Social Influence', and 'Disposition to Trust'. The finding that the perceived usefulness (i.e., 'Performance Expectancy') played the greatest role in user decisions in and of itself is not surprising, given that adoption studies frequently see this factor playing a significant role. Thus, the quality of the search results are what users look to first with respect to adoption. In other words, if DuckDuckGo is to compete with the major search engines, such as Google, Bing, and Yahoo, it must ensure a comparable quality in the results it returns.

The next factor was DuckDuckGo's reputation (i.e., 'Firm Reputation'), indicating that, with such a product, users look to the brand when deciding whether to use, and then subsequently assess their initial trust in the technology (i.e., 'Initial Trust'). Hence, it is crucial for DuckDuckGo to maintain the quality of its brand and trust in the technology that they offer if they want to preserve and expand their user base. This also opens the door to future research, which may seek to identify the tradeoff between the quality of the result and the firm's reputation and trust in the product.

Next on the list was the role that the opinion of their peers (i.e., 'Social Influence') plays in user decisions on whether to adopt. Accordingly, DuckDuckGo should seek to promote its technology through existing users (e.g., peer pressure) and marketing. The final factor examined was an individual's unique disposition to trust (i.e., 'Disposition to Trust'). Thus, whether a user is, by their nature, trusting would influence whether they use such a product, with those that are not trusting being more inclined to adopt. Consequently, DuckDuckGo may want to focus its efforts on such individuals.

In conclusion, our findings explain the rising usage of DuckDuckGo; while the quality of search results is a strong factor in determining adoption, DuckDuckGo's reputation, the trust placed in the technology, and an individual's disposition to trust, also play a prominent role in users' adoption decisions.

Table 3. Results of hypothesis testing.

Hypothesis	Causal path	Remarks
H1	Performance expectancy → Behavioral intention	Supported
H2	Effort expectancy → Behavioral intention	Not Supported
H3	Social influence → Behavioral intention	Supported
H4	Facilitating conditions → Behavioral intention	Not Supported
H5	Perceived risks → Behavioral intention	Supported[1]
H6	Initial trust → Behavioral intention	Supported[1]
H7	Firm reputation → Initial trust	Supported
H8	Firm reputation → Behavioral intention	Supported
H9	Initial trust → Perceived risks	Supported
H10	Initial trust → Performance expectancy	Supported
H11	Initial trust → Effort expectancy	Supported
H12	Trust of the government → Perceived risks	Not Supported
H13	Disposition to trust → Trust of the government	Supported
H14	Disposition to trust → Initial trust	Supported

[1] Supported via total effect

4.1 Limitations and Future Research Directions

With respect to this work, we note three limitations that should be highlighted. Tangentially, we present how these limitations also offer direction for future research on the topic. The first limitation relates to the effect that participant culture can have on consumer intention to accept a technology. Clearly, there is evidence (e.g., [1, 15, 17]) that raises this as an area of concern. In this paper, we restricted our sample solely to participants from the United States. Accordingly, the study of other cultures may lead to different findings and broaden our research. The second limitation refers to the method through which we exposed participants to the technology. Rather than having them interact with the DuckDuckGo search engine, they were offered a vignette and animated gif that highlighted the characteristics of the solution. It is possible that actual interaction with the technology could lead to different user perceptions and that, over time, those perceptions could change. The third limitation is with respect to our research focusing on users' intention to adopt, and accordingly did not investigate their actual usage. These limitations also identify how this work can be further developed: looking at users from different cultures; having participants actually interact with the DuckDuckGo product; and investigating how that interaction actually transforms into usage.

Acknowledgments. This research was funded in part through the New York University School of Professional Studies Full-Time Faculty Professional Development Fund.

References

1. Bandyopadhyay, K., Fraccastoro, K.: The effect of culture on user acceptance of information technology. Commun. Assoc. Inf. Syst. **19**, 522–543 (2007). https://doi.org/10.17705/1CAIS. 01923
2. Bélanger, F., Carter, L.: Trust and risk in e-government adoption. J. Strateg. Inf. Syst. **17**(2), 165–176 (2008). https://doi.org/10.1016/j.jsis.2007.12.002
3. Burnett, A.: A Baker's Dozen of Tips for Better Web Searches. Digital Commons @ University of Georgia School of Law (2020). https://digitalcommons.law.uga.edu/cgi/viewcontent.cgi? article=1077&context=cle. Accessed 05 Apr 2022
4. DuckDuckGo: DuckDuckGo Traffic. https://duckduckgo.com/traffic. Accessed 25 May 2022
5. Duò, M.: 21 Alternative Search Engines to Use in 2022. https://kinsta.com/blog/alternative-search-engines/. Accessed 05 Apr 2022
6. Falk, R.F., Miller, N.B.: A Primer for Soft Modeling. University of Akron Press, Ohio (1992)
7. Hair, J.F., et al.: PLS-SEM: indeed a silver bullet. J. Mark. Theory Pract. **19**(2), 139–152 (2011). https://doi.org/10.2753/MTP1069-6679190202
8. Kim, G., et al.: Understanding dynamics between initial trust and usage intentions of mobile banking. Inf. Syst. J. **19**(3), 283–311 (2009)
9. Kite-Powell, J.: This New Privacy-First Search Engine Keeps Your Searches Private. https://www.forbes.com/sites/jenniferhicks/2020/02/12/this-new-privacy-first-search-engine-keeps-your-searches-private/. Accessed 28 Jan 2022
10. Lancelot Miltgen, C., et al.: Determinants of end-user acceptance of biometrics: Integrating the "Big 3" of technology acceptance with privacy context. Decis. Support Syst. 56, 103–114 (2013). https://doi.org/10.1016/j.dss.2013.05.010
11. Oliveira, T., et al.: Extending the understanding of mobile banking adoption: when UTAUT meets TTF and ITM. Int. J. Inf. Manage. **34**(5), 689–703 (2014). https://doi.org/10.1016/j.iji nfomgt.2014.06.004
12. Pasquale, F.: Privacy, antitrust, and power. George Mason Law Rev. **20**(4), 1009–1024 (2012)
13. Ringle, C.M., et al.: SmartPLS 3. Bönningstedt: SmartPLS. (2015). https://www.smartpls. com/. Accessed 2 May 2022
14. Saravanos, A., Zervoudakis, S., Zheng, D., Stott, N., Hawryluk, B., Delfino, D.: The hidden cost of using amazon mechanical Turk for research. In: Stephanidis, C., et al. (eds.) HCII 2021. LNCS, vol. 13094, pp. 147–164. Springer, Cham (2021). https://doi.org/10.1007/978-3-030-90238-4_12
15. Srite, M., Karahanna, E.: The role of espoused national cultural values in technology acceptance. MIS Q. **30**(3), 679–704 (2006). https://doi.org/10.2307/25148745

16. Venkatesh, V., et al.: User acceptance of information technology: toward a unified view. MIS Q. **27**(3), 425–478 (2003). https://doi.org/10.2307/30036540
17. Yuen, Y.: Internet banking acceptance in the United States and Malaysia: a cross-cultural examination. Mark. Intell. Plan. **33**(3), 292–308 (2015). https://doi.org/10.1108/MIP-08-2013-0126

Providing Access to Educational TV
for Children Using RFID Technology

Mireya Zapata-Rodríguez[1]([✉]) [iD], Jorge Álvarez-Tello[2] [iD], and Hugo Arias-Flores[1] [iD]

[1] Centro de Investigación en Mecatrónica y Sistemas Interactivos – MIST, Universidad Tecnológica Indoamérica, Machala y Sabanilla, 170103 Quito, Ecuador
{mireyazapata,hugoarias}@uti.edu.ec
[2] Centro de Transferencia de Tecnología e Innovación – CTTI, Universidad Tecnológica Indoamérica, Machala y Sabanilla, 170103 Quito, Ecuador
jorgealvarez@uti.edu.ec

Abstract. Television is a communication medium found in most homes, facilitating accessibility to educational content through the reading-learning process.

This paper presents a control system for educational television that allows the selection and playback of pre-recorded videos in a television decoder using RFID tags. This has been designed based on a controller that allows replacing the commands sent by a conventional remote control.

To meet this educational objective, a prototype is developed from the mechanical, electronic and computer concept, to integrate a technological proposal that facilitates reading-learning, through a televised program and satellite transmission, integrating an instrument of personalized pedagogical assistance to an Ecuadorian spectacled bear for the assistance of children of a young age or with any type of disability that prevents them from handling a remote control.

As a result, we obtained the experimental development of a basic prototype for learning-reading that works with connection to satellite equipment and activates the components for learning through television by means of an RFDI system.

A unique tag is used for each pre-recorded program. When the RFID reader reads a tag that has been previously assigned, the TV module will transmit the sequence of signals needed to the TV decoder to play the specific movie or report.

Keywords: Educational television · Remote control · RFID technology

1 Introduction

Television is an audio-visual communication medium, which since its origins has been inserted more and more in the homes of families around the world, with a growing number of hours dedicated to this activity at younger ages. In this sense, there are studies such as Hudson [1], who state that subjects who have spent more time watching television in their childhood obtain higher scores in certain curricular subjects, as well as in certain attitudes. It is stated that this influence is related to variables such as the selection of programs allowed by parents with educational content, and the accompaniment of parents to explain certain controversial scenes, etc. [2]. These factors have underpinned the concept of the so-called educational television as a means of positive influence in the teaching-learning processes of children and adolescents under academic supervision [3].

There are detractors who claim that this type of medium has little value, that it also restricts the development of other activities, and constitutes a passive medium with which one cannot interact, which prevents the active construction of knowledge [4].

With a framework for the synthetization of evidence from the learning sciences and educational research regarding technological strategies that support the kinds of learning opportunities needed to promote children's well-being, healthy development, and a transferable learning process [5].

In this regard, it is important to point out that these criticisms are framed in the medium itself, limiting its educational potential to the technological aspect, but not to the content that is transmitted and that can affect a greater number of people under accessible time and space conditions, audio-visual multimedia technology and a matrix of programs (news, sports, cultural, contests, entertainment) [6, 7].

In this sense, there are initiatives promoted by paid television companies, which as an activity to contribute to vulnerable sectors of society, have implemented special education channels specifically designed to enrich the primary and secondary school curriculum, focused on rural communities that contribute to reducing the technological gap by promoting access to information with channels approved and regulated by government entities with transmissions of educational content in different subjects, which can be used to carry out distance training.

In this context, there is the challenge of looking for operational alternatives that allow TV integration in the educational field as a teaching-learning tool. The proposed prototype is especially attractive to young children, who, without having to manipulate the keys on a remote control and interact with the text messages displayed on a TV to select a film, simply use the pre-recorded tags and can quickly play the program of their choice; and even more so if we think of children with some type of disability, whose main commitment will be to stimulate their senses in order to achieve better results in the assimilation of knowledge.

2 Methodology

The proposed prototype is aimed at young children or those with some kind of disability, who have problems manipulating the remote control for channel selection. The sequence of steps that are selected through the keys of a remote control until reaching the movie or program, is automated by our proposed system.

When it reads a previously assigned RFID tag, it is responsible for sending the commands that allow the TV decoder to reproduce the selected program, without the need to manipulate the remote control. In this proposal, the set of available pre-recorded programs is selected by the teacher or tutor in charge, according to the development of the educational content to be treated.

2.1 Design Concept

This section presents a hardware and software co-design that allows the user to easily configure the system.

Hardware Design

Figure 1 shows the components that make up the proposed system, which is detailed below:

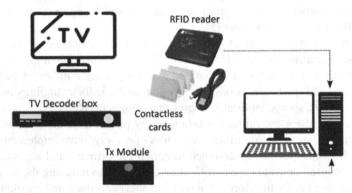

Fig. 1. System hardware components

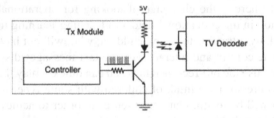

Fig. 2. Infrared modulation with Tx Module

- **TV**: digital television with TV decoder box compatible peripherals
- **TV decoder box**: is connected to the TV set in order to receive pay channels. For rural areas without communications infrastructure, a satellite connection is usually used to receive the signal. For this approach, the set-top box must have recording capability.
- **PC:** used to run the developed software application, so that the user can manage the database information of the stored educational programs, as well as link new RFID tags with their corresponding films.
- **Tx Module:** consists of a controller card that acts as an infrared transmitter at a carrier frequency of 38 kHz, emulating the operation of a remote control (see Fig. 2). Each button on the remote control has a unique digital code. The IR receiver of the TV decoder box recognizes each modulated signal as an individual button action. (see Fig. 3) Playing the correct sequence of IR signals performs the educational channel selection.

Table 1, shows the buttons used to navigate through the pre-recorded movie selection options, as well as the associated binary codes to be transmitted by the IR. It is important to mention that codes may vary depending on the brand of remote control.

Table 1. Codes associated with the remote control buttons

Remote control button	IR codes (Hex)
EXIT	0xC26F
LIST	0xc2a2
DASH	0xc127
DOWN ARROW	0xc22C
SELECT	0xc25E

The Tx Module must be located at a maximum distance of 2 m from the TV decoder box ensuring that the emitting IR LED points directly towards the IR receiver of the decoder. In its normal operating mode, the user, when approaching a previously assigned RFID tag to the reader, will give way to the playback of the video associated with it in the TV decoder box.

The Tx Module controller manages the storage in a non-volatile internal memory of the binary code sequence, which allows the educational program to be played back.

- **Contactless access cards:** are factory programmed with a unique 4-byte ID that cannot be changed. The ID is used to identify each unit and assign IR codes in the system database.
- **RFID reader**: reads proximity cards, the frequency depends on the type of card. In the case of the prototype presented, cards working at 13.56 MHz are used. Once the reader detects a card, the corresponding ID is sent via serial connection to the PC which uses this information through a customized API to search in the system database, or otherwise assign a sequence of IR codes.

Software Design

The proposed system includes besides the hardware, an API developed in Python so that the teacher can educational programs with the RFID tags. When executing the user application and performing the pairing of the serial ports, the system is ready to be used. Pressing the letter M on the keyboard, the user can access the main menu, which allows, among its functions:

- Task 1: Enter new educational programs, and associate each of them to an RFID card. For this it is necessary to approach the new card to the RFID reader.
- Task 2: Display the list of educational programs stored in memory.
- Task 3: Delete items from the list

Once the contactless cards ID are assigned to a educational pre-recorder educational program, the user only has to approach the cards to the RFID reader, and then the corresponding video will be played.

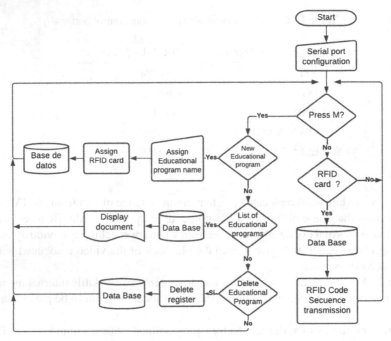

Fig. 3. Software application flowchart

Figure 3, shows the flowchart of the API developed for the system hardware, which shows the functions executed with each of the 3 configuration options detailed above. It is important to highlight that since it is developed in Python, it is a free access platform. In addition, it presents a friendly and easy to use interface.

3   Results

Table 2, presents the operating parameters of the developed hardware. As for the software, its usability was evaluated by measuring the efficiency of the application with respect to the configuration of the tasks implemented in the API. Based on a sample of 10 teachers of basic initial education, all of them with basic computer knowledge. The use of the platform was assessed with respect to whether the participants completed the task; left the task incomplete; or failed to complete the task. The results obtained are shown in Fig. 4, where it is observed that the main difficulty is presented in Task 1, which consists of assigning an RFID card to a pre-recorded educational program, which shows that it is necessary to simplify the steps required to complete this activity (it is proposed as future work). In turn, Tasks 2 and 3 showed similar results where most of the participants of the study were able to complete the task successfully.

Table 2. Hardware operating parameters

Parameter	Value
Voltage	5 V
Current (máx.)	500 mA
Distance between Tx Module and decoder (aprox.)	2 m
Viewing angle	20°

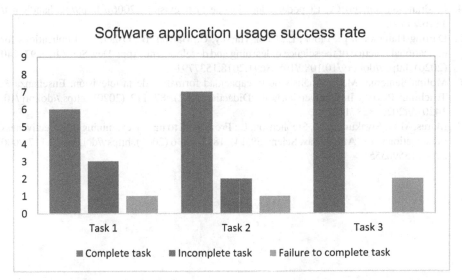

Fig. 4. Measuring the effectiveness of the software application

4   Conclusions

The results obtained with this proposal, present an alternative focused on children of preschool age as well as in children with disabilities, providing them with a control option over the contents of the educational programs that they most like to watch. Another important feature is that both, the RFID tags and the reader have been personalized, in such a way that they are more attractive to children. The RFID card reader is located in the teddy bear, which makes it more attractive for children to use. Regarding the usability of the application, the majority of users successfully completed the 3 tasks that make up the system options. Given that an initial prototype is presented, the results obtained from the usability-efficiency measurement have allowed us to identify the critical task that needs to be simplified for the user and that is proposed as future work.

References

1. Huston, A.C., Wright, J.C., Marquis, J., Green, S.B.: How young children spend their time: television and other activities. Dev. Psychol. **35**(4), 912–925 (1999). https://doi.org/10.1037/0012-1649.35.4.912
2. Rodríguez-Castro, M., López-Cepeda, A.M., Soengas-Pérez, X.: La televisión educativa en España: la oferta de Atresmedia, Mediaset y RTVE. RIED-Revista Iberoamericana de Educación a Distancia **25**(1), 203–221 (2022). https://doi.org/10.5944/RIED.25.1.30952
3. Adelantado-Renau, M., et al.: Association between screen media use and academic performance among children and adolescents: a systematic review and meta-analysis. JAMA Pediat. **173**(11), 1058–1067 (2019). https://doi.org/10.1001/jamapediatrics.2019.3176
4. Medrano-Samaniego C.: El poder educativo de la televisión (2006). http://hdl.handle.net/11162/45402
5. Darling-Hammond, L., Flook, L., Cook-Harvey, C., Barron, B., Osher, D.: Implications for educational practice of the science of learning and development. Appl. Dev. Sci. **24**(2), 97–140 (2020). https://doi.org/10.1080/10888691.2018.1537791
6. Molina Santonja, M.D.: Análisis de la capacidad formativa de la televisión. Enseñanza & Teaching: Revista Interuniversitaria de Didáctica **38**(2), 87–112 (2020). https://doi.org/10.14201/et202038287112
7. Mares, M.L., Sivakumar, G., Stephenson, L.: From meta to micro: examining the effectiveness of educational TV. Am. Behav. Scient. **59**(14), 1822–1846 (2015). https://doi.org/10.1177/0002764215596555

The Expression of Multi-sensory User Experience on Interactive Packaging Design-Emotional Design of Children's Food

Shijie Zhou[1] , Lv Bin[1], and Ting Wen[2(✉)]

[1] Commodity Planning Center, Beijing New Energy CO. LTD, Beijing, China
liarss@yeah.net
[2] Institute of Psychology, University of Chinese Academy of Science, Beijing, China
wentin1234@126.com

Abstract. In view of the era of experience economy, product packaging not only plays a role in protecting goods, but also is a media in communicating with the audience and the products. Compared with the traditional product packaging, interactive packaging design can better meet the needs of user experience. Especially in the field of children's food, packaging design should give full consideration to children's cognitive characteristics and psychological needs, and carry out the emotional design to provide the kids with better user experience. Based on the interactive concept of product packaging, this paper constructed the emotional design of children's food packaging experience on multi-sensory channels, so as to promote children's physical and mental health.

Keywords: User experience · Interactive packaging design · Multi-sensory senses

1 Introduction

With the goods becoming rich and diversified, the experience economy has changed people's consumption patterns and aesthetic preference. The industry has also developed continuously to meet with this transformation of the economic model. As a consequence, the consumers want to get more communication with goods in the process of consumption, in which the product packaging design is a direct medium of interaction between consumers and products.

In addition to protecting goods, packaging is also a intermediary of communication to the audience [1]. Modern packaging design not only needs to protect goods for good preservation and easy portability, but also needs to provide a way of emotional experience between the commodities and consumer groups [2]. Therefore, the traditional packaging noly to protect goods and convey information as the main function can not adapt to people's diverse emotional requirements. As a marketing strategy, we need to integrate some interactive elements into the packaging design, delivering more direct and rich information to make the product more absorbing and attractive [3].

© The Author(s), under exclusive license to Springer Nature Switzerland AG 2022
C. Stephanidis et al. (Eds.): HCII 2022, CCIS 1654, pp. 699–703, 2022.
https://doi.org/10.1007/978-3-031-19679-9_89

An excellent product packaging design should not only meet functional needs, but also give consumers mental pleasure. Through the emotional integration of packaging design, it stimulates the consumer's multi-sensory senses, meets the consumer's psychological needs in culture, so that the consumers can obtain interactive association, cognitive association and emotional resonance in the process of purchasing and using product. Therefore, in the general trend of dematerialization, interactive packaging design can enrich the connotation of user experience, wich not only strengthens the relationship between consumers and products, but also promotes the sustainable development of modern packaging industry [4].

2 Interactive Packaging Design

As a product packaging, the most important role is to protect the product. On the one hand, it allows the product to be sealed and stored in order to keeps its quality stable from the factory to the consumer. On the other hand, it also makes the product easy to carry, keeping it from damage caused by human factors or force majeure, so as to be sold in good condition to the people's hands. However, in the user-centered experience economy, product packaging should not only meets the above functional needs, but also need to satisfy more psychological needs of the consumer [5].

Kurokawa Masayuki, a Japanese design master, said that the 21st century is a design era that reflects the characteristics of body senses [1]. Therefore, a new packaging design concept, namely the interactive packaging design has appeared, which originate from the concept of interaction design firstly proposed by Bill Moggridge in 1984 [6]. Then scholars refine the interactive design method and apply it to the product packaging industry. Wang Anxia, a professor of Jiangnan University, defined interactive packaging design as follows: through the implementation of packaging materials and packaging means, it establishes a closer connection and formes an interactive relationship between products and consumers. This design breaks innovatively the pattern of single information dissemination of packaging in the past, but promotes the development of packaging design from unilateral and static to experiential and interactional.

According to the target people's physiological characteristics and behavior characteristics, interactive packaging design is an emotional design method, which bases on the reference of the existing interaction to set up a new bridge between the consumer and the product [7]. Its design concept pays more attention to the user experience, which not only considers the usability of the packaging, but also notes the user's feeling when they opened the wrapper through the multi-sensory perception [8].

Humanized packaging design has become a trend, and the emotional design should be truly different for a variety of people [9]. Especially for the vulnerable groups of children, we should explore those cognitive and emotional needs so as to offer the attentive care and promote their user experience. Therefore, this article discusses the principle and explians the application from the perspective of multi-sensory senses, in order to provide a new strategy for the development of innovative packaging design.

3 Multi-sensory Senses of Emotional Design Method

Before children choose and use the product, the first thing that attracts them is the packaging outside the product. Children in the stage of cognitive development need to experience the world through different sensory forms such as vision, hearing, touch, smell and taste. The stimulation of various sensory experiences can deepen children's understanding of the products. So embedding a variety of sensory design into children's product packaging can enable children to get a comprehensive perception in the process of opening the wrapper.

Vision. Eighty percent of our information acquisition comes from vision, which has a wide range, diverse functional values and different expression forms. The combination of graphic, text and colors is called packaging visual image, which is the most important arrangement of packaging design to display of product external image [10].

Graphic is the most important part of packaging, which have stronger visual expression to convey the information and attract the consumer. Therefore, most of the patterns of children's food packaging are mainly cartoon, because children are easy to abstract by the strange shapes, novel patterns.

Text is one of the elements of commodity packaging, which plays the role of annotation of commodity, providing consumers with the basic information and use requirements of the product. The design of text should conform to the age of consumers, take the kid's product for example, the font in packaging should be more childlike.

Color can arouse various emotions, express feelings, and even affect people's physiological cognition [12]. Because itself has certain temperature and emotional characteristics, different colors can be used to convey different feelings to consumers [13]. For kids, bright colour can convey a kind of lively experience to easily attract the attention of children.

Hearing. Auditory sense is completed by the joint activities of the ear, auditory nerve and auditory center [14]. Compared with vision, sound has the advantages of fast transmission and flexible acquisition, which can create an atmosphere and trigger emotions so as to leave a deep impression on consumers [15].

Therefore, the auditory interactive design of packaging is of great significance to attract consumers' attention. For example, in daily celebrations, children often choose the way of "opening" the beverage. Here, "opening" is not only an action, but also refers to the accompanying sound in the process of opening the drink package, which often creates a joyful atmosphere for people [16].

Touch. For individuals, the sense of touch is the most sensitive and real perception of human beings, of which tactile nerves are found throughout the body. By touching the object, we can get incredibly subtle messages. Hence, when consumers touch the product, the packaging material is easy to leave a deep impression on consumers, increasing consumers' sensory understanding of the product.

The selection of children's packaging materials, such as the different texture (soft of hard) will bring them various feelings, of which the feedback is direct and natural [17]. So children's food packaging is mainly made of paper and plastic. Because warm and moist material touch will make children closer to the product, while the cold and solid material will make children stay away. In addition, for children whose mobility is still developing, smooth surface is not easy to grasp, while rough texture is easier to control [18].

Smell. The sense of odor can leave person the most lasting impression, which generate powerful associations and strong emotions even before it has been edited. Some experiments have shown that a good olfactory experience can make the person produce positive and relaxed psychological feeling.

The method of interactive packaging design to convey taste is to extract the smell of food and then smear it on the outer packaging with special materials [19]. Without affecting the preservation of the quality of the food inside, children can feel the delicious food through the smell on the outer packaging. The olfactory experience in packaging design can not only satisfy consumer's curiosity, but also establish a good atmosphere.

Taste. Taste transmits the perceptional information from the sensory to the brain, where saliva triggers the taste experience. Compared with the other sensory channel, taste is the most difficult to integrate into the packaging design, because generally unsold goods cannot be tasted. Therefore, the expression of taste mainly relies on visual stimulation. Specific elements and visual skills are used to produces synesthesia of consumers and deepen the taste sensitivity vividly.

For example, shapes such as circles and ellipse often give people a feeling of soft and moist, while triangles and rectangles give them a feeling of hard and crisp. For the food packaging, its color is usually bright, which means to reflect the taste of food, sucha as red representing "spicy", orange representing "sour" and green representing "fresh".

4   Conclusion

In general, compared with the traditional packaging design, interactive packaging design is more "user-centered", which provides consumers the better user experience. As a new design direction, interactive packaging design can not only protect and sell products, but also satisfy the consumers' cognitive and emotional needs and enhance the product's brand competitiveness effectively, so as to promote the interaction and communication between consumers and products.

This paper discussed the future development trend of packaging design, and innovatively integrated the sensory sense as an interactive concept into the interactive packaging design of children's food. From the perspective of sensory channels (including vision, hearing, touch, smell and taste), the emotional design provides multiple dimensions of enriching the interaction mode between consumers and products. The research results have successfully practiced the application of multi-sensory senses on interactive packaging design of children's food. It not only provides scholars meaningful inspiration of user experience evaluation on packaging design, but also provides designers reliable guidance for emotional design methods of children's products.

References

1. Liu, R., Xiao, Y.: Expression of multi-sensory experience in the form of packaging design (2021). https://doi.org/10.19362/j.cnki.cn10-1400/TB.2021.08.017
2. Sun, Y.: Instant visual effect of sensory design experience in packaging design (2022). https://doi.org/10.19362/j.cnki.cn10-1400/TB.2022.01.012
3. Li, M.: Expression of multi-sensory design concept in products. Pack. Eng. (20) (2012)
4. Sun, Y., Wang, Y.: Application research of interactive packaging design from the perspective of experience economy. Hunan Pack. (02) 71–73 (2021). https://doi.org/10.19686/j.carol carrollnkiissn1671–4997.2021.02.019
5. Yuan, Y.: Discuss the application of interactive concept in the packaging design (a master's degree thesis, Qingdao university) (2017)
6. Guo, X.: Based on the interactive packaging design of the experience of users (2021)
7. Jiang, T., Fan, L.: Current situation and development trend of Beverage packaging design in China. Pack. Eng. (14), 74–78+83 (2019). https://doi.org/10.19554/j.cnki.1001-3563.2019.14.013
8. Sania, Zhang, X.: Research on interactive packaging design factors affecting user experience. Art Des. (Theory) (03), 41–43. https://doi.org/10.16824/j.carolcarrollnkiissn10082832.2022.03.030
9. Wen, L.: Research on humanized design of children's packaging under emotional experience. West. Leather **11**, 67–68 (2021)
10. Yizhan, Z.: Application analysis of interactive Concept in packaging design. Art Sci. Technol. **12**, 180–181 (2018)
11. Mou, Y.: Research on interactive Experience construction in packaging design. Think Tank Times (31), 174+176 (2018)
12. Sheng, Z., Xiaoyan, A.: Expression and thinking of humanization trend of design. J. Shaanxi Univ. Sci. Technol. **01**, 127–130 (2004)
13. Zhang, D.: Industrial Product Modeling Design. Chongqing University Press
14. Lv, G.-W.: Medical Neurobiology, 2nd edn. Higher Education Press, Beijing (2004)
15. Diana, A.: The Natural History of sensation, trans. M1 Lu Danjun. Flower City Press, Guangzhou (2007)
16. Wang, Y., Zhou, Y.: Research on the form of multi-sensory interactive packaging design. J. Pack. **03**, 88–92 (2020)
17. Fang, Y.: Research on extended function design of children's toy packaging. China Pack. Ind. **9X**, 1 (2014)
18. Li, C.: Research on the Extension design of The Qizhi Toy Packaging Function. (Research Dissertation, Wuhan University of Technology)
19. Xiao, J.: Application research of Interactive Concept in packaging design. Literary life: the next ten days (2014)
20. Liang, Q., Cong, Y.: Research on modern art design based on "Five senses" experience. Pack. Eng. **37**(20), 4 (2016)

An Initial Attempt to Build a Natural Sounds Library Based on Heuristic Evaluation

Xiuqi Zhu[1,2,3], Jingyu Zhang[1,2(✉)], Tongyang Liu[4], and Gang He[4]

[1] CAS Key Laboratory of Behavioral Science, Institute of Psychology, Beijing, China
737872253@qq.com
[2] Department of Psychology, University of Chinese Academy of Sciences, Beijing, China
[3] School of Animation and Digital Arts, Communication University of China, Beijing, China
[4] Chongqing Changan Automobile Company Limited, Chongqing, China

Abstract. Attention restoration theory (ART) predicts that the natural environment can restore consumed attentional resources. Previous studies also found presenting natural scenes visually can also have such an effect but whether natural sounds may also have this effect has not been fully examined. In this study, we used an exploratory approach to build a library of natural sounds. We surveyed 204 people by asking them to name ten different types of 'natural' sounds and the ten types of 'relaxing' sounds. The collected more than 1,800 answers were then coded according to the source and the characteristics. Finally, twenty-one categories of sounds emerged from these responses. Among them, six categories were considered to be both relaxing and natural (e.g. birds' songs). For other categories, they were only natural (e.g. thunder) or only relaxing (e.g. music). We discussed how to use this sound library in future studies.

Keywords: Attention restoration · Natural sounds · Human cognition

1 Introduction

Attention Restoration Theory (ART) predicts exposure to natural environments may lead to an improved cognitive performance by restoring attentional resources [1, 2]. In recent years, studies have begun to investigate whether created natural environment may also have such an effect. For example, by asking people to walk on a treadmill while watching videos of natural scenes, researchers found that their attention can be recovered [3]. Similarly, findings were also discovered in using images [7], videos [11], and virtual reality [9].

While most studies have found the effectiveness of using the visual form of natural scenes, whether presenting the natural sound in an artificial environment may also have such effect has not been fully explored. In an early paper, Ratcliffe and colleagues suggested that some bird sounds might be restorative, but they did not test it empirically [4]. Some later studies have found a few specific natural sounds (e.g., fountain, tweeting birds) do have such restorative effect [6, 8].

© The Author(s), under exclusive license to Springer Nature Switzerland AG 2022
C. Stephanidis et al. (Eds.): HCII 2022, CCIS 1654, pp. 704–710, 2022.
https://doi.org/10.1007/978-3-031-19679-9_90

However, it is still not known whether the restorative effect occurred because these sounds were natural or because they possess other more important features to restore attention. More importantly, it is not ready to equate these few kinds of sound to all the natural sounds without a systematic exploration. As a result, it is valuable to find out whether all the natural sounds may have the restorative effect or only a few very special sounds have this unique function. To do so, it is important to establish a library of natural sounds. In this study, we described our initial attempt to do such work.

2 Methods

To collect a comprehensive set of natural sounds which people are familiar with, we used a questionnaire to collect people's responses. As we also wanted to discriminate restorative sounds from natural sounds as a whole, we asked the participants to report sounds that they considered to be natural and sounds they considered to be restorative separately. We wanted to find the overlap and non-overlap of the two categories.

2.1 Participants

A total of 262 people participated in our survey. After eliminating the invalid answers, such as adjectives without meaning or ordinary numbers, we collected 204 valid responses with a mean age of (M = 24.91, SD = 5.02).

2.2 Design and Questions

The participants were asked to write down 10 specific natural sounds and 10 specific sounds that they feel relaxed. People were asked to provide details of the named sounds as many as possible so that readers can find and record them according to their description.

2.3 Procedure

We used a questionnaire to get the information we wanted. The questionnaire was posted on social media platforms and campus forums, and to attract more people to fill it out, we set a fee of 10 RMB for each person who filled it out.

This questionnaire contains some basic personal information (e.g., gender, age, occupation, and undergraduate major) and two completions. To improve the efficiency of our questionnaire collection, these questionnaires were set to be opened by scanning the QR code, and only one of these two questions would appear at random. After a week of questionnaire collection, these questionnaires were divided into two different questionnaires according to whether they answered the "natural sound" (n = 89) question or the "relaxed sound" (n = 115) question.

2.4 Response Coding

There were a total of 2040 entries from all the responses. First screening found that 180 meaningless entries were not clear or incomplete for us to find the actual source of the sound. For example, some entries were onomatopoeic words (e.g., buzzing, boing, etc.) or sound adjectives (e.g., elegant, slow-paced, etc.). Excluding these entries produced a set of 1860 entries for further analysis.

In the next step, we combined all the entries using different words to describe the same sound. For example, 'the sound of raindrops falling on the water surface when it rains' and 'the sound of dripping rain' were recoded as 'the sound of light rain', while 'the sound of a kitten meowing' and 'the meekness sound of a cat' were recoded as 'the sound of a cat', respectively. Using this approach, 141 different specific sounds emerged from the 1860 sound descriptions.

We further grouped these specific sounds into even larger categories based on their sources, amounts, and characteristics (the three elements of sound: loudness, pitch, and timbre). For example, 30 different types of animal sounds were merged into five types (birds, insects, aquatic animals, small pets, and big mammals) according to the morphology of the animals and the sound features. A similar approach was used for other sound types. Finally, all the 141 specific sounds were put into 21 different categories. The names, definitions, and examples of these 21 categories were listed in Table 1.

Table 1. Names, definitions, and examples of the 21 categories

Sound types	Definition	Examples
Wind	The sound of the wind	The rustle of the wind blowing through the leaves; The soft sound of the wind; The sound of wind echoing in the valley
Water flow	The sound of water flowing	Sound of flowing stream; Sound of water drops; Sound of spring water
Insects	The sound made by insects	Frog's call; The buzzing of bees; The humming of insects in the grass in the evening
Rain	The sound related to rain	Light drizzle; The sound of raindrops falling on the water; The sound of rain hitting the window
Birds	Sounds made by bird animals	Crisp bird calls; The chirping of birds; The sound of birds echoing in the forest
Thunder	The sound related to thunder	Rumbling thunder

(*continued*)

Table 1. (*continued*)

Sound types	Definition	Examples
Human Voice	The sound made by humans	The sound of chewing food; Uniform breathing sound; Clean and nice vocals
Pet	Sounds made by animals that people breed	The gentle purring of cats; Puppy barking; Kitten snoring
Loud Friction	Loud sound produced when objects rub against each other	Suddenly a crisp thud (e.g. something falling); The sound of chopping and cooking; The sound of the board erasing the blackboard
Artifact	Sounds made by human-made objects	The sound of turning pages; Telephone ringing; The sound of the wind blowing the wind chimes
Ocean	Sounds made by the ocean	The sound of waves lapping the beach; The sound of the ocean waves surging
Mild Friction	Mild sound produced when objects rub against each other	The rustling sound of sand flowing; Soft footsteps; The sound of rubbing between clothes
Music	Melody and rhythm through vocal and instrumental expression	Relaxing pure music; Soothing Piano Pieces; Class bell rings; Fast-paced drumming
Plants	Sounds made by the plant	The sound of growing plants; The sound of persimmons falling from the trees; The sound of a branch snapping
Ice&Snow	Sounds made by ice and snow	The sound of snow falling; The sound of footsteps walking in the snow
Vehicle	The sound made by the movement of transportation	Car hooting; The sound of a car driving; The sound of a bicycle chain turning
Mammals	Sounds made by mammals	Cow's call; Pig's call; Mouse's bark; The sound of galloping horses
Fire	Sounds made by fire	The sound of a burning campfire; The sound of burning fire; The sound of burning firewood
Aquatic Animals	Sounds made by animals living in the water	Dolphins singing in the sea; The ethereal call of the whale; The sound of fish spitting bubbles
Meaningless	Sound with no specific meaning	The Sound of Silence; Unclear sound
White Noise	Noise with equal noise energy contained in each band of equal bandwidth	White noise

3 Results

We further described the percentage of these sound categories mentioned as either natural or relaxing (see Fig. 1).

In the natural sounds, the top eight most frequently mentioned sounds were wind (16.07%), water (12.34%), insects (10.51%), rain (8.61%), birds (8.35%), thunder (5.91%), human voices (5.4%), and pets (4.24%). In the relaxing sounds, the top eight mentioned categories from highest to lowest frequency were music (16.35%), human voices (16.16%), water flow (8.08%), rain (7.68%), wind (7.00%), the artifact (6.80%), loud friction (5.81%) and birds (5.42%).

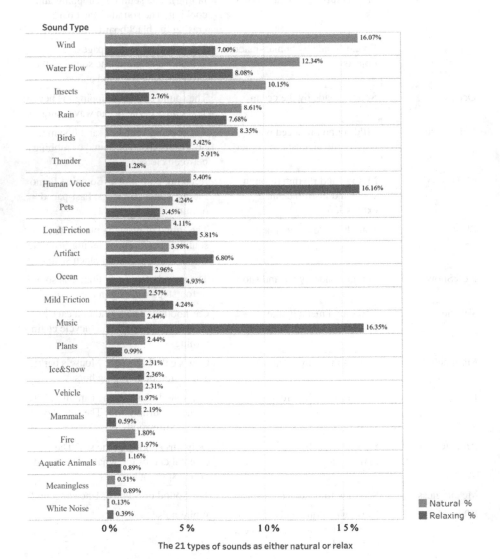

Fig. 1. The 21 types of sounds as either natural or relax

4 Discussion and Conclusion

Using a questionnaire to elicit people's concepts about natural and relaxing sounds, this study makes an initial attempt to build a sound library for investigating the effects of attention restoration. Twenty-one categorizations of sounds were created by coding the named sounds. Among these sounds, we found that some natural sounds were considered restorative by the participants, such as wind, water flow, rain, birds, and pets. The beliefs held by laypeople, somehow, match the findings of experimental studies of Alvarsson et al. [8] who found sounds of fountain and birds can have restorative effects.

In addition, the results of the questionnaire show some interesting findings. Some categories of sounds were mentioned much more often in one type than in the other. For instance, human voices and music were mentioned more often as relaxing than natural. So we treated these sounds as unnatural sounds with restorative properties. However, sounds of insects and thunder were mentioned often as natural sounds but not so as relaxing. It seems to indicate that not all natural sounds are created equal in their ability to assist people in restoring their attention. But do these believed-to-be-natural-and-unrelaxing sounds have no restorative effect? Further experimental studies are needed. The answer can tell us whether all the natural sounds have restorative effects or only certain sounds are restorative.

Some limitations must be mentioned. The first is related to the sampling issue. In the current study, most of the participants were female. As gender differences may exist in understanding and preferences of sounds [5], future studies may benefit from using a more gender-balanced sample. Second, we only asked ordinary people to list the sounds. People might only recall the most frequently experienced sounds. Future studies may benefit from using experience sampling methods by asking people to name the restorative sounds when they were exposed to the natural environment.

To conclude, we have established an initial library to test the restorative effect of sounds. In future work, these specific sounds can help us conduct further experiments and explore the therapeutic properties of natural sounds. In the longer-term plan, we wanted to design a CAVE [10] by listening to these sounds in a virtual natural environment and measuring their attention recovery effect.

Acknowledgment. This study was supported by the National Natural Science Foundation of China (Grant No. T2192932).

Reference

1. Kaplan, R., Kaplan, S.: the experience of nature: a psychological perspective (1989)
2. Kaplan, S.: The restorative benefits of nature: toward an integrative framework. J. Environ. Psychol. **15**, 169–182 (1995)
3. Crossan, C., Salmoni, A.: A simulated walk in nature: testing predictions from the attention restoration theory. Environ. Behav. **53**, 277–295 (2021)
4. Ratcliffe, E., Gatersleben, B., Sowden, P.T.: Bird sounds and their contributions to perceived attention restoration and stress recovery. J. Environ. Psychol. **36**, 221–228 (2013)
5. Spence, J.W., Peak, D.A.: The impact of sound on information recall: an investigation of gender differences (1998)

6. Van Hedger, S.C., Nusbaum, H.C., Clohisy, L., Jaeggi, S.M., Buschkuehl, M., Berman, M.G.: Of cricket chirps and car horns: the effect of nature sounds on cognitive performance. Psychon. Bull. Rev. **26**(2), 522–530 (2018). https://doi.org/10.3758/s13423-018-1539-1
7. Hicks, L.J., et al.: Restoration of sustained attention following virtual nature exposure: undeniable or unreliable? J. Environ. Psychol. **71**, 101488 (2020)
8. Alvarsson, J., et al.: Stress recovery during exposure to nature sound and environmental noise. Int. J. Environ. Res. Public Health **7**, 1036–1046 (2010)
9. Li, G., et al.: Closed-loop attention restoration theory for virtual reality-based attentional engagement enhancement. Sensors **20**, 2208 (2020)
10. Blach, R., et al.: A highly flexible virtual reality system. Futur. Gener. Comput. Syst. **14**, 167–178 (1998)
11. Jiang, B., et al.: Perceived green at speed: a simulated driving experiment raises new questions for attention restoration theory and stress reduction theory. Environ. Behav. **53**, 296–335 (2021)

Author Index

Printed in the United States
by Baker & Taylor Publisher Services